PENGUIN BOOKS

AFRICAN AND CARIBBEAN PEOPLE IN BRITAIN

'I've waited so long to read a comprehensively researched book about Black history on this island. This is it: a journey of discovery and a truly exciting and important work' Zainab Abbas

'The most comprehensive and accessible guidebook on what has come to be known as "Black British history". Suited for all readers, it provides a useful insight into how this history has developed, and the struggles to push for its expansion. It also inspires us to consider how we might contribute to the ever-growing understanding of this historical field' *Young Historians Project*

'An essential work that, in exploring national values, inter-cultural alliances and the politics of racialised identity, shines a light on the acts of the remarkable people across time who epitomised a universal struggle for the rights of all' Toyin Agbetu

'British historian and scholar Professor Hakim Adi has spent decades trying to correct what he calls the Windrush myth – the idea that Black migration to the UK began in 1948, when the famous ship landed with several hundred Jamaicans at Tilbury docks. His latest book, *African and Caribbean People in Britain*, is his crowning achievement' Kehinde Andrews, *Guardian*

'The Windrush narrative now overshadows all other narratives about people of African descent in the UK. Hakim Adi's *African and Caribbean People in Britain: A History* is a welcome and much needed corrective, improving understanding of the length and depth of the African and Caribbean presence in Britain . . . Magnificent' Onyekachi Wambu, Writers Mosaic

'His telling of British history characterises the diverse, multi-centred chronology of African and Caribbean landmarks, crises, progress, organisations, communities and, most importantly, individual experiences in Britain' *History Matters*

T0333130

ABOUT THE AUTHOR

Hakim Adi is Professor of the History of Africa and the African Diaspora at the University of Chichester. Hakim was the first historian of African heritage to become a professor of history in Britain. In January 2018, he launched the world's first online Masters by Research (MRes) degree programme on the History of Africa and the African Diaspora. Hakim is also the founder and consultant historian of the Young Historians Project. http://younghistoriansproject.org/

He has appeared in many documentary films, on TV and on radio and has written widely on the history of Africa and the African Diaspora, including three history books for children. His publications have been translated into French, Spanish and Portuguese and include: *West Africans in Britain 1900–60: Nationalism, Pan-Africanism and Communism* (Lawrence and Wishart, 1998); (with M. Sherwood) *The 1945 Manchester Pan-African Congress Revisited* (New Beacon, 1995) and *Pan-African History: Political Figures from Africa and the Diaspora since 1787* (Routledge, 2003).

His most recent books are *Pan-Africanism and Communism: The Communist International, Africa and the Diaspora, 1919–1939* (Africa World Press, 2013), *Pan-Africanism: A History* (Bloomsbury Press, 2018) and, as editor, *Black British History: New Perspectives* (Zed, 2019), *Black Voices on Britain* (Macmillan, 2022) and *New Perspectives on the History of African and Caribbean People in Britain* (Pluto, 2023). https://www.hakimadi.org

HAKIM ADI

African and Caribbean People in Britain

A History

PENGUIN BOOKS

PENGUIN BOOKS

UK | USA | Canada | Ireland | Australia
India | New Zealand | South Africa

Penguin Books is part of the Penguin Random House group of companies
whose addresses can be found at global.penguinrandomhouse.com.

First published in Great Britain by Allen Lane 2022
First published in Penguin Books 2023
003

Printed and bound in Great Britain by Clays Ltd, Elcograf S.p.A.

The authorized representative in the EEA is Penguin Random House Ireland,
Morrison Chambers, 32 Nassau Street, Dublin D02 YH68

A CIP catalogue record for this book is available from the British Library

ISBN: 978-1-802-06068-3

Contents

Preface   vii

1 The Early African Presence   1
2 African Tudors and Stuarts   11
3 That Infamous Traffic   29
4 Freedom Struggles   98
5 Struggles for the Rights of All   145
6 War, Riot and Resistance: 1897–1919   207
7 The Interwar Years   272
8 The Second World War and After   327
9 The Post-war World   378
10 Black Liberation   434
11 Into the New Century   489

Acknowledgements   521
Notes   523
Index   639

Preface

My original aim in writing this book was to provide not just an overview of the history of all those of African and Caribbean heritage in Britain, but also an introduction to the latest research. For many years the key work on the subject was Peter Fryer's *Staying Power: The History of Black People in Britain*, first published in 1984. That was almost forty years ago and there has been a considerable amount of new research since that time, as well as some rethinking about the subject.[1]

Fryer used the term 'Black' to include those of South Asian origin in a way that was common at the time but unusual today. Research on those connected with the Indian subcontinent has subsequently been greatly developed by Rozina Visram in her two books, *Ayahs, Lascars and Princes: The Story of Indians in Britain 1700–1947* and *Asians in Britain: 400 Years of History*, as well as by other historians.[2] Rather than using the well-established terms 'Black' or 'Black British', I have chosen to use the phrase African and Caribbean people for the title, and throughout I have written about the history of those of African and Caribbean heritage. That is because, even though I have edited a book entitled *New Perspectives on Black British History*, I'm not any more comfortable with that term than I would be with the term 'White British History'. It might be argued that there is only British history, with no other qualifiers, but unfortunately those of African and Caribbean heritage have too often been excluded from it. All people, including those of dual heritage, have a specific geographical cultural heritage, based on their places of origin, or that of their families, and I do not see why this should be denied to those of African and Caribbean heritage who have made such an impact on the history of Britain.

I take for granted that those who were born or have resided in the country can be considered British, or citizens of Britain and part of the history of Britain, irrespective of what modern racist legislation might declare to the contrary.

Fryer was not the first to attempt a general survey on the subject. As early as 1948, at a time when some people erroneously consider that this history began, Kenneth Little, a British anthropologist, published his book *Negroes in Britain: A Study of Racial Relations in English Society*. Although this focused mainly on 'the Coloured Folk of Cardiff', it also included an entire chapter 'The Negroes in Britain – 1600 A.D. to the Present Day'. A century before Little, in 1848, Wilson Armistead, a Leeds-based abolitionist, produced his *A Tribute for the Negro*, which, although not a history in the modern sense, contained much historical material on Africans in Britain, as well as elsewhere.[3] Since that time there have been many others who have contributed to our knowledge, such as pioneering writers Nigel File and Chris Power, who with their *Black Settlers in Britain* responded to demands from school students during the 1970s for more representative textbooks, as well as James Walvin, who published his *Black and White* and other work during the same decade.[4] One of the most prominent historians has been Marika Sherwood, who began writing about this history in the mid-1980s and has been a prolific writer and researcher ever since. She has written on almost every aspect of this history from the Tudor period onwards and has publications too numerous to mention.[5] Just as importantly, she has been a champion for this history over many years, one of the founders of the Black and Asian Studies Association in 1991 and for many years the editor of its *Newsletter*. For over thirty-five years she has been a tireless campaigner for changes to the National History Curriculum in schools, as well as for changes in the preservation and to the presentation of historical sources in museums and archives. She has probably done more than anyone to encourage the study and teaching of this history, as well as being a mentor to many, and has been largely unacknowledged for her efforts.

As a result of the work of Marika Sherwood, as well as many others, in recent years this history has become much more visible. In 2017 the broadcaster David Olusoga presented his acclaimed prime-time television series *Black and British*, followed by a book of the same title.[6] Olusoga is part of a long line of researchers of African and Caribbean heritage who have addressed the fact that standard presentations of Britain's history have often neglected or excluded those of African and Caribbean heritage. One of the earliest scholars was a self-educated Jamaican, J. A. Rogers, who lived and worked in the United States. His research and publications were designed to combat Eurocentric and racist views of history. In several of his works he writes about the history of African and Caribbean people in Britain, although his focus is often on prominent individuals. A meticulous researcher, his best-known works include *World's Great Men of Color* and *Nature Knows No Color-Line*, which were first published over seventy years ago.[7] Another important scholar was Edward Scobie (1918–1996), a Dominican writer and publisher who produced one of the first surveys of the subject in *Black Britannia: A History of Blacks in Britain*, first published in 1972. During the 1970s, two pioneering books were published by the Nigerian historian Folarin Shyllon: *Black People in Britain, 1555–1833* and *Black Slaves in Britain*.[8] Ron Ramdin, a Trinidadian historian based in Britain, published another important survey, *The Making of the Black Working Class in Britain*, which first appeared in 1987.[9] More recently there have been significant contributions from the African American historian Gretchen Gerzina, most notably her book, *Black England: Life Before Emancipation* and the radio series, *Britain's Black Past*.[10]

The historian working on the subject today therefore benefits from the work of numerous predecessors and I have endeavoured to draw on the work of as many researchers as possible. However, although there has been important new work, the focus of many historians remains firmly on the twentieth century. There is still a lack of research on the period before 1500 and on the seventeenth and nineteenth centuries, as well as the period after 1985. In short, there is still much research that remains to be done to strengthen our knowledge of this history.

The modern historian is also able to make use of the many historical sources and records that are now online, a particularly important resource in the midst of a pandemic. These include, for example, the University of Glasgow's database Runaway Slaves in Britain: Bondage, Freedom and Race in the Eighteenth Century, as well as some of the digitized material held at the Black Cultural Archives and the National Archives in London.[11] In 2003 the Chief Executive of the National Archives admitted 'it has recently been acknowledged the archives contain rich sources of African and Asian heritage', and then added 'once it has been determined what there actually is, the best way to promote it must be determined'.[12] However, in the years since, progress has been painfully slow. Unfortunately, government departments have destroyed many important documents relating to this history and still withhold many others.

It is a great shame that other repositories that hold important sources for the study of the history of those of African and Caribbean heritage in Britain do not make much more of it widely available online. The British Library, for example, has digitized some important interviews, but these are only available to readers who are physically at the library. Today, those outside the universities and major archives, such as the historian Jeffrey Green, are making some of their research available online.[13] So too are many others, such as African Stories in Hull and East Yorkshire, the Black Coal Miners Project and the Young Historians Project, which are collecting important oral histories and other historical material, often relating to neglected subjects such as histories of African women.[14]

In writing the long history of people of African and Caribbean heritage in Britain, historians can now utilize a variety of sources. DNA records and archaeology have proved illuminating for the period before 1500, although here great caution is required with the interpretation of scientific evidence, as recent discoveries relating to the appearance of Cheddar Man have shown. Much more attention needs to be paid to court and parish records for the early history of Africans in the British Isles. Indeed, a variety of sources can and must be used. The sources for this history are not only to be found in Britain. To give one example, the papers of twentieth-century London-based organizations, such as the Nigerian Progress Union and West African Students' Union, are to be found in Nigeria, although I also recall finding a rare West African Students' Union poster from the early 1930s almost hidden in archives in Washington, DC

It was more than forty years ago when I first began my own historical research and there have been many significant developments during that period. However, even when I first began my research on the history of Africans in Britain there was a tendency for this history to be reduced to the one that began only in 1948 with the arrival of a certain ship from the Caribbean. We felt then that such an approach not only obscured a much longer history, but also gave prominence only to the experiences of those who migrated to Britain from the Caribbean in the post-war period. In short, it did more to obscure than to enlighten us about Britain's past. Today, when the majority of Britain's Black population have migrated from or are connected with the African continent, it is even more vital that what has come to be referred to as 'Black British' history reflects the experiences and struggles of all those of African and Caribbean heritage. This history is always part of Britain's history, just as it is part of the wider history of the African diaspora and of Britain's colonial connections with Africa, the Caribbean and the United States as well as other parts of the world.

Despite the efforts of researchers and campaigners this history has remained largely hidden or obscured for too long. It has only been taught by a few dedicated school teachers and seldom in universities. In 1995 I was appointed to one of the few, and perhaps the first, academic posts in 'Black British' history at Middlesex University. There were few others by the time I became the first person of African heritage to become a professor of history in Britain twenty years later. It was not until after the Black Lives Matter protests in 2020 that there was a significant increase in the numbers of academic posts in this field. Indeed, for much of the last forty years this is a history that has largely been developed and researched by those outside academia. It has been sustained by community historians, through heritage walks and initiatives such as the Black Cultural Archives in London, as well as other independent archives and regional initiatives. Not only has the history of people of African and Caribbean heritage in Britain often been centred around their struggles, but to firmly establish this history requires a significant struggle as well.

I

The Early African Presence

In January 2016, *Mail Online* and several other media outlets in Britain announced that a new GCSE history course for Britain's school pupils, focusing on migration, was likely to teach them that 'the nation's earliest inhabitants were Africans who were in Britain before the English'.[1] The *Mail* lamented what it referred to as 'the extraordinary rewriting of our island's history', which it explained had 'been branded pro-immigration propaganda by critics'. One such critic described this presentation of history as 'indoctrination', others as 'disturbing and dangerous'.[2] The *Mail* claimed that such plans had provoked 'uproar', although it did acknowledge that, prior to the arrival of the Anglo-Saxons, a Roman legion of North Africans was stationed at Hadrian's Wall in Cumbria during the third century. However, having consulted an eminent historian, who concluded, to the *Mail*'s evident satisfaction, 'there is no evidence they ever settled here', the *Mail* exposed the individual responsible for such so-called 'indoctrination', a 'Marxist writer and journalist' called Peter Fryer. Concerned readers were perhaps reassured by V. S. Naipaul's view that 'This absurd supposition of Africans inhabiting Britain before the English only goes to show how our once esteemed centres of learning, Oxford and Cambridge, have been insidiously eroded by a dangerous dogma that, very like IS today, wrought misery and havoc in Russia, China and the Eastern bloc, where for all practical purposes it has failed.'[3]

Fryer, the author of *Staying Power: The History of Black People in Britain*, first published in 1984, and continually in print since that time, began his carefully researched survey of 2,000 years of British history with the sentence, 'There were Africans in Britain before the English came here.'[4] He was not alone in this view. In a paper presented to the

International Conference on the History of Blacks in Britain held in London as long ago as 1981, but published much later, a distinguished academic, Paul Edwards, had opined 'it would be a nice irony against racist opinion if it could be demonstrated that African communities were settled in England before the English invaders arrived from Europe centuries later'.[5]

The presence of Africans in Britain during the Roman period has been established by historians for many years. It is therefore correct to say that Africans were present before the settlement, centuries later, of Angles, Saxons and Jutes, although perhaps incorrect to say that these migrant communities are the main ancestors of the modern English.[6] The latest DNA evidence also suggests that the Angles and Saxons played a less important part in the ancestry of the English than had previously been supposed and that African migrants had reached Britain perhaps a thousand years before the Romans. Much of the evidence for an early African presence comes from tooth enamel oxygen isotope evidence, which can be used to determine the geographical source of water drunk by an individual in childhood, but it is evidence that needs to be considered with caution.[7] However, when used with other archaeological evidence it presents interesting questions regarding an early African presence in Britain. There is also even more interesting speculation, such as the possibility that the name of the Isle of Thanet in Kent might be derived from a Phoenician word. Enamel oxygen isotope evidence from human remains again suggests that the area might have received North African migrants in the Bronze Age.[8] There has long been speculation about ancient African populations throughout the Britain Isles both before and after the Roman period and clearly much more research needs to be done to establish the veracity of such claims.[9]

A significant development in understanding this early history was the revelation in February 2018 that those who might be considered some of the first Britons – that is the first to provide genes that can be found amongst some of the modern inhabitants of Britain – had 'dark to black' skin, as well as dark hair and blue eyes. Indeed, one newspaper headline boldly proclaimed that according to the latest DNA study 'the first Britons were black'.[10] The research, conducted by the Natural History Museum, analysed the skeletal remains of Cheddar Man, first discovered in a cave in Somerset in 1903, who is thought to have lived in England some 10,000 years ago amongst a population of only 12,000. The almost complete skeleton of Cheddar Man is the oldest so far discovered of a modern human in Britain. The study showed that migrants who originated in Africa, and came to Britain via western Asia and Europe, maintained darker skin pigmentation for much longer periods than was previously thought and that the development of pale skin pigmentation took place much more recently. The research into the origins and appearance of Cheddar Man suggests that the population of western European hunter-gatherers of that period almost certainly looked similar to Cheddar Man, with 'dark to black' skin. The earliest Europeans, just like the earliest Britons, could also be considered Black people. Notions of Britishness and Englishness once more need to be rethought.[11] The analysis of the skeletal remains of Cheddar Man also demonstrated significant scientific advances. Although the analysis of DNA has been possible for several years, techniques have markedly improved in the twenty-first century and created the possibility for new revelations about the ancient population of Britain in the future.

It has long been known that Britain was the place of cremation of the 'African emperor', Septimius Severus, who was Libyan-born and of Berber origin. Britain was also governed by several other Africans, including Quintus Lollius Urbicus, who came from what is Algeria today, was Governor of Britain from 139–142 CE and supervised the building of the Antonine Wall in Scotland. Several other African Roman governors also originated from what is today Libya, Tunisia and Algeria, as did numerous military commanders and soldiers.[12]

For some years, historians have known that Africans were part of the Roman army of occupation in Britain, especially connected with the period when Severus and his sons ruled the Roman empire.[13] There was a unit of North African soldiers, known as the *Numerus Maurorum Aurelianorum*, stationed at the western end of Hadrian's Wall, near what is today Burgh-by-Sands in Cumbria, as is evident from Roman records and several inscriptions found in the area. It is recorded that one of the Black soldiers in this unit presented a garland of cypress boughs to Emperor Severus, although according to Severus' modern biographer, this source, which also mentions the human sacrifice of 'black victims', cannot be entirely relied upon as established historical fact.[14] Archaeological evidence dating from the second and third centuries CE also includes the especially distinctive 'Roman head pots' said to be unquestionably of North African design, found at Chester, York and other sites, including some in Scotland. This shows not just that some of those serving in the Roman army of occupation were recruited from Africa but that it is likely that there were either 'soldier-potters', or African potters accompanying the army.[15] Referring to samples of cooking vessels found near York, one expert concluded that they were made 'by Africans for the use of Africans'.[16] Other evidence of an African presence in Roman Britain has been found from tombstones and other archaeological finds, including writing in what has been described as 'neo-Punic script'.[17] In short, there is much evidence of the presence in Britain not only of African soldiers but also civilians from what are today Libya, Tunisia and Algeria, all part of the Roman province of Africa at the time (itself a place name possibly derived from a language spoken in the region that was subsequently applied to the entire continent).

The latest archaeological and scientific techniques have been utilized to analyse human remains found in what was the Roman city of Eboracum, now York, where Emperor Septimius Severus died in 211 CE. At the beginning of the twentieth century people digging in a street in York discovered a 1,700-year-old stone coffin of a woman. She had been buried with jewellery, including jet and ivory bracelets, as well as other valuable possessions, and was undoubtedly of elite status. It was not until 2010 that archaeologists were fully able to analyse the skeleton, which they discovered to be that of a young woman, probably between eighteen and twenty-three years old and of North African origin.[18] The archaeologists were even able to make a reconstruction to show us what this African 'Ivory Bangle Lady' may have looked like.[19] This and other research has shown that those of African heritage, including African women of all classes, were a settled population before the arrival of the Angles and Saxons. Such findings prompted one leading archaeologist to conclude that analysis of the 'Ivory Bangle Lady' and others like her, contradicts common popular assumptions about the make-up of Roman-British populations, as well as the view that 'African immigrants in Roman Britain were of low status, male and likely to have been slaves'.[20]

Another young woman from North Africa has been discovered by archaeologists and scientists analysing human remains from the Roman period at the Museum of London. Tests showed that the 'Lant Street Teenager', who was only fourteen at the time of her death, had been born in North Africa but probably had ancestors from south of the Sahara. The teenager had only been living in London for a few years, prompting questions about the circumstances of her migration. Another skeleton found in London is of a middle-aged African man who had probably grown up in London and suffered from diabetes.[21] DNA analysis of such remains shows the diversity of Roman towns and cities, but also the fact that Africans could be found living in many parts of Britain. Recent analysis of human remains suggests that not only those of North African origin found their way to Britain but others from further south in Africa such as 'Beachy Head Lady' as well. This name refers to skeletal remains first discovered near Eastbourne in southern England in the 1950s which are thought to date from the mid-third century CE, in the middle of the Roman period, and are of a young woman. Although she is thought to have grown up in the area, analysis of her remains suggests that her origin was clearly from a region of Africa that was not part of the Roman empire, but that she was probably either born in Sussex or brought to Britain at a very young age. Such evidence poses fascinating questions about the past and the possibility of families of Africans living in Britain in ancient times.[22]

THE EARLY MEDIEVAL PERIOD

Although we are learning more about the presence of Africans and those of African descent in ancient and Roman Britain, at present we have very little knowledge of this presence for almost one thousand years following the main Roman exodus. This is partly because an African presence is not immediately visible, although there are certainly a few pictorial representations, and partly because very little research has been carried out. There are, however, numerous myths and legends about Africans during this early period, most notably that of Gormund, 'King of the Africans', who it is said ruled Ireland and invaded and 'ravaged England' with thousands of African troops in alliance with the Saxons. The legend of Gormund is mentioned in many sources, including Geoffrey of Monmouth's *The History of the Kings of Britain*, written in the twelfth century.[23] According to Geoffrey:

> After Malgo succeeded Careticus, a lover of civil war, and hateful to God and to the Britons. The Saxons, discovering his fickle disposition, went to Ireland for Gormund, king of the Africans, who had arrived there with a very great fleet, and had subdued that country. From thence, at their traitorous instigation, he sailed over into Britain, which the perfidious Saxons in one part, in another the Britons by their continual wars among themselves were wholly laying waste. Entering therefore into alliance with the Saxons, he made war upon king Careticus, and after several battles fought, drove him from city to city, till at length he forced him to Cirencester, and there besieged him. Here Isembard, the nephew of Lewis, king of the Franks, came and made a league of amity with him, and out of respect to him renounced the Christian faith, on condition that he would assist him to gain the kingdom of Gaul from his uncle, by whom, he said, he was forcibly and unjustly expelled out of it. At last, after taking and burning the city, he had another fight with Careticus, and made him flee beyond the Severn into Wales. He then made an utter devastation of the country, set fire to the adjacent cities, and continued these outrages until he had almost burned up the whole surface of the island from the one sea to the other; so that the tillage was everywhere destroyed, and a general destruction made of the husbandmen and clergy, with fire and sword. This terrible calamity caused the rest to flee withersoever they had any hopes of safety.

Other early historical reports, such as those from the Venerable Bede, record that the North African abbot Hadrian was sent by the Pope to accompany the new Archbishop of Canterbury to England in 668 CE. Hadrian, it is reported, was initially asked to become archbishop himself, but refused the post. He later become the Abbot of St Peter and St Paul's in Canterbury. Bede described him as 'vir natione Afir', which has been translated as a 'man of African race'. His exact origins are, however, unknown and some historians suggest that he was a Berber from today's Libya. It is thought that Hadrian, who spoke both Latin and Greek as well as Old English, had a major influence on the structure of the Christian church in England, which he helped to reform, and on education and Anglo-Saxon literature. He has recently been referred to as 'the African who transformed Anglo-Saxon England'.[24] It is thought that he brought with him some important North African literary works, at a time when Christianity was more established there than it was in Britain, and introduced students to new ideas in various subjects from astronomy, medicine and law to history and philosophy. As a later writer put it, England's cultural roots come from four strands, the learning of Greece, Rome, as well as the Hebrew tradition, 'and the light that came out of Africa'.[25] Recent archaeological isotopic analysis of the human remains found at a seventh-century cemetery in Ely, at sites in Wales dated earlier than the seventh century, and at a burial site in Northumberland, dated from the seventh to ninth centuries, have also identified skeletons of men, women and children that may have a North African origin, suggesting that links between England and the African continent might have been more common than previously thought.[26]

Once again it is DNA analysis of skeletal remains which reveals that Africans were certainly living in Britain in the early medieval and medieval periods. In 2013, a skeleton found in a Gloucestershire river was identified as that of an African woman dating from between the late ninth to early eleventh centuries CE, that is, before the Norman conquest. At present, however, nothing more is known about how she arrived or her status. No doubt our knowledge will increase as more research is undertaken.[27] Another young African woman has been identified from a Saxon burial site at North Elmham, in Norfolk, dated around 1000 CE, but again nothing is definitely known of the circumstances that place her there.[28] Such evidence of the presence of African women in pre-medieval England has in the past been linked to slavery, or at least capture. Historians have suggested that this presence might be the result of Viking raids on North Africa, or Muslim Spain, which ancient annals in Irish and Arabic report brought African captives, 'blue men', to Ireland.[29] There now seems to be other corroborating evidence for these reports, although no evidence that Vikings brought enslaved Africans to England.[30] Others, in rather more racist tones, have suggested that the young woman at North Elmham originated in Ancient Ghana and was trafficked across the Sahara, but with even less evidence to support this speculation.[31] It might just as plausibly be argued that these African women came from Africa to Muslim Spain and from there to Britain, since there is evidence from coins, real and imitation, as well as other sources, that trade between England and the Muslim world existed long before the Norman conquest.[32]

In the late twelfth century a monk named Richard of Devizes produced his *Chronicon* or chronicle of the reign of Richard I. In one descriptive passage he refers to his dislike of the city of London because 'all sorts of men crowd together there from every country under the heavens'. These include 'Moors' or 'Garamantes', a term specifically referring to Africans, who are the only 'sorts of men' described by geographical origin.[33] What is particularly interesting about Richard of Devizes' description is that it suggests that 'Moors' were fairly numerous in London and quite commonplace. A few years after this description, in 1205, King John 'gave a mandate to the constable of Northampton to retain Peter the Saracen, the maker of crossbows, and another with him, for the king's service and allow him 9d a day'.[34] Saracen was a vague term, but one that was often used to describe Africans. It is not clear if this mandate refers to two 'Saracens' or two crossbow-makers, but it suggests that those of probable African heritage could provide useful skills. This reference is in stark contrast to the disparaging remarks of Richard of Devizes, who appears to regard Africans as a social nuisance and a blight on the city of London.

There is also the skeleton of 'Ipswich Man' found in the cemetery of Greyfriars monastery and buried between 1258–1300 CE. It seems likely that Ipswich Man was another North African, probably from Tunis, the capital of modern Tunisia. Historians think this is the case because the Greyfriars monastery was built by Robert Tiptoft, a colleague of Richard de Clare, and both men went on a crusade together in 1270. In the *Flores Historiarum*, a medieval history, it states de Clare brought 'four captive Saracens' with him to England from Tunis in 1272. It may be that Ipswich Man was one of those four captured during the Crusades, but he is just as likely to have been a free man and possibly even a friar by the time of his death.[35] It was during the thirteenth century that we find one of the earliest pictorial depictions of an African man in England. This occurs in the *Domesday*

Abbreviato, an abbreviated version of the famous Doomsday Book, the survey of the country demanded by William the Conqueror in 1085. One of the illustrations in the *Domesday Abbreviato* from about 1241, accompanying the capital letter for the entry for Derbyshire, shows a man of African descent, from his dress probably not someone of noble status. It is not known if he represented a living person, nor exactly why he is depicted. Perhaps his image suggests that Africans were not unknown to the artist or scribe responsible.

Evidence of Africans in England during this period has sometimes been connected with slavery but often without compelling evidence. One of the earliest records of an enslaved African is, however, from the thirteenth century. It is recorded in the Calendar of Patent Rolls of Henry III for 21 June 1259 that the king sitting at Windsor had issued a 'Mandate to all persons to arrest an Ethiopian of the name of Bartholemew, sometime a Saracen, slave (*servus*) of Roger de Lyntin, whom the said Roger brought with him to England, the said Ethiopian having run away from his said lord, who has sent an esquire of his to look for him: and they are to deliver him to the said esquire to the use of the said Roger.'[36] The fate of Bartholemew is unknown, but it is important to note that this early record of an enslaved African is also a report of an African engaged in the struggle for self-liberation. His act of resistance is one that would be adopted by many other enslaved Africans in Britain in later centuries.

More evidence has now been discovered about the diversity of England in the medieval period from an analysis of the remains of those in cemeteries associated with the Black Death in fourteenth-century Smithfield, London. From the analysis of forty-one sets of human remains, it seems likely that several may have been African, or had African ancestry, suggesting a very diverse population in fourteenth-century London, with perhaps almost 30 per cent of the population 'with non-White European ancestry'. Such results clearly suggest that in future and with more research we will have much more extensive knowledge of African populations in the British Isles before 1500.[37] Our knowledge about the diversity of the population in medieval England has been aided by new techniques in bioarchaeology and DNA analysis in recent years, but also by the fact that since the 1990s researchers have become more aware that Africans were present in the British Isles before 1500 and therefore have begun to research and record their presence. As two of the researchers explained in 2019:

> for the past 15 years, colleagues and visiting researchers to the Museum of London and Museum of London Archaeology have been anecdotally observing the presence of people with Black ancestry and dual heritage in the medieval cemetery populations from London. Writing today, we can see that by not formally recording their presence, we have significantly contributed to their 'official absence' and further served to marginalize them from mainstream knowledge and academic discourse.[38]

2

African Tudors and Stuarts

For many years, any discussion concerning the presence of Africans from the late fifteenth to early seventeenth centuries in England and Scotland began with the same question: when did the first enslaved Africans arrive? Some historians considered that for England this was in 1555, while others suggested a date slightly later in the century, when English trafficking of Africans was initiated by Hawkins, Drake and others.[1] These opinions were countered by those who advanced the argument that England's involvement in the transatlantic trafficking of enslaved Africans did not properly commence until the mid-seventeenth century, or by those who expressed the view that it began much earlier but had remained largely hidden from the gaze of historians.[2] As we will see in this chapter, it is misleading to connect the presence of Africans only with human trafficking in this period. Most historians now consider that the status of Africans in the British Isles was more likely to be one of relative liberty rather than enslavement. Nevertheless, it was undoubtedly a period when Europe's relationship with Africa and Africans was already undergoing a fundamental change and was becoming increasingly exploitative.

By 1500 the trafficking of Africans to Europe, and across the Atlantic to the newly discovered American continent, had already been initiated by the Portuguese government and developed by private licence holders in Portugal, Spain and elsewhere. By the late fifteenth century, it was also the case that Africans, with royal approval, had organized their own confraternities in several Spanish cities and were purchasing the freedom of other Africans.[3] Historians hold differing views with regard to how many Africans were enslaved and transported from Africa in this early period, but it was certainly several hundred per year and possibly as high as several thousand. Total Portuguese trafficking figures for the period from 1450 to 1520 are likely to be well over 150,000 individuals.[4]

Both Spain and Portugal had a longer history of contact with Africa and from the eighth century onwards some Africans had entered Iberia, not only as enslaved people but also as conquerors, part of the Moorish invasion and occupation of what became known as al-Andalus. Once called 'Africa's kingdom in Europe', al-Andalus at one time included all of modern Spain and Portugal, as well as parts of France.[5] Such was the power and splendour of these African Muslim rulers, that in the early thirteenth century England's King John was reported to have sent a delegation seeking an alliance with Caliph Muhammad an-Nāsir, even proposing his own conversion to Islam. The caliph contemptuously rejected such overtures.[6] In fact, the modern history of both Spain and Portugal, including their overseas expansion, was forged during their attempts to expel these Muslim occupiers. Historians estimate that Africans comprised at least 5 per cent of the total population of Portugal in the sixteenth century and at least 10 per cent of the population of its capital, Lisbon. Significant numbers of Africans also resided in Spain. In the period from 1445 to 1516, records suggest the arrival of more than 6,000 enslaved Africans into the Spanish port of Valencia and that Africans may have numbered 10 per cent of the total population of Seville.[7]

A few English merchants based in Spain in the late fifteenth century were human traffickers and owners of enslaved Africans based in that country and in some of its newly acquired colonies. However, there is no evidence at present that they extended their trafficking and ownership of enslaved Africans to England during that early period, although it is likely that at least a few Africans reached England from that source. It is also likely that the practice of keeping African domestic servants may have originated in Spain and Portugal before spreading to England. We know that some Africans arrived in England in the late fifteenth century, such as the 'Black man that was a taboryn', a drummer, said to be the victim of an assault in Southampton in 1491 or 1492.[8] Another example from Southampton is that of the young African woman, Maria Moriana, who arrived with her Italian employer from Venice some time before 1470. In that year, her employer 'hatched a base plot to have her sold' to another Italian in Southampton. The precise nature of Maria's status is unknown. What is known is that she spoke no English, or Latin, and it seems that this led her employer to try to exploit her and make her sign a document she could not read. Once she was made aware of her predicament, she spoke up to demand her rights, which were subsequently upheld by the authorities.[9] This case appears to show how difficult it was to establish the institution of slavery in England in the late fifteenth century. A century later, in 1587, there was a legal case in which the 'owner' of an enslaved African unsuccessfully asked the court to compel the enslaved African to serve him, or to force the trafficker to refund his money. The court was unable, or unwilling, to take either course.[10]

It seems likely that these early African arrivals in England came from Spain and Portugal, or, like Maria, from southern Europe.[11] Some were referred to as Moriscos, a term used in Spain for those Muslims forced to convert to Christianity, some of whom were expelled from Spain. It is probable that some of these Africans made their way to Tudor England.[12] However, exactly where Africans came from and exactly who brought them to Britain remain questions to be more fully answered. At present, what we know is something of the lives and circumstances of Africans living in England and Scotland during this period. It is certainly possible that some were brought as enslaved people but it appears that it was not a status that could be easily, nor legally, maintained.

By the late sixteenth century English involvement in the trafficking, or seizing, of Africans had increased, largely as a consequence of England's economic difficulties, its conflict with Spain and the enthusiasm for privateering, or plundering the goods of enemy merchants (which was organized with full government support). This was also the period of England's overseas expansion, following the principles of mercantilism, which sought the amassing of national monetary wealth based largely on the acquisition of gold and silver bullion, and also, in England's case, by the development of exports, particularly of woollen cloth. It led to English merchants seeking new overseas markets and necessitated the construction of a national navy.

Mercantilism also contributed to a growing rivalry with foreign competitors, such as Spain, and the looting of their shipping. Spanish ships often carried Africans on board and, as part of their looting, some Africans might have been re-kidnapped and transported back to England. In 1601, it was reported in the proclamation of the Privy Council that 'great numbers of Negroes and blackamoors . . . are carried into this realm of England since the troubles between her highness and the King of Spain'.[13] Some historians have argued that Africans brought to England in these circumstances were the victims of human trafficking, at least in Europe, and that these circumstances provide the context for the infamous Privy Council warrants of 1596 and 1601 that appear to demand the rounding up of Africans and their transportation abroad.[14] However, it is unlikely that the English were engaged in large-scale trafficking in this period, although they were making increasing efforts to do so. The numbers of enslaved Africans transported to the Americas by English traffickers before 1580 are estimated at about one thousand and, in the next sixty years, about 4,000. It is only after 1640 that the numbers rise dramatically.[15]

By the late sixteenth century England was also in direct contact with the African continent, including what is today's South Africa. Diplomatic and economic relations had been established between Elizabeth Tudor and Morocco and there was a Moroccan embassy in London. By 1600 English merchants and seafarers had also established links with some kingdoms in West Africa, where they began to develop a trade in ivory, pepper and gold. As early as 1558, the first year of Elizabeth Tudor's reign, the Guinea Company was granted a royal monopoly of trade with West Africa for ten years. Links with West Africa led to the ruler of at least one African state sending his son to England to be educated in the early sixteenth century and thus begin a tradition of wealthy Africans educating their children, and especially sons, in Britain, a tradition which has continued ever since. After 1531, English adventurers such as William Hawkins, his son John Hawkins, Thomas Wyndham, John Lok and others made numerous sailing voyages to Africa, some of them clandestinely, and it is evident that some Africans began to arrive in England as a result.[16] John Hawkins began his human-trafficking activities in 1562. Elizabeth Tudor is supposed to have warned him that 'if any Africans should be carried away without their free consent, it would be detestable, and call down the vengeance of Heaven upon the undertakers', but it is difficult to imagine she did not know the nature of his maritime activities.[17] Clearly the monarch had the capacity to investigate further before heavily investing in such activities. Elizabeth Tudor, like many monarchs who succeeded her, was engaged in the human trafficking of Africans.

In 1555, the English merchant John Lok returned with five African men from Sharma, a town in what is now Ghana in West Africa. It seems that the men were kidnapped but there is no evidence that they were transported as slaves.[18] One was the son of 'the captain' of the town and the others are reported as bringing gold with them. The names of three of these men are recorded as Anthonie, Binne and George, which perhaps suggests that two of them were baptized. Contemporary reports describe them as tall and strong men who 'coulde well agree with owr meates and drynkes' although 'the coulde and moyst ayer dooth sumwhat offende them'.[19] Three of the five returned to Africa after about one year in London, so it seems likely that they were taken as emissaries and to learn something of the ways and language of the English, so that they could facilitate further trading relations. One of the Africans is even reported to have married an English woman.[20]

Other Africans, such as Walter Annerby, the son of an important official in the West African kingdom of Dungala, were sent to England for similar purposes during this period, or simply to broaden their minds. Annerby was also baptized during his visit in London in 1610.[21] These tourists included 'two chief young Negroes ... sons to the chief justice of that country' brought to London in 1592.[22] In this instance the idea that the Africans had travelled of their own free will was questioned in the Admiralty Court. It was decided that the men had come 'by consent of their friends to see the country'.[23] Other Africans clearly were kidnapped, including the South African known as Coree, brought to England by the East India Company in 1613, but returned to his homeland the following year. In this case, it appears that Coree returned with an increased knowledge of English goods and trading practices that was somewhat to the detriment of the East India Company, established by royal charter in 1600 to expand England's trade east of the Cape of Good Hope.[24]

BLACK TUDORS

Thanks to the work of modern historians, we now have sufficient evidence to conclude that most Africans who lived in England and Scotland in the sixteenth century were not enslaved.[25] Historians have discovered records showing that there were well over 300 Africans living in Britain in the sixteenth and early seventeenth centuries, in large towns and cities such as London, Plymouth and Barnstable, but also in much smaller towns and villages such as Blean in Kent. Some may have been brought to the country in service, or in servile status, probably from Europe rather than directly from Africa, but the majority were in paid employment of various kinds. There were 'Black Tudors' in the households of Sir Walter Raleigh, Robert Dudley (Earl of Leicester), the Earl of Northumberland, and William Cecil (Lord Burghley). Africans were employed as gardeners, cooks, laundresses and other types of domestic servants in the homes of aristocrats and other wealthy individuals.[26] Sir Francis Drake was even accompanied by an African man named Diego on his famous voyage of circumnavigation.[27]

Others were independent craftsmen such as the silk weaver Reasonable Blackman and the African needle-maker who prudently maintained a monopoly of his craft, of whom we shall hear more later on. Most Africans appear to have been male, but some were women and there are also a few examples of African men and women marrying, such as the trumpeter Anthonie Vause and his wife Anne, whose burial in 1618 is recorded.[28] It was, however, more common for relationships to be established between Africans and English people, both inside and outside marriage. Such 'mixed' relationships are nothing new.[29] We also have evidence, especially during the sixteenth century, of Africans and those of African descent being born and raised in the British Isles, such as the 'baseborn blackamoore', christened at St Margaret's, Westminster, in 1595.[30] Reasonable Blackman, an African 'silk-weaver', an independent craftsman with a new and much sought-after skill, lived in London's Southwark with a wife and children. The records show both the baptism and deaths of three of his children, although the origin of his wife is unknown.[31] There is also evidence that some sixty Africans converted to Christianity.[32] Others may have lived in England for a considerable time, such as 'Anthony, a poore ould Negro aged 105', who died in Hackney, London, in 1630.[33]

Two of the recorded baptisms in the late sixteenth and early seventeenth centuries are of young women. There was Marye Fillis, described as 'a Blackamore', about twenty years of age, the daughter of an African basket-and-shovel-maker baptized in London in June 1597, who was probably from Spain and worked for a seamstress, and Julyane, 'a blackamore servant' who was twenty-two years old when she was baptized in 1601. The young women may have been encouraged to be baptized by employers, or others, as was the custom of the times in a devout society. Clearly there was no impediment to them doing so in the same manner as everyone else.

These as well as other records relating to London suggest that there were a significant number of female African residents, mothers, wives and daughters during this period.[34] At one time historians suggested that significant numbers of African women worked as prostitutes during this period but there seems to be very little evidence to substantiate this view. The only known prostitute was Anne Cobbie, described as a 'tawny Moor' working in a well-known brothel in London and noted for her 'soft skin'. She enters the historical records because of the court case brought against the owners of the brothel in 1625.[35] Other African women lived outside the main towns and cities and there are a few records of those who lived in rural Suffolk, Somerset and Gloucestershire. An African 'singlewoman' named Cattalena is recorded as living in Almondsbury, a village near Bristol, in the early seventeenth century. At the time of her death in 1625 her most valuable possession was a cow and, besides a few domestic items and clothes, she owned little else. However, her possessions were valued at over £6 (three months' wages for a skilled craftsman) and this, and the fact that they were recorded, show that she was self-supporting and independent, and recognized as such by the local authorities.[36]

The general view of Africans and Europeans appears to have been that slavery did not exist in England in this period. For example, Diogo, an African taken to England in 1614, later reported that when he set foot on English soil 'he immediately became free, because in that Reign nobody is a slave'.[37] Africans in Tudor England gave evidence in court and this is generally seen as a sign that they were not enslaved. In later centuries, enslaved Africans in Britain's North American and Caribbean colonies were prevented from testifying in legal matters. However, in Britain, even in the eighteenth century, when the status of African servants was more often contested, it was not uncommon for those brought to the country with an enslaved status to give evidence in court.[38] In a court case in 1587, in London, a Portuguese doctor even complained that he had bought an 'Ethiopian' from an English mariner but that the African 'utterly refused to tarry and serve' him. He asked the court to assist in the recovery of the cost of the transaction, which was refused, since the institution of slavery was not sanctioned in English law.[39] As long ago as 1490, English law and custom seems to have opposed the institution of slavery. In that year, an African known as Pedro Alvarez obtained his freedom from Henry VII. Alvarez had previously lived in Portugal, where he was described as a slave. Whatever his former status, he was not only free in England but was able to maintain his new liberated status which was recognized when he returned to Portugal.[40]

AFRICANS AT COURT

The best known of those Africans living and working in England in the Tudor period is the 'blacke trumpet', as he was called, a trumpeter at court who we now know as John Blanke. It is generally assumed that the name was something of an 'ironic jest', the irony being that *blanc* in French means white. Whatever the case, Blanke is twice pictured on a horse in the Westminster Tournament Roll of 1511, which illustrated a royal procession and was created to celebrate the birth of a son to Catherine of Aragon and Henry VIII. His is the first illustration of an identifiable African for many centuries and he has therefore become widely celebrated.[41] Blanke is shown wearing a turban, and again historians have speculated as to the reason for this headgear; some suggesting that it was to cover his African hair, others that it relates to his religious beliefs, or was simply the fashion.[42] There is similar speculation that Blanke may have accompanied Catherine of Aragon to England as part of her entourage in 1501, but there is no evidence to support this view. What we do know is that he was the first recorded African wage earner in Britain, paid 8d a day (the wage of a skilled craftsman) by Henry VII in late 1507 and that he continued to receive regular payments throughout 1508. He therefore occupied something of a privileged position, since he enjoyed not only a regular wage, but also board and lodging and a clothing allowance and was paid at a rate that was significantly greater than most servants or workers. In 1509, when Henry VII died, John Blanke continued to be employed at court. The records show that he attended both the funeral of the late king and the coronation of Henry VIII and was given appropriate livery for both occasions. It is also recorded that John Blanke petitioned the new king for higher wages, in fact for a doubling of wages, a request that proved successful and perhaps tells us something about his status. We know little more about his life. The last report we have indicates that he married in 1512 and was presented with a wedding gown by the king.[43]

It seems likely that John Blanke entered England from Spain, where many Africans were to be found both as a result of the North African occupation of Spain, which had recently been brought to an end, and the beginnings of Spain's involvement in the transatlantic trafficking of Africans that commenced in the mid-fifteenth century. One of Catherine of Aragon's retinue was an African woman from Motril, in the kingdom of Granada, called Catalina, who acted in the important position of 'lady of the bed-chamber', and came to England with Catherine in 1501. Indeed, it seems quite possible that several of Catherine's retinue were African women. According to an eyewitness account by Sir Thomas More, 'except for three or four of them, they were not much to look at: hunchbacked, undersized, barefoot pygmy Ethiopians'.[44] Historians have been reluctant to accept that this account provides evidence of African ladies-in-waiting. Catalina is known to have been of Moorish origin and so it is quite possible that Thomas More was reporting exactly what he had seen in a derogatory way, four young African women, perhaps wearing sandals. Catalina assumed much more importance when she was sought as an expert witness many years later to testify that Catherine of Aragon had entered her marriage as a virgin. This was at the time when Henry VIII was attempting to dissolve his marriage, and when Catalina had already returned and spent many years in Spain as the wife of a Moorish crossbow-maker named Oviedo.[45]

Some historians consider that Catalina had been an enslaved woman when she entered Britain, although the evidence is far from conclusive. It is even possible that she was of noble birth but had a servile status imposed upon her resulting from the conquest of Muslim Granada by Christian Spain in 1492. What *is* clear is that such enslavement was not a status that had any legal sanction in England at the time, although slavery did exist in Spain and Portugal. Even a century later this seems to have been the case, as the Portuguese doctor mentioned above lamented the fact that he 'hath not an ordinarye remedie at and by the course of the common Lawes' and could not compel the 'Ethiopian' to serve as his slave.[46] Historians have concluded from this incident that there was an absence of a specific law on slavery in England; that even if Africans were brought to the country as slaves from abroad, it might have been difficult for their owners to maintain that servile status.

Although some records describe Africans as 'belonging' to their masters, this might not denote enslavement. It seems likely that slave status only affected a very small number of people and the evidence points towards an African population that was overwhelmingly free. During the Tudor period, England had no overseas colonies reliant on slave labour and was for most of the century unable to compete with Spain's and Portugal's domination of the lucrative trafficking of Africans across the Atlantic. The royal tradition of employing Africans at court may have continued with Katherine's daughter Mary Tudor and her half-sister, Elizabeth. Mary Tudor employed an African known as Fraunces Negro in the royal stables. Elizabeth Tudor kept a 'little black a More', an African child, at her court, since records show that during the 1570s she ordered two suits of clothes to be specially made for him by the royal tailors.[47]

AFRICANS IN SCOTLAND

Africans were also popular at the Scottish court of James IV. He directly employed seven African men and women, who included drummers and dancers, although royal accounts mention African children in Edinburgh, Dunfermline and elsewhere as well. Peter the More, or Moryen, and Margaret and Elen More were part of the retinue of Margaret Stewart, James IV's daughter.[48] These Africans may have been seized from the Portuguese by Scottish privateers. According to one report, attacks on Portuguese ships returning from Africa led to the 'unwonted appearance of blackamoors at the Scottish court, and sable empresses presiding over the royal tournaments'.[49] Or perhaps these 'blackamoors' made their way to Scotland by other means. What is significant is that whatever their former status was they were now paid employees or retainers and, it seems, highly regarded.

Peter the More not only received regular wages but also had his travel costs, clothes and lodgings paid by the crown. He was given permission by the king to travel freely throughout the kingdom and even to France, where his expenses were paid.[50] Similar payments are recorded for 'the More lassis', both for travel and servants, and even for a baptism ceremony for one of the young women in 1504. It is evident that some of the Africans at court were children and the king even made payment for a nurse for an African baby. In 1507, the king made financial provision on several occasions for his 'More taubronar' (African drummer), as well as his wife and child. The drummer had clothing, transport and other expenses paid on his behalf, including medical care.[51] In 1508 the king also made living expenses available for two African friars.[52]

Moreover, Africans at the Scottish court were part of significant ceremonies. In 1507 and 1508, the Scottish king himself took part in jousting tournaments for the favour of the 'Black Queen of Beauty', who it is thought was one of the African women at court. The tournaments were accompanied by sumptuous banquets lasting three days at the court at Holyrood House, during which the 'black lady' was also the centre of attention. The position of Africans at the Scottish court, which seems to have been one of respect, to judge from the financial records, has been thrown in doubt by the existence of William Dunbar's poem 'Ane Blak Moir', which appears to be openly racist, since it makes derogatory remarks about the physical appearance of an African woman, and suggests that she was the victim of sexual assaults. But the evidence shows that even in this instance the

African woman was dressed expensively and had two female attendants.[53] The accounts record that she 'was arrayed in a gown of damask flowered with gold, trimmed with green and yellow taffety; she had sleeves and gloves of black "semys" leather, and the sleeves were themselves covered with "pleasance," of which material she also had a kerchief about her arm ... She road in state in a "chair triumphal" covered with Flemish taffety, one hundred and sixty ells of this stuff – white, yellow, purple, green and gray [sic] having been purchased in Flanders at a costs of £88.'[54] Whatever the exact circumstances, the financial records and the poem are yet further evidence of the significant presence of African women at the Scottish court. Records of payments to similarly highly regarded Africans at the Scottish court were made throughout the sixteenth century.[55]

STUDENTS AND WORKERS

On New Year's Day 1611, Prince Dederi Jaquoah was baptized as John Jaquoah at St Mildred's Poultry in east London. Jaquoah was the son of a minor king in today's Liberia, and was about twenty years old at the time. He had journeyed to England on the return voyage of John Davies, a London merchant and haberdasher, the previous year. Jaquoah had been sent by his father King Caddi-biah to be baptized and remained in London for two years. He lived with Davies and his wife and evidently made an impact in London. One scholar has even suggested that Shakespeare was inspired by his father's name to name one of his characters Caliban, in *The Tempest*, first performed at the end of 1611.[56]

It is quite likely that between Dederi's father and Davies there was the expectation that he would be educated during his stay in London and would act as a useful intermediary in the growing trade relations between West Africa and Britain. Such trade may have included pepper, ivory and gold, but it may also have included human trafficking.[57] In this fashion began a tradition for West African notables to send at least one of their children overseas to learn the ways of their trading partners. Why Dederi, the 'king's son from Guinea' and his father, should desire to become Christian, can only be a matter of speculation.[58] It was not unusual for African rulers in contact with Europeans to adopt the names, religion and even dress of their partners, perhaps as a form of diplomacy.

The hundreds of Africans residing in England in the sixteenth century were employed in a variety of occupations. Perhaps the most important of these African workers was the unnamed African living in Cheapside, London in the mid-sixteenth century. He was reported to have been a craftsman 'making fine Spanish needles . . . but would never teach his art to any'. This African craftsman is thought to have introduced the art of making fine steel needles in England.[59] African workers also include Jacques Francis, who was a head diver, employed as part of a team of Africans divers to salvage the wreck of Henry VIII's flagship, *Mary Rose*. He became one of the first Africans to give evidence in court and his testimony has been preserved in the records of the Admiralty High Court. We can conclude from his court appearance as a witness and from other records that Francis was a free man, although there were efforts by the prosecution to cast doubt on the right of an African to testify. There were allegations that he was a 'morisco', a Spanish term sometimes used to describe a Muslim convert to Christianity, an infidel and 'commonly reputed' to be a slave. The High Court appears to have accepted that Francis, who was born on an island off the coast of Mauritania, was a man able to freely present evidence, a wage earner, not one bound to a master.[60]

Francis was based in Southampton and was about eighteen when he was first employed as a diver by a Venetian salvager living in that city. We do not know how he arrived in England, although it is likely that he came via Spain, Italy or Portugal, which had the largest African populations in Europe at the time. When he gave evidence in court on behalf of his employer in February 1548, he required an interpreter, but it is not known what language he spoke. Of his diving ability, there is no doubt. He had aquatic skills that most people in England did not possess and probably led the team of divers.

Several other Africans were employed as sailors during the Elizabethan period and probably before then too, as we have seen that at least one of Drake's crew, who was perhaps also his navigator, interpreter and oral historian, was Diego, an African. He served with Drake during his circumnavigation voyage and after, until his death in

1579.[61] The rapid expansion of the royal navy and privateering, as well as closer links with Africa and the Americas, led to an increase in the employment of African mariners, some of whom were also pirates. Some Africans may have been captured on board Spanish ships raided by the English. In the early seventeenth century, African sailors such as John Anthony and John Phillip both served with Sir Henry Mainwaring, a former pirate. Anthony, who was for some years based in Dover, has entered the historical records because in 1619 he successfully petitioned for the payment of outstanding wages, a clear sign of his status.[62]

Another of the Africans living in England in the late sixteenth and early seventeenth centuries was Henrie Anthonie Jetto (c.1596–1627). Nothing is known of his parentage but he was described as a 'Blackamore'. He was initially employed as a gardener but, by the time he wrote his will in 1626, one of the first Africans to do so, he had the status of a man of property, was a yeoman of Worcestershire, and a married man with several children. As a yeoman, Jetto would have been a landowner who had voting rights and perhaps other political rights and responsibilities too.[63]

THE STATUS OF
AFRICANS IN ENGLAND

Towards the end of the reign of Elizabeth Tudor, the Privy Council issued three documents relating to the standing of Africans in England. In July 1596, the Privy Council drafted an 'open letter' to the mayor and aldermen of London and to all other mayors and sheriffs claiming that Elizabeth Tudor's understanding was that 'there are of late divers Blackmoores brought into the Realme, of which kinde of persons there are all ready here to manie'. The queen apparently believed that population increase and 'to manie' Blackmooores led to unemployment and therefore 'that those kinde of people should be sent forth of the land'. The letter concludes by giving authority to a certain Edward Banes to transport out of England only 'those Blackmoores that in this last voyage under Sir Thomas Baskerville were brought into this Realme to the number of Tenn'. Although the 'open letter' is signed by the queen, there is no evidence that its demands were implemented. Its main historical importance is that it suggests that 'divers Blackmoores' were being brought into England, most likely as a result of England's wars with Spain and the activities of Baskerville and his associates, and the fact that some considered that there were 'to manie' of 'those kinde of people'.[64]

A few days after the first letter, there was a second, this time an 'open warrant' addressed to the Lord Mayor of London, along with 'all other vyce admeralles', mayors and public officers. This warrant, issued by the Privy Council, empowered a merchant from Lubeck, Caspar Van Senden, to 'take up so many Blackamoores here in this Realme and to transport them into Spaine and Portugall'. The aim of Van Senden appears to have been either to sell African residents abroad to defray the costs he had incurred liberating English prisoners-of-war, or to exchange them for these prisoners. But the 'open warrant' had added the stipulation that Africans residing in England could only be taken 'with consent of their masters', in other words with the agreement of their employers. Since most were trusted servants and retainers, often with scarce skills, this agreement was never likely to be given. Van Senden later reported that he had travelled throughout the kingdom on a doomed mission since 'the masters of them, perceiving by the said warrant that your orator could not take the Blackamoores without the master's good will, would not suffer your orator to have any one of them'.[65]

This royal edict, too, was doomed to failure. Rather than necessarily expressing the views of Elizabeth Tudor, the 'open warrant' shows something of the machinations of Van Senden and those in the Privy Council.[66] Once again its main significance is to demonstrate the presence of significant numbers of Africans in Britain and that their employers would not part with them. This letter too presents the view that the large numbers of Africans in England may be preventing other Christian subjects from finding employment and encourages employers to favour 'their own countrymen' rather than 'those kynde of people', in other words, Africans. However, the evidence shows that they did not and no Africans were transported by Van Senden.

A few years later, in 1601, there was a further draft of a royal proclamation expressing the view that Queen Elizabeth was 'highly discontented to understand the great numbers of Negroes and black-moores which (as she is informed) are carried into this realm since the troubles between her highness and the King of Spain; who are fostered and powered here to the great annoyance of her own liege people'. Again, the queen commanded Van Senden to transport the Africans, especially because they were 'infidels', out of her realm. This proclamation added that if anyone had 'possession' of these Africans and refused to deliver them to Van Senden their names should be given to the Queen so that she 'may take further course therein as it shall seem best in her princely wisdom'.[67]

This proclamation is a draft. It was no more successfully implemented than previous documents drafted by the Privy Council and appears to be a rather feeble response to petitions by Van Senden's dubious patrons there. It contains several interesting references, specifically to the period of the Anglo-Spanish War (1585–1604) and has a particular concern with non-Christians, who were apparently consuming 'the relief' provided for the Queen's subjects. There were clearly those who had such views but there is no evidence that Elizabeth Tudor held them. Most importantly, they were not implemented and, as is evident from the Privy Council's open letter of 1596, could not be.

It used to be thought that these documents and proclamations were official efforts to expel Africans from England. Historians have presented differing views as to how they should be interpreted.[68] The view that they refer to mass expulsions and state racism is now under scrutiny, but some historians have claimed that they may have indicated that human trafficking between England and Europe existed in this period.[69] However, there were no anti-African laws in Elizabethan England. The evidence suggest that Africans were treated in much the same way as all others living in England, who were not subject to feudal dues.[70]

In recent years, historians have been much less concerned with establishing an African presence in Britain in this period and rather more with discussing the status of those Africans who were present. If Africans were not slaves, what was their status and how were they viewed by their Elizabethan and Jacobean contemporaries? One view has been that Africans were perceived as unusual, exotic strangers, mainly of servile status, who in the records are often simply referred to by their first names, often not baptized, as their neighbours generally would have been, and clearly labelled as Blackamores, a word that seems to have first appeared in 1547, or by other similar distinctive terms.[71] This view is associated with the idea that what we would now call racism was already well established during the Reformation as exemplified in such notions as the divine 'curse of Ham' (to explain the skin colour of Africans, as presented in the writings of the Elizabethan adventurer George Best).[72] Best refers to the fact that Africans lived in Britain and reports that he has personally seen an 'Ethiopian as blacke as cole brought into England, who taking a faire English woman to wife, begat a sonne in all respects as blacke as the father was, although England were his native country and an English woman his mother'. He considered this a matter for some further investigation.[73]

Some of the interest in the presence of Africans in Tudor and Stuart England has arisen from the fact that African characters appear in the drama and writing of the time. Shakespeare's *Othello* is the most famous example, but there are others, both in his plays and the writing of his contemporaries, Thomas Kyd, Christopher Marlowe and Ben Jonson. There has also long been speculation about the identity of the 'dark lady' who is lovingly described and addressed in several of Shakespeare's sonnets. Some historians have suggested that this woman may have been someone called Lucy Negro, also known as Black Luce, a brothel keeper from Clerkenwell, London. However, it not certain that the women described in Shakespeare's sonnet was African, or of African heritage. In Sonnet 130 she is described with the lines 'If snow be white, why then her breasts are dun; if hairs be wires, black wires grow on her head', hardly a conclusive description. Moreover, Lucy Negro is never described in any of the records as a Blackamoore, or even as a Negro, so there is no conclusive evidence from those sources either.[74]

WHAT'S IN A NAME?

Some historians have argued that even the names used to describe Africans contain a hidden negativity, a 'racialization process because it essentializes a physical attribute'.[75] However, more recently such views have been brought into question by the possibility that Africans were perceived as a normal part of Elizabethan and Jacobean society. They worked in a variety of occupations, lived in towns and villages throughout England and Scotland and intermarried, or had sexual relations, with their British contemporaries. They were subject to no special laws and had a very similar status to their neighbours.[76]

Africans who lived in England and Scotland during Tudor and Stuart times were known by several descriptive terms. Blackamoore, spelt in various ways, is perhaps the most common, but other terms such as Negro, Moor, Black, Aethiopian, Morisco, were also employed and in some cases may even have been suggested, or used, by Africans to describe themselves.[77] Historians now consider that these terms were applied to Africans without any particular derogatory connotations. Certainly, people in Europe were interested in the fact that Africans had a different skin colour to their own, that this colour was transferred to children even when they did not live in a tropical climate and might even be transferred to children born of European women. However, in this period modern notions of racism had not yet been developed, especially in England. An African might sometimes be described as 'a stranger', indicating that they were foreign-born, but in other respects Africans appear to have been generally treated as other residents and subjects of the monarch.

As England's and Europe's relationship with Africa and Africans became increasingly exploitative, so too the status of Africans, and the way that they were referred to, underwent a significant change. The history of Africans in the British Isles is therefore an important one, not only in its own right but also because it may help us more fully to understand the source and nature of modern racism. That racism developed as a consequence of the human trafficking of Africans that began in England with Hawkins' first voyage of 1562 and the transportation of hundreds of enslaved Africans from their homeland to the Caribbean.

3

That Infamous Traffic

In the early seventeenth century England's global expansion entered a new phase with the acquisition of overseas colonies. In 1609, English adventurers occupied Bermuda in the Caribbean and, soon afterwards, Virginia and Massachusetts in North America. In 1625 Barbados was seized and by 1632 England had also occupied the Caribbean islands of Antigua, Nevis and Montserrat. The seizure of such important overseas possessions necessarily demanded a supply of labour so that they might be fully exploited. By 1619 English settlers began importing enslaved Africans into the newly acquired North American colonies, and then to England's Caribbean possessions. England's human traffickers also began consolidating their position in West Africa, so as to more effectively enslave members of the local population.

The English mariner Richard Jobson declared in 1620 that the English were a people 'who did not deale' in slaves, 'neither did wee buy or sell one another, or any that had our own shapes (sic)', but he expressed an increasingly old-fashioned and erroneous view.[1] England certainly did deal in enslaved Africans, but, when possible, would also send indentured labourers, convicts, political prisoners and other undesirables from the British Isles, especially from Ireland, to colonies in the Caribbean and elsewhere. This led to the seventeenth-century expression to 'barbadoes' a person. As early as 1617 a Puritan writer noted that what he referred to as 'slavish' servants were 'perpetually put under the power of the master as blackamores are with us'.[2] This supply of labour from the British Isles was, however, insufficient to meet the demands of what soon became large-scale crop production in an increasingly capital-centred economy.[3] As early as 1642 the English cleric and writer Henry Fuller presented the following amongst the characteristics of a 'good sea-captain', suggesting that the kidnapping of Africans was already commonplace:

> In taking a prize, he most prizeth the man's lives whom he takes, – Though some of them may chance to be Negroes or savages. It is the custom of some to cast them overboard, and there is an end of them: for the dumb fishes will tell no tales. But the murder is not so soon drowned as the men. What, is a brother by false blood no kin? A savage hath God to his Father by creation, though not the church to his mother; and God will revenge his innocent blood. But our captain counts the image of God, nevertheless, his image cut in ebony as if done in ivory; and in the blackest Moors he sees the representation of the King of heaven.[4]

Enslaved African labour was evidently more plentiful and more profitable than European labour. Nevertheless, as Eric Williams, the famous Caribbean historian on the subject, concluded, 'white servitude was the historic base upon which Negro slavery was constructed'.[5]

Following the introduction of sugar production in the newly acquired colonies, especially those in the Caribbean, the demand for enslaved African labour soared and soon became the major preoccupation of the English abroad. This was particularly the case in 1655 when England, under Cromwell's leadership, seized Jamaica from Spain. Several state monopolies were then established to conduct the trafficking of Africans to the new colonies, the best known being the Company of Royal Adventurers Trading in Africa, established after the restoration of the monarchy in 1663, and the Royal Africa Company established in 1672. It seems likely that in the period before 1662 England's human traffickers had already transported at least 100,000 Africans away from their homeland. In the ten years following that date at least 10,000 more Africans each year suffered the same fate.[6] The wealth that flowed from this great crime and the 'Africa trade' led to the creation of a new coin, the golden 'guinea', first minted in 1663 with African gold and afterwards stamped with the elephant and castle, the crest of the Royal Africa Company.

The Stuarts retained the same interest in human trafficking as their predecessors. The Duke of York, the brother of the monarch, became the first president of the Company of Royal Adventurers Trading in Africa (the royal monopoly established for the trafficking of Africans in 1660), while Charles Stuart and many of those close to the royal family were its main investors. So too were many others, including the diarist Samuel Pepys and the philosopher John Locke.[7] When the Royal Africa Company was formed, the Duke of York became its first governor and no less than fifteen lord mayors of London were amongst its early shareholders, as was Locke, who was yet to embrace his later defence of 'original liberty'.[8] In 1677 'several members' of the Royal Africa Company asked for a legal opinion as to whether human trafficking was in keeping with the Navigation Acts, mercantilist laws which required all trade to be carried out in British ships. The Solicitor-General reassured them that 'Negroes ought to be esteemed goods and commodities within the Acts of Trade and Navigation', thus dehumanizing Africans in the process.[9]

The new business of Great Britain, formed by the Act of Union in 1707, was human trafficking, and it provided the backdrop for the most popular novel of the period, Daniel Defoe's *Robinson Crusoe* (1719), as well as the main source of the hero's eventual wealth. Great Britain's emergence into the world was inextricably linked to its role as a major human trafficker and slaving power. The creation of the Bank of England and the National Debt, in 1694, were the necessary means for raising the finance for carrying out the trade and colonial wars of the later seventeenth and early eighteenth centuries, waged mainly against France. By 1713 these wars led to the famous Treaty of Utrecht, by which Britain secured Gibraltar from Spain, but even more importantly secured the *asiento* to supply Spain's American colonies with enslaved Africans. Queen Anne even boasted of the fact that 'I have insisted and obtained that the asiento or contract to supply the Spanish West Indies with Negroes shall be made with us for thirty years.'[10] The government promptly sold the rights for £7.5 million to the South Sea Company, an early and ultimately unsuccessful rival to the Bank of England, whose first governor was also employed as the Chancellor of the Exchequer.[11]

Between 1721 and 1730 British ships carried some 181,000 enslaved African men, women and children to the American continent. From 1701 to 1807 it is estimated that British ships transported

2.5 million enslaved Africans to the Americas, which means the traffickers were responsible for the deaths of millions more than that number, including those lost at sea and those killed in the course of violent kidnapping in Africa.[12] Britain dominated human trafficking in the eighteenth century and was responsible for a third of all African men, women and children forcibly transported across the Atlantic. By the end of that century, British ships not only supplied enslaved Africans to Britain's colonies in the Caribbean and North America, but also to the Spanish and Portuguese colonies and even to those of its major rival, France.

The slave system therefore cannot be separated from every aspect of Britain's economy and society in the eighteenth century. It is sometimes referred to as the 'triangular trade', denoting the three separate voyages from Britain to Africa, across the Atlantic from Africa to the Americas, and then the final side of the triangle from the American continent back to Britain. Each side of the triangle could produce a profit for those who had invested in this great crime against humanity. The 'trade' supplied the luxury items that defined the age – sugar, tobacco and coffee. This created the conditions for the emergence of the coffee houses where global trade was conducted and on occasion enslaved Africans were publicly sold. Lloyds of London began as a coffee house and was involved in insuring slave ships and their cargo, as well as Caribbean plantations. It was also advertised as a location in London where absconding enslaved Africans might be returned to those who claimed to be their owners.[13]

Profits from the 'trade' fuelled the development of banking, as well as insurance, since credit was vital for the expansion of all forms of human trafficking and related industries. The Bank of England and its first directors were all involved in financing and profiting from human trafficking, therefore establishing the financial system which enabled it and Britain's empire to expand. The financiers of human trafficking were also based in Liverpool, which emerged as the greatest port in the world for this crime in the eighteenth century, and established the Heywood Bank in 1773 (later part of Barclays Bank) to advance their interests. Barclays Bank dates from 1736, started by members of the same family, many of whom were connected with slavery, not just through banking, but also trafficking and the ownership of plantations.[14] Most modern banks can trace their history to this period and the financing of slavery and human trafficking.

The 'trade' produced great wealth, both from human trafficking itself, the plantation system and the slave production of luxury items, as well as the production in Britain of all the means to continue the slave system, for example, ships, guns, and all the other goods to be exchanged for human beings. Human trafficking usually realized almost 10 per cent in annual profits despite widespread rebellions and resistance from enslaved Africans. It inevitably produced a 'state of war' between the enslaved and enslavers, as Equiano later called it, and in the Caribbean a '200 Years' War' of liberation.[15] The maritime nature of human trafficking created the possibility for the expansion of shipbuilding and related industries, not least the development of the textile industry, but also the production of manacles and other instruments of torture, as well as the production of firearms. Then there was the production of all those items used to exchange for human captives, from alcohol to iron bars. As Eric Williams explained, 'it was finance from the West Indian trade that financed James Watt and the steam engine.'[16] More recent research has established that James Watt and other members of his immediate family were directly engaged in human trafficking and slavery, and in 1762 even imported to Britain a young enslaved boy, known as Frederick, who soon liberated himself from enslavement. Although James Watt later condemned slavery, his family's business interests continued to profit from it even in the nineteenth century.[17]

The Watt family's connection with human trafficking and slavery is hardly surprising, as there was little in eighteenth-century Britain that was untouched by it. The Church of England had numerous connections with the slave system, most notably through the Society for the Propagation of the Gospel in Foreign Parts, which owned the Codrington plantations in Barbados and some 300 enslaved African men, women and children. The governing body of the 'Society', which branded this word onto the bodies of enslaved Africans with a red-hot iron, was headed by the Archbishop of Canterbury. In 1760 he complained to one of his colleagues, 'I have long wondered and lamented that the Negroes in our plantation decrease & new supplies become necessary continually. Surely this proceeds from some Defect, both of Humanity, and even of good policy. But we must take things as they are at present.'[18] Many of Britain's stately homes and country houses were directly financed from the profits that accrued from this great crime, a fact that is increasingly being recognized by such bodies as the National Trust and Historic England.[19] One of the most notable is Harewood House in Yorkshire, one of the 'treasure houses of England' built between 1759 and 1771 for the Lascelles family who made their fortune from enslaved Africans in the Caribbean. Some infamous human traffickers, such as Bristol's Edward Colston, a leading figure in the Royal Africa Company, even became noted for their philanthropy.[20] Others, such as Thomas Guy, the founder of Guy's Hospital, were major investors in the South Sea Company and made fortunes from its involvement in human trafficking, or found themselves bankrupt when it collapsed. In 1720 over 500 members of both Houses of Parliament were shareholders in the South Sea Company, so too the royal family, Kings College, Cambridge, and the poet Alexander Pope.[21]

London was the first port to grow rich from human trafficking, for many years enjoying a monopoly position. In the mid-eighteenth century its dominance was challenged by Bristol and then by Liverpool, which began regular trafficking voyages in the early eighteenth century. Indeed, both Liverpool and Bristol were champions of 'free trade', successfully arguing that they too should participate in human trafficking.[22] By the 1740s Liverpool surpassed both of its rivals and by 1795 slave ships from Liverpool constituted the majority of such ships sailing from Britain and over half of all of Europe's slave ships.[23] Liverpool became the world's most important slaving port, with one in five enslaved Africans transported across the Atlantic in its vessels, although it cannot be forgotten that other British ports were also involved, including Whitehaven, Lancaster, Chester, Preston and Glasgow.[24]

It is estimated that in the eighteenth century the port of Liverpool employed more than 3,000 shipwrights, alongside many other ancillary producers of ropes, guns and other provisions. The triangular trade based in Liverpool also provided employment for the emerging industries of Lancashire and Yorkshire, the producers of textiles, brass, metalware, alcohol and other commodities. Human trafficking accounted for some 40 per cent of Liverpool's trade and employed one in eight of its population.[25] Africans were even incorporated into

Liverpool's architecture. African heads adorned the Customs House, built in 1740, and the town hall, constructed during the 1750s.[26]

According to the eighteenth-century English economist Malachy Postlethwayte, one of the main defenders of human trafficking, 'the Negroe-Trade and the natural Consequences resulting from it, may be justly esteemed an inexhaustible Fund of Wealth and Naval Power to this Nation'.[27] Karl Marx, a nineteenth-century economist, explained the connection between slavery and the industrial revolution, 'Without slavery you have no cotton; without cotton you have no modern industry. It is slavery that gave the colonies their value; it is the colonies that created world trade, and it is world trade that is the pre-condition of large-scale industry.'[28]

AFRICANS IN THE BRITISH ISLES

It was this growing involvement in human trafficking abroad that had a significant impact on the numbers and status of Africans in England, since some of those trafficked across the Atlantic were subsequently brought to the British Isles. In 1651, the investors in the London-based Guinea Company instructed one ship's captain – 'We pray you buy fifteen or twenty lusty negers of about 15 years of age, bring them home with you to London.'[29] The gradual change in the numbers and status of Africans in England may also have had some impact on how their presence was reported. In April 1645, during the English Civil War, the *Moderate Intelligencer*, a contemporary publication, complained about some of those who gathered in 'Lincolne's Inn-fields not far from the Portugall Ambassadours house'. There, it was said,

> gathers many hundreds of men, women, maids and boys together, then comes Negars, and other of like ranks, these make sport with our English women and maids . . . why these black men should use our English maids and women upon the Lords day, or any other in that manner, we know no reason for: but the truth is the fault is wholly in those loose people that come there, and in the Officers of those Parishes where it is done.[30]

The report is an intriguing one, suggesting that a critical mass of 'black men' were now present in London and behaving in an unseemly manner, but blaming others for their alleged behaviour. What is perhaps even more interesting is that 'these black men' are not regarded or described as being of servile status and are clearly popular with the 'English women and maids'. The relations between African men and English women were a subject frequently commented upon in later centuries.

However, it is also clear that African women were in England too, such as the 'Blackymore mayde named Francis', a servant in Bristol. It was reported to be 'somewhat rare in our dayes and Nation to have an Ethyopian or Blackmore to be truly convinced of sin'. Francis, however, was evidently a devout Christian, for much of her life, a 'Memmorable member' of a Bristol Baptist church in the mid-seventeenth century who made much of her faith when she was about to die. Another African woman connected with the radical Baptists during the 1640s, a period of great revolutionary change in England, was 'Dinah the Black', a servant probably living in London. Dinah was also described as a 'Blakmor', and is mentioned in the memoir of Sarah Wight, a Baptist visionary of that time. Dinah appears to have been ill, both physically and mentally; she might have had difficulty reconciling Christianity with her African identity and might even have been contemplating suicide.[31] Such accounts suggest that African women and men were fully part of the religious, political and personal turmoil so typical of that revolutionary period, when the 'world might be permanently turned upside down'.[32]

The status of some African men at the time is demonstrated by the case of Martin Francis, 'a blackamoore', who took three young women to court in 1658 for attempting to defraud him of £17 – a considerable sum – by their false promises of marriage to him by one of them. Although the result of the case is unknown, it is an interesting instance of a relatively wealthy African seeking to use the law to defend his interests.[33] Perhaps Francis was a seafarer, as was John Anthony, a Dover-based mariner and former pirate. Anthony had sailed with the infamous pirate Henry Mainwaring and probably arrived in Dover in 1615, at a time when James I had ordered that further piratical activities should cease. A year later the king pardoned Mainwaring and his crew and the former was later knighted. We know that Anthony was still living in Dover in 1619, when he was one of the crew of the *Silver Falcon* owned by Lord Zouche, warden of the Cinque Ports and a member of Privy Council. In March 1619, Anthony had not been paid for his services and became 'indebted for his diet, lodging and washing'. He therefore petitioned Zouche and the Privy Council, 'for payment of £30 wages due to him for services onboard the ship Silver Falcon, which the mayor of Dover is ordered not to pay without warrant'. In a second petition, it was suggested 'that the money may either be paid to himself or to Sir Henry Mainwaring, his present master'. Anthony was eventually paid only 17s 6d, although apparently with 'half a year's interest'. He was one of several African seamen who were wage-earners during this period.[34]

The status of these relatively wealthy and evidently free Africans might be contrasted with that of 'a Negro boy' who was reported 'lost' in the pages of a London publication in 1659. In this instance a reward was offered for his safe return. However, what may be inferred is that the unnamed child had absconded, perhaps providing an indication of his status.[35] In this period the kidnapping of children from Africa to be used as 'pets' became fashionable. Samuel Pepys, the diarist, records how in 1662 the Earl of Sandwich returned from a trip abroad with presents for his daughters including 'a little Turke and a Negro', while a ship arriving from West Africa in 1667 carried an official, formerly based in that region, who 'brought with him a great many small blacks'.[36] Indeed Pepys records several encounters with Africans, both alive and dead, during this period. In the latter category, he mentions one associate's continued possession of 'a black boy that he had that had died of consumption; and being dead he caused him to be dried in an oven, and lies there entire in a box'.[37] It seems that Pepys was also attracted to an African woman, whom he describes as a 'comely black mayde', and that he employed at least one African woman servant.[38]

SLAVERY AND FREEDOM

What conclusions can be drawn about the status of Africans in England in the second half of the seventeenth century? Habib reports that in 1662, for the first time, an African in England, one Emanuell Feinade, is recorded with the unambiguous status of 'slave'.[39] Africans were initially being brought into Britain by those connected with enslavement and the Africa trade, the captains and officers of ships and those who profited from the colonies in North America and the Caribbean. Some Africans clearly had slave status when they were imported from the colonies, even if the law remained ambiguous. Others, for example those who were employed on ships, may have been free or able to exercise some elements of freedom. In this period, the best-known legal case concerned with the subject of slavery was *Butts v. Penny* in 1677. That dispute centred on whether Africans could be considered property, since the plaintiff in the case alleged that his property, a hundred Africans, had been stolen from him. The judgment in the Court of King's Bench was that 'Negroes being usually bought and sold among Merchants, and so Merchandise, and also being infidels, there might be property in them.'[40] In the same year the Solicitor-General, Sir Francis Winnington, expressed the legal opinion that 'Negroes ought to be esteemed goods and commodities within the Acts of Trade and Navigation.'[41]

The *Butts v. Penny* judgment emphasized the importance of the absence of Christian faith, but what was addressed in legal terms normally occurred outside Britain, that is, the buying and selling of enslaved Africans, so it may not say much about the status of Africans within Britain. Indeed, it highlights a legal ambiguity, that English law was increasingly required to recognize the existence of slavery and the ownership of enslaved Africans in the North American and Caribbean colonies but did not formally acknowledge the existence of slavery within the British Isles. Enslaved Africans were increasingly brought to Britain from this period onwards, but their status remained an ambiguous one. Nevertheless, from the late seventeenth century onwards, there are increasing numbers of examples of enslaved Africans being bought and sold in the British Isles, being forced to wear collars like pet animals and referred to as slaves. By the early eighteenth century, the sale of Africans in London, as well as elsewhere, became increasingly commonplace.[42]

However, there are also many examples of Africans running away, or in other ways refusing to accept an enslaved status. In 1691, the *London Gazette* reported the escape and recapture of a 'Black boy

named Toby, aged about 19', only to have to report, shortly afterwards, that he had escaped yet again. In 1694, an advert in the same
publication admitted that an African it described as a 'Tannymore
with short bushy hair, very well shaped, in a grey livery suit with yellow, about seventeen or eighteen years of age, with a silver collar
around his neck' had run away. The advert offered forty shillings
reward to whoever might deliver him.[43] Such advertisements were not
uncommon in the late seventeenth century and became even more
common in the century following. Indeed, researchers at the University of Glasgow have recorded over 800 such adverts in the period
from 1700 to 1780, detailing those who self-liberated themselves
from moored ships, as well as towns and cities throughout the British
Isles.[44] The majority of these Africans who attempted to liberate themselves were men, but there were also some women whose exploits
have been recorded, such as an eighteen-year-old woman called Ann,
who with her 'green gown and a brass collar around her neck' ran
away from her owners in Glasgow in 1727.[45]

In these freedom endeavours, Africans' challenging conditions,
even when held as slaves, differed little from those facing many English people of similarly servile status.[46] Africans were sometimes aided
by the uncertain legal position regarding slavery and the fact that they
might find alternative waged employment. Just as in the period before
1677, many Africans sought baptism, but increasingly they did so to
establish that they were not 'infidels' and therefore could not be
legally enslaved. There is therefore also evidence that those who
asserted their ownership of Africans attempted to prevent their baptism. In 1701, it was reported in the *Weekly Journal or British
Gazetteer* that a 'Negro servant' to a 'lady of distinction' in Lincolnshire was 'severely lashed' for having himself secretly baptized
after growing impatient for a service promised but unfulfilled.[47] In
1760, *Lloyds Evening Post* published a report of a 'Negro girl about
nine years old' who had 'eloped from her mistress on account of ill-
usage'. The girl seems to have been befriended by 'two housekeepers'
who brought her to a church in Westminster to be baptized. However,
in the midst of the service she was kidnapped by her 'mistress', who
told the assembled congregation that 'the girl was her slave' and she
would 'use her as she pleased'. The newspaper account was written in

protest, but also to ask whether such a situation was lawful in England. No reply to this question was published.[48] There is, however, also evidence that some 'owners' had their servants/slaves baptized, such as Margaret Lucy, who was baptized in Idlecote, Warwickshire, on New Year's Day of 1690 and who was recorded as 'belonging to ye Lady Underhill'.[49] In 1710 *The Tatler* received the following intriguing correspondence:

> Sir—I am a black-moor boy, and have, by my lady's order, been christened by the chaplain. The good man has gone further with me, and told me a great deal of good news; as that I am as good as my lady herself, as I am a Christian, and many other things; but, for all this, the parrot who came over with me from our country is as much esteemed by her as I am. Besides this, the shock dog has a collar that cost almost as much as mine. I desire also to know whether, now I am a Christian, I am obliged to dress like a Turk and wear a turban. I am, Sir, your most obedient servant, Pompey.[50]

The *Butts v. Penny* case was followed by other cases concerning the legality of slavery: *Lowe v. Elton* in the same year and *Gelly v. Cleve* in 1694. In the latter case, enslavement for a non-Christian 'Negro boy' was again judged lawful 'because they are heathens, and therefore a man may have property in them'. However, in a series of judgments, *Chamberlain v. Harvey* (1696), *Smith v. Brown and Cooper* (1701) and in *Smith v. Gould* (1706), Lord Chief Justice Holt made a contrary ruling, arguing that there could not be an action for 'trover', the recovery of the value of property unlawfully taken from an owner, because English law, unlike that in the colonies, did not recognize the buying and selling of slaves.[51] In 1696 Holt did acknowledge what was referred to as the status of 'a slavish servant' but made no judgment on whether the baptism of an enslaved African in England led to freedom.[52]

The Chamberlain case concerned a young African who had been taken to England from Barbados. After his owners died, he was baptized and worked for wages for several employers. The plaintiff in the case was the son of the African's late owner, who brought a case of trespass against his current employer, but the court rejected his claim.[53] In 1701, in a case that concerned the sale of an enslaved African in London, Holt went so far as to assert that 'as soon as a Negro comes into England he becomes free, one may be a villein in England but not a slave'.[54] These judgments recognized that servile status still existed, whether from feudal times or from the peculiar nature of colonial occupation. The right to the labour of another human was legal, whereas chattel slavery, which gave owners the right of life and death over their slaves, was legal in the colonies but in England it was not. In 1706 Holt ruled that 'by the common law no man can have a property in another', but he did not rule out the right of a master/mistress to the unpaid labour of a servant, or that of those enslaved overseas. Moreover, the ruling argued 'if I imprison my Negro, a Habeas Corpus will not lie to deliver him', thus granting slaveholders in English significant powers to detain enslaved Africans.[55]

Legal judgments did not alter the fact that enslaved Africans brought to Britain remained enslaved and could be bought and sold throughout the country. Researchers at the University of Glasgow have compiled a list of newspaper advertisements for the sale of enslaved Africans, although often the terms used refer to Africans who were to be 'disposed of' at such a place and date, mainly in London, Liverpool, Edinburgh and Bristol. These were generally sales of individual Africans by those who claimed ownership, but slave auctions, as well as sales of multiple Africans, were not unknown. For example, in 1766, *Williamson's Liverpool Advertiser* carried the following from a broker: 'To be sold at the Exchange Coffee House, in Water Street, this day 12 September instant at one o'clock precisely ELEVEN NEGROES imported by the Angola.' In the same city in October 1768 the *Liverpool General Advertiser* announced the auction of 'A Handsome NEGRO BOY, From ANGOLA, about 9 Years of Age'.[56] It is evident that several such auctions took place in the city and undoubtedly elsewhere and involved children brought directly from Africa, as well as from the Caribbean and the American colonies. One street in Liverpool was apparently known as 'Negro Row', as 'Negro slaves were occasionally sold by auction in the shops, warehouses and coffee houses, and also on the steps of the Custom House'.[57]

Normally such adverts offered young African men for sale, but young women featured too. Many of those offered for sale were children, often as young as five or six years old, and in at least one case there was a mother and child. African children, or in some cases

Indian children, became a fashion accessory, in the same style as pet animals, and were often provided with fitted collars. They were a sign of wealth and sometimes appeared in portraits with their owners. Sale advertisements reflected the tastes of wealthy owners at the time. In 1705, for instance, the *Post Man and the Historical Account* carried the following advert: 'A Negro Boy about 12 years of age, that speaks English, is to be sold. Enquire of Mr Step. Rayner, a Watchmaker, at the sign of the Dial without Bishopgate.' In 1744, the *Daily Advertiser* issued a warning: 'To be SOLD, A Pretty little Negro Boy, about nine years old, and well limb'd. If not disposed of, is to be sent to the West Indies in six days-time.' In 1766, the *Edinburgh Evening Courant* carried the following: 'To be disposed of A NEGRO WOMAN, named Peggy, about nineteen years of age, born and brought up in Charlestoun, in the Province of South Carolina, speaks good English, an exceeding good House-wench, and washer and dresser, and is very tender and careful of children. She has a young Child, a Negro boy, about a year old, which will be disposed of with the mother.' [58]

What is most remarkable about many of these adverts is that African children are often included amongst a host of other merchandise,

From an eighteenth-century newspaper in Liverpool

not as the main item of sale, as if their disposal was not in any way particularly significant. In October 1743, for example, 'one Negro boy' was listed for sale, after alcohol, ribbons and candles, at a coffee house near the Royal Exchange in London. While in 1757 in Liverpool 'a Negro boy' was advertised for sale alongside wine and cider. [59] Most advertisements did not employ the term slave to describe their merchandise, but some did. A 'NEGRO SLAVE FOR SALE' was to be found in the *Public Ledger* in January 1761 and in the *Felix Farley Bristol Journal* of January 1768 could be found this advertisement – 'TO BE SOLD, A healthy NEGRO SLAVE, named PRINCE, 17 Years of Age'. Prices are seldom mentioned; perhaps this was considered bad taste. However, an advertisement in the *Edinburgh Evening Courant* in April 1768 showed that the sale price of 'A Black Boy' was £40. [60]

THE LAW

What is perhaps most significant is that Africans, whether they arrived directly from Africa, or from North America and the Caribbean, challenged their servile and slave status. One of the best-known legal cases is that of an African woman, Katherine Aukur, who had been brought to England from Barbados by a Robert Rich in about 1684. Her master and mistress 'tortured her and turned her out; her said master refusing to give her a discharge, she could not be "entertained in service elsewhere"'. Katherine's master then had her arrested and imprisoned. She, therefore, took her case to court, where it was heard at the Middlesex County Court in 1690. Katherine had been 'baptised at the parish Church of St. Katherine's, near the Tower', but this clearly did not exempt her from servitude, nor, it seems, did it make much impression on the court's ruling, although she is described as Rich's servant, not his slave. The court 'ordered that the said Katherine shall be at liberty to serve any person, until such time as the said Rich shall return from Barbados.'[61] The records provide no more information about Katherine, nor what occurred when Rich returned. What information we do have suggests that Africans could petition the courts and seek redress, but perhaps tells us more about the ambiguity of their servile status. In many ways, they were neither totally enslaved nor absolutely free. In the case of another African, John Caeser, in 1717, it was his wife Elizabeth who claimed that he had been held as a slave in Whitechapel for fourteen years, 'without any wages', even though he had been baptized for seven years. Elizabeth was forced to petition the courts, so that he might be set free to earn a livelihood for them both. The basis on which her petition was made was that she was 'advised that Slavery in England is inconsistent with the laws of this Realm'.[62]

In 1729, apparently in answer to demands for clarification from Bishop George Berkeley and other religious interests concerned to reassure slave owners that baptizing enslaved Africans did not automatically lead to manumission, the Attorney General, Sir Phillip Yorke, and Solicitor-General, Charles Talbot, gave a legal opinion on the status of slavery in Britain:

> We are of opinion, that a Slave, by coming from the West Indies, either with or without his master, to Great Britain or Ireland, doth not become free; and that his master's property or right in him is not thereby determined or varied; and baptism doth not bestow freedom on him, nor make any alteration to his temporal condition in these kingdoms. We are also of opinion, that the master may legally compel him to return again to the plantations.[63]

Although only a legal opinion, this position was reconfirmed in 1749 when Yorke, Lord Chancellor Hardwicke, ruled in the case of *Pearne v. Lisle* that regarding the legality of enslaving Africans, there was no distinction between the law in England and that in the colonies.[64] The legal opinion of Yorke and Talbot remained extremely influential and was still being published as a definitive view in the London press as late as 1762.[65] However, earlier in the same year, when legal action was again taken against an African in England the judgment was rather different. In that year in *Shanley v. Harvey*, the main defendant was an African, Joseph Harvey, who had been brought to England as a slave by Shanley around 1750, at the age of eight or nine. Shanley had then given him as a present to his niece, who had him baptized and changed his name. On her deathbed, in 1752, the niece had given Harvey seven or eight hundred pounds in cash, telling him to tell nobody but 'make a good use of it'. Although Shanley was represented by the Attorney General, the case was dismissed by the Lord Chancellor, who simply proclaimed, 'As soon as a man sets foot on English ground he is free: a Negro may maintain an action against his master for ill-usage and may have a habeas corpus if restrained of his liberty.'[66] However, legal judgments which denied Africans their rights and rejected the precedent established by Holt also occurred during the period between 1729 and the Mansfield judgment in 1772. Imperial law enacted in 1732 which decreed that enslaved Africans might be considered as property in the payment of debts throughout the empire led to the public auction of an African boy in London in 1763, although not without opposition from outraged Londoners.[67] This particular case, as well as several others, show that the fate and status of enslaved Africans in England was not simply determined by legal opinion and judgments, but also by challenges to slave status and ill-treatment by the supporters of Africans in Britain and most importantly by the actions of Africans themselves. All these laudable efforts were a precursor to those actions mounted later on in the eighteenth century in what can truly be described as a mass abolitionist movement.

AFRICAN ABOLITIONISTS

Even before the eighteenth century, individual Africans such as Katherine Aukur had made efforts to defend their right to appropriate payment for work, or services provided, and often made efforts to completely liberate themselves from servile status. During the eighteenth century, Africans also applied to the courts for recognition of their rights and protection from arbitrary detention and human trafficking. In 1730, for example, it was reported in the *Country Journal or the Craftsman* that a 'Negro Servant' had won a court case demanding wages from the captain of a naval vessel. The court awarded the plaintiff £42 in addition to legal costs.[68] In many instances Africans had public support, and on the few occasions when public slave auctions occurred these did not take place without some opposition. It is difficult to assess the extent of this opposition during the early part of the eighteenth century, but there is often evidence of its occurrence in contemporary publications.[69] Running away, or self-liberation, was also practised frequently. On one day in October 1732, the London-based *Daily Post* carried two advertisements from separate 'masters' offering rewards for the safe return of two 'Negro servants', Tobias Fortuyn and Christopher Corydon. Readers were warned not to 'harbour or entertain' these young African men who, it was suggested, might well try to seek alternative paid employment on more favourable terms.[70]

In 1764, the *Gentleman's Magazine* complained that the importing of African servants had created 'a grievance that requires a remedy'. The article explained that 'the main objection to their importation is that they cease to consider themselves as slaves in this free country, nor will they put up with an inequality of treatment, nor more willingly perform the laborious offices or servitude than our own people, and if put to it, are generally sullen, spiteful, treacherous and revengeful'.[71] A similar complaint appeared in the *London Chronicle* in the same year concerning the 'folly which is become too fashionable, of importing Negroes into this country for servants'.[72] A year later a letter-writer complained that 'Negro and East India servants' were 'estimated at the lowest to be thirty thousand in the whole kingdom'.[73]

In 1768 Sir John Fielding, a London magistrate echoed these earlier complaints when he wrote that enslaved Africans:

> Having no right to wages; they no sooner arrive here than they put themselves on a footing with other servants, become intoxicated with liberty, grow refractory and either by persuasion of others, or from their own inclinations, begin to expect wages according to their own opinion of their merits.[74]

According to Fielding there were, 'a great number of black men and women who have made themselves so troublesome to the families that brought them over as to get themselves discharged'. Fielding complained that 'they no sooner come over, but the Sweets of Liberty and the Conversation with Free men and Christians enlarge their Minds.'[75] These self-liberated Africans then 'enter into Societies and make their business to corrupt and dissatisfy the mind of every black servant that comes to England'. They encouraged others to become baptized or married, in the belief that this would prevent continued slave status.[76]

The liberating effect of marriage was demonstrated by several eighteenth-century court cases, the most famous of which is the case of Mary and John Hylas. Both had formerly been enslaved and were separately brought from Barbados to England. There they met and, in 1758, with their owners' consent, were married. John Hylas was freed and the couple lived together for eight years. However, in 1766 Mary was kidnapped by agents employed by her former owners and transported back to the Caribbean to be sold. John Hylas, with the assistance of the English abolitionist Granville Sharp, took the case to court, where he was victorious. The former slave owner was compelled to return Mary to her husband and John was awarded nominal damages. However, the case centred more on the rights of a husband than it did on the rights of an African woman. Indeed, the nominal damages awarded showed that even the rights of a husband were not fully upheld when he was an African as well.[77] A similar judgment was made in another case, around the same time, by the Attorney General. He argued that the marriage contract entitled the husband to the company of his wife, whereas a slave owner had no legal contract which could override that right.

There is thus some evidence that Africans were taking action to decide their own status, in England at least, and becoming organized for that purpose. Fielding's comments were echoed by the Jamaican owner of enslaved Africans and leading racist, Edward Long, who also complained about Africans brought to England. Amongst other things he lamented the fact that 'A Negroe running away from his master here is not by statute declared liable to imprisonment for any such offence.' Long continues:

> these servants soon grow acquainted with a knot of blacks, who having eloped from their respective owners at different times, repose themselves here in ease and indolence, and endeavour to strengthen their party, by seducing as many of these strangers into their association as they can work to their purpose.[78]

Long also makes it clear that these self-liberated Africans were assisted in their efforts to remain at liberty by 'vicious white servants and abandoned prostitutes'. These 'zealous friends' then assisted them to find paid employment, often with 'persons of rank and fortune'. Long particularly condemned those Africans who worked for low wages in Britain, arguing that they are denying employment to 'our white servants'. He was even more troubled about those who had 'eloped' in London and enjoy the company of 'the lower class of women in England', with whom they might produce 'a linsey-wolsey race'. He was greatly alarmed that Africans might subsequently be able to buy their way into Parliament, or become landowners.[79] Gilbert Francklyn, a human-trafficker and owner of enslaved Africans, also complained that Africans in England were encouraged and enticed to run away and that 'they found themselves upon a perfect equality, at least, with the inferior white people'. This status as well as 'the ideas of liberty . . . could not fail of having pernicious effects upon their minds, and great numbers ran away from their masters'.[80] Francklyn claimed that as many as 20,000 might have been 'lost to their owners' in this way, although this figure is clearly an exaggeration.

In comments directed at slave owners, Fielding made it clear that they could not rely on the courts for the safe return of fugitive Africans. Such reliance he explained 'is a Mistake, for Justices have nothing to do with Blacks but when they offend against the law'.[81] He also pointed out that attempts to reclaim Africans who had run away were fraught with danger because they had 'the Mob on their side'; in other words, the support of the ordinary citizens of London, especially the workers, who were starting to play an increasingly significant political role, whether in support of the radical politician John Wilkes or, in later years, during such events as the Gordon Riots which broke out in London in June 1780. Commencing as anti-Catholic demonstrations led by the Scottish protestant MP Lord George Gordon, who was also opposed to slavery, the 'riots' became a major insurrection lasting several days and were directed mainly against the rich and symbols of authority, including the houses of Fielding and Mansfield, as well as Newgate and other gaols. Thousands of troops were required to restore order and hundreds of Londoners were killed or wounded. Three of those arrested were described as 'black' in the records: Charlotte Gardiner, John Glover and Benjamin Bowfry. Glover, a servant, was found guilty but later reprieved. The fate of Bowfry is unknown, but Gardiner, who appears to have had nobody to intercede for her, was executed in July 1780.[82]

In what was soon to become an era of revolutions, Fielding warned of the dangers of people power in both London and in the Caribbean colonies. In the latter, he explained that:

> there is great Reason to fear ... those Blacks who have been sent back to the Plantations, after they have lived some Time in this Country of Liberty, where they have learned to read and write, been acquainted with the Use, and entrusted with the Care of Arms.

These Africans, he claimed, were responsible for 'those insurrections' occurring in the Caribbean.[83]

Although there is no strong evidence to suggest a link between Africans becoming organized in England and insurrections of the enslaved in the colonies, it is a fascinating possibility. It is not surprising that during the 1760s and thereafter the defenders of slavery and human trafficking were becoming increasingly concerned about their property and the system that provided their wealth. The 'state of war' between the enslaved and their enslavers had led to major battles in Jamaica in the early 1760s, a 'national liberation struggle' in Berbice in 1763, and several uprisings in Honduras in 1765 and 1768. Such rebellions continued in the Caribbean, in particular, before the outbreak of the revolution in the French colony of St Domingue in the 1790s. As we can see from the testimony of Fielding, Francklyn and Long, as well as from press reports, Africans contested their slave and servile status, organized and liberated themselves from bondage and, in all these endeavours, were aided by other poor and working people in England. White servants too could be harshly treated, might be denied wages and in response might run away and be sought after. However, it was unlikely that they would be kidnapped and sent to the colonies as chattels, although they might be press-ganged into the navy. In this important respect, the lives and status of significant numbers of Africans in Britain were very different, since many of them were brought from colonies where chattel slavery existed.[84]

COMMUNITY OF INTERESTS

We have clear evidence of what the historian Folarin Shyllon referred to as a 'community of interests': Africans 'banded together' to provide welfare and comradeship, to assist each other in the struggle for emancipation, since most Africans in Britain faced common problems stemming from the existence of slavery. This 'community' might well also have included the English wives of Africans, a group that highly alarmed Long, as well as other English supporters of slavery. In addition, there is evidence that Africans met together socially. A visitor to the house of Samuel Johnson, the famous writer, reported that when the door was opened by 'Francis Barber, his black servant . . . a group of his African countrymen were sitting round a fire in the gloomy anti-room'. Such gatherings at Johnson's house might also have included the African servant of his friend, the artist Sir Joshua Reynolds. It seems likely that this man was John Shropshire, who was robbed in a case that was later heard at the Old Bailey. Shropshire was robbed by another African, named Thomas Windsor, who was subsequently sentenced to death, but he kept the details of the case secret from his master. When Reynolds read of the incident and the sentence in the press he was appalled. He ordered new clothes to be taken to the prisoner and instructed Shropshire to take regular meals to Windsor. Reynolds prevailed upon his friend, the MP Edmund Burke, to lessen Windsor's punishment and as a result his sentence was changed to transportation.[85] In this instance the community of interests seems to have included non-Africans too.

We also know of other African social gatherings, in London at least. In February 1764, the *London Chronicle* reported:

> Among the sundry fashionable routs or clubs, that are held in town, that of the Blacks, or Negro Servants is not the least. On Wednesday night last, no less than fifty-seven of them, men and women, supped, drank, and entertained themselves with dancing and music, consisting of violins, French horns and other instruments, at a public house in Fleet-street, till four in the morning. No Whites were allowed to be present, for all the performers were Blacks.[86]

From 1726, there are reports of a christening ceremony of 'Guiney Blacks', as well as reports of 'Black guests' at the funeral of a Black servant.[87] In 1773 when two Black men were incarcerated for begging, the press reported that they were visited by 300 of their compatriots, who contributed towards their upkeep.[88] Later on in the century the Sons of Africa was established to campaign specifically against the trafficking of Africans. In the 1770s there is also evidence of the existence of something referred to as the Black Society. In 1772, a letter appeared in the press from a certain Mungo, who claimed to be the Secretary of the Black Society, enquiring as to the well-being of the 'Black servant maid of Captain Hughes Lady' who was to be sold as a chattel. Mungo made it clear that he, the Society and 'all our brethren' were aware of the judgment by Lord Mansfield and were 'desirous of knowing what has become of our poor sister'.[89] Although Mungo might be considered a derogatory name, following the blackface portrayal of a character of the same name in the comic opera *The Padlock*, which premiered in London in 1768,[90] nevertheless, the appearance of such a letter suggests that slavery in Britain remained in the spotlight. The Black Society's concern about the fate of a 'sister' is another example of the 'community of interests' working together for one of their own.

STRONG, LEWIS AND SOMERSET

In 1765, the predicament of Jonathan Strong, an African formerly enslaved in Barbados, came to the attention of a Granville Sharp, at that time a minor civil servant who would soon become one of the leading campaigners against slavery. The young man called at the London surgery maintained by Sharp's brother for the poor and needy. Strong had been beaten and nearly blinded by his former owner, who had brought him to England and then thrown him out on the street. The Sharp brothers supported Strong during the four months he spent in hospital, as well as during his convalescence, and found him new employment, a position he held for some two years. He was then by chance discovered by his former owner, who had him imprisoned.

Strong managed to contact Granville Sharp, who demanded his release, but not before his former owner had sold him to another, who was preparing to ship him overseas. Initially Strong was released from custody, as he had not committed any crime, but then Sharp was charged with having robbed Strong's former owner of his property.

The case of Jonathan Strong is significant for many reasons, not least Sharp's entry into the anti-slavery cause. He began to study the legal rights and position of Africans in England when he was advised by one eminent lawyer that the 1729 Yorke-Talbot opinion had the force of law and that therefore he was unlikely to win his case. Sharpe therefore embarked on his own two-year study of the law, although he had no legal training, and found no legal basis for slavery in England. He refuted the Yorke-Talbot opinion and published the results of his research in 1769 as *A Representation of the Injustice and Dangerous Tendency of Tolerating Slavery or of Admitting the Least Claim of Private Property in the Persons of Men, in England*. By such means, Sharp forced those who wished to re-enslave Strong to desist and, at the same time, he began campaigning against slavery and the trafficking of Africans. As the reader may recall, in 1768 Sharp became involved in the case of John and Mary Hylas. In 1769, he condemned an advertisement for the sale of an eleven-year-old 'black girl', who was described as the 'property' of the vendor: 'extremely handy, works at her needle tolerably, and speaks English perfectly well; is of an excellent temper, and willing disposition'.[91]

Sharp then became involved in the case of George August, known as Thomas Lewis, an enslaved African from the Gold Coast living in London, whose former owner attempted to kidnap him and send him to Jamaica to be sold as a slave. In this case, the kidnapping was witnessed and several people attempted to aid Lewis. As Sharp had gained a reputation in such matters, he was invited to help secure a writ of *habeas corpus* and Lewis' freedom. The case was eventually heard in a court presided over by Lord Chief Justice Mansfield, where a jury found in favour of Lewis, on the grounds that he was not property. Although in this case Mansfield made no judgment regarding slavery in England, his summing up centred on whether evidence could be produced to prove the ownership of Lewis. In this regard, he added 'his being black, will not prove the property'.[92] However,

Mansfield was opposed to any action being taken against the kidnappers and had tried, unsuccessfully, to get the case settled outside court, so as to avoid any judgment on slavery itself.[93]

It was during another similar case that Mansfield was compelled to make a more explicit judgment. This was the case of James Somerset, an enslaved man brought to England from Virginia in 1769. Somerset subsequently left his master but was kidnapped to be resold into slavery in Jamaica. The case assumed some prominence, not least owing to the fact that the owner of Somerset was backed by those 'West Indian merchants' who were the defenders of the enslavement of Africans.[94] Somerset was supported not only by Sharp but also by a legal team that freely provided their expertise. The importance of the case drew in others, including those in North America, such as the abolitionist Anthony Benezet, a zealous supporter of 'the Negro cause', who hoped for a definitive judgment against the existence of slavery in England. Mansfield's final judgment was that 'the claim of slavery never can be supported, the power claimed never was in use here, or acknowledged by the law. Upon the whole, we cannot say the cause returned is sufficient by the law; and therefore the man [Somerset] must be discharged.'[95]

This judgment was momentous and appeared to substantiate earlier pronouncements that as soon as a slave set foot in England s/he became free. It was certainly seen in this light by many at the time and as a result celebrated, not least by Africans themselves, in Britain and elsewhere. As the *Morning Chronicle* noted:

> Several Negroes were in court yesterday, to hear the event of a cause so interesting to their tribe, and after judgement of the court was known, bowed with profound respect to the Judges, and shaking each other by the hand, congratulated themselves upon the recovery of the rights of human nature, and their happy lot that permitted them to breathe the free air of England. – No sight upon earth could be more pleasingly affecting to the feeling mind, than the joy which shone at that instant in these poor men's sable countenances.[96]

Following the court case nearly 200 Africans held a ball 'at a public house in Westminster', while the *Public Advertiser* reported 'a Subscription is now raising among a great Number of Negroes, in and about this Metropolis, for the purpose of presenting Somerset with a handsome Gratuity, for having so nobly stood up in Defence of the natural Rights of the sable Part of the human Creation.'[97] Ten Africans wrote a letter of thanks to Sharp, referring to themselves as 'those who were considered slaves, even in England itself, till your aid and exertions set us free'.[98] Moreover, Somerset's former owner received notice from another owner of enslaved Africans that Somerset had written about the case to a Mr Dublin, an enslaved African in Bristol Wells, who had concluded that Mansfield 'had given them their freedoms', and therefore immediately absconded.[99] One modern historian has even claimed that the judgment contributed to the demands for American independence and the rebellion of July 1776.[100] However, Mansfield made the judgment with some reluctance. There was no legal basis for slavery in England but, he warned, 'the setting of 14,000 or 15,000 men at once loose by a solemn opinion is very disagreeable in the effects it threatens'. Whether such numbers of enslaved Africans existed or not, Mansfield did not liberate them. During the case of Charlotte Howe, a Black woman claiming poor relief, in which Mansfield presided in 1785, he upheld her status as a slave, explaining that the judgment in 1772 went 'no further than that the master cannot by force compel the slave to go out of the kingdom'. As an enslaved woman brought to Britain, Mansfield maintained that Charlotte Howe had neither right to poor relief, nor right to wages.[101]

Some Africans remained enslaved in England for many years after this judgment, as can be judged from reports in the press.[102] Two years after the judgment, Olaudah Equiano found that he, Sharp, and the law were powerless to prevent the kidnapping and transportation to the Caribbean of a former enslaved man, John Annis.[103] Sharp himself was sent an advertisement from a Liverpool newspaper in 1779 which announced 'to be sold at auction ... a Black boy about fourteen years old, and a large Mountain Tiger cat'.[104] Nevertheless, the judgment set an important precedent and was clearly influential during subsequent cases, including those heard in Scotland.

The Somerset case was widely reported in the press and stirred more debate about the question of slavery, not only in Britain but also in the colonies. It was perceived to be in favour of the rights of Africans in Britain and against the interests of the slave owners.[105] Its significance can be judged by the fact that one of the leading owners of enslaved Africans, the infamous Edward Long, found it necessary to immediately publish his *Candid Reflections Upon the Judgement Lately Awarded by the Court of King's Bench, in Westminster-Hall, on What Is Commonly Called the Negroe-Cause by a Planter.* Long argued that the laws of England were not designed for 'Negroe-slaves', who, he stressed, were an 'absolute necessity' for the wealth of Britain and its colonies. He emphasized that Parliament had passed numerous laws upholding the legitimacy of human trafficking and the ownership of enslaved Africans. Long clearly understood that the struggle of Africans in Britain to liberate themselves, which had been recognized by Mansfield's judgment, also undermined the right he and his friends had to own Africans as property in the colonies. Africans, he lamented, would conclude that they were held in bondage 'by no other obligation than the laws of the colony, and an exertion of illegal force over them by their masters'.[106]

AFRICANS IN SCOTLAND

African men, women and children were brought to Scotland in much the same way, although in smaller numbers, as they were brought to other parts of Britain.[107] We find the same type of advertisements in the press for the sale of Africans, and examples of those who attempted to liberate themselves by running away, although there were far fewer than in England.[108] Such notices show that there were African fugitives in Glasgow, Edinburgh, Arbroath, Greenock and other towns and cities throughout the eighteenth century. Ann, the eighteen-year-old 'Negro woman' who ran away in 1721, was perhaps uncommon as a female self-liberator, but there was much that was common about the description in the Edinburgh press, 'a brass collar about her neck, on which are engraved these words Gustavus Brown in Dalkeith, his Negro'.[109] The self-liberation of Africans also seems to have taken a similar course as in England. The same struggle between Africans and those who wished to own them also existed in Scotland and was evident in the Scottish courts, which had a different legal system from that of England.

One such case was brought by Jamie Montgomery, an African, who had been bought for a little over £56 in Virginia as a child in 1750, and then brought to Beith in Scotland. There he had himself baptized, according to his legal owner 'to free himself of my lawful service'. The owner, objecting to the baptism, attempted to send him back to Virginia and so Montgomery absconded but was subsequently arrested and imprisoned in Edinburgh. His case was then heard before the Court of Session, effectively the supreme court in Scotland, but he died before a judgment was given, although again the significance of baptism seems to have been the main focus of the case.[110]

In 1770 baptism was also key in the case of David Spens, formerly known as Black Tom, who had been bought as a slave in Grenada for £30 about ten years previously, and then brought to Fife by his owner David Dalrymple, who planned to send him back to Grenada – but not before agreeing to his baptism in 1769. It seems likely that Spens adopted his surname from Reverend Dr Harry Spens, the minister at the Parish Church of East Wemyss, where he was baptized. The owner later claimed that Spens had also been strongly influenced by a local farmer, John Henderson, a resident of Wemyss and church elder, who had 'put it into the Negroes [sic] head that Baptism by the Law of this Country would emancipate him from his servitude'.[111] Following the baptism and on the day when he was supposed to be returned to Grenada, Spens withdrew his labour and with Henderson's support wrote to his owner to affirm his freedom and threaten legal action to defend it:

> I am now by the Christian Religion Liberate and set at freedom from my old yoke bondage & slavery and by the Laws of this Christian land there is no Slavery nor vestige of Slavery allowed nevertheless you take it upon you to exercise your old Tyrannical Power over me and would dispose of me arbitrarily at your despotic will & Pleasure and for that end you threaten to send me abroad out of this Country to the West Indies and there dispose of me for money.[112]

Spens was arrested, but later freed and his owner died before the case could be heard. What is perhaps most significant about the case is the support that Spens received, not only from Henderson but also from the miners, salters and agricultural labourers of Wemyss. Indeed, Henderson wrote to Dalrymple that if he were to surrender Spens, 'the whole country would be inflamed'.[113] In Wemyss, 'a great amount of interest was taken in the case, and a great sum of money raised to enable Spens to defend what were considered to be his just rights and privileges as a British subject.' Evidently much of this money was raised through the churches in Wemyss and other local parishes.[114] This is particularly significant, since at the time the status of many Scottish miners and salters was legally described as one of 'slavery or bondage'.[115] It was reported that in total five lawyers were hired on Spens' behalf and all refused to accept any fee for their services. Two of these lawyers, William Ferguson and William Chalmers, paid bail of £30 to release Spens from gaol. When the case collapsed and Spens was granted his freedom he returned to Wemyss to work for Henderson.

These two cases were not settled in court, but the case of Joseph Knight was. Knight was an African sold into slavery in Jamaica and in 1769 brought to Scotland as the personal servant of a wealthy Scottish aristocrat named Wedderburn. Although Knight had been educated by his owner, he took note of the Somerset judgment to demand his freedom. His desire for freedom was made even more necessary by the fact that he had a child with Ann Thompson, a Scottish woman servant in the employ of Wedderburn. Wedderburn gave Knight money to support Thompson during her pregnancy but dismissed her from his service. When the child died, Wedderburn stopped any further financial support, but this did not prevent the marriage of Knight and Thompson in 1773. When Wedderburn refused to re-employ Thompson, or pay Knight, the latter withdrew his labour and left his former master to seek employment in Dundee. Wedderburn then had Knight arrested and the latter took his case to court in 1784. The case was initially decided in favour of Wedderburn but in 1788 it was heard in Scotland's supreme court. That court ruled that:

> the dominion assumed over this Negro, under the law of Jamaica, being unjust, could not be supported in this country to any extent: That, therefore, the defender had no right to the Negro's service for any space of time, nor to send him out of the country against his consent.[116]

Joseph Knight's successful case highlighted that Scottish law did not recognize the enslaved status of those brought from the colonies and was as significant as the Somerset case in England. Just as important as the legal arguments were those that presented the enslavement of Africans as morally unjust. According to the *Caledonian Mercury*, 'the rights of humanity were weighed in the scales of justice,' and it concluded 'it must give a very high satisfaction to the inhabitants of the United Kingdom, that the freedom of Negroes has obtained its first general determination in the Supreme Civil Court of Scotland.'[117]

AFRICAN WRITERS

James Albert Ukawsaw Gronniosaw

Shortly after the Somerset case the first book by an African was published in Britain. *A Narrative of the Remarkable Particulars in the Life of James Albert Ukawsaw Gronniosaw, An African Prince, related by himself*, was published in Bath in 1772.[118] James Albert, as he was known in England, dictated his *Narrative*. It was recorded for him 'by the elegant pen of a young lady from Leominster, for her private satisfaction'. The reason for its publication seems to have been partly financial, 'to serve Albert and his distressed family', and no doubt because the plight of enslaved Africans had increasingly become of public concern. There was also a strong religious incentive, since the book demonstrated Gronniosaw's great Christian faith, even when severely tested by adversity. The book is introduced by Walter Shirley, a key member of the Christian revivalist movement of the day, and dedicated to Selina Hastings, Countess of Huntingdon, perhaps the most prominent female revivalist in Britain at the time.

Gronniosaw's *Narrative* is mainly significant because it is one of the first of such 'slave narratives' to be published. It was preceded by Briton Hammon's *Narrative*, which appeared twelve years before but was published in Boston, at that time a British colony. These narratives were autobiographical accounts, which related at first hand the experience of slavery and liberation and often provide important information about the everyday challenges facing Africans in Britain. Gronniosaw was, by his own account, of royal birth. He was born c.1705 in the kingdom of Bornu, in what is today northern Nigeria. Tricked into enslavement, he was transported to Barbados and then

New York, where he was freed after the death of his owner. He later served in the navy and army before arriving in England, where he married a silk weaver, who was a widow and the mother of a child. The remainder of the *Narrative* relates his impoverished existence in several locations in England, periods of unemployment, the death of one of his children, but also his constant and strong Calvinistic faith. He died in Chester in 1775, where a short obituary appeared in the local press.[119] Despite its brevity and limitations, Gronniosaw's *Narrative* was undoubtedly influential and was mentioned by one of his successors, Ottobah Cugoano, in his *Thoughts and Sentiments on the Evil of Slavery*, as well as by Phillis Wheatley. It was published in at least twelve editions in the eighteenth century, including three in North America and two in Ireland, and several more before the British edition of 1840.[120]

Phillis Wheatley

Another writer connected with Selina Hastings was Phillis Wheatley, an enslaved woman possibly of Fulani heritage from West Africa. She was trafficked to North America as a child and purchased by a family in Boston, who taught her to read and write and named her after the slave ship that had brought her from Africa.[121] Wheatley became the first African woman to have her work published in English, and is today celebrated as the first female African American writer. Acknowledged as a child prodigy, she learned to read, write and speak English within a few months of her arrival in Boston and later learned Latin. She published her first poem at the age of thirteen.

Her *Poems on Various Subjects, Religious and Moral*, encouraged by and dedicated to Hastings, were published in London in 1773. Wheatley had already become well known in Boston before she sailed for London in June 1773, and her poem *On Recollection* had been published in the *London Magazine* in 1772.[122] She only remained in the city for just over a month, recalled to Boston because of the illness of her owner's wife, and so left before the publication of her *Poems*.[123] Her presence in London, and the imminent publication of her work, drew further attention to her enslaved status as well as the institution of slavery in both Britain and its colonies. She was only freed after her

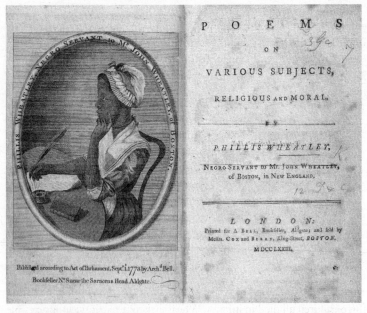

Phillis Wheatley, *Poems on Various Subjects, Religious and Moral*

return to Boston, probably as a result of her reception in London or, as she expressed it, 'at the desire of my friends in England'.[124]

The *Gentleman's Magazine*, for example considered it 'disgraceful' that she was still enslaved, and commented, 'Youth, innocence and piety, united with genius, have not yet been able to restore her to the condition and character with which she was invested by the Great Author of her being.'[125] The *Monthly Review* pointed its criticism at the people of Boston and stated, 'We are much concerned to find that this ingenious young woman is still a slave.'[126] In London, she spent time in the company of Granville Sharp, as well as other eminent personalities, and was seen as an example of what an African could achieve. One London review described her as 'this extraordinary Negro', another as a 'literary phenomenon', whose writing 'would do no discredit to an English poet'. The review concluded, 'the whole is indeed extraordinary, considered as the production of a young Negro, who was but a few years since an illiterate barbarian.'[127]

Her poetry was presented in the form of rhyming couplets and employs many classical and biblical allusions, although some have found evidence of an Islamic heritage.[128] She commented on her own status in 'On Being Brought from Africa to America', and on her homeland as 'pleasing Gambia' and 'Afric's blissful plain'.[129] Her attitude to enslavement can perhaps be gauged by the lines:

> I, young in life, by seeming cruel fate
> Was snatch'd from Afric's fancy'd happy seat:
> What pangs excruciating must molest,
> What sorrows labour in my parent's breast?
> Steel'd was that soul and by no misery mov'd
> That from a father seiz'd his babe belov'd:
> Such, such my case. And can I then but pray
> Others may never feel tyrannic sway?[130]

While she was initially feted and corresponded with many eminent figures, she then struggled to have a second book of poetry published. In 1778, she was married to African American John Peters. The couple's three children all died in infancy. Wheatley was a patriotic supporter of the American War of Independence, which she hoped would bring liberty to all including African Americans. Although she died in poverty in 1784, she is now celebrated as one of America's finest early poets.

Ignatius Sancho

In 1782, two years after his death, the letters of another eighteenth-century African, Charles Ignatius Sancho, were published in London. Sancho has been described as responsible for many African firsts in Britain: 'playwright, theatre critic, art critic, composer and patron of the arts; the first literary critic of Phillis Wheatley's poetry, the first direct attack on slavery, the only documented Afro-British voter during the eighteenth century'.[131] Sancho was born on a slave ship crossing the Atlantic Ocean around 1729. His mother soon succumbed to disease in South America, while his father committed suicide to escape from slavery. He was baptized Ignatius and brought to England at the age of two and given to three sisters in Greenwich, London, who surnamed him Sancho. They refused to educate him because their 'prejudices had unhappily taught them that African ignorance was the only security for his obedience, and to enlarge the mind of their slave would go near to emancipate his person'.[132] However, the sisters' attempts to deny Sancho an education were thwarted by their neighbour, the Duke of Montagu, who took a liking to the young boy, whom he met by accident. When the duke died, in 1749, Sancho absconded and sought refuge with his widow, who eventually hired him as her butler. When the duchess died, three years later, she left Sancho an annuity of £30 and a year's salary.

Sancho was then a relatively wealthy man, with savings of about £70.[133] He squandered his wealth, reportedly on women and gambling, but was fortunate to be re-employed by the new Duke of Montagu as his personal servant. He then settled down to a life of 'frugality', and in 1758 married Anne Osborne, an African woman, in St Margaret's Church in Westminster. They subsequently had seven children, 'Sanchonets', as their father called them, although only four survived to adulthood. In 1768, the duke employed the artist Thomas Gainsborough to paint Sancho's portrait. The portrayal of African servants was often a means to draw attention to the wealth of their employers. Five years later, ill health forced Sancho to retire from the duke's service, and he and his wife opened a grocery shop, next to their new home in Charles Street, Westminster.

Sancho's portrait has brought him some fame, but he became known during his lifetime, and since, chiefly for his letter writing, which he began during 1766. He was also a composer and a writer, although his two plays and a book entitled *Theory of Music* have not survived, and something of a literary critic. His first letter was to Laurence Sterne, using the latter's own writing style. It cannot be a coincidence that this was to encourage Sterne 'to give one half hour's attention to slavery as it this day practised in our West Indies', and Sancho writes of his 'miserable black brethren'. He adds that he is writing as 'one of those people whom the vulgar and illiberal call "Negurs"', and infers that his appeal is written on behalf of 'thousands of my brother Moors'. Sterne, who had already begun writing on the subject, wrote a sympathetic reply and the two men became friends.[134]

In some of his other correspondence Sancho commented on slavery, or his own status as an African in Britain, but he was otherwise politically conservative. His horror at the Gordon Riots led him to exclaim 'I am not sorry I was born in Afric'. Regarding his status in Britain, he once described himself as 'only a lodger – and hardly that'. On another occasion, he refers to Britain as 'your country' and criticizes 'your country's conduct' as 'uniformly wicked in the East-West-Indies and even on the coast of Guinea'. Although he also criticizes African involvement in transatlantic trafficking, he pointedly refers to 'the Christian abominable traffic for slaves' and the fact that Africa's 'petty kings' were 'encouraged by their Christian customers'. It is possible that some of Sancho's other comments on slavery and his own status have been removed by his editor, but nonetheless he was the first African to have his opposition to slavery published. In the eighteenth century, letter writing was considered almost an art form and it was clearly something which Sancho took seriously. Since some of his letters were published during his lifetime, it is likely that Sancho wrote for the public as well as for individual correspondents.[135]

A well-read and enlightened man, 'a man of letters', Sancho was familiar with the literature, music, art and politics of his time. He commented positively on the work of Phillis Wheatley and he also wrote of his own family life, everyday racism and life in general.[136] He corresponded with artists and actors, the literati, as well as members of the aristocracy, and included amongst his friends the actor David Garrick and the sculptor Joseph Nollekens. His first biographer claimed that Dr Johnson 'had promised to write the Life of Ignatius which afterwards he neglected to do'.[137] In short, he was a well-known figure. He wrote to other Africans, such as the musician Charles Lincoln as well as Julius Soubise, the notorious dandy and servant to the Duchess of Queensberry. Sancho's first letter to Sterne was published in 1775, together with the author's response, and it subsequently appeared in several contemporary newspapers.[138] The following year the press advertised the publication of some of Sancho's music, 'A Collection of Cotillions and Dances Dedicated to the Princess Royal'.[139] News of the death in 1780 of 'Mr Ignatius Sancho, grocer and oilman', probably from complications associated with gout, also received extensive press coverage.[140]

Following Sancho's death some of his letters were collected for publication by one of his correspondents, 'motivated by the desire of shewing that an untutored African may possess abilities equal to an

European'. The first edition of Sancho's *Letters* was published in August 1782. Here again there was significant press coverage, not least because there were over 1,200 subscribers to the first edition, including 'the names of the greatest characters of the present day'. This was evidence, one report suggested, that the country could 'surmount all the hardened and inhuman prejudices of slavery'.[141] Subscriptions to the first edition are thought to have realized £500 for his widow and family. There were several press reviews from August 1782 onwards, as well as extended obituaries. One newspaper prefaced an extract from the *Letters*, which it described as written by 'a Negro self-tutored', with the following: 'they have the ease of epistles written in the openness of nature, and in the playful familiarity of friendship. They breathe unaffected piety and have the ardour of genuine patriotism.'[142]

Sancho's letters are today of interest for his views on the culture and issues of his times, including slavery, as well as for the fact that they were written by an African. This was also the case in the eighteenth century, although then Sancho's writing was combatting the virulent racism of the period, when the defenders of the slave system denied the humanity of Africans. Sancho was one of those who showed that the moral sentiments and feelings of Africans were no different from other humans and, by so doing, he helped to undermine anti-African racism. He was recognized for this important contribution by his contemporaries, both the supporters of the slave system and those who opposed it.

EIGHTEENTH-CENTURY AFRICANS

Estimates of exactly how many Africans lived in England during the eighteenth century vary. The lawyer for Stewart in the Somerset case suggests that 'about fourteen thousand slaves' were in Britain, while Lord Mansfield himself put the number at '14000 or 15,000 men', whom he valued at £50 each.[143] The slave-monger Gilbert Francklyn refers to 15,000 to 20,000 African servants who, he alleged, freed themselves as a result of the case. More modern estimates suggest that the entire African population was between 10,000 and 15,000, with the majority living in London, out of a total British population of about 8 million.[144] The number of black Londoners was increased in the

1780s by an influx of several hundred 'Black Loyalists' from North America. Often formerly enslaved, they had fought for or otherwise aided Britain in the American war, sometimes in return for freedom. In Britain they became destitute, were referred to as the 'Black Poor' and were encouraged to travel as colonists to Sierra Leone in 1787, although discouraged by Lord George Gordon and by Olaudah Equiano, one of the most prominent Africans in London at the time.[145] Whatever the precise numbers and status of those in Britain, all would have felt the impact of slavery, since Britain was the world's leading human trafficker and British citizens owned more enslaved Africans than their European rivals. However, not all those of African heritage were enslaved and far fewer had that servile status towards the end of the eighteenth century, largely through their own efforts. Although they faced many struggles, black people can be found pursuing a variety of occupations and many would have faced similar challenges to other working people living at the time.

Some Africans who were connected with human traffickers in the

FOOT PAD'S - OR MUCH ADO ABOUT NOTHING.

An African woman appears in this drawing by Isaac Cruikshank (1795)

African continent were generally treated rather differently in Britain. Ayuba Suleiman Diallo (c.1701–1773) was from a leading Muslim Fulani family in what is today's Senegal. He was also engaged in human trafficking when he himself was kidnapped, along with his interpreter, on the African coast in 1731, sold to the Royal Africa Company (RAC) and transported to Maryland. Whilst in captivity, Diallo wrote a letter to his father in Arabic which was intercepted by the director of the Royal Africa Company, who had it translated. As Diallo was of noble birth, his freedom was secured and in 1733 he was brought to England by the RAC. Even in England, Diallo did not trust the RAC, and his supporters arranged for £59 to be paid to free him from any dependence on its good offices. The most notable of these was Thomas Bluett, the author of a biography of Diallo, who was known in England as Job Ben Solomon.[146] Diallo was feted in England, not least for producing three written copies of the Quran from memory and for translating Arabic texts for Hans Sloane, the founder of the British Museum. Diallo's portrait was painted – perhaps the first African to have this distinction – his biography published and 'he was graciously received by the royal family, and most of the Nobility, from who he received distinguishing Marks of Favour'.[147] He is said to have received gifts worth £500, including a watch from the royal family and, when he returned to Africa in 1734, to have carried a letter from the RAC which 'order'd their agents to show him the greatest Respect'.[148] It was reported that on Diallo's return he also secured the release from captivity of his interpreter with assistance from his friends in Britain.

There is also the case of William Ansah Sessarakoo (c.1736–1770) who was sent by his father, a leading figure in the government in the port of Anomabu in modern-day Ghana, to be educated in Britain along with a companion. The port was central to Britain's human-trafficking operations in the region, as was William's father. Rather than arriving directly in Britain, Sessarakoo and his compatriot were kidnapped by the sea captain entrusted with their safety and sold into slavery in Barbados. As a consequence, his father refused to continue relations with the RAC, preferring instead to engage with its French rivals. The RAC and the British government were compelled to pay for the liberation of William from enslavement and to take him to London where he and his companion were placed under the protection of the

Earl of Halifax, 'first commissioner of trade and plantations', the government minister responsible for human trafficking, 'who gave orders for clothing and educating them in a very genteel manner'.[149] Sessarakoo became quite a celebrated figure in London. The writer Horace Walpole recorded, 'there are two black princes of Annamaboe here who are the fashion at all assemblies, of whom I scarce know all the particulars ... though all the women know of it and ten times more than belongs to it.' The two Africans were baptized and received at court, Sessarakoo had his portrait painted and attended the theatre where his appearance was greeted with applause. He was even the subject of poems and 'memoirs' about his life. He remained in England for two years. In 1750 he returned to his father, who promised his support for the building of what became Fort William, the centre of British trafficking operations on the Gold Coast. Sessarakoo was subsequently employed by the RAC.[150]

Sessarakoo's reception in London suggests that there was a recognition from the government and those it represented that human trafficking was to some degree a partnership, the courtesies of which needed to be observed. Some Africans were treated better than others – if this was to the advantage of Britain's commercial interests. Images of the two 'African Princes', Diallo and Sessarakoo, appeared alongside each other in the *Gentleman's Magazine* in 1750.[151]

There were other Africans of noble birth in England during the eighteenth century. As was the case with William Ansah Sessarakoo, some African notables wished their sons, and sometimes daughters, to be educated abroad, or, in some cases, these African students were educated by the human traffickers in Britain. In 1788 those representing commercial interests in Liverpool, including those involved in human trafficking, reported that there were 'about fifty Mulatto and Negro Children, Natives of Africa, in this town and its vicinity, who have been sent here by their parent to receive the advantage of a European education'. This report added that an unknown number were also likely to have been sent to Bristol and London 'to learn sense and get a good head'.[152] In 1781 the Swedish abolitionist Carl Wadström reported that 'the desire of the Africans to have their children educated in Europe, appears from the voluntary sending them over for that purpose. There are generally from fifty to seventy of these children at school in

Liverpool, besides those who come to London and Bristol.' Wadström mentions two West African human traffickers educated in England in this manner. He was himself responsible for the education of Peter Panah, the son of the King of Mesurado, in present-day Liberia, West Africa, whom he had rescued from enslavement. The King of Mesurado had himself been educated in Liverpool. Panah was educated 'in the rudiments of Christianity' in Mitcham, Surrey, before dying of tuberculosis at a young age at Wadström's London home in 1790.[153]

The son of the Temne ruler, Naimbana, was entrusted to the care of Granville Sharp when he was sent to Britain to be educated in 1791. On one occasion the young man 'broke out into violent and vindictive language' when someone who had made derogatory comments about Africans was mentioned in his presence. He is reported to have said, 'I cannot forgive the man who takes away the character of the people of my country.'[154] On other occasions African children were brought to England as hostages in order to secure trading advantages, but were educated and treated lavishly during their captivity.[155]

It seems that these students did not remain long in England and would return to West Africa on the ships of the captains who acted as their guardians, 'where they endeavour to live and dress in the European manner'.[156] There were females, as well as males, studying the '3 Rs', although the girls might also learn domestic duties and needlework. They were then often reluctant to return to Africa. One who did, a Miss Norie, was said to have spent some time in England as a 'lady's maid in a genteel family'. Both African and British merchants thought that such education was beneficial to their commercial interests, but it was clear that the Africans generally took what was useful to them, which did not always include Christianity.[157]

By the end of the eighteenth century, it had also become the policy of the Church of England to educate some Africans in Britain. The most notable of these was Philip Quaque [Kweku] (1741–1816) who was recruited by the Society for the Propogation of the Gospel in Foreign Parts, sent to England in 1754 at the age of thirteen and later married an English woman, Catherine Blunt, during his stay. Quaque was one of three 'young lads' recruited for training as an Anglican priest, but one of his companions, Thomas Coboro, soon died 'under inoculation of the smallpox', while the other, William Cudjo, was 'seized with madness' and died after some years in Guy's Hospital. Quaque lived in London, was baptized in Islington Parish Church, and in 1765 became the first African to be ordained, at a service in the Chapel Royal, St James's Palace. He was appointed a missionary to Africans in the Gold Coast.[158] His mission in West Africa had limited success. Upon his return there he was shunned by his own family and 'has never been able to fulfil the object of his mission'. In short, he was unable to convert many Africans to Christianity and he was seen as 'paying more attention to the purposes of trade than to religion'.[159] As the society worked closely with those engaged in human trafficking, such as the Company of Merchants Trading to Africa, Quaque's predicament is not difficult to understand. Still, he maintained contact with the society until his death in 1816 and at least two of his children were also educated in Britain.[160]

THE AFRICAN ACADEMY

A new step in the provision of education for Africans in Britain was taken with the founding of the African Academy in Clapham, London, in 1799. Macaulay, Wilberforce, Granville Sharp, the leading members of the Clapham Sect of social reformers, as well as Hannah More and others, were involved, as members and supporters of the Society for the Education of Africans, to provide education for the sons and daughters of prominent Africans in what was becoming Britain's first colony in Africa, Sierra Leone. The short-lived academy aimed to provide Christian education, including teaching 'industrial habits', such as boat building, that might prove useful in the development of the colony under the direction of the Sierra Leone Company. This envisaged that Christianity, civilization and commerce might be spread throughout Sierra Leone and perhaps more widely in Africa. About twenty boys received training at the academy and four girls nearby. Accompanying the girls was Mary Perth (1740–c.1813), who had been born enslaved in Virginia and had moved to Sierra Leone via Nova Scotia in Canada (as had many of the other early African colonists, often referred to as Black Loyalists for their allegiance to Britain during the war with the American colonies).[161] Most of the students were the sons of West Africans, but the children of Nova Scotians and Maroons from Jamaica were also included. Several died while in London, but at least ten returned to Sierra Leone, although the academy closed down in 1806, perhaps because of the high mortality rate.[162]

Another notable student during this period was Francis Williams (c.1690–1762), the son of free and wealthy Jamaicans, who were also themselves the owners of enslaved Africans. It was reported that Williams had a patron, the former governor of Jamaica, the Duke of Montagu, who had him educated in Britain, first at a grammar school and then at Cambridge University, as an experiment, but there are no records of his time there. He studied law, entered Lincoln's Inn in 1721, and remained in England for some years, probably working in his father's import and export business, before returning to Jamaica, where he opened a school and was known as a great defender of the rights of the free people of colour. His only surviving work is in Latin and is dedicated to flattering the new governor of Jamaica; however, it contains the lines 'Worth itself and understanding have no colour; there is no colour in an honest mind, or in art.' Despite being a slave owner himself, his writing and educational accomplishments were widely seen at the time as a refutation of racist views about the inferiority of Africans.[163]

Dido Elizabeth Belle (c.1761–1804), was the daughter of an enslaved African woman brought to Britain, Maria Belle, and Sir John Lindsay, the nephew of Lord Chief Justice Mansfield. Some reports suggest that she was already pregnant when she arrived in Britain. Lindsay later freed Maria Belle and bequeathed land in Florida to her. Dido Belle lived with Mansfield in London and also at his suburban residence Kenwood House. Although unmarried, she lived a somewhat privileged existence. She was educated, provided with an allowance and acted as a companion to Mansfield's great-niece, with the two appearing in a famous portrait together, although she also had some of the responsibilities of a favoured servant. When Mansfield died in 1788, he left her a significant sum in his will. He also made it clear that she was a free person, which shows once again that ultimately slave status was still legal in England.[164]

Africans in Britain pursued a variety of occupations, although the majority were household servants. Some, like Sancho, Francis Barber and Julius Soubise had relationships with their employers that were advantageous for them (although even Barber appears to have temporarily absconded), while others were not so fortunate. Some formerly enslaved servants *were* freed, for example, Kate Coker, 'a Negro woman servant', and Frances Coker (1767–1820), a trained seamstress, who both worked for the family of John Pinney, a Bristol plantation and slave owner.[165] Others were not always so lucky. Another African, Pero Jones (c.1753–1798), who was brought to Britain from Nevis by the Pinney family, was not freed and is reported to have remained enslaved until his death.[166] Even those apparently legally free might be bound to employers or, on occasions, have had their free status disregarded. Ann Dennis or Williams, a servant who appeared as a witness in a matrimonial dispute in the House of Lords, claimed that her employer 'stole her freedom' as she had been brought to London from the Caribbean against her will in 1766. The sources tell us that Ann, who some considered a slave, was allowed to provide evidence before the House of Lords but nothing more about her ambiguous status.[167]

One historian has listed actress, barrister, cabinet maker, fencing instructor, gardener, highwayman, minister of religion, prostitute and victualler amongst the many other occupations undertaken by Africans in the eighteenth century.[168] In the early nineteenth century, William Sancho (1775–1810), the son of Ignatius Sancho and his wife Anne Osbourne, worked with his mother and became (probably) the country's first Black publisher and bookseller. He was based initially in his father's shop and then in Castle Street, near Leicester Square. He published his father's letters and works by others, including Wilberforce and Voltaire.[169] The records of cases heard at the Old Bailey also show Black people as victims, criminals and witnesses and even, as early as 1746, a 'Negro constable', of Clerkenwell, who arrested and interrogated a woman charged with theft and gave evidence against her.[170] Africans lived predominantly in London, as well as other port cities such as Bristol and Liverpool, but they were recorded in many other towns and cities in England as well as in Scotland and Wales. As early as 1676 John Mills was recorded as the churchwarden in Wolstanton in Staffordshire. Cesar Picton, of Kingston-upon-Thames in Surrey, was a coal merchant. There only appears to be one example of open discrimination against African employment. By an order of 14 September 1731, Africans were banned from apprenticeships in the

City of London, after John Satia, apprenticed to a 'joyner', was admitted to the Freedom of the City of London and thereby became eligible to vote. The Court of Alderman decided that Satia's admission should not be 'for the future drawn into precedent and that no Nigros or other Blacks be at any time admitted into the freedom of this City'.[171]

Scipio Kennedy (a.k.a. Douglas (d.1794)), was an enslaved African who was brought to Glasgow in 1704. He later learned to read and write and appears to have been employed partly as a smuggler. In 1725 he was freed and probably continued his smuggling activities before combining them with weaving. He married a local woman with whom he produced eight children, and died at an old age.[172] George Scipio Africanus (c.1762–1834), who was brought to Britain from Sierra Leone as a child, had a variety of occupations including waiter and labourer. He was baptized in Wolverhampton in 1766, while apprenticed to a brass founder, but by the early 1790s had married a local woman and established Africanus' Register of Servants, an employment agency in Nottingham. He became a successful entrepreneur, later owned several properties in the city and voted in elections.[173] John Ystumllyn (d.1786) probably arrived as a child in North Wales in the 1740s. His precise origins are unknown but it is likely that he was kidnapped in Africa. He is said to have learned to speak both Welsh and English, married a local woman and was employed as a gardener and land agent. His portrait was painted before his early death.[174]

THE ARMY AND NAVY

During the eighteenth century, the British army and navy began to recruit increasing numbers of African soldiers and sailors. It also became more fashionable for African military bandsmen, trumpeters and drummers to be recruited to some elite cavalry regiments, including the monarch's household regiments. This was a practice that dated back to Tudor times. By the end of the seventeenth century many African drummers and trumpeters, some of them enslaved, had been employed by English regiments in the Caribbean. Africans had also been employed as personal servants by some army officers, largely to add to their prestige, and were sometimes included in artistic representations, just as they were outside the military. Within elite regiments there are pictorial representations such as the African drummer shown in a picture of the Battle of Blenheim in 1704, or the African trumpeter of the Horse Guards, painted by the artist David Morier c.1750.[175] The use of African musicians, although long established, seems to have become even more popular with the craze for 'Turkish music' in the eighteenth century. One authority suggests that the use of a leopard skin by drummers and the flourishes associated with drum sticks are traditions introduced by, or related to, African drummers.[176] After 1757 Black musicians were recruited into most British Army regiments and African bandsmen remained a key feature until the 1840s.[177]

There was a more widespread use of African soldiers in general, who were mostly recruited from the Caribbean. One of the earliest such recruits was John Macnell, from Antigua, who enlisted in the 29th Foot Regiment at the age of just twelve in 1756. He was discharged as disabled in London, with a pension, twenty-two years later.[178] Another recruit whom we met earlier in this chapter was Ukawsaw Gronniosaw, who joined the 28th Foot Regiment about 1762 as part of his plan to come to England.[179] By the end of the century about 40 per cent of foot regiments employed Caribbean-born soldiers, in addition to those who originated from Africa, North America and the British Isles.[180]

Briton Hammon, Gronniosaw, Equiano and Thomas Lewis all served in the navy and it became almost commonplace for Africans to be employed as sailors. Both the Royal Navy and the merchant fleet suffered from a manpower shortage and Africans were an important reserve. Although recent research suggests that numbers may have been much lower than the 25 per cent of all mariners previously suggested, there were well over a thousand 'black tars' by the end of the eighteenth century.[181] A very few mariners of African heritage were officers, but in the early nineteenth century the Admiralty issued instructions that such men should be dismissed.[182] However, Africans were employed in many maritime occupations including as workers at the naval docks. An African sailor is often represented in artistic works at the side of Nelson at Trafalgar. In 1815, an African woman from Antigua disguised herself as a man and called herself William Brown.

She served for over a month on HMS *Queen Charlotte*, while she was still docked, before being dismissed because of her gender.[183]

Some Africans were even employed as sailors on slave ships, which could be a hazardous occupation during the eighteenth century. In 1779, an African sailor called Amissa brought a case against a ship's captain from Liverpool who had sold him into slavery in Jamaica, even though he had been paid wages and recruited as a pilot off the coast of what is today Anomabu in Ghana. Amissa was himself enslaved after being asked to row ashore several enslaved Africans. The captain of the ship returned to Africa and proclaimed that Amissa was dead. By chance, another African returned to the continent from Jamaica and alerted Amissa's friends. The King of Anomabu commissioned the captain of another ship to buy Amissa's freedom and sent an emissary to identify him. After three years of enslavement, he was initially brought to London. There, with the aid of the African Company of Merchants, responsible for human trafficking in Africa, a case was brought on his behalf and heard before Lord Mansfield at the Guildhall. The jury in the case only deliberated for fifteen minutes before finding in favour of Amissa and awarding him £300 in damages.[184]

After the 1772 judgment, which made it illegal for former owners to re-enslave those who had liberated themselves and transport them out of the country where they had found freedom, there was an even greater incentive for Africans to join the navy and come to Britain, in the belief that freedom reigned there. The commencement of the American Revolution and the proclamation of freedom for enslaved African 'loyalists' only increased the numbers from North America who ran away to sea. Hundreds of such mariners found their way to London only to swell the ranks of the Black Poor. Even before that time enslaved Africans used the navy as a passage to freedom. In 1751 William Castillo, sailing off the coast of Boston, had convinced a ship's captain to purchase him, agreeing to work for several years to repay the purchase price. Five years later he absconded, but in 1758 met his former owner in Portsmouth and was arrested and placed in an iron collar. The captain threatened to re-enslave and sell him in the Caribbean, but Castillo, who was literate, wrote to the Admiralty in protest. The Admiralty in turn wrote to the navy's commanding officer in Portsmouth as follows:

'the laws of this country admit no badges of slavery therefore the lords hope and expect whenever he discovers any attempt of this kind he should prevent it'.[185]

There are many instances of the Royal Navy employing 'slave mariners', but also instances of such mariners being returned to slavery, even if they had previously made their way to England. On other occasions, docking at an English port could lead to freedom, as was the case for the four Black mariners originating from West Africa, the Caribbean and North America on board the New England-built ship *Lawrence*, which arrived in Portsmouth in 1776. In that instance, port officials and local mariners intervened to secure their freedom.[186] In 1784 the Admiralty issued orders, 'Of the Government of Negroes', which gave instructions regarding the 'purchase of Negroes' aged twelve to fourteen years old, who were to serve apprenticeships in the navy. According to the document their 'treatment shall be considerate and humane' and they were only to be 'flogged for flagrant crimes and then in the manner practised in the Navy'. When they were not working, such apprentices were to be placed under superintendence and 'for their morals and behaviour to be taught to read and attend church'. It seems, therefore, that their numbers were sufficient for such regulations to be required.[187] Many other mariners were of free status and appear in the historical record as relatively affluent individuals who were sometimes the prey of those less fortunate than themselves. In 1736, John Guy, an African sailor on the *Newcastle*, alleged that he had been robbed of over seventeen guineas by several women in London soon after he had received his back pay.[188] In 1764 the *Gloucester Chronicle* reported 'the most barbarous murder committed on the body of George Harford, a Negro ... a sailor on board the Stag man of war'. Harford was apparently murdered for his wages and prize money. His murderer was subsequently executed.[189] In 1781, John Williams, an African sailor also on board a 'man of war' was robbed of five guineas by Ann Read in London, soon after he had received six months' pay. The accused in this case was sentenced to death.[190]

MUSICIANS AND COMPOSERS

African musicians were not just to be found in the British Army. Joseph Emidy was born c.1775 in Guinea but enslaved as a child and taken by Portuguese traffickers to Brazil. He was then taken by his owner to Lisbon, where he was taught to play the violin. He became so proficient that within a few years he was playing in the orchestra of the Lisbon Opera. In 1795, he was kidnapped, 'violin and all', by British sailors on the orders of the commander of the *Indefatigable*, Sir Edward Pellew, who wanted 'a good violin player to furnish music for the sailors' dancing'.[191] Emidy's kidnapping provides a further example of the dangers faced by Africans during this period, although kidnapping or 'impressment' was a common means of providing men for the navy even in England. Emidy was kept on board ship for seven years, to prevent his escape, until he was finally put ashore in Falmouth. He soon found employment as a musician and music teacher. According to one of his former pupils he, 'taught equally well the piano, violin, violoncello, clarinet and flute'. He was 'an exquisite violinist', and 'a good composer, who led all the concerts in the county'. Indeed, within a short time, Emidy was engaged in concerts throughout Cornwall and became the leader of the Truro Philharmonic Orchestra. In 1802, he married a local woman and the couple had eight children. He was known not only as a virtuoso violinist, but also a prolific composer, yet today nothing remains of his compositions, which included symphonies and concerti. It was said at the time that a career as a major composer was impossible since, 'his colour would be so much against him'.[192] Emidy died on 24 April 1835 and is buried in Truro. His obituary in a local newspaper referred to his compositions as evincing 'not only deep musical research, but also those flights of genius which induce regret that that his talents were not called into action in a more genial sphere than that in which he moved'.[193]

Although today Emidy is sometimes remembered as one of the first African composers in Britain, he was preceded by Ignatius Sancho, many years before, and by George Polgreen Bridgetower, who gave his first violin concert in England at the age of nine in 1789. Bridgetower was the son of a Barbadian father and an Austrian mother who was born in Poland. After arriving in England, he soon came under the protection of the Prince of Wales, who financed his musical and general education. Known as a child prodigy, he performed in numerous concerts in England and was included in the prince's private orchestra. He later became a friend of Beethoven, who described him as a 'very able virtuoso'. Beethoven initially dedicated what became known as the Kreutzer Sonata to Bridgetower, before a falling-out. Bridgetower and Beethoven gave the first performance of the work in Vienna. Bridgetower later studied at Cambridge University and had an illustrious career before dying in poverty in Peckham, London, in 1860.

THE SONS OF AFRICA

Two of the most famous Africans of the eighteenth century were the writers and abolitionists Olaudah Equiano and Quobna Ottobah Cugoano, both leading members of the Sons of Africa, one of the first African political organizations in Britain. Both men had formerly been enslaved and they may have had the same owner at different times.[194]

Cugoano was born in about 1757 in a Fanti coastal village in what is now Ghana. Almost everything that we know about him is from his own account and was initially published in his famous work of 1787, *Thoughts and Sentiments on the Evil and Wicked Traffic of the Slavery and Commerce of the Human Species*. In 1770, when he was about thirteen, Cugoano was kidnapped with about twenty others by African traffickers who sold him to Europeans. He was initially transported to Grenada and then in 1772 was taken to England where, it seems, he taught himself to read and write, but was also sent to school by his master. Cugoano lived in London and in 1773, at the age of sixteen, he had himself baptized John Stuart, at St James's Church, Piccadilly. According to his own account, he was 'advised by some good people to get myself baptized, that I might not be carried away and sold again'.[195] He does not say how he freed himself but subsequently he worked as a servant for the painters Richard and Maria Cosway, in Pall Mall, and appears in their etched self-portrait in 1784. In 1785 Richard Cosway, who moved in fashionable society, was appointed Principal Painter to the Prince of Wales, and through him Cugoano met artists such as

Joshua Reynolds and Joseph Nollekens, as well as other notable figures like Granville Sharpe. Cugoano began to organize with other Africans in London around the time that the Committee for the Relief of the Black Poor was established in 1786. In July of that year Cugoano and William Green, another prominent African in London, asked Sharp to assist them in saving a fellow African, Harry Demane, who had been forced aboard a ship bound for the Caribbean.[196]

Olaudah Equiano was born in about 1745 in 'Eboe' in the kingdom of Benin, now in south-eastern Nigeria. He was the youngest of six sons of an elder with the title *Embrenché*, a term 'importing the highest distinction and signifying in our language the mark of grandeur'.[197] When he was about eleven Equiano and his sister were kidnapped by other Africans. They were separated and, after passing through several African owners, Equiano was sold to Europeans who transported him to Barbados and then to Virginia, where he was sold and eventually bought by an officer in the Royal Navy. This owner named him Gustavus Vassa, after a Swedish king, and took him to London in 1757. Equiano served in the navy during the Seven Years' War but was then sold again in 1762. He managed to buy his own freedom in 1766 and remained in North America for a year before returning to London. He then worked as a mariner and hairdresser, joined an expedition to the Arctic, converted to Methodism, and was for a time a buyer and overseer of slaves in Central America. He seems to have begun his anti-slavery activities in 1774 by coming to the aid of a ship's cook, John Annis, whose former owner was attempting to kidnap him. In his efforts to free Annis, Equiano approached Granville Sharp but was not able to secure his friend's freedom.

The fate of Annis, who Equiano reported died as a re-enslaved man in St Kitts, shows the limitations of the Mansfield judgment of 1772. In the years after this defeat, Equiano continued to show concern for the fate of his fellow Africans. In 1779, he applied to become a missionary and return to Africa and, in 1783, he reported to Granville Sharp an infamous court case, in which Mansfield was also the judge, relating to the slave ship *Zong*. From this ship 132 enslaved Africans had been thrown overboard, allegedly because of a water shortage but in fact to claim their insurance value.[198] In the late 1770s Equiano also began to write regularly in the press, although not always on the question of slavery.[199] From 1788 onwards he wrote several newspaper articles arguing for the abolition of the trafficking of Africans on moral but also economic grounds. He argued that if Africans remained in Africa as consumers and producers this would be more advantageous to commercial interests in Britain.[200] He wished to influence matters in Parliament as well; in July of 1788 he and Cugoano co-signed a letter to the parliamentarian Sir William Dolben, along with four of their 'brethren', those who had previously styled themselves the Sons of Africa.[201]

The Sons of Africa has become the best-known organization of Africans in Britain in the eighteenth century and perhaps the first named political organization in Britain's history. The title Sons of Africa first appeared in a letter of thanks written to Granville Sharp in December 1787, although Equiano had co-written similar letters of thanks with other Africans earlier than that, in 1785. The letters were sometimes sent privately, but on other occasions appeared in the press. They seem to have been designed to encourage greater efforts 'towards breaking the yoke of slavery'. The signatures, sometimes from as many as twelve Africans, were often accompanied with the phrase 'For ourselves and Brethren', suggesting that they represented a much wider collective of Africans in Britain who were organized as abolitionists.[202]

THE ABOLITIONIST MOVEMENT

We have already seen that those in Britain most interested in an end to the enslavement of Africans were Africans themselves and that they adopted a variety of strategies (baptism, marriage, running away, collective organizing) to liberate themselves and their compatriots. Africans were active abolitionists, sometimes demanding wages for their labour, writing to defend their humanity and to condemn the entire slave system, as well as organizing themselves in bodies such as the Sons of Africa. They were aided by other working people and by those sympathetic to their cause, including doctors, lawyers, clergymen and men like Granville Sharp in England and Anthony Benezet in North America, who devoted themselves to the abolitionist cause. Legal judgments, especially the famous Somerset case, also assisted them and increasingly there were discussions in the press concerning slavery. In 1773, an influential poem was published by John Bicknell and Thomas Day, 'The Dying Negro, a Poetical Epistle, from a Black, Who Shot Himself on Board a Vessel in the River Thames, to his Intended Wife'. Day was influenced by the French philosopher Jean-Jacques Rousseau, to whom the poem is dedicated, but it is based on a tragedy that occurred in London. In May of 1773, it was reported that 'a black servant' had run away from his master and been baptized 'with the intent to marry his fellow servant, a white woman'. Having been forcibly kidnapped and placed aboard his master's ship in the Thames 'he took an opportunity of shooting himself in the head'.[203] In 1784 Day published his *Fragment of an Original Letter on the Slavery of the Negroes*, an attack on the hypocrisy of those who demanded the 'rights of man' in America but denied rights to Africans.[204] There was perhaps a heightened awareness of the barbarity of slavery, at that time, following the infamous *Zong* case. In 1776 there was even a motion introduced in the House of Commons 'that the Slave Trade was contrary to the laws of God, and the rights of men', although it was defeated. There was also evidence that many religious denominations, as well those seeking parliamentary reform, were opposed to the slave system and the trafficking of Africans.[205]

There had long been a questioning of the slave system by many of the leading figures of the European Enlightenment. Some like Montesquieu and Edmund Burke favoured reforms and amelioration, in the belief that the existing system created the danger of slave insurrection that could eventually destroy it. Others feared that immediate emancipation in the colonies was unworkable and there needed to be a slow transition.[206] In 1780 Burke drafted a plan for the reform and regulation of the slave system and in 1792 presented a 'Sketch of a Negro Code' to the government.[207] What was perhaps most important about the Enlightenment, however, was not the views of individuals but the fact that all existing institutions were questioned, and subject to criticism and analysis. Even Eurocentrism came under scrutiny in the work of Voltaire and others. This was most popularly done through debates and essay-writing contests, such as that which first encouraged the writing of the English abolitionist Thomas Clarkson. It was also an age when it was increasingly asserted that all men were born free and equal, and therefore it followed that the enslavement of Africans was a violation of 'natural rights'. The very notion that humans had inalienable rights first assumed popularity during this period, largely through the work of Montesquieu, Raynal, Diderot and the Encyclopedists in France, with their defence of 'natural rights' and the brotherhood of man.

Such views also had supporters in Britain. In opposition to the views of Locke and Hume, who found justifications for human trafficking and slavery, there were the religious views of Richard Baxter and Morgan Godwyn, as well as those of the Irish philosopher Francis Hutcheson. Baxter condemned slavery in his *Directions to Slave Holders* of 1673, arguing that Africans 'are of as good a kind as you, that is, they are reasonable creatures as well as you, and born to as much natural liberty'. He concluded, 'to go as pirates, and catch up poor Negroes, or people of another land, that never forfeited life or liberty, and to make them slaves and sell them, is one of the worst kinds of thefts in the world, and such persons are to be taken for the common enemies of mankind'.[208]

Godwyn, an Anglican minster in both Virginia and Barbados but not an abolitionist, nevertheless used the publication of his *The Negro's & Indians Advocate* in 1680 to argue against those who asserted that Africans were not as fully human as Europeans. Hutcheson, in his *System of Moral Philosophy*, published in 1753, defended the view that 'the natural equality of men chiefly consists in this, that these natural rights belong equally to all,' and found 'all notions of slavery . . . horridly unjust.'[209] The Scottish advocate George Wallace went even further in his book *A System of the Principles of the Laws of Scotland* (published in 1760). He declared that 'every one of those unfortunate men, who are pretended to be slaves, has a right to be declared free, for he never lost his liberty . . . This right he carries about with him and is entitled everywhere to get it declared. As soon therefore as he comes into a country in which the judges are not forgetful of their own humanity, it is their duty to remember that he is a man and to declare him to be free.'[210] An even more radical anti-slavery position was adopted in an anonymous pamphlet published in London in 1760 and entitled *Two Dialogues on the Man-trade*. The author condemns the fact that 'we Englishmen, we Christians' for over a hundred years had been 'at war and enmity with mankind' and destroyed 'many of the human race

who never did us any injury'. The author demanded immediate emancipation of all the enslaved and concluded:

> And so all the black men now in our plantations, who are by unjust
> force deprived of their liberty, and held in slavery, as they have none
> upon earth to appeal to, may lawfully repel that force with force, and
> to recover their liberty, destroy their oppressors: and not only so, but it
> is the duty of others, white as well as blacks, to assist these miserable
> creatures, if they can, in their attempts to deliver themselves out of slav-
> ery, and to rescue them out of the hands of their cruel tyrants.[211]

Others subjected the slave system to an economic analysis and
found it to be costly and unproductive. Perhaps the most notable of
these was as the Scottish political economist Adam Smith, best known
for his famous work *An Inquiry into the Nature and Causes of the
Wealth of Nations*, first published in 1776. In an earlier work, Smith
had referred to Africans as 'nations of heroes'. The 'rights of man', or
'natural rights', were not just moral and philosophical questions, they
were increasingly seen as life-and-death matters. This was particularly
the case during the American and French Revolutions, but also in
Britain, since such rights were not recognized by the existing political
system. Between 1765 and 1783 the American Revolution led not just
to the loss of Britain's colonies, but it also gave a voice to the stirrings
of an emerging English radicalism. It became increasingly difficult to
consider the rights of some men without considering the rights of all.

There was also religious opposition to the slave system, even amongst
some in the Church of England. Many evangelical Christians, such as
John Wesley, the founder of Methodism, were opponents. Wesley published his *Thoughts on the Slave Trade* in 1774 and later wrote, 'I would
do anything in my power to the extirpation of that trade, which is a
scandal not only to Christianity but to humanity.'[212] On both sides of
the Atlantic the Quakers, led by Benezet and John Woolman, had
become particularly active campaigners against the slave system and
they led by personal example. Benezet was in contact with both Wesley
and Granville Sharp and an inspiration for the writing and activism of
Thomas Clarkson. [213] The first Quaker petition to Parliament regarding
the abolition of colonial slavery was delivered in 1783, and their subsequent agitation may well have been widely influential. In October of

1785, Equiano and some other Africans presented the Quakers with an 'address of thanks' on behalf of 'the poor, oppressed, needy, and much-degraded black'.[214] In 1784, Reverend James Ramsey published *An Essay on the Treatment and Conversion of African Slaves in the Sugar Colonies*, the first direct attack on the slave system by a former slave owner. Two years later Thomas Clarkson published his anti-slavery *Essay on the Slavery and Commerce of the Human Species, Particularly the African*. Such abolitionist writing led to a backlash which meant, at least, that few in Britain and its colonies could remain ignorant about the issues of slavery and human trafficking.

The racist view of Hume, who in 1753 wrote, 'I am apt to suspect the Negroes, and in general all the other species of men (for there are four or five different kinds) to be naturally inferior to the whites', was only the most eminent summary of the justifications that slavery, human trafficking and empire demanded. Modern anti-African racism often developed within the context of a struggle to find such justification and reconcile it with Christianity. It is for this reason that early critics of slavery were often Quakers, Puritans, or others who found their faith at odds with the inhumanity of trafficking humans in pursuit of the profit that surrounded it and it was to become an inherent feature of the new capital-centred societies. It is also interesting that the early critiques of slavery and human trafficking began to refer to 'Whites' as well as 'Blacks'. As early as 1684 Thomas Tryon, an English philosopher and writer, launched a vigorous attack on the principle that might is right and posed the question from an African perspective:

> Have not you variety of Complexions amongst your selves; some very *White* and *Fair*, others *Brown*, many *Swarthy*, and several *Cole-black*? And would it be reasonable that each sort of these should quarrel with the other, and a man be made *a Slave* forever, meerly because his Beard is *Red*, or his Eyebrows *Black*? In a word, if our *Hue* be the only difference, since *White* is as contrary to *Black*, as *Black* is to *White*, there is as much reason that *you* should be our *Slaves*, as we yours ... And is not this a fine imployment think you, for Christians, to run to remotest Regions, to get their innocent Fellow Creatures and make Slaves of them [sic].[215]

Tryon opposes slavery and human trafficking on the basis that it is unchristian, unjust and inhuman and carried out purely for profit, and he refuses to accept any spurious racist justifications.[216] The defenders of such crimes against humanity, including the Church of England, therefore had to use all the means at their disposal to counter such cogent arguments and continually to reinforce anti-African views, not only in the colonies, but also in Britain. In the eighteenth century, as the abolitionist movement gathered momentum, and as Africans throughout the diaspora increasingly attempted to liberate themselves, leading racists found it even more urgent to state the case for the human traffickers and owners of enslaved Africans and also expedient to attack Africans in Britain.

In 1785, for example, James Tobin, an owner of enslaved Africans in Nevis who wrote in opposition to abolition in the colonies, was also of the opinion that 'Negroes' in Britain were lazy and 'those who are not in livery are in rags; and such as are not servants, are thieves or mendicants'. What for Tobin was even worse was that 'the great number of Negroes at present in England, the strange partiality shewn for them by the lower order of women, and the rapid increase of a dark and contaminated breed, are evils which have long been complained of, and call every day more loudly for enquiry and redress.'[217] The following year Gordon Turnbull produced *An Apology for Negro Slavery*, which he also based on the views of Hume and others 'who imagined the Negro-race to be an inferior species of mankind'. Turnbull asserted that enslaved Africans remained enslaved in England, but regarding the Black poor in London (whom he referred to as 'black objects') were those who, 'were it not for the outstretched hand of heaven-born charity would perish, miserably perish, with hunger or with cold. They are freemen.' Their fate, Turnbull concluded, would be much better in the Caribbean.[218] The leading English defender of the slave system, Edward Long, also produced every possible racist justification for the trafficking of enslavement of Africans, not least their 'barbarous' and inferior nature. He too was not only concerned with the abolitionist movement in Britain, including the self-liberation of Africans, but also the insurrections that were occurring in Jamaica and wherever enslaved Africans were held in bondage. Long pays particular attention to Tacky's Rebellion and the other major rebellions in Jamaica in the 1760s, which he attempts to explain not by the oppressive nature of slavery but by blaming them on the particularly 'martial temper' of the 'Coromantins', a reference to those Africans kidnapped from modern-day Ghana.[219]

The racism and such justifications did not derail the abolitionist movement of the day. Equiano, for example, attacked both Tobin and Turnbull in a series of articles in the press in 1788.[220] However, racism in general was entrenched not only in the views of the owners of enslaved Africans, but more importantly in the institution of slavery, as well as in the nature of the expanding empire and colonial rule itself. These inherently racist creations were not based on the views of individuals, but were the preferred policies of the rich and powerful in general, implemented by the entire machinery of the state. They were based on the premise that Africans (and others) were inferior subjects to be enslaved and ruled, and their homelands to be invaded and exploited for the benefit of others. Such justifications would be further developed in the nineteenth century.

The American Revolution and the demand for self-government by the American colonists also had an unintended impact on the struggle against slavery. During that conflict, the British government was compelled to grant emancipation to those Africans in the North American colonies who aided the Crown. Hundreds of these 'Black Loyalists', as well as African American sailors and others connected with the conflict ended up in London. They were legally free but impoverished, and their plight resulted in a Committee for the Relief of the Black Poor being established in 1786. Granville Sharp and others then conceived of a plan, which received support from some of the 'Black Poor', as well as from government, that they might be transported to establish the colony of Sierra Leone, Britain's first colonial acquisition in Africa.[221] Olaudah Equiano was temporarily appointed 'commissary' for this resettlement project, which was soon mired in controversy. Equiano alleged corruption and was subsequently dismissed from his post. Nevertheless, it was reported in one newspaper that support for the Black Poor was so widespread that white beggars disguised themselves in blackface to increase their incomes.[222] In this period, there was also evidence of an increasing awareness of the plight of Africans and growing public opposition to the slave system, initially stimulated in Britain by the actions of Africans themselves. In 1787 Granville Sharp and a group of Quakers formed the Society for the Abolition of the Slave Trade, in which they were soon joined by Thomas Clarkson. Through Clarkson, the society contacted William Wilberforce, the MP for Yorkshire, as well as others in Parliament.

The new abolitionist campaign burst into mass protest when the citizens of Manchester began petitioning Parliament to end the slave trade in 1787. By the end of 1788, Parliament had received more than a hundred such petitions and Prime Minister William Pitt had insti-gated a parliamentary inquiry into the 'slave trade' by the Privy Council Committee for Trade and Plantations. From Manchester alone there were nearly 11,000 signatures, almost 20 per cent of the city's population. From York there were 1,800 signatures, nearly 40 per cent of the adult males, and in Sheffield 2,000. Petitioners in Shef-field included 769 cutlers who lamented the fact that 'cutlery wares made by the freemen' of that city were being sent to Africa 'in part, as the price of Slaves'. Their opposition to such trade was based on the principle that they considered 'the case of the nations of Africa as their own'.[223] This sense of common oppression is also evident in the songs of Joseph Mather, the eighteenth-century balladeer of Sheffield. He included in 'The File Hewer's Lamentation' this verse:

> As Negroes in Virginia
> In Maryland or Guinea
> Like them I must continue
> To be both bought and sold
> While Negro ships are filling
> I ne'er can save one shilling
> And must, which is more killing
> A pauper die when old.[224]

It is estimated that between 1787 and 1792, 1.5 million people in Britain signed anti-slave trade petitions, about one-sixth of the total population. In 1791–2, more than 500 of these petitions were pre-sented to Parliament.[225] Nearly all the major towns and cities were represented and slavery became a matter of national concern, widely discussed in Parliament and the press.[226]

Other forms of propaganda were employed as part of the abolitionist campaign: poems such as William Cowper's 'The Negro's Complaint', soon popularized as a song, and Josiah Wedgwood's medallions and

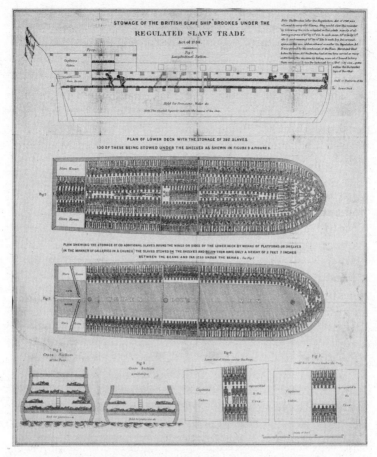

Diagram of the Liverpool slave ship *Brookes*, 1787

pottery portraying a supplicant African with the slogan, 'Am I not a man and a brother?' That image appeared in various forms, from household items to brooches and hairpins and became an essential fashion accessory. In addition, the famous schematic plan of the slave ship *Brooke*, which showed the terribly cramped conditions in which Africans were transported, was printed in thousands of copies to be hung on the walls of public houses and people's homes. There were also public lectures and debates, sometimes involving African speakers, who gave first-hand accounts of the nature of the slave system. In February 1788, for example, the Westminster Forum in London advertised the presence of 'A Native of Africa, many years a slave in the West Indies', who would recount 'a number of very remarkable circumstances respecting the treatment of Negro Slaves, and particularly of his being forcibly taken from his family and friends on the coast of Africa, and sold as a slave'. [227] At a debate in London in May 1789 a sole opponent of abolition was replied to 'by an African', who the press reported was 'not Gustavus Vassa' [sic], who 'discovered much strong natural sense, and spoke with wonderful facility'.[228] These were probably the first occasions on which Africans had spoken in public in this way. As newspapers reported, anti-slavery meetings were also the first occasions when women not only attended but spoke in public on such political matters.[229] Abolition ushered in the start of modern politics in Britain in which all the population was involved.

Within a few years, women and children were more personally involved in the campaign, since in 1791 all were encouraged to boycott the use of sugar. It was estimated that 300,000 families were involved in the boycott campaign, which also extended to rum and other slave-produced products, and included Scotland, Wales and Ireland. The abolitionist movement became perhaps the first national mass movement and one of the biggest political movements in Britain's history, involving all sections of the population including workers, women and Africans.[230] It united those demanding political reform and suffrage, all those concerned with the 'Rights of Man'. Rights were seen as indivisible; those campaigning for the rights of Africans were also concerned about the rights of ordinary people in Britain. Granville Sharp, for example, was not only an abolitionist, but also a member of the Society for Promoting Constitutional Reform, and Equiano a member of the radical London Corresponding Society.

The mass campaign culminated, in April 1791, in a parliamentary defeat for the first abolition bill introduced by William Wilberforce. But the campaign continued, both hampered and propelled by the outbreak of the revolution in France in 1789. For the British government, the revolution became an excuse to suppress agitation for political reform at home. For many reformers, it was inspirational, not least when the French revolutionaries temporarily halted the trafficking of Africans in 1794. As early as 1790, abolitionists in Manchester advertised in all the local papers, which were often reprinted nationally, urging the lobbying of all Members of Parliament on the issue of abolition during the next general election and reporting on abolitionist initiatives in Ireland and France. Regarding the latter, the Manchester abolitionists, led by the cotton merchant Thomas Walker, expressed the view that a nation 'so enlightened' by 'the great principles of Universal Liberty', would 'not forget the rights of others while they are so laudably endeavouring to secure their own'.[231]

In 1792 the Abolition Bill was passed in the House of Commons, but delayed and finally voted down in the House of Lords. After 1793 Britain's war with revolutionary France prompted government repression and attacks on leading radicals, as well as intervention in the Caribbean to maintain slavery in the French colonies and suppress the Haitian revolution. Thomas Clarkson later provided his own interesting analysis of what he considered to be the new unconducive conditions,

> Many looked upon the abolitionists as monsters. They became also terrified themselves. The idea with these was, that unless the discussion on this subject was terminated, all would be lost. Thus, under a combination of the Rights of Man, the rise and progress of the French revolution, and the insurrections of the Negroes in the different islands, no one of which events had anything to do with the abolition of the Slave trade, the current was turned against us.[232]

On the contrary, however, the 'insurrections of Negroes' were some of the main engines for change.

Abolition Bills were still regularly introduced in Parliament by Wilberforce, in 1795 and 1796, for example, but in general the campaign reached a low point, only to be revived in 1804, when it was strongly influenced by the victorious conclusion of the Haitian Revolution.

Cugoano and Equiano

It was in the context of this national mass abolitionist movement of the 1780s that the writing and other activities of Cugoano, Equiano and the Sons of Africa must be understood. Cugoano published his *Thoughts and Sentiments on the Evil and Wicked Traffic of the Slavery and Commerce of the Human Species, Humbly Submitted to the Inhabitants of Great Britain, by Ottobah Cugoano, a Native of Africa* in 1787, possibly with Equiano's assistance. Equiano published his *Interesting Narrative of the Life of Olaudah Equiano, or Gustavus Vassa the African, written by himself* in 1789, just before Wilberforce made his first abolitionist speech in Parliament and after the investigations and hearings organized by the Privy Council's committee, from which he and other Africans had been excluded.[233] Cugoano's book appeared in three different editions in 1787, and in a French edition the following year, before the author published a shorter edition entitled *Thoughts and Sentiments on the Evil of Slavery; or the Nature of Servitude as Admitted by the Law of God, Compared to the Modern Slavery of the Africans in the West Indies; In an Answer to the Advocates for Slavery and Oppression, Addressed to the Sons of Africa by a Native* in 1791. However, the books seem not to have been reviewed and little more is known of Cugoano's life, although there are indications that he toured Britain and travelled to 'upwards of fifty places', perhaps as a speaker.[234] The latter title was clearly addressed to the Sons of Africa from the author, 'merely to convey Instructions to his oppressed Countrymen', and with the intention that the remainder should be published 'in a short time'. Nothing further was published. Cugoano asked Granville Sharp to send him to Nova Scotia to recruit more settlers for Sierra Leone but he also expressed a wish to open a school 'for all of his complexion', to acquaint them with 'the Christian Religion and the Laws of Civilization'. There no evidence that he did either and there are no other records of his life after 1791.[235]

The importance of Cugoano's writing is that he directly attacks not only the trafficking of Africans, the 'slave trade', but also slavery itself and he calls on the enslaved to liberate themselves. He refuted contemporary pro-slavery arguments and condemned European 'pirates' and the entire slave and colonial systems. He blamed all who were not opposed to slavery for condemning Britain to future divine retribution and was one of the first to raise the need for reparation for the crimes committed against Africans. He went as far as to look forward to 'the world turned upside down' when the 'pirates, thieves, robbers, oppressors and enslavers of men' got their just punishments.[236] He wrote from a non-Eurocentric perspective, in that he posed the question of how Europe might respond to the African enslavement of Europeans. His work is part autobiography, part sermon denouncing the enslavers and traffickers, as well as their apologists, by employing biblical scripture to condemn the slave-mongers. Perhaps Cugoano was the 'Native of Africa' who 'arose and communicated to his attentive hearers' at the debate at the Coachmakers Hall in London in February 1788, 'several circumstances within his own experience relative to the treatment of his Countrymen in the West Indies; and endeavoured by a reference to scripture to prove the impropriety of the traffic in question'.[237]

Equiano's *Narrative* of 1789 was well received.[238] Mary Wollstonecraft reviewed it soon after its publication.[239] Two further editions were published the following year and nine in total between 1789 and 1794. During Equiano's lifetime, there were translations and more editions in the Netherlands (1790), New York (1791), Germany

From the frontispiece of Equiano's *Narrative*

(1792) and Russia (1794). The *Narrative* is extremely well written and it is particularly important because an African gave a first-hand account of life in Africa, his capture and the notorious 'Middle Passage' across the Atlantic, as well as testimony concerning his life as a slave. In recent years one of Equiano's biographers has found evidence to suggest that he may have been born in South Carolina, rather than in West Africa, but this evidence is contested by other historians.[240] If he was indeed born in North America, Equiano's non-African birth surely enhances his creative and literary ability. It also makes his *Narrative* an even greater work of designed anti-slavery propaganda. Whatever the case, it was undoubtedly influential during his lifetime and had a major influence on later slave narratives.

Equiano travelled throughout the country speaking about his *Narrative* and in favour of the abolitionist cause.[241] He spoke in Birmingham in 1790, and was associated with the members of the radical Lunar Society in that city. The Lunar Society included Thomas Day, Josiah Wedgwood, Erasmus Darwin, noted for attacking the slave system in his poetry, and James Watt.[242] It also included Joseph Priestley, whose *Sermon on the Subject of the Slave Trade* was published in 1788.[243] These men considered 'all mankind as brethren and neighbours' and Wedgwood, Darwin, Priestley and Day in particular acted accordingly, although Watt evidently did not.[244] From May 1791 to January 1792 Equiano visited Belfast and Dublin and spent several months in Ireland, where he came into close contact with those engaged in establishing the Society of United Irishmen, and where he sold nearly 2,000 copies of his *Narrative*.[245] In Belfast, Equiano stayed with one of the most radical members of the United Irishmen, Samuel Neilson, editor of the *Northern Star*, who organized amongst the working people of Ireland. In short, from 1789 to 1794, Equiano travelled the length and breadth of the British Isles, visiting more than twenty towns and cities, including those in Wales and Scotland.[246] During his tour, Equiano spoke, sold and signed copies of his book, distributed other abolitionist material and established a network of subscribers and booksellers. It is evident that many of the latter were drawn from the working class. Equiano visited several mines, and his supporters also included political radicals.

Although the work of Equiano was known to Wilberforce, and

other parliamentary campaigners, neither he, nor Cugoano, nor other Africans, were called to give evidence before Parliament. Nevertheless, Equinao used his *Narrative* to influence public opinion and he and Cugoano acted jointly with several other 'Sons of Africa', writing to prominent parliamentarians, abolitionists and, from 1785, the press, when they presented an 'address of thanks' to the Quakers.[247] The Sons of Africa became one of the first named African political organizations in Britain's history and one of the first Pan-African organizations anywhere in the world. In 1788 Equiano states that he wrote to Queen Charlotte 'on behalf of my African brethren', attempting to get support for Dolben's Amelioration Bill, which was opposed by the monarchy. The Sons of Africa often used both African and European names, for example, Cojoh Ammere, or George Wallace; Yahne Aelane, or George Sanders. They provide further evidence of Africans organizing themselves not just for their own freedom but also for that of other Africans in the period.[248]

Equiano also worked alongside some of the most radical political activists in Britain at the time, including Thomas Walker in Manchester, Samuel Eric Neilson and the United Irishmen and Thomas Hardy, the founder and Secretary of the London Corresponding Society (LCS). The LCS campaigned for 'a radical reform of the representation of the people', that is, for universal male suffrage, and was influenced by the writing of Thomas Paine and the American and French revolutions. It was one of the first political organizations of working people. Its members were mainly artisans, like the shoemaker, Hardy. It sought to unite other radical organizations, was feared by the government, which accused it of fomenting revolution, was infiltrated by spies and, in 1799, was eventually banned. It is not surprising that Equiano would move in those circles most likely to support the abolitionist cause, those engaged in other popular movements seeking political change and empowerment. It seems likely that Hardy and Equiano had known each other for some time before the founding of the LCS and it is known that Equiano lived with Hardy and his wife while he was editing the fifth edition of his *Narrative*. He was an early member of the LCS and writes to Hardy from Edinburgh: 'My best respect to my fellow members of your society. I hope they do yet increase.'[249] It is recorded that the first letter written by Hardy on behalf of the society was to someone Equiano had introduced, a Reverend Bryant in Sheffield. Hardy's letter contained the following:

> Hearing from my friend Gustavus Vassa, the African, who is now writing memoirs of his life in my house that you are a zealous friend to the abolition of that cursed traffic, the Slave Trade, I infer from that circumstance, *that you are a zealous friend to freedom on the broad basis of the RIGHTS OF MAN*. I am fully persuaded that there is no man, who is, from principle, an advocate for the liberty of the black man, but will zealously support the rights of the white man, and *vice versa* [emphasis in original].[250]

As Equiano was himself a member of the LCS, we may assume that he adhered to this very enlightened political position, which reflected the view long held by radicals. It may be that the arrests of Hardy and other leaders of the London Corresponding Society, as well as other acts of government repression, led to Equiano's own silence after 1794. However, it may also have been because of family responsibilities. In February 1792 Equiano married an Englishwoman, Susanna Cullen, who accompanied him on his tour of Scotland. She soon gave birth to two daughters and died in 1795. Equiano died just two years later, ten years before the Abolition Bill was passed by Parliament in 1807, which was designed to end the trafficking of Africans by British citizens.

The cause of abolitionism in Britain culminated first with this Act of Parliament in 1807 and then with another in 1834 which abolished slavery throughout the British Empire. Before the mid-twentieth century, historians were mainly concerned with celebrating the movement that had developed from the 1780s onwards, especially its parliamentary aspects, and therefore have concentrated on prominent men of property such as William Wilberforce, who introduced the Abolition Bill in Parliament, as well as his colleagues, sometimes collectively known as 'the Saints'. Since that time, and particularly following the publication in 1944 of Eric Williams' famous book *Capitalism and Slavery*, earlier views extolling the activities of Wilberforce and other 'saints' have been challenged. Williams argued that economic factors in Britain and throughout the empire were of much greater importance in bringing the slave system to an end than the activities of a few great men. He also questioned why the world's leading slave-trafficking power in the eighteenth century should suddenly become the champion of abolition in the nineteenth. Following Williams, some have pointed out that the commercial interests represented by the British government were more concerned with the development of slave-based economies in Brazil, Cuba and even the United States, rather than those in Britain's colonies in the Caribbean. Others have pointed out that Britain's championing of an anti-slavery position allowed it to restrict the economic activities of other rival powers, since it was British traffickers who transported and supplied most enslaved Africans to their economic competitors, such as France. It was such arguments that cleared the ground for a restriction of human trafficking even before the Foreign Slave Trade Act of 1806.

A key factor in this significant shift was the revolution that took place in the French Caribbean colony of St Domingue, where, from 1791, enslaved Africans and their allies fought for their liberation, not only against the French but also against the forces of Britain and Spain, the three major European armies. In January 1804 the island of St Domingue declared its independence from France and was renamed Haiti. The revolution in Haiti contributed to, and occurred alongside, other major insurrections of enslaved Africans across the Caribbean, in Jamaica, Grenada, St Vincent and elsewhere, which severely threatened the entire slave-based colonial system. Even some of those Africans forcibly recruited into Britain's West India regiments mutinied in Dominica in 1802.[251]

Toussaint L'Ouverture and some of the other leaders of the Haitian revolution became nationally known figures in Britain. Those close to Wilberforce, such as James Stephen and Henry Brougham, commented at length on the revolutionary events in the Caribbean. Stephen's *Buonaparte in the West Indies, or the History of Toussaint L'Ouverture, the African Hero* (1803) was influential and strongly in favour of the Haitian revolution and commenced with the sentence 'Everybody has heard of Toussaint, the famous Negro General.'[252] The creation of the new Haiti led many in Britain to realize that the Caribbean had changed for ever.[253]

The possibility of a more general abolition of the trade in enslaved Africans came to be viewed by some in Britain as a means to press home a naval and economic advantage over France and its allies. It was a means to limit the numbers of Africans imported into British colonies, and thereby prevent the likelihood of further revolutions and maintain the slave system. The revolutionary events in Haiti gave greater impetus to the Abolition Committee in Britain, which was re-formed in 1804, with Stephen and Brougham, alongside Wilberforce, as its leading members. They argued that since Britain controlled so much of transatlantic human trafficking and held more enslaved Africans than its rivals, abolition would harm the importation of enslaved Africans to its rivals, particularly Bonapartist France. In 1806 Britain's commercial interests and partial abolition were secured by the Foreign Slave Trade Bill, introduced into the Lords with the words 'if we give up the trade [in Africans] it was not possible for any other state, without our permission, to take it up'.[254] This Act banned the export of enslaved Africans to Britain's economic rivals, a measure that effectively ended about 60 per cent of Britain's trafficking of Africans across the Atlantic.[255] The following year even the monarch and the royal family, the greatest defenders of human trafficking, as their predecessors had been, acquiesced and abolition was embraced as being 'sound policy', that is to say, in the general interests of the rich and powerful.

In the period just before 1807, the victorious revolution of enslaved Africans and their allies in Haiti had a major impact on the entire slave system, as did other rebellions of the enslaved which continued throughout the nineteenth century. Ending human trafficking, some British abolitionists argued, would be a security measure to prevent the importation of future African revolutionaries. African resistance to slavery in the Caribbean and elsewhere was not just restricted to major rebellions but also continued in a constant 'state of war' and undermined the slave system from within. The struggles for liberation by Africans and their allies in Britain also played a significant role in its demise, as is clear from the efforts of the enslavers to oppose any legal challenges to slavery.

There is no doubt that for many in Parliament, and outside too, the demand for abolition was based largely on a variety of economic, geopolitical and security motives. Prime Minister Pitt and others had been concerned about competition from St Domingue and other Caribbean colonies even before 1791, and had unsuccessfully sought agreement from both France and Holland to prohibit the trafficking of Africans. Others in Britain were more concerned about what they saw as the subsidies given to slave owners and sugar producers in the

Caribbean, and government support for economies and a trade that was in relative decline in importance by the end of the eighteenth century. Still others in Britain became more interested in developing direct trade links with India, Brazil and other Spanish American colonies. The trafficking of Africans to Britain's colonies was no longer so important and was seen as being an impediment to important trading links elsewhere. Although these economic motives for abolition have long been associated with the name of Eric Williams, in fact very similar views were expressed by British historians of the late nineteenth and early twentieth centuries. Most importantly, economic justifications for an end to 'the trade' were strongly advanced in the period preceding the Abolition Act which was finally passed in 1807. All these circumstances mean that the Parliamentary Act of 1807 abolishing the trade in enslaved Africans was passed not mainly for humanitarian reasons but because it was in the interests of the rich and their representatives in Parliament to do so.

It is important to note that it was the actions of people, and most importantly of the enslaved themselves, in the Caribbean, Britain and beyond, that had made enslavement and trafficking increasingly unpopular, inefficient, unprofitable and dangerous. The conditions for this significant change in policy were brought about by Africans themselves, in Africa, in Britain's colonies in the Caribbean and North America, as well as in Britain and elsewhere. The struggle against human trafficking and slavery was truly international and in the late eighteenth century it became a mass political movement, often connected with a wider struggle for political rights.

4

Freedom Struggles

In the early 1970s, James Walvin, now an eminent British historian, wrote about the 'disintegration' of the African population in Britain in the nineteenth century. He asserted that by the 1850s and 1860s there were 'very few Negroes in evidence'.[1] Walvin argued that 'black immigration' had slowed down and that the 'trickle into England of black students, freed slaves, domestic servants or sailors was not sufficiently strong to compensate for the steady numerical decline of the local black population'.[2] In addition, he suggested, the small numbers of Black women in Britain led to 'interracial breeding' and the inevitable 'process of disintegration'. Although a government census was conducted from 1801 onwards, it provides little indication of the numbers of those of African or Caribbean heritage. We now have the benefit of more research on this period, but fewer articles and books on the subject compared with those relating to the previous century. Historians seem to have found the nineteenth century of less interest, or perhaps less accessible, than the previous one, even though important communities were established, and numerous significant individuals were active during this time. Much more research is needed to gain a fuller picture of this period.[3]

The presence and status of 'Negroes' in the nineteenth century in Britain was clearly a subject that was of concern to some Victorians. In 1875 Charles Dickens' periodical *All the Year Round* published a significant article entitled 'The Black Man', which discussed the history of both those of African and Asian descent in Britain.[4] The author speculated on when Africans might first have arrived; suggested that 'Negro serving boys' first became the fashion after 1659; commented on the term 'black-a-more'; provided early examples of the public auction of Africans, as well as examples of their tendency to liberate themselves from enslavement. The article lamented the fact that 'the Negro footman is now rarely seen; and indeed, it would appear that there has been a considerable departure of the "black man" from among us. He fills no longer the place he once occupied in our English domestic life.' It expressed the view that 'prejudice has dealt severely altogether with the black man', and wondered, 'can it be that when it was firmly established, not so very long since, that the Negro was "a man and a brother", he forthwith ceased to be a friend?'[5] Dealing with such 'prejudice' was just one of the challenges facing those of African and Caribbean heritage in the nineteenth century, as they still waged a struggle against human trafficking, enslavement and their consequences. As Britain's empire expanded throughout Africa during the century it precipitated new forms of migration, but also presented the need for struggles against the new imperialism and colonial rule. Moreover, throughout the century most of those referred to as 'Negroes' were part of an impoverished working class that was waging its own struggles for political rights in Britain.

THE ABOLITION ACT

As we know from the previous chapter, in 1807 Parliament was persuaded to pass the Abolition Act, partly on the basis of economic concerns, partly on the basis that limiting the importation of enslaved Africans would tend to limit the likelihood of future revolutions and preserve slavery throughout the Caribbean colonies. It was also persuaded because abolition was seen as a way of diverting attention away from an unpopular war against France and its allies and persuading the people that such a war was being fought in the interests of a noble cause. After the Foreign Slave Act in 1806 it could be argued that most of 'the trade' had ended already. Even some of the major established Caribbean planters were in favour of abolition, since this worked against the interests of their commercial rivals, both foreigners and those who had acquired newly captured territory in the Caribbean from Britain's enemies. They reasoned that this might be especially advantageous if abolition could be forced upon other countries as a consequence of Britain's military and naval supremacy.

Other representatives of the rising bourgeoisie supported the measure as a means to limit the economic and political power of those who had arrested the development of industrial capitalism and 'free trade', and prevented its representatives from dominating Parliament.[6]

The 1807 Act was subsequently used as the representatives of the rich envisaged: to advance Britain's interests, not least by relying on the Royal Navy Anti-Slave Trade Squadron to interfere in international shipping across the Atlantic. However, it did not end British citizens' involvement in the trafficking of Africans, nor slavery itself.[7] Following major insurrections in the Caribbean, and as a consequence of other economic and political considerations, slavery was only made illegal in 1834, but continued in some areas of the British Empire for another century. The trafficking of Africans in general increased during the nineteenth century and many British human traffickers sailed under foreign flags of convenience. Nor did the 1807 Act end Britain's dependence on slave-produced goods, such as cotton, the mainstay of the Industrial Revolution. Even the so-called 'legitimate commerce' subsequently developed with Africa, such as the extraction of palm oil, was largely produced with enslaved labour. As one eminent historian has written: 'the flow of British resources into the slave trade did not cease in 1807. After this date British subjects owned, managed and manned slaving adventures; they purchased newly imported Africans into the Americas; they supplied ships, equipment, insurance and most of all trade goods and credit to foreign slave traders.'[8] In short, British subjects continued to be fully involved in the human trafficking of Africans, especially in such countries as Cuba and Brazil.[9]

The Abolition Act increased rather than diminished Britain's interference in Africa, since it subsequently led to the deployment of the Royal Navy's Anti-Slavery Squadron, and other political and economic interventions, as well as the acquisition of colonies and culminated in the so-called 'scramble' for Africa at the end of the nineteenth century. The 'scramble', or 'new imperialism', in Africa refers to the contention between all the major European powers for colonial acquisitions, spheres of influence, sources of raw materials, markets for manufactured goods and investment, leading to the sustained invasion of the continent, followed by its partition, and ultimately the imposition of colonial rule.[10] However, the Abolition Act did affect the importation of Africans into Britain's Caribbean colonies and therefore also into Britain. Maintaining Africans as household servants in Britain also became less popular in the nineteenth century and contributed to the impoverished state of many African residents.

SLAVERY STILL UPHELD IN ENGLAND

Some have argued that the judgment of Lord Chief Justice Mansfield, in the case of James Somerset in 1772, completely ended the institution of slavery in England. It is true that Mansfield's judgment made it unlawful for Africans to be compelled to leave England and be returned to a status of slavery in the colonies, but that was not the end of the matter. It might be said that Mansfield was forced unwillingly to provide a legal judgment which supported the self-liberating activities of the enslaved and their allies in England. However, there were several legal judgments after this time which underlined the fact that slavery in Britain was still upheld by the law. And even those formerly enslaved who resided in Britain found it impossible to challenge colonial laws. Elizabeth Newton was an enslaved woman in Barbados, who was literate and had something of a favoured status. Both her sisters had manged to buy their freedom, or have it bought for them. Elizabeth was initially a 'house slave', but after a series of disputes with her owners was sent to the fields, beaten and her life threatened. She decided to run away to London, where, she presumed, after the Mansfield judgment she might be free, and from where she might petition her owner. She was forced to flee without her three children and first made her way by ship to the neighbouring island of St Vincent by paying the ship's captain. Then, by similar means, she sailed from St Vincent to London in 1795. There she found a husband and, as Mrs Miler, appeared in person before her former owners demanding a manumission paper, so that she could return to her children in Barbados. She claimed that her entire family had been freed before the death of her previous owner. When she failed to gain satisfaction, she took legal action, but was again unsuccessful. It seems that she remained in England where she sadly died before her children were emancipated by the legislation of 1838.[11]

The 1807 Act therefore made no immediate impact on the institution of slavery in the colonies, or even in Britain, as several important cases make very evident. For example, in 1802, there was the case of *Williams v. Brown*. Williams, an African from Grenada, had escaped from slavery in Grenada and made his way to London. There in 1797 he entered into employment as an 'ordinary seaman' on a voyage to Grenada on board the *Holderness*, a ship captained by Brown, the defendant. When Williams reached Grenada, he was claimed as a 'runaway slave' by his former owner. An agreement was then reached between the three men. In return for a payment by Brown, the ship's captain, the former owner would free his slave. Williams, describing himself as a 'free black man on the island of Grenada', then entered into an indenture, whereby he agreed work for Brown and 'during the term of three years to faithfully serve in the capacity of a sailor', but for lower wages than other seamen. On his return to England, Williams pursued a case against Brown on the grounds that he was owed unpaid wages for his previous voyage to Grenada. The judgment in this case was simply to uphold that whatever status Williams might have enjoyed in England, in Grenada he was a slave. When he returned to Grenada, before his legal manumission, he remained a slave and was therefore 'unable to fulfil his contract with the defendant'. The judgment made clear that an enslaved African did not become for ever free by residing temporarily in Britain.[12] It was a significant judgment and was referred to in subsequent cases.

Further proof that the Mansfield and other judgments did not grant freedom to the formerly enslaved is provided by the case of Grace Jones. In 1822 a young enslaved woman called Grace Jones was brought to Britain from Antigua by her owner, a Mrs Allan. Grace is referred to in the legal reports as a 'female attendant' and as 'by birth and servitude a domestic slave'. The legal, or indeed moral, basis for her enslavement is not considered nor contested in the reports. The two women returned to Antigua the following year. Grace, it is reported, did so 'voluntarily'. In Antigua, she remained in servitude until August 1825, when she was seized by the Antiguan customs 'as forfeited to the King, on the suggestion of having been illegally imported in 1823 in violation of the 1807 Act'.[13] A court case ensued in which the Vice-Admiralty Court of Antigua ruled that Grace should be returned to her owner. On appeal by the Crown the case was heard in London. The question to be answered was whether Grace, having lived in England, was 'divested' of her slave status, or whether on return to Antigua she returned to servitude.

The case was heard by William Scott, Baron of Stowell, Judge of the High Court of Admiralty who referred to himself as 'a friend to abolition generally'. Relying on earlier judgments by Talbot and Yorke, and the more recent case of *Williams v. Brown*, Scott ruled that Mansfield's judgment had been an anomaly that had been forced upon him and which had never been invoked since that time. Scott also argued that Mansfield had never clarified the precise meaning of his judgment and that 'it has never happened that the slavery of an African, returned from England, has been interrupted in the colonies in consequence of this sort of limited liberation conferred on him in England'.[14] Under the law Grace Jones remained enslaved.

In the 1820s there were several cases of enslaved women brought to Britain from the Caribbean, who then found themselves impoverished, or in difficult circumstances. One was a young woman from Buenos Aires brought to Britain by an admiral's wife, who had heard from sailors that she would become free once she landed. Her case was championed by Quaker abolitionists who paid for her board and education in London. Another woman named Polly was brought to Kent from Trinidad by her owner in 1827. She 'knew she was thought free in England, but she thought she was more a slave than in the West Indies.' Polly was eventually employed as a servant in Britain, but when it was discovered that she was from Sierra Leone she was returned there, where she was also employed as a servant.[15]

SOME NOTABLE INDIVIDUALS

Sara Baartman

Although not enslaved, the treatment of Sara Baartman, an African woman exhibited in Britain in the early nineteenth century, also gives some indication of how even nominally free Africans were sometimes treated. Sara, or Saartjie, Baartman (c.1777–1816) was a Gonaqua woman born in the Cape Colony, in what was to become South Africa. Her birth names are unknown and she later became known by the derogatory title 'the Hottentot Venus'. Modern historians have done much to reclaim her early life in Africa and she is now in many ways a celebrated figure.[16] In 1810 she was brought to London by Hendrik Cesar, a 'free black' sometimes referred to as her 'keeper', and Alexander Dunlop, an unscrupulous Scottish doctor, in order that her body, in particular her large buttocks, could be exhibited to the paying public.

Sara was one of many Africans who were exhibited in various ways throughout the nineteenth century. These Africans were sometimes displayed alongside other 'freaks' of nature, as well as for allegedly educational or scientific purposes. Such exhibitions were common. In 1899, for example, there was an exhibition of 'over 200 hundred natives of South African tribes, a number of Boer families, representatives of mounted police and a number of animals', which toured the country. It was called 'Savage South Africa' and aimed to present scenes from Britain's war against the Zulus in 1879. There were several complaints made about the show at the time, including some from Africans, but the government claimed that it was powerless to intervene.[17] In the modern period, Sara Baartman has again become famous, viewed more as a victim of racism and sexism and as a symbol of the new post-apartheid South Africa, where her remains were reburied in 2002.

It is not clear whether Sara originally agreed to come to London, nor how much she knew of the reason for her journey. Her previous status had been somewhere between slave and servant and for a time she had been employed as a wet nurse. She was first exhibited in London in 1810 as 'the Hottentot Venus ... a most correct and perfect Specimen of that race of people', at the Egyptian Hall in Piccadilly, for the admission charge of two shillings.[18] She was exhibited in a cage, 'produced like a wild beast', apparently under duress and threats of violence. Although she was never exhibited nude, she was in clothing that made the shape of her body obvious. According to *The Times* she was 'dressed in a colour as nearly resembling her skin as possible. The dress is contrived to exhibit the entire frame of her body, and the spectators are even invited to examine the peculiarities of her form'.[19] According to one account, her body was pinched, poked and prodded. According to another, her 'master declared that she was as wild as a beast and the spectators agreed with him, forgetting that the language of ridicule is the same, and understood alike in all countries, and that not one of them could bear to be the object of derision without an attempt to revenge the insult.'[20] She also sang and danced.

Her public exhibition created a scandal, letters of protest were written to the press and there were allegations that she was 'in a state of slavery in England'. Cesar was forced to respond by claiming that she 'is as free as the English'. Her case was eventually championed by Zachary Macaulay, the well-known abolitionist and former governor of Sierra Leone, and other members of the African Institution, which had ironically been established for 'the civilisation of Africa' rather than the civilizing of Britain. Macaulay had himself gone to Piccadilly to see whether Sara 'was made a public spectacle of her own free will and consent or whether she was compelled to exhibit herself'. Two other members of the African Institution had also made visits, including one who had unsuccessfully attempted to communicate with Sara in Dutch. The African Institution pledged to enable her to return to Africa, if she so wished, and instituted court proceedings to determine whether she was a willing participant. Before the court case, it was revealed that Dunlop had initially tried to sell the right to exhibit Sara to the proprietor of the Liverpool Museum in London. The offer had been declined, but this suggested that Sara was enslaved and forced to exhibit herself.[21]

The case was heard in the Court of King's Bench in November 1810, with the Attorney General acting on Sara's behalf, and was widely reported in the press.[22] She was interviewed in the presence of Dunlop and in Dutch for three hours and appeared to confirm that she had willingly agreed to come to Europe and to be exhibited for payment for a period of six years. She claimed that she did not wish to return to Africa even to visit her siblings, that she had two African boys to wait on her and that she was paid half of the proceeds every Sunday. Her only complaint was that she needed warmer clothes. However, all this was in the presence of Dunlop and those who interviewed her stated that she was illiterate and understood very little of the agreement made with him. They concluded: 'To the various questions we put to her whether if she chose at any time to discontinue her person being exhibited, she might do so, we could not draw a satisfactory answer from her.'[23] In the absence of any evidence of duress the case was dismissed, although the exhibitors were warned not to engage in any 'immodest on indecent exposure of this female stranger'.[24]

However, this court case and Sara's apparent willingness to be exhibited only added to her celebrity, as well as to the view that only in Britain could such a person be protected by the law. She travelled around in a carriage, met the aristocracy and had poems and songs composed about her. There were many caricatures and other representations of her body and she held the copyright for some of them.[25] Her exhibition in London continued for eight months, then she appeared throughout Britain and in Ireland and was even baptized in Manchester in December 1811. In short, she became a celebrity, perhaps the single best-known African woman of her time, but one who was exhibited as a freak and used by some to make racist and sexist generalizations about the inferiority of Africans in general, and African women in particular. Nothing more seems to be known about the two enslaved

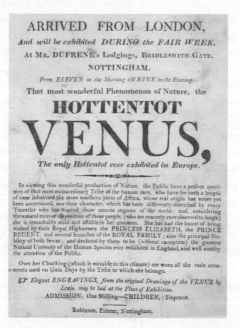

Advertising Sara Baartman as an exhibit in Nottingham

African boys that accompanied her. Cesar, another African who has been forgotten by history, seems to have been ruined by the court case and it is believed he died in London the following year.[26]

In 1814 Sara Baartman was taken to Paris where, if anything, her treatment was even worse than it had been in Britain. In addition to being publicly exhibited, she was an object of lurid fascination for artists and anatomists, including Georges Cuvier. When she died of an unspecified illness in 1815 Cuvier conducted the dissection of her body, but did not perform an autopsy. A cast was made of her body parts, including her genitalia, and these and her brain and skeleton were retained and displayed in museums until the last quarter of the twentieth century, when complaints forced their removal. Her body was used in death, as in life, to argue that she and other Khoekhoe women were closer to apes than to humans. Sara Baartman's remains were finally returned to South Africa in 2002 following an official request from President Nelson Mandela.[27]

Sara Baartman was, unfortunately, not unique. In 1838 another 'Hottentot Venus', named as 'Kaitus Vessula from the Cape of Good Hope', was performing in London and subsequently elsewhere in Britain. It is possible that this woman was Elizabeth Magnes, a Black woman born in London, who had been exhibited for six and a half years at several Leeds fairs and was known for her extraordinary strength.[28] Nor was it only the bodies of women that aroused interest and fascination. A man only known as Wilson, a Boston-born African American seaman, was used as an artist's model in London in the early nineteenth century, and chiefly employed for his physique. His body was exhibited in paintings such as George Dawe's *A Negro Overpowering a Buffalo* (1810). Sir Thomas Lawrence declared he was 'the finest figure he had ever seen, combining the character and perfection of many antique statues', another artist that he was 'a perfect model of beauty and activity'. Black models became something of a vogue, at a time when Black was generally not considered beautiful.[29]

Fanny Eaton

Another celebrated artist's model in the nineteenth century was Fanny Eaton (1835–1924), who became famous as a model for the

Pre-Raphaelites and their circle. She was born Fanny Antwistle in St Andrew, Jamaica, to a woman of African heritage called Matilda Foster, who possibly had been formerly enslaved, and an unknown father, presumed to be a European.[30] Little is known of her early life, or the origin of her surname at birth. Mother and daughter came to London during the 1840s and by 1851 appear in the census living in the St Pancras district, London. It seems likely that Matilda worked as a laundress and Fanny as a servant, they lived in some poverty. In 1857 Fanny married James Eaton, a horse-cab owner and driver from Shoreditch, and they eventually had ten children. As a married woman Fanny continued to live in the St Pancras area and to work as a charwoman but, from about 1859 onwards, she subsidized her income by posing as an artist's model. She first appeared in the work of Pre-Raphaelite artist Simeon Solomon in 1859 in his painting *The Mother of Moses*, where she was the model for two of the depicted figures. The work was publicly exhibited at the Royal Academy the following

Fanny Eaton c.1859

year. She subsequently appeared in work by Dante Gabriel Rossetti, John Everett Millais, Walter Fryer Stocks and several other artists. Eaton also worked as an artist's model at the British Academy itself, although it is not clear how, nor when she first became a model. She was clearly desired for her beauty – Rossetti described her as having a 'fine head and figure' – but often used to add exoticism to paintings and to represent a non-European, although seldom, except in sketches, represented as herself. Eaton continued modelling for almost a decade and there is no evidence to suggest exactly why she retired.

Fanny Eaton's life continued to be one of some hardship. In 1881 her husband died and as a widow, with seven children to care for, she could only find employment as a 'needle woman'. By 1901, at over sixty years old she had moved to Oakfield, Isle of Wight, and was working as a cook for a wine merchant and his wife. Ten years later she was back in London, living with the family of one of her daughters in Hammersmith. She died in London at the age of eighty-nine.

Mary Prince

The precise status of enslaved Africans in Britain, even after the 1807 Act and the general public sympathy for the enslaved, was brought into focus by the case of Mary Prince in 1828, just a few years before Britain's Parliament finally abolished the institution of slavery throughout the British Empire. Mary Prince was born a slave in Bermuda in 1788. She was subsequently separated from her family and siblings and sold to different owners several times during her early life. In 1815 she was sold to a man named Wood for 300 dollars and taken to Antigua. There she joined the Moravian church and in 1826 was married to Daniel James, a 'free black' and carpenter of that country, without asking her owner's permission. In 1828 Mary Prince was taken to England by her owner and later that year, after refusing to labour for her owner any longer, she left, and some months later reported to the Anti-Slavery Society in London that she was being mistreated. There she was told that if she remained in England, she would be free, but a return to her husband in Antigua would entail slavery. It seems that Prince and her husband had hoped that by coming to London she would be freed by her owner. Prince tried to eke out an existence in London for about a year on her own, as a char-woman, before returning for assistance to the Anti-Slavery Society, and in 1829 she was employed as a domestic servant by its Secretary, Thomas Pringle. In the same year, the Anti-Slavery Society unsuccessfully petitioned Parliament on her behalf, having failed to convince Wood to sell Prince her freedom. Two years later, in 1831, she dictated her life story to Susanna Strickland, a friend of Pringle. The result was the *History of Mary Prince*, first published in 1831, which appeared in three editions during that year. It was the first 'slave narrative' to be written by a woman in the English language and the only one by a woman who was a slave in Britain. Its publication led to several court cases – one in which Pringle sued the publisher of *Blackwood's Magazine* for challenging the honesty of Prince's account and one in which Wood brought a libel case against Pringle, which he won.

Prince's account was clearly edited by Pringle for use as abolitionist propaganda, but her *History* is substantially accurate. It not only presents the 'horrors of slavery' in the Caribbean colonies but also how that institution could still exist in London in the early 1830s. Prince might legally have been free in London, but initially knew nobody and had no means of support. She could not compel her owner to grant her freedom in Antigua, nor to sell her manumission. There is no reason to doubt Pringle's assertion that 'the idea of writing Mary Prince's history was first suggested by herself, and that it was done so "that good people in England might hear from a slave what a slave had felt and suffered".'[31] Prince's *History* shows the difficulties that even a former slave in London befriended by the Anti-Slavery Society might experience. In this regard, it is worth noting that Pringle lists Prince's 'chief faults' as 'a somewhat violent and hasty temper, and a considerable share of natural pride and self-importance', the very qualities vital to her life of dignity and resistance.[32] Indeed, Pringle's commentary tells us something else about the status of Black people in London, since he explains that he is as used to employing Black servants as he is white ones. He also tells us that 'the case of Mary Prince is by no means a singular one, many of the same kind are daily occurring', as well as reminding his readers that it has been a mistake to believe 'that no slave can exist within the shores of Great Britain'.[33] Nothing more is known about Prince's life, nor about her death.

Mary Prince was not the only Black woman in contact with the Anti-Slavery Society in the 1830s. An African woman known as Polly was brought from Trinidad to serve an abusive owner in Ramsgate, Kent. Polly considered herself free in England, but initially found herself alone and friendless. She found employment with a female member of the Anti-Slavery Society, who recorded that Polly often thought of the enslavement of 'my people' and broke down in tears. She still spoke Twi and clearly remembered 'being stolen' in Africa when 'she was gathering shells on the sea-shore, under the direction of her grandfather.'[34] There were many other women with similar experiences.

Nathaniel Wells

Not all those who came to Britain from the Caribbean were enslaved or impoverished, as the life of Nathaniel Wells (1779–1852) demonstrates.[35] Wells, a landowner, slaveowner and perhaps Britain's first Justice of the Peace and sheriff of Caribbean heritage, was born in St Kitts.[36] He was the son of William Wells, a Welsh plantation owner and merchant, and an enslaved house servant known an Juggy, who after manumission was known as Joardine Wells. Nathaniel was one of several of William Wells' children born to enslaved mothers, but the only son. In his will William Wells freed four of his 'house Negro women' and other favoured house slaves. He also left each of them a pension and bequeathed considerable wealth to his daughters. Evidently Nathaniel, Wells' 'natural and dear son', was well cared for. He was educated in London from the age of ten, under the care of his paternal uncle, and inherited the majority of the estate, including three plantations and monetary wealth valued at around £120,000 following his father's death in 1794.[37] He was then in a position to free four enslaved people, two of them his mother's nephew and niece, the only such action he ever took.[38]

In June 1801 Nathaniel married Harriet Este, the only daughter of the former chaplain to George II, and had ten children, seven of whom died before him. In 1802 bought the 3,000-acre Piercefield estate (now Chepstow Racecourse) for £90,000, with grounds that were open to visitors. One of these visitors referred to a 'Mr Wells, a West Indian of large fortune, a man of very gentlemanly manners, but so much a man of *colour*, as to be but little removed from a Negro'.[39] He was also described as 'a Creole of a very deep colour,' who was 'very exact about admission to see the grounds'. In other regards Mr and Mrs Wells were said to be of 'charitable and good disposition', and Mr Wells 'very kind as a neighbour'.[40] He acted as a local church-warden from 1804 until 1843 and, along with others, paid for improvements to St Arvan's Church. He seems to have been fully inte-grated into high society in the area and was made a Justice of the Peace in 1806 and Sheriff and Deputy Lieutenant of Monmouthshire in 1818, probably the first time someone of African heritage had held such positions.[41] In 1819 he sent official condolences on behalf of the county of Monmouthshire to the Prince of Wales following the Queen's death.[42] In 1820 Wells received a commission as a lieuten-ant in the local Chepstow Troop of Yeomanry. Two years later he is recorded to have taken part in military action against striking min-ers and iron workers in South Wales and resigned his commission soon after.[43] Nathaniel Wells enjoyed a status in Britain that he would have been legally denied in St Kitts. There, 'free coloureds' were denied the vote and public office.

When his first wife died, Wells married another clergyman's daugh-ter in 1823 and had a further ten children. He moved to Bath in 1844 and died there in 1852. Following his death, his estate was divided amongst his children. Despite Wells' 'charitable and good disposition' he remained a slave owner for much of his life. He owned two estates containing over 200 enslaved people until the mid-1820s, and a fur-ther estate with more than 80 enslaved people remained in his possession until the Emancipation Act of 1834. In 1837, as a slave owner, he received more than £1,400 compensation from the British government for the loss of eighty-six enslaved people.[44]

Sarah Forbes Bonetta

Following the parliamentary abolition of the slave trade in 1807, the trafficking of Africans continued, since other nations continued to ply the trade and many countries, especially those in Latin America, con-tinued to require the labour of enslaved Africans. Even when other countries, such as the United States, also declared bans on human trafficking, they did not abolish slavery itself and so smuggling was rife and profitable. British investment in slavery and its products continued throughout the nineteenth century, including providing ships, equipment, insurance and credit to those directly responsible for the enslavement of Africans. The Industrial Revolution continued to be sustained by slave-produced cotton from the United States, and British citizens continued their investment in slave economies such as those of Cuba and Brazil.[45]

The British government did institute its anti-slavery squadron of Royal Navy ships, often with African crew members, which intercepted suspicious vessels, interfering in the maritime activities of the citizens of Britain and other countries in the Atlantic. As a result, some enslaved Africans were freed and around 50,000 taken to Sierra Leone, which in 1808 became Britain's first African colony. There they endeavoured to rebuild their lives and some became a significant influence throughout Britain's future colonies in West Africa. Some were employed as labourers in the Caribbean, others enlisted in Britain's navy and army, often for lengthy terms, in ways that were seldom based on their own free will. Some were 'indentured' in other parts of Africa.[46] However, there were also cases of Royal Navy officers colluding with human traffickers, and selling them confiscated slave ships. *The Narrative of Louis Asa-Asa*, published in the same volume with *The History of Mary Prince*, shows that foreign ships engaged in human trafficking were often returned to their owners for future use, even when those enslaved were released from captivity.[47] There appear to be numerous cases of the British government either permitting continued human trafficking, or colluding to allow it, well after 1807 and even after 1834.[48] 'Legitimate commerce' from West Africa, such as the groundnuts and palm oil much sought after in Britain, was often grown by enslaved labour.[49]

One of the consequences of the activities of the anti-slavery squadron was the famous rescue of Aina (c.1843–1880), born in the kingdom of the Egbado people of Yorubaland, who now refer to themselves as the Yewa. Although claims were later made that she was a princess, there seems to be no solid evidence to support this view.[50] At the time of her birth the Egbado were engaged in the Okeadan War and subject to raids by the powerful neighbouring kingdom of Dahomey. In one of those raids the young Aina's parents were murdered and she was captured and taken to Abomey, the capital of Dahomey. From 1849 to 1850 Frederick Forbes, a young naval officer in the anti-slavery squadron and the captain of HMS *Bonetta*, had been sent on a mission to Gezo, the King of Dahomey, to discuss bringing human trafficking to an end. While at court he had been presented with Aina, who had been held captive for some two years. Forbes argued that not to accept this 'present', whom he renamed after himself and his ship, 'would have been to have signed her death warrant.' Forbes had Aina baptized Sarah Forbes Bonetta at Badagry, whilst still in West Africa. He seems to have regarded her 'as the property of the Crown' and therefore she was brought back to England.[51]

Shortly after their return Forbes reported that the child was, 'a perfect genius; she now speaks English well, and has a great talent for music. She has won the affections, with but few exceptions, of all who have known her, by her docile and amiable conduct, which nothing can exceed.' Forbes tellingly added comments that say much about the period in which he lived:

> She is far in advance of any white child of her age, in aptness of learning, and strength of mind and affection; and with her, being an excellent expression of the Negro race, might be tested the capability of the intellect of the Black: it being generally and erroneously supposed that after a certain age the intellect becomes impaired and the pursuit of knowledge impossible – that though the Negro child may be clever the adult will be dull and stupid. Her head is considered so excellent a phrenological specimen, and illustrating such high intellect that Mr Pestrucci, the medallist of the mint, has undertaken to take a bust of her, intending to present a cast to the author.[52]

Sarah initially lived with the Forbes family but received an audience with Queen Victoria as early as November 1850. Victoria recorded that the 'poor little Negro girl' was 'sharp and intelligent and speaks English', and although 'dressed as any other girl', when 'her bonnet was taken off her little black woolly head and big earrings gave her the true Negro type.'[53]

Subsequently the monarch 'arranged for the education and subsequent fate of the child'. She called her Sally and clearly saw much of her new protégée. The queen recorded in her diary in January 1851: 'After

luncheon Sally Bonita, the little African girl came with Mrs Phipps, &
showed me some of her work. This is the 4th time I've seen the poor
child, who is really an intelligent little thing.'[54] The following year, and
under the monarch's patronage, Sarah/Sally was sent to be educated at
the Church Missionary Society School for girls in Freetown, Sierra
Leone, which was established in 1849. This was partly because it was
felt the climate would suit her better but also because both Forbes and
Victoria viewed Sarah as a future missionary.[55] However, for reasons yet
unknown, Sarah returned to England in 1855, still under royal patronage, this time to live with Dr James Schoen, a missionary and linguist,
and his family, in Gillingham, Kent. She continued to be a regular guest
of Queen Victoria and the royal family. She is reported to have spoken
French and other European languages and to have been musically gifted.

By the early 1860s Sarah was sent to live in Brighton to finish her
education and perhaps to encourage her to marry. In 1862, with

Sarah Forbes Bonetta

Victoria's permission and active encouragement, she married Captain James Davies, a wealthy African merchant, in Lagos, Nigeria, apparently despite her own misgivings.[56] The wedding, also held in Brighton in August 1862, attracted considerable interest from the press and was reported as an event of political and social significance, especially to those 'interested in the African race', but also as an anthropological curiosity.[57]As a married woman Sarah lived with her husband, first in Sierra Leone, then in Lagos, but in 1867 returned to London with her eldest daughter, named Victoria after her royal godmother. She returned again in 1875 with her children at a time when her husband's business was failing and he was facing bankruptcy. She subsequently returned to Lagos, but financial difficulties may have contributed to her own ill-health and she died in debt in 1880 in Madeira. Her children continued to enjoy a close relationship with Victoria and the royal family until the monarch's death in 1901.

Prince Alemayehu

Sarah/Aina was not the only African child who was of interest to Victoria. She was also involved in the education and early burial of Prince Alemayehu (1861–1879), the orphaned son of Emperor Tewedros II of Abyssinia, now Ethiopia. Alemayehu was orphaned at the age of seven in 1868, when the British Army invaded Ethiopia and his defeated father committed suicide. His mother also died soon afterwards. The invasion was an example of a 'punitive expedition'. The British Army took the opportunity to loot the Abyssinian capital, Magdala, even removing Christian religious items and illuminated manuscripts, as well as parts of the emperor's body, which found their way to such institutions as the British Museum and British Library. Alemayehu was also taken back to London by his self-appointed guardian, although without any of his royal entourage. He lived first on the Isle of Wight with his guardian, where he was introduced to the queen and, under official patronage, was later sent to various public schools, including Cheltenham College. He was photographed, had his portrait painted on numerous occasions and, thanks to his royal patron, was later enrolled at the Royal Military College, Sandhurst.

At the age of eighteen he caught pleurisy and subsequently died, never having the opportunity to visit Ethiopia again. He was entombed by royal command at Windsor Castle. Victoria expressed her grief and shock at his premature death and added, 'All alone, in a strange country, without a single person or relative, belonging to him, so young, & so good, but for him one cannot repine. His, was no happy life, full of difficulties of every kind, and he was so sensitive, thinking that people stared at him because of his colour, that I fear he would never have been happy.'[58] In the twenty-first century some doubt has been cast on the official narrative about his life, with some claiming that he was effectively abducted. The government of Ethiopia has on many occasions unsuccessfully requested the repatriation of his remains, as well as the return of all the cultural artefacts looted from Magdala.

THE LIBERATION WARS OF 1816 AND 1823 AND THE ABOLITIONIST MOVEMENT

In 1814 a new abolitionist movement developed in Britain, mobilized initially to protest against the decision of the government and its European allies to permit defeated France to recommence the trafficking of Africans for a period of five years. Within a few weeks of the announcement more than 800 petitions containing over 1.5 million names poured into Parliament and the government was minded to put pressure on the French government again to abolish the slave trade.[59] However, just as in the past, the anti-slavery movement in Britain was only one aspect of the struggle against slavery; the other was the activity of the enslaved themselves, especially in Britain's Caribbean colonies. These two struggles against slavery were often interconnected and influenced each other.

In April 1816 a major liberation struggle broke out in Barbados. Often known as Bussa's Rebellion, it involved thousands of the enslaved on seventy plantations, who armed themselves and set fire to large swathes of the island. It was led by Bussa, who was African-born, and several others, including the famous 'revolutionary ideologue', Nanny Grigg, a literate enslaved woman who was 'informed about the successful Haitian Revolution, and who was an advocate of the military solution to ending slavery'. Grigg, it was reported, told other enslaved Africans that 'the Negroes were to be freed on Easter Monday, and the only way to get it was to fight for it, otherwise they would not get it; and the way they were to do, was to set fire, as that was the way they did in St Domingo.'[60] Other enslaved people believed that freedom was on its way 'through a black woman who was a Queen', perhaps a reference to Queen Charlotte, the wife of George III.[61] Free people 'of colour' were also involved and those who were literate were especially important conveyers of information from newspapers.

This major rebellion, lasting some four days, was savagely repressed by the colonial authorities with more than 200 killed or executed. It was partly inspired by the efforts of the abolitionists in Britain to campaign for the monitoring of the enslaved population through regular registration under an Imperial Registration Bill.[62] It showed that debate, discussion, campaigning and legislation in Britain also had some influence on the resistance of the enslaved in the Caribbean. 'The insurrection has been quelled but the spirit is not subdued,' wrote the Speaker of the Barbados Assembly, 'nor will it ever be subdued whilst these dangerous doctrines which have been spread abroad continue to be propagated amongst the Slaves.'[63] Other major liberation struggles followed, including that of 1823 in Demerara, partly inspired by the creation of a new anti-slavery society in Britain and the motion for abolition announced in Parliament, partly by the reforms and amelioration demanded by the government, as well as the refusal of the plantocracy to accept reforms. The leaders of the enslaved declared at the time that, 'God had made them of the same flesh and blood as the whites, that they were tired of being slaves to them, that their good King had sent Orders that they should be free and they would not work any more.'[64] The rebellion involved some 13,000, led by Quamina and Jack Gladstone, named after his owner, the father of the future prime minister, and was mainly a consequence of the enslaved being encouraged by demands for reform in Britain and heroically fighting for their rights in opposition to the slave system.[65] The fact that an English missionary was implicated in the rebellion and subsequently died in prison, before the issuing of a royal pardon, only added to the impact of the episode and growing demands in Britain for emancipation.[66]

Anti-slavery sentiment remained popular in Britain, but the

abolitionist movement was headed by men who viewed the eventual ending of the institution of slavery as a gradual process, that might be brought about largely through the auspices of an enlightened Parliament. The full title of the Anti-Slavery Society was Society for the Mitigation and Gradual Abolition of Slavery Throughout the British Dominions. Its leaders were also fearful of reviving the mass working-class activism of the late eighteenth century. In early 1823 the abolitionist movement burst into life again with the founding of the new society and the formation of hundreds of branches throughout the country. In 1824 more than 700 petitions were presented to Parliament, and between 1828 and 1833 over 5,000 petitions signed by more than 1.5 million people in Britain were sent there too. The popular demand in the country was for immediate abolition and taking action, such as a boycott of sugar, to bring it about. Although these demands were rejected by the leaders of the movement, they were often made by women such as the radical Quaker, Elizabeth Heyrick.

In 1824 Heyrick published a widely read pamphlet called *Immediate Not Gradual Abolition*, as well as several others in the next few years.[67] She took an uncompromising position: 'The West Indian planter and the people of this country stand in the same moral relation to each other as the thief and the receiver of stolen goods', she wrote, and therefore urged people to boycott slave produce and become the 'active opposers of slavery' rather than just to sign petitions.[68] She argued that 'free labour' was more productive than slave labour but that this view must be forced upon the slave owners. Her arguments became influential on both sides of the Atlantic, and Frederick Douglass is said to have acknowledged her influence.[69] She also argued, 'the slave has a right to liberty, a right which is a crime to withhold, let the consequences to the planters be what they may', and she demanded compensation for the enslaved.[70] Heyrick was prepared to argue against the prevailing view of the leading abolitionists. She called the notion of gradual emancipation the 'wily artifice of the slaveholder', and 'the very master-piece of satanic policy'. She expressed her sympathy for the enslaved who had rebelled in the Caribbean, likening them to the Greek patriots who were supported by the British government in their war of liberation against the Ottoman Empire.

Heyrick was particularly influenced by the 1823 slave rebellion in Demerara. In 1824 she anonymously published *An Enquiry Which of the Two Parties is Best Entitled to Freedom? The Slave or the Slaveholder?* The rebellion, Heyrick argued, had started as a legitimate strike because the slave owners, and the colonial authorities, had refused to implement a new law from Britain banning corporal punishment. Heyrick contrasted the initially peaceful protests of the enslaved with the violent retribution meted out to them by the colonial authorities, which led to several hundred deaths, including executions.[71] Naturally Heyrick was also concerned about injustices closer to home, such as the plight of the impoverished working people who were nevertheless the producers of wealth. She was a supporter of a minimum wage and the right to strike. She felt that it was the working people who must play a central role against slavery since they too 'had tasted the cup of adversity', and she pointedly addressed her writing to the people rather than the government.[72]

Heyrick's argument that people should rely on their own activism, not on petitioning Parliament, as well as the example of her activism in Leicester and elsewhere, inspired others and led to the creation of more than forty women's abolition committees.[73] It was one of these, the women's committee in Sheffield, that became the first anti-slavery organization in Britain to demand immediate abolition. The women's societies often went from door to door, gaining support for the movement, and were generally more likely than those organizations led by men to support immediate abolition. They soon formed the backbone of the abolitionist movement. Nevertheless, abolitionist political action in Britain was still mainly designed to pressure Parliament, which at that time was highly unrepresentative. To give one example, a large city such as Manchester had no representatives there, and only those who were major property owners were eligible to stand as MPs. Demands for abolition, even of a gradual kind, were thus often connected with the demand for parliamentary reform.

THE BAPTIST WAR

By 1830 the demand of the abolitionist movement was for immediate abolition, at least for those newly born into slavery. A new campaign was started, based on the experience of the women's committees and the employment of paid advocates. In a year there were more than 1,200 local committees.[74] The revived movement had its influence in the Caribbean too, most evidently in Jamaica, where reports appeared in the press, especially in the *Watchman and Jamaica Free Press* published by Edward Jordan and Robert Osborn.[75] As in previous times, rumours circulated in Jamaica concerning emancipation, and in December 1831 a major liberation struggle broke out. Known as 'the Baptist War' and led by Samuel Sharpe, an enslaved but literate man, it was based on the premise that the enslaved must fight for their freedom. More than 20,000 enslaved people took part in the insurrection, which was one of the largest ever in the Caribbean. It caused over one million pounds of damage, and was savagely repressed by the colonial authorities. About 500 participants were killed or executed, while some English missionaries were criticized for allegedly inspiring the revolt. Sharpe, it was reported, was fully informed of what was happening in Britain, having read for himself accounts of the abolitionist movement. Like Nanny Grigg, he determined that the enslaved must act for themselves.[76] Before his execution Sharpe is reported to have said: 'I would rather die on yonder gallows than live in slavery.' It was said of him that he 'was such a man, too, as was likely, nay certain, had he been set free, to commence another struggle for freedom: for he felt keenly the degradation and the monstrous injustice of the system, and was bent upon its overthrow.'[77]

The insurrection in Jamaica had a powerful impact on the lawmakers in Britain just at the time when Parliament was being reformed. Amelioration clearly was not effective and it became clear that without emancipation, other more powerful insurrections would take place that might succeed, like the revolution in Haiti. In addition to the uprisings of the enslaved in the Caribbean, there were also economic forces at play. Some argued that low-wage labour could more profitably produce sugar, especially in India, than enslaved labour, especially since the plantation owners and the sugar trade were effectively subsidized through high duties on sugar. Others found greater returns on investments in the slave societies of Cuba and Brazil than in the British colonies in the Caribbean, and pointed to the declining role played by Caribbean trade in the national economy. Many raised a demand for free trade against the monopoly on sugar exercised by the Caribbean plantocracy. The parliamentary reforms of 1832 also gave voice to new powerful industrial interests in Parliament. As Eric Williams wrote, 'the capitalists had first encouraged slavery and then helped to destroy it'.[78]

The new Parliament finally agreed to gradual 'emancipation' and on terms most favourable to the 46,000 slave owners, who received 20 million pounds in compensation, paid for by the British taxpayer until 2015.[79] Heyrick argued that compensation ought to be 'first made to the slave, for his long years of uncompensated labour, degradation and suffering'.[80] There were many other abolitionist critics too, as well as those representing workers denouncing both the compensation and the Government's plans for 'apprenticeship'. Some of the enslaved, the 'field hands' allegedly emancipated in 1834, were forced to labour for another six years without pay, while others were made to do the same for a total of four years. In response a new Central Emancipation Committee organized hundreds of petitions of opposition in Britain, as well as its own inquiry in Jamaica.[81] One 'apprentice', James Williams, had his freedom purchased and was brought to London, where he published *A Narrative of Events Since the First of August 1834*.[82] The government was eventually forced to limit 'apprenticeship' to four years for all, although not without further criticism from those who not only condemned forced labour and chattel slavery in the Caribbean, but also wage slavery in Britain.

It was not until August 1838 that 800,000 enslaved Africans in the Caribbean were legally freed, as well as those in Britain and other parts of the empire such as Canada and Cape Town. However, slavery continued in what were to become Britain's African colonies. It was not finally abolished in the Gold Coast, for example, until 1928. British citizens also continued to invest in slave societies in countries such as Brazil and Cuba and to benefit from slave-produced cotton from the United States.[83] Nevertheless, from this period onwards Britain officially became an 'anti-slavery nation', and assumed the moral high ground. Rapidly forgetting its own crimes, it was in a position to criticize others and to develop its 'civilizing mission', in Africa in particular, which led to increasing economic and military intervention in that continent. It was in the cause of abolition, and free trade, that African villages were bombarded and Lagos in West Africa was violently seized in 1861.[84] This growing intervention and Britain's contention with the other big powers eventually led to the invasion and partition of Africa at the end of the nineteenth century.

THE AFRICAN POOR

Many of those Africans living in London in the early years of the nineteenth century lived in poverty. As early as 1805, under the direction of William Wilberforce, Zachary Macaulay and others, an African and Asiatic Society was established for the 'Relief and Instruction of Poor Africans and Asiatics' and their descendants, in London and the vicinity. Most of the Africans were formerly domestic servants with no trade, who for a variety of reasons found themselves unemployed and facing the 'general prejudice against their colour'.[85] The society provided schools, employment, support in old age, as well as religious instruction, but also the possibility of repatriation for those 'desirous of returning to their own country'.[86] Perhaps the most significant aspect of the society's charitable work was that it was focused on families, some of them with numerous children. The society's reports suggest that it also aided many women, one of whom had been brought as a servant from South Africa, another who had come with her family from the United States. Yet another was Elizabeth Cooper, a widow with seven children, who originated from Nova Scotia. She had previously travelled to Sierra Leone where her husband had died. Returning to London destitute, she was eventually aided to travel to the United States. The reports of the society suggest the existence of an extremely diverse group of Africans, at least in the first twenty years of the nineteenth century, which included the elderly as well as women and children. It used to be thought that in the early nineteenth century, African males strongly outnumbered females and that the population was overwhelmingly young, most being under forty years of age. But the evidence from the early years of the century suggests otherwise.[87]

One hostile commentator expressed concern about the political aims of the society, which, on at least one occasion in 1815, appears to have provided a dinner for its members and friends, including a 'medley of blacks and mulattoes . . . many of them mendicants'. Joseph Marryat, a notorious pro-slavery MP and banker, criticized such a gathering, at which James Stephen and others toasted the health of Henri Christophe, the president of Haiti, the equality of all was extolled, and a 'black man led in a white woman with a partly coloured child'. Marryat considered such occasions were likely to encourage those in the colonies 'to overthrow the established order of things'.[88]

The existence of the society pointed to the extreme poverty of many Africans, especially in the capital. This is also evident from the first report of the Society for the Suppression of Mendicity, formed in 1818, which refers to 'the wretched condition of many Africans and other persons of colour', many of whom had formerly been in the armed services.[89] It seems likely that many of these would have been sailors discharged from service at the conclusion of the Napoleonic Wars, often without the pensions to which they were entitled.[90] Vagrancy and begging were seen as particular problems in this period and led to investigations by Parliament and intervention by such bodies as the Society for the Suppression of Mendicity. A parliamentary select committee report of 1814–15 mentions several African beggars, including one who it was said 'retired to the West Indies with a fortune', but a year later the report maintains that 'there do not appear to be many Africans amongst the vagrants', possibly because many had been repatriated to the Caribbean.[91]

Some African beggars, such as Joseph Johnson, a former seaman who wore a model of HMS *Nelson* on his head; Billy Waters, the 'king of the beggars', a busker whose portrait was painted; and Charles M'Gee, were well known in their day and became better known as a result of their portrayal in John Thomas Smith's *Vagabondiana: Or, Anecdotes of Mendicant Wanderers through the Streets of London, with Portraits of the Most Remarkable Drawn from the Life*, first published in 1817. On his death M'Gee was also reported to have bequeathed a considerable estate, much of it to the daughter of an alderman who had been particularly kind to him.[92] The reports of the Society for the Suppression of Mendicity appear to show that most of those Africans with whom it came into contact were male, several were married, and came from the Caribbean as well as from the African continent. Some were denied support, if it can be so called, by the parish workhouse and often from the society itself, which viewed begging as a vice to be suppressed. Others, even those reduced to begging through illness, might be imprisoned for what was considered their crime. The society often encountered strong resistance and a clear sense of solidarity amongst impoverished Africans. According to one report, 'a native of St Domingo was apprehended in Park Lane by four of the Society's officers, after a most desperate resistance, during which, the constables were compelled to use their staves, in consequence of five other blacks attempting a rescue.'[93] Some beggars were former soldiers, or seamen, whose services were no longer required in the immediate post-war period.[94] It is worth quoting the opinion of the journalist and social reformer Henry Mayhew, who published four volumes of a famous report on those impoverished in London in the middle of the nineteenth century:

> There are but few Negro beggars to be seen now. It is only common fairness to say that Negroes seldom, if ever, shirk work. Their only trouble is to obtain it. Those who have seen the many Negroes employed in Liverpool, will know that they are hard-working, patient, and, too often underpaid. A Negro will sweep a crossing, run errands, black boots, clean knives and forks, or dig for a crust and a few pence. The few imposters among them are to be found among those who go about giving lectures on the horrors of slavery, and singing variations on the 'escapes' in that famous book Uncle Tom's Cabin. Negro servants are seldom read of in police reports, and are generally found to give satisfaction to their employers. In the east end of London Negro beggars are to be met with, but they are seldom beggars by profession.[95]

Where beggars existed, they were part of a larger impoverished working-class population in London as well as in other cities. All the evidence suggests that Africans and those of African heritage in Britain in the nineteenth century pursued a variety of occupations. In the early part of the century men and women continued to work as domestic servants, while many other men were employed in the Royal

Navy and Merchant Navy and were particularly to be found residing in Britain's port cities.[96]

CONVICTS

The records of convicts and trials, such as those held at the Old Bailey in London, may focus mainly on unfortunate individuals, but they tell us something of the lives of poor people of African and Caribbean heritage in London in that period. However, not all records indicate that individuals were Africans and much more research is needed. Historian John Ellis has analysed the records of Newgate Gaol between 1817 and 1856 and found well over 300 examples of 'inmates of colour', the vast majority originating from Britain, Africa, the Caribbean and the United States.[97] The nearly 200 male African convicts transported to Australia and analysed by historian Ian Duffield were overwhelmingly from London and mainly employed as mariners and domestic servants. However, they also came from Liverpool, Bristol, Plymouth and other port cities, as well as from Surrey, Kent and elsewhere. Most had been born in North America or the Caribbean but over 20 per cent were British-born. One of these, Joseph Williams, was a cook and butler born in Bath who had migrated to New Zealand where, in 1847, he was convicted of theft and receiving stolen property. Another was Charles Hall, a sailmaker, ploughman and labourer who was born in Newport, on the Isle of Wight, but who had migrated to Adelaide, Australia, where he was arrested and convicted for burglary in 1842.[98] Another transported convict was Jacob Morris, a fifty-seven-year-old cook and former seaman who robbed another African mariner named Joseph Uxbridge. Morris had originally been sentenced to death, but his sentence was commuted to transportation. The court proceedings shine a light on the differences that might exist between two such African workers, the one forced into crime, perhaps by difficult circumstances, and the other, who had served on board HMS *L'Aigle* and disembarked at Woolwich in August 1815 with over £84 in back pay and prize money in his pocket.[99]

The proceedings of the Old Bailey barely refer to the origins of Uxbridge and Morris. They were only once mentioned by a single witness as 'two coloured men', although Uxbridge is referred to as 'a man of my own colour' by Morris.[100] In some cases origins of both accused and witnesses are omitted, as in the case of George Barrett in May 1801. Barrett, a forty-year-old servant sometimes known as Barrott, was accused of theft from his employer. He shared some of the stolen goods, giving 'a pair of nankeen pantaloons', to his friend John Stuart, who was a bandsman in the Duke of York's regiment. Stuart was an African American originally from Virginia, and Barrett was born in St Kitts, but these details are never mentioned at the Old Bailey. Barrett was sentenced to seven years' transportation but died in Newgate Gaol in December 1801.[101] Another Old Bailey case was that of Marian Mitchell, a 25-year-old African woman from Martinique, a young mother and laundress, transported for ten years in 1838 after being convicted of stealing seven shillings from a man she had allegedly been trying to importune in London.[102] In 1838, 24-year-old Elizabeth Jones, referred to as a Black woman, a mother and cook, was transported for seven years for the theft of clothing and money worth just over £2 alongside her alleged accomplices.[103] The details of working-class African women are more limited in this period. Most appear to have been domestic servants, but again were often forced into a life of crime, or prostitution, to make ends meet. In 1801 Ann Holman, 'a black woman' who was described in the court proceedings as 'one of the most infamous prostitutes to be found in the night about the Hay-market', and 'an infamous and dangerous whore' who 'ought to have been hanged years ago', was perhaps not unexpectedly unsuccessful in bringing her case for assault.[104]

It seems likely that most women of African and Caribbean heritage would have been domestic servants, 'in service', especially in the period before 1870. That category would include cooks, laundresses, maids, seamstresses and nurses. Adverts by, or for, 'coloured' women in these occupations appeared in the press.[105] They were also increasingly sought after as attractions in the entertainment industry, as barmaids, for example, or as singers and musicians, as well as novelties in circuses, stage shows and music halls.[106] Another important archive for shedding light on the lives of the poor is associated with Thomas Barnardo, who first established residential homes for homeless and poor children in east London in 1870. The archival material shows the extreme poverty and exploitation that existed for many poor people, including those of African and Caribbean heritage, but also the struggles faced by children. One moving account from the 1870s illustrates how Elizabeth Williams, a widowed 'Negress, who was a sack stitcher at Stratford Jute works and paid 1s 8d for every one hundred sacks, was forced to clothe her three children in sacks'. They were subsequently admitted to a Dr Barnardo's home, where two of the children died. The mother also died of tuberculosis within a few years of their admission.[107]

SOLDIERS AND SEAMEN

In the nineteenth century men from Africa, the Caribbean, and North and South America continued to be recruited into the army, as well as the merchant fleet and Royal Navy, just as they had been in the eighteenth century. Black soldiers served throughout the Napoleonic wars – at least eight saw action at the Battle of Waterloo – but their services were less in demand after 1815. By the end of the nineteenth century there is some evidence of a colour bar in the army. Nevertheless, there are many examples of servicemen of African heritage after 1815, wherever the British Army was to be found. With the expansion of imperial trade and naval activity throughout the nineteenth century recruitment of sailors from Africa, the Caribbean and the United States increased. Although Black servicemen originated from diverse backgrounds, many enlisted in Britain and most appear to have originated from the Caribbean. Employment in the navy remained an important means for Black people in America and the Caribbean to travel and make a living. However, mariners, as well as navy tailors, cooks and carpenters, were recruited all over the world. Employment on British ships, or ultimately in Britain itself, provided the opportunity of a relatively safe haven for those fleeing slavery and racism elsewhere in the Atlantic world.

William Afflick, originally from St Kitts, somehow found his way to Britain and, in 1801, enlisted in the 10th Hussars, one of the British Army's 'premier regiments', serving alongside several other Black soldiers in the dangerous role of a trumpeter.[108] In 1811 he was a married family man. His first son Charles was baptized in Brighton, and he had already seen action in France and Spain before his regiment was despatched to Belgium and took part in the Battle of Waterloo. A highly decorated soldier, Afflick was discharged with a pension of nine pence a day in 1816 and settled in London, where he worked as a barber in St George's Hospital. In 1831, his son, the twenty-one-year-old Charles, was found guilty of the theft of a dressing gown and transported. William died in the hospital where he had worked in 1851, but many of his descendants are today in Australia.

Some men, such as Thomas Rackett, born in Demerara, in what is modern-day Guyana, enlisted in both the navy and army. Rackett had served in the Royal Navy before joining the Coldstream Guards, as a musician, aged about twenty-five, in Middlesex, in 1811. His history provides some information about the lives of the Black poor in London in that period. In 1811 he married at St Marylebone and eight years later appears as a witness and a concerned citizen in a court case, later heard at the Old Bailey, involving theft at a London brothel. In 1821 he was discharged from the Guards on a meagre pension of six pence a day. In 1828 his wife, Margaret, was witness to the wedding of another soldier, Joseph Aguirra, from Guadeloupe, who was in the Grenadier Guards, suggesting some camaraderie amongst Black soldiers and their spouses at that time. In 1830, Rackett, who was living near Drury Lane, London, was racially abused and assaulted by Aby Belsaco, a prize fighter, bouncer and brothel-keeper, allegedly over a two-pence debt owed to Margaret Rackett. Thomas Rackett died of asthma in August 1837 and was buried at St Giles in the Fields.[109]

Another African American soldier, Israel Waterford, joined the army after being incarcerated as a prisoner-of-war. Waterford was apparently born free in Philadelphia in 1785 and worked as a seafarer. He was captured in Guadeloupe, in 1810, during the Napoleonic Wars, along with another crew member of a merchant ship. The circumstances of the arrest are unclear, but Waterford was imprisoned in Porchester Castle in Hampshire.[110] This particular prison had also been the place of internment for more than 2,000 Black prisoners-of-war, many of them formerly enslaved, who had fought for the liberation of Guadeloupe, St Vincent and St Lucia in the 1890s and been captured by Britain's interventionist forces in 1896. The prisoners included nearly a hundred women and children, as well as 300 French soldiers, another almost one hundred having died on the voyage from the Caribbean to Portsmouth. Although many were later repatriated to France, it seems likely that some of them joined the British army and navy.[111] Certainly this was the fate of Waterford, who, a year after he arrived, volunteered to join the East Middlesex Militia, probably as a bandsman as this was the fashion at the time. He was one of several Black bandsmen serving with militias. A year later he joined the 74th Regiment of Foot and served as a private throughout the Peninsular War and in France. He later returned to his family in Philadelphia.

During the late eighteenth century, enslaved soldiers and auxiliaries were recruited directly in the Caribbean, such as the so-called 'King's Negroes', the forced labourers attached to British fortifications in the region. In the 1790s more than 13,000 enslaved men were dragooned into the West India Regiments.[112] Enslaved soldiers played an important role in maintaining Britain's interests in the Caribbean during the wars against France from 1793 to 1815. Indeed, one historian has claimed that one of the reasons for a delay in the abolition of the slave trade until 1807 was that the British government needed to supply enslaved soldiers to these regiments. Other enslaved men were used for military purposes in East Africa and in the Royal Navy.[113] Even after 1807, enslaved Africans 'liberated' by the Royal Navy from human traffickers were often designated to be employed by those same military and naval authorities.[114] A law of 1807 declared that 'all Negroes purchased by or on account of His Majesty, His Heirs and Successors and serving in any of His Majesty's Forces, shall be taken to be free . . . and that such Negroes shall also to all intents and purposes whatever, be considered as Soldiers, having voluntarily enlisted in His Majesty's service.' This law was interpreted to apply not just to those in the West Indian Regiments but more generally throughout the army and navy and may have encouraged enlistment.[115]

Although military service could be brutal and was generally unpopular, it offered an escape from poverty and a certain status for Black soldiers, who received equal pay and pensions to their white counterparts. It was common for such soldiers to be discharged from one regiment and re-enlist in another. However, pensions were often inadequate and many former soldiers, even those who were designated 'Chelsea Pensioners', were forced to supplement their meagre incomes, to beg, or to enter the workhouse.[116] Those free men recruited directly into the British Army were often restricted to musical roles and were very seldom promoted above the rank of non-commissioned officer. Alex Figaro, an African American labourer from New York who joined the 4th Dragoons in Lancashire, was promoted to trumpet-major before his retirement in 1824, as was James Godwin, a veteran soldier and carpenter of Jamaican origin who had served at Waterloo, who held the rank from 1836 until his retirement in 1840, at the age of fifty-two, after thirty-one years of service.[117] It seems that only one man, George Rose, a Jamaican veteran of Waterloo, reached the rank of sergeant. He was not a musician and was a member of several regiments, including the kilted Scottish regiment, the Black Watch. Formerly enslaved, he had managed to escape and had somehow made his way to Britain, where he enlisted in 1809. Wounded several times, he served in Ireland, Germany, the Netherlands, Gibraltar and elsewhere before retiring in Glasgow in 1837. In 1849 he returned to Jamaica, possibly as a missionary, and died there in 1873.[118]

Many other soldiers were drummers, trumpeters and cymbalists recruited into such regiments as the 4th Dragoons and the 29th Foot, the latter also known as the Worcestershire Regiment.[119] One of these drummers, the Barbadian John Sampson, had enlisted in England in 1798 as a teenager, and was in his mid-twenties when he was murdered in 1807 in Aberdeen by other soldiers.[120] The reasons for his murder are unclear. He was known as 'as a great boxer' who had often challenged and beaten soldiers from the same regiment as those who killed him. Moreover, he was alleged to have killed one of his adversaries in a previous fight. The court case which ensued concluded there had been a 'grudge', although no pre-meditation.[121] Many others also enlisted at an early age, probably to escape poverty. George Wise, from Nova Scotia, enlisted in the 29th Foot at the age of ten in 1805 and served in numerous conflicts for the next thirty years. John Freeman, from Antigua, enlisted in Berkshire in 1800 at the age of fourteen. He was discharged in 1818, having seen service in the Napoleonic wars in Spain.

Another young drummer was Peter Askins from St Domingo, who also enlisted in Berkshire at the age of eight. He was discharged in 1841, the most decorated enlisted man in the regiment, and drew his army pension until his death in 1852.[122] Child soldiers of Caribbean origin were also recruited in Ireland in the early nineteenth century, like Charles Arundell from St Kitts, who enlisted at the age of ten in Dublin in 1799. A veteran 'journeyman soldier', who was based in Ireland, he served as a bugler and drummer in several regiments for some thirty years. Several other Black soldiers also enlisted in Ireland, some of them in Irish regiments of the British Army, evidence of an African population in Ireland probably several thousand strong.[123] What such young children were doing in the British Isles, and whether they were with their families, remains as yet unknown.

Soldiers faced the challenges of racism as did other Black citizens. Stephen Blunman was born in Barbados but enlisted in the Scots Guards as a musician in London in 1802, when he was about twenty. A hairdresser by trade, he was married with a young child, when, in 1818, he was abused and attacked in a public house in London's Elephant and Castle. According to the report at the ensuing trial, the landlord would not serve him 'but called him names reflecting on his colour and country'. When he left the premises, he was attacked by the landlord and another man, but the assault was seen by a watchman, and other witnesses, and the two attackers were taken to court, found guilty and each fined 17s 4d. There is, however, no evidence of Blunman receiving any compensation. He continued his military career until 1824 when he was discharged and became a Chelsea Pensioner, with a pension of one shilling a day, until his death in London in 1837 at the age of sixty.[124] Much earlier, in 1807, several newspapers carried the following report: 'One of the Black musicians belonging to the Guards, being accosted in the Strand a few days since, with "Well blackie, what news from the devil?" knocked the fellow down who asked the question with this appropriate and laconic answer: "He send you dat – how you like it?"'[125] That incident reflected the experience of many.[126]

There were hundreds of Black soldiers, recruited and enlisting in the British Isles, or retiring there in the nineteenth century. They formed something of a fraternity, as a leading military historian explains:

> Relationships between Black soldiers were formed both before and during military service: Black recruits enlisted together, and serving Black soldiers recruited Black civilians. Black soldiers named each

other as next of kin on campaign service. They established relationships with each other that transcended regimental rivalries, and this included their wives and children. They acted as witnesses to each other's marriages, became godparents to each other's children, saw their sons enter the same regiments and their daughters marry soldiers (both Black and White).[127]

By the 1840s the tradition of Black musicians seems to have become less favoured and slowly died out. In 1830, for example, the Commanding Officer of the 78th Highlanders Regiment wrote indicating that former musicians who were 'Africans by birth' had subsequently been 'sent to the ranks'. However, 'on account of their Colour according ill with the Highland dress', he 'considered them rather an incumbrance on the Regiment', and had therefore proposed them for discharge.[128] It is difficult to judge whether such views were widespread, or in any way had official support, although the racist views of Viscount Garnet Wolsey, Adjutant-General to the Forces, appeared in the press in 1888.[129] Two years previously, European non-commissioned officers in the 2nd West India Regiment had written to the press, complaining that they were 'being passed over for promotion by Native Sergeants'.[130] In 1896 a newspaper article lamented the fact that since the 1870s 'Negro Musicians' had completely disappeared from the army – a view that was corroborated by Charles Dickens in *All the Year Round*.[131]

Few other Black soldiers were recruited in the late nineteenth century before the enlistment of Jimmy Durham. Durham was a Sudanese child named Mustapha, born in about 1885, who was orphaned by the military action of the Durham Light Infantry in Sudan. His father had been killed during the Battle of Ginnis and his mother fled on a boat with him and another child. The vessel was also attacked by British troops and Mustapha was abandoned in the panic and adopted by the men of the regiment. He was renamed after two of them as Jimmy Francis Durham, and remained in the care of the regiment until, aged about fourteen, he enlisted in 1898 as a bandsman. He served in the regiment until his death in Ireland in 1910.[132]

Just as in the eighteenth century, many Africans served in the Royal and Merchant navies. A marine life enabled travel and also payment, however meagre, as well as accommodation and food. Many of those from Africa, the Caribbean and America would have found their way to Britain by working their passage on board ships, while for many others it provided their main occupation. Political activists such as Robert Wedderburn and William Davidson were both mariners, as was Chatham Cuffay, the father of the Chartist William Cuffay. Wedderburn relates how on two occasions he was press-ganged into naval employment, a fate that would befall many others. By the late 1830s thousands of mariners of Caribbean origin were registered as merchant seamen on British ships, the majority of them based in Britain, as well as hundreds more 'men of colour' from Africa, Canada, the United States and elsewhere. Many of these mariners would have spent much of their lives at sea. Perhaps the best example is a Jamaican, Henry Sinclair, who went to sea as a six-year-old in 1776 and was still a mariner sixty-nine years later in 1845 at the age of seventy-five. He was a ship's cook based in Poplar, East London, a common area of residence for seamen, although some would have been based in other ports, such as Liverpool. Sinclair is recorded as working until he was seventy-eight but perhaps continued for longer. His employment included fourteen years in the Royal Navy.[133] Many others were also cooks, or stewards, but a few rose through the ranks to become mates, or even chief mates, although the majority remained ordinary seamen. Alexander Francis was a Jamaican who spent more than twenty years in the Royal Navy from the 1850s onwards. He retired in 1878 as a Petty Officer First Class and then lived and worked in the Medway towns in Kent.[134] There are, however, some indications that in the Royal Navy in the early nineteenth century seamen 'of colour' who aspired to be junior officers and ships' surgeons were discriminated against and that some may even have been dismissed from service.[135]

By the early nineteenth century there were hundreds of these sailors 'of colour' in British ports, such as Liverpool and London, consolidating these cities as places of African settlement. It was often very harsh employment. A Barbadian seaman, William Jordan, was effectively starved and frozen to death on a ship which lay at anchor in the River Medway in Kent in 1861. Despite a local outcry and the prosecution of the ship's captain, the court decided he had no case to answer. It was also not unknown for 'coloured' seamen to successfully sue their ships' captains for non-payment of wages.[136] In 1870 it was recorded that, since 1840, some 3,212 West Indians and 1,200 Africans had been admitted to the Dreadnought Hospital Ship at Greenwich. The hospital catered for both merchant seamen and those in the the Royal Navy and its records give some indication of how common African and Caribbean seafarers were.[137] Because of their maritime skills, sailors could also work in the merchant fleet, or even on board slave ships. Records show, for instance, that in the decade before 1805, Liverpool slave ships recruited more than seventy such seamen from Africa, the Caribbean and Liverpool itself.[138] As what was called 'legitimate trade' with West Africa developed throughout the nineteenth century, there was a demand for more African sailors and even all-African crews, thought to be essential before vaccines were found for tropical diseases. Liverpool, Cardiff, London, South Shields and elsewhere gradually became known as ports where entire Black crews could be recruited.

Liverpool became especially important for the trade with West Africa after the development of steamships in the 1840s. Following the repeal of the Navigation Act in 1849, a measure largely designed to ensure the importation of cheaper raw materials into Britain, the employment of a cheaper foreign and especially a colonial labour force became increasingly common in the Merchant Navy. The most notorious example were seamen from India, commonly called lascars, who were paid lower wages and given poorer conditions of service than other seamen. Such discrimination was enshrined in the Lascar Act of 1823 and the Merchant Shipping Act of 1894.[139]

Black crews from Cardiff can be found in newspaper reports from the 1850s. These often detail the cruel treatment they received, especially on American ships. When the first and second mate on board the *Gleaner* attacked six 'coloured seamen' as the ship pulled out of Cardiff docks in 1851 the police were called and the perpetrators punished with sentences of transportation and hard labour.[140] There was also a demand for stokers and trimmers who both worked in the boiler-rooms of the new steamships. Africans, and those from the Caribbean and colonial seamen in general were assumed to be more suitable for this gruelling work below deck and were often paid less than others. Ship owners sometimes argued that Caribbean, or other colonial seamen, were more obedient and hard-working and attempted to create divisions which they could exploit.[141] The development of so-called tramp shipping which moved from port to port, seeking cargo, soon constituted 60 per cent of all British shipping, and led to the recruitment of more Black seamen, including those from Somalia, as well as Kru seamen from West Africa.

By 1901 there were well over a thousand seamen from the Caribbean alone working on British ships.[142] Much earlier in the nineteenth century, African seamen in Liverpool had chosen to frequent their 'own' boarding houses and also learned to join together to seek legal redress if they felt wronged by their employers.[143]

Employment in the Royal Navy for sailors of African descent seems to have become less typical after the Napoleonic Wars, but was clearly of importance before 1815. The most notable example is that of Captain John Perkins (c.1745–1812), 'Jack Punch', as he was known, a Jamaican, reportedly of mixed heritage and possibly of slave origin, who had an illustrious career as a Royal Navy officer and spy before 1800. Known for his daring capture of enemy ships and as a supporter of the revolutionary events in Haiti, Perkins was forced to resign through ill-health in 1804. He was unique, not only because of his background, but also because he reportedly never visited Britain.[144] Perkins was unusual. Most men from Africa and the Caribbean remained ordinary seamen.

Another famous figure was twenty-one-year-old William Brown, from Grenada, who registered as a sailor on HMS *Charlotte* for a month in Chatham, Kent, in 1815, before being discharged 'for being a female'. The story was subsequently reported in *The Times* and elsewhere, by which time it had been so embellished that Brown was presented as a married African woman willing to leave her husband for the navy, and a veteran with eleven years' service, including 'for some time as captain of the fore-top'. *The Times* also reported that she also had a significant share of prize money, was 'a smart well-formed figure . . . possessed of considerable strength', and her features were said to be 'rather handsome for a black'.[145] Women sailors were uncommon but not unknown at the time and, if only for a month, it seems that the woman known as 'William Brown' was the first female from the Caribbean to join the Royal Navy.

Those from Africa and the Caribbean were more regularly employed by the Royal Navy as Britain's maritime activities expanded in the eighteenth and nineteenth centuries. These seamen included those who escaped from slavery, since the Royal Navy encouraged such escapes.[146] What may have begun as an expedient became commonplace and it is estimated that during the late eighteenth and early nineteenth centuries, sailors of African descent comprised between 3 and 25 per cent of Royal Navy crews.[147] Several seamen of African descent sailed with Nelson on board HMS *Victory* at Trafalgar, for example, including nine from the Caribbean and one from Africa. George Ryan, African born, is often credited as being the Black sailor pictured with Nelson at his death, immortalized in paintings and on Nelson's Column in London. Another of the ships in Nelson's fleet, HMS *Bellerophon*, included ten sailors of African heritage from the Caribbean and North America. Others, including those born, or based in Britain, would also have worked as crew in other ships during the Battle of Trafalgar and other naval battles throughout the period. In later years they might well have returned to Britain, like the Jamaican sailor John Simmonds, to marry local women and retire as a Greenwich pensioner, although it seems that some Black mariners struggled to obtain pensions.[148] One such was Samuel Michael (c.1768–1833), an African American originally from Philadelphia, who had joined the Royal Navy in 1792, after spending ten years as a merchant seaman. He served until 1812 in several ships, the last being HMS *Ethalion*. During his service he lost a leg and was discharged by Greenwich Hospital as an out-pensioner (i.e., non-resident), but with a pension for life of £16 a year. Unable to survive on this, he took employment as a cook in the Merchant Navy for the next twenty years before being admitted to the Dreadnought Seamen's Hospital in 1831 after fifty years at sea. A married man with three children, based in London, he spent the last year of his life at Greenwich Hospital.[149]

One notable Black mariner was William Hall (1827–1904), who joined the Royal Navy and became the first Black man to be awarded the Victoria Cross, Britain's highest military honour for bravery. Hall was the son of former enslaved parents, who had been brought to Canada by the Royal Navy during the Anglo-American War of 1812. Hall's parents both worked for Sir William Cunard, the shipping tycoon. Hall volunteered for the Royal Navy in 1852 and served in the Crimean War, where he was promoted to 'captain of the fore-top' and also decorated. He later saw action during the First Indian War of Independence in 1857, during which his bravery was cited, and he received the Victoria Cross in 1859. He remained in the Royal Navy and was subsequently promoted to the rank of Petty Officer.[150] Towards the end of the nineteenth century it was reported that the Admiralty banned the employment of 'black or coloured men and boys' in the navy 'without the special sanction of the Admiralty', probably as the result of an increasing colour bar in the armed forces.[151]

MARY SEACOLE

Perhaps the most prominent figure to be associated with the armed forces was Mary Seacole (1805–1881), the Jamaican-born 'doctress', hotelier and entrepreneur, whose widespread fame arises from her role as a carer for British soldiers during the Crimean War and the publication of her autobiography, *Wonderful Adventures of Mrs Seacole in Many Lands*.[152]

Born Mary Jane Grant in Kingston, Jamaica, Seacole was the daughter of a Scottish lieutenant in the British Army and a Jamaican woman. She spent most of her life outside Britain. She claimed that she learned 'the Creole medicinal art', including the use of herbal remedies and hygiene, from her mother, but she also learned other medical skills from military and naval surgeons in Jamaica. She followed in the footsteps of other Jamaican women healers who used traditional remedies such as pomegranate, cinnamon bark and mustard seeds, including some brought from Africa, to treat a variety of ailments. Contemporary Jamaican doctresses included Coubah Cornwallis and Sarah Adams. 'The African Couba', also referred to as 'the motherly lodging-house-keeper', was reported to have treated Horatio Nelson when he contracted dysentery, and the young William IV. The wife of the latter is said to have sent Couba an expensive gown as a token of thanks, which she refused to wear, but reserved for her burial in 1848.[153] Sarah Adams, who was for a time the matron of the Royal Naval Hospital in Port Royal, Jamaica, who died in 1849, appears to have been as much admired for her looks as her doctoring skills, but her responsible position speaks for itself.[154]

Seacole gained medical experience in Jamaica and considerably more during her stay in Panama. There she combatted cholera by using a combination of 'mustard plasters and emetics and calomel', as well as 'mercury applied externally', together with 'massages of warm oil, camphor and spirits of wine,' and by these and other such remedies managed to save some of her patients.[155] She travelled widely, including throughout the Caribbean, and also experienced racism, mentioning it as one of her most vivid memories of 'London street-boys', as well as an experience suffered at the hands of Americans in Panama. It is evident that by the time she travelled to the Crimea she had considerable experience of life, had been married and widowed, as well gaining experience in the treatment of patients suffering from a variety of ailments.

Britain's military conflict against Russia during the Crimean War (1853–6) was part of what was often referred to as the 'Eastern Question': a concern that Russian expansion at the expense of Turkey would harm Britain's imperial interests in the Mediterranean, as well as throughout Asia. Nursing and medical provision for British troops was rudimentary and this led the War Office to appoint Florence Nightingale to recruit nurses at the start of the conflict. Seacole later wrote 'no sooner had I heard of war somewhere, than I longed to witness it', and, turning her back on the gold-mining investments she was pursuing in London, she attempted to join a second contingent of Nightingale's nurses bound for the Crimea, so as to be 'useful to my own "sons", suffering for a cause it was so glorious to fight and bleed for'.[156] Seacole applied to the War Office, other government departments and to Nightingale's representatives, but her offer of service was rejected, causing her to reflect 'was it possible that American prejudices against colour had some root here? Did these ladies shrink from accepting my aid because my blood flowed beneath a somewhat duskier skin than theirs?'[157]

In response Seacole decided to make her own way to the Crimea and to open 'an hotel for invalids', subsequently named the British Hotel, intending 'on her arrival at Balaclava to establish a mess table and comfortable quarters for sick and convalescent officers'. According to her autobiography, Seacole was received with courtesy by Nightingale, although the latter is reported to have written 'I had the greatest difficulty in repelling Mrs Seacole's advances, and in preventing association between her and my nurses.'[158] With the support of her business partner, Thomas Day, and using military contacts whom she knew from Jamaica, Seacole built her 'hotel' from scrap and salvaged material and opened for business in March 1855. She provided meals and sold everything from 'a needle to an anchor', as well as providing medical care. William Russell, *The Times'* famous war correspondent, referred to her as a 'warm and successful physician, who doctors and cures all manner of men with extraordinary success. She is always in attendance near the battlefield to aid the wounded and has earned many a poor fellow's blessing.'[159] The *Illustrated London News* reported:

> Perhaps at first the authorities looked askant [sic] at the woman-volunteer; but they soon found her worth and utility; and from that time until the British army left the Crimea, Mother Seacole was a household word in the camp ... she attended many patients, nursed many sick, and earned the good will and gratitude of hundreds.[160]

An even more telling report appeared in the *Morning Advertiser*, which, after praising her activities, concluded: 'Mrs Seacole is, moreover a highly intelligent woman, and a further proof that the race from which she sprang is one capable of high intellectual development.'[161]

When the Crimean War came to an end, Seacole found herself in a precarious financial position and on her return to England was declared bankrupt. Several fundraising events were held to support her, including the Seacole Fund Grand Military Festival in July 1857, which was supported by major military figures, including the dukes of Cambridge and Wellington and Major-General Lord Rokeby. It reportedly attracted an audience of 40,000, but only raised £57 for Seacole. Her autobiography was published the same year and is often credited as the first by a woman of African or Caribbean heritage. However, it is unclear whether, like Mary Prince, whose *History* appeared a quarter of century earlier, Seacole dictated her narrative to an unnamed editor.[162] In his preface William Russell tellingly wrote 'I should have thought that no preface would have been required to introduce Mrs. Seacole to the British public,' and he concluded:

I have witnessed her devotion and her courage; I have already borne testimony to her services to all who needed them ... I trust that England will not forget one who nursed her sick, who sought out her wounded to aid and succour them, and who performed the last offices for some of her illustrious dead.[163]

Seacole returned to Jamaica in 1859 and subsequently travelled to Panama, but soon found herself in a difficult financial position again. Funds for her support were raised in London under the auspices of the Prince of Wales and senior military figures, which enabled her to buy land and property in Jamaica. When she returned to London in 1865, she was able to purchase property in Marylebone, her portrait was painted in 1869, and, increasingly, she moved amongst the elite. In 1871 a bust of her was sculpted by Count Gleichen, a nephew of Queen Victoria, and she reportedly became the private masseuse of the Princess of Wales. At the time of her death in London she left an estate valued at £2,500.[164]

There were several other women from the Caribbean and from Africa who were nurses in Britain during the nineteenth century. One such was Annie Brewster (1858–1902), who was born in St Vincent, although her father was Barbadian, but migrated to Britain with her parents and family in the 1860s. In 1881 she started her training at the London Hospital and later worked there as the nurse in charge of the ophthalmic wards until her death.[165]

PRIZE-FIGHTERS

Seafarers were known for being able to take care of themselves, and in the nineteenth century several famous boxers found their way to Britain by working their passage on board ships. They include the African Americans Tom Molineux (or Molineaux), Henry Sutton, Jemmy Robinson, Bob Smith and Sam Robinson, as well as 'the Morocco Prince', James Wharton, and John Perry from Nova Scotia, who followed his father into the Royal Navy as a sailor.[166] Boxing, or prize fighting, provided a spectacle for thousands and was linked to gambling. It was sometimes frowned upon by the authorities, but became an increasingly popular professional sport amongst all classes during the nineteenth century.

The first record of a Black prize-fighter is that of Joe Lashley, 'an African Black' who fought and defeated his opponent at Marylebone Fields, London, in June 1791. No other information has yet been found on this historic fight or its victor. The most notable of the nineteenth-century African American boxers, or prize-fighters, was undoubtedly Bill Richmond (c.1763–1829), who became so well known that he was given a role at the coronation of George IV.[167] There is much that remains unclear about his early life. Born into slavery in New York, he was taken under the wing of Brigadier-General Hugh Percy of the British Army in about 1776, during the armed struggle for America's independence, in circumstances that remain obscure. Richmond accompanied Percy to England, where he was for a time educated and apprenticed to a cabinet-maker in York. It appears that he practised this trade in London during the 1790s before receiving the patronage of Thomas Pitt, the notorious Lord Camelford, finally becoming a professional boxer when he was over forty years old, in 1804. Many of Richmond's earliest amateur contests had resulted from racist insults directed at him, or at white women with him for accompanying a 'man of colour'. Richmond subsequently married one of these women during the 1790s, and they had four children together.

Richmond also had to overcome racism in his early professional career. A report of one fight in London indicated that the spectators 'were very clamorous against the black'.[168] He managed to overcome such challenges and became one of the first successful Black boxers, often competing against men much younger than himself, including the celebrated prize-fighter Tom Cribb. To supplement his income from boxing, Richmond also found employment as an 'enforcer', providing security for the politician and playwright Richard Sheridan during the 1806 general election, and he worked in a similar capacity for the Covent Garden Theatre. In addition, he often acted as a trainer and sparring partner, and offered boxing tuition to anyone who could pay.[169] By 1810 he had acquired sufficient funds to become the landlord of the Horse and Dolphin public house, in London's St Martin's Street. He soon focused his energy on mentoring and training another African American boxer, Tom Molineux (1784–1818).

Much mystery surrounds the early life of Molineux, including whether he was born free or enslaved. Whichever was the case, he arrived in England in around 1810 and after a few months under Richmond's direction was in a position to challenge the boxing champion of England, Tom Cribb. This challenge created some unease in those who feared 'lest, to the dishonour of our country, a Negro should become the *Champion of England*' (italics in original). Another publication remarked, 'what alarmed natives most was the prospect that an African had threatened to decorate his sooty brow with Cribb's title'.[170] It was reported that nearly 10,000 spectators arrived for the fight, which was held in appalling weather on Copthall Common, near East Grinstead, in December 1810. What happened next is the subject of controversy. Cribb eventually won the fight but, according to one report, only after about 200 people invaded the ring and 'if one of the Moor's fingers was not broken, it was much injured by some of them attempting to remove his hand from the ropes'.[171] Although the fight continued for another fifteen rounds after this incident, it was also reported that on another occasion Cribb failed to beat the count but was still declared the victor.[172] Some concluded that Cribb had won unfairly, either because of racism or the actions of those who had placed large bets on him.[173]

Molineux alluded to the issue of racism in a public challenge to Cribb, probably written by Richmond, in which he expressed 'a confident hope, that the circumstance of my being a different colour to those of a people amongst whom I have sought protection will not in any way operate to my prejudice'.[174] Both Richmond and Molineux were subject to insults from individuals and further evidence of crowd 'antipathy against a man of colour' before Cribb accepted the challenge and a rematch was scheduled with a purse of £400 for the winner.[175] Richmond placed all his financial resources on the outcome of the rematch, which took place in September 1811, and attracted an even larger audience, of some 20,000. There was clearly a climate of antipathy towards Molineux, produced by those who feared that 'the laurels of a British champion were in danger of being wrested from him by a Baltimore man of colour'. The latter was sometimes referred to as 'the Moor' in the press.[176] In the event Cribb won decisively, Richmond was financially ruined and blamed by Molineux for his defeat.

Richmond and Molineux were never reconciled. The former, out of financial necessity, continued to box, even though he was over fifty years old, and in 1814 became one of the founders of the Pugilistic Club, which attempted to professionalize the sport. Molineux also continued to fight, initially in Scotland and later in Ireland, but he was racked by illness. He died in Galway in August 1818, '"very humanely attended" by three people of his colour', in a room occupied by the 77th Regiment, then stationed in Ireland. These soldiers also paid for his funeral. Richmond continued his involvement with pugilism. In 1820 a leading commentator of the sport remarked 'we know of no pugilist better calculated to teach the science than RICHMOND; not only from his superior knowledge of boxing, but from his acquaintance with men and manners, and civility of deportment on all occasions'. Indeed, Richmond had become known as the leading 'scientific teacher of the art of self-defence'. The following year, at his own insistence, he represented all 'gentlemen of colour' when pugilists were invited to attend George IV's coronation in 1821, allegedly to provide added security. Like others, Richmond was affected by the severe economic conditions in the country during the 1820s. In 1826 he arranged an unsuccessful benefit for the Lancashire weavers, following the so-called 'power loom' riots, while in 1828, aged sixty-five, he declared his willingness still to fight (for a purse of £100). In his last years several benefit events were arranged to keep him from complete destitution. He died in London in December 1829.[177]

In the early nineteenth century people of African and Caribbean heritage were to be found pursuing numerous and varied occupations, but the vast majority lived in difficult social and economic conditions, as did most of their British contemporaries. For some, enslavement was still a fact of life in Britain, even in the 1830s, just as it was for those in the Caribbean. It is not surprising, therefore, that in the same way as in the eighteenth century, those of African and Caribbean heritage concerned themselves not only with their everyday struggle for survival, but also with the major political struggles of their time.

5

Struggles for the Rights of All

The many struggles facing Africans and the working class in Britain, a consequence of their common oppression, led to a strong tradition linking the demand for abolition, and for the rights of Africans, with radical politics and the struggle for the rights of all working people. The politics of Equiano's London Corresponding Society (LCS) is the most significant example, but there were many others. It is noteworthy that the Haitian Revolution was often used as an inspiration to encourage working people in Britain to liberate themselves. Such views were expressed in Wordsworth's sonnet 'To Toussaint L'Ouverture' (1803) and in Thomas Rickman's 'An Ode in Celebration of the Emancipation of the Blacks of Saint Domingo' (1804). It was an age when many like Cugoano wanted 'the world turn'd upside down'. The LCS came under attack by the government in the late 1790s, as did other radical organizations in Britain and Ireland, but the movement endured, not least because of the poverty and unemployment facing many working people, who, in this period, had few political rights and were not even permitted to vote.

Among the early-nineteenth-century radicals there was a Jamaican woman, Catherine Despard, married to Edward Despard, an impoverished former colonial official. When he returned to Britain from Honduras, in 1780, she accompanied him. They were an unusual pair. A colonel from a prominent Irish family, Despard became a leading figure in the LCS and was closely connected with the Irish republican Robert Emmet, as well as the United Irishmen, who demanded and fought for Ireland's independence from England. Emmet was a defender of the 'levelling principle of universal equality' and was executed for treason in 1803, a consequence of his revolutionary activities with disempowered and exploited workers, as well as alleged plans to assassinate the monarch. Catherine was the daughter of Sarah Gordon, who described herself as 'a free black woman'. Sarah Gordon had reportedly bequeathed her daughter four enslaved Jamaicans in her will, although their subsequent fate is unknown. Catherine was also described in police reports as 'a black woman' and by Despard's family as 'a poor black woman who called herself his wife'.[1] When her husband was arrested, on numerous occasions, she became a major campaigner, demanding an improvement of prison conditions and the reintroduction of the law on *habeas corpus*, as well as becoming an important intermediary between Despard and his friends and comrades still at liberty.[2] The government was particularly concerned that she was the main courier for Despard's writing, which, they feared, would subsequently be published and used to promote further subversive activities.[3] Despard was arrested for the last time in November 1802 at a meeting of workers in London. He was tried for treason, found guilty and sentenced to be executed and disembowelled. Catherine successfully campaigned that he should not be disembowelled and that he be accorded an appropriate funeral. She may even have aided him in the composition of his final speech from the gallows.

One of the most important strands of the radical movement was that associated with Thomas Spence, 'glorious old Tom Spence' as the German revolutionary, Friedrich Engels called him.[4] In his plan first outlined in *Property in Land Everyone's Right*, Spence advocated revolutionary change and what has been referred to as 'agrarian socialism': the redistribution of privately owned land for rent by the landless and the funds accruing to be used for the benefit of the general population.[5] One of Spence's most enthusiastic followers was a Jamaican, Robert Wedderburn (c.1762–c.1836), who faced imprisonment several times throughout his life. He not only advocated revolution in Britain, but also called for the enslaved in the Caribbean to rise and liberate themselves.

Wedderburn was born in Kingston, Jamaica, in 1761 or 1762, the son of an African-born enslaved woman, named Rosanna, and a Scottish plantation owner, Dr James Wedderburn. Although he was born free, Robert Wedderburn witnessed the torture of both his mother and maternal grandmother and was largely disowned by his father.

He joined the Royal Navy and arrived in England in 1778. There he joined the 'underworld' of the working poor and unemployed people of London and eventually found work as a tailor, a precarious occupation at that time. He was no doubt radicalized by his upbringing in Jamaica, his harsh naval experiences and the conditions facing the poor in London. He witnessed and perhaps participated in the Gordon Riots of 1780, was influenced by radical Methodism and by 1813 had joined the circles of the Spencean Philanthropists, or Spenceans, as Thomas Spence's followers were known.[6] The Spenceans, in many ways the radical successors to the LCS, appealed to artisans and other working people and often met in taverns. They blended elements of religion and millenarianism with their revolutionary doctrine 'that the earth belonged to the children of men, making no difference to colour or character, just or unjust'.[7]

Wedderburn believed that Spence's revolutionary plan might be adopted in both Britain and the Caribbean, since, following in the tradition of Hardy and the LCS, Spence also linked the rights of the enslaved in the Caribbean with those of working people in Britain. In 1814 his periodical published William Cowper's anti-slavery poem *The Negro's Complaint*.[8] In 1816 the Spenceans played a prominent role in the demonstrations at Spa Fields in London, held to demand political reforms, and where their leaders made common cause between the working people in Britain and 'African slaves in the West Indies'.[9] One of those arrested and transported for his part in the 'riots' that erupted after a second major demonstration at Spa Fields was 23-year-old Richard Simmonds, an African American pastry cook, who led a group of men who ransacked a gunsmith's shop and stood his ground, sword in hand and 'more bold than the rest', when a cavalry troop arrived to suppress the rebellion.[10] During his interrogation Simmonds claimed that several others of African descent had also been involved in the rebellion.[11] The 'riots' were themselves an attempt at insurrection, demonstrating the desperation of many working people in London.

The period following the Napoleonic Wars was not only the time of the demobilization of half a million soldiers and sailors, but also one of economic hardship, as well as social and political unrest. Many organizations demanding political reform and the right to vote were created and hundreds of petitions sent to Parliament. There were also protest meetings, marches and attempts at rebellion. In this climate, the government took draconian measures to suppress popular discontent and opposition, including imprisonment without trial. Opposition to unemployment and poverty was widespread and those speaking out against it ranged from luminaries such as Wilberforce and the Archbishop of Canterbury to radicals and revolutionaries like Wedderburn and William Davidson. In 1817 the government passed the so-called 'Gagging Acts' – the Treason Act and the Seditious Meetings Act. The latter aimed to prevent all meetings of more than fifty persons, as well as preventing the planning of smaller meetings. It also made it illegal to belong to certain organizations, such as the Spenceans, that promoted the 'confiscation and division of the land'.[12]

It was in this period that Wedderburn became the de facto leader of the Spenceans for about a year and first published his periodicals *Forlorn Hope* and then the *Axe Laid to the Root or a Fatal Blow to Oppressors, Being an Address to the Planters and Negroes of the Island of Jamaica*. The second edition of the *Axe Laid to the Root* was an 'Address to the Slaves of Jamaica', and several further editions focused on slavery in the Caribbean. However, these publications were sold to the working poor of London, and there is no doubt that Wedderburn was appealing to their revolutionary sentiments.[13] He was an opponent of slavery, landowners, the rich and the established Church. An advocate of abolishing private property in land, he demanded redistributed land for all, universal suffrage and peoples' empowerment in Britain and the Caribbean. His revolutionary method included the idea of the general strike, but he also discussed the merits of the guerrilla warfare as practised by the Maroons, as well as the revolution in Haiti. The publications show that Wedderburn was both a writer and poet. He also preached revolutionary sermons in the Haymarket and Soho that soon established him as the 'notorious firebrand' of the most radical Spenceans.[14] In addition to sermons, or 'lectures' presented twice on Sundays, Weddurburn hosted twice-weekly public debates, on contemporary political issues such as the role the established church played in inculcating passivity amongst the enslaved and the working poor, at which several hundred paid sixpence to attend and participate.[15]

In August 1819 Wedderburn, billed as 'the offspring of an African slave', debated the question – 'Has a Slave an inherent right to slay his master who refuses him his liberty?' According to police reports, he explained to his audience of 200 of 'the lowest description' that the government sent armed men to Africa to kidnap men and women for profit, just as they employed workers as slaves in cotton factories. Wedderburn concluded that death was as acceptable as slavery. He specifically named those who had died for political activity, and said if he was to die for liberty, he hoped it would rouse those left behind to kill their masters and gain their liberty. He presented biblical support for such views and claimed that he had written to the enslaved in the Caribbean not to slay their masters until a vote had been taken at the meeting. When the meeting voted overwhelmingly in favour, Wedderburn allegedly told the audience that he would write 'home and tell the Slaves to Murder their Masters as soon as they pleased'.[16] The government subsequently arrested Wedderburn and prosecuted him for blasphemy.[17]

Another important Jamaican Spencean was William Davidson (1786–1820), who would play a central role in the ill-fated Cato Street conspiracy and was finally to be executed for his political activities. Davidson was born in Kingston, Jamaica, the son of the Scottish Attorney-General of the island and a 'woman of colour'. He was sent to Scotland to be educated and for three years he was apprenticed to a lawyer in Liverpool. He tired of the law, ran away to sea and was subsequently press-ganged into the Royal Navy. He then served an apprenticeship before working as a journeyman cabinet-maker in Lichfield. He also received an allowance from his mother. With her support he bought a large house in Birmingham, intending to establish his business there, but was unsuccessful. He then worked in London and became a Sunday-school teacher in Walworth. In about 1816 he married a widow with four children and later moved to Marylebone. It was reported that he joined the Marylebone Union Reading Society, although he was too poor to pay the weekly subscription of two pence and attend regularly.[18] This was one of several such societies where members read and discussed the work of radicals such as Thomas Paine, as well as books and newspapers about parliamentary and political reform. Davidson is reported to have spoken at one radical meeting in London and to have attended several others.[19] Like many other working people at the time, he wanted democratic political change, parliamentary reform and the right to vote.

William Davidson

It seems that it was around this time that he was introduced to Arthur Thistlewood, the leader of the more revolutionary faction of the Spenceans in London. He was subsequently befriended by a police spy who encouraged his involvement in a conspiracy to assassinate the members of the Cabinet and provoke a revolutionary uprising. It would follow in the aftermath of the infamous Peterloo Massacre in Manchester in 1819, which had provoked mass protests throughout the north of England and elsewhere, and had incensed radicals and many working people throughout the country. Many felt that such a repressive government had to be overthrown, since working people had no political rights and were denied the vote. Wedderburn was one of those preaching the need for armed revolution during this period and was a strong supporter of Thistlewood.[20] Nationwide protests had been met with the introduction of the 'Six Acts' by the government, laws that sought to suppress radical meetings, publications and speeches, and expressly made military training for civilians a criminal offence. In short, the government feared revolution and took measures to prevent it, including the infiltration of radical organizations.[21] In December 1819, to prevent his growing influence, Wedderburn was arrested.[22] It was in these circumstances that a group of conspirators, including Davidson, planned to meet in a hayloft in Cato Street, central London, to prepare to assassinate members of the Cabinet who, they believed, would be dining at a house in Grosvenor Square. A police spy and agent provocateur had encouraged the conspirators and provided them with weapons. The police entrapped the conspirators, who were apprehended and charged with high treason.

The police portrayed Davidson as a militant and resolute figure. When he was arrested he swore, 'Damn the man who would not die in Liberty's cause, I glory in it.' At his trial at the Old Bailey, he professed his innocence, claimed that he knew nothing of the conspiracy that he was 'a stranger in a strange land' and that he had been given weapons by others. He also asked the court 'if my colour be against me' and claimed that 'one man of colour may be mistaken for another'.[23] His main defence was that he had been entrapped and that witnesses were fabricating evidence against him. He maintained this stance in letters written to his wife and to Lord Harrowby, Lord President of the Council and a former employer, who had been targeted by the conspirators as the host of a dinner for other Cabinet members.[24] His evidence to the court and demeanour at his trial contrasted greatly with the evidence presented against him.[25] The jury at the Old Bailey took only thirty minutes to find Davidson guilty and he was publicly hanged and decapitated on 1 May 1820.

The conviction of Davidson and his comrades was widely seen in radical circles as a miscarriage of justice and the consequence of entrapment, false evidence and a political trial. Unsuccessful efforts were made to apprehend the police spy, who was subsequently spirited out of the country by his paymasters.[26] The so-called 'conspirators' claimed not only that they had been entrapped and framed, but also were denied the ability to produce witnesses in their defence. Several defended their political aims while condemning the government and the travesty of justice, whereas Davidson spoke mostly of his innocence and his family. The charge of high treason was clearly intended to be a deterrent against radical political change, since the conspirators were charged under a law of 1795 which declared it illegal to force the sovereign to 'change his measures or counsels' or 'to put any force or constraint upon, or to intimidate, or overawe, both Houses, or either House of Parliament'.[27] What was more, the government took measures to limit reporting of the trial and the speeches of the defendants and assembled a great show of military might at their place of execution outside Newgate Prison.

Wedderburn had been close to Thistlewood as well as Davidson, but had had no opportunity to participate in the Cato Street conspiracy, since he had been arrested for blasphemous libel the month before.[28] Wedderburn had by then a growing reputation as a preacher, an espouser of the liberation theology of his day and a 'notorious firebrand' and revolutionary. He was well known enough to feature in an engraving by the caricaturist George Cruikshank.[29] While he was in prison he was visited by Wilberforce and, after his release, continued with his political activities. In 1824 he published his autobiography, *The Horrors of Slavery*, dedicated to Wilberforce, but containing a trenchant attack on the institution of slavery and its practice by members of his own family. There is evidence to suggest that he maintained his political view on the identity of interests between those enslaved in the Caribbean and the working people of Britain, as, in his old age, he was imprisoned once again and he declared 'I am a West Indian, a lover of liberty and would dishonour human nature if I did not shew myself a friend to the liberty of others.'[30] He was in short, a fighter for the rights of all.

The third of these important Black radical figures was William Cuffay (1788–1870), 'a scion of Afric's oppressed race', one of the leaders of the London Chartists.[31] The Chartists were named after their support for the People's Charter, first drafted in 1838 by the London Working Men's Association, an organization founded two years previously by William Lovett, a carpenter. The charter emerged following the 1832 Parliamentary Reform Act, which failed to grant working people political rights and the vote. It raised six political demands: universal suffrage; vote by secret ballot; no property qualification and payment for anyone to become a Member of Parliament; annual parliaments; and equal representation of constituencies. The proposers were supporters of the view that the franchise should be genuinely universal and include women, but decided not to make the latter element a major demand, 'lest the false estimate man entertains of this half of the human family may cause his ignorance and prejudice to be enlisted to retard the progress of his own freedom'.[32] However, there were many women Chartists and supporters of Chartism, including Cuffay's third wife. The six points were drafted into a parliamentary bill which was endorsed at mass meetings of working people all over the country. The plan of the Chartists was to campaign by petitioning Parliament, but also, if the petition was rejected, to declare a general strike. They were the first national working-class organization in Britain's history, and one of their campaigning tactics was to organize an elected national convention of worker's delegates. The first of these was held in London in 1838.[33] The Chartists and their demands were greatly feared by the governments of the day. The Chartist petition was initially presented to Parliament in 1839, with 1.25 million signatures, but was rejected, leading to major unrest. A second petition

William Cuffay

with over 3 million signatures was presented in 1842, and again rejected. A third petition in 1848 was also rejected by Parliament. Cuffay was to become one of the leaders of the Chartists in London.

William Cuffay was born in Chatham, Kent, one of five children, although his first biographer claimed that he was born 'on board a merchant ship'.[34] He was the son of a former enslaved man named Chatham Cuffay, from St Kitts, and a local woman, Juliana Fox. It appears that Chatham Cuffay and a woman called Lynda Myra Cuffay, possibly his mother, were both baptized in Chatham in 1772, so it is possible that three generations of the Cuffay family had made their home in the Medway area.[35] William Cuffay's grandfather was said to have been 'an African dragged from his native valleys in the prime of his manhood', and it would appear that his descendants maintained their connection with Africa through their surname.[36] Chatham was an important naval dockyard and the area has records of an African population from the mid-seventeenth century onwards. Chatham Cuffay worked in the dockyards and also as a cook on board a Royal Navy ship. As a young man William Cuffay was apprenticed to a tailor, and in 1819 he moved to London to ply his trade. His small stature, and reported deformity, were probably a result of rickets, but it was said that 'he took great delight in all manly exercises'.[37] Like many working people of that era, Cuffay lived in some poverty and his first two wives died within a few years of marriage. He married for a third time in 1827.

His first entry into politics was in 1834, when he joined an unsuccessful tailors' strike in support of improved wages and conditions. The failure of the strike, and the lack of employment which followed, no doubt propelled Cuffay to take further action. By the time the first Chartist petition was presented to Parliament, in June 1839, he had joined the movement. At the end of that same year he spoke at a meeting of the Metropolitan Tailors' Charter Association. Cuffay moved a resolution opposing the imprisonment of Chartist leaders and the death sentences passed on those defending the Newport Rising (which had been launched to secure their release). He vigorously condemned the 'injustice and cruelty' of the government.[38] In 1842 he was unanimously elected chair of the Great Public Meeting of the Tailors, who adopted the second national petition in support of the new People's Charter. Significantly, this also called for Ireland's independence, and was eventually signed by about a third of the adult population. According to reports, Cuffay spoke in 'beautiful and manly language', recited a poem and pledged that 'he would stand like a man until the last and, if he died, he would die like a martyr gloriously in the cause'.[39] It appears from reports that Cuffay's wife Mary Ann was also an active Chartist.

Parliament's rejection of the people's petitions and the Chartists' renewed demands led to widespread demonstrations, strikes and other protest actions that culminated in a general strike. Hundreds of Chartists, men and women, were arrested, imprisoned and transported for their political activities. Cuffay was one of the signatories of a letter sent to the *Northern Star* on behalf of the Chartist Metropolitan Delegate Meeting calling for support for those arrested and condemning 'the manner in which capitalism has encroached on the rights of labour'.[40] It was during this period when so many leaders had been arrested that Cuffay was elected to the Chartists' National Executive. It was also at this time that Cuffay's opposition to the Anti-Corn Law League, which attempted to lower the wages of workers in pursuit of free trade, led *The Times* to refer contemptuously to him as 'the Black Man and his party'.[41] He was often attacked by those publications which represented the interests of the rich and powerful, but his political aims remained constant, to 'secure the people their just and inalienable rights'.[42]

It seems that on occasions Cuffay spoke of his African ancestry and the enslavement endured by his father and grandfather. He also recognized the struggles waged by the working people of Britain against human trafficking and enslavement. On one occasion he is reported to have thanked the workers at a meeting in London for what they had done for those in the Caribbean and to have concluded that 'whilst he had life and reason he would do his best to aid them in return'.[43] Cuffay clearly made much of his heritage and was well known as a 'descendant of Africa' – he also often addressed his audiences of workers as 'my fellow slaves'.[44] He was also recognized as an accomplished chairman at meetings, a witty and often humorous speaker, an actor in Chartist plays, and as a vocalist who led the singing of Chartist songs. At the 1845 Chartist National Convention he proposed the resolution in support of Fergus O'Connor's land plan, an attempt to provide workers with smallholdings on which they could become self-sufficient. Cuffay was regularly elected as joint auditor of O'Connor's Land Company, which was wound up in 1851 when it failed to gain legal recognition. He was generally applauded for his honesty and hard work and was clearly an internationalist. He supported the right of Ireland to independence and was a member of the executive of the Democratic Committee for Poland's Regeneration. In 1848, at a demonstration of thousands in London to welcome the revolution in France, Cuffay seconded a motion, proposed by the Chartist leader Ernest Jones, opposing any interference in France by the British government.[45]

It was following this demonstration that large crowds of people were engaged in disturbances that ended up in looting in Camberwell, in which two Black men, David Anthony Duffy and Benjamin Prophett, were arrested and, with many others, tried and convicted at the Old Bailey. It is difficult to conclude, as Fryer seems to have done in his account, *Staying Power: The History of Black People in Britain*, that the two were 'leaders of a demonstration'.[46] Although, at the Old Bailey, both men were identified as 'heading the mob', and may have been some of the most active participants in the looting that reportedly took place on 13 March 1848, they seem to have just been part of a crowd of hundreds. What is clear is that the government were determined to make an example of all those arrested as being connected with the Chartists.[47] Prophett, known as 'Black Ben', a 29-year-old, was identified by several witnesses. Although he protested his innocence, he was convicted of two charges of housebreaking and larceny, along with several others. He was sentenced to fourteen years' transportation, but appears to have subsequently been imprisoned and paroled in 1855. Duffy, a 21-year-old labourer and beggar, was also accused of housebreaking and burglary, identified by several witness, convicted and sentenced to seven years' transportation. Duffy's defence was that it was a case of mistaken identity and that he was accused 'because I am a coloured man'. According to witnesses, when he was arrested he claimed that he was being mistaken for Prophett.[48]

The last Chartist petition was delivered to Parliament in April 1848, and Cuffay was elected one of three London delegates to the National Convention, which met on a daily basis to prepare a mass demonstration in support of the petition. The government, fearing insurrection, readied police, troops, cavalry and artillery under the command of the Duke of Wellington to disperse the demonstrators.

Even the queen was removed from London because of alleged government fears concerning her safety. It is now thought that about 150,000 people, including significant numbers of Irish demonstrators, marched to Kennington Common on 10 April 1848. They carried a variety of banners including: 'Labour the source of all wealth' and 'Ireland for the Irish'. The crowd were addressed by the Chartist leaders and informed that the government had banned any mass presentation of the petition to Parliament. Cuffay, the chair of the 'Demonstration Committee', also addressed the crowds, denouncing some of the Chartist leaders for not making the government ban known before, since consequently the demonstrators were not in a position to march to Parliament. He had wanted to confront the military in order to expose the undemocratic nature of the ruling class. Indeed, the sixty-year-old Cuffay had argued that if Parliament should again reject the petition, 'the Executive should be prepared to lead on to liberty or death'.[49]

It was also following this great demonstration that Mary Ann was dismissed from her employment – simply for being Cuffay's wife. Both the government and the Chartists now prepared for a trial of strength. Several Chartist leaders were arrested, demonstrations banned, and new draconian legislation enacted. It was in these conditions that Cuffay eventually joined the 'Ulterior Committee' of Chartists, preparing an insurrection in London, and was elected its secretary. However, within the ranks of the revolutionary Chartists were police agents and agent provocateurs and Cuffay was first entrapped, then arrested and tried, for 'levying war on the queen'.[50] A contemporary wrote that he had become 'convinced of the hopelessness of the undertaking . . . and a chivalrous sentiment of honour withheld him from withdrawing from it alone. He went on, therefore, against his own judgement.'[51] Even his arrest presented evidence of his character.[52] He was arrested at home, 'whence he had refused to fly, lest it should be said that he abandoned his associates in the hours of peril'.[53] He was also armed, not to avoid arrest, but as he related because of the many death threats he had received from the enemies of the workers. Cuffay unsuccessfully demanded 'a jury of my equals' and he remained defiant in court. He condemned the press for the 'great prejudice that has been raised against me': there had been many racist insults, and he declared that in the circumstances he expected no mercy from the jury.[54] He also condemned the agents provocateurs and explained, 'this is no more than I have expected for some time. As certainly I have been an important character in the Chartist movement, I laid myself out for something like this from the first. I know that a great many men of good moral character are now suffering in prison only for advocating the cause of the Charter.' He concluded:

> I have the fortitude to bear any punishment your lordship can inflict upon me. I know my cause is good, and I have a self-approving conscience that will bear me up against anything, and that would bear me up even to the scaffold; therefore, I think I can endure any punishment proudly. I fear no disgrace at being called a felon.[55]

Cuffay was sentenced to be transported for life to what is now Tasmania, and arrived at the penal colony in November 1849. His wife, who had been supported by public donations from Chartists and other well-wishers, joined him in 1853. Both received significant public support and Cuffay was accorded many testimonies regarding his steadfast, loyal and honest character. He was, wrote one historian, 'the most renowned of the transportees of 1848'.[56] Although he was later pardoned, Cuffay remained in Tasmania and continued his political activities, one of few exiled Chartists to do so. Following his death in 1870 one obituary commented, 'He always supported the people's side, and opposed everything that tended to cripple the rights of the people.'[57]

LIVERPOOL

One of the most important developments occurring throughout the nineteenth century was the consolidation of distinct Black communities in several towns and cities in Britain, including London, Liverpool, South Shields and Cardiff. However, those of African and Caribbean heritage could be found throughout the country. For example, John Kent (1805–1886), credited by some as having been one of Britain's first Black policemen, was born in Cumbria. He was the son of a formerly enslaved African from the Caribbean who was a seafarer, and a locally born mother. Kent was admitted to the Carlisle City Police in 1837, although dismissed for drunkenness seven years later. Known as 'Black Kent', he also worked as a paver, court bailiff and as a railway signalman. He was well known in the area and his death was the occasion for obituaries in several local papers.[58] At the other end of the country an African of unknown origin, variously known as Makippe, Watto and George Watteau, settled in Chislehurst, Kent, in 1875. There he worked as a gardener, became something of a local celebrity as a result of his claimed association with David Livingstone, was recognized a pillar of the local Methodist church and died at the age of eighty-seven in 1931.[59]

A distinct Black community in Liverpool probably dates back to the 1730s and perhaps before. It was connected with the growth of Liverpool as a major port as a result of the human trafficking of Africans across the Atlantic. By 1771 one in three British ships engaged in transporting enslaved Africans came from Liverpool and by the end of that century 60 per cent of British slaving vessels came from that city. At the time when Britain was the world's leading trafficker of enslaved Africans, Liverpool became the major European port engaged in human trafficking.[60] As in other parts of Britain in that period, Liverpool's African population comprised both free and enslaved people, personal servants, seafarers and young students, including children, the latter often sent 'to learn sense and get a good head' by their parents, some of whom were engaged in human trafficking on the west coast of Africa. According to a contemporary account, 'there are generally from fifty to seventy of these children in Liverpool, besides those who come to London and Bristol'. Indeed, the Swedish abolitionist Wadström mentions that several West African traffickers were themselves educated in Liverpool as children.[61] A report of 1788 concluded, 'there are several of these children in Liverpool, who are boarded and educated by the merchants and masters of ships trading to Africa.'[62]

The African population was somewhat enlarged as a result of an influx of Black loyalists from North America, following the struggle for independence of the United States, although most of this population remained in London.[63] Liverpool's prominence in maritime trade, especially that with Africa, continued after the parliamentary abolition of the slave trade in 1807. Young Africans in Liverpool were forced to play a part in the struggle between abolitionist MP William Roscoe, and his pro-slavery successor in the early nineteenth century. Two young people were paraded around the city bearing signs saying 'The African Trade Restored', while two others held an alternative sign – 'We thank God for our freedom'.[64] In 1809 Roscoe was instrumental in the rescue of nine African mariners in Liverpool, including a boatswain, who had been imprisoned for debt in the borough gaol, but in fact in the interests of the captain of a Portuguese ship who wished to confine them until his ship was ready to sail. Roscoe attempted to arrange bail for the men, but the gaol was surrounded by the armed agents of the ship's captain, who hired a lawyer to enable the mariners to be released into his possession. The gaoler informed the nine men that they were free to leave, but also to stay as long as they wished, while their fellow prisoners vowed that they would not be taken by force. By these circumstances, their liberty was ensured, after which, it was reported, Roscoe was instrumental in arranging an official inquiry. Although the Portuguese captain agreed to pay costs and the local magistrates took a dim view of this use of the gaol, it appears that the case was not so unusual and the captain had formerly been advised to take this particular course of action. Subsequently, the Liverpool magistrates took measures to prevent further incidents of this kind while most of the mariners found employment in the Royal Navy.[65]

One prominent visitor to the city in June 1811 was a former enslaved man named Mohammed, who had originally been purchased in 1798 by a man called Daniel Hill, in Antigua. Hill soon recognized that Mohammed was a devoted Muslim and 'had acquired a considerable share of Arabic literature'. He showed his slave some kindness and eventually agreed to free him. Mohammed made his way to Liverpool, where he remained for two or three months before returning, with the assistance of the African Institution in London, to Goree, in West Africa, and from there to his home village.[66] Some other visitors to Britain in this period were not so fortunate. The report of the Directors of the African Institution detail the story of John George Whiston, a free man from St Vincent, who had been liberated in 1799, along with his mother, by his former owner in Martinique, who bore the same surname. The manumission was legally recorded and John Whiston subsequently made his way to St Vincent, where he was employed as a merchant's clerk for two years. In 1809 he applied to become a steward on a British ship and sailed for Britain, where he remained for a further two years, almost certainly spending some time in Liverpool. He then returned to the Caribbean in 1812 and, after thirteen years of liberty, was arrested and claimed as a slave by representatives of his former owner. He was defended by Henry Perry Keane, a leading barrister and the son of the attorney general of the island, who managed to temporarily halt the ensuing legal proceedings by himself paying £100 for Whiston's release, pending further legal action.[67]

By the nineteenth century many of the Black population in Liverpool were seafarers and their trials and tribulations were regularly reported in the local press.[68] Employment as a seafarer could prove hazardous for those of African heritage on certain routes and there were several reports of seafarers who were Liverpool residents being enslaved in the United States. In 1822, in the wake of the suppression of the rebellion led by Denmark Vesey, South Carolina passed a Negro Seamen's Act stipulating that any free sailor of African descent entering a South Carolina port had to be imprisoned until his ship was ready to sail.[69] Similar laws were then passed in other southern states.[70] Some Black seamen continued to be employed by the Royal Navy, including those born in Liverpool such as Henry Steward. However, in 1830 Steward was also imprisoned in the southern United States and the British government unsuccessfully attempted to secure his release. The government had more success with the case of William Houston, who had moved to Liverpool with his entire family, including his mother (who ran a boarding house for Black seafarers in the city during the 1840s and 1850s). He too was kidnapped and sold into slavery in the United States but the Foreign Office successfully paid £500 for his release.[71] In 1852 it was reported that sixty-three Black British sailors were imprisoned in the United States.[72]

In January 1857 the *Liverpool Mercury*, and other newspapers in Britain and the United States, reported a 'mutiny' by the crew of 'coloured men' on board the USS *James L. Bogart* moored in the River Mersey. It was reported that some of the crew had been misled about the destination of the ship, which was bound for Alabama. When they refused to work and proceed with the voyage, for fear of imprisonment and enslavement when the ship docked, they had been attacked by the ship's mates and one man, James Christie, was shot and wounded. The crew vigorously defended themselves and one of their attackers had also been injured. The ensuing court case led to a strong legal defence of the crew, who clearly had much local support, and the eventual conviction and transportation of the assailant who had shot one of the mariners. The *Liverpool Mercury* referred to the case as 'nothing more or less than the revival of the slave trade' and demanded government action to avoid any future incidents of kidnapping. *The Times* pointed out that such atrocities were not uncommon and that in the previous year nearly seventy mariners had been kidnapped in similar circumstances.[73]

In the 1820s, for example, John Glasgow, a free-born seafarer from Demerara, settled in Liverpool and married a farmer's daughter from Lancashire. In order to maintain regular income, he continued to work as a mariner, while his wife tended their farm. In 1830, aged about twenty-five and now a father of two, he set sail for Georgia in an English vessel destined to collect a shipment of rice. Once he landed in Savannah he was arrested and incarcerated, pending the return voyage of his ship. As the ship's captain failed to pay the fee for his release, he was auctioned as a slave and sold for 350 dollars. He apparently remained in that condition, his story only being known from the narrative of John Brown, a fugitive from slavery in Georgia.[74] Brown himself finally managed to escape to Lancashire, but admitted, 'I worked hard here until I found that there is prejudice against colour in England, in some classes, just as there is in America.'[75]

However, an American visitor writing in the mid-nineteenth century presented the following alternative view of the status of Black seafarers in Liverpool:

> Speaking of Negroes, recalls the looks of interest with which Negro sailors are regarded when they walk the Liverpool streets. In Liverpool indeed the Negro steps with a prouder pace and lifts his head like a man; for here, no such exaggerated feeling exists in respect to him, as in America. Three or four times I encountered our black steward, dressed very handsomely, and walking arm in arm with a good-looking woman. In New York such a couple would have been mobbed in three minutes, and the steward would have been lucky to escape with whole

limbs. Owing to the friendly reception extended to them, and the unwonted immunities they enjoy in Liverpool, the black cooks and stewards of American ships are very much attracted to the place and like to make voyages to it.[76]

The possibility of such conditions even led some African Americans to stow away on ships bound for Liverpool. One who did so in the 1840s, a former enslaved man named James Watkins, soon reported that 'the leprosy of racial hatred had affected some on British soil, especially those who came into contact with American merchants and captains'.[77] Nevertheless, many African Americans made the voyage to Liverpool and some stayed in the city. After the Fugitive Slave Law was passed in 1850, it appears that many African Americans made efforts to reach Britain, with many relocating to Liverpool. Several became destitute and had to seek the support of the Reverend Francis Bishop and the Liverpool Town Mission.[78] Another visitor to Liverpool in 1855 was Mohommah Gardo Baquaqua, an African Muslim who had been enslaved in Brazil before his liberation in the United States. Baquaqua converted to Christianity and studied for three years in New York before moving to Canada and writing his autobiography, the sole example by an enslaved African from Brazil. He apparently remained in Britain for two years, but nothing is yet known about this period, nor the rest of his life.[79]

A free-born man from New York, William Powell, relocated his entire family, a wife and seven children, to Liverpool in 1850. They resided there for ten years and William was employed by a ship's broker. Thereafter he aided many of his compatriots who arrived in Liverpool and was a key figure linking the anti-slavery movements in Britain and the US. Amongst other activities, he wrote and found subscribers for the American anti-slavery press, sent goods to the Boston Anti-Slavery Bazaar and imported books and pamphlets on the subject. He was one of those who worked to establish the Warrington Anti-Slavery Society in 1859. His children were educated locally and his eldest son, William Jr, studied medicine in London and Dublin and became a surgeon at two Liverpool hospitals, before returning to the US as one of only thirteen African American doctors in the Union army. Powell was an active anti-slavery campaigner and many African

Americans stayed at his Liverpool home. He was evidently one of many 'coloured friends' who supported the young fugitive slave, known only as 'Josephine', who had escaped from New Orleans and was hidden on board by the boatswain of a ship that arrived in Liverpool in 1856.[80]

As steamships became more common all-Black crews were regularly recruited by shipping companies, especially by Elder Dempster, a company founded in 1868 which dominated shipping to West Africa. Liverpool became a centre of settlement for seafarers from West Africa, as well as those from the Caribbean and North America, a development that was a consequence of the expansion of the British imperial interests in Africa in the nineteenth century. African seafarers also included Somalis, as well as Kru seamen from Sierra Leone and Liberia who, from the early nineteenth century onwards, began to settle in Liverpool and other British ports, such as London and Cardiff.[81] African seafarers often constituted a transient community, because of the nature of their employment. Nevertheless, over time their relationships with local women in Liverpool contributed to establishing a distinct and enduring Black community that by the early twentieth century numbered several thousands.[82]

Reports on this community and its members are numerous. In 1861 the author Charles Dickens commented on a public house in Liverpool in which 'the jovial black landlord presided over a scene of merriment and dancing', and the customers were mainly Black. Dickens was told that this community 'generally keep together, these poor fellows ... because they were at a disadvantage singly, and liable to slights in the neighbouring streets'.[83] Another contemporary commentator, Henry Mayhew, writing in a similar period, observed that: 'It is only common fairness to say that Negroes seldom, if ever, shirk work. Their only trouble is to obtain it. Those who have seen the many Negroes employed in Liverpool, will know that they are hard-working, patient and too often underpaid.'[84]

By the mid-nineteenth century African seamen, as well as those from the Caribbean and North America, were already dwelling in an area close to the docks and by 1871 constituted one of the largest Black populations outside London. By the turn of the century, they were still to be found in the poorest areas of the city and were a pool of cheap labour for the shipping companies, often facing periods of unemployment between voyages. Many of them worked on tramp ships with irregular routes, searching for cargoes throughout the world. The shortage of African women meant that this maritime population continued to intermarry, or cohabit, with local women and produced a unique community in Liverpool, whose descendants exist to this day.[85] Sometimes advertisements in the *Liverpool Mercury* and other newspapers requested a 'coloured lady' or similar, particularly in the field of entertainment, and it is evident that Black women also made their way to Liverpool, or were born in that city.[86] By the end of the century there was even at least one 'coloured' tattoo artist, known as Professor Johnson, who worked out of a public house near the Sailor's Home, a charitable institution.

It was this community that produced James Brown and also John Archer, the future Black mayor of Battersea, who was born in Liverpool to Barbadian and Irish parents in 1863.[87] It is clear that many of those of African heritage arrived in Liverpool from other countries looking for work, from Canada, for example, as well as those from Africa, the Caribbean and the United States. Some individuals, such as Jacob Christian, an Antiguan seaman who arrived in Liverpool in the mid-nineteenth century, managed to rise above their impoverished origins. Christian married a local woman and became a timber merchant. One of his sons, George William Christian (1872–1924), became a merchant trading with West Africa and was reportedly a millionaire.[88]

In 1880, Jacob Christian was one of those who attended a 'meeting of coloured seamen' in Liverpool to complain about the racism suffered by those who manned ships docking at the port, but were then denied further employment to enable them to return to their countries of origin. E. G. Fairchild, who chaired the meeting, complained that the previous year 'an address' had been presented to the Mayor of Liverpool to investigate the conditions faced by the seamen, but no action had been taken. He added that many seamen were forced to work on tramp vessels, or enter the workhouse, and many were sleeping rough on the docks. Jacob Christian reported that when he had approached ship owners he was told 'I want no coloured man', and that seamen were routinely abused. Christian was one of the nine men who formed a committee to provide relief and seek redress for the seamen.[89]

James Brown

One of Liverpool's most successful sons was James Brown (1815–1881) who became one of the first Black journalists and newspaper owners in Britain and a champion of the free press. He was born in Liverpool in 1815, the son of David Brown, a Black mariner and later a blacksmith, and Elizabeth Gough, said to be a member of the prominent Liverpool merchant family. The couple had married in Liverpool in 1810. (It is now thought that David Brown's father was a man known as Cato, formerly enslaved in North America and liberated, or self-liberated, during the American War of Independence. Cato then moved to Nova Scotia, Canada, and has since become a legendary figure who is reputed to have fought at the Battle of Trafalgar, but his connection to the Browns of Liverpool is not entirely certain.)[90]

James Brown was an apprentice to a Liverpool printer before he was variously employed as a compositor. He also managed a Liverpool public house. He married a woman with links to the Isle of Man, which led him to pursue his trade as a printer on that island in 1846.[91] Brown printed the *National Reformer*, the paper of the leading Chartist, James Bronterre O'Brien. Before a change in the law in 1848, newspapers printed in the Isle of Man were not taxed, as they were in the rest of Britain, and were eligible for free postage to the mainland. Several publishers, including O'Brien, took advantage of this loophole to enable working-class readers in England to have access to cheap newspapers. In 1848, after the *National Reformer* had folded, Brown started his own paper, the aptly named *Manx Lion*. It seems that it was in these circumstances that Brown first developed his crusading approach and support for a free press. He and his growing family lived in some poverty for many years, but he supplemented his income in various ways, as well as sometimes performing as an amateur bass singer. By printing advertising circulars his income gradually improved and in 1861 he became the proprietor of the *Isle of Man Times and General Advertiser*, which started as a four-page paper, with Brown's son, J. A. Brown, as its editor from 1863.[92]

'Darkie' Brown, as he was often referred to, must have faced severe challenges on the island, but he soon used the *Isle of Man Times* to campaign for democratic reforms to the House of Keys, the self-elected

Manx Parliament. He demanded that such a body should be representative of 'the source of all power – the people themselves'. However, his trenchant editorials and condemnation of the 'tyranny' and 'despotic power' of the House provoked the anger of many of its members, whom he referred to as 'self-elected noodles'. In 1864 Brown was summoned to appear for 'contempt' of the House and 'a breach of its privileges' and, although he ably defended himself, claiming that the House had no right to try him, he was subsequently sentenced to six months' imprisonment. Whilst in prison he kept a diary and continued to denounce the House. His son helped him to find a lawyer and the Court of Queen's Bench soon ruled that his imprisonment was unlawful, and he was released after only seven weeks. He then sued the House of Keys and was awarded over £500 in compensation. Two years later the House of Keys accepted the principle of elections, a reform which clearly owed something to Brown's campaigning.

Brown's business as a printer flourished in his later life and was worth more than £7,000 in 1877, four years before his death. One of his sons continued his printing business, which was rewarded with government contracts, and the *Isle of Man Times* became one of the most successful newspapers on the island. Nevertheless, it is clear that James Brown and his eldest son faced many racist incidents and abuse, including that published in the local press, and he was singularly unsuccessful on the two occasions he stood for public office in 1863 and 1864.[93] Brown died in March 1881 at the age of sixty-five, but was remembered long afterwards not least because he was associated with the democratic reform of the House of Keys.[94]

AFRICAN AMERICANS IN BRITAIN

Despite the difficulties faced by many African and Caribbean people in Britain, African Americans, especially those who were fugitives from slavery, often viewed it as a safe haven. 'The change is so sudden ... that I can hardly believe my senses. I feel for once in my life a man indeed,' reported William Powell, who, although free, was forced to find asylum in Liverpool with his family in 1850.[95] Much could be made of Britain's abolition of slavery in its Caribbean and some other colonies, although

African American abolitionists were often forced to face the fact that many regarded British 'wage slavery' as little better than the enslavement of African Americans, and they were expected to condemn both forms of exploitation and oppression and not just encourage the building of a 'moral cordon' around the United States.[96] Some African Americans came to Britain to seek a refuge, or to find employment, but it has been estimated that about a hundred of those who arrived in Britain before 1861 participated in anti-slavery activities.[97]

Some refugees and fugitives simply stowed away on ships, or like Mary Ann Macham were hidden by supportive mariners. Born in 1802 in Virginia, Macham arrived at Grimsby as a stowaway in 1831 and then spent the rest of her life in North Shields, where she worked as a servant and later married a local rope maker. In 1875 she dictated the first part of her life story and added to the account in 1890. She died at the age of ninety-three and is buried in North Shields.[98] Others purchased tickets, sometimes for first-class transport, but were discriminated against by Cunard or other shipping companies, as the abolitionist Frederick Douglass was, of whom more later. Such experiences demonstrated that Britain was a far-from-perfect haven, with its own forms of racism. African Americans were also routinely denied passports by the American authorities, a consequence of their status as non-citizens. Henry Highland Garnet, the prominent African American abolitionist, was perhaps the first to obtain one for his voyage to England in 1861.[99]

The first major African American campaigner in Britain was Nathaniel Paul, a Baptist minister, originally from New York, who visited in 1832 to raise money for various projects associated with those of African heritage in Canada and the United States.[100] Others soon followed, including Moses Roper, Charles Lenox Remond, Harriet Jacobs and Frederick Douglass. Many of the most notable African American abolitionists and campaigners of the nineteenth century, including William Wells Brown, Martin Delany, Alexander Crummell, Henry Highland Garnet, Sarah Parker Remond, William and Ellen Craft, and, at the close of the century, Ida B. Wells, spent time in Britain. During a period of more than thirty years leading up to the American Civil War, abolitionists could be found in towns and even villages throughout the British Isles and some, like Douglass and

William Wells Brown, became national celebrities. Brown, for example, estimated that in a period of five years he gave more than a thousand lectures.[101]

African Americans often strove to enlist and encourage anti-slavery sentiment in Britain, and many commented on the relative lack of racism they encountered. Some were engaged in fundraising activities to release others from slavery, or for other projects to assist African Americans, as well as those in exile in Canada. In 1860 the former slaves Theodore Gross and Lewis Smith raised enough money in Britain to purchase Smith's four eldest children from slavery.[102] About a dozen fugitives published their autobiographical 'narratives' whilst in Britain. Several wrote other books too, including William Wells Brown, who, whilst in London in 1853, published *Clotel*, regarded as the first novel by an African American.

By the mid-nineteenth century abolitionist organizations and networks of support had been established throughout the British Isles, in some cases largely owing to the activities of African Americans themselves. An entire lecture circuit was established, with some campaigners, such as William Wells Brown, delivering hundreds of lectures to a total audience of 200,000 people. Josiah Henson, one of the most famous African American abolitionists in Britain, was reported to have addressed more than 500,000 people during his visits in the 1870s. He was widely credited with inspiring the creation of the character of Uncle Tom in Harriet Beecher Stowe's famous novel, an association he was continually forced to deny. He was in fact a major anti-slavery activist, who not only smuggled his family out of America to freedom, but also many others. In 1851 he was the sole Black exhibitor at the Great Exhibition in London, toured Britain on several occasions and, in 1877, was invited to a private audience with Queen Victoria.[103] So numerous were the fugitives in London after 1850 that special organizations were established for their support. Some created their own ad hoc organization – American Fugitive Slaves in the British Metropolis, which first met in August 1851 to commemorate Emancipation Day in the Caribbean. At that time four leading African American abolitionists, Wells Brown, Crummell, Garnet and J. W. C. Pennington were simultaneously touring Britain.[104] In 1861, during his first visit to Britain, John Sella Martin, an African American minister from Boston, claimed 'there is no end to colored people here.

Some are begging money to build churches, buy relations, establish Newspapers and build schools. Indeed, they are as much a nuisance as they are in Boston. And what is painful the white people are tired of them', although he also admitted that 'there are some here doing a first-rate business'.[105]

In 1859, William and Ellen Craft, who opened their west London home to many visiting American abolitionists, became two of the members of the executive of the London Emancipation Committee (LEC), which worked to influence British public opinion on the question of slavery. The LEC also supported the African Aid Society, which included amongst its leading members Garnet and the Jamaican Robert Campbell.[106] William Craft was a leading activist in London and also a member of the John Anderson Committee (formed to invite that famous fugitive slave to Britain and to provide him with an education. Anderson had killed a slave-catcher during his flight from Missouri and a reward was offered for his capture. He eventually reached Canada but was subsequently betrayed and threatened with extradition to the US. After triumphing in court, he came to Britain and spoke to what was reported to be the largest anti-slavery audience in London, about 6,000 people, in July 1861.)[107]

William Craft had travelled throughout Britain with his wife Ellen to describe their audacious escape from slavery, she disguised as a white man and he as her slave. The Crafts spent nearly twenty years in Britain and were not alone in being part of the London anti-slavery movement. Sarah Parker Remond, one of the most prominent African American women activists, was a member of the executive of the Ladies' London Emancipation Society established in 1863.[108] Other African Americans who participated, or formed organizations in Britain included: James McCune Smith, who studied medicine at Glasgow University and from 1833 was actively involved in the Glasgow Emancipation Society, and J. W. C. Pennington who helped organize the Glasgow New Association for the Abolition of Slavery in 1853.[109]

Several other African Americans besides Anderson and McCune Smith were educated in Britain during this period. Alexander Crummell enrolled at Queens' College, Cambridge, in 1849 and from 1851 until 1854 William and Ellen Craft lived and studied at Ockham

School in Surrey. Between 1853 and 1856 Francis Anderson, another fugitive, enrolled in the Voluntary School Establishment, a teacher-training institute in London.[110] Sarah Parker Remond enrolled at the Bedford College for Ladies from 1859 to 1860.[111] The three children of the successful fugitive James Watkins were all educated at Birmingham Grammar School.[112] Wells Brown's two daughters were also partly educated in Britain and both graduated as teachers in 1853, one later becoming headmistress of a school in Woolwich.[113] William G. Allen, a free-born 'professor of the Greek language and of Rhetoric and Belles Lettres', was forced to flee to Britain from the United States, along with his white wife, and both opened schools in Islington during the 1860s.[114] Dr George Rice (1848–1935), the son of formerly enslaved parents, studied medicine at Edinburgh Royal Infirmary and later worked and lived in Kent. He was appointed superintendent of Woolwich Union Infirmary in 1878. In 1884 he became the medical officer at a school for poor and orphaned children in Sutton and soon commanded a salary of over £450 per year. He later became the District Medical Officer for Sutton and Cheam.[115]

The African American refugees often commented, not just on issues relating to slavery in the United States, but also on the condition of the British workers, on temperance and other matters, including racism in Britain. In 1863 in Newcastle William Craft became known for his rebuttal of the racist views of James Hunt, President of the London Anthropological Society. Hunt was one of those leading efforts at the time to give racism a 'scientific basis', and find proof of the alleged inferiority of the 'Negro race', which, he claimed, was closer to the ape than the European. In August 1863 he and a colleague presented such views to the annual meeting of the British Association for the Advancement of Science, where they were challenged, and skilfully and humorously refuted, by Craft. Alluding to the well-known African fable of the lion and the hunter to affirm that those who write history often favour themselves, Craft then drew on his own recent experience in Dahomey, the enslavement and history of his own family, the lives of Sarah Forbes Bonetta and Bishop Samuel Crowther, as well as the independence of Haiti, to refute the racism of Hunt.[116] It was reported at the time that Craft's 'clear, open, generous and manly countenance contrasted most successfully with that of his bitter opponent'.[117] In his

Three Years in Europe: or Places I Have Seen and People I Have Met, published in 1852, Wells Brown denounced the racism of the author Thomas Carlyle for 'his recent attack upon the emancipated people of the West Indies, and his laborious article in favour of the re-establishment of the lash and slavery'.[118] In the aftermath of the Morant Bay Rebellion in Jamaica, in 1865, when nearly 500 Jamaicans were executed and hundreds more flogged, Sarah Parker Remond felt compelled to write to the London press 'to say a word in defence of the most hated race in the world, the Negroes and their descendants', who, she argued, were held in contempt by 'Southern Confederates' and 'former West Indian planters', by the London press as much as by the 'pro-slavery newspapers in the United States'.[119]

Although African Americans often collaborated with each other and, of course, with a range of British organizations and individuals, there is very little evidence that they formed strong connections with other Black people in Britain. Some interaction must have taken place in Liverpool and London, or perhaps at various universities, but there is no record of it. Frederick Douglass, for example, famously identified himself with the Chartists, but there is no evidence that he ever met William Cuffay, and the two men would probably have had some political differences.[120] William Wells Brown described his experiences in Britain at length and, in particular, in relation to other Black people. In one letter to Frederick Douglass, he wrote: 'In an hour's walk through the Strand, Regent, or Piccadilly streets in London, one may meet a half a dozen colored young men, who are inmates of the various Colleges in the metropolis. They are all signs of progress in the cause of the sons of Africa.' However, it is not clear if such meetings led to discussion between Brown and these students from Africa and the Caribbean.[121] Indeed, in his well-known memoirs, which chronicled his travels throughout the British Isles, Brown only mentions one African, whom he refers to both as Selim the African prince and Joseph Jenkins, whom he describes as 'the bill-distributor of Cheapside, the crossing-sweeper of Chelsea, the tract-seller and psalm-singer of Kensington and the Othello of the Eagle Saloon'. This individual, Brown claimed, was also a part-time clergyman in Cheapside, a band-leader and 'the greatest genius' that he had met in Europe.[122]

It seems that Brown's report of Jenkins may have been an amalgamation of several individuals, including the actor Ira Aldridge. These might have included Selim Aga, a former enslaved man from the kingdom of Taqali, in Sudan, who spent much of his childhood in Scotland, and who had one (and possibly two) children there, and whose autobiography *Incidents Connected with the Life of Selim Aga: A Native of Central Africa* was first published in Aberdeen in 1846. Aga, who was also known as a singer and poet and ended his life as a surgeon, is thought to have lectured on Egypt and lived in London for several years, from 1849 until 1857, before returning to Africa. He remained concerned about Africa, and in 1853 published a pamphlet entitled *Africa Considered in Its Social and Political Condition, with a Plan for the Amelioration of its Inhabitants*. His plan was for a transcontinental railway which would run from West to East Africa.[123] On his return to Africa, he accompanied the expeditions of William Baikie and Richard Burton, spent time in Lagos, Kano and Liberia, and was recognized as a leading explorer in his own right. Unfortunately, he was murdered in Liberia in 1875.[124]

There were many other African Americans in the country, many of them entertainers, such as the dancer William Henry Lane, known as Master Juba and billed as the 'Greatest Dancer in the World', who toured for many years, but died in poverty in Liverpool in 1854.[125] Another was Aaron Banks, a comedian who performed throughout Britain for twenty years. Others were associated with various stage productions of the anti-slavery novel *Uncle Tom's Cabin*, which became popular in Britain from the 1850s onwards (the book sold well over one million copies), or with various groups of 'jubilee' singers, whose songs became popular after the American Civil War. The most famous of the latter were the Fisk Jubilee Singers, a choir from Fisk University in Nashville, who first visited Britain on tour in 1873.[126]

The US also sent another form of entertainment to Britain in the mid-century years, the 'black-face' minstrels, a form which was popular in Britain for well over a century. Lane (and other African American performers.) was compelled to wear black make-up at times. Such was the popularity of the spectacle of white men presenting insulting stereotypes of African Americans (especially via their songs, dances and accents), so that even Black performers were sometimes required to do so as well. Such 'black-face' performances in Britain dated from the 1830s and reached new heights of popularity in the 1840s with the arrival of five white performers, the so-called 'Ethiopian Serenaders'.[127] Like the exhibition of Africans, such as Sara Baartman, 'minstrelsy', as it was often known, generally ridiculed those of African heritage. Its appropriation and distortion of some aspects of African American culture no doubt contributed to Eurocentric and racist thinking, although some have seen it as a kind of recognition of that culture.[128] Frederick Douglass described such performers as 'the filthy scum of white society, who have stolen from us a complexion denied to them by nature, in which to make money, and pander to the corrupt taste of their white fellow citizens'. He contrasted them unfavourably with the Hutchinson Family Singers, who also toured Britain, but their singing was about abolition, temperance and women's rights.[129]

The Civil War itself was a matter of some importance in Britain, not least because an embargo by the US government cut Britain off from vital supplies of raw cotton, which led to mass economic disruption and unemployment, especially in Lancashire and the north of Britain. The war was fought, as Frederick Douglass pointed out, because there were 'two direct, point-blank and irreconcilable antagonisms under the same form of government', which were 'slavery' and 'free labour'.[130] Despite great economic hardship, the cotton workers of Manchester met at the Free Trade Hall on 31 December 1862, where they were addressed by 'the fugitive slave', John Anderson, and other speakers including William A. Jackson, the formerly enslaved coachman of Jefferson Davis and Union spy.[131] The workers met to discuss their own stand in relation to slavery and it is clear that 'their talk was of the "sacred and inalienable rights of every human being", and of "the common brotherhood and sisterhood of mankind" – words big with the hopes of many, but an offence and foolishness to the privileged few.' The workers denounced the slave owners and their own 'governing classes' and pledged their support for the embargo, the 'Free North' and President Lincoln, on the day before the abolition of slavery was proclaimed in the US. In so doing they also stood against the mill owners and the press which supported them, as well as leading political figures in Britain. The stand of the mill workers was subsequently acknowledged by Abraham Lincoln and led to the sending of essential supplies from the US. The 'citizens of Manchester' made it clear that it was the responsibility of the working class of Britain to stand on the side of freedom and prefaced their address to Lincoln with the words, 'Let all who have laboured to glorify the Slave Power, the most monstrous outgrowth of the modern world, read it, and see how vain have been their efforts to corrupt the minds of the working classes, and how wide a gulf is fixed between them and the great body of people.' The address included the following:

> one thing alone has lessened our sympathy for your country and confidence in it – we mean the ascendancy of politicians who not merely maintained Negro slavery, but desired to extend and root it more firmly. Since ... the war, which has so sorely distressed us ... will strike off the fetters of slaves, you have attracted our warm and earnest sympathy ... You have procured the liberation of the slaves in the district around Washington, and thereby made the centre of your Federation visibly free. You have enforced the laws against the slave trade, and kept up your fleet against it, even while every ship was wanted for service in your terrible war. You have nobly decided to receive ambassadors from the Negro republics of Hayti and Liberia, thus for ever renouncing the unworthy prejudice which refuses the rights of humanity to men and women, on account of their colour.[132]

Welcoming the imminent emancipation proclamation, the workers concluded: 'Heartily we do congratulate you and your country on this humane and righteous course. We assume that you cannot now stop short of a complete uprooting of slavery. It would not become us to dictate any details, but there are broad principles of humanity which must guide you.'[133] Lincoln's response, addressed to the 'workingmen of Manchester', referred to their 'sublime Christian heroism which has not been surpassed in any age or any country'. Lincoln concluded, 'it is indeed an energetic and re-inspiring assurance of the inherent power of truth, and of the ultimate and universal triumph of justice, humanity, and freedom.'[134]

The Manchester meeting led to the founding of the Manchester Union and Emancipation Society, which soon organized more than forty local branches and over 150 meetings throughout the north of England with the aim of 'enfranchising black labour in America and ... white labour in England'.[135] Similar meetings, often involving several thousands, were held throughout the country and produced a regular commentary from Karl Marx, then living in exile in London. He was full of praise for the 'English popular masses' who, despite constant propaganda in the press, remained solidly in support of the anti-slavery cause in the US and opposed to any intervention by the British government.[136]

THE CHURCH

Several African Americans played a prominent role in churches and missionary work in Britain during the nineteenth century at a time when abolitionism was sometimes closely connected with Christianity. In 1852, Henry Highland Garnet was appointed as a missionary to Jamaica by the United Presbyterian Church of Scotland. In 1863, J. Sella Martin was appointed pastor of the free Christian Church in Bow in East London and was a founder of the English Freedman's Aid Society and many of its local chapters.[137] Thomas Lewis Johnson (1836–1921), formerly enslaved in Virginia, who later published his autobiography *Twenty-Eight Years a Slave*, left Britain in 1878 for the Cameroons and spent three years in Africa before he returned to live in Bournemouth.[138]

Peter Stanford, formerly enslaved in Virginia, became a Baptist minister in Canada and arrived in Liverpool in 1883 to raise money for his church. He travelled throughout Britain and subsequently moved to Birmingham, married a local woman in Smethwick and, in 1889, was asked to become the pastor of the Hope Street Baptist Church in Birmingham, by the unanimous decision of the congregation. Stanford later wrote, 'I was not allowed to take my position however until after a stern fight . . . today notwithstanding my birth as a slave and the colour of my skin, I am the pastor in this great city of Birmingham.'[139] Stanford, sometimes referred to as 'England's Coloured Minister', who was also a Freemason, then went on to establish the Wilberforce Memorial Church in Sparkbrook.[140] In 1894 that church resolved that he be sent to the United States 'in the interests of the philanthropic and Christian public of England', to investigate lynching and other 'alleged outrages' perpetrated against African Americans and to plead 'with the prominent white Christians to induce them to exert their influence in preventing further reprisals, and in insisting upon the enforcement of law and order'. It was this journey, on behalf of his mainly working-class congregation in Birmingham, but also with the support of numerous local minsters, aldermen and counsellors, that subsequently led to his book *The Tragedy of the Negro in America*, published in Boston in 1897.[141] Stanford was clearly much more than a Baptist minister; he was also connected with the anti-racist Society for the Recognition of the Brotherhood of Man and probably played a part in establishing a local branch in Birmingham.[142] He was not, however, the first Black Baptist minister in Britain – a Jamaican, George Cosens (1805–1881) had preceded him. Cosens came to Britain as a student and had apparently converted to Methodism. Initially a Methodist minister in the north of England and the Channel Islands, he subsequently became a Baptist in Weymouth in the 1830s. He was then appointed Pastor of Cradley Heath Baptist Church in the Midlands in 1837, before later moving to Brierly Hill in Dudley.[143]

One of most significant missionaries and churchmen of the nineteenth century was British-born, the Reverend Thomas Birch Freeman (1809–1890), who was hailed as 'the greatest pioneer missionary West Africa has ever known'. Freeman was born in Twyford, near Winchester, to an African father and Amy Birch, his English mother, who was reportedly a domestic servant.[144] Little is known about his early life or his father, a gardener, reportedly of Caribbean enslaved origin, who died when he was just six years old. Thomas was the fourth child of his mother, but the only son of his father. Whatever his circumstances, he somehow managed to receive a good education. As a young man he initially followed in his father's footsteps and became 'botanist and head gardener' to Sir Robert Harland at Orwell Park near Ipswich. However, he had already become a Methodist and in 1837 offered his services to the Wesleyan Missionary Society. He was ordained in Islington Chapel in London, in October 1837, and sent to the Gold Coast with his first wife, who died shortly after arrival. In 1840, on his return to England, Freeman married a second English wife who also died shortly after reaching West Africa.

Freeman became 'one of the most successful missionaries' of his time and remained in West Africa until his death, founding many Methodist churches, as well as schools, on the Gold Coast and what was to become the British colony of Nigeria, and gaining thousands of converts. One of his main qualities was the strength of his constitution and thus his longevity, as death from various tropical diseases usually ended the lives of other missionaries from Britain. Freeman was also known as a skilled diplomat, able to work with African rulers, such as the kings of Asante and Dahomey, as well as colonial officials, but he was particularly successful amongst educated Africans and 'recaptives' (those liberated from slavery by the Royal Navy). His reports of travels to various African kingdoms were first serialized and then published in 1843 as his *Journal of Various Visits to the Kingdom of Ashanti, Aku and Dahomi, in Western Africa.*[145]

Often criticized for his 'slovenly' book-keeping, although also renowned for his honesty, he was forced to resign in 1857 because of accumulated debts. He was immediately offered employment as the Civil Commandant of Accra by the colonial governor. In his later life Freeman became a farmer and amateur botanist. He also wrote a novel entitled *Missionary Enterprise, No Fiction: A Tale Founded on Facts*, which was semi-autobiographical, in order to encourage more missionaries from Britain. This was published anonymously in London in 1871. In 1873, at the age of sixty-four, he temporarily returned to his duties as a missionary, before in 1875 retiring to live in Accra with the Fanti woman who was to become his third wife.

THE THEATRE

One of the first African Americans to gain national prominence in Britain was the actor Ira Aldridge (c.1807–1867), who arrived as a young man, in 1824, after finding his career blocked due to racism in his birthplace. Aldridge claimed to be of Senegalese heritage but was born in New York. He became one of Britain's leading Shakespearean actors, making his debut on the London stage in 1825 at the Royalty Theatre in east London, where he played several roles and became the first Black actor in British history to play the role of Othello. Billed as 'a Man of Colour', Aldridge soon appeared at the Royal Coburg

Theatre (now the Old Vic) in London in a number of different roles. In 1825 he is reported to have enrolled in courses at Glasgow University and he married Margaret Gill, a woman from Yorkshire.[146] He subsequently spent forty years in Britain and, in 1863, officially became a British citizen in order to purchase and bequeath property.[147] He was noted for his ability to play both tragedy and comedy, including all the major Shakespearean roles: Shylock, Lear, Macbeth, Hamlet and Richard III, for which he used special white make-up. He also sang and played the guitar.[148] As early as 1827 he was awarded an honorary army commission as 'the first man of colour in the theatre' by the government of Haiti. A contemporary explained that this honour was 'complimenting him on his successful progress in contradicting the assertion that his race is incapable of mental culture'.[149] Aldridge was considered important enough for a biographical sketch, or *Memoir*, to be anonymously written and published about him in 1849. It is evident from this that his acting and achievements were seen as a major vindication of Africans everywhere, demonstrating that 'the swarthy African is as capable of cultivation as the fairest son of Albion', and that 'a great amount of the highest order of human intelligence is to be met with in people of colour'.[150]

However, in his early career, Aldridge often received a hostile and racist press reaction in London, but played to great acclaim elsewhere in the country.[151] This was at a time when slavery and its abolition was a very topical issue and perhaps Aldridge had drawn even more attention as a result of his marriage to a white woman.[152] Although pro-slavery and racist attitudes were evident in sections of the press, audiences were almost always enthusiastic about Aldridge's performances, and he was supported by other actors, including the celebrated Edmund Kean.[153] Such was his popularity and reputation that he was made manager of the Coventry Theatre in 1828, just four years after arriving in Britain at the age of twenty. Aldridge was often billed as 'the African Roscius' (named after a Roman slave), or the 'African Tragedian', or simply as 'the African'. He excelled in plays such as *The Revolt of Surinam*, *The Death of Christophe, King of Hayti*, *The Padlock* and *Obi or Three-fingered Jack*, the latter written especially for him, as well as other plays in which he played African characters and could emphasize anti-slavery themes. Aldridge recited poems as well, such as James Bissett's 'The Negro Boy' (which was also written especially for him). He later adapted Shakespeare's *Titus Andronicus*, 'turning the central villain of the play, Aaron the Moor, into a hero', and there is strong evidence that he played parts and performed material that allowed him to address the issue of slavery and present the dignity of Africans in opposition to the prevailing racism of the press. One press report claimed that he 'has the power to present in strong, broad, effective bearing, the injuries, sufferings, and passions of the much abused African', another that 'his appearance ... is a "great moral lesson" in favour of anti-slavery'.[154]

Aldridge had a significant impact on the cause of abolition amongst the people of Coventry at a time when they were petitioning Parliament for an end to slavery in Britain and throughout its colonies.[155] He also regularly spoke directly to audiences, using his farewell address to comment on racism and abolition. It seems that the enthusiastic responses he received from audiences were not only a result of this tremendous acting ability but also his political stand. There are several reports that he donated part of his income to support the abolitionist movement in the US and one account, that in 1854 he personally intervened to buy the freedom of a family of five African Americans who had fallen foul of the Fugitive Slave Law in New York.[156]

In his later career Aldridge toured Europe and was honoured in many countries. He visited France, Germany, Sweden, Serbia and elsewhere, sometimes performing Shakespeare's plays in these countries for the first time. He was particularly respected in Poland and Russia for his realistic acting style. He was awarded many honours in Europe, and was recognized by the *Illustrated London News* as 'the only actor, native or foreign, so decorated'.[157] He died on tour in Łódź, Poland.

ALL KINDS OF PERFORMERS

Aldridge was not the only prominent African American on the stage in Britain during the nineteenth century. His compatriot Morgan Smith was also successful as an actor in a variety of roles. In 1837 Frank Johnson, the celebrated African American bandmaster and composer, toured Britain with his own group of musicians.[158] In the

1850s, following the success of the anti-slavery novel *Uncle Tom's Cabin*, several theatrical versions of the book were performed throughout Britain, involving both African American and black British actors.[159] In the latter part of the century, the Boston-born singer, comedienne and actress Amy Height (1866–1913), who first appeared on stage in Britain in 1883, became highly popular, especially in variety shows and pantomimes. Height appeared in *Uncle Tom's Cabin*, later shared the bill with famous music-hall comedian George Robey, and also played straight roles. Often based in London, she died in Camberwell.[160]

Another famous performer was William Darby (1796–1871), born in Norwich as one of four children to John Darby and Mary (née Stamps).[161] He seems very likely to have been the first Black circus-owner in Britain. A century later he was immortalized in song by John Lennon under his stage name, Pablo Fanque. Almost nothing is known of his parents, although John Darby is reported to have been a butler. William was orphaned at a young age and apprenticed to a circus proprietor. He initially performed in circuses as a 'leaper and rope walker', but then later also as an 'equestrian' and horse trainer, billed as 'the Young Darby'. At some point he adopted the name Pablo Fanque, to which was sometimes added the description 'from Africa'. By the 1830s Fanque was touring the country with William Batty's circus and in about 1834 married Susannah Moore, the daughter of a Birmingham button-maker. The first Mrs Darby was later killed in a tragic accident when part of a circus venue collapsed. Fanque married his second wife, Elizabeth Corker, an equestrienne from Sheffield, in 1848. Fanque's children from both marriages were to become circus performers, as did his nephew, Billy Pablo, a 'man of colour' who was a tightrope dancer and bareback rider. Circus performers of African and Caribbean heritage were not unusual in Victorian Britain. George Christopher (1826–1881), a tightrope dancer known as 'Herr Christoff, the World's Wonder', also performed with Fanque and for a time headed his own circus company.[162] Joseph Hiller was another Black circus artist who later did the same.[163] Another famous circus performer was the Afro-German Miss LaLa (1858–c.1919), born Anna Olga Albertina Brown in Stettin. Best known as a trapeze and 'iron jaw' artist, Miss LaLa was sometimes titled 'the African princess'. She appeared all over Europe, including London and Manchester, and was immortalized in a painting by Degas.[164]

In 1841 Fanque started his own circus and within a few years 'by his own industry and talent, he got together as fine a stud of horses and ponies as any in England'. He seems to have been particularly successful in Lancashire and surrounding counties and received support from all sections of the population. He also became well known for his benefit performances and 'acts of benevolence' for local charities. One letter to the *Blackburn Mercury* in 1843 stated:

> Ministers of religion, of all denominations, in other towns, have attended Mr Pablo Fanque's circus. Such is his character for probity and respectability, that wherever he has been once he can go again, aye and receive the countenance and support of the wise and virtuous of all classes of society. I am sure that the friends of temperance and morality are deeply indebted to him for the perfectly innocent recreation which he has afforded to our population, by which I am sure hundreds have been prevented from spending their money in revelling and drunkenness.[165]

Indeed, Fanque's circus was said to be so popular in some towns that local publicans complained that 'the cash normally spent in their houses is diminished'.[166]

By the late 1840s Fanque was successfully employing two separate companies of circus performers, but by the end of the 1850s he was facing bankruptcy. Fanque subsequently recovered somewhat from this financial setback and both revived his circus and performed for others almost until the end of his life. Although he had become famous as a 'thorough master of his profession', it was reported that at the time of his death in Stockport in 1871 'he died in great poverty'.[167]

There were undoubtedly many other performers of African and Caribbean heritage, as well as those who migrated from the United States. Advertisements that describe 'Negro' performers sometimes referred to those who simply used 'burnt cork'. However, Tom Lucette appears to have been an exception. He described himself as the 'original black drummer, Negro comedian, dancer and instrumentalist' and was sometimes even referred to as 'the N— Paganini'.[168] None of this is decisive in proving exactly who he was as there were several 'Negro comedians' during the 1860s and 1870s who were not necessarily people of African heritage. Whoever he was, he was clearly in demand in the music halls of the period and sometimes performed with a Miss Lucette, regarding whom no details are given. Whatever the case, in 1886 the following report appeared in the theatrical press concerning an incident in a Brussels café.

> Two swells who had been dining not wisely but too well, interrupted a N— dwarf, Tom Lucette, in one of his songs with cries of 'Va au Congo' ('Go to Congo') and 'Va te Laver' ('Go and wash yourself'). The dwarf stood it as long as he could, and then asked his tormentors to be quiet, but without the desired result; so at the end of this song he quietly walked up to the principal disturber and gave him a blow on the nose, amid the applause of the audience.[169]

AFRICANS UNITE

By the mid-nineteenth century the struggle to end slavery in many of Britain's colonies appeared to have been won, or, at least, the argument had been won (since slavery continued in many parts of Africa well into the twentieth century). The European exploration of Africa was well under way, which would create the conditions for the subsequent scramble for colonies. The idea of the inferiority of Africans as enslaved people, largely propagated by the slave owners and their supporters, began to be replaced by new 'pseudo-scientific' forms of racism, as Peter Fryer has termed them.[170] This racism was based on allegedly scientific measurements, or investigation, but merely amounted to new justifications for the conquest and subjugation of Africa, or continued colonial rule in the Caribbean (and elsewhere, including Ireland). Ironically, a further source of racism emerged from the alleged aims of the state to abolish slavery both within and outside the British Empire. These professed aims of governments, churches and humanitarians would lead to a 'civilizing mission', a shouldering of what would be called the 'white man's burden' in Africa (as well as in Asia and other parts of the world). What was deemed to be progress for 'the Negro' would require the wholesale adoption of Euro-centric values, culture and institutions. This 'new imperialism' and the extension of the

British Empire which gathered pace towards the end of the nineteenth century assumed, and, indeed, promoted African inferiority as well as Anglo-Saxon superiority. Thereafter, racist notions justified a divine 'dual mandate' for Britain to rule the 'dark continent' and develop (and profit by) its abundant material resources. As Cecil Rhodes concisely expressed it in 1877:

> Africa is still lying ready for us it is our duty to take it. It is our duty to seize every opportunity of acquiring more territory and we should keep this one idea steadily before our eyes that more territory simply means more of the Anglo-Saxon race, more of the best, the most human, most honourable race the world possesses.[171]

In the mid-nineteenth century the resistance of colonial subjects to Britain's expanding empire building was met with savage repression and many deaths. These too then required racist justification. This was openly expressed after the outbreak of the First Indian War of Independence in 1857. Acts of violent repression were also evident following the Morant Bay Rebellion in Jamaica in 1865. In this instance some justified the violence against Jamaicans in an openly racist manner. *The Times*, for example, referred to the 'original savagery of African blood', and concluded that whenever the 'black man' attains 'a certain degree of independence there is the fear that he will resume the barbarous life and fierce habits of his African ancestors'.[172] However, it has long been noted that although the government, much of the ruling class and its press supported the violence of Governor Eyre, working people and many leading intellectuals, such as Charles Darwin, Charles Buxton and John Stuart Mill, condemned him.[173] Those on both sides of the debate were concerned with liberty and repression in England, as much as they were with Jamaica. There was a vociferous demand that Eyre should be prosecuted, both for the murder of George William Gordon, a local politician and critic of colonial government, as well as for the deaths of hundreds of other Jamaicans.[174] In September 1866 it was reported that 10,000 working men met at Clerkenwell Green in support of their 'brother proletarians'. After declaring 'the monster ex-governor' and 'wholesale murderer' guilty, they burned a 'well got-up effigy' of Eyre.[175] When, in 1867, two Jamaicans, Dr Robert Bruce and Alexander Phillips, brought charges against Eyre and

Brigadier General Nelson for 'assault, battery and false imprisonment', the Lord Chief Justice and the English courts declared that neither man had the right to seek redress in Britain for acts committed by the Jamaican colonial authorities.[176] There were those for whom the lives and rights of colonial subjects did not matter and were not protected by the law in the late nineteenth century, any more than they had been during the era of slavery. Nevertheless, opposition to empire continued, at home and abroad. In 1884 Sudanese resistance to British imperialism was referred to in racist terms by some, yet there were also those who opposed Britain's military intervention in Africa. The most notable example was 'The Socialist League's Manifesto on the Soudan War', signed by William Morris, Eleanor Marx and their comrades. Amongst other things, the League declared, 'the victory gained by the Soudanese is a triumph of right over wrong by a people struggling for their freedom.'[177] Just as there was imperialism and racism, there were evidently anti-imperialists and anti-racists.

One of the most remarkable of the latter was Wilson Armistead, a Quaker merchant born in Leeds in 1819. Armistead founded and became the first president of the Leeds Anti-Slavery Association and devoted his short life to supporting those of African heritage. He was a fierce opponent of slavery in the United States and provided accommodation for William and Ellen Craft, as well as other African Americans. He was, to use his own expression, a 'compiler', although today he might be considered more of an anti-racist campaigner and a historian. He produced more than eighty anti-slavery publications, and also wrote in defence of the Haitian Revolution. His most famous work, *A Tribute to the Negro: Being a Vindication of the Moral, Intellectual, and Religious Capabilities of the Coloured Portion of Mankind; with Particular Reference to the African Race*, was published in 1848. In more than 500 pages, Armistead presented a thorough refutation of anti-African racism, as well as biographical and historical accounts of the lives of many Africans, including Olaudah Equiano, Ottobah Cugoano, Phillis Wheatley, Ignatius Sancho and Toussaint L'Ouverture. Armistead also provided a history of the rebellion on board the slave ship *La Amistad*, as well as accounts of contemporary figures such as Frederick Douglass and William Wells Brown. He introduces his work by condemning those whom he refers to as powerful 'White men, civilized savages' who invade and enslave others, 'and then, pointing to their colour, find their justification in denying them to be men'. He concludes:

> The most extensive and extraordinary system of crime the world ever witnessed, which has now been in operation for several centuries, and which continues to exist in unabated activity, is NEGRO SLAVERY ... The hapless victims of this revolting system are men of the same origin as ourselves – of similar form and delineation of feature, though with a darker skin – men endowed with minds equal in dignity, equal in capacity, and equal in duration of existence – men of the same social dispositions and affections, and destined to occupy the same rank in the great family of Man.[178]

Despite the activities of Armistead and others, the extension of empire and colonial rule continued to fuel racism in Britain, as well as throughout the colonies. The emergence of a 'colour bar', and various other forms of discrimination, became increasingly commonplace by the end of the century. The continuation of colonial rule in the Caribbean, and what was to become the scramble for colonies in Africa, also meant that larger numbers of African and Caribbean people were drawn to Britain. Some came as workers: seafarers, for example, vital to Britain's merchant fleet, who soon began to establish distinct communities in the port cities, such as Liverpool, London, Cardiff and elsewhere. The presence of increasing numbers of African and Caribbean workers in Britain was often viewed by trade unions, and even organizations claiming socialist leanings, as competition from cheap labour. Employers such as shipping companies found that it was greatly to their advantage to exacerbate any divisions amongst their workforce so as to weaken any joint protests over wages or conditions of work.

Other migrants were drawn to England by the prospect of education, since higher or professional education was not provided in the colonies. The emergent elites in both Africa and the Caribbean, if they could afford it, increasingly sent their children to Britain to be educated in the manner of Victorian ladies and gentlemen at schools and universities. As always, the minds of students were open to a variety of ideas and influences and some of those educated in Britain began to challenge the increasingly strident imperialism and racism during the latter part of the nineteenth century, both individually and, by the end of the century, from within their own organizations.

One of earliest attempts at an 'African Association', an early Pan-African organization of those from Africa and the Caribbean, together with African Americans, started to take shape in the late 1850s. The idea may have been proposed by Thomas Hodgkin, an English anti-slavery campaigner who had helped to fund the Aborigines Protection Society in 1837 and was also connected with the African Aid Society. The latter society promoted the voluntary repatriation of those of African heritage in North America to Africa as agents of moderniza-tion and the 'Christian civilization of the African races', although it suggested that 'destitute Negroes' arriving in London from the US should also be assisted to relocate to Africa.[179] In this period the eco-nomic development of Africa was viewed as the most suitable means to rid the continent of the ills of human trafficking and slavery. It also accorded well with the commercial interests of various bodies in Brit-ain. As was the case with the anti-slavery squadron, the 'civilizing mission' and intention to aid economic development in Africa led to greater British intervention there, and eventually the 'scramble' for colonial possessions and the invasion of the continent. The society also produced its own newspaper, the *African Times*, which became the mouthpiece of those intent on the civilizing mission (including those from the African diaspora). The *African Times* was edited by Ferdinand Fitzgerald, an Irish Protestant, who was assisted by Wil-liam Rainy, originally from Dominica, a leading journalist and editor in West Africa. In 1861 Hodgkin convened a meeting of those inter-ested in such an African association, including the chargé d'affaires of the Haitian government in London. However, at this stage it appears that such plans came to nought.[180]

Hodgkin was also in contact with the African American Martin Delany, and Robert Campbell, a Jamaican, during their visit to Britain, as well as with Thomas Hughes, a local politician in Cape Coast, West Africa. Delany and Campbell had just returned from Abeokuta (in modern-day Nigeria), where they had acted as 'commissioners for the African Race', exploring the possibility of those in the diaspora repat-riating to Africa. Whilst he was in London, Delany, one of the most distinguished African Americans of the nineteenth century, who is often associated with the slogan 'Africa for the Africans', attended the annual meeting of the International Statistical Congress (an early attempt to standardize measurements). There, in the presence of Prince Albert, he was seated next to the US ambassador to Britain. The latter was reminded of Delany's presence by the words of Lord Brougham, who stated, 'there is a Negro present, a member of the Congress'. Delany is said to have replied, 'I assure your Royal Highness and your lordship that I am a man', a response, so *The Times* reported, that was greeted with 'loud laughter and vociferous cheering'.[181]

Africanus Horton

For some, education in Britain could well be a path to advancement. William Fergusson, a Jamaican, became the first student of African descent educated at the University of Edinburgh and qualified as a doctor in 1809. He was then commissioned as an officer in the British Army and served for many years in Sierra Leone, Britain's first African colony, where he eventually became governor, the only person of African descent to fulfil this role. Another Caribbean returnee from Trinidad, John Carr, became Chief Justice of Sierra Leone and provided a scholarship for twelve-year-old James Horton (1835–1883) to become a boarder at the missionary-run CMS Grammar School in Freetown.[182] Horton was the son of 'recaptives', enslaved Africans who had been freed by the Royal Navy's anti-slavery squadron and resettled in Sierra Leone. In 1855 he was chosen as one of three students to be sent to King's College London, and subsequently the University of Edinburgh, to train as army doctors at the expense of the War Office. By the time he reached Edinburgh, where he became the first graduate from Africa, Horton had already adopted the name Africanus to signify pride in his African identity. He also became connected with the African Aid Society and its monthly publication the *African Times*, launched in 1861.

The society and its publication were mainly concerned with the abolition of slavery, encouraging African American migration to West Africa and establishing the growing of cotton in that region, as an alternative to slave-produced supplies from the United States. These aims were supported by a coalition of abolitionist and commercial interests in Britain, but they provided an opportunity for the new class of Western-educated Africans and their counterparts in the diaspora to exchange views and opinions and to use the *African Times* as a 'public advocate'. By 1866 the paper would boast that it should be regarded 'as the organ in England of the civilised blacks of the British settlements', and that both African Americans in the United States and 'their brethren' in West Africa were 'demanding the responsibilities of constitutional government'.[183] The *African Times* became the first English newspaper to regularly present the views of Africans.

Horton, who was commissioned as Staff Assistant-Surgeon in the British Army in West Africa, began to use the *African Times* to present his own views on a variety of issues including the notion of self-government for Britain's coastal colonial settlements in West Africa. This right appeared to be promised by the recent report of the Select Committee of the House of Commons on Africa. In 1865 Horton wrote an address to the African Aid Society entitled *Political Economy of British West Africa: with the Requirements of the Several Colonies and Settlements (the African View of the Negro's Place in Nature)*, which was first published as a pamphlet and favourably reviewed in the *African Times*.[184] Horton subsequently elaborated his views in his famous work *West African Countries and Peoples*, which was subtitled *A Vindication of the African Race* and published while he was in London in 1868.[185] Horton had already written to the *African Times* to refute the racist views of James Hunt and the London Anthropological Society, which had been presented in an infamous publication of 1863 titled *The Negro's Place in Nature*. Like Craft before him, Horton concluded that Hunt 'knows nothing of Africa and the Africans'.[186] Horton was a great supporter of what he viewed as Britain's potentially positive influence on Africa, which he thought would lead to the 'progressive advancement of the Negro race', but he was also a defender of Africa itself, which he argued, in ages past, 'was the nursery of science and literature: from thence they were taught to Greece and Rome'.[187]

In *West African Countries and Peoples*, he openly attacked Hunt's Anthropological Society and other 'Negrophobists', including Robert Knox and Richard Burton, 'the most determined Africa hater', who were developing new forms of anti-African racism. Horton established himself as one of the first Africans not only to argue against the emerging pseudo-scientific racism of the period, but also to endeavour 'to prove the capability of the African for possessing a real political Government and national independence'.[188] In his writings he called for a host of improvements and political reforms throughout Britain's settlements in West Africa, including a demand that Fourah Bay College, in Sierra Leone, should become the 'University of Western Africa'.[189] Almost immediately he had an influence on the Fanti Confederacy formed on the Gold Coast to establish a modern African state, which he championed in his *Letters on the Political Condition of the Gold Coast* in 1870.[190] He is one of the most significant figures in the early history of Pan-Africanism and he has been described as 'the father of modern African political thought'.[191]

Edward Blyden

Horton may have been the first African to champion the capacities of his compatriots and oppose pseudo-scientific racism, but perhaps even more influential was his friend and contemporary Edward Blyden (1832–1912). 'The most articulate and brilliant vindicator of Negro and African interests in the nineteenth century', Blyden was born in the Danish colony of St Thomas in the Virgin Islands.[192] When his attempts to enrol at colleges in the United States met with rejection, he was encouraged by supporters of the American Colonization Society (ACS) to migrate to Liberia. Under the auspices of the ACS, Liberia had become an independent state in 1847, with a ruling class composed of African American settlers. Blyden completed his education in Liberia, where he became a teacher and then a school and college principal. In order to develop his school and further his own education, Blyden began corresponding with several eminent people in Britain, including William Gladstone, at the time the Chancellor of the Exchequer.[193]

Blyden first wrote to Gladstone in April 1860 asking for a copy of the recent Budget, seeking his help with his own study of Latin and Greek, and inquiring whether he might be supplied with a 'small library' of books on classical studies and English literature to assist with his learning and the teaching in Liberia of 'men of enlightened minds, of enlarged views, of high-toned character'.[194] Blyden's letter, which included quotations in Latin, soon became famous as Gladstone shared it with the well-known reformer and abolitionist Henry Brougham. Brougham then alluded to it in a speech in the House of Lords, applauded 'the Negro gentleman in Liberia' for his study of ancient and modern languages and suggested that the letter might be made public since, he concluded, 'a better composed or better reasoned letter was never written'.[195] Blyden also began corresponding with Brougham and, when he first visited London in 1861, presented him with an ebony walking stick mounted with ivory and gold from the 'young men of Liberia', for 'the valuable services ... rendered to the cause of Africa and her oppressed descendants'.[196]

Blyden cultivated several other influential friends during his visits to Britain, including Thomas Hodgkin and the wealthy banker and MP Samuel Gurney, President of the British and Foreign Anti-Slavery Society. He subsequently became the friend of bishops, government ministers, colonial governors and wealthy capitalists. His friendship with Alfred Lewis Jones, owner of the Elder Dempster shipping line, is reported to have allowed him free passage on any of the company's steamships.[197] Blyden also had a lifelong friendship with R. B. Smith, who taught classics at Harrow School, and often stayed at Smith's home when he visited Britain. Smith described Blyden as 'an African of the purest Negro blood, a man of great ability and an accomplished linguist'.[198] He used these friendships partly as a means to elicit support for the general advancement of Liberia, which he linked to the progress of Africa and Africans. He returned to England regularly, first in his role as a professor of Greek and Latin, then from 1877 as Liberia's official but unpaid ambassador to Britain, as well as on numerous other occasions.

Reportedly, when Blyden first met Gladstone they spoke to each other in several languages, including French, Latin, Greek and Arabic.[199] For some twenty years they maintained their correspondence, Blyden clearly unperturbed by the fact that the politician's great wealth had come from his family's ownership of enslaved Africans, that Gladstone's maiden speech in Parliament, in June 1833, had been used to defend the enslavement of Africans, that he had been a strong supporter of compensation for slave owners, following abolition in 1838, and that he considered Africans 'the less developed race'.[200] They regularly exchanged views on Latin and Greek scholarship, but also on a variety of other matters, with Blyden often asking for Gladstone's publications and sending his own. On one occasion he expressed to Gladstone his admiration for 'the popular feeling manifested on behalf of the weaker side in the recent Jamaica disturbances', a reference to his perception that 'the English heart' had been critical of Governor Eyre's savage suppression of the Morant Bay Rebellion.[201] Blyden also wrote to Gladstone for 'sources of information on the Ancient Ethiopians' in preparation for his article on 'The Negro in Ancient History'.[202]

Blyden was a politician, a newspaper editor, an internationally known writer in defence 'of that peculiar type of humanity known as the Negro, with all its affiliated and collateral branches'.[203] He wrote thirteen books and numerous articles, was an advocate of an independent African church, demanded a West African University 'run by Negro scholars', was concerned with 'the redemption of Africa and the dis-enthralment and elevation of the African race', and has been seen as one of the 'fathers of Pan-Africanism'.[204] He regularly gave public lectures in Britain in defence of Africa and Africans. Many of his most famous writings were published in Britain, including *Christianity, Islam and the Negro Race* (1886) which, with its positive assessment of Islam as 'the form of Christianity best adapted to the Negro race', created consternation in missionary circles and a major debate in *The Times*.[205]

A great anglophile, Blyden was much admired by the Colonial Office in London for his support for British expansion in West Africa. In 1871 he moved to Sierra Leone to teach Arabic and later was employed by the British government as an official explorer of Sierra Leone and as 'Government Agent to the Interior'. On several occasions Blyden also acted as an unofficial Liberian representative in London, until August 1877, when the President of Liberia made him the country's first ambassador to Britain.[206] He served as ambassador in 1877–9, in 1892, and again in 1905–6. It was during his first period as ambassador, in 1878, that he was elected a temporary honorary member of the Athenaeum Club in Pall Mall, which included amongst its membership Charles Darwin and Charles Dickens. Blyden, who was proposed for membership by the Dean of Westminster, almost certainly became the first African to receive such an honour.[207]

Blyden became even better known in England in 1892, when he and Alfred Jones were able to arrange for 78-year-old Liberian Martha Ricks, a former enslaved woman, to have lunch with members of the royal family and present the Queen with a quilt.[208] As ambassador, one of Blyden's tasks was to seek a treaty of protection with Britain during the period of the scramble for African colonies. He clearly felt that 'England was the power from which his country had most to hope from and least to fear'.[209] It was perhaps in light of these views that from 1896 to 1899 the British government appointed him Political Officer, or Agent for Negro Affairs in the British colony of Lagos, with special responsibility for education, and, in 1901, as director of Mohammedan Education in Sierra Leone (although in 1898 the government ignored Blyden's critical views on Britain's role in the Hut Tax Rebellion there).

Blyden had the unique position of being as well known amongst the ruling class in Britain as he was amongst young intellectuals in Africa and throughout the diaspora. Amongst the latter he was widely celebrated. 'The work of Edward Wilmot Blyden is universal, covering the entire race and the entire race problem' was the conclusion of J. E. Casely Hayford, an eminent African contemporary.[210] Blyden was, however, a man of many contradictory views, but in his day was perhaps the foremost champion of Africa, African institutions and Africans. He was firm in his belief that Africa could be regenerated and developed only by Africans themselves and that those in the diaspora were destined to play a vital role.[211]

Samuel Celestine Edwards

While Blyden seemed to welcome some aspects of European imperialism and colonial rule, there was another influential figure in Britain who had a different view and a different audience. Samuel Jules Celestine Edwards (c.1857–1894) was born either in the British colony of Dominica, or in Antigua, where he was partly educated.[212] As a teenager he ran away to sea, against his mother's wishes, and spent some time in the United States, both in New York and in San Francisco. In the late 1870s he settled in Britain, first living in Edinburgh and then in Sunderland and Newcastle. He worked in several occupations, including as a builder's labourer, before becoming a lecturer for the Independent Order of Good Templars (IOGT), one of many temperance societies popular at the time. Although originating in the United States in the 1850s, the IOGT had a membership of over 200,000 in Britain by the early 1870s. It included several Black members, most notably in Liverpool, where the Toxteth lodge boasted more than fifty by 1884. Indeed, at the time that Edwards joined, the organization had undergone a split over the inclusion of African American lodges in the United States.[213] Edwards also joined the Primitive Methodist Church and, although he expressed a desire to be sent to Africa as a missionary, was instead sent to preach in east London. There he was for a time a medical student at the London Hospital, and a student of theology at King's College, but his main occupation was as a lecturer, one who combined a devotion to temperance with his own unique brand of Christian socialism, anti-racism and anti-imperialism. He was known to be 'proud of his colour and his people', and once admitted

Samuel Celestine Edwards

that his greatest temptation' as he travelled through England was a cutting response to racist remarks to 'floor "mean whites"'.[214]

Edwards is reported to have attracted audiences of hundreds, and sometimes thousands, of people and he spoke not just in London, but throughout the country, from Plymouth to Edinburgh, on issues including opposition to racism and British imperialism in Africa and India, as well as lynching and other forms of racism in the United States. He was also connected with the Christian Evidence Society, speaking against the growing trend for atheism amongst the working class, and helping to establish new branches of the organization, which reached the peak of its popularity in the early 1880s. One of Edwards' lectures, *Political Atheism*, was published in London in 1890 and accounts of his lectures in the local press indicate that they were often lively affairs.[215] One contemporary commented:

> There was something so unique in a black man teaching white men Christianity, and in knowing more about it than themselves, that at first one would feel inclined to be angry and resent it, but you could not. He was so happy in his method, so agreeable in his manner, so witty in his argument, so choice in his illustrations, so scathing in his remarks, that he insensibly won you to his side.[216]

Edwards' major publication was a biography of Bishop Walter Hawkins, of the British Methodist Episcopal Church in Canada, entitled *From Slavery to a Bishopric* (1891). 'I undertake this work', Edwards commented, 'because I think it will probably act as a stimulus to the young men of my race, who though physically free have not yet realized the duty they owe to themselves and to humanity at large and especially to the British public, to whom I feel we owe a great deal of gratitude for leading the way for our emancipation in the New World.'[217] Whatever his limitations as a historian, Edwards was perhaps one of the first African or Caribbean people in Britain to write a historical account of slavery. His concerns were clear, whether in his writing, or in public lectures, which were often delivered to working-class audiences.

In 1892 Edwards became the editor of *Lux: A Weekly Christian Evidence Journal*, the first Black person to fulfil such a role, while he also continued his nationwide lecturing. In 1893 he gave his support to the national speaking tour of the African American Ida B. Wells, the famous anti-lynching campaigner, and to the establishment of the Society for the Furtherance of the Brotherhood of Man (SFBM) that was being formed in Britain by anti-racist campaigners Catherine Impey and Isabella Mayo. Edwards and Wells often spoke from the same platform, while in *Lux* he encouraged readers to give their support to the anti-racist and anti-lynching campaigns of the SFBM.[218] Wells was the most prominent African American to speak out against lynching and racism in the United States at the end of the nineteenth century, and was invited to speak in Britain by Mayo and Impey. The latter was already publishing the anti-racist journal *Anti-Caste* and had met Wells in the United States.[219] In addition to her tour of Britain in 1893, Wells returned for further speaking engagements the following year, partly financed by Edwards. He also published, and wrote an introduction to, a collection of Wells' lectures entitled *United States Atrocities – Lynch Law*.[220]

Wells' tour in 1894 received significant attention from the British press, including an interview with newly elected MP Keir Hardy for his *Labour Leader*. Wells also met at least seven African students who helped her during her time in London, including J. E. Casely Hayford, at that time training as a barrister, Oguntola Sapara, a medical student, and two unnamed women.[221] The culmination of the tour was the formation of an Anti-Lynching Committee in London with Passmore Edwards as secretary. It had many illustrious supporters, including Ben Tillett, Keir Hardie, Tom Mann and Dadabhai Naoroji, as well as several MPs and newspaper editors. It also received a donation of £14 'sent by a dozen Africans who were residing at that time in London'.[222] It was evident that those Africans attracted to the capital were starting to involve themselves with matters of Pan-African concern.

In this period, the SFBM became the Society for the Recognition of the Brotherhood of Man (SRBM), with Edwards as executive secretary and editor of its new monthly publication, *Fraternity*, whilst he also remained editor of *Lux*. His editorials in *Fraternity* included denunciation of lynch mobs in the United States and imperialists such as Cecil Rhodes in Africa, as well as vigorous defence of human rights in India, Russia, Australia and elsewhere.

Edwards wrote with particular vigour against British imperialism and the 'scramble' for African colonies during this period and was equally critical of missionaries, whom he described as 'Salaried Officers of the State'. In response to Britain's planned annexation of Uganda he wrote:

> If the British nation stole no more, they have stolen enough and have sufficient responsibility at home and abroad to occupy her maternal attention for the next hundred years. If the British nation has not murdered enough, no nation on God's earth has. Those who are crying aloud for Uganda are not her best friends, for she cannot occupy the country without more blood and additional injustice.[223]

Edwards' anti-imperialism was not just personal opinion but reflected a wider critique of empire, both in Britain and in the colonies, that was often supported in the pages of *Fraternity* by letters from its readers and the eyewitness accounts of local correspondents.[224] However, he was one of the first to establish a connection between slavery and the contemporary colonial invasions and partition of Africa. Most importantly, he highlighted the emergence of contemporary racism, 'Anglo-Saxonism', as he termed it, as well as exposing the hypocrisy of Britain's so-called 'civilising mission in Africa'. Edwards maintained a gruelling schedule of activities, lecturing, editing, and organizing the SRBM, as well as having financial responsibility for the success of *Fraternity*, all of which soon had a negative impact on his health. In June 1894 he was forced to travel to the Caribbean to recuperate, but never returned and died a few weeks after his arrival.[225]

It now seems possible that Edwards was the author of another book, *Hard Truth*, which was published just before he left for the Caribbean. The author was listed as Theodore Thomas, 'a coloured gentleman now residing in this country', but recent research has questioned whether such a person ever existed.[226] *Hard Talk* presented a dialogue between Christ and Satan, including a commentary on racism in Britain and British imperialism in southern Africa. The book bears all the hallmarks of Edwards. 'Britain', Satan concludes, 'is the birth-place of the very essence of the seed of prejudice against the Negro race.'[227] *Hard Talk* was also the first book by a 'coloured' author in Britain to critique the minstrel shows in which 'Britons black their faces to buffoon the Negro', as well as the everyday racism affecting medical students and other Black people in Britain.

STUDENTS, STUDENT POLITICIANS AND TEACHERS

Edwards does not appear to have been influenced by the publication of John Jacob Thomas' *Froudacity*, which was published in London two years earlier in 1889. The book was reviewed in some British papers and clearly had some impact on the Colonial Office officials.[228]

J. J. Thomas (1841–1889) was a Trinidadian teacher, educationalist and linguist (and a member of the London Philological Society), who responded to the Eurocentric and anti-African views of J. A. Froude, Regius Professor of Modern History at Oxford University, as outlined in his book *The English in the West Indies* (1888), with a counterblast in *Froudacity* (1889). Froude had only visited the Caribbean once, fleetingly, and was far from being an expert on its history, but was arrogant enough to pontificate on it and to argue, in an openly racist manner, against any democratic rights for the majority of its population in the future. Thomas referred to Froude's views as 'the baseless assertions of this conjuror-up of inconceivable fables', which he refuted one by one.[229] Thomas wrote parts of *Froudacity* in the Caribbean, where it was published as a series of articles in the *St George's Chronicle and Grenada Gazette*, but it was completed during his visit to London between 1888 and 1889. It was published in London, in 1889, the same year as Thomas's death in that city from tuberculosis at the age of forty-nine.

One of the questions posed by J. J. Thomas in 1889 was the following:

> The intra-African Negro is clearly powerless to struggle successfully against personal enslavement, annexation, or volunteer forcible 'protection' of his territory. What, we ask, will in the coming ages be the opinion and attitude of the extra-African millions – ten millions [sic] in the Western Hemisphere – dispersed so widely over the surface of the globe, apt apprentices in every conceivable department of civilized

culture? Will these men remain forever too poor, too isolated from one another for grand racial combinations? Or will the naturally opulent cradle of their people, too long a prey to violence and unholy greed, become at length the sacred watchword of a generation willing and able to conquer or perish under its inspiration.[230]

It is evident that those of African descent in Britain began to consider how to answer this question, and students from various countries often played an important role. Throughout the nineteenth century the numbers of students from Africa and the Caribbean had grown steadily, especially as Britain's colonial possessions in Africa increased. There were no higher education institutions in the colonies, with the exception of those that offered some training for the clergy, and few other educational institutions. Parents who could afford to do so sent their children to schools in Britain, where they enrolled alongside those studying for such professions as law and medicine.[231] They were sometimes joined by those from humbler backgrounds as well.

As a result of missionary endeavour in Africa, several Africans came to Britain to train as missionaries. They included the South African Tiyo Soga, who spent several years in Scotland during the 1840s and 1850s, studied at the University of Glasgow, was ordained as a minister in the United Presbyterian Church of Scotland and later married a Scottish wife. All of his seven African-born children returned to be educated in their mother's homeland, just as their father had been. Soga expressed his developing Pan-African views in regard to his sons, who returned to Africa during his lifetime. He asserted 'that although their mother is white, they were to consider themselves black men, and that they were to take their place as Kafirs – a race of which they never need be ashamed'.[232] A. K. Soga, his youngest son, was to become one of the leading figures in the early South African Native National Congress (later the ANC). Another son, J. F. Soga, later became South Africa's first veterinary surgeon. Their sister Jessie Margaret Soga (1870–1954), who remained in Britain, became a classical singer and music teacher, and later a suffragette, a leading member of Glasgow's Women's Social and Political Union.[233] Several South African students attended training at St Augustine's Missionary Training College in Canterbury during the nineteenth century, while a number of other young Africans from various parts of the continent began to receive secondary education at such schools as Queen's College in Taunton, which was connected with the Methodist Church. Many of the Soga children were educated at Dollar Academy in Scotland, as was James Risien Russell, the son of a wealthy sugar planter from British Guiana, who attended, along with at least one of his brothers, in the early 1880s. Russell then studied medicine at Edinburgh University before becoming a distinguished researcher on nervous disorders and later a professor at University College London.

Numerous West Africans, some of them formerly enslaved, also trained as missionaries in Britain. They included two from the Yoruba kingdoms of what is now Nigeria: Joseph Wright, who studied in Britain in the 1840s, and Samuel Ajayi Crowther, educated in Islington during the 1820s and 1840s respectively.[234] In 1864 Crowther became the first African bishop in the Anglican church and in the same year received a Doctor of Divinity degree from the University of Oxford. He was also an important linguist, producing important works on the Yoruba, Igbo and Nupe languages, as well as a *Narrative* of his early capture and travels.[235]

One particularly notable schoolboy from the Caribbean was Richard Hill (1795–1872), who was the son of a father from Lincolnshire and a Jamaican mother. At the age of five Richard was sent to be educated with his father's relatives in Cheshunt and thereafter at the Elizabethan Grammar School in Horncastle. He returned to Jamaica after the death of his father in 1818. It is reported that Richard's father was opposed to slavery and that on his deathbed he made his son solemnly pledge himself to devote his life to the cause of emancipation and never to rest until slavery itself had been abolished.[236]

Richard devoted himself to that cause and was noted as one of the leading advocates of the interests of the 'free people of colour' in Jamaica, lobbying both the government and the abolitionists on their behalf from the early 1820s onwards.[237] He later returned to England, first to present the petition of the 'free coloureds' to the House of Commons and subsequently to work with Clarkson, Wilberforce and others in the anti-slavery movement to hasten its abolition. Hill was later sent by the Anti-Slavery Society to investigate conditions in Haiti before he returned to Jamaica in 1832. He appears to have been the author of *Haiti and Spain: A Memorial*, which upholds the rights of those in both Haiti and the Dominican Republic.[238] He was for many years a magistrate, who defended the interests of the newly emancipated, and was derogatorily referred to as the 'Black Viper' by the plantocracy there.[239] Wearing another hat, as a naturalist, he wrote several scientific papers and corresponded with Charles Darwin. Members of the American Anti-Slavery Society said of Hill that:

> He is a colored gentleman, and in every respect the noblest man, white or black, whom we met in the West Indies. He is highly intelligent and of fine moral feelings . . . His manners are free and unassuming, and his language in conversation fluent and well chosen . . . He is highly respected by the government in the island and at home, and possesses the esteem of his fellow citizens of all colors . . . Though an African sun has burnt a deep tinge on him he is truly one of nature's nobleman. His demeanor is such, so dignified, yet so bland and amiable, that no one can help respecting him.[240]

Darwin's Tutor?

John Edmonstone was born enslaved in Demerara (now part of Guyana), but almost nothing is known of his early life except that his Scottish owner was a Charles Edmonstone. He was taught taxidermy by Charles Waterton, an English naturalist and explorer who was related through marriage to Edmonstone's owner. However, Waterton's account suggests 'that John had poor abilities, and it required much time and patience to drive anything into him'.[241] Whether this was the case, or not, Waterton reports that John was later taken to Scotland, freed by his owner and was able enough to be 'employed in the Glasgow and then the Edinburgh museum'.[242] It is probable that John Edmonstone was in Edinburgh around 1817 and found employment as a 'bird-stuffer', or taxidermist, for many years. During the early 1820s, he lived in Lothian Street, close to Charles Darwin, who was beginning his study of medicine at that time, as a young man of seventeen. Darwin later wrote 'a Negro lived in Edinburgh who had travelled with Waterton, and gained his livelihood by stuffing birds, which he did excellently: he gave me lessons for payment, and I often used to sit with him, for he was a very pleasant and intelligent man.'[243] After forty lessons, for which Edmonstone was paid a guinea an hour, Darwin gave up his medical career and began the career as a naturalist for which he became famous. He used the skills he learned from Edmonstone, who may also have encouraged his anti-slavery and anti-racist beliefs.[244] Nothing appears to be known of Edmonstone's later life, nor the place and date of his death.

Thomas Jenkins

One of the most remarkable students of the early nineteenth century was Thomas 'Tom' Jenkins, whose original name has remained unknown. He was the son of an African king in the region of the Little Cape Mount River, in today's Liberia. The king wished that his son could be educated abroad for a few years and made an arrangement with a Captain Swanstone (or Swanson), a trader from Hawick in Scotland to take his son there. In 1803 Swanstone transported the boy to Scotland via Liverpool on board his ship, the *Prudence*, and renamed him during the journey. It is reported that soon after arrival at Hawick, Swanstone died and the young Thomas was eventually adopted by a local farmer, a relative of the deceased captain. He apparently soon learned to speak as the locals did and busied himself around the farm as a cowherd and transporter of peat. After some years he was then adopted and employed by a man called Laidlaw and it was at this time that he began to educate himself, studying by candlelight, and he also received a basic education at an evening school. Not content to stop there, he began to teach himself mathematics, Latin and Greek, and used all his meagre savings to buy a Greek dictionary. He was described both as an 'extraordinary specimen of African intellect ... one of the most popular characters in Upper Teviotdale', and as resembling 'in every respect except his skin an ordinary peasant of the south of Scotland'.[245]

When Tom was about twenty years old, a vacancy appeared for a schoolteacher in Teviothead, for which he applied and was judged 'the best fitted for the situation' but rejected as a 'Negro and born pagan'. However, Tom also had his local supporters and they decided to open a rival school in a local smithy and to pay him the appropriate salary.

As a result, the first established school remained empty and Tom Jenkins became the first African schoolteacher (and presumably headmaster) in Britain, serving at the school for several years from 1814. He still wished to pursue his own studies and later also studied Latin, Greek and mathematics at the University of Edinburgh (although he was not the first student of African descent at that university).[246]

By June 1818 Tom Jenkins was in London, enrolling for a teacher-training course at the Borough Road College, Southwark, and receiving the recommendation of William Allen, a leading abolitionist. He subsequently became a professional teacher, establishing a school in Pimlico and later teaching at the Fitzroy Sabbath and Day School in Grafton Street, in central London. In 1821 he was invited by the Governor of Mauritius to teach on that island. He became initially an inspector of schools and then, in 1823, took charge of his own school. Thomas Jenkins died in Mauritius in June 1858.[247]

Sir Samuel Lewis (1843–1903), a Sierra Leonean and the first African to be knighted in 1896, studied law at University College London from 1866, and thereafter at the Middle Temple. He returned to Sierra Leone, was for a time acting Chief Justice, and later wrote the biographical introduction to Blyden's *Christianity, Islam and the Negro Race*. Another Sierra Leonean, Christian Frederick Cole (1852–1885) graduated from Oxford University in 1877 and was probably the university's first African graduate. Forced to supplement his income by teaching and giving music lessons, he eventually became a barrister, the first African to practise law in England. In 1879 Cole thought it necessary to present his views both on racism and British imperialism in a pamphlet, *What Do Men Say about Negroes and Reflections on the Zulu War by a Negro, B.A., of University College, Oxford, and the Inner Temple*, which he wrote in poetic form and dedicated to W. E. Gladstone.[248] Cole's reflections included:

> Ye white men of England
> Oh tell, tell, I pray,
> If the curse of your land,
> Is not, day after day,
> To increase your possessions

> With reckless delight,
> To subdue many nations,
> And show them your might.[249]

He also looked forward to the future Africa, when Africans –

> Will with stunning pride assert their claims
> And put to silence all opprobrious names,
> The world with eyes open shall then exclaim
> Afric! Thy sons have won eternal fame.[250]

Joseph Renner Maxwell (1857–1901), who studied law at Merton College, Oxford, from 1876 onwards also originated from Sierra Leone and was another of that university's first African graduates. Maxwell came from an elite family, but like many educated Africans in this period he was acutely aware of the ongoing contest between the European powers for colonial division and control of the African continent. He was best known for his controversial book advocating marriage between educated Africans and Europeans, *The Negro Question or, Hints for the Improvement of the Negro Race, with Special Reference to West Africa*, published in London in 1892, and written after Maxwell had risen almost to the top of the colonial civil service in the Gambia. However, in 1881, the year after he became a barrister, Maxwell delivered an address at St Jude's Institute in London on 'the advantages and disadvantages of European intercourse with the West Coast of Africa'.[251]

It has been estimated that between 1880 and 1919 well over a hundred students came to Britain from the new West African colony of the Gold Coast. Some like John Mensah Sarbah (1864–1910), later a founder of the Gold Coast Aborigines' Rights Protection Society and an important writer on traditional African legal systems, were initially schooled in Britain. In 1880 Sarbah went to Worthing School and then Queen's College, a school in Taunton, before studying law in London and becoming one of the Gold Coast's first barristers. His *Fanti Customary Laws*, an early attempt to write Africa's history from an African perspective, was published in 1897.[252] Several other prominent Gold Coast families sent their children, especially sons, to Queen's College, or other favoured schools such as Dulwich College in London. Then, like Mensah Sarbah, J. E. Casely Hayford and other prominent men, they embarked mainly on legal and medical careers.[253] J. E. Casely Hayford (1866–1930), who studied at Cambridge University, became one of the most prominent Gold Coast politicians and journalists, also writing *Gold Coast Native Institutions*, which was published in 1903.[254] He was later a founder of the National Congress of British West Africa and a financial supporter of the *African Times and Orient Review*, one of the first Pan-African newspapers in Britain. Arthur Wharton (1865–1930), later a famous athlete and the 'first black footballer' in the world, also came from the Gold Coast to Britain, originally to train as a missionary at Cleveland College in Darlington.[255]

Such students were often joined by other West Africans, who came for business, political, missionary or other matters to the centre of the empire. Although male students often later became better known, female students, such as Arthur Wharton's sister Clara, and Eve Nancy Sarbah, Mensah Sarbah's sister, were also educated in Britain, as was Casely Hayford's wife, the former Adelaide Smith.[256] By the end of the century, a significant colony of highly educated West Africans, including doctors and lawyers, were residing in London and other cities throughout the British Isles. For example, between 1874 and 1895, six Yoruba students (several born in Sierra Leone) qualified as doctors in London: Nathaniel King (1874), Obadiah Johnson (1884), John Randle (1888), Orisadipe Obasa (1891), Akinsipe Leigh-Sodipe (1892) and Oguntola Sapara (1895).[257]

Other Africans were sponsored for missionary training by the various British-based missionary societies. In Colwyn Bay, Wales, for example, the African Institute was established to provide African missionaries with practical skills. Many of these were young Africans from the Congo. In total the institute trained nearly a hundred students, who pursued a variety of careers, and some of whom remained in Britain. One of the most notable was Lulu Coote (1890–1964), the daughter of a Dutch father and Congolese mother, who arrived at Colwyn Bay in 1897. She later became one of the first African nurses in Britain, training at Ashton-under-Lyme Infirmary, where, from 1911, she was employed. The institute also gave rise to several prominent student politicians, including Kwesi Ewusi, who became one of the founders of the Ethiopian Progressive Association in Liverpool in

1904, and Oladipo Lananmi, who founded the African Students' Association in London in 1916.[258]

By the end of the nineteenth century professionals and students from Africa and the Caribbean could be found not only in London, but also in other towns and cities throughout Britain. Although some might initially have welcomed colonial expansion in Africa, many came to realize that this was to create severe limitations, even for the most highly educated, since it denied Africans the right to govern themselves just as colonial rule did in the Caribbean. They also grew increasingly concerned about other forms of racism and Eurocentrism in the colonies, in the US, and in Britain itself.

6

War, Riot and Resistance: 1897–1919

One of the most important aspects of the history of African and Caribbean people in the twentieth century has been the formation of political organizations. Although there had been many efforts by those of African and Caribbean heritage to aid each other over the centuries, there is very little evidence of people working within organizations in order to do so until the twentieth century. Political organizations became vitally important at the turn of the century, not only because of the oppressive nature of colonial rule in Africa and the Caribbean but also because Black people in Britain were subject to various forms of racism and often regarded as inferior to other citizens.

THE AFRICAN ASSOCIATION AND THE
FIRST PAN-AFRICAN CONFERENCE

The growing political concerns of African and Caribbean intellectuals in Britain during the last part of the nineteenth century culminated in the founding of the African Association in London in September/October 1897.[1] It was founded by Henry Sylvester Williams (1869–1911), a Trinidadian law student enrolled at the Inns of Court in London, who became its first secretary, Thomas J. Thompson from Sierra Leone, another law student, Charles Durham, a Trinidadian solicitor, and an Antiguan, Reverend Henry Mason Joseph, who had formerly been connected with the Society for the Recognition of the Brotherhood of Man.[2] Although membership of the Association was only declared open to 'Black Men', its joint-founder, and first treasurer, was an African woman, Alice Victoria Kinloch (c.1863–c.1946) from South Africa, who came to Britain in about 1895 and had been lecturing throughout the country, as well as writing, on the 'slave-like' conditions and oppression of Africans in her homeland perpetrated by capitalists and missionaries alike.[3]

It seems likely that Kinloch had some connection with *Fraternity*, and her important role was made clear by Williams when he explained that 'the Association is the result of Mrs Kinloch's work in England and the feeling that as British Subjects we ought to be heard in our own affairs'. Kinloch herself explained that 'with some men of my race in this country, I have formed a society for the benefit of our people in Africa by helping them to bring some of the dark side of things in Africa and elsewhere to light.'[4] It is noteworthy that such an important British political organization was founded and inspired by an African woman. Kinloch, who was the African Association's first treasurer before her return to South Africa in 1898, also appears to be the first African woman to have her views on African exploitation published in Britain, with the release of her pamphlet *Are South African Diamonds Worth Their Cost?* in 1897. Kinloch clearly had a major influence, since some of the earliest activities of the African Association were its protests to the British government about conditions in South Africa. She presumably also influenced Williams, who later temporarily relocated to South Africa and became the 'first black person' to practise law in the Supreme Court in the Cape Colony.[5]

Although the association claimed that 'no one not of African descent' could be a member, it appears that a later treasurer of what became the Pan-African Association was Frank Colenso, another South African and the son of the Anglican Bishop of Natal. He was of European descent, but, like his father, was a strong campaigner for the rights of the Zulu people and other Africans in South Africa.[6] The other officers and committee members were mainly law students or lawyers from the Caribbean and from West Africa. The association's supporters included Liberal Party MPs and members of the Anti-Slavery Society and Aborigines' Protection Society, although the latter appears to have been a most reluctant supporter.[7] The association also received support from the press in West Africa, the United States and the Caribbean. Its most notable supporters were Dadabhai Naoroji, who had been Britain's first Indian parliamentarian, and Alfred Webb, the Irish nationalist and former MP.[8]

The African Association was mainly concerned with various injustices in Britain's African colonies, as well as the Caribbean. Its aim was:

> To encourage a feeling of unity to facilitate friendly intercourse among Africans in general; to promote and protect the interests of all subjects claiming African descent, wholly or in part, in British Colonies and other places, especially in Africa, by circulating accurate information on all subjects affecting their rights and privileges as subjects of the British Empire, by direct appeals to the Imperial and Local Governments.[9]

It also worked to influence British public opinion so that 'Members of Parliament could be instructed that the better treatment of Native Races should command greater attention in Parliament'. It had some contact with the Liberal Party, engaged in a nationwide lecture programme, published letters in the press and declared that it wished to be a representative body on 'matters affecting the destiny of the African Race'.[10] Most importantly it wanted African self-representation. As Williams later asserted, 'No other but a Negro can represent the Negro.'[11]

The association was opposed to the violence and racism of the European colonial powers in Africa, as well as economic conditions in the Caribbean, although not necessarily opposed to colonial rule itself, nor the 'civilizing' mission. It was particularly concerned that educated Africans were not consulted and had no say regarding the fate of their compatriots and the African continent. Here it is important to note that it used the term 'Africans' to include both those from the continent and from the diaspora. While it lobbied the British Parliament about conditions in the Caribbean and southern Africa, as well as the promotion of racism in Britain, and submitted proposals for reforms, it also concerned itself with the colonies of the other European powers in Africa. Although it received some support from enlightened opinion in Britain, it was viewed with contempt by the British government.[12]

By early 1899 the association, which referred to itself as the Pan-African Conference Committee and mainly comprised students and professionals, had announced the convening of such a conference the following May. This would be timed to coincide with the Paris Exhibition and 'would be the first occasion upon which black men would assemble in England to speak for themselves and endeavour to influence public opinion in their favour'.[13] The committee consulted Booker T. Washington as well as other leading African Americans about their intention to hold a conference. Plans for the conference, which was still mainly aimed at influencing enlightened public opinion in Britain, were also widely reported in the African American press, as well as in Anglophone Africa and the Caribbean. It seems that after Williams met with the Haitian writer and Pan-Africanist Benito Sylvain, in Paris, the scope of the conference was broadened to include 'the treatment of native races under European and American rule', so lynching in the United States could also be discussed.[14]

The first Pan-African Conference was finally held in Westminster Town Hall, not far from the Houses of Parliament, from 22 to 24 July 1900, 'under the auspices of the African Association'.[15] The discussions focused on slavery, colonialism and racism – all forms of oppression against Africa and Africans – and how they might be removed. There was also a focus on possible forms of reparation for Africa and Africans. The conference was chaired by Bishop Alexander Walters, from the United States, and included speakers from that country, the Caribbean and Africa, in addition to those based in Britain.[16] Among key British-based participants were John Archer (1863–1932), Samuel Coleridge-Taylor (1875–1912), who composed music for the event, Richard Akiwande Savage (1874–1935) and John Alcindor (1873–1924), both of the latter representing the Afro-West Indian Society at Edinburgh University, as well as Frederick and Harriet Loudin, who directed the Loudin Jubilee Singers. Benito Sylvain, who delivered one of the main speeches as the representative of Emperor Menelik of Ethiopia, and W. E. B. Du Bois were amongst the distinguished international participants at the conference, which also included female African American speakers. The conference's 'Address to the Nations of the World', which condemned racial oppression in the United States, as well as throughout Africa, and demanded self-government for the colonies, was drafted under the chairmanship of Du Bois and included the famous phrase, 'the problem of the 20th century is the problem of the colour-line'.[17]

The press in Britain, the United States, West Africa, South Africa and the Caribbean reported on the conference. It condemned anti-African racism, recognized the importance of the 'three sovereign states', Haiti, Liberia and Ethiopia, sent a 'memorial' to Queen Victoria calling her attention to the conditions imposed on her 'native subjects', and announced its intention to establish branches of a new Pan-African Association (PAA) in Africa, the Caribbean, and North America.[18] The PAA was presided over by Bishop Walters, with an executive committee that included Williams, Archer, Coleridge-Taylor and Frederick Loudin.[19]

Plans for a second conference in the United States in 1902 and a third in Haiti in 1904 were announced and Williams launched the first few issues of a magazine, the *Pan-African*, which focused on Africans within the British Empire. There were also plans for a 'bureau in London with the object of watching the interests of the African races all over the world'.[20] Despite Williams' strenuous efforts, both the Pan-African Association and the *Pan-African* soon collapsed and no further conferences were organized.[21] Nevertheless, Williams' activities and those of the African Association should not be considered a failure. They established the ideas behind the new terms 'Pan-African' and 'Pan-Africanism' and initiated the modern Pan-African movement by convening the London conference.[22] Williams continued his political activities in Britain. In 1902 he published *The British Negro: A Factor in the Empire*, a pamphlet based on two lectures, one condemning racism throughout the empire and the other extolling the history of Ethiopia.[23] He later joined the Liberal Party and the Fabian Society and, in 1906, successfully stood as Progressive Party candidate for Marylebone Borough Council in London, at the same time as John Archer was successfully elected to Battersea Borough Council. This was three years after the Bahamian, Dr Allan Glaisyer Minns (1858–1930), was elected as a member of Thetford town council in Norfolk. In 1904, Minns, who represented the Conservative Party, was elected Mayor of Thetford, 'the first black Briton to achieve such an office'.[24]

ARCHER AND COLERIDGE-TAYLOR

The most prominent Black politician of this period was John Archer (1863–1932), born in Liverpool to a Barbadian father, who was a ship's steward, and an Irish mother. Archer is thought to have been a seafarer in his early life and to have travelled the world. He returned to Britain in 1894 and established himself as a professional photographer in Battersea. Archer became a member of the Battersea Labour League, and a supporter of the radical MP John Burns. He was also reportedly a member of the United Irish League and from 1906 to 1909 served on Battersea Borough Council. In 1912 he was re-elected to the council and in 1913 elected Mayor of Battersea. In his acceptance speech Archer declared:

> For the first time in the history of the English nation, a man of colour has been elected mayor of an English borough. That will go forth to all the coloured nations of the world and they will look at Battersea and say 'It is the greatest thing you have done. You have shown that you have no racial prejudice, but recognize a man for what you think he has done.'[25]

Although Archer was preceded by Minns in his appointment as a mayor, he was generally believed to have established an historic first and received congratulations from around the world. After attending an event at the Guildhall with other London mayors, Archer told a friend that 'it filled my heart with joy – the first time one of our race has done so as mayor'. His victory was especially important in the Unites States and was reported in *The Crisis*, the official magazine of the National Association for the Advancement of Colored People edited by W. E. B. Du Bois, as well as other publications.[26] In response to a letter of congratulation from the African American John Edward Bruce, Archer replied that he hoped his election would,

> encourage you over in America where for so many years you have been suffering the injustice of inequality . . . I'm afraid that I would not have a very long life in the USA because I seem to be peculiarly formed, in other words I have more of the fighting than the peaceful quality within me, and I could not put up with the indignities that our people have to put up with in the land of their birth.[27]

Another highly important British-born figure at the London conference of 1900 was Samuel Coleridge-Taylor (1875–1912), born in London to a father from Sierra Leone (who returned to Africa before his birth), and an English mother who raised him in Croydon. At the age of seventeen Coleridge-Taylor won a violin scholarship to the Royal College of Music and became best known as the composer of *Hiawatha's Wedding Feast*, which was first performed in its entirety in 1901, became extremely popular and a standard in the choral repertoire. Coleridge-Taylor received no royalties for his most popular work and continued to work as a composer and conductor, while also teaching at both Trinity College of Music and the Guildhall School of Music in London. He also made three visits to the United States, initially invited by the African American Coleridge-Taylor Choral Society, where he performed at the White House.

In 1905 Coleridge-Taylor completed *Twenty-Four Negro Melodies Arranged for the Piano*, which was published in the United States with a preface by Booker T. Washington. Coleridge-Taylor explained the aim of his composition: 'What Brahms has done for the Hungarian folk music, Dvorak for the Bohemian, and Grieg for the Norwegian, I have tried to do for these Negro melodies.'[28] He also wrote an *African Suite*, a symphonic poem entitled 'Toussaint L'Ouverture' and collaborated with African American poet Paul Laurence Dunbar on several works. Many of Coleridge-Taylor's musical compositions and his participation in the Pan-African Conference, where he arranged the musical programme, give an indication of his sympathies. It is evident that he faced racism himself on several occasions and took a public stand against it in several letters to the press. In one written in February 1912 he wrote: 'the fact is that there is an appalling amount of ignorance amongst English people about the Negro and his doings . . . Personally I consider myself the equal of any white man who ever lived, and no one could ever change me in that respect.'[29]

Coleridge-Taylor had already completed over a hundred musical compositions when he died of pneumonia at the age of thirty-seven. His funeral was an occasion for collective grief. One wreath was shaped as a map of Africa, bearing the inscription 'From the Sons and Daughters of West Africa at present residing in Britain'. Another from Dusé Mohamed Ali's *African Times and Orient Review* had more than seventy African subscribers.[30]

Samuel Coleridge-Taylor

BLACK EDWARDIANS

It might be thought that students and professionals, such as Williams and Allan Minns, were only temporary sojourners in Edwardian Britain, but many lived and worked in Britain for years. Minns arrived in 1879 and, like his elder brother, studied medicine at Guy's Hospital in London. Both brothers, as well as their sister, then made their home in Norfolk. Minns became a magistrate, married twice and lived in Britain until his death in Dorking in 1930.[31] Some professional families, such as that of John Barbour-James (1867–1954), who originated from British Guiana but worked as a colonial civil servant in West Africa, were perhaps unusual, but they merely show the diversity that existed at the time. The London-based Barbour-James family, which included eight children, was headed by their Guianese mother, Caroline. They shared their Acton home with the family of Samuel Cambridge, a barrister who also originated from British Guiana.[32]

The professionals were undoubtedly exceptional, but there were many others who, although less well known, were part of permanent communities of African and Caribbean heritage that had already established themselves by Victorian times, especially in Britain's ports, such as Liverpool and Cardiff. Most of the males in these cities were employed as seafarers, or in other maritime trades, but their British-born children, as well as other migrants, might undertake a variety of working-class occupations, from tram and bus drivers to domestic servants. Women might be employed as house servants, while, as in the previous century, the entertainment industry was open to all. Napoleon Florent (1874–1959), for example, arrived from St Lucia in 1907 and worked as an actor for most of his life. His family of five children was also supported by the work of his English wife, who sought employment wherever she could find it.

In addition to Lulu Coote, whom we met in the previous chapter, another African woman who trained as a health worker during this period was Oreoluwa Green (1885–?), who travelled to London in 1912 to study midwifery, music and pharmacy. She studied at the London College of Music and Clapham School of Midwifery and she was the first West African woman to qualify as a chemist when she obtained the Apothecaries Certificate from the London Pharmaceutical Society. She later worked as a dispenser at the Soho Royal Ear Hospital before returning to Nigeria in 1917.[33]

Black people were to be found living throughout the country during this period, whether as students and professionals, workers, or impoverished inmates of the workhouses.[34] One historian has estimated the total Black population at the time may have been in the region of 50,000.[35] Some made a significant impact in sport, such as Salford-born James 'Jimmy' Peters (1879–1954), who was the son of George, a Jamaican lion-tamer, and his English wife. James Peters also reportedly started life in the circus, performing as a bareback rider. After his father was mauled to death by a lion, he was abandoned by his mother and admitted to a London orphanage at the age of eleven. Although he worked as a carpenter, he was soon recognized as a promising athlete and played rugby union at all levels. In 1907 he became the first Black player to be capped for England, winning several caps. He later played rugby league and joined St Helens in 1914 on the eve of war.[36]

Another prominent sportsman of working-class origins was Walter Tull (1888–1918), who was born to a Barbadian father and English mother in Folkestone. Both his parents died whilst he was a child, and Walter and his brother, Edward, were placed in an orphanage. Edward was later adopted, moved to Scotland and as Edward Tull-Warnock later trained to become 'probably the first black dentist in Britain'.[37] Walter was an apprentice printer, but also excelled at football and played initially as an amateur for Clapton FC in London, and then from 1909, at the age of twenty-one, professionally for Tottenham Hotspur. He suffered from racist abuse in several games and in 1911 joined Northampton Town. When war broke out, Tull became the first member of his team to enlist. He served in two football battalions and in 1917 was promoted to second lieutenant, one of the first

Walter Tull photographed as a player at Tottenham Hotspur

British-born people of Caribbean heritage to be made an officer at a time when this rank was barred to those not of 'pure European descent'. Decorated for gallantry and mentioned in dispatches, he was killed in action during the Second Battle of the Somme in 1918.[38] In 2018 a campaign was initiated to demand that the Military Cross denied to Tull should be posthumously awarded.[39]

As in the past, several Black men found employment as boxers during the period leading up to the First World War. William Johnson, a Sierra Leonean who may have begun his working life as a mariner, was next employed as an engineer in Manchester and then as a waiter in Leeds. He provided for his British-born children by touring in a boxing booth, an occupation adopted by several former mariners. His sons also became boxers, the most notable being Len Johnson, of whom more will be said later.

There were numerous African American men and women who performed in British music halls in this period, such as Bert Williams and George Walker, others performing various forms of minstrelsy, as well as those performing in the still-popular *Uncle Tom's Cabin*. There were singers and performers from the Caribbean and Africa, as well as British-based entertainers of African and Caribbean heritage. One of the latter was Dusé Mohamed Ali (1866–1945), in 1902 a struggling actor in Yorkshire, billed as the 'distinguished coloured reciter', and the 'only coloured actor and dramatic author in the world'. Ali later worked as an electrician on the Franco-British Exhibition, subsequently opened a theatrical agency and acted as an impresario for different shows as well. Later still he would re-emerge as an important political figure, journalist and editor.[40]

Children of wealthy or professional families from the colonies would often be educated in Britain. By this time at the turn of the century Queen's College in Taunton had already become a popular destination for those arriving from West Africa. It was normally the sons, and more rarely the daughters, of such families who would continue their university education in Britain, most often in law, or medicine. There were however, notable women students such as Kathleen Easmon (1891–1924), who originated from West Africa but was educated at Notting Hill School for Girls, and lived in Shepherd's Bush. The Easmons were closely connected to the Casely Hayfords and other elite West African families in Britain, including that of Samuel Coleridge-Taylor. Kathleen Easmon had a somewhat unusual career path for a young African woman at this time. She attended South Kensington College from 1910 until 1914, where she studied fashion design and then became an associate of the Royal College of Art, later performing as both a dancer and musician.[41] Colonial rule offered few educational opportunities and almost none in higher education. Those who wished to pursue a professional career were forced to train overseas, mainly in Britain. For example, many medical students trained in Scotland, at such universities as Glasgow, Aberdeen and particularly at Edinburgh.[42]

In the early years of the century Edinburgh University already had its Afro-West Indian Literary Society, established for 'the promotion of social life and intellectual improvement among African and West Indian students', which sent its president, Richard Akinwande Savage, and two other delegates, John Alcindor and William Meyer, to the 1900 Pan-African conference.[43] In 1902 West African students protested against the openly discriminatory policies of the West African Medical Service, which banned from appointment those of 'non-European parentage' and persuaded the Dean of the Medical Faculty at Edinburgh University to write in complaint to the Colonial Office.[44] Another example of student politics at Edinburgh is connected with the appearance in 1906 of Keir Hardie's 'Zulu Letter'. The 'Zulu' in question was actually the Sierra Leonean medical student H. R. Bankole-Bright, who was at Edinburgh from 1905 to 1910, later to become one of the founders of the National Congress of British West Africa and the West African Students' Union. Bankole-Bright had written to Hardie, approving of his criticisms of British misrule in Africa and giving the impression that he was a Zulu student. In his reply Hardie included a fiery denunciation of British imperialism and expressed the hope that 'the day will speedily come when your race will be able to defend itself against the barbarities being perpetuated against it by hypocritical whites'.[45]

What was also clear was the high level of political activity amongst African and Caribbean students in Edinburgh at this time, who lobbied politicians and wrote to the press, both in Britain and in West Africa. It was this kind of activity that was to occupy Prince Bandele Omoniyi, another Nigerian student in Edinburgh, in the early years of the twentieth century. Omoniyi is best known for his book *A Defence of the Ethiopian Movement*, which was published in Edinburgh in 1908. Unlike many West African students, and despite his royal title, Omoniyi lived in poverty and conducted nearly all his political activities independently. He wrote to the Scottish and West African press and in the *Labour Leader*, the paper of the Independent Labour Party (ILP); and he corresponded with the ILP's Ramsay MacDonald, as well as with members of the government, including Prime Minister Campbell-Bannerman. Known at the university as 'a genuine enthusiast in the cause of the Negroes', most of Omoniyi's student life in Britain and his book were devoted to defending the interests of Africans throughout the British Empire. As a result, like many who would follow him, he was seen as a trouble-maker by the Colonial Office, and official indifference probably contributed to his early death at the age of twenty-eight from beri-beri, following brief imprisonment in Brazil.[46]

Bandele Omoniyi

ETHIOPIANISM

Ethiopianism, another name for early Pan-Africanism, was popular amongst African and Caribbean students in Britain during the first years of the twentieth century. The name 'Ethiopia' was often used as a synonym for Africa. The term 'Ethiopian movement' was used to refer to an independent church movement in parts of Africa in the nineteenth century and to those advocating 'Africa for the Africans'. By 1904 there was an Ethiopian Association in Edinburgh and in Liverpool in the same year the Ethiopian Progressive Association (EPA) was founded 'by West African and West Indian natives, students at the various colleges', although its constitution shows that at least two of its founding members were physicians and one member, C. Bartels-Kodwo, was based in Cornwall.[47] The EPA published at least one edition of a journal, *The Ethiopian Review*, and its president, Isaac Augustus Johnson from Sierra Leone, and secretary, Kwesi Ewusi from the Gold Coast, were in contact with Booker T. Washington and W. E. B. Du Bois in the United States. The association aimed:

> To create a bond of union between a) all other members of the Ethiopian race at home and abroad, b) to further the interest and raise the social status of the Ethiopian race at home and abroad; and to try to strengthen the friendly relations of the said race and the other races of mankind.[48]

Africans and those from the Caribbean often joined together to further their interests, established organizations that were Pan-African in orientation, as well as creating links with prominent African Americans and their organizations. For example, Moses Da Rocha, another student at Edinburgh, was in correspondence with the African American journalist John Edward Bruce. South African Pixley Seme and African American Alain Locke, who were both students at Oxford, formed an African Unity Society during 1908–9, 'open to all men of African or Negro extraction who are interested in the general welfare of the Race both in Africa and other parts of the world'.[49] As the EPA expressed it, these students were concerned with 'matters of vital importance concerning Africa in particular and the Negro race in general'. They were also concerned with racism and the 'colour bar' in Britain, which was evident at universities such as Edinburgh and Cambridge, but also throughout the country, as the EPA clearly reported.[50]

THE GROWTH OF RACISM?

In this period, and indeed until 1965, there were no laws against racism in Britain. Racism was perfectly legal. It was continually fuelled by the existence of colonial rule. A widespread 'colour bar' was already in existence, which often made in difficult for Black people to find accommodation, as well as employment. In addition, 'foreign' and colonial workers were routinely seen as a threat to the jobs and wages of other workers in Britain and their presence in Britain and marriage to local women were viewed by the state as a threat to the established colonial and racist hierarchy. At the turn of the century some Africans were still being exhibited throughout the country as exotic curiosities from the 'dark continent', such as the 'Savage South Africa' exhibition which toured Britain at that time, the six Congolese Mbuti people brought to Britain and exhibited in 1905, as well as during the Franco-British Exhibition in London in 1908, which contained what was described as a Senegalese 'village'.[51] The use of racist epithets in public was also common, as was the view that Africans and those of African descent were inferior to Europeans. As British publisher and editor W. T. Stead commented on the London Pan-African conference, 'the notion that even black men have rights is no doubt novel to most of us'. As late as 1910 the *Encyclopedia Britannica* declared that 'the Negro would appear to stand on a lower evolutionary plane than the white man'.[52] The insults and other forms of discrimination were well described by Augustus Merriman-Labor (1877–1919), a Sierra Leonean writer and barrister, in his *Britons through Negro Spectacles, or a Negro on Britons with a Description of London*, published in 1910. Merriman-Labor spent fifteen years in London, qualified and was then debarred as a barrister, worked at the Woolwich Arsenal and finally died in Lambeth Workhouse Infirmary in 1919, so he had rich experience on which to draw for his writing. In his book he explained that 'In the lower-class suburbs a black man stands the chance of being laughed to scorn until he takes to his heels ... bad boys will not hesitate to shower stones or rotten eggs at any passing black man ... The so-called fairer sex are no less venomous. White factory girls ... will make fun of you by throwing kisses to you when not making hisses at you, whilst others shout "Go wash your face guv'nor or sometimes call out n——! n——! n——!"'[53]

Several others, including Williams and Omoniyi, wrote about their experiences of racism in Britain and in the colonies. The latter complained that: 'The treatment accorded to Africans in the Nativeland and abroad by the ignorant classes of white men and those who ought to know better generally makes one's blood boil.'[54] Perhaps the most prolific writer on the subject was Dr T. E. S. Scholes (1856–c.1940), a Jamaican who had probably arrived in London as early as 1878 and subsequently studied medicine at Edinburgh University from 1880 to 1884, but may not have practised in Britain.[55] Scholes later became a missionary in Africa, had some connections with the Colwyn Bay Institute and also visited the United States. In 1896 he started to devote himself to writing. One of his books, *Chamberlain and Chamberlainism: His Fiscal Policy and Colonial Policy*, was written under the pseudonym of Bartholemew Smith. His best-known works were: *The British Empire and Alliances: Britain's Duty to her Colonies and Subject Races* (1899) and *Glimpses through the Ages; Or the 'Superior' and 'Inferior' Races, So-Called, Discussed in the Light of Science and History*, published in two lengthy volumes in 1905 and 1908. In the latter work Scholes declared that his purpose was to inquire 'into the circumstances in which the colourless people designate themselves the "superior race" and in which they designate the "coloured races" as inferior races'.[56] It was, therefore, a vindication of Africa's history, as well as a refutation of both racism and colonial rule. Drawing on the history of ancient Egypt, Scholes asserted that the 'Negro has been shown to have been the chief pioneer and founder of European civilization'.[57] However, Scholes went much further and condemned the violence, looting and rape that accompanied the 'new imperialism of the period, whether in Africa or Asia'. He did so by presenting evidence of such crimes in over 800 detailed pages, by quoting from the speeches of imperialists such as Joseph Chamberlain, Britain's Colonial Secretary, and highlighting the everyday racism that he and others experienced in Britain and through-out the colonies. Moreover, Scholes also predicted the likelihood of revolutions, future wars between the imperialist powers, and increasingly strident demands for colonial freedom.[58] He was certainly one of the most notable critics of racism and imperialism in Britain but, like others at that time, he argued for a change of government policy, not the end of colonialism.[59]

It is evident that Scholes was in contact with Williams, Seme and Locke, as well as with the US-based Negro Society for Historical Research. Williams, after his South African sojourn, had also got to know Seme and another South African law student, Alfred Mangena. Mangena, who entered Lincoln's Inn in 1903, later on convened a meeting 'to promote friendly intercourse' and 'mutual help' amongst 'coloured folk' residing in London, and in order to establish a society to work for the 'progress of Africans and the advancement of the interests of Africans' in March 1906.[60] This is more evidence that important Pan-African networks were continually developing amongst those in Britain, as well as between them and those in Africa and throughout the diaspora. Like Williams, Seme, Mangena and others used their legal training to represent those protesting against various colonial abuses in the colonies. Most notable in this regard was Mangena's unsuccessful attempt to stop the execution of those convicted of leading the Bambatha Rebellion and to seek justice for all Africans in South Africa. He was, however, successful later when he sued Sir William Arbuckle, the Agent General of Natal, in the Court of King's Bench. He made legal history in several ways, most notably in becoming the first Black South African barrister. He later represented a South African delegation which included Gandhi that visited Britain in 1909 to petition Parliament.[61] After they left Britain, Seme and Mangena both became founders of the South African Native National Congress, now known as the African National Congress (ANC), alongside another law student, George Montsioa, who had also been a student in Britain, first at the Colwyn Bay Institute and then, from 1906 until 1910, at Lincoln's Inn.[62]

Those students who became professionals often remained in Britain. Dr John Alcindor, for instance, found work in hospitals throughout London before opening his general practice in Paddington around 1907.

Barrister Edward Nelson (1874–1940), originally from British Guiana and a student at Lincoln's Inn until 1904, worked in the legal profession for many years in Manchester and the surrounding area, where he was elected to and served on the local council until 1940.[63] Some faced discrimination, as did Jamaican physician Harold Moody (1882–1947), who was rejected by the Camberwell poor-law guardians on the grounds that 'the fastidious poor would refuse to be attended by a Negro'. Moody went on to establish his own practice in Peckham and would later play a major role in British politics as the founder of the League of Coloured Peoples.[64]

Other former students, like Scholes, maintained their links with Britain in order to publish their work. Two of those whom we met in the previous chapter, Casely Hayford and Sarbah, were particularly successful in this regard, with Casely Hayford using some of his experiences in Britain to write his semi-autobiographical novel *Ethiopia Unbound: Studies in Race Emancipation* (published in London in 1911),[65] and Sarbah publishing both his *Fanti Customary Laws* and then his *Fanti National Constitution* there in 1897 and 1906 respectively.[66] (Such publications were mainly intended for an African readership, although they also aimed to inform colonial officials.) The years immediately before the First World War produced a new kind of publication which can be considered the real start of an African press in Britain – the launch of the *African Times and Orient Review*.

DUSÉ MOHAMED ALI AND THE
AFRICAN TIMES AND ORIENT REVIEW

Dusé Mohamed Ali (1866–1945) claimed to be of Egyptian-Sudanese origin and to have been sent to England in 1875 at a young age to study. He later became a much-travelled actor, in Britain and the United States, as well as a writer and journalist who had visited the Caribbean and even parts of Asia.[67] Ali took small parts in plays throughout Britain and also secured work as a jobbing journalist. From as early as the 1880s he had contributed letters to the press on the 'Egyptian Question', then a topical subject following Britain's armed occupation of the country in 1882, which Ali claimed had led to the death of his father. In 1899 he settled for a time in Hull, working as an actor, docker, journalist and teacher of elocution.[68] He later established his own theatre company and became a theatrical agent.[69] Between 1909 and 1911 he wrote regularly for a new socialist journal, the *New Age*, and began work on his major but often plagiarized book, *In the Land of the Pharaohs*, which was published in 1911.[70]

In 1911 Ali became connected with the first Universal Races Congress held in London. Organized by Gustav Spiller, of the South Place Ethical Society, it purported to be a learned conference discussing the concepts of 'race' and 'races', as they were then understood, and its delegates included W. E. B. Du Bois and Mojola Agbebi, a Baptist minister from Nigeria.[71] Du Bois' visit prompted him to write about the 'thousands of colored people in the city' and to comment that 'London is polite and considerate to its colored brothers. There is color prejudice and aloofness undoubtedly here, but it does not

Dusé Mohamed Ali

parade its shame like New York or its barbarity like New Orleans'.[72] Ali was involved with publicity for the event and entertaining the delegates invited to it, and it seems that it was the event which partly inspired him to launch the journal the *African Times and Orient Review* (*ATOR*), first published in 1912. Ali later wrote, 'the recent Universal Races Congress ... clearly demonstrated that there was ample need for a Pan-Oriental, Pan-African journal at the seat of the British Empire'.[73] The publication of the *ATOR* in July 1912 was eventually a partnership between Ali, who wanted a journal 'dealing with social and political issues in Africa and the Orient at large' and a Sierra Leonean businessman, John Eldred Taylor (c.1880–1924), who desired a publication reflecting his trading interests throughout West Africa and abroad.[74] Most noteworthy was the new publication's cover, designed by the English artist Walter Crane, a leading figure in the Arts and Crafts movement, who modified a motif he had earlier designed for the Universal Races Congress 'to embody the idea of concord between Europe, Asia, and Africa'.[75]

Although the new publication hoped to find support amongst the eminent delegates who had attended the Universal Races Congress, it was clear that it also aimed to speak for and appeal to 'coloured people'. Indeed, in its first edition Samuel Coleridge-Taylor called for it to be 'heartily supported by the coloured people themselves, so that it would be absolutely independent of the whites as regard circulation'.[76] Ali wrote in the first issue:

> As for YOU of the Black race, the Brown race and the Yellow race, this is YOUR VERY OWN JOURNAL [sic]. The more humble you are, the more need you have of us and the more readily shall we extend our sympathy and advice.[77]

This was the beginning of an entirely new kind of publication, one controlled by Africans and promoting African-Asian unity many years before the famous Bandung Conference in 1955. However, the *ATOR* was immediately in need of financial support and, after a rapid takeover, backing was soon in the hands of a consortium of influential West African entrepreneurs, doctors and lawyers, many of whom, like Joseph Casely Hayford, were campaigning against the most blatant injustices of colonial rule.

The *ATOR* was published on a monthly basis from 1912 to 1918 and then was revived as the *Africa and Orient Review (AOR)* throughout 1920. For five months in 1914 it was published on a weekly basis, a remarkable achievement, before publication was suspended during the war until January 1917. Much of its coverage was of events in West Africa, but it also covered other colonies, as well as the United States, Turkey and Japan. It was particularly eager to highlight injustices in the colonies, such as the public flogging of two Nigerians for failure to prostrate themselves before a British colonial official, a story which featured in the first edition. Ali initiated a campaign to stop such practices, questions were raised in Parliament and he wrote an open letter to the Colonial Secretary on the subject, a ploy that would be adopted by other anti-colonial campaigners in Britain. Although it pointed out colonial and other abuses, the *ATOR* promoted both universal brotherhood and the view that the British Empire should be supported, but at the same time reformed. Ali could also be critical of what he referred to as a current 'super-colour prejudice in Britain', and nostalgic for the Victorian era when, he claimed, 'there was no colour bar'.[78]

Ali was regarded by leading figures in the Colonial Office as a 'notorious disseminator of sedition and lies ... a strong supporter of "Pan-Ethiopianism" or "Africa for the Africans"'. His political stance and links with the Jamaican Pan-Africanist, Marcus Garvey, were viewed apprehensively by the authorities and the *ATOR* was regularly monitored by the Colonial Office, MI5 and the Special Branch of the Metropolitan Police. Ali was also a strong supporter of Pan-Islamist causes and his fellow Muslims throughout the world, whether in the Balkans, India or Britain. His support for the Ottoman Empire only caused still greater concern to the security services. Even though he remained essentially loyal to the British Empire, during the First World War he was placed under surveillance and the *African Times and Orient Review* was banned in British colonies.[79]

The *ATOR* was distributed internationally, throughout Africa, the American continent, parts of Asia, and even on steamships, and in Britain by professional distributors including WH Smith & Sons. Its notable contributors included Du Bois, Garvey, Coleridge-Taylor, Booker T. Washington, Annie Besant and John Edward Bruce. Garvey worked at the *ATOR*'s office in London's Fleet Street as a messenger while he was in Britain in 1913. The *African Times and Orient Review* featured a regular women's page and showed itself to be supportive of the movement for women's suffrage. The *ATOR* also inaugurated the first international beauty contest specifically for women of African origin in 1920, offering a prize of £100 for the 'most beautiful coloured woman in the world', and a prize for the photographer of the winning entry. The *AOR* folded before the winners could be announced, but twelve photographs of entrants were published, about a third of them from Britain.[80]

Dusé Mohamed Ali left Britain for the United States in 1921 but he and the *African Times and Orient Review* had certainly made their mark. He can be credited with launching and sustaining a publication which spoke to and for 'coloured people' and in particular for Africans. Ali and the *ATOR* were particularly well known in West Africa and amongst West Africans in Britain. They provided both a focus and a meeting place. Ali also acted as a guardian for some young Africans visiting Britain, an adviser on appropriate schools and accommodation, and many visitors stayed with him and his wife in their home in Clapham. He kept in contact with all the main African, Asian and Muslim organizations in the country, as well as with many significant individuals and organizations throughout the world.[81]

AFRICAN STUDENTS START TO ORGANIZE

Just before the outbreak of war, there were several attempts by Africans resident in Britain, both students and others, to organize themselves into a political force, stirred by such indignities as the announcement by London University Graduates' Club in 1914 that it would operate a colour bar so Africans would be ineligible for membership. British commercial and humanitarian interests, represented by such organizations as the African Society and the Anti-Slavery and Aborigines' Rights Protection Society (ASARPS), were alarmed at the development of Ethiopianism, especially after the 1906 rebellion against the colonial authorities in South Africa. They were worried that racism and the colour bar in Britain might provoke anti-British feelings amongst African students and visitors, which they would then transmit to their compatriots in Africa. They were also concerned that African students might follow in the footsteps of Indian students, who had formed the Indian Home Rule Society in 1905. In 1909, one member of that society, Madan Lal Dhingra, assassinated Sir William Curzon Wyllie, an assistant to the Secretary of State for India, despite police surveillance. Sir Harry Johnston and other imperialists therefore saw the need to 'foster a more sympathetic spirit', and 'to remove certain social disabilities', as they expressed it, in order that anti-colonial sentiments might be extinguished and the British Empire preserved. Various schemes were suggested: a 'Universal Races Club' for example, or some other way of bringing African students into contact with 'the better side of British life'. The aim of these 'well-wishers', such as ASARPS, to shield African students from untoward or subversive influences, remained a major goal for government, religious and humanitarian organizations throughout the colonial period. However, this goal was pursued in the face of the colonial system, as well as other forms of state racism and from these it was impossible to shield the students.[82]

In 1912, after consultation with the Colonial Office, the ASARPS and the African Society began to plan for a conference of all African students in the country, to discuss how to deal with the colour bar, even though African students had already begun to organize themselves independently. The aim was to establish accommodation and a meeting place for students in London, so as to keep them away from what were viewed as 'the worst influences of our modern civilisation', and to encourage loyalty to the empire. The 'Conference for Africans', held in April 1913, included only about forty Africans, and of those most were professionals rather than students, or older male residents such as Dusé Mohamed Ali. Many examples of the colour bar were discussed, as well as the organizers' fears about sexual relationships between African men and British women. Initially there was some support for the idea of hostels, or residential clubs, but those at the meeting gradually turned against the idea, as it became clear that this would lead to increasing governmental control of Africans' lives. In the *African Times and Oriental Review*, the proposed hostel was unflatteringly described as 'a sort of rounding up place for West Africans'.[83]

In this way, on the eve of the Great War, the stage was set for the confrontations which would continue until the 1950s. The idea of a student hostel was at the heart of the matter, for who would assume control of it: the students themselves, the Colonial Office, or those posing as humanitarians? African attitudes would undergo a radical change as a result of the war years, the international demands for self-determination and the racist violence which broke out in many British cities after the war. Increasingly, after 1918, African students realized that in order to attempt to change conditions in Britain and West Africa, they had to become more proactive. They would need allies, but at the same time it was imperative that they should seek to preserve their independence and self-reliance.

Even during the war, African students began to form new organizations. The first of these was the African Students' Union, founded in December 1916, primarily as a social organization. The founding president was E. S. Beoku-Betts, a Sierra Leonean law student at the Middle Temple. In August 1917, the *African Times and Orient Review* published Beoku-Betts' presidential address to what was now referred to as the African Students' Union of Great Britain and Ireland, although the union does not seem to have lasted for long, and probably ceased its activities when its president returned to Africa later that year.

The West African Christian Union was also formed in 1916 by the Nigerian Oladipo Lahanmi. It soon collapsed but was re-launched under the auspices of the Student Christian Movement (SCM) 'as a joint union of West African and West Indian students', becoming known as the Union of Students of African Descent (USAD). According to the SCM, the new union devoted 'a good deal of time to the consideration of race and colour questions', and its members exhibited 'some rather undefined bitterness on the score of exploitation and bad government at home'. These organizations often achieved very little and it was not until 1918 that an organization was founded with a much broader membership.[84]

THE FIRST WORLD WAR

The Great War can be said to have started in Africa on the 12 August 1914, in what was then the German colony of Togoland (now comprising both Togo and Ghana) in West Africa. The first shot fired by a 'British soldier' was by Sergeant-Major Alhaji Grunshi, one of more than 7,000 men in the Gold Coast Regiment of the West African Frontier Force, after the British invasion of Togoland.[85] There is also evidence that some of the last shots during the war were fired in Africa, in the British colony of Northern Rhodesia (present-day Zambia) on 13 November 1918, but it took another twelve days for German troops to surrender on 25 November. The war was a global conflict, but it has all too often been portrayed as one that only occurred in Europe and only involved Europeans.[86] The involvement of Africa and Africans highlights something else of importance – the war was principally one fought between the major powers for geopolitical advantage; indeed, for a redivision of the world in their interests. When the war ended, Germany's colonies in Africa, such as Kamerun (Cameroon), Togoland and Tanganyika, became spoils of war divided between the victors, France and Britain, with repercussions that are still felt today. Africans' opinions were not consulted on this, nor on the fact that the wealth of the colonies was harnessed for the imperial war effort.

There was much opposition and several rebellions against African involvement in the First World War, most notably that led by Reverend John Chilembwe in the British colony of Nyasaland in 1915. Chilembwe had objected to various aspects of colonial rule even before 1914, but he became particularly opposed to the forced conscription of more than 200,000 African men as porters, many of whom were later wounded or killed. Soon after the outbreak of war Chilembwe wrote in a local newspaper:

> We understand that we have been invited to shed our innocent blood in this world's war which is now in progress throughout the wide world. On the commencement of the war we understood that it was said indirectly that Africa had nothing to do with the civilized war. But now we find that the poor African has already been plunged into the great war.

A number of our people have already shed their blood while others are
crippled for life . . .

Let the rich men, bankers, titled men, shopkeepers, farmers and
landlords go to war and get shot. Instead the poor Africans who have
nothing to own in the present world, who in death, leave only a long
line of widows and orphans in utter want and dire distress are invited
to die for a cause that is not theirs.[87]

However, this anti-colonial rebellion was rapidly suppressed by the
colonial authorities. Chilembwe was killed and more than forty other
participants executed.

Nevertheless, despite the inter-imperialist nature of the conflict,
thousands of African and other colonial troops volunteered, or were
conscripted into Britain's armed forces. About 55,000 Africans served
as soldiers and hundreds of thousands of men and women served as
auxiliaries, or porters. More than 10,000 lost their lives and the first
was probably an African, one Private Bai of the Gold Coast regiment,
who lost his life on 15 August 1914.[88] Some Africans within the
empire clearly believed that the war offered an opportunity to counter
prevailing Eurocentric views about their inferiority (and that of other
colonial subjects). Others may have enlisted out of a sense of patriotism, particularly following George V's appeal to the empire in 1915,
or for adventure, or from a variety of motives.[89] Conscription was
widespread in Africa, but also existed in the Caribbean and Canada,
as well as in Britain.

Those in the Caribbean were directly recruited into the British West
Indies Regiment (BWIR) formed in 1915, and some served as combat
troops in Africa and Palestine. The BWIR was only established after
several protests about the exclusion of recruits from the Caribbean.
All the men received basic military training at Seaford, in Sussex.
There they were poorly housed and many hospitalized as a result of
the dreadful conditions they were subjected to there. Nearly 300 men
were subsequently dismissed because of frostbite and nineteen died
from that condition.[90] Poor conditions and lack of pay led to a strike
at Seaford in October 1915, and several of the ringleaders were repatriated to the Caribbean.[91] In 1916 another 600 Jamaicans suffered
from exposure and frostbite caused by freezing conditions while on

their way to Europe by ship. Five died and more than a hundred were forced to have limbs amputated.[92] More than a thousand of the 10,000 troops in the BWIR that left the Caribbean never returned; they died in action or as a result of illness. The poor treatment and lower pay given to soldiers of the BWIR, as well as the racism they suffered, led to a mutiny by some troops in Taranto, Italy, in 1918.[93]

Colonial troops might be deployed in combat in Africa and Palestine, but there was resistance to their deployment in Europe to fight against Europeans. When the BWIR was deployed in Europe, it was mainly as auxiliaries, although sometimes they were on the front lines. The British attitude differed from that of the French, who did use Africans as combat troops in Europe, and was largely based on racism and the view that Africans should not be armed to fight against Europeans. Before the outbreak of war Brigadier-General Sir James Willcocks, a leading British military figure, had explained his approach to Black troops: 'it is always judicious . . . never to give the black man an idea that you seek his assistance against other white men'.[94] In 1902 the Committee of Imperial Defence had issued a memorandum stating that the 'main burden of a great struggle between the British Empire and one or more states of European race or descent must be borne by white subjects of the king', adding, 'military contingents therefore of other than men of European descent need not be considered'.[95]

However, as the war became more prolonged, regiments from Bermuda, Mauritius and South Africa became involved, as well as Black Canadian troops led by white officers, who arrived in Britain on their way to serve in non-combat roles in Europe. Canada established a Black 'construction battalion' based in Nova Scotia, although a few Black Canadians also managed to join regular army regiments. South African troops were also deployed within Africa, but more than 20,000 in the South African Native Labour Contingent served in Europe, often in the worst conditions and required to perform various types of manual labour. They suffered the greatest single loss of lives when the troopship SS *Mendi* was accidentally rammed in the English Channel in January 1917, with the resulting loss of more than 600 men, including many of the ship's crew.[96]

Some of those in the colonies stowed away on ships, or found other ways to make the hazardous journey to Britain, and sought to enlist directly in the British armed forces.[97] One of these was Lionel Turpin from British Guiana, the father of the famous boxer Randolph Turpin, who joined the Royal Warwickshire Regiment, almost lost his life after being gassed in France, and after the war died prematurely in 1928.[98] Others from the Caribbean found that they were rejected, even after the journey to Britain, but might eventually be admitted to the BWIR. Some men of Caribbean heritage born, or long resident, in Britain were only admitted to the BWIR, rather than regular regiments in the British Army. Such was the fate of Private Francis, who was described as 'a coloured man who worked in the shipyard at Liverpool'.[99] Some of those who served in the BWIR were buried in graves in Britain, suggesting that they and their families were residents in the country at the time.[100]

Evidently racist attitudes, from the government downwards, often existed towards the recruitment of 'coloured volunteers' in Britain but there was no clear policy to exclude their enlistment.[101] There is one example of a policy of outright segregation. In 1916 a Royal Engineers Coloured Section was established to which many seafarers in Britain's port cities were consigned.[102] Government departments and the Manual of Military Law (1914) permitted enlistment by 'any Negro or person of colour', as long as 'British subjects' outnumbered such 'aliens' by fifty to one. However, a 'person of colour' was not permitted to become an officer.[103] The policy was clarified in 1918, when the Army Council 'decided that British subjects of colour may be enlisted into combatant or other units of the British Army' provided that there were no problems in regard to language or food.[104] However, the Army Council privately made it clear to colonial governors that 'it is not considered desirable to post coloureds to regular British units'.[105]

Recruitment in Britain, it seems, was largely down to the whim of the recruiting officer and might be based on how dark-skinned or light-skinned a potential recruit was. Two Jamaicans, Roy and Norman Washington Manley, who were students in Britain at the time, were evidently acceptable. Both served in France, where 21-year-old Roy was killed in action. Norman later wrote bitterly of the 'violent colour prejudice' he faced as a soldier in the Field Artillery in France.[106] Other Caribbean recruits were featured in the press of the time. Several newspapers carried articles, and there are even photos of a Jamaican recruit in the Staffordshire Regiment, while the *Daily Mirror* showed a picture of one Edward Jones, a Barbadian recruit to the Cheshire Regiment, in Trafalgar Square.[107] However, in some places it was difficult for 'men of colour' to enlist. There are numerous examples from Cardiff, where significant numbers of African and Caribbean men resided.[108]

The latest research not only shows that Black people in Britain participated in the war, often in much the same way as other volunteers, but also tells us something about the lives and families of those involved. Some of the most important information has been passed down through families, or been discovered through a photo found by chance showing an unknown 'Black Tommy' or, in one case, through the diary and memorabilia of one of those who served, which was also found completely by accident.[109]

Arthur William David Roberts (1897–1982) had left his history in a cardboard box in an attic and it was only found in 2012, twenty years after his death. He was born in Bristol to a Caribbean father who was a ship's steward and an English mother. As a child he moved to Glasgow with his father and was educated in that city. He later became a marine engineer. As a volunteer, in February 1917, he joined the King's Own Scottish Borderers and then the Royal Scots Fusiliers and thus became one of the few Black soldiers to see front-line action in a Scottish regiment and the only one to have left his memoirs, a diary, as well as sketches and even some photos of his experiences.[110] These experiences ranged from the mud, trenches, barbed wire, gas, shelling, dysentery and no-man's-land of Flanders, to the Battle of Ypres and French brothels. Although he wrote of 'my own poor efforts as a scribbler', his writing is often moving. He wrote fatalistically of death in the trenches:

> As we plunged on, one of our section who was walking at my left shoulder suddenly collapsed with a groan. A splinter had struck him in the abdomen. Some stretcher bearers were following our party but before they came up the poor chap had expired ... Strict orders had been issued before the battle that nobody but stretcher bearers were to stop for the wounded ... We therefore after a sympathetic glance pushed on, besides it might be anybody's turn next.[111]

On his own survival he commented:

> What a night last night. We were shelled to blazes. I had a very narrow shave. One fellow in front of me had his head blew off. The chap beside him was severely wounded. The chap next to me was wounded and one of the chaps behind him was killed and the fellow beside him was wounded. I completely escaped. That was everyone round me were either killed or wounded. We lost about a dozen all told. We moved forward this morning.[112]

Roberts was just one of the soldiers originating from a British port city. Research in Liverpool has uncovered the story of Marcus Bailey, who served in the Royal Navy, and Walter Colebourne, who joined the King's Liverpool Regiment and was killed in action at the Battle of the Somme in 1916. Ernest Marke and Tommy Macauley, who both originated from Sierra Leone, also volunteered for the army in Liverpool, but were fortunate that the war ended after their basic training.[113] Liverpool-born Albert James, whose father was a sailor from Bermuda, left behind his infant son to serve in the Royal Field Artillery in Egypt and Palestine, while his brother William served in the Merchant Navy.[114]

THE BLACK BATTALION
AND OTHER WARTIME ROLES

In Cardiff there were proposals to establish what was at different times referred to as a 'battalion of dark-skinned Britishers', 'a 'coloured race battalion', a 'Black Battalion', or, as it was called in a poem, a 'coloured brigade', in part because local Black volunteers had previously been rejected by the recruiting sergeant.[115] In 1914 it had been reported that eager volunteers from Jamaica and Barbados who tried to join the Welsh Guards had been turned away. One commented that he would go to France because there 'they are taking the blacks as well as the whites'.[116] In May 1915, 'about thirty stalwart coloured men ... anxious to join the army' were interviewed by the chief recruiting officer, after initial authorization from the War Office.[117] Locals had promised that 'a thousand would rally to the colours' from Cardiff, Barry, Port Talbot and Swansea, if the War Office approved the proposal for a special battalion. It seems that long-established Black residents of Cardiff, such as Edward Wiltshire and Harry O'Connell, supported the proposal and some may even have initiated it.[118] Wiltshire, a Barbadian who had been in Cardiff for nearly forty years, complained that hundreds of volunteers in Cardiff had been told 'we have no room for black men in the Army'. He believed that elsewhere Black men had been recruited and gave the example of three who had enlisted in the Welsh Guards. He concluded a press interview by indignantly asserting 'we are as much Britishers as the Ghurkhas or the colonials'.[119] According to one press report, as many as fifty Black volunteers from various ports, frustrated at the delay in forming the 'coloured battalion', successfully enlisted in the Durham Light Infantry instead.[120]

The most enthusiastic recruiter for such a battalion was Edward Tupper of the National Sailors' and Firemen's Union (NSFU).[121] He envisaged that the battalion would recruit men from all the ports including London, Liverpool and North and South Shields. However, James Henson, a union official from Bristol, suggested that after fighting to safeguard Cardiff from German conquest, the shipowners would be more likely to provide the seafarers with better wages than the army or the navy.[122] In October 1915 Tupper announced that the ban on recruitment had been lifted, as men were no longer required by the 'merchant service'. He declared that the Admiralty had authorized him to recruit 'all coloured men willing to serve the country', that men could even be directly recruited at the offices of the Seamen's Union.[123] Tupper soon claimed to have recruits from Cardiff, Newport, Liverpool and London and even suggested that a second battalion could soon be formed.[124] But no battalion ever seems to have materialized, perhaps because of continued opposition from the Admiralty.[125] Tupper subsequently announced that he still had the names of '1500 coloured Britishers who offered to serve', a clear indication that their offers had not been accepted.[126] When nine stowaways from Barbados appeared in court in east London in May 1915, claiming that they came to enlist, the magistrate ordered that they be sent to Cardiff in the care of the West India Committee to join the 'coloured battalion'.[127]

Others volunteered in towns and cities throughout the country.

Lionel Turpin, a nineteen-year-old former seaman from British Guiana, was living in North Shields when he enlisted in the York and Lancashire Regiment in 1915. He served in France and was wounded and gassed during his four years of service. Invalided out of the army, he settled in Leamington Spa, worked in a foundry and married a local woman, but died in 1929 from his wartime injuries. Turpin was the father of the well-known boxers Randolph, Jackie and Dick, as well as two daughters.[128] Richard Dickie Barr (1888–1955) was born in Cornwall, but his miner father was of African origin. He appears to have worked as a steward in the merchant fleet before he joined the Royal Naval Volunteer Reserve at the outbreak of the war. Eventually he fought with the Royal Navy Division and saw action at Gallipoli and in France, where he was wounded. After the war Barr returned to Cornwall and worked as a builder's labourer.[129]

Several men enlisted in London, such as Henry Solomon from West Africa, a former pupil at St Paul's School. Harold Brown from east London, the son of a Jamaican seaman and an English mother, served in the Royal West Surrey Regiment and was awarded the Military Medal for his bravery. Brown subsequently worked as a seaman and docker.[130] John Williams, who enlisted in 1914, was awarded the Distinguished Conduct Medal, the Military Medal and French Légion d'honneur. The *African Telegraph* referred to him 'the man whom white soldiers call "The Black V.C."', since he was said to have single-handedly killed four German officers disguised as spies, 'which would earn any European the V.C.' However, Williams was not awarded the Victoria Cross.[131]

Those who served also included Joe Clough (1887–1977), a Jamaican, who was a London bus driver who had been resident in Britain since 1903. Married, and with two children, he volunteered for the Royal Army Service Corps in 1915 and drove a field ambulance in France for four years. This was despite the racist view of those at the War Office who declared that, 'neither women nor coloured troops could be used in Field Ambulances', because 'strength, coolness and courage, in addition to training, are required'. After the war Clough settled in Bedford and continued to drive buses and taxis.[132] The number of Black soldiers in London led to the establishment of their own club in Drury Lane, which was visited by the Jamaican writer Claude McKay and described in his memoirs and several articles. He recalled 'a host of coloured soldiers', including those 'from the West Indies and Africa, with a few coloured Americans, East Indians and Egyptians amongst them'.[133]

Others with an African heritage who served included J. Egerton Shyngle, the son of a Nigerian father and an English mother; Patrick Freeman from Sierra Leone, who first joined the French Navy and then the British Army; as well as Bob Collier and George Williams, the latter of whom was twice wounded and gassed in France.[134] Brighton-born Frank Dove, son of a lawyer from Sierra Leone, joined the Royal Tank Regiment straight from Oxford University, where he had studied law, and was later awarded the Military Medal for his bravery at the Battle of Cambrai in France in 1917. In 1918 Dove joined the RAF, later became a successful lawyer and went on to box for Britain at the 1920 Olympics.[135] Other African students who enlisted included Nigerians Eugene and John Brown, who both joined the 5th North Staffordshire Regiment. The former of the two was killed in action.[136]

Frederick Njilima, from what was then Nyasaland (today Malawi), was attempting to gain admission to Cambridge University when war broke out. His father had been hanged by the colonial authorities as one of the leaders of the 1915 rebellion in Nyasaland. Njilima was apparently told by the former Bishop of Nyasaland that to enhance his chances of admission to higher education he must 'purge his father's offence' and 'enlist in the British army'. According to his own account, while waiting for admission he 'was struck by war fever. I decided to join the white war', and he added, 'because I am a brave man and for fun.' Whatever his exact reason, he enlisted in the Irish Rifles, trained in Nottingham and then transferred to the Machine Gun Corps, apparently under the name of Frederick Gresham. Wounded in action in France, he was awarded the Military Medal and a disability pension after the war.[137]

Another soldier who made a substantial contribution during the First World War and to soldiers more generally via his support of the British Legion was the twenty-four-year-old George Roberts (1891–1970), a Trinidadian who enlisted in the Middlesex Regiment in 1915 and became perhaps the first Black sergeant in the British Army. He saw action in the famous battles on the Somme and in the Dardanelles and was used by the military to recruit more men from Trinidad. After the war Roberts became one of the earliest members of the British

Legion, and led thousands of ex-servicemen in a march to Parliament to demand their rights and appropriate pensions for their service. Their route across Westminster Bridge was blocked by police who attacked them with truncheons, but the veterans fought back and continued their protest. According to George Roberts' own account, this 'militant action' and the 'Battle of Westminster Bridge' played 'a great part in unifying the various ex-Service organizations into the British Legion and bringing nation-wide pressure to bear on the Government'. Roberts remained in Britain for the rest of his life, working as an electrician, and he was a leading member of the British Legion for many years. In 1931 he was to become one of the founding members of the League of Coloured Peoples.[138]

The sporting triumphs of 'coloured soldiers' were also acclaimed at the time, as several news reports attest. A Private Steuart of the Shropshire Light Infantry, a public-school boy 'belonging, we believe to the West Indies' was reported to have won a cross-country race at Aldershot held for soldiers of Kitchener's army in 1915, in the presence of the king and other members of the royal family.[139] Private 'Darkie' Duncan of the Welsh Guards, 'a typical Negro of the West Indies, born in Jamaica', won a middleweight boxing championship held at Caterham Barracks, Surrey, in 1915. Duncan, a former docker, had enlisted in Cardiff, proof that some Black soldiers could enlist in the area. Asked about the origin of his pugilistic skill he is reported to have replied, 'You have to do a bit of it at Cardiff, or you go under.' Of Duncan it was said that there was 'no man more popular' at Caterham.[140]

Those in uniform might still face racism, as is clear from a case reported in the *Liverpool Echo* in 1915 concerning Private Frank Nelson. Described as 'a black soldier in the King's Liverpool Regiment', Nelson was abused by a drunk who was initially sentenced to prison for his actions but subsequently successfully appealed against his conviction.[141] Others, such as the Jamaican James Slim, who had joined the elite Coldstream Guards in France, seem to have been dismissed from that regiment due to racism.[142] Another man, Obadiah Coles, whose previous employment was as an actor in Nottingham, used racism as his defence when charged with being an absentee from military service in 1917. He simply stated that all recruiting officers had rejected him because of his colour.[143]

Officers

Although Walter Tull has often been credited as the first and only soldier not of 'pure European descent' to become an officer during the war,
there are several other examples. Unlike Tull, they came from privileged
backgrounds. George Bemand (1892–1916) came from a wealthy
Jamaican and English family and was educated at Dulwich College in
London. He applied for a temporary commission in the Royal Field
Artillery, appears to have lied about his Jamaican background and,
although described as 'dusky', was recruited as a second lieutenant.
Bemand was killed in action in France in 1916, like his younger brother,
who was killed in 1917 fighting for the same regiment.[144] John Smyth
was the son of a clergyman from Sierra Leone and his English wife.
Brought up in London, he was given a commission in the Royal West
Kent Regiment in 1914 and in 1916 became a second lieutenant in the
Machine Gun Corps. He was killed in action in June 1918.[145] Both
Bemand and Smythe were commissioned as officers before Walter Tull.

Another who became an officer was Reginald Collins, who was
born in Jamaica in 1894. He clearly stated that he was not of 'pure
European descent' when, at the outbreak of war, he travelled to England to join the Royal Fusiliers and subsequently served in France. He
was approved for officer training in Oxford and applied to join the
British West Indies Regiment. Although his request was initially
denied, 'owing to his colour', he was eventually appointed second
lieutenant in the BWIR in 1917 and served in Egypt, Palestine and
Italy before returning to Jamaica at the end of the war.[146] David Louis
Clemetson was a Jamaican of mixed heritage born in Port Maria in
1893. He was partly educated in Bristol and was studying law at Trinity College, Cambridge, when he volunteered for the Royal Fusiliers
in 1914, also openly stating that he was 'not of pure European descent'.[147] He was wounded in Salonica and while he was being
evacuated to Britain suffering from shell shock, his ship was torpedoed and sunk. Clemetson survived and, after being hospitalized in
Scotland, was subsequently commissioned as second lieutenant in the
24th Welsh Regiment in October 1915, several months before Walter
Tull, and was later promoted to lieutenant. He was killed in action in
Péronne, France, in September 1918.[148]

Medics

Those who were qualified as doctors were entitled to a commission when they joined the Royal Army Medical Corps (RAMC), but some doctors of African heritage were refused admission, or the rank of officer to which they were entitled.[149] Even G. O. Rushdie-Gray, the Jamaican government veterinary officer who had also served as a vet to the West India Regiment, and was sent to Britain with the support of the Jamaican government, was refused a commission in the Army Veterinary Corps on openly racist grounds.[150] Dr Ernest Jenner Wright (1892–1955), the son of a Sierra Leonean lawyer and an English mother, was born and educated in Britain, but rejected by the RAMC and told to 'go home' to Sierra Leone, where he subsequently served in the inferior position of Native Medical Officer. Dr M. C. F. Easmon, also of Sierra Leonean heritage, suffered a similar fate when he was initially rejected for the West African Medical Service, even though he had been educated in London and his father, Dr John Easmon, had been Chief Medical Officer in the Gold Coast. Easmon continued to campaign against such discrimination in West Africa for many years. When war commenced, he was awarded 'an ungazetted rank of temporary lieutenant and served in the Cameroons campaign for nine months'.[151] In similar fashion, Dr James Jackson Brown was only offered the rank of Warrant Officer by the RAMC rather than the commission he was entitled to.[152]

Others were more fortunate. Dr James Risien Russell (1863–1939) was born in British Guiana, the son of a Scottish plantation owner and a Guyanese woman. He was educated in Scotland and studied medicine at Edinburgh University, as well as in Berlin and Paris. He became a leading neurologist and as early as 1908 was awarded a commission in the RAMC, where he served until 1918. Following the war Dr Risien Russell had a distinguished career, becoming a professor of clinical medicine and serving at the National Hospital and University College Hospital, London.[153] Dr J. McDowall from St Vincent was also given a commission when he enlisted in Britain in November 1917. Subsequently transferred to Ambulance Transport as a captain, he was rejected for the position by his commanding officer, who wrote to the Surgeon-General, demanding the transfer of the 'West Indian Negro' whose presence was resented in the wards.[154]

Munitions Workers

There are also reports of the welcome that some Black men received in Britain, where they were often seen as a novelty, especially by the press. Most importantly, those from the colonies gained new experiences and formed new views about Britain and the British. In 1915, Aubrey Williams, a Trinidadian, wrote of all the wonders that he had seen in England, including underground trains. He concluded, 'I have been so lucky that a white lady has adopted me and the life I am living is too grand to describe.'[155] A Jamaican, Charles Bryan, is reported to have married and had a child with an English woman, whilst he was working at an ordnance factory in Sheffield.

Relationships between African and Caribbean war workers and local women boomed during the war. In 1917 it was reported in the press that the influx of war workers from West Africa in the docks and factories in east London had led to an 'epidemic' of more than a hundred weddings between them and local women. An 'income of £10 to £12 a week' was reported to be an 'attraction to a girl of humble birth', as well as the buying of presents for such 'sweethearts' and their parents. One young woman, it was alleged, had 'renounced a private in a London regiment and transferred her heart to a Negro', whom she had married within three weeks of first meeting him. A local clergyman, who 'deplored' such marriages, stated that 'the real attraction is the money which the Negroes are able to command in munition factories throughout the country', and lamented that his warnings had gone unheeded.[156] Sensational nationwide reporting of such issues no doubt had a negative influence and, in some areas such as east London, led to racist attacks. Relationships between the BWIR and local women appear to have prompted preventive measures by the army, which restricted the movement of these soldiers in such towns as Plymouth.[157] Women also worked producing munitions and, as press reports make clear, it was likely to have been a source of employment for many workers of African and Caribbean heritage as well, especially in such cities as London and Manchester.[158]

Seafarers

Many years ago, Peter Fryer wrote of the huge sacrifice made by 'black seamen' during the war, reporting that from Cardiff alone, a thousand were killed at sea and another 400 'rescued after their ships were sunk, went back to the port, to die of exposure'. In fact, the original newspaper report Fryer cited refers to more than 'seventeen hundred ... sailing out of Cardiff and South Shields [who] had been lost to enemy action', although the figures also included 'Hindoos, Malays, Somalis, Arabs etc'.[159] Contemporary reports suggest that about 700 Yemeni seamen from South Shields lost their lives.[160] Historian Edward Scobie quoted a Cardiff-based clergyman who commented on the fact that submarine warfare had 'turned the sea into a sailors' grave'. In those circumstances, he reported, the authorities 'transferred two hundred men from the coloured troops in Mesopotamia to work in the Merchant Navy ... It was a time of national crisis; and they were jolly brave, these coloured sailors. They brought food to Cardiff at the greatest risk of their lives.'[161]

Yet, surprisingly, very little has subsequently been written about the role and fate of such seafarers, who were such an important part of Britain's African and Caribbean population and vital to the wartime economy, until the centenary of the First World War provoked new interest in 2014. Somali, West African and Caribbean seafarers shipped out of British ports such as Liverpool, Glasgow, Southampton, South Shields and Cardiff, as well as African and Caribbean ones, and many gave their lives as merchant shipping was attacked by German ships and submarines There are well over a thousand wrecks from the First World War around the coast of Britain alone. Ernest Marke, a fourteen-year-old stowaway from Sierra Leone at the time, vividly described two such encounters with submarines, one of which sank his ship, in his autobiography.[162] The latest research has indicated that the Butetown (Tiger Bay) area of Cardiff alone lost about 100 African and Caribbean merchant seamen.[163]

African and Caribbean seafarers served in both the Royal Navy and the Merchant Navy during the war. The best-documented and -photographed is Marcus Bailey (1883–1927), a Barbadian who left his homeland in 1902 and for several years worked in the Merchant

Navy, as well as on board fishing vessels based in Hull, Grimsby and Fleetwood, before he volunteered for the Royal Navy and joined HMS *Chester* in 1916. He had already qualified as a mate, married and, by the end of the war, had a young family. It seems likely that he served during the Battle of Jutland and survived, while many of his crewmates were killed or wounded. After the war, he continued to work at sea, but died at a relatively young age.[164] Another seaman, a nineteen-year-old Trinidadian, Louis Anchoy, was recruited to the Northumberland Fusiliers in Newcastle in November 1914, but dismissed for health reasons a month later. He returned to serve in the Merchant Navy and sadly died of a heart condition in 1918.[165]

Several men already resident in Britain joined the navy. Barbados-born Lewis Walcott lived in London and joined the Royal Navy as a stoker in 1906. In 1914 he was conscripted to serve in the Royal Naval Division, a light infantry unit comprising Royal Navy and Royal Marine reservists and volunteers. He was wounded during the Gallipoli campaign but during the war he was again employed as a stoker on Royal Navy ships. Decorated for his wartime duties, it seems likely that he returned to live in London after the war. Walter Moore, a mechanical engineer probably born in Trinidad, enlisted in the Royal Naval Division and also saw action at Gallipoli and at the Battle of the Somme before being transferred to the BWIR, where he was promoted to sergeant. After the war he returned to Trinidad. George Reeves was a Sierra Leone-born stoker or fireman based in Hull who enlisted in the navy in 1917. Transferred to the Royal Naval Division, he saw action in the trenches in France before being demobbed in 1919. He then became a merchant seaman and later served on convoys during the Battle of the Atlantic in the Second World War.[166]

Many other West African seamen were lost when two passenger liners were torpedoed by German submarines off the coast of Wales, and recent research has provided names and details for some of these human losses. SS *Falaba* was sunk in 1915, one of the first passenger ships to be attacked, resulting in the deaths of more than a hundred passengers and crew. The SS *Apapa* was sunk in 1917, with the loss of more than seventy passengers and crew. The racist thinking of the time considered that Black seafarers were generally only fit for intense physical labour in the worst working conditions. West African seamen were therefore generally employed as firemen and trimmers in the ships' engine rooms and were often the most vulnerable to enemy torpedoes. At least ten of the crew members of SS *Falaba* who died were based in Liverpool, but had been born in Africa or the Caribbean, most of them from Sierra Leone. Another ten men from Sierra Leone and Nigeria were lost on the SS *Apapa*. Most resided in Liverpool and one, John Thomas, had an English wife. Both ships belonged to the Elder Dempster Company that operated between Liverpool and West Africa, and employed many West African seamen. Throughout the duration of the war the company lost more than forty ships and approximately 140 Black seafarers.[167] Another ten West African seamen were drowned with the sinking of the troop carrier SS *Mendi* in 1917.[168]

African and other non-European seafarers were generally paid less than white British crews, especially if they were recruited outside Britain, and often were not even recognized as British. John Liverpool Torbotoh, a 27-year-old Sierra Leonean merchant seaman, was killed when his ship, the SS *Harmattan*, was torpedoed in 1917. When his family tried to claim compensation, they were informed that he was not classified as a British subject.[169] Such different conditions of employment clearly created problems. In June 1915 the *Milford Haven Telegraph* reported that sixteen seamen had refused to continue to work there when 'three coloured men' were added to the crew.[170]

Prisoners-of-War

African and Caribbean seafarers often found themselves at risk of capture by the Germans, especially those whose ships were berthed at such ports as Hamburg and Bremen after war was declared. Others arrested included the crew of a South African warship sailing in German territorial waters. The best-known examples are those who were amongst the 300 'men of colour' who were incarcerated at the Ruhleben Camp in Spandau near Berlin. Not all the men of colour were seafarers and the most notable was 'Prince Monolulu' (Peter Karl McKay, 1881–1965), the well-known racing tipster who originated from St Croix. Another was Noel Sylvester (also known as Sylvester Leon (c.1880s–?)), the noted Jamaican actor and later one of the first to broadcast on BBC radio in Jamaican dialect.[171] At Ruhleben, men of African, Caribbean, Yemeni and Asian origin were housed in segregated facilities within the camp, even though they participated in some general camp activities, sports and music-making in particular. In the case of West African internees, the shipping companies often refused to pay them wages while they were detained, so their families suffered along with the men. The family members of William Savory, a Barbadian trawlerman based in Grimsby, were forced to enter the workhouse during his internment as they had no other means of support. The British government did provide some financial assistance to the families of those who were captured, but this had to be repaid when the men were released.[172]

Savory later explained the circumstances of his capture. He sailed out from Grimsby on 24 August 1914, on a fishing trawler, the *Seti*, which was sunk two days later by German naval gunfire. In just two days nineteen trawlers suffered the same fate. Savory wrote that 'Civilians crowded round us prisoners, broke through the line of soldiers and with their connivance, spat in our faces and threw stones and lumps of coal at us ... I was also kicked and called a "Black pig of a mine-layer".' He and his shipmates were taken to a naval prison, interrogated at gunpoint and cajoled to confess that they had been engaged in laying mines. They were then transported across Germany, and Savory remarked that he was singled out for public exhibition and maltreatment everywhere. He later contracted pneumonia and was hospitalized for two months and suffered in many other ways before eventually being transferred to Ruhleben in September 1915. He only remained at the camp for two months, where he was well treated, and was repatriated to Britain in November 1915, along with 120 other prisoners.[173]

Conscientious Objectors

Perhaps the most significant event in Britain during the war was the introduction of conscription in January 1916. One of the most notable opponents of this policy was a skilled Jamaican carpenter, the 6-foot-6-inch Isaac Hall, who had arrived in the country at the age of thirty-five, shortly before the declaration of war in 1914. Thereafter Hall had tried to return to Jamaica, but, probably because of wartime conditions, was unable to do so. Described as 'the grandchild of a slave on a sugar plantation' and, even less politely, as 'a simple-minded Christian, taught in a little mission hall to believe the bible literally', he nevertheless became a vigorous conscientious objector – as over 18,000 pacifists and others who refused military service were referred to at the time.[174]

Hall ignored the summons to report for military training and was subsequently arrested and forcibly taken to the training camp. Once there, he still refused to serve and was dragged around the parade ground until he was unconscious. He refused to obey all orders and even to accept alternative war work. He was subsequently court-martialled and sentenced to two years' hard labour in Pentonville Prison. He was ordered to work, but refused time after time, so was kept in solitary confinement and forced to exist on bread and water. He became so ill that it was feared that he had contracted tuberculosis and questions about his condition were asked in Parliament.[175]

Hall was rescued from prison by Alfred Salter, a physician in Bermondsey and a member of the pacifist No Conscription Fellowship, who later wrote: 'I was horrified at the spectacle of a living skeleton – a gaunt, bent, starved, broken man, a coal-black man with ashen lips and sunken eyes. But he was broken only in body; his soul and spirit were as resolute as ever. One of the warders told me that Isaac Hall was the bravest man he had ever met.'[176] Hall may have endured much more, as did many other conscientious objectors who were imprisoned, tortured and threatened with execution. Salter's subsequent complaint to the government apparently led to Hall's release. He was taken to Salter's home to recover for several months until he was well enough to return to Jamaica. Hall's bravery is not as well known as that attributed to those who fought in the war, such as Walter Tull and Arthur Roberts, but it is perhaps even more noteworthy.

Hall may not have been the only Jamaican conscientious objector. The following words appeared in the pages of *The Tribunal*, the publication of the No Conscription Fellowship, in October 1916:

> I am a Negro of the African race born in Jamaica. My parents were sent
> in bondage to Jamaica. They were torn from their home. My country is
> divided up among the European powers (now fighting each other), who

in turn have oppressed and tyrannized over my fellow-men. The allies of Great Britain, i.e., Portugal and Belgium, have been the worse oppressors, and now that Belgium has been invaded, I am to be compelled to defend her ... As a people the Negroes are the last among men taken into consideration in this country, although we be regarded as British. Even Germans or any aliens who are white men are preferred to us. I am not given ordinary privileges as a citizen. I have tried to find work and I have been refused solely on account of my colour ... I have been buffeted from one labour exchange to another ... Businessmen claim that their employees would not work with me. Others hold ... they may lose their customers because I am a negro. In view of these circumstances, and also the fact that I have a moral objection to all wars, I would sacrifice my rights rather than fight, for to subdue one with might can never destroy the evil.[177]

These words were taken from the written statement of 'a negro who was recently arrested as an absentee, and who had been under the impression that his colour exempted him' from conscription and are often attributed to Hall, but his situation appears to have been rather different. Moreover, Salter's biography, written many years later, refers to Hall as a man of 'simple Christian faith, and stated that that he "knew nothing of the issue of the war. He knew only the commandment 'Thou shalt not kill' "'.[178] This may, or may not, have been true, but as these words were published anonymously, it is doubtful that they can be attributed to Hall. This begs the question, if these are not the words of Isaac Hall, then who was this other Jamaican who spoke out against conscription? There might well have been more widespread opposition to recruitment. The *Cambria Daily Leader* reports an incident in September 1916 when a certain Robert Ebenezer Vanloo, described as a 'coloured man' and a boarding-house keeper, was charged with 'making statements likely to be prejudicial to recruiting'. The defendant had allegedly disrupted a meeting outside the Shipping Office at Barry where attempts were being made to 'recruit a battalion of coloured men'.[179]

THE AFTERMATH OF THE WAR

Whatever limited progress might have been made during the war towards greater equality between Britain's white and Black citizens, the end of the war brought it to an abrupt halt. British troops and seamen of African and Caribbean heritage were not invited to the peace parade in London in 1919, even though Africans from French colonies were and did participate. During the 1920s, African and Caribbean servicemen were excluded from the commemorative efforts of the Imperial War Graves Commission (IWGC) and were not commemorated in Britain. Seamen 'of colour', for example, those of African and Caribbean heritage, initially only appeared on memorials in India. Thus, a memorial in Portsmouth to men lost at sea might mention white Royal Navy seamen, but not those of Caribbean origin who had sailed and died alongside them. Where there are memorials that include the names of all merchant seamen, for example, at Tower Hill in London, this was not the original intention of the IWGC.[180] Other seamen, such as the West Africans in the crew of the torpedoed SS *Mendi*, are not visibly commemorated at all in Britain, even though the 'native' South African troops they were transporting to battle were awarded this distinction.[181]

It was only in 2021, more than a century later and after a lengthy inquiry, that the Commonwealth War Graves Commission accepted and acknowledged what had happened after the First World War:

> In conflict with the organization's founding principles, it is estimated that between 45,000 and 54,000 casualties (predominantly Indian, East African, West African, Egyptian and Somali personnel) were commemorated unequally. For some, rather than marking their graves individually, as the IWGC would have done in Europe, these men were commemorated collectively on memorials. For others who were missing, their names were recorded in registers rather than in stone. A further 116,000 casualties (predominantly, but not exclusively, East African and Egyptian personnel) – but potentially as many as 350,000 – were not commemorated by name or possibly not commemorated at all.[182]

THE RIOTS OF 1919

Between January and August 1919 there were large-scale racist attacks on African, Caribbean and other 'people of colour' in nine towns and cities throughout Britain. Over 250 people were arrested, scores were injured, and five lives were lost. Since 1919 these attacks have always been described as riots, which disguises their aim and their victims. The attacks began in Glasgow and subsequently occurred in South Shields, Liverpool, Newport, Barry, Cardiff and London. Some attacks, such as those in Liverpool and Cardiff, occurred at the same time, while the disturbances in Hull and Salford were initially on a smaller scale and had different characteristics, at least to some degree.

The term 'race riot' was first used in reports by the contemporary Scottish press.[183] The common denominator is evident – all of these locations were ports and had long-established communities which included African, Caribbean and Yemeni men, many of whom were seafarers. Many of these locations also had, since the late nineteenth century, seen conflicts between British and other 'foreign' seamen, the former accusing the latter of undercutting wages. As long before as the late 1870s, 'coloured' seamen in Liverpool had been complaining that the ship owners discriminated against them and had organized themselves to try to seek a remedy.[184] Traditionally, the so-called Lascar seamen, most of whom were from India, were paid at lower rates and employed in poorer conditions than British seamen. This was legally sanctioned. Chinese, Adenese, West African and Somali seamen faced such discrimination too, while Greek and other European seamen might be paid at lower rates as well. Such accusations of undercutting wages were made by the seamen's unions, but often misdirected at fellow workers, rather than levelled at the employers. These allegations also frequently resulted in the targeting of 'coloured' British seamen, including those designated as Chinese and 'Arab', even though they generally did not receive lower pay. The employers benefited by setting one group of seamen against another, exploiting the lower wages and poorer conditions of some in order to attack the wages and conditions of all.[185]

These riotous attacks occurred during a period of severe economic crisis and political unrest in Britain, when millions of former servicemen were being demobilized and there was acute competition for employment, especially as the post-war shipping industry contracted. 1919 was a year of riots and mutinies, when even the police went on strike and the government feared the possibility of revolution. The attacks were part of a wider problem of racism and fear of 'aliens', especially the fear that British workers were facing competition from what was seen as cheap foreign labour. These animosities were initially mainly directed towards Chinese seamen, even by Black workers in ports such as Cardiff, but they could just as easily be manipulated and directed towards all 'coloured' seamen and people, especially those of African, Caribbean and Yemeni heritage, who lived in these port cities.

By April 1919, the government had received several 'well-written representations from coloured seamen' complaining of racism in the ports of Glasgow, South Shields, Newport and Barry, and the unhelpful attitude of the Seamen's Union.[186] 'Every morning we go down to shipping offices to find ourselves work so as to make an honest bread and are bluntly refused on account of our colour,' Winston Samuels, a sailor in Cardiff originally from British Guiana, had informed the Colonial Office in December 1918, '[w]hereas, foreigners of all nationality get the preference.'[187] There were, of course, other examples of a more general racism arising from Britain's position as the world's leading colonial power, a situation which fostered manifestations of white supremacy. In April 1919, two soldiers wrote to the *Yorkshire Post* complaining of the casual racism they had often experienced and reported that on several occasions they were referred to as 'n——' while on leave for a few days in Leeds.[188]

What made the situation worse was that in many instances racism and racist attacks were encouraged by the seamen's unions, the National Sailors and Firemen's Union and the British Seafarers' Union, as well as other unions, which should have been defending all workers. In 1915, for example, the Admiralty succumbed to pressure from the NSFU to exclude Chinese seafarers from British ships, at this time numbering over 9,000 men, several thousand of whom were based in Britain.[189] In response an order was issued that all crews should be British or 'British coloured persons'.[190] In 1916 the Triple Alliance of mine, rail and transport workers, including seamen, passed a resolution demanding a halt to what was referred to as 'the sinister movement to import coloured labour into this country'.[191] It was rumoured that the government might be considering encouraging the migration of war workers from South Africa to Britain. The Parliamentary Labour Party passed a resolution voicing its opposition.[192] Behind such opposition was the strongly held view that 'men of black and yellow races ... work under conditions repugnant to white labourers', but not the belief that trade unions and their allied political parties should defend the rights and conditions of *all* workers.[193] Only the press of revolutionary organizations in 1919, such as the Workers' Socialist Federation's newspaper, the *Worker's Dreadnought*, and the Socialist Labour Party's the *Socialist*, condemned the attacks on Black workers.[194]

During the course of the war and in response to demands for labour to replace those at the front, migration from Africa, the Caribbean and elsewhere increased, as did the visibility of Black workers in industry and the wider society. There was also an increasing incidence of relationships and marriages between Black men and white women, which led to outrageous reports in the press. In 1917 the Manchester-based *Daily Despatch* carried a series of articles complaining of the 'black peril', which prompted the Salvation Army to commission an investigation into what it referred to as 'the danger attendant upon this coloured invasion'.[195] Elsewhere, reporting was less sensational and in Cardiff the *Western Mail* conducted interviews with local women, who generally reported that they were happily married to 'coloured men'.[196]

Glasgow

In January 1919, in Glasgow, Emanuel Shinwell of the British Seafarers Union (BSU), one of the leaders of the Red Clydeside workers' revolt (later a well-known government minster and subsequently Baron Shinwell), specifically condemned the hiring of 'Chinese and other coloured labour'.[197] Such views were expressed at several mass meetings of seafarers, as part of the campaign for a forty-hour week and a general strike in Clydeside, and were published in the local press. As in the past, Shinwell linked the employment of Chinese and Black seamen with the unemployment of recently demobilized white workers, while the BSU in Glasgow refused to admit 'coloured' seamen.[198]

On 23 January, just a few hours after one such meeting, and near to its location, some white seamen began attacking Black seafarers, veterans of the recent war, driving them from the docks towards their boarding houses. In the course of this attack Tom Johnson, a Sierra Leonean seaman, was stabbed and forced to shoot at his assailants in self-defence. Rather than being immediately taken to hospital, he was subsequently arrested by the police.[199] Boarding houses in James Watt Street and Broomielaw Street were then attacked by a large crowd, and Black seamen were compelled to defend themselves and their homes. Shots were fired on both sides before the police arrived. In what was to become a familiar scenario in other cities throughout the country, the police arrested thirty seamen, all of whom were from Sierra Leone.[200] Eventually only three were charged and convicted of a breach of the peace. The sole white man arrested was charged and convicted of the same offence, even though he had assaulted a policeman aiding a Chinese man who was also being attacked.[201] This 'riot' in Glasgow was the earliest of the racist attacks in 1919 and was widely reported.[202] It was not the only example of racist violence in the city during that year.

South Shields

In January and February 1919 similar tensions over employment culminated in attacks on mainly Yemeni seamen in South Shields. They were part of a population of several thousand Yemenis and Adenese, as well as Somalis and others, who had been encouraged to migrate to Britain to support the war effort, but most of whom had in fact first settled in the area in the late nineteenth century, the majority as seafarers.[203] In 1916 the local press had carried an anonymous letter claiming that, at the shipping office, 'Arabs are being signed on every day to the disadvantage of Britishers'. At this time the term 'Arab' was used to describe Sudanese, Adenese, Somalis, Yemenis, Zanzibaris and Egyptians in Britain.[204] A letter in response from a local Yemeni pointed out that the 'Arabs' were 'British subjects', but the nature of the tension was clear.[205] In January 1919 'a large crowd of white men', in fact naval seamen, attacked a Yemeni café in South Shields owned by Abdul Naggi and, in the following days, there were further attacks on the same café, the owner and his house.[206]

As in Glasgow, it was two union officials, John Fye and James Gil-roy, who discriminated against the Yemenis, abused them even though they were also union members, and incited white seamen to attack them and prevent them from working on board ship. Fye reportedly shouted, 'Come on you black bastards, you are not going to join the ship.'[207] Once again, this dispute became a major incident in the Mill Dam dockside area, involving hundreds of people, some armed with revolvers. The Yemenis and other Black residents fought back, attacking the shipping office and the union officials. Eventually military and navy forces were deployed to restore order. The local press labelled the attack an 'Arab riot', but it also reported that such racist discrimination against seamen had occurred for some time and that Fye had discriminated against Yemeni seamen years earlier in 1914.[208] Fifteen Yemeni seamen were subsequently charged with 'unlawful riotous conduct', but the union official was also charged and eventually convicted of using 'language likely to cause a breach of the peace'.[209] Twelve Yemenis were convicted, but no other people were arrested for their involvement in the disturbances.

Hull and Salford

Disturbances in these two areas were less violent, prolonged or widespread than in Scotland, but in Salford there was a struggle between large numbers of Black seamen and the police in March 1919, which indicated deep mutual mistrust.[210] A fight between Black and white men was reported in the press in April 1919. No explanation was provided, but three Black men were convicted of assault. The newspaper report itself is of interest since it mentions that at a 'negro concert party' in a lodging house 'N—— were strumming banjos while white girls danced.'[211] In Hull the press reported one incident in May where there was a fight between a small group of 'coloured' and white men. Then in June of that year 'coloured' sailors chased Chinese seamen from the shipping office. A few days later Black and white seamen were involved in a fight.[212] An attack by a 'crowd of fishermen' on two 'coloured seamen' on a ferry in July was reported in the press as a 'colour riot', and the two victims were fined for allegedly attacking a policeman.[213] Such incidents continued, and in 1920 a 'coloured man' chased by a hostile crowd fired a warning shot, then a second which wounded one of his pursuers. After that, a crowd attacked a Black sailors' boarding house. The police had some difficulty restoring order and found it necessary to take several Black people into protective custody. The attacks continued the following day and one man was seriously wounded when he attacked a house belonging to a Black man.[214] Once again the Black men who were being attacked and defending themselves were the ones arrested, often for firearms offences. Such incidents were often reported as relating to 'white women', in a judgement ignoring wider economic issues, unemployment and the role of the unions. Both cities had a relatively small Black population. That of Hull was estimated at the time as no more than a hundred.[215]

London

The disturbances that broke out in Cable Street, east London, in April 1919, appeared to have been initially of a different character from those elsewhere in the country. Some press reports suggested that they occurred between 'Arabs and some young Englishmen' because the former 'objected to English girls visiting an Arab eating house'. Some claimed that the young women working in this establishment were 'subject to insulting remarks' but no further details were provided.[216] However, others made it clear that the main participants were seamen and that the incident arose because of an unexplained 'feud' existing between 'white and coloured seamen arriving at the Port of London'.[217] It is certain that a dispute arose within a café and, according to one record, a soldier attacked a 'coloured' man, who defended himself.[218] As a consequence the café was then attacked, reportedly by a 'crowd including soldiers, sailors and women', which forced the 'Arabs' to defend themselves. Several accounts refer to the fact that 'the coloured seamen present were thoroughly frightened by the attitude of the crowd'.[219] According to press reports, a fight ensued 'in which revolvers, knives and bottles were used'. One mentioned that there were attempts to set the café alight and that it was besieged for two hours. Several people were seriously wounded before the police managed to quell the attack.[220]

Again, the attack was labelled a 'riot', especially in the press, and some headlines, 'Riot over white girls', and 'Arabs and English girls', for example, were clearly inflammatory and reported throughout the country.[221] One newspaper claimed that the attack was a consequence of 'a growing evil in the cosmopolitan quarters of London'. That 'evil', it was suggested by an apparently well-informed police officer, was that the 'coloured sailor' was 'successful with English girls', because he dressed in the latest fashions and spent a lot of money. His 'dashing debonaire manner' and 'generosity' were said to 'overcome the colour bar in the estimation of girls of a certain class'. It was said that his popularity was 'increased by the fact that he rarely gets under the influence of liquor'.[222] Several papers added that there were regular disputes relating to English women in the area, and that 'white men' resented the attention paid by coloured men to some waitresses at some of the cafés.[223] The subsequent court proceedings suggest that only four wounded 'Arabs' were arrested and convicted of various offences, and that three of them were imprisoned for short periods, even though the evidence suggested that they were acting in self-defence.[224]

The Cable Street 'riot' is the first in 1919 in which the role of women is mentioned, and it set a precedent for later reporting on events in Liverpool and Wales. However, earlier racist attacks on Black people's dwellings in Canning Town, east London, in 1917, labelled 'colour riots' in the press, had also been described by the police as the 'consequence of the infatuation of white girls for black men'. One newspaper reported that 'a crowd of about a thousand people', women as well as men, was involved, that Black seamen used weapons, including a revolver, to defend themselves and at least one English woman was also under attack.[225] Three Black men were arrested, but only one was eventually charged.[226]

The events in Cable Street in 1919 were linked in one press report with an incident in Edgware Road, west London, in which a soldier from the Caribbean serving in the Dorset Regiment was charged with wounding a labourer. The paper reported that the incident arose following an argument in a public house 'between coloured men and a girl'.[227] In May 1919 there were reports in the press of fighting between American and 'black troops' serving in the British Army, at a camp in Winchester. Again, the dispute was meant to be 'over a woman' and involved scores of men on both sides, the Black soldiers apparently parading the streets shouting, '[W]e are as good as any white men.'[228] A local eyewitness erroneously claimed that 'two of the darkies' were dead, but mainly complained that the American troops, who had threatened to lynch them, were being leniently treated.[229]

On May Day 1919, the *Daily Herald* reported growing tensions in London, Liverpool, Cardiff and Glasgow, owing to the employment of 'thousands of Asiatics' at a time when thousands of 'British or British coloured' seamen, often ex-servicemen, were unemployed. It also alleged that during the war ship owners had broken the agreement of 1915 and had employed 'Chinese' rather than 'British' crews. This situation, the newspaper commented ominously, had already led to 'disturbances and incipient rioting'.[230]

Further attacks on 'coloured' seamen occurred in Commercial Road and Whitechapel Road in east London on several nights in May 1919, when many men were hospitalized with serious knife and gun-shot wounds. One report claimed, as usual, that the responsibility lay with women 'whose association with coloured men has aggravated the ever-present hostility between whites and blacks in the district' and provocatively described 'the rout of the black men' by 'the East End lads'. Some white women, it was reported, were also attacked. It appeared, however, that the main origin of any hostility was again occasioned by competition between seamen for employment.[231] Thousands participated in the attacks, which the police reported had clearly been launched on the 'coloured' men.[232] The following month there were attacks on Chinese residents in the area and their English wives, after a march by unemployed white seamen, and isolated attacks on Black men and their dwellings continued into the summer of 1919 and reoccurred the following year.[233]

Liverpool

The attacks in Liverpool which broke out in June 1919 were some of the most serious.[234] They involved thousands of people and resulted in scores of arrests, many houses being severely damaged, and the tragic death of Charles Wootton, a 24-year-old seaman from Bermuda, who had served in the Royal Navy. In Liverpool, as well, there was pressure from the trade unions to maintain employment for white seamen and to exclude Black sailors. The population of African and Caribbean heritage in Liverpool was one of the largest in the country. According to one contemporary estimate it might have included about 5,000 people.[235] Many were employed as merchant seamen, but during the war some were in the army, others in the munitions industry, or were employed in sugar refineries, or in other factory work. At the close of the war, many were demobilized and unemployed.[236]

There had been some confrontations over racism at the end of the war. For example, at the Royal Military Hospital, where a Black sergeant and amputee in the BWIR, John Demerette, known as 'Demetrius', was involved in a dispute with a military police guard. The fight escalated until fifty Black troops, and some of their white comrades too, had been forced to defend themselves from racist taunts and violence from hundreds of others. The police had been summoned to restore order and a nurse had later died as a result of shock and subsequent pneumonia.[237] Other incidents, in which racism evidently played a part, had also occurred before June.[238] In April, for example, two injured 'coloured' soldiers, patients at another war hospital and part of a crowd of fifty, were arrested by the police. In court the two men protested that they had been victimized, 'simply because they were coloured men'. One stated: 'I am as good as any white man . . . I have done my bit just as Mr Lloyd George has done, for king and country.'[239]

At the beginning of June, according to press reports, more than a hundred Black seamen were made redundant and there had already been complaints that they faced competition, not only from other British workers, but also from other European seamen who descended on the port.[240] Some community leaders in Liverpool such as D. T. Aleifasukure Toumananah, the secretary of the Liverpool Ethiopian Association, had even suggested that destitute colonial seamen might be paid to encourage their voluntary repatriation.[241]

Some of the earliest confrontations were between European and Black seamen. Newspaper reports mention 'Russians and Scandinavians', after a vicious attack left John Johnson, a Black sailor, hospitalized. These confrontations led to police intervention and then, since the police blamed the Black sailors for the violence, to further arrests of Black seamen and their determined resistance. Several were arrested in the house where 24-year-old Charles Wootton lived. He evaded arrest, but was pursued by a large crowd, pushed, or forced, into the water in the docks and then, although police were present, hit on the head with stones thrown from a crowd who were chanting 'Let him drown'.[242] National press coverage of these attacks mentioned the tragic death of Charles Wootton, but also generally suggested that the violence had been caused by 'West Indian Negroes', who were also the majority of those arrested, or that the cause of the violence was due 'to the familiarity which exists between many of the Negroes and white girls'.[243]

A few days later, there was more violence as Liverpool's Black community came under attack for several days by organized gangs and crowds numbering as many as 10,000. According to one police report, these gangs 'commenced savagely attacking, beating and stabbing every Negro they could find in the street'.[244] Both people and houses were attacked and there were attempts to set fire to houses and their contents. The police now had to provide 'protective custody' for hundreds of Liverpool's Black population, men, women and children. Liverpool's Assistant Chief Constable wrote to the Home Office, fearing further loss of life and asking if steps could be taken to intern 'or remove the black population', which he estimated at several thousand, 'by compulsory repatriation or otherwise'.[245] One newspaper headline even proclaimed 'N—— to be interned at Liverpool'.[246] A young Ernest Marke (1902–1995), in Liverpool at the time, was caught up in the attacks being perpetrated by those he referred to as 'John Bulls'. One of his friends was 'beaten unconscious and left for dead' and Marke was also attacked but saved by local women factory workers, who 'rushed at the mob shouting and screaming madly'. According to Marke, following the war 'those who didn't get their jobs back started taking it out on the Negroes, any Negro', and he records how Black seamen 'started carrying guns and razors to defend themselves'.[247]

These shocking and tragic attacks were largely fuelled by the impact of military demobilization as well as the essentially racist approach of the trade unions. In addition, the press often condemned the presence of Black workers, as did the Lord Mayor of Liverpool and the police.[248] As they did in London, the police often blamed violence on Black men's propensity to 'swank around in smart clothes', or the fact that their white female partners engaged in 'boasting to other women about the superior qualities of the negroes compared with those of white men'.[249] Thus the blame was placed on the victims of both unemployment and racist violence. Press reports generally adopted a similar approach and, although scores of people were arrested, generally focused attention on the sentences meted out to a few seamen of West African origin. There was, for example, a particular focus on a ship's fireman, who police alleged had been brandishing an iron bar and shouting, 'Down with the white race – I will kill the first white man who touches me.'[250] Other press reports largely justified the riots. In June 1919, the *Reynolds News* commented:

> It was a blunder to let a crowd of negroes [sic] loose on our cities. They were bound to cause trouble. A foolish woman and a negro may easily cause a serious riot, for white men will not put up with it. These blacks should have been kept at work until ready to be shipped home. If all our years of experience in dealing with racial problems have not taught us these things, then we are very stupid.[251]

The *Western Mail* went further and appeared sympathetic to US-style lynching:

> In the United States the force of public opinion, reinforced by unofficial public action of a ruthless kind, is sufficient to prevent the mischief. In our own country the tolerance which is exhibited towards the problem is due not to far-fetched ideas of racial equality, but to slackness . . . it exhibits either a state of depravity or a squalid infatuation; it is repugnant to all our finer instincts in which pride of race occupies a just and inevitable place.[252]

The violence justified by the press was followed by government attempts, including financial inducements, to repatriate many 'British coloureds' (but not those with white wives). It was feared that racist attacks in Liverpool, and elsewhere, would have a detrimental impact throughout the empire and might contribute to anti-colonial rebellion. Although repatriation was presented as a measure to prevent further violence in Liverpool, as ever blame was placed on the victims of the attacks (who were presented as a problem the country needed to get rid of) rather than the perpetrators. Plans were also announced to repatriate some Chinese and other 'aliens'. Aleifasukure Toumananah appeared to speak for many of the victims when, in a press interview, he highlighted the role that Black servicemen and seafarers had played during the recent war. 'We ask for British justice', he said, 'to be treated as true and loyal sons of Great Britain.'[253]

Despite estimates that Liverpool's Black population was in the thousands, the police only produced a list of a few hundred men who might be repatriated. Almost 200 were of West African and mainly Sierra Leonean origin. About sixty were still employed, almost all as seamen. The rest were unemployed, but had generally been employed as mariners during the war. Another hundred were unemployed former seamen of Caribbean origin, the majority from Jamaica and Barbados.[254] Ernest Marke was one of those who was offered money by the government to leave Liverpool, but he was only given the opportunity to go to British Guiana (not back to Sierra Leone, his birthplace). There he was forced by economic necessity to escape by stowing away on another ship.[255]

The attacks on the African and Caribbean population of Liverpool also highlighted the discriminatory actions of the police, their view that 'in every case the coloured man was the aggressor', and the fact that in many cases little was done to prevent attacks on the homes of the Black population. Indeed, people were ordered to leave their homes and seek police protective custody.[256] The police arrested almost as many Black people as they did white people during the riots, but nearly half of the arrested Black people were found not guilty in subsequent court cases. It was clear that even those who were eventually convicted were often acting in self-defence. While most of the white rioters were subsequently found guilty, they were frequently given more lenient sentences than the Black people involved.[257]

Newport, Barry and Cardiff

In Wales attacks occurred in three different locations in the same month, in Cardiff, Barry and Newport, during June 1919. All three were important ports that had grown both in size and diversity in the late nineteenth century, largely as a result of the area's coal-mining industry. Employment on the tramp steamers that delivered coal was insecure and unattractive to many British seafarers and therefore provided work for increasing numbers of 'coloured' seamen. By the end of the First World War there were long-settled populations of African and Caribbean seamen in these Welsh ports, as well as those from Aden, China and elsewhere. As in Liverpool and London, these sailors had often married local women and established distinct dockland communities. These communities had continued to grow throughout the war as Britain required additional merchant seamen and other workers. As elsewhere, wage increases which benefited 'coloured' seamen as well as whites may have contributed to their matrimonial eligibility. It is unlikely that these communities had a combined population greater than a few thousands by 1919. However, many sailors continued to complain that in the aftermath of the war they faced unemployment because of discrimination. Winston Samuels, originally from British Guiana, who had served during the war, wrote to the Colonial Office:

> We do not want any favour all we want is fair play. Every morning we go down to shipping offices to find ourselves work so as to make an honest bread and are blatantly refused on account of our colour. Whereas foreigners of all nationality get the preference. This is not only in Cardiff but throughout the United Kingdom.[258]

By April 1919 'coloured seamen' who wrote to the Colonial Office complained that over 800 of them were suffering from unemployment and racism.[259] Long before the war, there had been hostility to 'foreign' seamen. Racist attacks had occurred in Cardiff during the late nineteenth century.[260] Such antipathy continued in the pages of the press. During the 1911 seamen's strike racist attacks were particularly directed at Chinese seamen and even organized by local trade union leaders.[261] As the war drew to a close, there were also those who expressed various moral concerns. The dislocation caused by the post-war economic crisis and demobilization created significant unemployment, as well as a housing shortage in South Wales, and led to trade union animosity. It is likely that, as it did elsewhere, this created some of the conditions for the events in June.[262]

The first large-scale disturbances began in Newport, where the numbers of 'coloured' seamen would have been quite small. Nevertheless, there had been fights between white American and Black British seamen a few months before June. Contemporary accounts present differing causes for the violence, but competition for housing and jobs featured prominently. Eight boarding houses where Black seamen resided were clearly targeted by large crowds during the affray, with their furniture being ransacked and burnt in the street. This continued for several days.[263] There were also attacks on a Black-owned restaurant, a Chinese laundry and an 'Arab' boarding house, as well as significant resistance to these attacks.[264] When the police finally intervened, 'over twenty black men were arrested' – the great majority of those arrested during the disturbances.

One peculiarity of the Newport riots was that one of the suspected ringleaders arrested was a Black soldier, Percy White, serving in the local Monmouthshire regiment. His presence allowed the police to claim that the cause of the attacks was mere 'hooliganism', rather than tensions over a scarcity of jobs at the docks. However, another one of the ringleaders clearly stated that he had acted 'for the benefit of the seamen of whom I am one'. Both men were sentenced to three months imprisonment with hard labour. Disputes between seamen in Newport continued in following years, but such was the competition for employment that in 1921 violence even occurred between different groups of so-called 'Arab' seamen from Newport and Cardiff gathering around the Shipping Office.[265]

In Barry disturbances occurred in June 1919 following the death of a demobilized soldier, Frederick Longman, at that time a dock worker. He, with two other men, became involved in a fight with 'two negro seamen' one of whom was Charles Emmanuel, originally from the French Caribbean. At the start of the altercation Longman had apparently said to Emmanuel, '[W]hy don't you go down your own street?'[266]

The fatal stabbing of the dock worker by Emmanuel, who seems to have been defending himself from a racist attack, was reported to be the cause of subsequent violence when 'crowds of hundreds of people made for the streets in which the negro sailors live'. Attacks on both property and persons ensued and continued sporadically for another day when a fish-and-chip shop owned by a Jamaican man and his Welsh wife was attacked and damaged by a crowd. However, strong police and military intervention prevented further attacks.[267]

In Cardiff the disturbances that broke out in June were some of the most serious in the country, leading to three deaths, dozens injured and hospitalized and thousands of pounds worth of damage to property.

There have been several studies of these disturbances, the first of them in 1947.[268] There had been clashes between seamen before June. In May, for example, Black seamen had fired shots at white American seamen from the local naval base. There had been other incidents too. Police reports cannot be relied upon, but the Chief Constable of Cardiff reported to the Home Office that it was the racism of 'American sailors' that had spread to 'soldiers and demobilised men'.[269] There is some evidence that even in government circles the racism of American and other foreign servicemen in Cardiff was seen as provoking events in Cardiff.[270]

The incident which led to violence in June 1919 was a dispute between several Black men who, returning home in carriages with their white wives, responded to racist abuse. A fight ensued during which the Black men reportedly fired shots and other weapons were used on both sides, leading to one Black man being stabbed.[271]

RACIAL RIOTS AT CARDIFF.

A "man of colour" addressing a crowd in the Tiger Bay district on Friday. He advised his countrymen to do nothing likely to cause trouble.   [Western Mail photo.

A newspaper account of the attacks in Cardiff

Violence continued for three days following this initial incident, with hostile crowds, including many ex-servicemen, besieging houses and assaulting individuals in the streets in Bute Town, the area where most of the Black community lived.[272] One newspaper report refers to a Hadji Mahomet, a 'Somali priest', who was forced to clamber onto the roof of a house in Homfray Street 'and with stoicism watched the wrecking of his premises'.[273]

One account of the violence has been provided by Ibrahim Ismaa'il, a Somali seaman who had recently arrived in Cardiff. He was not sure of the reason for the violence, but was told that 'the trouble was started by the arrival of American soldiers who had very strong colour prejudices'. In his autobiography Ismaa'il explains that when the riots began all the Somalis went to defend their boarding houses. According to his report:

> In Millicent Street the fight started about 7:30 pm. and lasted a fairly long time. Seven or eight Warsangeli defended the house and most of them got badly wounded. Some of the white people also received wounds. In the end, the whites took possession of the first floor, soaked it with paraffin oil and set it alight. The Somalis managed to keep up the fight until the police arrived. One of them was left for dead in the front room and was later carried to the hospital where he recovered; some escaped through a neighbouring house and came to tell us the story of what had happened, the others gave themselves up to the police and we did not see them for a long time.[274]

Once again, Black people defended themselves by any means necessary, including using guns and knives. An elder told the press that the inhabitants of the Bute Town were well armed: 'It will be hell let loose if the mob comes into our streets,' he said. 'We are ready to obey the white man's laws, but if we are unprotected from hooligan rioters who can blame us for trying to protect ourselves.'[275] In the course of this violence two white men were killed, one an ex-serviceman shot as part of a crowd setting fire to a house. Nine of those in the house were subsequently acquitted of the assailant's murder. In the same way as in other areas of the country, police action during the disturbances tended to view the Black community less as the victims than as a cause of the problem, and so they constituted the majority of those arrested, although most were subsequently acquitted. Other deaths followed, including that of Mohamed Abdullah, allegedly killed by a blow to the head from a policeman or another attacker, for which nobody was arrested.[276] Several hundred 'negroes of all types' attended Abdullah's funeral and there was similar unity at protest meetings held in the wake of the violence involving 'Arabs, Somalis, Egyptians, West Indians and other coloured races'.[277]

As in Liverpool, some of the leaders of the Black community urged the repatriation of some men and their families as a solution to both rioting and post-war unemployment.[278] The Colonial Office implemented such a scheme, but with only limited numbers of 'distressed' seamen involved at first. The plight of those remaining worsened and in 1921 there were well over a thousand unemployed Black seamen in Cardiff, most of them with no financial means of support, and some 'at the point of starvation'. The only response of the government was to encourage these men to leave Britain and eventually 600 men were repatriated, several clearly believing that they had been effectively deported.[279]

Contemporary explanations as to the causes of the disturbances varied. Some reports in the press declared that the attacks were precipitated by 'a feeling of animosity against the coloured men because of their association with white girls'.[280] Others explained the cause as that 'some of the negroes in Cardiff own their own homes', and the fact that 'they seem to have grown more arrogant of late ... giving free rein to their love of display and ostentation', thereby 'making themselves more attractive in the eyes of a class of women who infest seaports'.[281]

REPATRIATION

The racist attacks and related disturbances in 1919 were a poor reward for those who had been willing to give their lives during the recent war. They had several significant consequences. One was that the seamen's unions continued to play a perfidious role in regard to their Black members. In June, at the height of the riots, the *Daily Herald* carried an interview with an official of the NSFU, in which he claimed that although 90 per cent of the Black seamen were union members and the union had 'tried to get them taken on', ships' captains were against their employment and he believed that 'the white men who have done the fighting should be shipped before the blacks'. In the official's view, 'they [the NSFU] are actuated only by patriot motives', and 'were doing perhaps what others ought to be doing in other spheres'. He claimed that 'there is nothing against the majority of the blacks', although he did remark that they had the 'habit of carrying razors and revolvers'. He also stated that he thought that the Home Office should intervene in east London where 'the white girls were fermenting trouble by their actions'. A different union official offered the view that 'the great numbers of coloured men' brought to Britain during the war should be repatriated by the government. Seamen were said to be particularly concerned about the impact of the 'coloured influx' on wage rates, and the official warned that, unless checked, the 'influx' would also have an impact on other industries.[282]

At the end of the war the government did little to reward those African and Caribbean seafarers, as well as other workers who had contributed to the war effort. Even during the war, three Adenese men in Britain with British passports had been arrested under the 1914 Aliens Act, a sign of how such legislation, which was supposed to be concerned with 'enemy aliens', could be used against 'coloured' seamen.[283] In time, the government did introduce a repatriation scheme, together with a small resettlement allowance, for all 'British workmen from overseas', who had arrived after 1914 for wartime work. Initially this was not aimed at 'coloured' seamen. When, from February 1919 onwards, seamen from Africa, the Caribbean, Aden and elsewhere *were* included, due to large-scale unemployment, they were only offered a free passage to their countries of origin.[284] Those who refused repatriation might also be denied unemployment benefit. The provisions changed again in the middle of June 1919, when a financial inducement was introduced, in order to rid the country of those who were seen as presenting a problem, whether they had arrived after 1914 or not.[285] It appears that the NSFU favoured such an inducement, and local repatriation committees were established in seven of the ports where there had been rioting, with the unions' participation. Even before June 1919 the NSFU worked with the government and the police to encourage the repatriation of 'coloured' seamen.[286]

Since many Black seamen had families and owned property, they considered Britain their home and refused to leave. However, at least

800 were repatriated, in the six months following June 1919, and hundreds more via various schemes over the next year. Some, like Ernest Marke, were sent to work in British Guiana. The total number who left is unknown: it may have been several thousand. Many others remained, refusing to accept a 'gratuity' that they considered paltry, nor wishing to be separated from their families. Men from Africa were specifically prevented from taking their 'white' wives or families with them if they returned there. Men from the Caribbean might receive permission to be accompanied in certain circumstances, and if they could produce a marriage certificate. It had been established that 'the coloured population whose presence here is causing so much trouble', in the words of the government, were not truly British and could be asked, or compelled, to leave the country. Furthermore, the Colonial Secretary claimed that the government could do little about the employment of 'coloured' seamen 'as the attitude of the white seamen's union makes it impossible'. Those who did remain would, in the years that followed, often find themselves without regular employment and sometimes destitute.[287] In April 1920 seven men wrote to the Colonial Office from Cardiff on behalf of over 800 'Coloured Seamen' who 'risked our lives in the Country's cause'. All the men had been unemployed for at least six months and complained that 'foreigners' were being employed in preference to 'British Subjects'.[288]

The problem of unemployment in the shipping industry arose not just because of post-war demobilization, but also because British shipping was in competition with foreign rivals, economically inefficient, and undergoing technological change. There were, for example, fewer jobs for ships' stokehold crews, roles traditionally performed by Black seamen, and those that did remain would mostly be given to white seamen.[289] Nevertheless, the shipowners still benefitted from having a pool of unemployed 'coloured' labour, while at the same time the NSFU was reluctant to represent all its members irrespective of nationality. Indeed, the union increasingly found itself in alliance with the government in a campaign against the employment of so-called 'alien coloured' seamen, principally Yemenis and Somalis.[290] In 1922 the NSFU secured official recognition of their so-called 'PC5' card system under which seamen had to have a card from the union to order to gain employment and where discrimination against those trying to obtain the card was often alleged by 'coloured' seamen.[291]

During the year of the riots the government introduced the 1919 Aliens Restriction (Amendment) Act, which included a clause that stipulated that 'alien' seamen could not be employed on British merchant ships 'at a rate of pay less than the standard rate of pay'.[292] The act also provided the government with powers to deport such 'aliens', and, although the act could also be applied to seamen from Europe, it was widely seen as applying to Chinese seamen, many of whom were based in Britain. Some newspapers also linked the riots directly to this legislation, although the vast majority of African, Caribbean and other 'coloured' seamen were British subjects, so the act should not have applied to them.[293] However, since they were often encouraged by the government to leave the country, they also became, by default, 'aliens', constituting a problem that the government needed to continue to remove. In 1920 the Aliens Order required all 'aliens' seeking residence, or employment, to register with the police and this directive was also used against 'coloured' seamen who did not possess a passport and could not prove that they were not 'aliens'. As one historian has pointed out, 'throughout the early 1920s the category "coloured alien" broadened to encompass men from Asia, Africa and the Caribbean, British or alien, seamen or not.'[294]

In April 1925 the government went one step further and introduced the Special Restriction (Coloured Alien Seamen) Order. It is still unclear whether this measure was designed to create divisions amongst seamen who might band together to fight for the rights of all, but it was again based on the premise that 'coloured seamen' were a problem to be got rid of. The legislation, which had been encouraged by the NSFU and the police, was initially aimed at 'Arabs', but nonetheless it effectively declared that all 'coloured seamen' were aliens, unless they could prove otherwise, and required them to register with the police.[295] Home Office statistics showed that those subsequently registered as 'aliens' under this order included Somalis, other Africans, West Indians, and many from Asia as well. It was blatantly racist legislation. Those designated as 'aliens' were forced to carry a passbook, could be denied entry to Britain and even deported. In some cases, those who were not seamen were detained and harassed under its provisions. Some who were clearly British subjects even had their passports confiscated by the police.[296]

The racist legislation led to immediate opposition from African, Caribbean and other 'coloured' seamen in such places as South Shields, Barry and other ports, especially those who had served during the First World War. Indeed, in 1917, earlier government attempts to rid some ports of 'Arabs' had led to a threatened strike by these seamen in South Shields and had therefore been stopped.[297] There was also a unanimous resolution of protest from the Cardiff Coloured Association as well as complaints from some government departments such as the Colonial Office.[298] But, at the same time, there were calls from some police forces for even more draconian powers. In fact, the Chief Constable of Cardiff argued that measures needed to be taken regarding sexual relations, as they were in South Africa, since in Britain 'our race has become somewhat leavened with colour strain'.[299]

The racist attacks in 1919 had one further impact on those who were repatriated. There were anti-colonial riots, strikes and protests in Trinidad, Jamaica and British Honduras involving some of the repatriated ex-servicemen and seamen. In September 1919 there was a mutiny on the SS *Orca*, a ship carrying repatriated seamen and military prisoners of the BWIR. There were several attempts to free those imprisoned during the voyage and threats of violence 'to all whites on board'.[300] One man was killed and another wounded in the course of this rebellion.[301] The events of 1919 led to further attacks on Britain's Black communities. Those who had contributed to the war effort saw the introduction of various hostile measures which, although aimed largely at 'coloured' seamen, had wider consequences and fostered a racism that was to the detriment of all.

7

The Interwar Years

During the interwar years several new political organizations were formed in which students and other intellectuals played a major role. Student numbers at the time were not large, although estimates range from about seventy West Africans and a similar number from the Caribbean to the claim that there were 300 African students and professionals in London alone. However small the figures, these new organizations and their members often played a key political role.[1] The war had led to a new political consciousness, as African and Caribbean servicemen had given their lives for Britain and the empire, and, as a result, they expected to be treated as equals and that the colonies be granted some form of self-determination. Increasing familiarity with white men, and especially white women, in wartime circumstances, had also fostered new attitudes towards intermarriage amongst African and Caribbean men, as well as encouraging them to challenge the use of the term 'native'. During the riots, for example, the police in Liverpool had offered the opinion that they were partly caused by:

> the arrogant and overbearing conduct of the negro population towards the white, and by the white women who live or inhabit with the black man, boasting to other women of the superior qualities of the negroes as compared with those of the white man.[2]

In the post-war period the re-emergence of a vibrant Pan-African movement and early forms of anti-colonialism in Africa and the Caribbean also had their impact on those in Britain. At the same time, racism in Britain and a wider experience of the 'colour bar' also had a lasting influence on those returning to the African and Caribbean colonies. In 1919 a Colonial Office official noted that 'racial feeling' was rising in the Caribbean. He thought that the causes were many:

> participation of coloured men in the war – slights and insults received by them, mainly from Dominion troops on account of their colour – in the USA race troubles – Liverpool and Cardiff riots – and in addition the general unrest all over the world.[3]

This new political consciousness was reflected in a more strident post-war Black press that built on the pioneering efforts of the *African Times and Orient Review*, itself revived for a year in 1920 as the *Africa and Orient Review*. It was a development which was viewed with alarm by the government and those concerned with the preservation of the empire. Disgruntled Black seamen, soldiers, students and others were increasingly seen as a problem within Britain and those who might potentially create even more significant problems in the colonies. There was a particular concern that the experience of racism encouraged 'seditious tendencies' amongst students and 'natural nationalist dissatisfaction with their position as subject races'.[4]

Some of the earliest opinion polls regarding 'race prejudice' were conducted in the 1920s. A study by the American sociologist Richard Lapiere, published in 1928, found that over 300 people surveyed in Britain were overwhelmingly 'with prejudice', a characteristic apparently less developed amongst the French. Lapiere helpfully concluded that 'no biological explanation can account for the difference found between France and England in their attitudes towards coloured peoples'.[5] Racism remained a problem throughout the period and the colour bar was ubiquitous. In 1935, for example, Southern Railway's booking clerks were instructed 'not to supply coloured people with special rail admission tickets to the Blue Lagoon swimming pool in Orpington, Kent'. The manager of the pool explained: 'It's not a question of the colour bar in the accepted sense. Our experience is that women bathers, in particular, do not like to be in the pool at the same time as coloured men.'[6]

THE AFRICAN PROGRESS UNION

One of the earliest and most influential new organizations was the African Progress Union (APU), launched in December 1918 at an inaugural dinner at the Great Eastern Hotel in London. The APU was established following a series of consultative meetings by Africans and 'descendants of African blood', with the aim of 'voicing African sentiments' and 'furthering African interests'. It declared that it was 'an association of Africans from various parts of Africa, the West Indies, British Guiana, Honduras and America', established not in rivalry with any other organizations, but 'actuated by love of country and race'.[7]

The APU's inauguration was attended by thirty founder members who elected John Archer, the former Mayor of Battersea, as chairman, Robert Broadhurst (c.1860–1948), a merchant from Sierra Leone, as honorary secretary, and the Trinidadian Felix Hercules (1889–1943), associate secretary.[8] Other officers included Kwamina F. Tandoh (c.1877–c.1932), a London-based businessman from the Gold Coast, as well as two Nigerians, the lawyer Montacute Thompson and Thomas H. Jackson, who would become a leading newspaperman and in 1920 established the short-lived *African Sentinel* in London.[9] Others attending included John Barbour-James (1867–1954) from British Guiana, who had formerly been a post office manager in the Gold Coast; Dr John Alcindor (1873–1924), a Trinidadian physician practising in London; Dusé Mohamed Ali; and John Eldred Taylor, the Sierra Leonean publisher of the *African Telegraph*.[10] Women participants included Trinidadians Audrey Jeffers and Sylvia Acham-Chen, Barbour-James' daughter Muriel and Cecilia Amado Taylor, a Sierra Leonean nurse and midwife.

Archer made a stirring speech at the event in which he drew attention to the role that African and Caribbean colonies, and their troops, had played in the war, but he predicted that the colonies would be denied any form of self-determination in the post-war world. He also mentioned the question of reparations, then being discussed by the victorious great powers, and he concluded that 'the Negro race here still need reparation to be made to us'.[11] Archer also outlined the main aims of the APU:

To promote the general welfare of African and Afro-Peoples ... to establish in London, England a 'home from home', where the members of the association may meet for social recreational and intellectual improvement ... to spread by papers ... and by means of a magazine or other publications, knowledge of the history and achievements of African and Afro-Peoples past, and present, and to promote the general advancement of African Peoples and to create and maintain a public sentiment in favour of brotherhood in its broadest sense.[12]

Archer declared that he was and had always been a 'race man', and the other officers made speeches showing that they too were equally concerned with such matters as the sacrifices made by Africans during the war, the need for a meeting place for Africans in London and contemporary problems of racism. Thompson condemned the use of such words as 'native' to describe Africans and complained that 'no other race has been described by colour'.[13] Tandoh declared that the colonies required a say in their own government and thought that demand might be aided by African representation at the League of Nations.[14] One of the union's first actions was to send a telegram to the government, pledging loyalty to the empire but also demanding that the Allied governments apply the principle of self-determination in relation to Germany's former colonies in Africa.[15] The APU also suggested that an African 'advisor' should be added to Britain's delegates to the post-war peace conferences. Through Broadhurst and W. F. Hutchison, originally from the Gold Coast, the APU also began to encourage increased activity amongst the newly formed committees of the National Congress of British West Africa (NCBWA).[16]

THE SOCIETY OF PEOPLES OF AFRICAN ORIGIN

Several of those present at the founding of the APU were also connected with the Society of Peoples of African Origin (SPAO) established at the close of the First World War by John Eldred Taylor. Its leading members included another Sierra Leonean businessman, Samuel Hughes, in addition to Felix Hercules. Taylor had first published the *African Telegraph* in London in 1914, not long after the emergence of the *African Times and Orient Review*. It became more widely known in December 1918 for exposing the public flogging of two naked women, which had occurred in 1914 under the jurisdiction of a colonial official in northern Nigeria. In 1919, the official, with government support, sued Taylor for libel and subsequently won the case, although the colonial authorities were forced to prevent further public flogging.[17] As the case was widely reported in the press in Britain, West Africa and the United States, in the view of the government the *African Telegraph* became 'a newspaper tending to promote racial hatred'. At the end of 1918, when Felix Hercules was appointed editor (as well as the general secretary of the SPAO), he became a subject for state surveillance.[18] The SPAO also stressed racial pride and the glories of Africa's past, as well as the importance of the role of women. Two of its leading members were Cecilia Amodo Taylor and Audrey Jeffers, who were designated joint honorary secretaries of the SPAO's ladies' committee. Jeffers was at the same time the Secretary of the London-based West African and West Indian Christian Union, an organization that spent much of its time in the 'consideration of race and colour questions', so evidently there were several organizations with similar concerns. Women also began to play increasingly important roles, and Jeffers' successor as Secretary of the Christian Union was a Nigerian, Aurora Fanimokun.

The SPAO's views, including their demand for limited self-government for Caribbean and African colonies within the British Empire, were presented in a series of articles entitled 'The African SOS' which appeared in the *African Telegraph* in early 1919.[19] It made it clear that such demands should always be 'pursued constitutionally', that the SPAO 'would have no truck with irresponsible agitators' and, it appealed, 'let us be moderate'. In February 1919 Taylor represented the SPAO at the Pan-African Congress convened by W. E. B. Du Bois in Paris. He continued to advocate moderate reforms for the colonies, but also an end to the colour bar and all discrimination, as well as equal educational opportunities for women.[20] The APU was represented at the Paris congress by Archer, who reportedly told the congress 'we must fight for our just rights at all times'.[21] Thereafter the APU developed an association with Du Bois that led it to play a key role in two subsequent Pan-African congresses.

THE 1919 RIOTS

All the existing organizations were compelled to respond to the racist attacks of 1919. The *African Telegraph* had initially called for everyone's 'best behaviour' in its 'Open Letter to Coloured Men in England' published early in 1919, but in April it condemned the 'race riots' as 'a disgrace to England,' and was scathing in its denunciation of trade-union racism, stating:

> The men now cast on the streets have paid their subscriptions as members of the Sailors and Fireman's Union, but the officials of the Glasgow branch have made and enforced a rule that no coloured man, even among its own members, be allowed to sail on British vessels.[22]

In June, Hercules was one of the speakers at an SPAO-organized public protest meeting in Hyde Park, London, at which he said that the SPAO had 'learned with horror and regret that large numbers of Africans and West Indians who came here either as seamen or in a military capacity to help the Mother Country during a critical period have been "signed off" and left stranded at various ports'. He also alleged that 'dangerous foreigners' were 'trying to sow dissension between the British working man and Black Britishers'.[23] At the same meeting John Eldred Taylor made a similar claim. He condemned 'the manifestations of race hatred and antagonism which have lately broken out in London, Liverpool and Cardiff, resulting in the ill-treatment, punishment, and death of negroes in those places', and demanded of the government:

> that adequate protection should be granted us as British subjects, especially as we are informed that agents-provocateurs are at the bottom of the movement. This meeting also protests against the preference shown to foreign seamen over negro seamen who have served the Empire in time of need.[24]

In the same month Leo Daniels, Secretary of the African Races Association of Glasgow, published a letter condemning the attacks on those who fought 'on the same battlefields with white men to defeat the enemy and make secure the British empire'. Daniels was an African Canadian, although in one paper he was described as 'of Egyptian descent', who had lived in Glasgow since 1886.[25] The association, formed at Glasgow University in 1917, had a membership of mainly students and professionals. Its first president may well have been a South African, S. M. Molema, a medical student and, in 1920, the author of *The Bantu Past and Present*. Molema reported that there were only seven 'coloured' students at the university, and probably for this reason the association also recruited non-students, several of them doctors. By December 1917 it had a membership of over twenty, mostly from the Caribbean, but also several from South and West Africa, including the Nigerian James Vaughan.[26] In 1919 the association clearly felt compelled to publicize its views on the 'unwarranted' attacks, questioning whether they were 'compatible with British teachings of justice and equity'.[27]

In June 1919 an APU delegation, led by Archer, visited Liverpool's deputy lord mayor to express its concern about those Black people who had been arrested. The APU subsequently contributed to the legal fees of several of those arrested, who were represented by one of its members, the barrister Edward T. Nelson. Hailing from British Guiana, Nelson had studied law at Oxford and in 1919 was practising in Manchester. Of the fifteen men whom Nelson defended, ten received prison sentences ranging from eight to twenty-two months.[28] Another Black barrister and APU member, W. S. Callander, also from British Guiana, represented Joseph Thompson, a Barbadian seaman, who was arrested for defending himself during rioting at West Indian Dock, London, in August 1919. Callander also defended Eldred Taylor during his libel case later that year.[29]

On behalf of the SPAO, Hercules wrote to the Colonial Secretary, asking whether the government intended to provide adequate protection for all its citizens, including Black men with white partners, and requesting an inquiry into the death of Charles Wootten, who had been killed after being attacked by a mob in Liverpool docks during the racist attacks in that city. Hercules also protested about the unemployment facing those Black seamen and the preference given to foreign workers. He then assumed even more prominence by responding to a letter in *The Times* from a former colonial administrator, who had justified the racist attacks on the basis that relationships between Black men and white women were 'such a thing of horror', that they 'revolt our very nature'. Hercules, in his published response, protested indignantly about the numerous colonial examples of what he referred to as the 'seduction of my women and girls by white men', and argued that if the repatriation of African and Caribbean servicemen was demanded to safeguard women in Britain, then British forces should also be evacuated from the colonies.[30]

In July 1919 Hercules was one of those involved in the temporary merger between the SPAO and the APU, which gave rise to a new organization, the Society of African Peoples (SAP), dedicated to the 'salvation of the people of the African race'.[31] Its inaugural meeting was attended by a delegation of the South African Native National Congress (led by Sol Plaatje) then visiting London. The delegation was accompanied by John Eldred Taylor and Thomas Jackson when they met with the Prime Minister, Lloyd George.[32] It appears that the SAP had encouraged the political activity of Dr Rufus Fennell (1887–1974) in Cardiff. Fennell was described in contemporary accounts as 'a coloured medical man', an ex-serviceman, and a US-trained doctor working as a dentist in Pontypridd. Fennell, it appears, was born in the US in 1887, although he may have been of Caribbean descent. When he arrived in Britain in 1915, he worked mainly on the stage as an actor and singer, and there is no evidence that he had any medical qualifications.[33]

Whatever his antecedents, Fennell came to prominence during the riots in Cardiff, where he emerged as 'the recognised leader of the coloured population in Cardiff'.[34] He organized two protest meetings, acted as the spokesman for the Black community, and called on people to defend themselves and their homes while remaining within the law. He also led deputations to the local council, where he was a strong advocate of repatriation. It was Fennell who accompanied 200 men who had agreed to be repatriated to Plymouth and who reported to the press how badly they were treated, as they had been denied the gratuities which they had been promised and denied food on their journey. In July 1919 he went to London to lobby the government concerning repatriation and it was at that time that he became associated with Hercules and the newly created Society of African Peoples. Fennell complained to government officials about the racism of the police and the way the repatriation process was being organized, but he was not opposed to repatriation itself.[35] John Eldred Taylor appears to have taken a similar approach when he was invited to a meeting of the London Committee for the Repatriation of Coloured Men, based at the police station in Poplar, east London. At one meeting, Taylor openly opposed William Connoll, a schoolteacher from Grand Cayman, who, as the representative of more than one hundred men in a hostel in Limehouse, had been demanding increased levels of government compensation to meet their expenses. Taylor explained that 'he and his society were advising the many coloured men who came to them for advice, to accept the Government Offer'.[36]

THE COLOUR BAR, COLONIALISM AND PAN-AFRICANISM

The APU aimed to establish a war memorial in London which 'would be a fitting token of the recognition of the services rendered by the sons of Africa'. Such a memorial, it was felt, would be 'educative' and might have some impact on the racism so prevalent at the time.[37] This was seen as even more important following the riots and the exclusion of colonial troops from the victory parade in London in 1919. As Hercules expressed it: 'Black men all the world over are asking today: "What have we got? What are we going to get out of it all? The answer, in effect, comes clear, convincing, and conclusive: '*Get back to your kennel, you damned dog of a n——!*' "' Hercules concluded that what he saw as the indifference and inactivity of 'the Imperial Government during the race riots drives home the fact they approve of them, that they are in line with Imperial policy'.[38]

During 1919 the APU and the SPAO separately concerned themselves with the challenge of establishing a meeting place, a 'home from home' for Africans in London. However, these plans were not realized and the situation developed into a contest between the APU and other African organizations on the one hand, and various missionary and government bodies on the other, as to who could first establish such a centre in London. This struggle came to symbolize African demands for self-government and self-reliance at the time and, for the APU, continued throughout its existence during the 1920s.[39]

Felix Hercules, who appears to have quarrelled with Taylor, Archer, Broadhurst and others, left Britain in the summer of 1919 for a tour of the Caribbean from which he would not return. Colonial Office officials considered the *African Telegraph* 'a wretched production almost entirely devoted to denouncing colonial government and their officers and stirring up hatred of Europeans', and were so alarmed by Hercules' tour that he was placed under constant surveillance.[40] In Jamaica he spoke on the 'Unity of the Coloured Race', just a few days before fighting broke out between Jamaicans and Royal Navy sailors, said to be 'due to the treatment which had been received by coloured sailors at Cardiff and Liverpool'. Hercules also promoted the proposal of the SPAO that a person of colour be appointed to a royal commission to investigate the government and economy of the colony. According to a letter sent to the Colonial Secretary, the SPAO considered it 'to be only fair that one of the commissioners should be of the same race as the majority of inhabitants of the colony'.[41]

The SPAO had also demanded economic and other social reforms in Jamaica as well as advocating a federation of the British West Indies.[42] Hercules' reiteration of these views during his tour clearly inspired members of the local Jamaica League, who made a special presentation in his honour. He also travelled to Grenada and British Guiana, where he promised the aid of the SPAO, and to Trinidad, where he was denied entry 'because his presence might endanger the public's safety', during strikes and other protests in that colony. Such was Hercules' notoriety that several parliamentary questions were asked about his tour and his being banned from Trinidad.[43] However, although he remained in contact with those in Britain for some years after this tour, Hercules never returned. By the end of 1919 John Eldred Taylor's legal fees and other debts terminated the SPAO's activities and the publication of the *African Telegraph*.[44] However, the short-lived SPAO showed that Black political organizations based in Britain had the possibility to exercise influence throughout the empire.

In 1920 the APU worked with the delegation of the newly formed National Congress of British West Africa (NCBWA) which had arrived in London to lobby the Colonial Office to reform colonial rule in the region. At that time, Broadhurst, who was the main point of liaison, wrote that the APU existed 'for the purpose of advancing the welfare of Africans in every possible way'.[45] In the summer of 1921, the APU was reorganized under the chairmanship of John Alcindor, following the resignation of Archer. In August of that year, Broad-hurst and the APU played a major role in organizing the opening session of the second Pan-African Congress, convened by Du Bois, which was held in London. The congress was opened by Alcindor, who told the more than one hundred delegates that 'Governments were not the enemies of the African races', but rather that 'they themselves were their own enemies because they lacked character, they lacked education, they lacked cohesion'. Nevertheless, in his view the task was to 'speed up' the awakening consciousness that all was 'not well with Africa and Africans', and 'galvanise it into activity by means of wise propaganda'.[46] One of the sessions of the congress was chaired by Archer, who introduced Shapurji Saklatvala, at that time a pro-spective Labour MP for Battersea, who spoke about the concerns of the Indian people. Many of the most notable African and Caribbean men in London attended, including Eldred Taylor, Barbour-James and Broadhurst. Notably, women were almost entirely absent from the recorded list of participants.[47]

One of the main issues discussed at the London session was the 'colour bar' and other forms of racism. It was an opportunity for speakers to give their heartfelt personal experiences and views. The session was mainly notable for producing a 'Declaration to the World', sometimes known as the 'London Manifesto', which demanded racial equality and limited self-government and other reforms in the colonies.[48] In November 1923, the first session of the third Pan-African Congress was also held in London. Alcindor and other leading APU members, such as Tandoh and the Sierra Leonean Emma Smith (1864–1928), were again prominent and assisted with the organization of the event.[49] Following the congress, Du Bois spoke at the annual meeting of the APU, an occasion, like the congress itself, which showed that the APU was concerned and informed not only about matters in Britain and the colonies, but also those in the US and throughout the African dias-pora.[50] The activities of the APU continued for several years and it remained committed to the creation of a meeting place and even offered a 'benevolent guardianship' to the 'hundreds of African stu-dents who go to England each year'.[51] However, its influence waned and by 1924 Barbour-James was to preside over a new association (the Association of Coloured Peoples).

NEW ORGANIZATIONS
AND NEW ACTIVISM

In the decade after the First World War student organizations such as the Union of Students of African Descent (USAD), and, most importantly, the West African Students' Union (WASU) became more prominent.[52]

The Union of Students of African Descent

The USAD established in London in 1922 grew out of the earlier West African and West Indian Christian Union, which had supplemented its membership with non-Christians. Its first president was a Trinidadian, Percy Acham Chen, and a Nigerian, Aurora Kayode (née Fanimokun) was another of its most prominent early members. By 1924 it boasted well over one hundred members and after 1923, when H. A. Hayfron-Benjamin from the Gold Coast became its president, it began to concern itself much more with matters of direct interest to West African students and to draw its membership from both England and Scotland. The USAD declared itself to be an apolitical, cultural and social organization 'believing that a premature participation in politics does not seem likely to serve the best interest of the average student'. Nevertheless, it soon found itself ranged against both the press and the Colonial Office as one of its Nigerian members, Ladipo Solanke (c.1886–1958), spearheaded a major anti-racist campaign.[53]

Solanke came to Britain in 1922 as a law student at University College London but, according to his diary, he was soon in debt and forced to teach the Yoruba language to other students to make ends meet. Nevertheless, he quickly began to make a name for himself as a leading spokesman for the growing number of West African students residing in the country. He was to remain a leading anti-colonial and anti-racist campaigner until his death in London in 1958. In March 1924 he wrote a letter to *West Africa*, the widely read British publication financed by those with commercial interests in the region, to complain about an article in the *Evening News*. The offending article, 'Empire making in Nigeria', had credited the colonial government with abolishing 'cannibalism' and 'black magic' within twenty years.

The article had also quoted from a recent speech by the Governor of Nigeria in which, it was claimed, he referred to areas of Nigeria where 'human meat was sold openly in the markets in quite recent times'.[54] Solanke had already complained to the *Evening News*, refuting claims of cannibalism and demanding that the truth be told. In his view such racist reporting could 'do serious harm to those of us from Nigeria who are now in London for educational purposes'.[55] He was supported by other African members of the USAD, including its Nigerian vice-president, Adegunle Soetan, who wrote his own protest letter to *West Africa*. However, the racism of the *Evening News* was quickly followed by derogatory articles in the *Sunday Review* and the *Sunday Express*, ridiculing the West African section of the Empire Exhibition being held at Wembley to promote Britain's imperial mission and colonial progress. In particular, press reports were full of offensive remarks about Akosua Baa, a princess from the Gold Coast, who was, like others, on display in a 'walled city' as part of the exhibition.

The Empire Exhibition was the occasion for many African dignitaries and other visitors to travel to London. It was an important national event, attracting over 26 million visitors, so it was a particularly opportune time for student protests.[56] The USAD passed a resolution condemning the articles, which it sent to the Colonial Secretary, calling the articles 'vulgar and offensive' and demanding that the Colonial Office take action to ban them. The USAD made clear its intention to send its resolution to the press throughout West Africa, as well as to various prominent individuals. Although the Colonial Office was reluctant to interfere with what it considered the freedom of the press, steps were taken to prevent further racist articles about the West African section of the exhibition.[57]

The students did not condemn the entire rationale for such an exhibition, but they had flexed their muscles, scored an important victory and shown what might be achieved. They had gained the support of *West Africa*, an influential publication that carried a front-page editorial demanding action to protect 'British West Africans from such outrages'. Such a victory could only encourage more student activism.[58] Indeed, Solanke suggested that the USAD 'begin a campaign to suppress the everyday ridicule against the Blacks in this country', and he regularly scoured the press for offensive material. He later wrote that it was the racism faced by Africans, and particularly the racist press coverage of the Empire Exhibition that spurred him to attempt to organize West African students in Britain. He wrote that he had a divinely inspired dream revealing that:

> Until Africans at home and abroad, including all persons of African descent, organize and develop the . . . principles of self-help, unity and cooperation among themselves, and fight it out to remove the colour bar, they would continue to suffer the results of colour prejudice and remain the hewers of wood and drawers of water for the other races of mankind.[59]

His protest letters received encouragement from Amy Ashwood Garvey (1897–1969), the former wife of Marcus Garvey, who was living in Streatham at the time. The two became friends and, partly due to her continuing enthusiasm, a new organization, the Nigerian Progress Union (NPU), was formed in Ladbroke Grove in July 1924.[60]

The Nigerian Progress Union

The NPU worked 'to promote the general welfare of Nigerians, from an educational not a political point of view', and this included the aim of establishing 'a much-needed hostel in London for all African students'. It also aimed to promote research into West African traditional laws, customs and institutions. Most of its thirteen male founder members were studying law, or medicine. Daniel Ekanem Esin (Middle Temple and London School of Economics) was elected president of the NPU, F. O. Lucas (Middle Temple) vice-president, F. O. Vincent (Inner Temple) became treasurer and Solanke honorary secretary. Amy Ashwood Garvey did not attend the inaugural meeting but Solanke wrote that the NPU was 'conceived, born and mothered' by her, so she was honoured with the Yoruba title of 'Iyalode' (traditionally a high-ranking female chief) of the NPU.[61] Although based in London, the NPU soon attracted members from other cities, including Bristol, Birmingham and Edinburgh. By 1925 it had more than thirty members, at least three of them women, including the two daughters of leading Nigerian politician and NPU patron, Dr Curtis Adeniyi-Jones. The union met monthly and became particularly concerned to find ways to

The Nigerian Progress Union

combat everyday racism. In the 1920s 'the colour bar' even existed within some universities, which were reluctant to admit African students.[62]

The NPU viewed Nigeria as a potential 'mighty Negro Empire or Republic', full of 'immense possibilities' and 'undeveloped resources and wealth'. Its development was arrested, it was argued, as a result of colonial rule, because its education system was 'not national enough', and because the Nigerian 'had been taught to hate all his institutions and customs'. The NPU wished to remedy this problem. Its approach seems to have been inspired by Amy Ashwood, who claimed that 'the Negro race . . . is not yet ripe for political emancipation', but the NPU's principles of 'self-help, self-sacrifice, self-control and self-knowledge' probably derived from her former husband. Solanke, who later worked with Marcus Garvey, claimed that he 'aroused in us . . . our race consciousness, although we may disagree with some of the methods of the great Negro organizer'.[63]

Despite apparently rejecting politics, Solanke published an 'Open

Letter to the Negroes of the World' and other information about the NPU in an African American journal called *The Spokesman* in 1925. Amongst other things, he argued that 'the Negro at home and the Negro abroad should find their way to understand each other better with a view to cooperating for the final emancipation of the entire Negro race'.[64] As well as directing appeals to African Americans the NPU kept abreast of political developments in Nigeria and throughout West Africa. It was often addressed by various visiting African dignitaries and soon came to the attention of the Colonial Office.[65] One of the main objectives of the NPU was the promotion of 'Negro or African literatures, culture and institutions through research' and Solanke was at the forefront of these efforts. In June 1924 he was the first person to make a radio broadcast in the Yoruba language in Britain, when he gave a speech entitled 'An Instance of Mortality' to a national audience.[66]

The West African Students' Union

African and Caribbean students often joined several organizations. In the 1920s those like the APU and USAD continued to function alongside the Gold Coast Students' Association and local associations such as the Africa societies at the universities of Edinburgh and Cambridge. These organizations were particularly necessary as a means of mutual support in the face of the ubiquitous racism of the time. However, in 1925, a Sierra Leonean politician, Dr Herbert Bankole-Bright, a former medical student at Edinburgh who was visiting London, urged the numerous students from the West African colonies to establish a new united organization to reflect the politics and formation of the National Congress of British West Africa. Solanke had already mooted a similar idea and, although some labelled them 'segregationists', he and twenty other male students founded the West African Students' Union at 5 Lancaster Road, Ladbroke Grove, in August 1925.[67] For the most part under Solanke's leadership, the WASU established itself as the main cultural and political forum for West Africans in Britain for the next twenty-five years. It served as a training ground for many of their future political leaders and functioned as a major campaigning organization in Britain against racism and colonial rule. Solanke became the WASU's general secretary, a post he held for many years, and J. B. Danquah, a philosophy student at University College London from the Gold Coast, its first president.

The union had several aims including, 'to present to the world a true picture of African life and philosophy', and to 'foster a spirit of national consciousness amongst its members'. It also quickly established major advances over earlier organizations. A monthly journal, *Wāsù* (a word with different meanings in various languages in West Africa, for example, 'to preach' in Yoruba) was published regularly from March 1926. Over the years *Wāsù* played a major role championing the concerns of West Africans in Britain, not least the mounting demands for independence from colonial rule. In its early years the journal was mainly concerned with African history, languages, culture and philosophy. It championed the notion of West African political and cultural nationhood, as earlier imagined by James Africanus Horton and Edward Blyden, as well as 'the equality of the races'.[68] These were also the dominant themes in two publications by WASU members, Solanke's *United West Africa at the Bar of the Family of Nations*, in 1927, and J. W. de Graft Johnson's *Towards Nationhood in West Africa*, published in 1928.[69] The WASU also managed to develop several international connections and was soon advertising that its journal was available in the United States, Brazil, the Caribbean, various parts of Africa and even in India.

The WASU also campaigned against the numerous examples of racism and the colour bar. Two of its members, Ekundayo Akerele and Adetokunbo Ademola (the latter was to become Chief Justice of Nigeria) were acquitted of charges of a breach of the peace in 1927, when it was revealed in court that a case had been fabricated against them. In 1928 the WASU objected to the use of the word 'n——' by the politician David Lloyd George during an election speech.[70] In 1929 the students campaigned against a display of 200 Africans in an 'African village' at an exhibition in Newcastle. The matter was subsequently raised in Parliament by the Indian MP Saklatvala, who pointed out that it would only be making an exhibition of the 'wretched way in which Africans were living'. He called on the government to make sure that exhibitions 'did not bring the Negro population into contempt or ridicule'.[71] In 1930 the new president of WASU, Dr Okunade Ajibade, complained that 'we cannot find rooms in hotels to lay our heads', and led a deputation to see Members of Parliament about the colour bar. He gained the support of the newly formed West Indian Students Association, students from India and Ceylon, and an increasingly prominent Jamaican physician based in Peckham, Dr Harold Moody.[72]

In such circumstances, the WASU was determined to establish its own base in London. During 1928 it was able to temporarily use Marcus Garvey's house, in Castletown Road, West Kensington, as its headquarters, but it continued with plans to establish its own hostel. In 1929 Solanke was sent on a fundraising mission to West Africa and he toured the four colonies for three years, founding over twenty new branches of the WASU as he went. The mission not only raised sufficient funds to rent a house on his return, but also allowed the WASU to claim that it represented public opinion throughout British West Africa through these branches. The WASU hostel was eventually opened at 62 Camden Road in March 1933 with Solanke's wife, Opeulu Obisanya, as its first 'matron'. One of the hostel's first guests was Fela Sowande (later to become a famous musician). One of its most important aspects was a restaurant which provided African food.[73] The need for a hostel was further highlighted by the court case involving Oluwale Alakija, the president of the WASU, who, in 1932, successfully sued a London hotel for refusing him admission because he was a 'man of colour'.[74]

Indeed, even the Colonial Office became concerned that the increasing numbers of students, the future leaders of Africa, as well as important African visitors to Britain, were becoming disaffected by their experiences of racism. The Colonial Office began its own attempts to establish a student hostel in London, in rivalry with the WASU. For this purpose, it convened a semi-clandestine committee of trustees, including the president of the newly formed League of Coloured Peoples.[75]

The League of Coloured Peoples

The League of Coloured Peoples (LCP) was founded in March 1931, at the central London YMCA, under the presidency of Harold Moody (1882–1947), a Jamaican GP who, from 1912 until his death, maintained a surgery in Peckham. Moody arrived in Britain in 1904 to study medicine at King's College Hospital, married an English woman and was very much a London resident. A devout Christian, he preached throughout Britain for the Christian Endeavour Federation and was in 1935 elected its president, probably the first time that anyone of African or Caribbean heritage was elected president of 'a British white national organization'.[76] He formed the LCP largely in response to the problems posed by the racism which he had on many occasions experienced himself or come across when he attempted to help other Black professionals in Britain.[77] Moody had been rejected for several hospital posts, on one occasion 'because the Matron refused to have a coloured doctor working at the hospital'.[78] Even when he was a well-established GP, he was rejected as a 'Poor Law' doctor (doctors provided free of charge to the poor before there was the National Health Service) in south London, since the poor 'would not have a n—— to attend them'.[79]

Although for most 'coloured' people racism was a daily occurrence, the colour bar had only assumed national prominence during the 1924 Empire Exhibition and did so again in 1929, when the famous African American performer Paul Robeson was ejected from the Savoy Grill in London. There were then several other reports of racism in the press which, by early 1931, prompted a meeting of the Missionary Council in London. It was at this meeting that the creation of a new organization specifically to deal with the colour bar was proposed. Moody then became the moving force behind the creation of the LCP, encouraged by a visiting African American historian, Dr Charles Wesley of Howard University.[80]

The LCP was subsequently led by professionals and students from the Caribbean and West Africa. By the early 1930s some 300 students belonged to it, but its membership was open to all, including members of missionary societies and sympathetic politicians.[81] As Moody explained, the term 'coloured' meant 'everyone' – 'because there are no WHITE people ... We therefore admit all people as members ... however our work is mainly confined to people of African descent ... although we have some Indians in our ranks.'[82] In 1933 the LCP produced the first edition of its 'official organ', *The Keys*, which proclaimed that the LCP 'has as its main object the purpose of stating the cause of the Black Man', but could not ignore 'the claims of the people of colour who owe allegiance to a flag other than our own'.[83] *The Keys* was named by LCP member Stephen Thomas after Dr James Aggrey's reference to the need for both black and white piano keys to make music, a metaphor for racial harmony. It regularly reported on the achievements of African Americans, as well as on the famous international campaign to free the 'Scottsboro boys', nine African Americans falsely convicted of rape, while also highlighting the triumphs of the West Indies cricket team and commenting on various aspects of British rule in the African and Caribbean colonies.

The LCP was a campaigning and pressure group, but it was just as well known for its garden parties, or for organizing summer outings to the seaside or Christmas parties for some of London's impoverished Black children. It gained a particular reputation for campaigning against the colour bar in the health service, but it took action on a variety of issues.[84] It also attracted a wide range of members: the Jamaican writer and broadcaster Una Marson (1905–1965); Stella Thomas (1906–1974), the first African woman barrister; the first Black student at the LSE, Arthur Lewis (1915–1991), who became a Nobel Prize-winning economist; radicals like the writer and activist C. L. R. James (1901–1989), as well as communists such as Desmond Buckle (1910–1964) and Peter Blackman (1909–1993).[85]

Marson occupied a particularly significant role in the early 1930s. Her play *At What a Price* was staged at the YMCA, as well as at the Scala Theatre in London's West End, in 1933. Although it made a financial loss, it was notable for its all-LCP cast, including the writer herself, Moody, Stella and Stephen Thomas, and Desmond Buckle.[86] Marson was also Assistant Secretary of the LCP, as well as Assistant Editor (and sometimes Editor) of *The Keys*, which soon had a circulation of several thousand copies. *The Keys* sometimes featured poetry, including Marson's 'Nigger', her own literary protest against the colour bar. She later wrote of the racism she faced finding employment as a stenographer: 'One agent told me she didn't register Black women because they would have to work within offices with white women. Another agent tried to find me a position and he told me that though my references were excellent, firms did not want to employ a Black stenographer.'[87]

Marson also took up the problem of racism faced by other Black women. At the British Commonwealth League conference in 1934 she spoke of 'a coloured girl nurse' who had applied for work at twenty-eight British hospitals and 'had been rejected in every case'. An investigation by the *News Chronicle* confirmed Marson's complaint and concluded, 'a coloured girl has a very poor chance of securing a nursing post in the average hospital'.[88] Some LCP members did succeed in completing their nursing training in Britain, such as Susannah Nylander, a Sierra Leonean, based at the Crumpsall Hospital in Manchester, while others such as the Ademola sisters, who were Nigerian members of the WASU, trained in London. However, her assessment in *The Keys* was that 'it is almost impossible for boys and girls of colour, born in this country', to obtain suitable employment.[89]

Many of the LCP's early members, such as Stella and Stephen Thomas and Desmond Buckle, were West African students, and its relationship with WASU during the early 1930s was often fraught. The most significant quarrel was over Aggrey House, the hostel for Black students in London established in October 1934 by the Colonial Office in Doughty Street, next to today's Dickens Museum. Even before the Colonial Office could open its hostel, in March 1934 the WASU had published a small pamphlet titled *The Truth about Aggrey House – An Exposure of the Government Plan for Control of African Students in Great Britain*.[90] Harold Moody and all those connected with Aggrey House were denounced as traitors and the WASU organized a boycott and issued an appeal 'to every lover of freedom to help us check this scheme of imperialism'. The students saw the involvement of the Colonial Office as connected with 'imperialist oppression in the colonies', and their campaign drew them closer to communist-led organizations in Britain: the League against Imperialism (LAI), the National Council for Civil Liberties and the Negro Welfare Association (NWA), the 'subversive elements' of most concern to the Colonial Office.[91] The dispute over Aggrey House created divisions between the WASU and the LCP and led to accusations against Moody. However, even earlier, in 1932, the *Negro Worker*, edited in Hamburg by Trinidadian communist George Padmore (1903–1959), had issued a warning:

> We appeal to all militant coloured students in London to break with the sycophantic leadership of Dr. Harold Moody, a typical 'Uncle Tom', whose coat strings are so tied up with the Colonial Office that he is out to have every self-respecting Negro kowtowing before his arrogant imperialist masters.[92]

Moody's label as a moderate stuck, and even though, for a time, the WASU and the communists were using similar language, the former's dispute with the LCP was resolved a few years later. The lobbying methods of the WASU and the LCP were not so different. Indeed, the LCP also was in close contact with the LAI and other communist-led organizations. In 1931, when David Tucker, a law student and publicity secretary of the LCP, was subject to the colour bar and refused admission to some tearooms in London's Strand, it was the LAI that wrote to the British government in protest.[93]

STRUGGLES OF THE SEAFARERS

The problems faced by 'coloured seamen' continued during the 1930s. In this period 'coloured' remained a term which might refer to those who originated from West Africa, Somalia and the Caribbean, as well as Yemen and other parts of Asia. It also included many who were long-term British residents, as well as their children. The numbers were significant. One survey of east London in 1932 estimated that there were 1,500 unmarried 'coloured seamen' in the Canning Town area, as well as 300 families headed by African or Caribbean men.[94] What is noticeable is that during the 1920s and 1930s racist attacks in the press and elsewhere were often made on the families of seamen and particularly on those referred to as their 'half-caste' children.[95] Underlying many of the problems faced by seamen and their families were the 1920 Aliens Order and the 1925 Coloured Alien Seamen Order, which effectively decreed that all 'coloured seamen' were aliens, unless they could prove otherwise, and made them liable to arrest and even deportation. By 1927 more than 8,000 'coloured seamen' had been forced to register with the police under the 1925 legislation. This encouraged the view that such seamen, although necessary in wartime, were in peacetime an unwanted social and moral problem.[96] The problems facing the seamen and their families during the 1930s led to sustained resistance involving several organizations created during that decade. Increasingly, these organizations formed a united front against racism and colonialism and for the rights of all 'coloured' people in Britain.

By 1930 the slump in the British shipping industry had already led to the unemployment of more than 20,000 seamen and severe competition for work. In some ports African, Caribbean and Yemeni seamen were supported by the Seamen's Minority Movement (SMM), formed in 1929 and affiliated to the communist-led National Minority Movement, which sought to establish a new union 'run by seamen for seamen'.[97] The SMM established its own 'committee of militant coloured seamen' which included Chris Braithwaite, known as Chris Jones (1885–1944), and Jim Headley in London, Harry O'Connell in Cardiff and William Brown in Liverpool.[98] The SMM battled against racism in the shipping industry, as well as the officials and policies of the National Union of Seamen (NUS), accurately described by one historian as 'effectively a company union for the British Shipping Federation'.[99] At a time of large-scale unemployment, the NUS, as well as other seamen's unions, continued to create divisions and incite racism against 'coloured seamen', especially those referred to as 'Arabs' (including Somalis, Sudanese, Adenese, Yemenis, Zanzibaris and Egyptians). The unions often claimed that they only intended to reserve 'British jobs for British seamen', including 'coloured seamen'. They maintained that they were only opposed to 'coloured aliens' because they undercut British wage rates. However, the unions did nothing to organize these workers, who were often British colonial subjects, nor to protest at the poor pay and conditions to which they were subjected. Government, as well as union campaigns against 'coloured aliens', tended in practice to be directed against all 'coloured' people, and therefore blatantly racist. The main consequence was to create divisions amongst workers, to act as a diversion from the common problems they faced and, by attacking 'coloured' workers, to attack the rights of all.

In 1929 there was a renewed racist campaign in the NUS' paper, *The Seaman*, which included a demand for stricter government application of the Special Restriction (Coloured Alien Seamen) Order of 1925, as well as encouraging attacks on 'Arab' seamen, their families and the growing numbers of so-called 'half-caste' children.[100] This was at a time when the union should have been defending the jobs and rights of all seamen. The racist campaign culminated in the summer of 1930 with the introduction of a rota system for the employment of 'Arab' and Somali seamen in Cardiff, South Shields and Hull, which was administered, to the great detriment of the seamen, by the NUS and the shipowners, under the auspices of the National Maritime

Board and with full government support until the start of the Second World War.[101]

In these circumstances there were many examples of seamen fighting for their rights in the ports. In the spring of 1930, thirteen Somali seamen from South Shields were prevented from boarding a ship docked in North Shields by sailors and other white men on the quayside. When the Somalis defended themselves, they were arrested and three subsequently imprisoned. The incident was reported in the press as a riot. In response, representatives of the SMM blamed the NUS and its policies for such divisions, claiming both in open-air meetings and in the press that the incident could have been prevented.

When the new rota system was introduced in August 1930, many so-called 'Arab' and Somali seamen rejected it, as well as attempts to create divisions between them and white seamen. They were supported by the SMM, which also began to campaign with them against the need for seamen to pay for the PC5, a form showing that they were fully paid-up union members, before they could obtain work. Somali and other 'Arab' sailors on Tyneside took the lead in this struggle, which consisted of a strike, with seamen picketing against the NUS and the shipowners, but all seamen in the area, both Black and white, were involved. At the same time, in Cardiff, Liverpool and some other ports, 'sympathy strikes' were organized.[102] At one mass meeting at the Mill Dam in South Shields it was reported that nearly a thousand 'Arabs' and Somalis attended and more than a thousand white seamen.

The SMM claimed that during this period almost one-third of its members were based in Tyneside and this would certainly have amounted to several hundred.[103] The NUS and shipowners, with police support, attacked the pickets, and several seamen were arrested, in what was referred to in the press as a 'racial riot'. In the aftermath many of the twenty arrested 'Arab' seamen were deported, despite support from the SMM and the International Class War Prisoners' Aid Committee.[104] Those that refused to join the rota were denied both employment and 'outdoor relief' from the Public Assistance Committee, and some were forced to enter the workhouse. Moreover, in 1931 a total of nearly sixty 'Arabs' unable to prove that they were British subjects were deported from South Shields.[105]

Cardiff

Unemployment in Britain rose by 76 per cent during the Depression decade of the 1930s. Workers of African and Caribbean heritage were particularly vulnerable. Between 1930 and 1933 it is estimated that a third of all seamen in Britain were unemployed, but in Cardiff the figure was higher: 40 per cent.[106] The figures for unemployment amongst Black seamen were worse still and in 1936 it was reported that 'out of a total of 690 unemployed firemen on the Cardiff Docks Register, 599 were coloured men'.[107] The Black population in Cardiff, mainly confined to Tiger Bay, in the Butetown dockland area, had continued to suffer from discrimination in the period following 1919. This was as a result of the racist Coloured Alien Seamen Order and the policies of the seamen's union.[108] Moreover, as early as 1929, a local survey of 119 employers in Cardiff reported that 80 per cent of respondents refused to employ Black people.[109] However, discrimination also occurred in many other ways. In 1941 it was reported that 'it has always been the policy of the local authority to favour the segregation of the coloured people in the dock area'. Segregation did not only occur in the United States and South Africa.[110] The Tiger Bay population was therefore amongst those most severely affected by mass unemployment during the 1930s and the least likely to receive financial support. Some 'coloured seamen' were also affected by the rota system introduced in August 1930.

In 1933 the first edition of *The Keys* reported 'it is the most difficult thing for a coloured British citizen, even though born in England, to obtain work of any kind in this country'. This was true throughout the UK. Coca Clarke recalled that during the 1930s her father, an unemployed seaman from Nigeria, organized 'African shows' in Blackpool to earn a livelihood. She remembered that, 'He did all sorts of things, illusions like changing a woman into a skeleton and back; fire-eating and walking on glass, hot coals dancing, methylated spirits makes the soles of your feet really hard.' He also employed 'about six English Black girls' from Cardiff and Liverpool as African dancers in this enterprise. According to Clarke, 'the girls sort of danced with African skirts, not specific African dance as they do today'. She explained, '[I]t was the only thing Black girls could do in them days really, because you could not get a job in a shop, or you know a decent job.'[111]

The LCP particularly focused on Cardiff and pointed out:

That in Cardiff alone there are 1800 seamen and labourers from the West Indies and West Africa and 500 Somalis and Arabs. That these men who were wanted during the Great War and who served their King and Country well, are now having a most difficult time from the local authorities. That these men, our fellow British citizens, are being subjected to the 'Colour Bar' (locally dubbed 'the means test') in unemployment relief.[112]

Unemployed Black seamen were regularly paid less 'unemployment relief' because it was argued 'coloured men needed less to live on than white men'.[113] The Tiger Bay population was also affected by other forms of racism. In 1929 the Chief Constable of Cardiff had even argued for legislation, modelled on South Africa's Immorality Act, to prevent local women engaging in sexual relations with Black men.[114] The Chief Constable complained that such relationships produced children who were 'half-caste with the vicious hereditary taint of their parents'.[115] The racism of the 1930s therefore increasingly focused not only on the undesirability of the employment of Black seamen, but also the very existence of their children, who, it was argued, were often unemployable and constituted a significant social problem. In 1929 the *Daily Herald* reported with alarm that 'hundreds of half-caste children with vicious tendencies' were growing up in Cardiff, while the following year the *Western Mail* lamented the fact 'that there were more than 500 half-caste children in Cardiff, and the authorities in the city were at a loss to know what to do with them'.[116]

Such racist scaremongering, which became widespread, led to the publication of a major report on the subject by the Liverpool Association for the Welfare of Half-Caste Children in 1930. Officially titled the *Report on An Investigation into the Colour Problem in Liverpool and Other Ports*, but known as the Fletcher report, it attacked both the seamen and their families and sought to establish that there was a 'colour problem' in Liverpool and elsewhere.[117] Openly racist in its outlook, the Fletcher report favoured the discriminatory policies of the NUS and restricted the employment of 'coloured seamen', whom it referred to as 'a real social menace'. It was warmly welcomed by the union.[118] Several other reports on the same subject and based on similar eugenicist arguments were produced in this period. A brief synopsis of the more sympathetic views of Nancie Sharpe, who in 1932 received some funding from the Methodist Church for a survey of conditions in the ports of Cardiff and London, subsequently appeared in *The Keys*.[119] In 1935 the Richardson report on 'coloured seamen' and their families published by the British Social Hygiene Council might even have been encouraged by the reported concerns of the LCP.[120] The Richardson report dwelt on the 'idleness' and 'ignorance' of the unemployed seamen, the prevalence of 'venereal disease' and tuberculosis amongst them and their families, the 'loose moral character' of their female partners and the resulting 'half-caste population'. The 'half-caste girl' was seen as a particular social and moral problem, unemployable and almost certain to be destined for a life of prostitution. The report concluded that in the dockland areas of London, Liverpool and Cardiff there were sufficient seamen 'mated to the white women of the districts to produce hundreds more of this unfortunate half-caste population as each year passes'.[121]

One of the differences between the WASU and the LCP was that the League took a much greater interest in the problems faced by Black workers during the Depression in cities such as Liverpool and Cardiff (and the LCP eventually established a branch in the latter). Moody first visited Cardiff in September 1934 and reported that the colour bar was denying a population of '5,000 coloured people' (half of the 'roughly ten thousand coloured people' in Britain, according to the LCP), employment, as well as unemployment benefit.[122] The LCP was then contacted by Harry O'Connell, a resident in Cardiff for many years, who had established the Cardiff Coloured Seamen's Committee to defend their interests. On the committee 'sat spokesmen of Malayan, Arab, Somali, West-Indian and African workers', who, once again, found that their interests were betrayed by the government as well as the National Union of Seamen.[123]

O'Connell, a former seaman himself, was a leading organizer for the communist-led Seamen's Minority Movement in Cardiff and had long been a spokesman for 'coloured seamen' in Cardiff, where he had first settled in about 1910.[124] As a member of the NUS he had protested against the discrimination faced by Cardiff seamen, as well as the discriminatory policies of the union, and in the late 1920s he helped to establish the Colonial Defence Association in Cardiff (an organization that appears to have been re-formed in 1937).[125] In 1932 he attended the congress of the communist-led International of Seamen and Harbour Workers, held near Hamburg, Germany, where he was referred to by George Padmore as 'the leader of the colonial seamen in England'. Following the demise of the SMM, O'Connell established the Cardiff Coloured Seamen's Committee, probably in 1933, to 'fight against' any discrimination in employment. On behalf of this committee, he travelled to London to confront the NUS and, later, to gain the support of the LCP, as well as others including Arthur Evans, the local Conservative MP.[126]

O'Connell was also a member of the Negro Welfare Association (NWA), which was most often represented by its Barbadian secretary, Arnold Ward (c.1886–c.1944), known to the authorities as 'one of the principal Negro agitators' in Britain.[127] The NWA had been formed in London in 1931 and was one of several initiatives by communists to establish 'negro' organizations in London, Liverpool and Cardiff, and in particular to organize seafarers to fight for their rights. Both Ward and O'Connell were regularly in contact with George Padmore, as well as other Black communists based in Europe and the United States, and contributed to and disseminated the *Negro Worker*, the publication of the International Trade Union Committee of Negro Workers. The NWA had fewer members than the LCP and was described as 'a fighting organization of class conscious, anti-imperialist Negro and white workers'. One of its most notable members was Jomo Kenyatta (1891–1978), the future leader of Kenya, who was based in Britain during the 1930s and 1940s. Other prominent activists included Chris Jones from Barbados, formerly an organizer for the NUS and the SMM, and Rowland Sawyer, a seaman from Sierra Leone. The NWA often worked with the League against Imperialism to highlight examples of the colour bar, or injustices in the colonies. It also campaigned on the Scottsboro case, in particular during the 1932 tour of Britain by Ada Wright, the mother of two of the accused.[128] The Scottsboro case was a cause célèbre during this period and Kenyatta, WASU member Kobina Kessie and African American performer Isaac Hatch were the three Black members of the London-based Scottsboro Defence

Committee chaired by Carmel Haden Guest, the wife of a Liberal Party MP.[129]

From 1933 onwards, Ward served on the editorial board of the *Negro Worker* and his letters condemning the 1935 British Shipping (Assistance) Act, the treachery of the National Union of Seamen and the plight of 'Negro and other coloured seamen', were often featured in that publication.[130] Ward was also concerned with the plight of the seamen's families during the Depression and the NWA regularly organized seaside outings for children who, it was reported, 'pass their childhood in the dark and damp slum areas'. Ward wrote that the children of Black seamen 'are treated as outcasts and "aliens" and they cannot get a decent job. Thus, the hardships of hunger, misery and squalor combined with segregation make life for our little ones as hard and sorrowful as it is for their parents.'[131]

'Probably the best piece of work done by the League so far', was how *The Keys* described the LCP's intervention in Cardiff 'on behalf of the coloured seamen'.[132] Two members of the League, P. Cecil Lewis from St Vincent, the League's secretary, and George Brown, a historian from the United States studying at the LSE, spent several weeks in Cardiff in 1935, interviewing over 200 people and investigating the conditions facing its Black population. They found that many of the seamen continued to face discrimination and even arrest from the police, even though they were British, because of the British Shipping (Assistance) Act of that same year and the 1925 Coloured Alien Seamen Order. The 1935 act provided subsidies to British tramp shipping during the Depression and encouraged shipowners to employ 'British' crews. As in the past, the term 'British', although often defined as 'natives of the United Kingdom', was widely interpreted to mean 'white'.[133] Some of the seamen who were discriminated against in Cardiff had distinguished military service careers, several had served during the First World War, others in the colonial conquest of Africa, and one during the Boer War. Many of those classed as 'aliens' by the police had been in the country for more than twenty years, several for over thirty years and had British passports, birth certificates and other official documents. The LCP contacted the local MP and subsequently questions were asked in Parliament.[134] It also contacted those administering the shipping subsidy, as well as the NUS, the Unemployment

Assistance Board and the Shipping Federation and managed to secure employment for some seamen.

However, the LCP's report concluded that the trade unions, police and shipping companies had collaborated to deny '3,000 coloured seamen residing in Cardiff ... their rightful claims to employment'. In addition, the report found that the families of seamen were suffering from lack of a balanced diet, and that their children, referred to as 'half-castes', were denied secondary education and employment and even rejected from churches. The LCP continued to campaign on behalf of those in Cardiff, believing that such blatant racism was bad for the empire.[135] It also began to concern itself with young people in several other cities including Swansea, Hull, South Shields and Glasgow.[136]

The Shipping (Assistance) Act led to protests in other port cities. More than forty Somalis and many other 'Arab' seamen in South Shields and other parts of the north-east complained to the government that they were being discriminated against. Two Somalis, Omar Mohamed and Adan Erobay, representing forty Somalis from South Shields, wrote to the government in March 1935:

> Shipping is not too bad here for the Foreigners such as German, Norwegian and other Nationalities, yet we are British still they never give us a chance ... we have all served in the last war and in the Navy also Army, we lost a lot of men in German East Africa. So now Sir I have done our duty [sic] for this Country ... [137]

Letters of protests from Somalis in South Shields continued. A deputation approached the local mayor and more than fifty wrote to the government again in August 1935.[138] A police investigation into the situation in South Shields reported to the government that the Somali seamen had 'always expressed dissatisfaction at being treated as aliens'.[139] The Somali Society of Great Britain and a group of forty-four Somalis based in Sunderland hired lawyers to defend their rights. Many seamen sought naturalization as British subjects: according to some press reports, as many as a thousand a day. Those without official documents sought ways to prove their 'British nationality'. The consequences of the act were draconian. One seaman, who had lived and worked in Britain for twenty years, was refused readmission after he went on pilgrimage to Mecca.[140]

But the work of the LCP in Cardiff was merely an intervention from those outside the area and its branch did not last long. O'Connell soon lost patience with Moody and he, as well as other Black communists such as Alan Sheppard and Jim Nurse, were often the main organizers and fighters for the rights of those in Butetown.[141] In this period many of the most active political activists were either Communist Party members, or connected with the international communist movement. It was the only international body that stood openly against racism as well as colonialism. Many were inspired by social, economic and political developments in the Soviet Union. Communism offered a worldview which argued that workers of all lands should stand together and fight for their rights. It was O'Connell who, in 1935, wrote a letter to the press strongly refuting the disparaging comments that had appeared in the Richardson report produced by the British Social Hygiene Association. Moody claimed that 'the coloured people of Cardiff are mainly communists, simply because no one else has seen fit to give them a helping hand'.[142] The problems facing the seamen and their families were not so easily solved, even with the support of the LCP, and others, such as the League against Imperialism, and their protests continued throughout the 1930s.[143]

In April 1935 'a special posse of police was rushed down to the shipping office' as protests erupted at the exclusion of West African and Portuguese seamen from the ship *Ethel Radcliffe*, 'on which they had served for nine or ten years'. In this instance the local NUS official suggested that since eight or nine thousand 'coloured men' had been 'imported' into Cardiff by the shipping companies, those no longer required should be 'repatriated' rather than 'put on the rates'. The government was no more supportive. In a response to the local MP, the Home Secretary declared that it was the seamen who were legally required to prove that they were British. If they could not, they were legally required to register as 'aliens'.[144] The Cardiff Coloured Seamen's Committee, led by O'Connell and representing West African, Caribbean, Somali, and Malayan workers, sent its representatives to London to confront the NUS about its support for the Shipping (Assistance) Act and condemned what they regarded as the union's hypocrisy and double dealing.[145]

Liverpool

During the 1930s unemployment in Liverpool rose by 106 per cent. In 1933 10 per cent of its entire population was receiving public assistance and many lived in great poverty.[146] The Black community in Liverpool had long suffered from discriminatory treatment, as events in 1919 had demonstrated. Ernest Marke's recollection of being attacked and arrested by three plainclothes policemen as he walked home one night in 1921, suggests that racism continued in many forms. 'The colour prejudice was still intense,' he wrote. 'I found that even some members of the Liverpool police force had become so prejudiced against coloured men that their behaviour towards them had become nothing less than hooliganism.' Even though he was eventually acquitted Marke wrote that he 'always had a feeling of apprehension walking the Liverpool streets'.[147]

Measures first introduced in Liverpool in this period to control 'alien' seamen, such as the use of fingerprints and special registration cards, were subsequently incorporated into the Coloured Alien Seaman Order of 1925.[148] Those who were seafarers, including the Kru (from Liberia and Sierra Leone), were largely employed by the Elder Dempster Company, which monopolized shipping between Liverpool and West Africa.[149] During the 1920s it concluded a series of 'agreements' with the government which effectively exempted West African seamen from the Coloured Alien Seaman Order but also, with government connivance, allowed Elder Dempster to keep men contracted to the company with poorer conditions and rates of pay than those of white seamen. Those whom Elder Dempster found troublesome could, again with government support, be deported, as was the case with John Zarlia. He had been 'called up during the War for service in the Army and was given exemption on the grounds that his work was of national importance'. But he was deported to Sierra Leone in 1928, leaving behind his English wife and a child who were dependent on the relief provided by 'Liverpool guardians'.[150]

Many seamen abandoned ship in Liverpool, establishing homes and families in the city, as well as their rights to British citizenship, relief and other social services.[151] The Home Office privately acknowledged such rights and that such migration was a 'penalty of being a mother country with a large mixed Empire'. However, it concluded 'the most that we can do is to discourage coloured seamen from obtaining British passports, so that we can treat them as aliens when they get here and prevent them from remaining.'[152]

The Ethiopian Association had been one early attempt by Africans to organize themselves. Another, established in 1920, was the National African Sailors and Fireman's Union, founded in Liverpool 8 with around a dozen members, mainly West Africans. Membership was open to 'all coloured persons' engaged in seafaring, and honorary membership was open to others. It clearly aimed at improving wages and working conditions, but another one of its goals was to 'promote amity and a better understanding between the coloured races and others of a different race'. The union was only in existence for a few years and by 1923 only its general secretary, S. S. Ross, was still at sea, other members having returned to Africa, or having been forced to seek work ashore. Nevertheless, it was an early effort to organize for the rights of seamen.[153] In 1930 a 'Negro Society' was established by the local branch of the Communist Party in Liverpool, which held meetings with more than eighty seamen, students and factory workers from West Africa, the Caribbean and the United States. Nothing seems to be known about this organization, nor other communist initiatives such as those connected with a branch of the Negro Welfare Association which was formed in Liverpool during this period.[154]

It was in Liverpool that Pastor Daniels Ekarte (c.1890–1964) emerged as an important provider of services for local people and in 1931 he opened the African Churches Mission, at 122–4 Hill Street. Ekarte had arrived in Britain from Nigeria in 1915, having worked his passage on a merchant ship. He first worked in mills and factories and seems to have drifted into gambling and crime before becoming an itinerant preacher. Somehow, he secured some funding and support from the Church of Scotland Foreign Missions Committee and his African Churches Mission was officially opened by the Bishop of Liverpool. Included amongst its aims was 'to promote and extend the adoption of the Mission principles among the Negroes and their children in the City', and 'to provide funds for the relief of members'.[155] Another reason why the mission was established was that the 'coloured people in Liverpool' were often denied admission to other churches. A Wesleyan African Mission, created in 1923, even had separate entrances, the 'white and coloured congregation being by municipal order quite distinct'.[156] The African Churches Mission also acted as a social centre and canteen. Ekarte reported that at that time 'almost the entire juvenile coloured population' were unemployed and the mission organized Scouts and Guides troops for children 'to impart some little measure of training'.[157]

Ekarte's mission was run on a shoestring, had meagre funding and was sparsely furnished, but it provided welfare, including free meals, and education, as well as religious services, for more than 500 men, women and children in Liverpool for over two decades.[158] In short, it was 'a haven of refuge for stranded Africans'. Ekarte became a friend to the friendless. According to the mission's publication, '[H]e attends the police court to intercede for those who get into trouble. He may pay a fine, or a lodging, or for medicine or even for a funeral.'[159] Ekarte seems to have first been in contact with the LCP in July 1934 when he addressed its conference with his speech 'The Negro in the World Today' alongside Harry O'Connell, Arnold Ward, Jomo Kenyatta (in Britain representing the Kikuyu Central Association) and other speakers.[160] *The Keys* suggested that Ekarte had established a branch of the LCP in Liverpool and sought 'affiliation', but it is not clear if such a branch was ever formed.[161]

ETHIOPIA AND A UNITED FRONT

The LCP's conference indicated an increasingly united approach to solving common problems. There were certainly differences in the life experiences of Moody, Marson, Ekarte, O'Connell and Kenyatta, but they were united in their concerns about the increasingly oppressive nature of colonial rule, as well as the ubiquitous racism that they all experienced in Britain, which affected students and professionals as well as workers and their families. The LCP conference included participation by the WASU and other organizations such as the NWA, plus a delegation from the Gold Coast led by Nana Sir Ofori Atta, visiting the country to lobby the Colonial Office, as well as Otto Huiswoud, the secretary of the International Trade Union Committee of Negro Workers (ITUCNW).[162] This growing unity amongst key Black political organizations was given a major boost by their joint opposition to the invasion of Ethiopia by the fascist government of Italy in 1934.

Ethiopia, or Abyssinia as it was then often known, was one of only three states in the world (alongside Haiti and Liberia) which was governed by Africans, or those of African descent. But it was coveted by the big powers. In 1925 Britain and France had signed a secret agreement to divide Ethiopia into separate spheres of influence and both Britain and Italy had launched various provocations against the country before the infamous Wal Wal incident in 1934, in which a further Italian provocation led to armed clashes and deaths on both sides. For those of African and Caribbean heritage in Britain, Ethiopia occupied a special place as a symbol of African independence and self-determination. Biblical references only added to its significance.[163] Kwame Nkrumah, the future leader of Ghana, who had recently arrived in Britain at that time, later recalled that when he first heard of the Italian invasion 'it was almost as if the whole of London had suddenly declared war on me personally'. The *New Statesman and Nation* warned that 'to coloured people everywhere, the war would seem a concerted attack of white against black'.[164] Fascist Italy's aggression heightened anti-colonial consciousness and Pan-African unity. There was worldwide condemnation of fascist Italy's warmongering too. The full-scale invasion of Ethiopia by Italy in October 1935 signalled a crucial stage in the drive towards a new world war and demonstrated the lengths to which the fascist powers would go to re-divide the world in their interests. The invasion also highlighted the weakness of the appeasement policies of Britain and France, especially after the infamous Hoare–Laval Pact in December 1935 in which the two countries secretly attempted to appease Italy by partitioning Ethiopia, which exposed the fact that the governments of two major colonial powers were conniving to support fascist aggression. The entire episode dealt a body blow to the credibility of the League of Nations, and contributed to the crisis that was engulfing the colonial world, calling into question the colonial system itself.

It was in these circumstances that many new Pan-African organizations and coalitions were formed in Britain.[165] One of the most significant was the International African Friends of Abyssinia (IAFA), formed in London in July 1935 by C. L. R. James, Amy Ashwood

Garvey, Chris Jones, Jomo Kenyatta, George Padmore and others 'to assist by all means in their power in the maintenance of the territorial integrity and political independence of Abyssinia'.[166] The IAFA and its successors re-employed the term 'African' to mean Africans from both the continent, the Caribbean and the wider diaspora, in the same way as the African Association and the APU had done. James was chairman, Dr Peter Milliard (1882–c.1953), a Guyanese physician working in Manchester, and T. Albert Marryshaw, a Grenadian trade unionist, were vice-chairmen, Jomo Kenyatta was the secretary and Amy Ashwood Garvey the treasurer. Ashwood Garvey's long-time friend, the Trinidadian actor/singer/impresario Sam Manning (1898–1960), Ras Makonnen (1900–1983) from British Guiana, the Somali Mohammed Said and George Padmore completed the executive committee.

Padmore (born Malcolm Nurse) was originally from Trinidad and had joined the Communist Party whilst a student in the United States. He soon rose to be a significant figure within the ITUCNW and was the editor of the *Negro Worker*, as well as the author of *The Life and*

Amy Ashwood Garvey speaking at Trafalgar Square

Struggles of Negro Toilers (1931). However, by 1934 he had parted company with the communist movement and moved to Britain, where he became a leading activist.[167] Cyril Lionel Robert James had arrived in Britain from Trinidad in 1932 at the invitation of his compatriot, the cricketer Learie Constantine (1901–1971), later to become Britain's first Black peer. James had worked as a journalist and was an avowed Marxist and a supporter of Trotskyism who involved himself in many organizations, including the Independent Labour Party and the LCP.[168] Makonnen, who claimed Ethiopian descent, changed his name from George Thomas Griffith during this period and had already taken up the Ethiopian cause in both the United States and in Denmark (he had been deported from the latter for his outspoken views).[169] Several others later became part of the IAFA, including the African American singer John Payne. J. B. Danquah, George Moore and Samuel Wood, the latter three representatives of two delegations from the Gold Coast visiting London at the time, were also involved. Moore and Wood were to wait nearly two years before the Colonial Office heard their petition on behalf of the Gold Coast Aborigines' Rights Protection Society. During 1935, with the assistance of the National Council for Civil Liberties, among other supporters, they campaigned in the constituency of the Colonial Secretary, Malcolm MacDonald, during the general election and may have contributed to his defeat.[170]

According to Padmore's account, the IAFA's origins were to be found in an 'ad hoc committee' that he had chaired which had been formed to offer support to the two delegations from the Gold Coast visiting Britain to protest against various 'obnoxious laws' that had been introduced by the colonial authorities.[171] What appears most likely is that the IAFA was formed by several African and Caribbean activists. Its founding highlights the significance of Pan-Africanism as an important political current amongst those whom Padmore referred to as 'politically minded Negroes', whether the focus was the Gold Coast, Ethiopia, the Caribbean, or events in Britain.[172] Indeed, in this period several activists called for a 'Black United Front', or common action to deal with common problems. Despite political differences, such shared action was not unusual and could involve the other principal African/Black organizations in Britain, such as the WASU, the LCP and the NWA, as well as others, for example the Gold Coast

A reconstruction of Cheddar Man who lived in Britain 10,000 years ago.

A reconstruction of the Ivory Bangle Lady who was buried in York in the third century.

A section of the Westminster Roll (1511) showing the royal trumpeter John Blanke.

The Duke of Perth with an unnamed African child (c.1700).

William Ansah Sessarakoo.

Ayuba Suleiman Diallo.

A portrait of Dido Elizabeth Belle with her cousin.

An eighteenth-century portrait of an unnamed
coachboy, from Erddig, Wales.

Portrait of a trumpeter from the 1st Troop of Horse Guards (*c.*1750).

Portrait of an African, possibly Ignatius Sancho (*c.*1760).

A portrait of Ira Aldridge playing Shakespeare's
Othello (1826).

A portrait of Mary Seacole (1869).

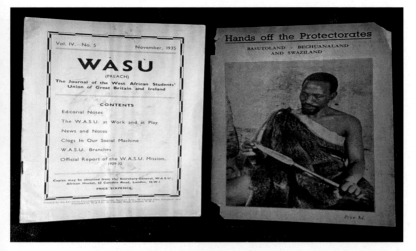

Publications of the West African Students' Union and the International African Service Bureau (1930s).

Publications of the Coloured Workers' Association, the Pan-African Federation and the Caribbean Labour Congress (1940s).

Ajibola Lewis (*right*) became a tireless campaigner after her son Olaseni (*left*) was killed by eleven police officers in Bethlem Royal Hospital in 2010.

Anti-racism protestors in 2020.

Students' Association. Although Makonnen claimed that the 'existing African and West Indian organizations in England at the time were very mild', he clearly arrived at a time of significant change.[173]

The IAFA established its headquarters at Amy Ashwood Garvey's International Afro Restaurant, at 62 New Oxford Street, London, itself an important new venue for '[r]ace intellectuals from all parts of the world'.[174] At its first public meeting, in July 1935, it resolved to support Ethiopia's struggle to maintain its independence. Subsequent meetings were held during the summer and autumn of 1935 throughout Britain, denouncing fascist Italy, calling on the League of Nations to intervene and raising funds to send to Ethiopia 'a body or bodies of men and women of African descent or race to be placed at the disposal of the Emperor to render service, military or civil'.[175] Many Black women volunteered for ambulance work and as nurses. However, as James pointed out at the time, 'most of us who were in the organization and who were supporting it, had a conception of politics very remote from debates and resolutions of the League [of Nations]. We wanted to form a military organization which would go to fight with the Abyssinians against the Italians.' It seems that James and other potential warriors were dissuaded from that course of action by Ethiopia's representative in London.[176]

All this shows that the politics of those residing in Britain during this period, partly as a response to the Italian invasion, demonstrated a new militancy that contrasted with the more measured protests of former times. In Cardiff, O'Connell was arrested and subsequently convicted for 'conduct likely to cause a breach of the peace', for allegedly calling on workers to 'wreck' the city's Italian consulate, a charge he denied.[177] The militant style was exemplified by the resolution passed at the IAFA's second public meeting in July, which called 'upon all Africans and people of African descent all over the world to ... pledge themselves to assist Abyssinia in her struggle by all means at their disposal'. It was also evident in the 'Hands of Abyssinia Manifesto' written by Kenyatta, as general secretary of the renamed International African Friends of Ethiopia (IAFE), published in the Communist Party of Great Britain's newsletter *Labour Monthly* in September 1935.[178]

Even the formerly more moderate LCP was radicalized by events in Ethiopia. According to an article in *The Keys* written by C. L. R. James, the invasion of Ethiopia had 'been of immense benefit to the race as a whole', since although 'unfortunate for Abyssinia' it had 'shown the Negro only too plainly that he has got nothing to expect from them [the governments of Britain, France and Italy] but exploitation, naked or wrapped in bluff'.[179] At the LCP's Annual General Meeting in September 1935 a resolution was passed declaring to all the colonial powers 'that the time is now right for them to consider a plan for the future of Africa which ... should be nothing less than the ultimate and complete freedom of Africa from any external domination whatsoever'.[180]

The WASU was also voicing its own protests and regarded the Italian invasion as almost tantamount to a 'racial war'. It too considered that Italy's aggression exposed not just the British government's policy of appeasement but also the illegitimacy of Britain's colonial rule and the 'spiritual bankruptcy of the West'. After an address by Amy Ashwood Garvey, the WASU established its own Ethiopian Defence Fund which was administered by an all-female committee chaired by Mrs A. M. Cole, and which included Irene Howe, Aderemi Ademola and Gladys Franklyne. There were also demonstrations of support for Ethiopia by Africans in Cardiff, Liverpool, and elsewhere, including in Edinburgh, where a relief committee was formed.[181] It was in this context that the WASU declared 'the Ethiopian disaster may yet prove a blessing in disguise if it succeeds in uniting the Black peoples of the world'.[182] At its annual conference in October 1935, the NWA could declare, with some justification, that 'a mighty movement of solidarity is growing day by day throughout the world in support of the Abyssinian people in their struggle for independence'.[183]

At this time, African and Caribbean workers in Britain also considered it necessary to form their own fighting organizations as exploited 'colonial' workers. Such organizations already existed in Cardiff and in North Shields, where the Coloured Nationals Mutual Social Club, established in 1934 by African, Caribbean, Indian and Malay seamen, had over a hundred members by the following year.[184] In 1936 the Colonial Seamen's Association (CSA) was formed in London, largely in response to the Shipping (Assistance) Act of the previous year. Led by Chris Jones, the CSA was formed by several organizations including the NWA, LCP, India Swaraj League (an organization led by Krishna Menon demanding independence for India) and LAI, and appears to have been linked to the Communist Party.[185] According to its secretary, Surat Ali, the CSA was established 'as the expression of the discontent existing amongst the colonial seamen and its aim was to redress their grievances'.[186] It held its first annual conference in November 1936 and, the following year, was one of the first organizations to protest against the demand by the Nazi government for a return of former German colonies in Africa. It also held meetings on the situation in Britain's colonies in the Caribbean.[187]

These organizations were often influenced by a wider internationalism, as well as the need to organize with other workers in Britain. It is significant that Padmore considered that one of the key tasks of the IAFE was to 'arouse the sympathy and support of the British public'.[188] In May 1936 several organizations from Britain, including the LCP and the African Churches Mission, attended the International Conference of Negroes and Arabs held in Paris, and the IAFE and WASU were both in touch with Ethiopia support organizations in France.[189] Solanke and Amy Ashwood Garvey were also in contact with Dr Willis Huggins, an African American who travelled via London to Geneva where, on behalf of organizations in the United States, he delivered a petition on Ethiopia to the League of Nations.[190]

THE INTERNATIONAL AFRICAN SERVICE BUREAU

While the Ethiopian conflict brought several organizations in Britain closer together, the IAFE did not endure long after the Italian conquest amidst several internal disagreements and the resignation of C. L. R. James in the summer of 1936.[191] In 1936, it was the IAFE and other Black organizations in Britain, including the WASU, the NWA, the LCP and the Somali Association that welcomed Ethiopia's emperor Haile Selassie, his daughter Princess Tsehai and other family members upon their arrival to exile in London.[192] Some of the emperor's subsequent statements and his sojourn in Britain found favour with another new arrival, the Jamaican Pan-Africanist Marcus Garvey, who also arrived in Britain during in the spring of 1935 and was to reside in London until his death in June 1940. Garvey later publicly censured

Selassie in his journal, *Black Man*, as a 'great coward' arguing that 'Haile Selassie has proved the incompetence of the Negro for political authority, but thank God there are Negroes who realise that Haile Selassie did not represent the truest qualities of the Negro race'.[193]

Perhaps as early on as 1935 Padmore had begun to form a new organization which was variously known in police reports as the Pan-African Brotherhood and Pan-Afro League, and eventually became known as the Pan-African Federation. It included amongst its membership Kenyatta, Wood, Moore and Mohammed Said from the IAFE and others including the veteran Pan-Africanist Robert Broadhurst, as well as Jones and Makonnen. Initially this group of activists held meetings and produced a publication entitled *Voice of Africa*, but they struggled financially. A not dissimilar group appears to have become consolidated after the arrival in Britain from West Africa of Isaac Wallace-Johnson, when it re-emerged as the International African Service Bureau (IASB), based at 94 Gray's Inn Road, London, in the early part of 1937.[194]

Isaac Wallace-Johnson (1894–1965) was a leading labour organizer and Pan-Africanist from Sierra Leone, who was politically active throughout Britain's colonies in West Africa. In 1937 he came to Britain after his conviction for 'sedition' in the Gold Coast following the publication of his anti-colonial newspaper article, 'Has the African a God?' After he lost the initial court case, which became very much a cause célèbre in West Africa and beyond, and received a fine, Wallace-Johnson decided to lodge an appeal with the Court of the Privy Council in London, an appeal which was ultimately unsuccessful.[195] In 1937 he was still close to the NWA and LAI, and was writing for the ITUCNW's *Negro Worker*, having spent some time in Moscow as a student. He also remained in contact with Padmore. Although police reports describe Wallace-Johnson as the 'principal founder' and 'driving force' behind the IASB, this may well be an overstatement, since Wallace-Johnson did not remain in London in the long term and appears to have been expelled from the IASB the following year.[196] Whatever the case, initially Wallace-Johnson was elected general-secretary and Padmore chairman of the IASB. While Kenyatta and Ashwood Garvey also played leading roles, Makonnen seems to have been the most important fundraiser, and treasurer too, Jones was

organizing secretary and James the editorial director.[197] Executive
committee members included those living outside Britain, such as the
Paris-based Garan Koutaté, who had formerly worked with Padmore
and the ITUCNW, Nnamdi Azikiwe from Nigeria, and two women,
Elsie Duncan from West Africa and Aidi Bastian, a Jamaican, who
was one of the founders of the Ethiopian World Federation in New
York in 1937. It seems likely that some of these were also involved
in Padmore's abortive attempts in 1934 to convene a 'World Negro
Unity Congress'.[198]

The IASB 'represented progressive and enlightened public opinion
amongst Africans and peoples of African descent', and aimed to 'support the demands of Africans, Asians and other colonial peoples for
democratic rights, civil liberties and self-determination'.[199] Full membership was open only to those of African descent, but 'Europeans
and others who desired to demonstrate in a practical way their interest in African welfare could become associate members'. Padmore
made it clear that the IASB were opposed to 'racial exclusiveness' and
that one of the 'chief functions of the Bureau was to help enlighten
public opinion in Great Britain ... as to the true conditions in the
various colonies, protectorates and mandated territories in Africa and
the West Indies'.[200] To this end he, together with James and Jones,
moved closer to and often spoke at the meetings of the Independent
Labour Party, and were involved with related organizations, such as
the British Centre against Imperialism.[201] For Padmore and the IASB,
activism in Britain had to be linked with internationalism in a common struggle to end colonial rule and other forms of oppression, and
many of those drawn to the organization considered themselves
Marxists.[202] According to Makonnen, the nature of the IASB was also
influenced by the experience of the British-based India League, which
was also internationalist in orientation and aimed to influence people
in Britain against colonial rule in India. Makonnen explained that the
aim of the IASB was to 'emphasise service to people of African descent in as many ways as possible'.[203] Another interesting feature in
this regard was the IASB's aim to work with 'other existing organizations which have the welfare of the African at heart', not just in Britain
but also in Europe and the United States. Indeed, the IASB strove to
coordinate the activities of such organizations 'which at present exist

in different parts of the black world and ... bring them into closer fraternal relation with one another'.[204]

The IASB initially produced two regular publications, *Africa and the World*, as well as the *African Sentinel*, both launched in 1937 and edited by Wallace-Johnson, and then subsequently *International African Opinion*, initiated in July 1938, at first edited by James and then by Makonnen. The *International African Opinion* carried the IASB motto: 'Educate, Co-operate, Emancipate. Neutral in nothing affecting the African people', but many of its articles were addressed to 'British workers'. The IASB organized itself as a Pan-African information bureau, collecting and disseminating information about the struggles of Africans globally. In addition, it organized public meetings and demonstrations and took a particularly keen interest in the labour rebellions in the Caribbean and the international campaign opposing any transfer of colonies to Nazi Germany. It also produced a series of pamphlets on important issues, such as *Hands off the Protectorates*, which focused on South Africa's attempts to annex the three British protectorates, Bechuanaland, Basutoland and Swaziland.[205] The IASB also managed to get questions asked in Parliament through sympathetic MPs, such as Ellen Wilkinson and the future Labour Party Colonial Secretary, Arthur Creech-Jones. Other sympathizers included such notable British figures as Nancy Cunard, Stafford Cripps, Victor Gollancz and Sylvia Pankhurst.[206]

PAN-AFRICAN PROTEST

The labour rebellions in the Anglophone Caribbean, often occasioned by poverty and unemployment, but also stirred up by anti-colonial sentiment, as well as the Italian invasion of Ethiopia, began in 1935, with strikes in St Kitts and then strikes and protests in Trinidad, British Guiana, St Vincent and St Lucia. In the years following there was again significant unrest, culminating in a general strike in Jamaica in 1938 and further rebellions elsewhere that were severely suppressed, leading to almost fifty deaths.[207] The strikes marked an important stage in the anti-colonial struggle in the Caribbean and showed the political strength working people had at their disposal. In response, in

1938 the British government established a royal commission, chaired by Lord Moyne, to investigate and make recommendations.

As was the case in regard to Ethiopia, events in the Caribbean provoked protests by the IASB, LCP and NWA, demanding political reform and even self-government. It was in this period that W. Arthur Lewis, a former editor of *The Keys*, wrote *Labour in the West Indies* (1939) and the three organizations presented a joint memorandum on 'economic, social and political conditions in the West Indies and British Guiana' to the royal commission led by Moyne. What is significant is the collective preparation of this document, involving the work of Padmore, James, Lewis, Blackman, Moody, Makonnen and others, as well as its reference to Ethiopia and the demand for an end to colonial rule.[208] It was one of several occasions when the organizations worked together, as well as with others, to draft critical responses to royal commissions enquiring into the consequences of colonialism in the Caribbean and African colonies.[209]

Another significant publication was Marcus Garvey's new monthly journal, *Black Man*. Garvey was often a popular speaker in London's Hyde Park, but he also faced criticism for his 'anti-labour bias' and his stand on Ethiopia, particularly from African students in London who, according to Padmore, 'attempted to break up his meetings'.[210] On behalf of the IASB, Wallace-Johnson openly criticized Garvey in the press for his political views and reported that he had been publicly challenged by Padmore and James for his attacks on Selassie and on striking Caribbean workers.[211] Wallace-Johnson also took issue with Garvey's claim that he was 'a capitalist and favoured the ruling class', and concluded that he had 'obviously outlived his usefulness in so far as leading the African people may be concerned'.[212]

Unrest in the Caribbean occurred at the same time as major protests in parts of Africa, including the 'cocoa hold-ups' in the Gold Coast (in which farmers refused to sell their crops to major European buyers) and opposition to a racist and expansionist South Africa, as well as more general concerns about Nazi Germany's demand for the return of former German colonies administered as League of Nations mandates by Britain and France. These demands, which also had supporters in Britain such as Lord Rothermere, again highlighted the iniquities of colonial rule and led to joint action by the IASB, the

LCP, the WASU and others. In 1938, the *African Sentinel* published resolutions and protests from fraternal organizations in Paris, including the Union des Travailleurs Négres and Rassamblement Coloniale.[213] This growing Pan-African unity was perhaps best illustrated by the Conference on African Peoples, Democracy and World Peace organized by the LCP, the NWA, the Gold Coast Students' Association, Coloured Film Artists Association and others on the eve of war in July 1939. The previous year O'Connell had written to Moody on behalf of the Colonial Defence Association in Cardiff to encourage such unity: 'We believe it is very important at this stage for the complete unification of all the coloured groups in Britain.'[214]

The conference aimed 'to show that the British people can ... safeguard their own liberties, extend the boundaries of democracy to embrace the peoples of Britain's colonial empire and, by so doing, lay the foundations for true freedom and lasting peace in the world'.[215] More than 250 people attended and were addressed by two leading British politicians, Arthur Creech Jones and Sir Stafford Cripps, amongst others. Conference resolutions condemned colonial rule, fascism and Britain's appeasement policy, while demanding self-determination for all those in Africa and the Caribbean. Increasingly, such resolutions stressed the important role of the working people and 'coloured labour' in anti-colonial struggle. As Makonnen expressed it, he and other Pan-Africanists insisted on 'seeing the colonial world as a whole'. They would demand rights for all colonial trade unionists, for example, and circulate their demands throughout the Caribbean, North America and West Africa. He added that the same approach 'brought us into close touch with other coloured groups in London' including students and others from Asia, with whom they 'found it profitable to co-operate'.[216]

The radical Pan-Africanism that emerged in Britain in the 1930s and early 1940s was propagated and disseminated in a host of periodicals and other publications, many of them banned by the colonial authorities. The publications of the WASU and the LCP also began to reflect a more radical approach by the late 1930s and Blackman, a communist, was for a time the editor of *The Keys*. The IASB which propagated its views through several publications, aimed 'to create a connecting link between the Africans at home (in Africa) and the Africans abroad

A demonstration in Cardiff against fascism and war

(in the West Indies, United States of America, and other Western countries)', and indeed with 'Negroes wherever they are'.[217]

Padmore often played a key role. He had been a prolific journalist and writer since his time as editor of *Negro Worker*. After his split with the communist movement, his writings appeared regularly in African American papers, and in the African and Caribbean press, as well as in socialist publications in Britain. He wrote or jointly authored several other books during the period, including: *How Britain Rules Africa* (1936), and *Africa and World Peace* (1937). James wrote *A History of Negro Revolt* (1937) and *The Black Jacobins* (1938), a major history of the Haitian Revolution, although, as he later acknowledged, throughout the book 'it is Africa and African emancipation that he has in mind'.[218] The IASB also produced a series of pamphlets during this period. All were written, as Padmore said of *How Britain Rules Africa*, to present things 'from the point of view of the blacks', and he added, 'the time has come for Africans to speak out for themselves'.[219] It might also be said that all these publications were collaborative efforts, examples of a new Marxist-influenced Pan-Africanism.

PERFORMERS, SPORTS
PLAYERS AND POLITICS

The most famous entertainer during the 1930s was undoubtedly the African American singer and actor Paul Robeson (1898–1976), who was considered one of Britain's favourite performers from 1935 to 1940.[220] Robeson had established himself in London during the late 1920s, at the time when he appeared in the stage version of the musical *Showboat*.[221] Thereafter he endeared himself to cinema and concert audiences throughout the country and he made several important films including the *Song of Freedom* (1936) and *The Proud Valley* (1940), a fictional portrayal which nevertheless reflected his close relationship with the coal miners of Wales. In January 1933, Robeson performed in Eugene O'Neill's play *The Emperor Jones* to support the Scottsboro campaign.[222] In 1935 he appeared in the play *Stevedore* at the Embassy Repertory Theatre in London, aided by George Padmore, who helped to find Black actors for a production which portrayed Black and white workers in the United States organizing together to defend their rights.[223] In 1936 Robeson played the lead in James' play *Toussaint Louverture: The Story of the Only Successful Slave Revolt in History*, at London's Westminster Theatre. This was the first time that 'black professional actors had ever performed on the British stage in a play written by a black playwright'.[224]

Robeson later repudiated some of the films he made in Britain, most notably *Sanders of the River* (1935), which attempted to present colonial rule in Africa in an entirely positive light. During the late 1930s he performed in *Plant in the Sun* at the working-class Unity Theatre in London, and thereafter tended to devote himself more fully to working-class audiences. He took a courageous stand against fascism and established an increasingly close connection with the communist movement. It seems likely that the NWA played an important role in Robeson's growing interest in the Soviet Union.[225] His interest in African languages and anti-colonialism was encouraged by his association with organizations such as the NWA, the LCP and particularly the WASU. Robeson became the patron of the WASU, and a regular visitor to its hostel, and later wrote that he 'discovered' Africa whilst in

Britain. He explained, 'That discovery, which has influenced my life ever since, made it clear that I would not live out my life as an adopted Englishman, and I came to consider myself an African.' As well as African students, Robeson wrote that he also met the African seamen of London, Cardiff and Liverpool, many of whom he worked alongside in his films.[226]

Securing work as film extras was one of the few casual occupations open to Black people in this period of mass unemployment and widespread racism. Women and children also often appeared as extras in the films of the day.[227] Even Jomo Kenyatta was sometimes employed in the film industry, as was Ernest Marke, and both appeared in *Sanders of the River*.[228] In 1935 the Coloured Film Artistes Association was founded in order to safeguard the interests of African and Caribbean workers in the industry and its membership included 'Asians born in the West Indies'. Registered as a Friendly Society in 1939, it was led by J. Cox and Peter Blackman and soon had more than 400 members. Described at the time as 'the first trade union of coloured people in this country', it worked closely with the NWA and included Arnold Ward on its executive committee.[229]

Robeson was clearly not the only performer involved in political activities during this period. Isaac 'Ike' Hatch (1892–1961), another African American who was also a member of the Scottsboro Defence Committee, hosted a benefit concert for the campaign in 1933. Originally from New York, he had settled in London in the 1920s and worked as a nightclub singer and manager, musician and recording artist. The Scottsboro benefit concert featured Black performers, including the Mississippi Page Boys and the Black Flashers, as well as the Gold Coast Quartet and Guyanese dancer Ken 'Snakehips' Johnson (1914–1941), alongside classically trained musicians such as the Guyanese clarinettist, conductor, composer and journalist Rudolph Dunbar (1899–1988), who made his home in London in the early 1930s and established his own 'coloured orchestra'.[230] In August 1934 the press announced the first ever BBC broadcast by an all-British coloured band led by Dunbar.[231]

Dunbar and other musicians regularly performed at Ashwood Garvey's nightclub, the Florence Mills Social Parlour at 50 Carnaby Street. Opened in 1936 and named after the African American singer who had taken London by storm in the mid-1920s, the Social Parlour has been described as 'a calypso club with bamboo decorations, creole food and the haunting melody of American jazz and blues'.[232] Makonnen remarked that it was one of the most famous of the Black clubs in London at the time: '[Y]ou could go there after you'd been slugging it out at for two or three hours at Hyde Park or some other meeting, and get a lovely meal, dance and enjoy yourself.'[233] Food was cooked by Ashwood Garvey, and music at the club was often supplied by her partner, the Trinidadian singer and comedian, Sam Manning, who performed mento and calypso in addition to jazz and blues. Manning could claim to have introduced calypso to Britain, as in 1927 he made some of the first recordings of this music released by a British recording company. He continued to record for Parlophone throughout the 1930s, often with his 'West Indian Rhythm Boys'.[234] In 1935 Manning and Ashwood Garvey were responsible for presenting *Harlem Nightbirds*, 'an all-coloured revue' and the 'first British negro revue', according to press reports, with musicians and singers recruited in such cities as Liverpool and Cardiff as well as in London. The revue played throughout the country from 1934 to 1935.[235]

Makonnen's comments make it clear that there were several Black nightclubs in London at the time. He mentions the Caribbean, where it was possible to hear famous musicians such as Ike Hatch, who established two of his own clubs during the 1930s: first, the Nest and then, in 1935, the Shim Sham in Wardour Street. Other Black-owned clubs in London included Friscos and Jig's. They were considered some of the best venues for authentic jazz and entertainment, as well as places where people of all nationalities and social classes, including celebrities, could meet and socialize.[236] Clubs for dancing, drinking and entertainment in which Black people played a major role were not only to be found in London, of course. Many towns and cities had their own. It appears that the authorities turned a blind eye to such establishments if they were only frequented by those of African and Caribbean heritage. In 1919 in Glasgow, for example, the police raided 'a Black Man's club' when it became a 'public dancing salon' and was 'attracting Glasgow men and young girls, as well as men of colour'.[237]

Musicians of African and Caribbean heritage often performed jazz during the 1920s and 1930s, and even earlier. Dan Kildare, a Jamaican, played in London with his own jazz band, the New York-based Clef Club Orchestra, as early as 1915.[238] British-based musicians can be said to have helped introduce live jazz music to Britain during the 1920s as members of such ensembles as the Southern Syncopated Orchestra which, in 1919, was led by Egbert Thompson, a Sierra Leonean raised in Jamaica, and soon included many other African and Caribbean musicians too. Other musicians came directly from Africa and the Caribbean, such as the Trinidadian Cyril Blake (1900–1951), who had served in the Merchant Navy, Jamaican Leslie Thompson (1901–1987) and Frank Lacton, a pianist from Sierra Leone. Even classically trained musicians, such as the Nigerian organist and composer Fela Sowande, who studied at Trinity College London, played jazz to support themselves, as did pianist Rita Cann, one of only a few British-born Black female musicians in this period.[239] Cardiff's Deniz brothers, Frank, Joe and Laurie, were British-born, the children of a Cape Verdean father and a mother of Anglo-African American descent, and all three became professional musicians.[240]

Cardiff became an important training ground for Black British musicians, many of whom went on to play calypso, jazz and other popular forms of music in London nightclubs. As well as the Deniz brothers, guitarist Victor Parker, George Glossop and Don Johnson also originated from Cardiff, as did two women pianists, Lily Jemmott and Clare Deniz. Emerging musicians in Cardiff could perform at the numerous local house parties at which calypsos were popular, as well as at public dances. Aside from seafaring, working as a performer, or in sports such as boxing were two of the few avenues of employment available for working-class African and Caribbean men during the Depression years.[241]

The musicians from Cardiff all eventually came to play in London's fashionable clubs, but would have initially performed at admission-paying all-night 'bottle parties' organized in homes or commercial premises that were designed to sidestep licensing laws. The venues were often under police surveillance, sometimes raided, and were regarded by the authorities as dens 'of vice and iniquity' where Black men were to be found in close proximity to white women and sexual proclivities were not restricted to heterosexuality. A police report on the Shim Sham Club concluded that amongst its clientele were to be found:

> Thieves, Prostitutes, Ponces, Lesbians, Homosexualists, Drug addicts, Coloured men and women and other very undesirable persons, all of whom visited these premises in order to satisfy their various vices.[242]

During this period calypso and other Caribbean genres were often as popular as African American ones as a result of the influence of Manning, Cyril Blake and his brother George, as well as Leslie Thompson. In 1936 Leslie Thompson and Ken Johnson joined forces to establish an all-Black jazz band, the Jazz Emperors.[243] Johnson subsequently formed his West Indian Dance Orchestra, which performed in some of London's most established nightclubs.[244] Those of African and Caribbean heritage in London and other areas provided their own cultural entertainment. By 1938 the WASU had purchased a second hostel at South Villas in Camden Town, London, after another successful fundraising campaign. Known as Africa House, it was opened by Lady Simon, the wife of the Chancellor of the Exchequer, and became an important cultural, political and social venue, providing African food and music as well as accommodation. Makonnen remembered it as 'a homely place where you could always get your groundnut chop and there would be dances on a Saturday night'.[245] From the mid-1930s onwards, a social committee of women led by Mrs Olu Solanke, which included many women studying nursing and midwifery, such as Aderemi and Adenrele Ademola, and Tinuade Adefolu, organized dances and concerts, many of them featuring musicians playing West African music. Africa House was perhaps one of the first modern African music venues in the capital, featuring O. A. Adeyin's 'orchestra', and various Nigerian Sakara bands, as well as recorded music.[246]

Boxing was another avenue of employment open to working-class Black men, just as it had been in the nineteenth century. In the twentieth century, companies deploying travelling boxing booths often employed Black boxers, such as Bill Johnson, an apprentice ship's engineer on the Elder Dempster line who arrived in Liverpool from Sierra Leone in 1897. The companies employed boxers to tour around Britain and take on volunteers from the paying audience as opponents in their fights (who could also earn some money if they lasted in the booth for a minimum of three rounds). Bill Johnson's Manchester-born son, Len (1902–1974) started work in the boxing booths in 1921 and would remain a professional boxer for the next twenty years, working in two booths and owning one himself.[247] He was joined in the profession by his two brothers and many others during the interwar period.[248] Len Johnson was talented enough to defeat several British and European champions, but although he was the best boxer at his weight, and a local hero, he was banned from fighting for a British title despite some support from the sporting press. In 1930 he announced his retirement, stating, amongst other things, 'the prejudice against colour has prevented me from getting a championship fight . . . I am willing to fight anyone . . . but the colour prejudice is against me . . . What can I do? I'm banned, and so I'm getting out.'[249] Another important family of boxers were the three Turpin brothers based in Leamington Spa, the eldest of whom, Lionel 'Dick' Turpin, became a professional in 1937.

From early on in the twentieth century a colour bar existed in boxing, as in other forms of employment in Britain. Black boxers were excluded from competing for the National Sporting Club's Lonsdale Belts after the legal ban on the world heavyweight champion Jack Johnson's fight in London in 1911. In 1922 the government banned a fight between the British champion and the new world light heavyweight champion from Senegal, Louis Phal. It was explained that 'such contests, considering that there are a very large number of men of colour in the British Empire, are considered against the higher national interest and they tend to arouse passions which it is inadvisable to stimulate'.[250] It was a view that was supported by the author Sir Arthur Conan Doyle and *The Times,* which complained that 'boxing matches between white men and blacks, to be photographed for the delectation of coloured races all over the world, have become a dangerous anachronism'.[251] In 1929 the British Boxing Board of Control (BBBC) formally banned all 'coloured' boxers from competing for British titles, a ban that lasted until 1948. The Secretary of the BBBC had explained that 'it is only right that a small country such as ours should have championships restricted to boxers of white parents – otherwise we might be faced with a situation where all our

British titles are held by Coloured empire boxers.'[252] In 1948, Lionel 'Dick' Turpin finally became 'the first black man to contest a British domestic title', and 'the first black man to win a Lonsdale Belt' when he won the British middleweight title.[253]

While Black professional boxers could earn a living, but not fight for British titles during the interwar period, other sportsmen found it still more difficult to break into the professional game. Learie Constantine arrived in Britain from Trinidad in 1928 with the West Indies cricket team and became the first Black professional cricketer when he joined Nelson Cricket Club in the Lancashire League. He remained at the club until 1937, although initially he faced a certain amount of racism. Under the influence of C. L. R. James, who stayed with him during the 1930s, Learie became more determined to take a stand against racism, joined the LCP and began his career as a writer. Constantine captained the LCP cricket team and the League staunchly championed his bowling, as well as the exploits of the West Indies cricket team, and arranged hospitality during the latter's tours of Britain.[254]

A few footballers were also successful. Jack Leslie (1901–1988), born in London's Canning Town, played for Plymouth Argyle from 1921 until 1935, and in 1925 was selected for England, but did not make the team. 'They must have forgotten I was a coloured boy', was how he explained his mysterious selection and then deselection to a journalist many years later.[255] His contemporary Eddie Paris (1911–1971), who was born in Chepstow and played professionally for Bradford Park Avenue, became the first Black player to be selected for Wales in 1931. Alfred Charles (1909–1977) played for the Trinidad national team, but only one 'first team' game for Southampton in 1937. He appears to have had more success in Britain as a professional magician.[256] Another player born abroad who represented his country was Tewfik Abdallah (1896–?), an Egyptian, who played for Derby County during the 1920s. He scored on his debut in October 1920, and also played for Cowdenbeath and Hartlepool. Mohamed Latif (1909–1990), another Egyptian, played a single 'first team' game for Glasgow Rangers in 1935, but probably as an amateur.[257] Roy Brown (1923–1989), who was born in Stoke, signed up for Stoke City's football team when he left school at the age of fourteen in 1937. However, the outbreak of war was to severely affect his career, and he served in the army until the Football League resumed fully in 1945–6. The previous war had ended the lives of his father and uncle, Eugene and John Brown, who had travelled to Britain from Nigeria in 1912 as students and enlisted in the North Staffordshire Regiment in 1914. Roy's Brown's Uncle John was killed in action and his father was invalided out of the army and subsequently died of his injuries.[258]

One of the most interesting developments in sport during this period was the founding of the All-Blacks football team in Cardiff, 'a team of clever coloured colonials known throughout Wales'. The team reportedly included 'Africans, West Indians, Indians, Somalis, Arabs and Egyptians, and they have played in all parts of the world'. They played friendly matches in Wales and, in 1938, also played two matches in England, against Cheltenham Town and Luton Town. According to one press report, Cardiff was merely the headquarters of this 'club for coloured men, and the members are principally drawn from seaports like Cardiff, Liverpool, London, Shields and Bristol'.[259] According to another report, the members were 'eleven coloured boys drawn from the suburban districts of Cardiff'.[260]

The interwar years presented many challenges for those of African and Caribbean heritage in Britain. Most were working people who faced unemployment and increasing impoverishment as a result of the global economic depression. All suffered from the effects of the ubiquitous colour bar and racism that was in large part a consequence of Britain's presumed right to govern an empire of people who were assumed incapable of ruling themselves. In Britain racism was given further official sanction through legislation such as the Coloured Alien Seamen Order which led to state-sanctioned discrimination, especially against seafarers and their families. During this period, African and Caribbean communities in the port cities also faced racist attacks, while racism was a social ill which even permeated boxing, one of the few sports in which Black men were prominent.

In response to such conditions, those of African and Caribbean heritage continued to build up their own communities, political organizations and publications. They struggled against racism and protested against the injustices of empire and colonial invasion. In the period leading up to the Second World War, organizations with a

Pan-African orientation became more prominent, partly as a consequence of the rise of fascism and the invasion of Ethiopia, but also as a result of Black people's common experiences in Britain and the colonies. Increasingly, these organizations found common cause with other enlightened people in Britain who took a stand against racism and colonialism and demanded a new world order in which all people might govern themselves.

8

The Second World War and After

In October 1938 the London-based International African Service Bureau (IASB) issued a 'Manifesto against War' in its publication *International African Opinion*. In a preface the IASB explained that although 'war seemed almost unavoidable', it was receiving communications from 'every corner of the colonial world . . . and the tenor of every one of them was opposition to any war fought by imperialist powers for a re-division of territory, a war in which the Black peoples would only be used as cannon fodder and from which it was a foregone conclusion that they would gain nothing'. As a consequence, the IASB distributed the manifesto widely and it was reprinted in several English journals. In September 1939, shortly after the declaration that Britain had entered the Second World War, the IASB reissued the manifesto in opposition to the war and military conscription, on behalf of itself and 'other associated anti-imperialist organizations' in Africa and the Caribbean. It also appeared, with a different title, in *The Crisis* and other African American publications, with George Padmore credited as the author.[1]

Addressing 'Africans and peoples of African descent', the manifesto reminded its readers of the 1914–18 war, how 'coloured races' had been used as 'cannon fodder', and the way in which they had been treated in its aftermath. The IASB asserted that the current war was not being fought for democracy, nor principally against fascism. It pointed out that the British government had done nothing to prevent fascist Italy invading Ethiopia, but that the war was being fought for the preservation of the colonial empires. Those in the colonies had not been consulted about their involvement and, 'enjoy less democracy in their own countries than they did in 1914'. The IASB asserted that

'Africans have as much freedom and liberty in their own countries as the Jews enjoy in Hitler's Germany'. They therefore demanded self-government for the colonies, arguing that this one act would give 'hundreds of millions of subject peoples something to defend' and inspire the workers of Germany to overthrow Hitler. In conclusion, it stated, 'if peace is to be achieved imperialism must be abolished'.[2]

Such views, which emphasized the nature of British imperialism and its appeasement of Nazi Germany, were not uncommon at the time and persisted until the war assumed a clearly anti-fascist character, especially after the intervention of the Soviet Union in 1941. Memories of the brutal suppression of the labour protests and strikes that occurred throughout the Caribbean colonies during the late 1930s were still vivid, as were everyday conditions in what were referred to as 'England's West Indian Slums'.[3] From 1935 until 1940, in Jamaica and Trinidad alone, nearly fifty people had been killed by the military during demonstrations and more than one thousand arrested. Some of the strike leaders in the Caribbean, such as Uriah Butler in Trinidad and Ken Hill in Jamaica, remained imprisoned during the war, since the colonial government feared their continued activism. Isaac Wallace-Johnson, a well-known trade-union organizer and anti-colonial activist in West Africa, was also interned until 1944. He was declared someone 'likely to prejudice "safety and defence" if permitted liberty'.[4] Britain's West African colonies had also seen mass anti-colonial protests and demonstrations involving hundreds of thousands during the 1930s.[5] Racism and segregation were still common in many British colonies during this period, and not just those such as South Africa and Kenya, which were dominated by European settlers.

In Padmore's view, there should have been no support for the war effort and he personally rejected military conscription.[6] For the IASB and other organizations in Britain, the war presented another opportunity for democratic demands, such as self-government in the colonies, as well as the elimination of racism and the colour bar everywhere. In July 1939 the League of Coloured Peoples (LCP), Negro Welfare Association (NWA), Gold Coast Students' Association and Coloured Film Artists Association convened a conference on 'African Peoples, Democracy and World Peace' in London. The conference was addressed by a diverse group of speakers including the future Labour Colonial

Secretary, Arthur Creech Jones, Sir Stafford Cripps, recently expelled from the Labour Party, Princess Tsehai, the daughter of Ethiopia's Emperor Haile Selassie, Krishna Menon of the India League, Padmore and others. Most importantly, the conference resolved to secure for Africa and the Caribbean a series of demands including: universal adult suffrage; universal free compulsory education; freedom of speech, press and organization; full rights for workers' and farmers' organizations; and the 'immediate abrogation of all existing oppressive legislation'.[7] Even during the first few weeks of the war, in October 1939, a delegation of the LCP, the West African Students' Union (WASU), NWA and others, including Sylvia Pankhurst, demanded a meeting with the Colonial Secretary to complain about repressive legislation in the African colonies. Apparently, this was not only an attempt to embarrass the government, but also to make it clear that African and Caribbean people in Britain expected some colonial reforms to be guaranteed and stated publicly in official war aims.[8]

Such aims were also evident in Padmore's and Nancy Cunard's 1942 publication *The White Man's Duty*, which, amongst other things, demanded legal penalties against racism.[9] Organizations such as the LCP and WASU had similar aims and did their best to advance them during the war. Moody called for self-determination for the colonies, but supported any sign that the British government was 'welcoming of aid from its "younger" brothers of the Empire'. He readily applauded government statements that it was 'training the people of the colonies for ultimate self-government'.[10] The demands of Padmore, the LCP and the WASU were not fulfilled, but there were some significant advances as a result of the war. Their demands were restated throughout the conflict and with particular vigour during the Manchester Pan-African Congress held in October 1945.

THE COLONIES AND THE WAR

As during the First World War, Britain's colonies and colonial subjects, as well as residents of African and Caribbean heritage, made an enormous contribution to the war effort, even though they did not enjoy the same rights as other British citizens. Well over half a million

Africans served in the military within the African continent, in the war against Japan and in Europe. In many cases men were conscripted into the services, including what were referred to as the Pioneer Corps, which were labour rather than combat units. African soldiers were still subjected to physical punishments and they received lower rates of pay than white soldiers. Nevertheless, many received awards and commendations for their gallantry and more than 15,000 lost their lives. African troops were not commissioned as officers, although Seth Anthony, from the Gold Coast, was an exception. He started the war as a private but was sent to Sandhurst in 1941 and by the end of the war he was a major.[11]

Many African and Caribbean countries were used for navy and air-force bases, including Nigeria, the Gold Coast and Sierra Leone. The United States established military bases in Caribbean countries such as Antigua, the Bahamas, British Guiana, Jamaica, Trinidad and St Lucia. The British government was reluctant to recruit military units from the Caribbean and it was not until 1944 that a Caribbean regiment was formed, drawn from over a thousand volunteers from all of Britain's Caribbean colonies. This regiment was deployed in Europe for 'general' duties rather than combat. Individuals based in Britain, or who managed to travel to Britain, did successfully enlist in the British Army, but there was no mass recruitment from the colonies. A few technicians were recruited to the Royal Engineers, but the War Office was reluctant to recruit troops from the Caribbean, citing climatic and accommodation difficulties.[12] The entire British Caribbean also provided over a thousand volunteers for the Trinidad Royal Naval Reserve. According to figures released in 1946, 219 service personnel from the Caribbean lost their lives, 265 were wounded and 96 became prisoners-of-war.[13]

The African and Caribbean colonies also made enormous financial contributions despite impoverished conditions. It is reported that of Trinidad's entire revenue from 1940 until 1946, 6 per cent went towards war loans and 12 per cent for 'military and naval service'. By 1943 its population had contributed £500,000 to various war funds and $3.5m to war loans at a time when many workers earned less than two shillings a day. Jamaica was reported to have raised enough money to fund eight aircraft. West Africans donated over £1.5 million for the war and both African and Caribbean colonies supplied raw materials, including food, often produced by conscripted labour working for private companies. In some places, wartime conditions led to strikes, such as those occurring in Rhodesia in 1940 and Nigeria in 1945.[14]

THE COLOUR BAR

Despite not enjoying full democratic rights in Britain, or its colonies, African and Caribbean people participated in the war as combatants, or contributed to the war effort in other ways. Although in 1939 the Colonial Office noted that 'it was essential to convince coloured people that their assistance is needed and valued', other government departments were not so keen. Governors of Britain's colonies were informed in 1939 that 'it is not desired that non-European British subjects should come here for enlistment'.[15] In Britain the colour bar continued, since there were no laws against discrimination. It was so ubiquitous that one West African, Rowland Sawyer, co-wrote a play about it on the eve of the war.[16] There were still different wage rates in the Merchant Navy for 'coloured' seamen, a ban on 'non-European' officers in the armed services and even some opposition to people of African and Caribbean heritage enlisting as war broke out.[17] In 1938 the Army Council had strengthened the colour bar, in order to restrict 'all army recruitment to men of pure European descent'.[18] Similar racist restrictions were also in place in the Royal Navy (RN) and Royal Air Force (RAF).

On the eve of war, in 1939, the government considered it expedient to remove the most blatant examples of racism, in words at least, in part because African and Caribbean students at Oxford, Cambridge and Newcastle universities, as well as others, had complained that they had been unable to enrol in the Officer Training Corps, or to gain commissions in the armed forces. Dr Robert Wellesley Cole, a Sierra-Leonean doctor practising in Britain recalled: 'I looked forward to the discrimination based on colour to disappear with the war', but he added, 'I could not join the Officers' Training Corps as a student, because though British I was not "of pure European Descent".'[19] After war was declared, and after much deliberation, the government finally decided in October 1939 that 'during the present emergency' it would look better to officially allow enlistment as well as commissions, for those 'not of pure European descent'. The new policy applied to 'all three services', but in practice the colour bar was retained in regard to commissions and was relaxed more generally only with extreme reluctance. As one government official noted, 'We must keep up the fiction of there being no colour bar.'[20]

The colour bar also operated in such auxiliary services as the Air Raid Precautions (ARP) services administered by local authorities. In September 1939 Reverend E. N. Jones (Laminoh Sankoh), a leading member of the WASU, was dismissed from his post as a stretcher-bearer in Paddington. Around the same time two 'other coloured men (an Indian and a Negro)' were also dismissed, allegedly because other stretcher-bearers complained of their presence. In a letter contesting his dismissal Jones wrote, 'at a time when the country is engaged in a war to destroy Hitlerism, one of whose doctrines is race discrimination, it seems strange ... that such abominable doctrine should be practiced in this country'.[21] However, the local authorities maintained that it was more expedient to 'sacrifice the coloured men' and retain those who held racist views. The WASU immediately took up the case by writing to several MPs, as well as government ministers, to demand that action was taken to 'see that this evil of Colour Bar is completely suppressed and stamped out before it spreads'. However, although questions were asked in Parliament and such cases were reported in the press, they were not satisfactorily resolved.[22] In Cardiff, on the other hand, it was reported that the ARP services included 'a number of West Indian, West African, Arab, Jewish and coloured men and women wardens and messengers'. The report adds that 'The ARP duties in the district appear to have brought about quite a strong sense of comradeship and co-operation.' One of these ARP wardens was Edward Bovell, a former seaman from Barbados, who had settled in Cardiff's Butetown in 1885.[23]

One African who successfully served as an ARP warden was E. I. Ekpenyon, a Nigerian and former student who had been in London since 1928. He wrote about his wartime experiences in St Marylebone in London during the Blitz.[24] Promoted twice and finally serving as Deputy Post Warden, he also made several radio broadcasts for the BBC Empire Service during the war. Ekpenyon reported:

> Once I had to help to evacuate people from a bombed shelter. As I was leading a lady to another shelter, a whistling bomb came sailing overhead, and I had to throw the lady down on the pavement and lie on top of her. I was pleased that she was not hurt, though she was very shaken. In the shelter to which I took her I noticed that there was uneasiness. But I assured the people that all was well, and that there was no need to be alarmed.[25]

However, he also sometimes faced difficulties in the public air-raid shelters. 'Some of the shelterers told the others to go back to their own countries, and some tried to practise segregation. A spirit of friendliness and comradeship was lacking. If this spirit had continued it would, as certainly as the night follows the day, have led to riots.' Ekpenyon had to develop a variety of means to unite people, but he also told them that if they didn't cooperate, they should seek shelter elsewhere. He found he had to educate them about the British Empire: 'I said that though I am an air-raid warden in London, I am still an African. I also said that I am one of many peoples of other countries that make up the Empire.'[26]

In January 1940, Edinburgh-born George Price, 'son of a British West Indian' who had served in the Royal Navy during the First World War, appeared before the Edinburgh Conscientious Objectors tribunal. Price, described as 'a 20-year-old Edinburgh mattress worker', had been rejected by both the RN and the RAF because of the colour bar. As a result, he told the tribunal, he had decided 'never to join up, or serve with the British forces'. The tribunal was sympathetic but eventually refused him permission to register as a conscientious objector. His case received some press coverage, was taken up by the LCP and questions were asked in Parliament by his MP, Arthur Woodburn, himself a former conscientious objector during the First World War.[27] Price was rejected because those joining the navy were required to be 'British-born sons of British-born parents'. Price therefore subsequently refused to join the army, stating that he would 'go to jail before they will get me', and he told the press that he had experienced racism since the age of twelve, when he and his sister were refused membership of an Edinburgh tennis club. He remarked that 'ever since that first experience we have come up against the colour bar, but thank goodness there are many people in Scotland who are not so narrow-minded as the government authorities appear to be'.[28]

In the same month, K. A. Ward, a Barbadian medical student in Edinburgh, who had previously worked as a motor engineer, wrote a letter of complaint to the Colonial Office because he had been rejected for enlistment as a flight mechanic in the RAF. Encouraged by the government to reapply, he was refused again.[29] Examples of the colour bar in the armed forces and auxiliary services can be found throughout the war. Even the Voluntary Aid Detachments, which provided nursing care for military personnel, had, earlier, demanded that State Registered Nurses had to be 'British subjects, daughters of British subjects and of pure European descent', although this formulation was removed at the start of the war.[30] Those of African and Caribbean heritage, as well as others affected by the colour bar, had to continue to struggle to serve and make their contribution to the war effort, a war ostensibly being fought against fascism. They faced not just occasional individual prejudice but the blatant racism of the state itself.

These and other similar incidents led to what George Padmore called the 'colonial defence organizations in London' – the WASU, the LCP, the NWA and the IASB – to jointly challenge the colour bar in the armed forces. According to Padmore, 'Meetings were organized and resolutions adopted. Letters were sent to the press and MPs lobbied in the House of Commons. A representative delegation also called at Downing Street and protested to the Secretary of State for the Colonies. Similar representation was made to the Air Ministry and War Office.'[31] Initially there was little obvious success, although Harold Moody continued to wage a campaign against racism in the media, even forcing the BBC to apologize for a 1940 broadcast in which the N-word was used.[32] Moody's children did manage to receive commissions in the armed services, two as doctors in the Royal Army Medical Corps and two who served in the RAF. Charles Arundel 'Joe' Moody, Moody's son, was one of the first to benefit from a change in government policy and in 1940 he was admitted for officer training. He eventually served with the Royal West Kent Regiment, but only after vigorous campaigning by his father and the LCP. However, as Joe Moody admitted, there were attempts to 'get me out of the way' and he was subsequently transferred to what was clearly considered the more appropriate

Caribbean Regiment. A very few other commissions were subsequently awarded, but clearly the War Office was reluctant to enlist 'coloured' service personnel. A Colonial Office official explained that changes in regulations did not 'mean that men of colour will in practice receive commissions ... only that the men will not be turned down on "Pure European descent" basis at recruiting offices'.[33]

THE RAF

In 1939 the RAF had also barred all enlistment to 'men of colour', arguing that although it was opposed to any discrimination, it could not ignore 'strong feelings of antipathy which are well known to exist and which we are powerless to remove'.[34] Dr Leo March, a Jamaican-born dental surgeon, was just one of those rejected when he responded to an RAF appeal for dental surgeons in September 1939.[35] Appeasement of racism thus became official policy and continued even after the announcement in Parliament in October 1939 that the colour bar had been abolished. In May 1940 an Air Ministry official insisted that 'the RAF did not want and would not absorb Black applicants'. A letter sent to colonial governors made it clear that 'the presence of a coloured man' amongst air crew 'would detract from efficiency'.[36] At the close of 1939 the LCP wrote to the Colonial Office to complain that several men including March, Babatunde O. Alakija, a Nigerian student, and Sydney Kennard, a qualified pilot from British Guiana, were still being rejected by the RAF.[37]

However, because of the great losses sustained during the early part of the war, and especially after the Battle of Britain, from the autumn of 1940 the RAF opened recruitment to Black people in Britain, as well as those from the colonies, although in some West African colonies this change in policy was not made public until the following year. It seems that the publicity value of such recruits was considered desirable by the government as well, especially if they could be drawn from the most prominent family backgrounds. In general, however, the RAF aimed to recruit skilled workers rather than pilots from the colonies. Similar changes were made to the recruitment policies of the army. As a consequence, Leo March and Dr Otto Wallen from

Trinidad were declared eligible for commissions in the Royal Army Medical Corps.[38]

The abrupt change in policy was noted by Padmore in an article in *The Crisis* entitled 'Hitler makes Britain drop color bar', which was published in the United States in March 1941. According to Padmore, 'The new policy is quite simply opportunistic. It is dictated by the imperialist needs and influenced by the present military problems confronting Britain since the collapse of France and other Continental allies.' He pointed to the £17 million donated by the Caribbean and other colonies for aircraft, noting that Jamaica was the first colony to start a Spitfire fund and that the Gold Coast alone had provided finance for fifty aircraft.[39] He argued that such changes in government policy were not 'to be interpreted as a manifestation that democratic freedom is being extended to the non-self-governing sections of the empire, such as India, Africa and the West Indies'.[40] Padmore also noted that the colour bar, both in Britain and the colonies, had recently come under attack, most notably from the Archbishop of Canterbury and other senior church leaders, who had written an open letter to *The Times* in September 1940. Amongst other things, they stated that 'the prejudice which erects a colour bar or prompts racial exclusiveness is, in fact, a denial of Christian principles'. The church leaders recognized the dangers of racism at a time when Britain needed the support of the 'coloured Empire', and was ostensibly fighting against an enemy 'pledged to a doctrine of race-superiority and race-domination'. In its hour of need, Britain needed its empire and racism could be seen as a hindrance.

At the close of 1940 a young Nigerian, Babatunde O. Alakija, the son of a member of the colony's Legislative Council and formerly a student at Oxford, was hailed in the press as the first African to be permitted to train as a pilot in the RAF.[41] Another Nigerian, 25-year-old Peter Adeniyi Thomas, had also been successful in his application, with support from the colonial government in Nigeria. Thomas, a member of one of the wealthiest families in Nigeria, arrived for pilot training in Britain in 1941. In 1943, according to press reports, he became the first African 'to get his wings in the RAF' and to gain a commission. That year a short propaganda film was made about him by the government's Colonial Film Unit. Unfortunately, Flight Lieutenant Peter Thomas' wartime flying ended in tragedy, as he became 'the first Nigerian pilot to be killed in action' in January 1945 while attempting to crash-land his plane in the Brecon Beacons in Wales.[42]

By March 1941 appeals for aircrew were being made in West Africa as well as in the Caribbean, yet very few Africans were ultimately selected for training in Britain, a situation that provoked outrage in the local press, especially in Nigeria. Air crew were recruited based on educational qualifications. During 1941 fewer than ten men had been selected from Nigeria and initially only five from Sierra Leone. By this time, travel to Britain for African and Caribbean volunteers involved an extremely hazardous sea voyage, on occasions lasting more than a month, in U-boat-infested waters. Some men, such as Claude Foster Jones from Sierra Leone, made their own way to Britain, even after being rejected by the colonial authorities. Foster Jones made a direct complaint to the Colonial Secretary in London and eventually succeeded in joining the RAF as an engineer. Another Sierra Leonean, William Leigh, worked his passage to England and was initially accepted as an RAF wireless operator/air-gunner. After four weeks he was selected for pilot training in Canada. Several men stowed away on ships bound for England. A Nigerian, Robert Naronje, stowed away in the coal bunker of a ship, but gave himself up after several days without food or drink. On reaching England he too finally joined the RAF. [43]

Another who joined the RAF was Sierra Leonean John Henry 'Johnny' Smythe (1915–1996), who, in 1940, travelled to Scotland to undertake training. He was one of only a few Africans trained as a navigator, was posted to 623 Squadron at Downham Market and later promoted to Flying Officer.[44] He flew in bombers and later recorded some of his experiences:

> We knew what lay ahead of us. Every day we counted the number that returned. We also knew that there was a good chance that we would not return. We met with our first serious trouble during an operation over Mainz in Germany. The plane had several times been pelted by flak and it was in a bad state. Although we lost one of our engines, we still managed to limp back home.
>
> On one occasion we were flying back over England when a German fighter began to dog us. I saw it first and yelled to the rear gunner, 'Frank, open up!' It was quite scary because we were flying so low that,

had the plane been actually shot down, we wouldn't have had time to bail out! The noise caused by the two aircraft brought our anti-aircraft fire from the ground, which fended off the German fighter, and we were able to land safely. Another lucky escape!

Unfortunately, his luck ran out on his twenty-eighth mission in November 1943. In his own words:

> We were flying at 16,000 ft when the fighters came out of nowhere. They raked the fuselage and there were flames everywhere. Then the searchlights caught us. I was hit by shrapnel. Pieces came from underneath, piercing my abdomen, going through my side. Another came through my seat and into my groin. I heard the pilot ordering us to bail out. We had some rough ones before but this seemed to be the end.

Flying Officer Johnny Smythe managed to parachute to the ground and hid in a barn.

> Men in uniform came into the barn where I was hiding behind some straw. Then they opened up, raking the place with automatic fire. I decided to give in. The Germans couldn't believe their eyes. I'm sure that's what saved me from being shot immediately. To see a black man – and an officer at that – was more than they could come to terms with. They just stood there gazing.

After initially being badly treated, Johnny Smythe was taken to the notorious Stalag Luft I, a prisoner-of-war (POW) camp for Allied officers, where he served on the escape committee. He made light of his own inability to escape, saying, 'I don't think a six-foot-five black man would've got very far in Pomerania, somehow.' He remained a POW for two years until liberated by the Red Army in 1945.[45]

Flight Sergeant Akin Shenbanjo, a Nigerian, had enlisted in 1941 and served for thirty operations with 76 Squadron as a wireless operator/ air-gunner. He is said to have flown in a Halifax bomber christened *Achtung! The Black Prince*. In 1943 the bomber was hit during a raid on Lille, but Shenbanjo managed to return to base. In 1944 he was awarded the Distinguished Flying Medal, was later promoted to Warrant Officer, and managed to survive the war. In 1944 Sierra Leonean Flight Sergeant Ade Hyde was a navigator based in Yorkshire with 640

Squadron. Wounded during a bombing raid over France, he kept silent about his injuries until the mission had been completed. He was hospitalized for three months and then returned to service. Hyde was promoted to Pilot Officer, and in 1945, for his 'tenacity and unfailing devotion to duty', he was awarded the Distinguished Flying Cross. Others were much less fortunate. Sergeant Bankole Vivour, a Nigerian bomb-aimer, was killed in March 1944 during a bombing raid on Nuremberg, one of more than 500 aircrew to lose their lives in a single night. In July 1944 another Nigerian, Sergeant Akinpelu Johnson, was killed when his plane struck a tree on take-off.[46]

Although it might appear that, having lowered the colour bar for Africans and those from the Caribbean, all was well, incidents of racism still occurred. Africans were barred from captaining planes, apparently in response to an incident when a white crew refused to serve with a Black captain. In another incident a West African fighter pilot was beaten up and thrown out of a public house by American pilots he had recently escorted into battle. Other West Africans faced discrimination and even assault when they were posted to colonial territories, including West Africa. In Britain great efforts were made to shield Africans from the worst aspects of racism by organizations such as the Victoria League, and many stayed in Britain after the war. Some received government assistance to remain as students, while Johnny Smythe became a liaison officer for the Colonial Office, later welcoming Caribbean migrants onto the SS *Windrush* before embarking on a legal career.[47]

However, the government had no intention of recruiting air crews from West Africa in any great number and only about sixty men joined the RAF. Recruitment in the Caribbean was very different, as about 450 aircrew and nearly 6,000 ground personnel were enlisted.[48] There were also about eighty women from the Caribbean who joined the Women's Auxiliary Air Force. Although the RAF argued that those from the Caribbean were better educated, and therefore more eligible, there were more students from Africa than from the Caribbean studying in Britain at the time. The RAF and the Air Ministry continued their reluctance to completely drop the colour bar and in 1944 all enlistment from the colonies was stopped. Although the colour bar was not officially reinstated, however, Air Ministry officials agreed that 'on paper, coloured troops [would] be eligible for entry ... but the process of selection [would] eliminate them'.[49]

Some of those who joined the RAF from the Caribbean have become well known in recent years because of their own memoirs of the war.[50] About a hundred were commissioned as officers, more than 250 served at the rank of sergeant or above, while at least a third of all volunteer aircrew were killed in action.[51] Some trained in Canada before arriving in Britain as aircrew, while some, such as eighteen-year-old Billy Strachan (1921–1998) from Jamaica, made their own way to Britain, knowing nobody in the country. He arrived in Bristol in March 1940, presented himself for enlistment a few days after his arrival, then trained as a wireless operator/air-gunner, but was, unusually, allowed to retrain and became a pilot officer flying Lancaster and Wellington bombers.[52] He later recalled the bravado that existed amongst aircrew at the time:

> We had several narrow escapes. Once when the navigator, who was also the bomb-aimer, was lying flat on his back looking down the aimer, a bullet flew over his head, under the pilot's backside and up the side of

A group of RAF officers including Johnny Smythe
(seated second from right) and Ulric Cross (seated third from right)

my leg – I still have the scar to prove it. Yet I was never terrified. In fact none of us was. I suppose we had the over-confidence of youth. We never thought it would happen to us. We were a tight unit – as crew we did everything together. We came back, had parties, checked up to see who were lost and heartlessly said things like – Oh, I'll have his bike.[53]

Under the influence of his mentor, Una Marson, herself the first Black female radio producer for the BBC's Empire Service, Flight Lieutenant Strachan was employed as a liaison officer investigating racism at various RAF bases.[54]

The most decorated flyer from the Caribbean was Trinidadian Ulric Cross (1917–2013), who served in Bomber Command and was awarded the Distinguished Flying Cross and Distinguished Service Order. Cross explained: 'The world was drowning in fascism and America was not yet in the war, so I decided to do something about it and volunteered to fight in the RAF.' He arrived in Britain in 1941 and after training as a navigator was posted to 139 (Jamaica) Squadron at RAF Marham in Norfolk. This unit was so named because it flew bombers paid for by the people of Jamaica. His wartime service included over eighty sorties and twenty bombing raids over Berlin, for which he was later promoted to the rank of Squadron Leader. He was one of more than 250 Trinidadians who served in the RAF during the war, of whom more than fifty lost their lives.[55]

Ivor De'Souza (1918–1996), a Jamaican, joined the RAF in 1940, trained as a pilot and was posted to an Australian squadron as Flight Commander, in charge of a squadron of twelve aircraft.[56] Jamaicans, Dudley Thompson (1917–2012), and John J. Blair (1919–2004) also served in Bomber Command, both as flight lieutenants. Blair, who trained as a navigator, was subsequently awarded the Distinguished Flying Cross. Thompson's family were opposed to him enlisting but he was determined to fight 'Hitler's racism'. In England he found other challenges: 'One of the questions on the form I had to fill in was "Are you of pure European descent?" I answered "Yes." When the recruiting officer queried me – thinking I hadn't understood the question – I challenged him to prove otherwise with a blood test. I think he gave up in disgust or frustration. This overt racism existed even under the stress of war, in the early stages.'[57] However, Thompson, who eventually joined the elite Pathfinder Squadron, looked back on the war years as a 'period of great friendship and warmth'.[58]

Cy Grant (1919–2010), from British Guiana, joined the RAF in 1941, trained as a navigator and was also commissioned as an officer with a bomber squadron. During his third mission in 1943 his plane was shot down over Germany and he was subsequently captured. His photograph appeared in a German newspaper with the caption, 'A member of the Royal Air Force of indeterminate race'. Grant spent the rest of the war as a POW in Stalag Luft III, the camp connected with the 'Wooden Horse' escape and the 'Great Escape'.[59] He later became well known as an actor, singer and cultural performer. Errol Barrow (1920–1987), the future prime minister of Barbados, was one of the first from the Caribbean to join the RAF in December 1940. Trained as a navigator, he was commissioned as an officer in 1944. He was posted to 88 Squadron and by the end of the war had completed forty-five bombing missions.[60]

Some of those who joined the RAF were British-born men and women such as Cardiff-born Arthur Young (1923–1944), who joined in 1941 at the age of eighteen and eventually became a wireless operator/air-gunner with Bomber Command. He too was killed, along with the rest of his crew and two civilians, when in July 1944 his Lancaster bomber developed engine trouble, crashed in Salford and exploded on impact.[61] Another was Sergeant Vivian Florent (1921–1944) who was born in London in 1921 to the St Lucian actor Napoleon Florent and his English wife. He joined the RAF in 1941 and trained as an air-gunner. He was twenty-three and stationed at RAF Pocklington in Yorkshire when, in June 1944, his plane crashed, killing all those on board.[62] In 1943, just over a year before his son was killed, Napolean Florent had written to the Colonial Office to complain that his local Labour Exchange had never found him a job. He said that he knew 'of many coloured men who were sent after jobs from labour exchanges, but when they go to the employer, the employers say, "I am very sorry but I did not know they were sending a coloured person," so they did not get the job.' He explained that when he had applied to the Assistance Board for financial support he was told to go back to his own country. He had applied for a state pension but had been told that he was not eligible, even though he had been in Britain since 1888.[63]

Lilian Bader (née Bailey) was born in Liverpool in 1918, but grew up in Fleetwood in Lancashire. Her mother was Irish and her father a Barbadian, Marcus Bailey, who served in the Royal Navy during the First World War. At the outbreak of the Second World War Lilian Bader worked in a Navy, Army and Air Force Institute (NAAFI) canteen in Catterick, Yorkshire, but was forced to leave because of the colour bar. As she explained, 'I had been employed for about seven weeks when I was called into the office of the district manager. Very apologetic, he explained to me that head office had ordered him to dismiss me; my father had not been born in the UK.'[64] She subsequently wrote to appeal against her dismissal, was interviewed and 'told to stop making a nuisance of herself'. In 1941 she was accepted into the Women's Auxiliary Air Force, at about the time that her brother was lost at sea. Bailey trained as an aircraft instrument repairer, and she eventually became a corporal.[65]

Those recruited to RAF ground crew from the Caribbean arrived in Britain in the latter stages of the war, between 1944 and 1945, while some women joining the Auxiliary Territorial Service (ATS) arrived in 1943. Six hundred women from the Caribbean volunteered to join the ATS, which was the female equivalent of the Territorial Army. Most remained in the Caribbean, 200 were posted to the United States and about 100 were stationed in Britain, although they had to pay for their own passage there.[66] The ATS was the only military service to recruit women from the colonies. Recruitment to the ATS was also affected by the colour bar. No Black recruits from the Caribbean were sent to the US and the War Office was extremely reluctant to allow them to come to Britain, or even to serve in the Caribbean.[67]

In 1941 the first Caribbean woman to volunteer for the ATS in Britain, a Ms L. Curtis, was accepted until the War Office found out that she was Black.[68] Strong pressure from the Colonial Office eventually led to thirty Black Caribbean women being allowed to join the ATS in Britain in October 1943. They were the first group of the 100 highly qualified women who would eventually be recruited. The journey across the Atlantic to Britain could be perilous during wartime, but Nadia Cattouse, one of the recruits from what was then British Honduras, recalled the perils of travelling via a segregated United States as well. She and other ATS recruits were instructed to move from a 'whites only' train compartment and forced to stay in a brothel, because no hotel would accept them, before they arrived in Britain in June 1944.[69]

The stories of RAF ground crew are less well known and their treatment was often very different to that enjoyed by officers such as Ulric Cross. A Jamaican, Sam King (1936–2016), has become the best known of these recruits and was later the Mayor of the London Borough of Southwark. He arrived in Britain in November 1944 and trained as a skilled aircraft engineer at Filey in Yorkshire. He was then posted to Hawkinge in Kent and later wrote a memoir of some of his wartime experiences, which were mainly positive and reflected the need for everyone to work together to defeat Nazi Germany.[70] However, some ground crew complained that 'they would give us ... all the skivvy work like sweeping up and cleaning lavatories. The next big group performed motor-driving duties and motor mechanic [sic], few did clerical work; only a very small minority of West Indian groundcrew airmen found themselves in the technical field.'[71] Others complained of a lack of promotion opportunities and of racism from American servicemen. However, the majority of experiences of the British public were positive, once initial curiosity had been satisfied and erroneous ideas dispelled. Still, friendships, or even conversations, with white women could often lead to conflicts and violence.[72]

The most notable case of this kind involved 23-year-old Donald Gerald Beard, a Jamaican airman, who was falsely accused of murder by police in Manchester's Piccadilly, just after the war in September 1946. The deceased had been involved with other civilians in a fight with Caribbean airmen. Apparently, this occurred because the civilians objected 'to the Jamaicans associating with white girls'.[73] A fight ensued and Beard was arrested. He later recalled, 'when the policeman realised he had no coloured man to hold, he turned around and said to me, "It's a fair country. You will get justice." Just like that, and then they took me to Strangeways prison that night in Manchester.'[74] Fortunately for Beard, the Jamaicans in Manchester got together with Ras Makonnen and the Pan-African Federation and arranged for Norman Manley KC, a famous barrister and a future prime minister of Jamaica, to lead the defence team. Manley 'made asses of the police', and their evidence, and the judge had to stop the case and acquit Beard.[75]

FORESTERS AND MUNITIONS WORKERS

While the government realized that it was expedient to recruit those from the Caribbean, not least because of feared political unrest in the colonies, officials had a low opinion of 'West Indian combatant units'. Although many in the Caribbean demanded to serve the 'Mother Country', the War Office was extremely reluctant to accept them. A breakthrough was made with the deployment of the British Honduran Forestry Unit in August 1941, partly to deal with 'starvation and social unrest' in what is modern-day Belize, as well as a chronic shortage of skilled workers in Britain.[76] There was, however, strong opposition in some quarters to their deployment there and concerns about their relations with local women. The voyage to Britain was difficult too, as some were torpedoed during the Atlantic crossing, and others were transported via the United States. One complained, 'we were confined like prisoners and made to work and were guarded over by white soldiers ... We felt more like prisoners-of-war than volunteers travelling to the United Kingdom to do war work.'[77] When they arrived, the foresters were provided with conditions that were inferior to those offered to workers from Canada, Australia and New Zealand, including a lack of warm winter clothes.

In total about 800 men eventually worked in Scotland in very poor conditions. There were several protests, including one by the LCP, after a delegation had visited the men. A senior Colonial Office official concluded that the conditions in both the camps provided for the Hondurans was a 'public scandal'.[78] They were also paid at the lowest rate and in 1942 several men went on strike, while others simply left and found alternative work in England. The most damning criticism of the camps was made by the journalist, musician and conductor Rudolf Dunbar in his 1942 *Report on Social Welfare Among Coloured People on the Tyneside*. Amongst other things, he wrote:

> the men are living in a deplorable condition ... They are deprived of all form of entertainment and, the harsh treatment of most of them by the authorities does nothing to alleviate their sufferings ... a great portion of the men are miserable and desperate ... and wish to return home.

The men are not provided with sufficient warm clothing and ... There seems to be a muddle under the terms on which the men were engaged. Married men find their wages insufficient. The men seem to have been enlisted in a haphazard fashion.[79]

By 1943 the government was seeking ways to repatriate the foresters, especially alarmed at the marriages and relationships that they had established with local Scottish women. Nearly a hundred men were sent back in August of that year, although many of them had severe medical problems. These men returned without proper documentation, via the United States, where they were imprisoned for a month before the British authorities arranged for their return home.[80] Several hundred were repatriated by the end of 1943.[81] Those that remained in Britain eventually found alternative employment, although they were rejected by the RAF and the Admiralty, which 'felt that colonial coloured volunteers were rather an embarrassment and difficult to place in this country'.[82]

Similar problems affected the employment of Caribbean munitions workers in Britain.[83] Conditions in Britain's West Indian colonies grew worse during the war, as did the shortage of labour in Britain. It was not until February 1941 that over a hundred Jamaicans were brought to Britain to be employed in the Royal Ordnance Factories and fifty other munitions works and factories in the north-west, mostly in and around Liverpool but also in Manchester and Bolton. Nearly 350 men in total from several Caribbean islands were employed in munitions work by the end of 1942, after the government agreed to provide limited training. One volunteer recalled, 'we young Jamaican lads viewed the call to work in British munitions factories with suspicion, although lots of us were out of work ... Nevertheless I was eager to see the mother country, the great seat of education to the world, the great London.'[84] Many of the men had difficult voyages and at least five were killed after being torpedoed in the Atlantic.[85] The first contingent to arrive in 1941 were officially welcomed by the government, and even provided with new clothes, but later arrivals received much less of a welcome. Many were housed in apparently 'segregated' hostels that remained unheated in winter. Some men complained to the LCP about the colour bar in Liverpool, and the difficulty of finding alternative accommodation. One later wrote, 'because we are black, we were not treated as humans'.[86] Another recalled, 'Prejudice was always a problem ... The prejudice was caused through ignorance.'[87] As a result, many of the volunteers attempted to find accommodation in the areas where Liverpool's Black population lived.

During the war, Learie Constantine, the West Indies cricketer, was employed as a welfare officer for the Ministry of Labour, with special responsibility for those from the Caribbean. From 1941 onwards Constantine was based in Liverpool and he recalled that even finding employment for the Caribbean volunteers was difficult, despite the existence of a chronic labour shortage at the time. 'Some firms either flatly refused to take on coloured men or put endless delays in their way, hoping to make them seek work elsewhere.'[88] At the Royal Ordnance Factories at Kirby and Fazakerley there were a series of complaints by Caribbean workers as well as West African ones. According to Constantine, 'in one area, a number of coloured workers came out on strike because one of them had suffered unpleasant discrimination'.[89] In August 1942 at Fazakerley there were complaints about racism and lack of promotion. The men at the factory first contacted the factory superintendent, explaining that although they were 'engaged in the common cause for Freedom and the recognition of all peoples and rights, we daily come up against the spirit of negrophobism ... Some refer to us as "n——" and "coolies"; others make it their duty to instruct operators not to speak to us, and a good few, by their actions and attitude to us, make it only possible for disaffection to bed forth.'[90] Others complained that trade unions would not accept them for membership, or that they were being paid at lower rates than promised, and they made Constantine, the LCP, the WASU and the government aware of numerous other grievances.[91] The LCP duly noted that the West Indian workers, 'refuse to appreciate anything that savours of colour discrimination'. While the Colonial Office tried to make arrangements that would prevent those from the Caribbean 'becoming "contaminated" by the rather unsatisfactory West African seamen population in Liverpool',[92] African workers had their own complaints, not least that the West Indians were given preferential treatment and were unfriendly.[93]

THE COLOUR BAR AGAIN

Throughout the war the participation of people of African and Caribbean heritage was made more difficult by the existence of the ubiquitous colour bar. Many, although not all, of the problems affecting volunteer munitions workers, foresters, RAF crew, ARP workers and even those employed by the NAAFI were a result of the existence of racism in Britain that was sanctioned and maintained by the armed forces and the government itself. Because the war was ostensibly fought against the racist ideology of Nazism, and also because of the need to maintain loyalty throughout the empire, ministers were eager to distance the government from any responsibility for the colour bar. Representatives of the Colonial Office argued for 'legislation to support the common law rights of persons of all races in obtaining refreshment and hospitality in hotels', but nothing was done to change the law. They also argued that more should be done to educate children and the general public, but found great opposition to their proposals.[94] At times the existence of the colour bar threatened to become a national scandal, as damning reports often appeared in the press.

In June 1942 the *New Statesman and Nation* drew attention to many of the problems facing Black volunteers: '[W]hat should shame us far more deeply is the social colour snobbery with which they are often treated . . . they are refused admission to dance halls, turned out of hotels, separated from white men in fire watching parties . . . people do not know where their own empire is nor who inhabits it.'[95] In September of that year Brendan Bracken, the Minister of Information, was compelled to make a statement on the issue after encouragement to do so by Rudolph Dunbar, who was already becoming famous in Britain as a conductor, as well as a musician, and was employed by the Ministry of Information. In April 1942 he became the first person of African heritage to conduct the London Philharmonic Orchestra. Later that year he also conducted the London Symphony Orchestra and the Liverpool Philharmonic Orchestra, playing works by William Grant Still and Coleridge-Taylor, including the latter's forgotten work *Toussaint L'Ouverture*. Dunbar was also widely known as a war correspondent and London editor for the *Associated Negro Press*.[96]

Bracken's article in the *Sunday Express* recognized that 'most coloured people in Britain come from the British colonies. They are therefore British citizens with, in theory, the same rights as any Englishman.' However, he added, 'it is in fact true that there is still some colour prejudice in this country and still social barriers against coloured people'. Bracken claimed that 'the British government is in favour of putting an end to this prejudice as quickly as possible', but he also claimed that legislation was not the answer and that the colour bar was simply due to 'ignorance' and the 'ancient insularity of the British people'.[97] Desmond Buckle, himself from the Gold Coast, surveyed the problem from the communist perspective and wrote that 'much remains to be done by the British workers in the armed services and in civil life to remove all obstacles to the development of full comradeship'. He called on the working class to do more and, referring to the Soviet Union's victory at Stalingrad, concluded, 'absence of artificial social and racial barriers is one of the sources of Soviet strength. Immense benefit would result to the war effort if all individuals both civil and military, were to learn that elementary fact.'[98]

In August 1943 the operation of the colour bar created an even bigger scandal when it affected Learie Constantine. He had just finished playing at an international cricket match at Lord's when he and his family were denied admission to the aptly named Imperial Hotel in Russell Square, London. His companion was told: 'We will not have n—— in the hotel because of the Americans. If they stay tonight, their luggage will be put out tomorrow and the doors locked.' The hotel was at the time occupied by 200 US Army officers. The managing director of the hotel stated: 'We prefer to cater for white people; I think that is not unreasonable.' Constantine subsequently sued the hotel for breach of contract and triumphed. He was awarded token damages of £5. The incident was also widely reported in the press, prompting a famous cartoon by David Low in the *Evening Standard*. Questions were asked in Parliament and the government was again forced to condemn the colour bar. The incident also gave Constantine the opportunity to speak about 'the sort of thing that happens to us every day', including the experiences of the West Indian munitions workers.[99]

A second infamous case in 1943 was that of Amelia King who was born in Stepney, London, in 1917. She attempted to enlist in the

THEY TRIED PUTTING A COLOUR BAN ON HARVESTS

This is Amelia King. She was refused work on the land because of her colour.

Colour doesn't prevent her father and brother fighting in the Merchant Navy.

Press and public clamour exposed this shameful treatment of a Stepney-born girl.

THAT IS ONE CASE, HERE IS ANOTHER.

Leary Constantine, well-known broadcaster and sportsman, was turned out of the Imperial Hotel.

Why? Because of his colour.

Coloured folk can die fighting for us, can help destroy Fascism, can help preserve our freedom, but they are not allowed to gather in the harvest or stay at certain hotels.

How long is this vicious discrimination to continue?

That depends on YOU. Depends on whether you are prepared to add YOUR protest to the growing demand that racial discrimination be ended for ever.

Issued by the Holborn Trades Council and printed by the London Caledonian Press Ltd. (T.U. all Depts.), 74 Swinton Street, W.C.1.—1948

A protest against racism during the war

Women's Land Army (WLA), which provided women workers for farmers, in an effort to increase food production during wartime. Amelia King reported that a WLA official immediately raised the 'colour question' and told her, '[I]t was the farmers who would object and then that perhaps it would be the billeting people.' The official reportedly added, 'I have had trouble with other girls coming like you, and I suppose if I went to your country the position would be the same.' In a press interview Amelia King said that 'I did not think it was fair. I had a brother in the Navy and my father was at sea. I thought we were fighting for freedom.' Amelia's father, Henry King, a seaman for thirty-seven years in the Merchant Navy, had come to London from British Guiana in 1906; her brother worked as a stoker in the Royal Navy. According to press reports, 'five generations of her mother's ancestors – all coloured folk – lived in Limehouse.' Amelia King was told that she had been rejected by the WLA. A few weeks later she was offered a job working in munitions but she refused, commenting that if her colour was not good enough for the WLA, she would not work in munitions. The Minister of Agriculture was then compelled to make a statement in Parliament, in which he claimed that Amelia King was encouraged to find alternative employment 'because of the extreme difficulties of finding her work on the land'.[100]

Amelia King's case was taken up by her local MP and a campaign started against the colour bar. Her photo appeared on the front page of the *Daily Mirror*. A leaflet with her photo, which also mentioned Learie Constantine's case, was produced by the Holborn Trades Council. Amongst other things it pointed out, 'Coloured folk can die fighting for us, can help destroy Fascism, can help preserve our freedom but they are not allowed to gather in the harvest or stay in certain hotels. How long is this vicious discrimination to continue? That depends on YOU. Depends on whether you are prepared to add YOUR protest to the growing demand that racial discrimination be ended for ever.'[101] A 'Londoners Protest Meeting against Racial Discrimination' was held in Conway Hall and people were encouraged to 'put an end to the colour bar and the nation's shame'. Amelia King was later accepted by the WLA.

THE WAR AT SEA

Amelia King and Lilian Bader both had family members who served at sea during the war. Both of Lilian's brothers served: Frank in the Royal Navy and James, who was lost at sea in 1941, in the Merchant Navy. In one tragic incident three men from Liverpool on just one ship, the SS *Sithonia*, lost their lives when it was torpedoed in the Atlantic in 1942.[102] Another to be torpedoed was Sid Graham, who had been born in Custom House, east London, to a Barbadian father in 1920. His ship, the *Scottish Star*, was hit in 1942, as he explained:

> I was having a bath in a bucket and when we got torpedoed, I went up in the air and hit my ribs on the washbasin . . . I got up on the companionway and that's when the submarine started to shell us. Wasn't going down quick enough for him. I was badly hit in the arm. I went in the

lifeboat and we got away from the ship and the ship went down ...
Luckily enough we were in the Caribbean, not in the cold, but we
didn't know where we were going.[103]

Sid Graham and twenty others survived for ten days in a lifeboat,
often surrounded by sharks, until they were found by a fishing boat
and landed in Barbados, where he eventually found one of his aunts.
However, he reported that 'in those days as soon as you got torpedoed
on them ships your money was stopped right away'. Six months later
he was able to return to his family in England, who had no idea what
had happened to him and who had lost their home in an air raid. Sid
Graham later took part in the D-Day landings in Normandy.[104] There
were also many acts of heroism by Black seafarers reported, and in
one instance immortalized by Richard Eurich's painting *Survivors
from a Torpedoed Ship*. As early as 1940, the *Daily Express* carried
the headline 'Coloured Hero' and explained that 'the hero of the story
is a coloured man, George Taylor, whose home is at Freetown, Sierra
Leone. With a bullet-wound in one eye and half-blinded in the other,
Taylor stuck to the wheel on the bridge, obeying his captain's orders.'[105]
Yet another to be torpedoed and killed was Wilmot Young, a seaman
from Jamaica, who had moved to Cardiff in the 1920s. His son Jocelyn, another merchant seaman, also lost his life during the war.
Wilmot's daughter, the jazz singer Patti Flynn, campaigned for nearly
thirty years to have a war memorial in Wales for them and for the
thousands of others of African, Caribbean and Asian heritage who
served in two world wars but had been forgotten.[106]

However, just as in the other services, there is evidence to suggest
that the Admiralty and the Ministry of Shipping were reluctant to
recruit in the African or Caribbean colonies during wartime. The
admission of 'men of colour' to the Royal Navy was based on
instructions issued by the Admiralty to recruiting officers in October
1940. This stipulated that 'coloured men are not accepted to serve
for long term engagements ... Whilst coloured men are not theoretic-
ally excluded ... in practice, no coloured man who is not
British-born and the son of British-born parents would be regarded
as suitable for acceptance.' Although this is somewhat ambiguous, a
few months previously the Admiralty had declared 'there is no need

for us to take coloured men now residing in England'.[107] In 1943 the recruitment regulations stated: 'black and coloured men and boys and any person in whom there is evidence of such parentage or ancestry, unless with the special sanction of the Admiralty, are absolutely ineligible for entry.'

In that same year *Picture Post* took up the case of a young man who had been rejected by the RN on the grounds that he was 'too dark'. In response the RN wrote, 'experience has shown that it is in the interests of the persons themselves that they should not be entered for a life's career in the Royal Navy unless their appearance is predominantly European. Otherwise ... attention and comment from shipmates ... is likely to cause distress and resentment.'[108] However, some men did manage to serve. Allan Wilmot, a Jamaican and the son of a master mariner, first joined the RN and then the RAF. He enlisted in Jamaica and served alongside other Jamaicans on HMS *Hawken*, a minesweeper. In 1944 he transferred to the marine section of the RAF, where, he explained, 'my unit picked up aircrews shot down or ditched at sea'.[109]

While African and Caribbean merchant seamen based in British ports served and gave their lives, hundreds appear to have remained unemployed during the war. In Liverpool and Cardiff, the National Union of Seamen remained opposed to any increased employment of 'coloured' sailors. Although the Colonial Office issued a call for volunteers in the Caribbean in 1940 and found more than 1,800 suitable recruits, deployment was limited by official reluctance 'to mix coloured and white races in the same department on board ship'.[110] African and Caribbean seamen were also paid lower wages, leading to strikes in several ports during the war. In 1940, when Elder Dempster, sailing between Liverpool and West Africa, continued to pay African crews lower wages than other seamen, a strike was declared on the *Abosso*. The seamen issued a statement which concluded, 'we have been told that this country is fighting on behalf of defenceless people. If so, we defenceless seamen are appealing to you to defend us from the tyranny of the shipping company.'[111] The strikers were supported by Pastor Daniels Ekarte and by some sections of the press, and eventually the government was forced to institute an inquiry which merely uncovered that the exploitation and impoverishment of African seamen in Liverpool, and elsewhere, had been ongoing for many years, with government and NUS approval.

During the war merchant seamen could not be conscripted into the armed services but had to continue to work as seamen. Those who were unemployed joined the Merchant Navy Reserve Pool, where they were paid subsistence wages while awaiting allocation to a ship. However, some 'coloured' seamen were prevented from joining the pool, while others, though admitted, were paid even less than subsistence wages. In 1942 eighteen West African seamen refused to sail on Elder Dempster ships because the company refused to pay them the appropriate wages. They were subsequently gaoled for a month with hard labour by Liverpool magistrates. After protests by the LCP, and others, the Colonial Office instituted an inquiry, but there is no evidence that the seamen were compensated, while efforts by Constantine and others to find them employment were unsuccessful. Similar discrimination operated on other shipping lines. African and Caribbean seamen had no union to represent their interests and only towards the end of the war were wage rates relating to the pool increased in their favour.[112]

THE HOME FRONT

When the war broke out, thousands of people of African and Caribbean heritage were living in Britain, many of them born in the country. Many joined, or attempted to join, the armed forces and other auxiliary services, like Lilian Bader and Amelia King, and some, like Vivian Florent, gave their lives serving the country. One of those who was called up was the Jamaican musician Leslie Thompson, who had migrated to Britain in 1929 and worked for many years as a jazz musician and bandleader. Some musicians and singers were able to continue working at their profession during the war, such as Adelaide Hall, who joined the Entertainment National Service Association (ENSA) and entertained troops in both Britain and Germany, while two well-known jazz musicians, the Guianese bandleader, Ken 'Snakehips' Johnson and his saxophonist, Dave 'Baba' Williams, lost their lives in an air raid during a performance at London's Café de Paris. Thompson joined the Royal Artillery and, as he later recalled, 'was the only coloured fellow in the brigade'. He trained as an anti-aircraft gunner and eventually became a sergeant, but still managed to spend much of his time playing the trumpet in army dance bands and eventually joined the War Office's Stars in Battledress and performed in Germany and Norway. In his memoirs he claims that as a sergeant the gun he was responsible for shot down 'the highest-flying German plane over Britain', some seven miles high.[113]

There were many others who volunteered as air-raid wardens, or in the Auxiliary Fire Service and in stretcher parties, or who worked as nurses and in many other roles. Fernando Henriques, who had lived in London since the age of three, attempted to join the RAF when war broke out but was told 'that "wogs", that is people of non-European descent, were not considered officer material'. He then joined the National Fire Service, responded to air raids for three years and later recalled that there was 'only one incident that made me conscious of my colour. That was being told by an irascible officer that my quarters were too good for a "n——"'.[114] In Manchester, former boxer Len Johnson's war service was in civil defence, where he was a rescue foreman, responsible for rescuing those trapped in houses after bombing raids. He later became a civil defence instructor in Cumbria, specializing in 'First Aid and Physical Training'.[115]

There were of course, many other contributions, such as that of Bill Miller (1890–1970), a veteran of the Royal Flying Corps in the First World War, who, as an air-raid warden in Plymouth, was arrested and found guilty of commandeering vehicles, without authority, to evacuate women and children to safety.[116] Several children of African and Caribbean heritage were evacuated from port areas likely to be subject to bombing raids such as in Liverpool, Cardiff and London.[117] Although their stories are not well known, two of these children, Stephanie and Connie Antia, featured in a wartime film called *Springtime in An English Village* (1944). They were the twin daughters of an African seaman and had both been evacuated from London to Stanion, a small village in Northamptonshire, in 1942. The film shows Stephanie being crowned 'a Dusky Queen of the May'.[118]

THE COLOUR BAR, PROPAGANDA
AND THE UNITED STATES

Throughout the war, the Colonial Office had taken the lead in encouraging government to take some measures to address both the colour bar and the increased numbers of people of African and Caribbean heritage living in Britain. First, it had been necessary for the government to relax the colour bar in the armed and auxiliary forces, largely to maintain the loyalty of the colonies. This had become more apparent after the fall of Singapore and after other military defeats in Asia in 1942. In September 1942, the Colonial Office established its Advisory Committee on the Welfare of Coloured People in the UK, which included Harold Moody as one of its members. This body, established to deal with the influx of African and Caribbean workers and service personnel, emphasized 'welfare' rather than dealing head on with the colour bar. One of its first measures was to open a new Colonial Centre in London where, because of the colour bar, accommodation was difficult to find. The Colonial Office also supported the creation of a hostel for 'coloured seamen' in North Shields, referred to as Colonial House. Established by the International Coloured Mutual Aid Society led by a Nigerian, Charles Minto, the hostel was opened in North Shields in May 1942.[119]

In addition to the wartime appointment of Learie Constantine at the Ministry of Labour, the Colonial Office's Public Relations Department also made much of the official appointments of other people of African and Caribbean heritage during the war, such as Ivor Cummings at the Colonial Office and Una Marson at the BBC, which was then under the direction of the Ministry of Information.[120] Marson, who also volunteered as an air-raid shelter warden, began broadcasting for the BBC in 1939 and made several radio programmes on colonial contributions to the war, as well as programmes featuring Caribbean music and poetry. From 1941, she was only officially employed as a 'programme assistant' for the Empire Service, but was very much a pioneer at the BBC. She produced and compèred the *Calling the West Indies* programme, as well as appearing in a short propaganda film with that title in 1943.[121]

It was not just those from the Caribbean who were encouraged to send messages 'home' to the colonies during the war. Several members of the WASU were asked by the BBC to make broadcasts, including Princess Adenrele Ademola, the daughter of the King of Abeokuta in Nigeria, who did so in 1942. The princess and her elder sister both studied nursing in Britain and were just two of the many African and Caribbean nurses who made important contributions during the war. Some, like Abioseh Pratt from Sierra Leone, were even required to provide medical care for German POWs.[122] For the government such contributions were a good example of colonial involvement in the war effort. Therefore in 1943 Adenrele Ademola became the subject of a film, *Nurse Ademola*, produced by the Ministry of Information's Colonial Film Unit (CFU), the first African nurse to gain such recognition. *Flying Officer Peter Thomas* was also made in 1943 and *Learie Constantine* in 1944. In 1941 the CFU produced *An African in London*, a propaganda film for African audiences designed to show that all were welcome and there was no colour bar. However, because it featured

Nurse Ademola

the Guyanese actor Robert Adams, the WASU objected to the casting. When another propaganda film, *An African in England*, was made in 1945, it featured members of the WASU. The music for the CFU's films was generally provided by its musical director, Fela Sowande, a Nigerian organist and composer who was a member of the WASU.[123]

The government's position on the colour bar was highlighted further after the entry into the war of the United States and the arrival of one million service personnel of the segregated US Army in Britain, including more than 130,000 African American troops.[124] The government decided to appease racism in the US Army whilst claiming that it was opposed to the colour bar in Britain and throughout the empire.[125] Its approach led to de facto segregation in some towns and cities where US troops were stationed, and to an upsurge of racism in Britain, including attacks on 'Black British' servicemen. The American Red Cross even operated a segregated centre for African American troops in Duchess Street in London.[126] Much has been written of the estimated one thousand, or more, babies born to British women and African American fathers during the war, which eventually became a major social problem for the government, since the children were born 'out of wedlock' and at a time when both US and British state racism was hostile to such mixed relationships and the children they produced.[127] Similarly, there are many accounts of racists attacks, either by American soldiers on African and Caribbean men in Britain, or on African American soldiers. There were also numerous occasions when discrimination led to major incidents, one of the most infamous being the so-called 'Battle of Bamber Bridge'. In 1943, at Bamber Bridge, near Preston, in 1943, one soldier was killed and several wounded when military police provoked retaliation from African American troops.[128]

In most areas African American soldiers seem to have been welcomed. In fact, it is reported that in Bamber Bridge public houses displayed 'Black troops only' signs to show their support for the soldiers and opposition to segregation.[129] In areas such as Liverpool, where there were already established Black communities, they were also welcomed not least for their relative affluence and were often invited to the homes of Black residents. However, there were also many instances of US Army servicemen attempting to import US racism into Britain, demanding that facilities be segregated and even attacking Black civilians and servicemen. Caribbean technicians in the north-west of England made several official complaints that after the US Army arrived, colour bars were introduced in bars and dance halls. In one incident in Warrington, in 1943, 'American soldiers demanded the ejection of one of the Jamaican technicians who was dancing with a white girl'. The manager of the dance hall rejected such a demand and told the Jamaican that 'as long as he paid his admission money the doors would be open to him and he would be welcome'. The US army subsequently wrote to the manager, 'it is not our intention to dictate the policies of privately owned establishments, but in the interests of eliminating trouble in which our troops may be involved we would appreciate your cooperation in prohibiting Negroes from attending the dances'.[130]

In another incident, in 1943, George Roberts, 'a trainee from the Leeward Islands' who had joined the local Home Guard was denied admission to Grafton Dance Hall in Liverpool by the police. He then donned his Home Guard uniform, but was refused entry a second time because American soldiers were attending the dance. Roberts reported the incident to the Mayor of Liverpool, saying that his uniform had been insulted and he was therefore refusing to undertake his Home Guard duties. He was subsequently prosecuted and fined £5 by the Liverpool Police Court. He appealed and the fine was reduced to a farthing, after the Recorder made a lengthy address against the colour bar and the prejudices of a 'noisy and intolerant minority'.[131]

There can be no doubt that the war, which increasingly assumed an anti-fascist character, also exposed racism and the colour bar in Britain. As we have seen, the government was generally reluctant to welcome Africans and Caribbeans to Britain as part of the war effort. It also tried, unsuccessfully, to prevent large numbers of African Americans coming to Britain. In the US the National Association for the Advancement of Colored People accused the British government of asking the US government not to station any African American troops in Britain. The government's opposition to African American troops was based on the premise that their presence would exacerbate racism and lead to dangerous and unwelcome liaisons with British women. The opposition to the large-scale recruitment of troops from the colonies was based on similar fears, as well as the view that it upset well-established colonial and racial hierarchies. In addition, there was a strongly held view that Black troops were inferior. The Secretary of State for War commented in 1942, 'while there are many coloured men of high mentality and cultural distinction, the generality are of a simple mental outlook ... In short they have not the white man's ability to think and act to a plan.' The following year he concluded: 'On purely military grounds I am afraid the drawbacks of so employing them, whether as combatant (e.g., anti-aircraft) troops or as labour units outweigh any advantages.'[132] No doubt such views and those presented in educational institutions and in the media had some influence on wider society. Many people still held strange and, by modern standards, racist views about 'Negroes'. Yet all the evidence suggests that the vast majority of people in Britain were opposed to any colour bar.[133] At the same time, one of the views most commonly expressed was a strong opposition to 'mixed' marriages and relationships, as if to suggest that they represented some form of sexual deviancy. Such views clearly existed at government level and even led to some discussion concerning the possibility of laws prohibiting 'miscegenation'.

The numbers of babies born to African American fathers during these years shows us that many had rather different views about such relationships. It was also the case that in some instances such relationships were celebrated as part of an 'international stream', or trend directed against fascism. In 1943, for example, *Picture Post* contained a photo-essay 'Inside London's Coloured Clubs', which certainly celebrated 'mixed' couples dancing at Frisco's and Bouillabaise. At these two fashionable jazz clubs, according to *Picture Post*, 'you see the light-skinned American and the black Nigerian. You hear the accent of Chicago mixing with cockney and Cardiff. Soldiers, Red Cross workers, students, factory workers, actors and swing fans. All come to the basement under White London.'[134]

CHARTER OF RIGHTS

The protests concerning colonial rule and the colour bar launched by the LCP, the WASU and others continued throughout the war. In 1943 both organizations unsuccessfully proposed that the government should establish an Anglo-colonial committee to address the colour bar. The WASU also vigorously criticized several propaganda films made by the government during the war, most notably *Men of Two Worlds*, for what it deemed their 'deeply-rooted erroneous views' and 'colour prejudice'.[135] During the war the WASU and its members acted as a contact point for African prisoners-of-war, such as Johnny Smythe, and Africa House was used to accommodate munitions workers. The WASU was also in contact with many other African organizations in Britain, in Edinburgh, Birmingham, North Shields and Liverpool, as well as with leading political figures in West Africa. One British-based publication even began referring to the WASU as 'the nearest approach there is to a British West Africa High Commission in London'.[136]

The WASU took advantage of the war to strengthen its position as the spokesperson of 'the views, the feelings and the prayers of not only the members of the WASU but also of our people in West Africa'.[137] It was used by many groups and individuals in West Africa to petition Parliament and in 1942 established its own parliamentary committee of Labour MPs for this purpose.[138] As early as 1940 the WASU demanded 'Dominion status' for West Africa, arguing that it should have the self-governing status that had recently been promised to India, and enjoy the same liberties that existed in Britain, including the right to establish trade unions. However, such hopes were dashed when Prime Minister Churchill explained that references to the right of self-determination in the Atlantic Charter, agreed between Britain and the United States in 1941 as a limited statement of war aims, only applied to Europe and not to the colonies.[139]

In 1943 the WASU became alarmed at the rumoured prospect of conscription for 'colonial peoples temporarily resident' in Britain. It immediately issued a public protest, arguing,

> that a people's government is a necessary prerequisite for popular conscription ... and while all West Africans fully support the prosecution of the war ... we seriously consider it in the interests of justice, democracy and freedom, for which it is proclaimed the war is being fought, that the Imperial Government grant the West African Dependencies internal responsible self-government now, as well as making the Atlantic Charter fully applicable to them, before introducing the burden of military conscription.[140]

By 1943 such demands were almost becoming commonplace. Pad-more's and Nancy Cunard's pamphlet, *The White Man's Duty: An Analysis of the Colonial Question in the Light of the Atlantic Char-ter*, which was published early that year, raised very similar demands regarding the need for freedom: 'if the people of India and the Colo-nies are to be asked to throw their weight into this conflict they must be given that incentive', they argued, and demanded a 'Charter for the Colonies' as well as legislation against the colour bar.[141] In July the following year the LCP held a conference at which the future Labour Colonial Secretary, Creech Jones, delivered a keynote speech entitled 'The Need for a Charter'. The LCP conference subsequently drew up a 'Charter for Coloured Peoples' calling for economic and political reforms leading to self-government for Britain's colonies, as well as an end to all forms of discrimination.[142] These demands were rejected by the government.[143]

The beginning of the end of the war can be dated to the victory of the Soviet Union's Red Army at the Battle of Stalingrad in February of 1943. Peter Blackman was assembling Wellington bombers during the war and that victory moved him to compose his powerful poem 'Sta-lingrad', which concludes with the words:

> Then Red Star spread your flame upon me
> For in your flame is earnest of my freedom
> Now may I rendezvous with the world
> Now may I join man's wide-flung diversity
> For Stalingrad is still a Soviet town.[144]

The global defeat of fascism, in which the Soviet Union played a key role, inspired optimism about the future, but also highlighted important developments within that country. George Padmore argued that the British Empire could never emulate what the Soviet Union had achieved because the people of the colonies had no right to self-determination and because imperialism exploited rather than developed colonial territories.[145] It was an argument he was to develop much further in the book he and Dorothy Pizer wrote at the end of the war, *How Russia Transformed Her Colonial Empire*.[146]

It was in 1944, as the war drew to a close, that Pan-African organ-izations based in Britain and Ireland, acting on the initiative of the

IASB, united in Manchester to form the Pan-African Federation (PAF).[147] The PAF declared that it was 'a federation of organizations of African Peoples and Peoples of African descent throughout the world', but the main organizations represented included the Negro Welfare Centre (Manchester); the Negro Association (Manchester); the Coloured Workers' Association (London); the Coloured People's Association (Edinburgh); the United Committee of Coloured and Colonial People's Associations (Cardiff); the African Union (Glasgow); the Association of Students of African Descent (Dublin); and the African Progressive Association (London). In addition, the PAF also included representatives of three African organizations: Jomo Kenyatta of the Kikuyu Central Association (Kenya); Isaac Wallace-Johnson of the West African Youth League (Sierra Leone) and Bankole Awooner-Renner (1907–1970) of the Friends of African Freedom Society (Gold Coast).[148]

This was the first occasion when so many of the key organizations in Britain had formally united. The PAF listed as its aims:

> To promote the well-being and unity of African peoples and people of African descent around the world; to demand self-determination and independence of African peoples and other subject races from the domination of powers claiming sovereignty and domination over them; to secure equality of civil rights for African people and the total abolition of all forms of racial discrimination; to strive to cooperate between African peoples and others who share our aspirations.[149]

Although the WASU and the LCP were not formally part of the PAF, they often allied with it on matters of general concern. During the latter stages of the war all these organizations were determined to formulate policies for the post-war world, which could place Africa and the diaspora at the centre of world affairs, bring about self-government for the colonies and a new world free from racism and the colour bar. As Padmore later explained:

> You would be surprised how easy it was to bring into existence the Pan-African Federation, which is a federated body comprising more than 14 constituent organizations composed of workers, students, intellectuals, Africans, West Indians, and other peoples of African descent. When it

comes to the struggle against imperialism, British or otherwise, these people feel as one. They do have their little petty squabbles, but they are never of a fundamental character.[150]

The new PAF was located in Manchester, at one of Makonnen's bookshops at 58 Oxford Road. Its president was Dr Peter Milliard (1882–1953), a local GP who was also the president of the Negro Association, while Makonnen acted as general secretary. The Manchester area's Black communities had developed significantly in the period after 1918, first in Salford and then in Moss Side. Initially these communities were largely formed of seafarers (and their families), as well as those who managed to find work in the area's factories, but they also included professional men such as lawyer Edward Nelson, who had a practice established in the area since 1910, and Millard, who opened his surgery in 1930. In that same year a deputation of mainly Nigerian men complained to the city's lord mayor about racism in the local press and that they were denied 'equality of opportunity in employment'. Other features of the colour bar were also present in Manchester, although the city was considered by many to be 'not as prejudiced' as other parts of the country.[151] During the Second World War, the Black population in the north-west increased but the colour bar was maintained, especially after the arrival of the US Army. The premises opened by Makonnen and others, restaurants and nightclubs such as the Ethiopian Teashop in Oxford Road, were therefore well frequented, as were local shebeens.

In such circumstances welfare organizations of various types were vital. The Negro Association was first formed in the 1930s as a welfare organization for seamen and their families. It was revived by Milliard in 1942 with a membership of about thirty, mainly Caribbean men. The Negro Welfare Centre appears to have had a mostly African membership and was established by Jimmy Taylor, from the Gold Coast, with financial assistance from Makonnen. According to Taylor, a Cambridge graduate, a former WASU member and owner of multiple nightclubs, its aim was to 'foster unity amongst the various Tribes of the Race; promote understanding between the Negro and other Races', and assist with the education of children. Taylor was aided by Eddie Du Plan, also from the Gold Coast, and by a Nigerian,

E. A. Cowan, and the centre opened premises in Liverpool, Manchester and, for a time, other cities as well.[152] Although the centre in Manchester did engage in some 'welfare', it also provided facilities for dancing and drinking and was regarded with some scorn by Makonnen. He claimed that 'the intention was not welfare but simply to bleed the fellows', and referred to 'the Negro club with its bunch of women packing the place from morning to night, catering to the Black Americans and later the Bevin Boys during the war'.[153] Nevertheless, Manchester had well-established communities and facilities that made it an ideal location for the Pan-African Congress in 1945.

The other organizations within the PAF reflected the presence of African and Caribbean students and intellectuals, as well as workers, in towns and cities throughout Britain and Ireland. Dublin and Edinburgh, for example, had long been important centres for the training of physicians. Some of the organizations were undoubtedly short-lived. Ernest Marke declared that the Coloured Workers Association was formed by him because 'an interest in furthering the welfare of my fellow Black men had always been with me, ever since the race riot of 1919'. The association, which included amongst its members James Nortey, a former boxer from the Gold Coast, met in one of the rooms of Marke's Soho nightclub. Commenting on its limited lifespan Marke explained years later: 'Possibly the climate wasn't yet ready for the organized societies we see today, and in any event, there were too many people with contradictory aims within it. But I like to think, perhaps a little fancifully, that within that organization a small breeze of independence sprang up, which years later became the "wind of change".'[154]

THE MANCHESTER PAN-AFRICAN CONGRESS

During 1944 the WASU and the LCP were both in contact with W. E. B. Du Bois in the United States and began to discuss convening a post-war Pan-African congress. However, it was the PAF which took the initiative, recognizing that it would be possible to confer with colonial trade-union representatives following the World Trade Union Conference held in London in February 1945. This conference emerged from the wartime alliance of Britain, the United States and the Soviet Union and was the first occasion when all the major trade-union centres would meet together. It also reflected the important role that workers and 'common people' had played in the defeat of fascism and the aspiration that they would play a major part in shaping in the post-war world. As the Transport and General Workers Union put it, 'Common people everywhere must unite in a great world drive to end this evil, outworn system of capitalism and lay the foundations of an economic order which will make ruinous crises and disastrous wars impossible.'[155]

For the PAF what was even more significant was that the emerging trade union movements in the colonies would also be represented for the first time, since they were transported to London under the auspices of the government. All four of Britain's West African colonies sent representatives, including Wallace-Johnson, who had been imprisoned throughout the war for his political activities. British Guiana and Jamaica also sent delegates, including Ken Hill, who had been a political prisoner in Jamaica during the war.[156]

Wallace-Johnson made a significant impact at the London conference, which effectively founded the new World Federation of Trade Unions in February 1945. On behalf of all the colonial delegates he proposed a 'Charter of Labour for the Colonies' which had as its first demand 'the abolition of the Colour Bar and all racial discrimination'.[157] The colonial trade unions sought the support of the international labour movement for the anti-colonial struggle and an end to colonial rule. Their speeches were widely reported in the British press.[158] The London conference declared 'that it is necessary to bring to an end the system of Colonies, Dependencies and subject countries as spheres of economic exploitation'.[159] The trade unions present also expected labour representation at the founding of the United Nations (UN), including in its Security Council.[160] The global defeat of fascism ushered in a post-war world of great expectations. The working people of all countries, including those in the colonies, who had made such great sacrifices, were determined that a new world order would be established, in which their rights would be upheld and their voices heard.

It was in these circumstances, in February 1945, that the PAF invited the African and Caribbean trade union delegates to a meeting in Manchester. At this meeting, Padmore suggested that after a second

World Trade Union Conference a Pan-African gathering should be held in Paris in September 1945. A provisional organizing committee was formed including Padmore, Kenyatta, Makonnen, James Taylor, Milliard and Wallace-Johnson, which had the task of producing a manifesto that would be both a 'call to action' and could be sent to the new United Nations. What became known as 'The Manifesto on Africans in the Post-War World' was originally drafted by Desmond Buckle and called for an end to 'the present system of exploitation' in Africa and for a new world economic order. It also demanded that the UN continue the struggle against racism and for the Allies to 'remove from their own territories those theories and practices for the destruction of which Africans have died on many battlefields'. It argued that 'International co-operation demands the abolition of every kind of discrimination: on account of colour, race and creed wherever such discrimination exists.'[161]

The PAF's organizational meeting in Manchester was followed by a public meeting attended by about 300 people, the 'largest Negro mass meeting in Manchester's history', according to one press report. It included African and Caribbean munitions workers as well as African American troops, and was addressed by some of the trade-union delegates, as well as by Constantine, Makonnen, Kenyatta, Milliard and Padmore. It was following press reports of this meeting that Du Bois first became aware of the PAF's plans for a Pan-African meeting in Paris. Padmore managed to placate him and explained that 'everything is tentative', that what was being planned might constitute a precursor to a later, 'much more effective gathering'. At the time both Du Bois and the WASU considered that the next Pan-African congress should be held in Africa. Padmore made it clear to Du Bois that the PAF's planned event 'was primarily concerned with the workers and peasants who must be the driving force behind any movement which we middle-class intellectuals may establish'. Padmore explained further that 'Today, the African masses, the common people are awake and not blindly looking to doctors and lawyers to tell them what to do'.[162]

The PAF was not only concerned with a new Pan-African congress. In June 1945 it convened the Subject Peoples' Conference at Holborn Town Hall in London in collaboration with the WASU, the Federation of Indian Associations in Britain, the Ceylon Students' Association and the Burma Association.[163] This conference, attended by both British and colonial trade unionists, issued its own manifesto, 'The Colonies and Peace', which declared that for those in the colonies Allied victory would have no real meaning 'if it does not lead to their own liberation from the tentacles of imperialism'. It pointed out that a lasting peace required the liquidation of imperialism, the root cause of wars, and stressed that since the colonial peoples had given their lives for the Allied victory, they could not be left out of the deliberations for peace. In particular it demanded that the UN took measures for 'the unconditional ending of all colonial systems within a definite and stipulated period'. Those in Britain seeking an end to colonialism had been encouraged by the stand taken by the Soviet Union at the founding meetings of the UN, when it had made a similar call for the end of colonial rule. Although the UN did not fully endorse such proposals, largely because of efforts by the British government to strengthen its colonial grip, it was clear that the post-war world increasingly viewed colonialism unfavourably.[164] The conference organizers clearly envisaged that those oppressed by colonialism should work together to free themselves and thus stressed the need not just for Pan-African but also Afro-Asian unity.[165]

Such unity was displayed in support of the general strike in Nigeria in July 1945, at the meeting organized by the PAF and the WASU in Conway Hall in London, 'one of the largest rallies of coloured peoples ever witnessed in the British capital'. The London meeting was followed by similar events organized by the PAF in Manchester and Liverpool, as well as a Strike Relief Fund organized jointly with the WASU.[166] All these events demonstrated the effectiveness of the PAF, which could speak for and coordinate the activities of African, Caribbean and Asian organizations in Britain. It was with this heightened sense of its own strengths that the PAF continued with its plans for what was now termed a Pan-African congress, with some agreement from the WASU and the LCP. By the late summer the venue had been switched from Paris to Britain, which was considered to have more conducive conditions to the organizers' aims, especially after the election of the new Labour government in July 1945, and that it would be held in October of the same year. All delegates were instructed to show credentials from 'workers' organizations, the co-operative societies,

peasant associations, labour parties and national liberation organiza-
tions' in the colonies and not 'the middle strata and professionals'.
Invitations were also sent to some British organizations such as the
Independent Labour Party.

The election victory of Attlee's Labour Party had temporarily
increased optimism amongst those of African and Caribbean heritage
in Britain. In September 1945 the PAF sent an 'open letter' to the
Prime Minister welcoming the new government, which, it considered,
'makes possible the inauguration of the century of the common man'.
The PAF demanded that the Labour government take a new path and
argued that 'To condemn the imperialism of Germany, Japan and
Italy, while condoning that of Britain would be more than dishonest,
it would be a betrayal of the sacrifice and sufferings and the toil and
sweat of the common people of this country. All imperialism is evil.'
Furthermore the open letter asked for several immediate reforms as
'an expression of Socialist goodwill', including the demand 'that discrimination because of race, colour or creed in Britain be made a
punishable offence'. The Labour government failed to respond and
the PAF continued with its congress preparations.[167]

The PAF also found time to organize a second Subject Peoples' Congress in October 1945 in London, where the main focus was on the
struggle for anti-colonial liberation in French Indo-China, India, Malaya
and other parts of Asia. Several of the delegates from the inaugural congress of the World Federation of Trade, recently held in Paris, also
participated and Afro-Asian unity was stressed throughout. Wallace-
Johnson emphasized that 'the unity among the coloured races, the vast
majority of whom are workers and peasants, may yet lay the foundation
for the wider unity among all workers and exploited and oppressed'.
Here, in essence, was the politics of what was soon to become the Manchester Pan-African Congress. Wallace-Johnson joined with others in
condemning the new Labour government's approach to colonialism. At
the last moment it was decided that the Pan-African Congress would
convene from 13 to 21 October in Manchester, the home of the PAF,
because there were better facilities for accommodation and catering.
Makonnen was also able to secure Chorlton Town Hall as the venue
through his contacts with the local Labour Party.[168]

The Manchester Pan-African Congress held in October 1945 has been described as the zenith of the Pan-African movement and perhaps the most important of all the Pan-African meetings held outside the African continent. It was also one of the most important political meetings ever organized by African and Caribbean people in Britain.[169] Kwame Nkrumah, newly arrived from the United States and registered as a student at the London School of Economics, became one of the main organizers, and he later referred to it as a 'tremendous success', where 'both capitalist and reformist solutions to the African problems were rejected'. Nkrumah argued that in contrast to previous congresses 'the delegates who attended were practical men of action'.[170]

The congress was attended by key figures, the majority originating on the African continent, such as Obafemi Awolowo, Jaja Wachuku, Hastings Banda, Jomo Kenyatta and Nkrumah himself, who would play a key role in subsequent anti-colonial struggles in Africa, as well as leading Pan-Africanists such as Amy Ashwood Garvey, Padmore, Makonnen, Robert Broadhurst and trade unionists such as Wallace-Johnson, Ken Hill and the Trinidadian Rupert Gittens. Du Bois arrived from the Unites States and was accorded the honour of presiding, but apart from his presence and that of the visiting trade unionists, most of the participants were based in Britain, although they might be delegates of organizations in Africa and the Caribbean. Gilbert Cargill and H. Lawson, for example, were two of the Honduran foresters brought to Britain during the war. At the congress they both represented the British Honduras Workers' League. Another Manchester-based delegate was Joseph Linton, who had worked in munitions during the war. Although a Jamaican, he represented the St Kitts-Nevis Trades and Labour Union. Alma LaBadie, a Jamaican who had come to Britain as a volunteer for the Women's Auxiliary Air Force, represented the Universal Negro Improvement Association.[171] The organizers reported that there were nearly 200 delegates 'representing 60 nations and groups of African descent'.[172]

The Manchester Pan-African Congress was arranged by the PAF and other British-based Pan-African organizations, and also by the local community in Manchester, who assisted with accommodation, catering, entertainment and administrative duties. Several notable Mancunians attended, included Len Johnson, a representative of the local branch of the Communist Party. The congress was in many ways the embodiment of the radical Pan-Africanism of the 1930s that had then been further developed in Britain by organizations such as the IASB. This Pan-Africanism stressed the important political role of the masses of the people and drew on the experience of the Caribbean labour rebellions and strikes, as well as strikes and boycotts in West Africa and elsewhere. It considered that it was the struggles of the working masses that would play a key role in bringing colonialism to an end and that these struggles were a part of the global struggle of all working people for empowerment.

The congress was opened by Amy Ashwood Garvey, who announced: 'We are here to tell the world ... that we are determined to emancipate ourselves.'[173] The opening session was devoted to the colour problem in Britain, and the congress held separate sessions on: imperialism in North and West Africa; oppression in South Africa; the East African picture; Ethiopia and the black republics; and the problem in the Caribbean. In addition, Amy Ashwood Garvey reminded the predominantly male delegates that 'for some reason very little has been said about the black woman', who 'has been shunted into the social background to be a child bearer'.[174] The overall political orientation of the congress was summed up in two resolutions. The first, 'the Challenge to the Colonial Powers', condemned imperialism, demanded independence and for the first time argued that it might be necessary 'to appeal to force to achieve freedom'. The second, a 'Declaration to the Colonial Workers, Farmers and Intellectuals', affirmed the right to be free from foreign domination, determined that attaining political power was 'the first step towards, and the necessary prerequisite to, complete social, economic and political emancipation'. It declared that 'colonial workers must be in the front of the battle against imperialism', and added 'Your weapons – the Strike and the Boycott – are invincible.' It concluded, 'Today there is only one road to effective action – the organization of the masses. And in that organization the educated colonials must join.'[175]

Another important document was a 'memorandum to the UN', drafted by Du Bois, which demanded the 'participation of designated representatives of the African colonial peoples' within the deliberations of the UN. It was supported by nearly forty organizations in the United States, the Caribbean, Africa and Europe, including the PAF, the LCP, the IASB, the National Council of Nigeria and the

Cameroons, the Non-European Unity Committee of South Africa, the Caribbean Labour Congress and the Kenya African Union.[176] The congress concluded with a public meeting in Chorlton Town Hall.

At the time, the congress received limited press coverage and was most memorably documented by Hilde Marchant and John Deakin in their article, 'Africa Speaks in Manchester' in *Picture Post*. Deakin's photos capture some of the main personalities at the event, such as Kenyatta, Du Bois and Amy Ashwood Garvey, as well as John McNair of the Independent Labour Party. Perhaps even more importantly, the article also captured the slogans that adorned the walls of Chorlton Town Hall, such as 'Down with Anti-Semitism', 'Oppressed Peoples of the Earth Unite', and 'Labour with a WHITE skin cannot Emancipate Itself while Labour with a BLACK skin is Branded'.[177] The Colonial Office also appears to have been largely unconcerned about the congress, although the event was monitored by the security

The Manchester Pan-African Congress

services, and they were relieved that it was not influenced by the Communist Party. One official wrote, 'the proceedings of the Congress were of little interest'.[178] Nevertheless, the proceedings and declarations of the congress remained of interest throughout the world. In Manchester, too, the congress made a profound impact. In old age Mancunian activist Kath Locke recalled meeting the participants as a young woman, 'you met all these important people . . . it took you out of the Uncle Tom's Cabin mentality into the strength and you realised we were not a minority, we were a majority'.[179]

THE WEST AFRICAN
NATIONAL SECRETARIAT

One of the immediate consequences of the Manchester Pan-African Congress was the founding soon after, by Nkrumah and the other West African delegates, of the West African National Secretariat (WANS) at a meeting held in London in December 1945. According to Nkrumah's account the WANS was established, 'in order to put into action the new Pan-African nationalism, with particular reference to West Africa and with the object of calling a West African National Congress and of directing the programme of self-government for the West African colonies, British as well as French.'[180] What was new for the WANS was that this would include all of West Africa, not just the British colonies, and have a socialist orientation.[181] Wallace-Johnson became the first chairman, Nkrumah its first secretary-general, and in 1946 they made a 'missionary tour' of Liverpool, Manchester and other parts of northern England to inform people of the WANS' aims.[182] Other members included Nii Odoi Annan, a student at Edinburgh University, Kojo Botsio, a student at Oxford University, Bankole Akpata, a WASU member, Bankole Awooner-Renner, a journalist and law student and Mrs Olabisi Awooner-Renner, who appears to have been the only woman.

In March 1946 the WANS established a monthly newspaper, the New African, with Nkrumah as editor.[183] He later wrote that through its pages he preached 'African unity and nationalism and attacked imperialism and the unjust laws in the colonies'.[184] However, only five editions of New African were published, the last in July 1946.[185] Although the

WANS was imbued with the spirt of Manchester, it was also influenced by the politics of the Communist Party of Great Britain (CPGB). According to Nii Odoi Annan, he, Nkrumah, Awooner-Renner, Akpata, Botsio and others were connected with the Communist Party and had also formed the 'Circle', a small, secret, organizing 'vanguard group' within the WASU and the WANS.[186] According to Nkrumah, who was the group's chairman, they 'began to train themselves in order to be able to commence revolutionary work in any part of the African continent'.[187] The Circle's ultimate aim was a 'Union of African Socialist Republics', and in 1946 the WANS published the collected thoughts of Awooner-Renner in a pamphlet entitled *West African Soviet Union*.[188]

The WANS immediately began to campaign for its aims, sending correspondence condemning colonialism to the newly formed UN and gaining support in West Africa and the United States, as well as in Britain and France. It often acted jointly with the WASU, as well as the LCP and PAF, and announced to the world that it stood for the 'complete liquidation of the colonial system', and looked forward to the independence and industrialization of West Africa as one united country.[189] Nkrumah's return to the Gold Coast in 1947, as well as the departure of other members, somewhat impeded further WANS activity. It continued its activities in Britain for some years, although they were rather curtailed. Cooperating with other organizations such as the WASU, the LCP and PAF, they demanded that the Labour government 'terminate immediately their imperialist domination' of the colonies and grant independence.[190]

THE PAN-AFRICAN FEDERATION AND PAN-AFRICA

The work of the Pan African Federation (PAF) following the Manchester Congress initially focused on promoting the resolutions of the congress as widely as possible, especially in the colonial press. A lengthy telegram was sent to the British government's Colonial Office outlining some of the demands made in Manchester. The PAF also established the Manchester-based PANAF Service Ltd., one of the first such publishing houses, with Makonnen, Padmore, Kenyatta and Milliard as directors and with capital from the numerous restaurants and clubs that Makonnen had established in Manchester.[191] PANAF published Padmore's edited accounts of the founding of the World Federation of Trade Unions and the Manchester Congress: *The Voice of Coloured Labour: Speeches and Reports of Colonial Delegates to the World Trade Union Conference, 1945* and *Colonial and Coloured Unity – a Programme of Action: History of the Pan-African Congress*, which included additional material written by Du Bois. The PAF also organized various public meetings and demonstrations. PAF activities often involved organizing local protest actions with the WANS and the LCP. In this period, much of the PAF's work was undertaken by Makonnen and Milliard in Manchester, as well as by Padmore, Peter Abrahams, and Dorothy Pizer, who provided unpaid secretarial services, in London.[192] International activities were organized with the WANS, the WASU and the LCP in relation to South Africa, with the Jamaican Trade Union Congress in support of striking workers in Jamaica, as well as in support of press freedom in West Africa.[193]

The PAF, and Makonnen in particular, was also involved in the case of the African seamen's strike on board the SS *Princesa*, an ageing refrigerated ship sailing to Britain from Argentina in 1946 with an all-Black crew (and Britain's meat ration). Conditions were so bad that the crew went on strike and the ship was eventually escorted into Bristol by the Royal Navy and the police. In total seven African seamen were arrested, six based in Liverpool and one in Manchester, and charged with various offences including 'continued disobedience to lawful commands' and assault.[194] The seamen claimed not only that conditions on board were bad, and that there was a shortage of fresh water, but that some of them had been beaten up, threatened with firearms and chained in the ship's hospital. The case, which was widely reported in the press, was significant because the arrested Africans received some support from the National Union of Seamen, and the charges against most of them were subsequently dropped. Three men, Joseph Kuya, the stepfather of well-known Liverpool activist Dorothy Kuya, Gilbert Cole and Olabode Odunsi did, however, receive short prison terms.[195] Makonnen later claimed that he organized the defence team for the men, although most of the details he provides appear to be at variance with the facts. He certainly did stand bail for the three men who appealed against their sentences.[196] The most interesting part of his account is the instruction to the men not to speak in English and only through interpreters, in order to aid their defence.[197]

Perhaps the most significant activity of the PAF was the publication, in January 1947, of *Pan-Africa: A Monthly Journal of African Life, History and Thought*. This was largely the work of Makonnen, aided initially by Peter Abrahams and subsequently by Dinah Stock. The latter was an English friend of Kenyatta, who had assisted him with the writing of *Facing Mount Kenya*. Although no women were listed as associate editors, they certainly wrote for the journal and the second edition includes an article on 'Colour persecution on Tyneside' credited to Mary Winters. Makonnen remained publisher and managing editor and established a mail-order Pan-African bookshop (as well as an actual bookshop, named the Economist, which was situated near Manchester University). The aim of *Pan-Africa* was 'to become a storehouse of information on African affairs and a field for the widest discussion of African views'.[198]

Indeed, *Pan-Africa* provides a useful indication of PAF activities and concerns at the time. One special edition in the autumn of 1947, entitled *Nigerian Prospect*, which was available in Britain and the United States, was devoted to information concerning the visit to Britain of a delegation of the National Council of Nigeria and the Cameroons (NCNC), headed by Nnamdi Azikiwe, to protest against attempts to impose an undemocratic constitution on Nigeria. The delegation received considerable support in Britain from the WANS, the WASU and others. Padmore and the PAF worked closely with it, publicized its aims and activities and supported a national speaking tour 'to appeal to the common people of Britain', when the Colonial Secretary rejected demands for a new constitution and 'immediate steps to self-government'. *Pan-Africa* provided an analysis of the tour and the NCNC's demands, a lengthy interview with the delegation and other relevant material.[199] *Pan-Africa* also included important articles relating to the PAF's activity in opposition to racism in Britain, especially that perpetrated by the police, 'local authorities and officials' against Somalis and other seamen.[200] Makonnen clearly aimed to make *Pan-Africa* and other associated publications widely available. However, it became unsustainable, not least because it had been banned in many colonies, and it ceased publication in early 1948 just as the PAF ended its activities.[201]

Thousands of people who came from the African and Caribbean colonies, as well as those based in Britain, contributed to the war effort. Many volunteered for active service and had to overcome official racism in order to participate in the struggle against fascism. Service during the war gave rise to great expectations, not only concerning the independence of the colonies, but also the removal of the colour bar and the status of African and Caribbean people in Britain. Throughout the Second World War people stood together against a common foe abroad, but this took place in Britain too. In 1941, for example, workers at the Swift Scale factory in London's Park Royal had staged an unofficial strike when their Jamaican trade-union leader was unjustly sacked.[202] African and Caribbean people had established influential organizations, had raised their demands for a new world order and were determined to take their rightful place in the post-war world.

9

The Post-war World

After the Second World War, many more African and Caribbean people came to live in Britain. Some service personnel and war workers remained in the country after 1945 and established small communities in towns such as Bolton. By 1948 they had already been joined by hundreds of students, from both the Caribbean and Africa, who arrived in Britain for training because of the new Labour government's plans for economic development in the colonies. The number of students from the Caribbean increased from fewer than two hundred in 1939 to almost a thousand by 1947 and nearly seven thousand by 1960.[1] The West African Students Union (WASU) welcomed what it happily referred to as 'the invasion of the UK by West African students'.[2] By 1948 there were also over one thousand students from the West African colonies, mainly from Nigeria and the Gold Coast, and this figure more than tripled in the next few years, standing at nearly four thousand by 1954.[3] In addition, there were increasing numbers of students from East and Central Africa, almost a thousand by the early 1950s.[4] By 1960 there were at least 11,000 African students in Britain and probably many thousands more. This trend continued as the designation 'student' allowed some to evade the restrictions of the 1962 Commonwealth Immigration Act, the first post-war legislation aimed at limiting immigration from Africa and the Caribbean.[5]

The West Africans included many more women students, around 600 by 1950, many of them arriving to train as nurses and to boost the new National Health Service (NHS) launched in 1948. It has often been forgotten that African nurses and health workers, as well as Caribbean ones, were some of the pioneers enabling the creation of the NHS.[6] Female nurses were often encouraged by the authorities

The West African Students' Union at Africa House

not to marry, and initially not to settle in Britain but to return to their countries of origin after training, such was the concern regarding 'coloured' immigration.[7] It is no coincidence that the West African Women's Association (WAWA), the first of its kind in Britain, was formed in 1946. Its first president was Irene Cole, a medical student from Sierra Leone, and Ayo Adeniyi-Jones, a Nigerian, was its first secretary. Seven years later, led by Fola Ighodalo, the Nigerian Women's League (NWL) was established in London to educate women, many of them student nurses, for 'good citizenship and feminine leadership'.[8] After 1955 the Colonial Office encouraged male African students coming to Britain to be accompanied by their wives, a policy which not only increased the numbers of African women in the UK but also gave rise to the wide-scale practice of many West African parents placing their children with English working-class foster carers, often for years and, on occasions, on a permanent basis. By 1968 it was estimated that some 5,000 children were fostered in this manner, a trend that was to continue for several decades.[9]

The increased number of students from the Caribbean led to the founding of the West Indian Students' Union (WISU) in 1946 to 'promote fellowship between West Indian students in the UK', but it was also concerned with the 'cultural, political and economic development of the West Indies', including the provision of higher education. The WISU was initially based at the colonial students' hostel at Hans Crescent, Knightsbridge, before the West Indian Student Centre, with government support, was opened in Collingham Gardens, Earls Court, in 1955. The centre became a major venue for cultural and political activities and the WISU a significant organization which included Forbes Burnham, Errol Barrow, Michael Manley and Maurice Bishop amongst its notable leaders.[10] However, many students still found it difficult to find accommodation and to support themselves in Britain in the post-war period. The existing hostels, including those provided by the WASU, were insufficient to meet the new demands and the colour bar often made it difficult for students to rent accommodation or to find employment. In 1949 a leading WASU member commented on the many destitute students forced to 'catch a bit of sleep' in the WASU's hostels. He added, 'It is not in every country of the world that Negro students find it hard to get jobs or acquire technical skills in factories and technical schools as is the case in Britain.'[11]

In addition to the students, who were generally considered to be temporary residents, there were hundreds of African and Caribbean stowaways who arrived in Britain looking for a better life and an escape from the unemployment and poverty that existed in the colonies. They were men like nineteen-year-old David Oluwale, an apprentice tailor from Lagos, Nigeria, who arrived in Hull on board the SS *Temple Bar* with two other stowaways in September 1949, was sentenced to a month's imprisonment in Leeds and, for the next twenty years of his short life, remained close to that city, initially living there with other African migrants.[12] Solomon Quarcoopome was another stowaway, arriving in Liverpool in 1949 from Accra, Ghana, on board SS *Llanwern*. Like Oluwale, he initially found work in Sheffield's steelworks, but, in 1958, moved to Manchester, which, unlike Leeds, already had a relatively large and well-established African population mainly based in the Moss Side area.[13]

Although hostile press reports sometimes suggested hundreds of stowaways were arriving, Home Office figures suggest that the total numbers entering Britain between 1946 and 1953 were about 1,500 Africans, overwhelmingly from West Africa, and 1,000 from the Caribbean.[14] Thousands of official migrants from Africa also arrived in Britain seeking work during the post-war period. The influx of African workers and students led to the emergence of many new organizations such as the Nigerian Union, and the African League, founded by Enrico Stennett and others, to unite Africans and those from the Caribbean.[15] The Communist Party, too, found it necessary to establish West African and West Indian branches during the late 1940s and 1950s.[16] Indeed, the Communist Party was one of the few organizations to openly welcome African and Caribbean migrants in this period, referring to them as 'brothers in the fight for a better life'.[17] One temporary Caribbean recruit recalled that joining the Communist Party 'was easy because they were the only white people who showed any sympathy to our plight'.[18]

In addition, there were hundreds of official migrants from the Caribbean hoping for improved prospects, arriving on ships such as the SS *Ormonde*, which docked in Liverpool in 1947. The *Ormonde* brought some ninety 'authorized coloured passengers' from the Caribbean, who had each paid £28 for the voyage. The ship also carried eleven stowaways, including Clement Rowland, who had served with the RAF, as well as two former sailors, Henry Peart and Frederick West, who had survived the sinking of the USS *Norfolk* in 1944. Several of the other passengers and stowaways, it was reported in the press, had also served in Britain during the war.[19] It is evident that such migrants, including stowaways, were well aware of the acute post-war labour shortage in Britain, estimated at more than 1.3 million job vacancies, as well as the availability of 'public assistance', and compared both favourably with the unemployment and poverty that they faced in the colonies.[20] Several stowaways subsequently appeared at Bristol Crown court and told similar stories. Eugene Thompson, a 24-year-old from Jamaica, claimed 'I stowed away because I can't get anything to do. All my shoes and clothes were worn out and I wanted to get a better living.'[21] Vincent Brown, another Jamaican formerly in the RAF, commented:

We had to get work or starve. The economic conditions in Jamaica are deplorable and there is absolutely no work. I am married with five children and I have been unemployed for three years. My life savings are diminished and I have parted with all my personal belongings. I have been at home empty-handed, only to see my wife and children go to bed without food. That is why I stowed away – to come to England to find work. As British subjects we think we should be given preference for work in this country over Germans and Poles.[22]

Vincent Brown had highlighted something significant: those from Africa and the Caribbean were British subjects, even before the 1948 British Nationality Act, and had every right to enter and reside in Britain. Moreover, they were arriving at a time when the British government had initiated a European volunteer workers scheme, to encourage the migration of workers, many from the Baltic States, Poland and Germany (and including some former enemy POWs and combatants), to fill job vacancies. More than 180,000 European workers were recruited, not least because, as 'aliens', they could be directed to work in specific industries and locations and, it was envisaged, would be swiftly assimilated into the population.[23] Those workers who made their way from Africa and the Caribbean and who had historic ties with the 'mother country', could not be so directed, nor assimilated so easily, so they were not encouraged, even when they were former service personnel and skilled workers. The contrast was obvious for all to see, as was the paradox of unemployment in the colonies and a shortage of workers in Britain.[24]

There were numerous press reports of the financial burden imposed on public assistance by stowaways (mostly from West Africa) in port cities such as Liverpool, Hull and London. However, there were also reports of those like 21-year-old Sammy Branch, from Lagos, a former stowaway studying to be an electrical engineer in Liverpool.[25] He was presented as a 'valuable citizen', someone who 'takes a great interest in the welfare of other coloured men in the city as an assistant scoutmaster'.[26] The SS *Almanzora*, a ship formerly used to transport Caribbean ex-servicemen back to the Caribbean, docked in Southampton in December 1947, bringing about two hundred migrants from the Caribbean, including thirty-one stowaways, and several former servicemen, including Alan Wilmot. He later wrote that, unlike those on later more famous voyages, 'there was no national publicity for the *Almanzora*'s passengers'.[27] What was perhaps most significant was that as British subjects, stowaways and 'authorized' passengers both had a legal right to live and work in Britain. Stowaways might face a few weeks in prison, but even George Stewart, dubbed 'coloured king of the stowaways' by the *Daily Mirror* as he had reportedly seen 'most of the world through portholes as an unauthorized passenger', was recognized as a British citizen.[28] These citizens often faced very challenging circumstances. Alan Wilmot could only find a place to sleep on London Underground trains when he first arrived and explained that he received a very different welcome to the one he had received during the war. He later wrote, 'I had never known what it was to be broke, hungry or homeless until I returned to England.'[29]

THE 'COLOUR BAR'

One of the consequences of the increased numbers of African and Caribbean people in Britain in the post-war period was that the existing colour bar affected increasing numbers of people. Racism remained legal and was given official sanction in numerous ways. In the British Army and Royal Navy, for example, recruitment was only open to those of 'pure European descent'. However, 1948 signalled the end of the colour bar in boxing. In February of that year, Lionel 'Dick' Turpin became the first 'coloured boxer' in over thirty years to win the right to compete for a British boxing title. In May 1948 he went one step further and won the British Empire Middleweight title and, on 28 June 1948, he won the domestic British Middleweight title in front of a crowd of 40,000 in Birmingham, the 'first coloured boxer in the annals of the ring to win a British boxing title'.[30] Two years later his brother, Randolph Turpin, won the same title and went on to win the European and world titles, beating Sugar Ray Robinson in the latter contest in July 1951.

Between 1911, when Home Secretary Winston Churchill prevented African American world heavyweight champion Jack Johnson from fighting in Britain, and 1948, the British Boxing Board of Control (BBBC) declared that contenders for British titles must be 'legally

The boxing Turpin brothers (from left to right) Jackie, Dick, Randolph

British subjects born of white parents'. This stipulation made British boxing more openly racist than it was in the US and prevented boxers such as Len Johnson from ever competing for a British title. Various protests against the boxing colour bar had been launched before 1948. During the war there were demands that Tommy Martin, a Black British boxer who served in the RAF, should be able to compete for a title, but they were rejected by the BBBC.[31] There were more protests in 1947 following two fights for the British Empire featherweight title in which Cliff Anderson, a boxer from British Guiana, was widely believed to have been discriminated against by the referees. Then, after a legal challenge lodged by the Turpin brothers, the racist regulation was finally removed.[32]

However, discrimination in other employment, over accommodation, hotels and public houses was still so commonplace that the Colonial Office was concerned that racism might make those from the colonies 'susceptible to Communist doctrines, and also gave rise to very unfavourable publicity in the colonies themselves'.[33] As the Cold War intensified, the Colonial Office was particularly concerned about the impact of the colour bar on students returning to the colonies. Several new student hostels were opened in an unsuccessful attempt to shield students, and public opinion in the colonies, from the consequences of racism in Britain.[34] However, despite such perceived threats and increasing demands, the government concluded that anti-racist legislation would be unworkable and its main aim remained to discourage large-scale permanent settlement in Britain by those from Africa and the Caribbean. Government officials therefore expressed concern about the arrival of the *Ormonde* and other ships. In 1947 a Colonial Office official, returning from a visit to the Caribbean designed to discourage further migration, reported that the government 'should not undertake the additional responsibility of organizing a scheme of recruitment in the West Indies'.[35]

The response of the government to the increase in the African and Caribbean population in the UK was not only to seek means to prevent further increases, but also to find ways to deport some of those already in Britain whom it considered undesirable. The government was generally opposed to African and Caribbean migration on the basis that it would contribute to what was increasingly referred to as the 'colour problem' in Britain, a view based on the premise that the presence of Black people provoked racism.[36] An environment was established during the late 1940s which was hostile to migration from Africa and the Caribbean, which created the conditions for further racism and several large-scale racist attacks. Such an approach was a continuation of what had been official policy during the 1920s and 1930s, after the partial relaxation of the official colour bar during the war years. Opposition to any influx of 'coloured workers' was also maintained by many trade unions, and especially by the National Union of Seamen (NUS), at a time when unemployment was again rife in Liverpool and other ports. Remarkably, there were also attempts to revive fascism after the war, such as the creation of Mosley's Union Movement which stirred up opposition to immigration from the Commonwealth.[37]

African and Caribbean organizations, such as the West African Students' Union, continued to oppose any manifestations of such prejudice and in the post-war period many new organizations were formed for this purpose. One was the Coloured Workers' Association, sometimes known as the Coloured Workers' Welfare Association (CWWA), established in London in August 1947 by Ernest Marke, Robert Matthews, J. L. Martin and Abdul Sessay. The CWWA claimed in its newsletter, *Progress*, that it was concerned with 'organising the subject peoples of the world', but for the most part it appears to have engaged in public protest meetings and producing small publications focusing particularly on racism. In one early publication in 1948 it drew attention to the fact that at the same time as a major labour shortage 'no jobs are available for coloured workers'. In another it protested to the government about the colour bar in employment – 'the Colonial workers have fought and given their lives in every battlefield in Europe and thus have the right to work and live in Britain'. Matthews was one of the political personalities of this period. He stood as an unsuccessful Labour candidate in the local council election in St Pancras, provided accommodation for the Trinidadian trade unionist Uriah Butler when he visited London, and often spoke at London's Speakers' Corner on a range of issues affecting African and Caribbean people in London from the late 1940s until the 1960s.[38]

African and Caribbean seafarers, stowaways and those in dockland areas faced particular problems in the post-war period as the shipping industry contracted and the colour bar prevented mariners from securing employment and accommodation, even in hostels designed for seafarers.[39] Colonial House, in Leman Street, Whitechapel, designed as a hostel for 'coloured' seamen during the war, became a meeting place for many, but was unable to meet the need for accommodation caused by the growth in numbers and was closed by the Colonial Office in 1949. The 'coloured' population of Stepney soon became the focus of numerous investigative reports, as well as articles in the press.[40]

The most important provision for African and Caribbean men in the area was the 'seamen's mission', a hostel established by an Ethiopian woman who had long been resident in Britain. Kathleen Wrasama was brought to Britain as a child by missionaries in 1917 and presented as an example of 'one of the heathens' from Africa. She experienced several traumatic years in a children's home in Yorkshire before escaping at the age of thirteen to work on various farms. She later worked as a film extra and settled in London. She and her husband, Suleiman

Wrasama, a Somali and former seafarer, opened a hostel for Somali and other African seamen in east London to help both those wounded during the war and post-war stowaways. The Wrasamas made numerous efforts to seek official support for African and Caribbean men in the area and, in 1951, after these proved fruitless, Kathleen took the lead in forming the Stepney Coloured People's Association, which fought for the rights of all 'coloured' people in Stepney, and provided welfare and taught literacy to adults and children alike until its demise in 1959. As Kathleen Wrasama explained:

> I was fed up with writing to the Colonial Office and going to the Colonial Office – they said I was nothing but an agitator and a communist. You know if you're doing anything and you're fighting for your people, they say you're a communist, and I didn't know the first thing about politics in my life. I didn't know what politics were, and they said I was an agitator and a communist and I wasn't, I was fighting for my people.[41]

THE WINDRUSH MYTH

Into the hostile environment being created by the government and some trade unions sailed HMT *Empire Windrush* in June 1948. Ironically, the ship had transported hundreds of former Caribbean service personnel back to the Caribbean, but then its captain had also been compelled by the government to recoup costs on the return journey.[42] It therefore returned to Britain with more than 1,000 passengers, nearly 500 of them Caribbean migrants (mostly from Jamaica), seeking a better life in Britain. The docking at Tilbury was captured on film, some of the passengers were interviewed and, over several decades, the *Empire Windrush* established itself as a symbol for all subsequent post-war migration. Perhaps the ship's most celebrated passenger was Aldwyn 'Lord Kitchener' Roberts (1922–2000), the famous Trinidadian calypsonian, who provided an a cappella version of his calypso 'London Is the Place for Me' for the waiting Pathé News film crew and for posterity. He was joined on the voyage by two other Trinidadian calypsonians, Egbert 'Lord Beginner' Moore (1904–1981) and Harold 'Lord Woodbine' Phillips (1929–2000). All three had been

Johnny Smythe welcoming passengers a board the *Empire Windrush*

touring Jamaica and contributed to a calypso revival in Britain during the 1950s. Phillips, formerly of the RAF, who eventually settled in Liverpool, has been credited as a significant mentor and influence upon the Beatles during their early years. Another significant performer on the *Empire Windrush* was Mona Baptiste (1928–1993), also Trinidadian, and one of only a few women onboard, a singer who subsequently became a successful film actress throughout Europe.[43]

Another of the notable passengers was Sam King (1926–2016), who later became the first Black Mayor of Southwark. He was one of several ex-servicemen on board, had friends in Britain and was able to rejoin the RAF. Others found work on London Transport, or moved out of London to work in the mines, or in other occupations where there was still a post-war labour shortage.[44] Even Eva Buckley, a stowaway on the *Empire Windrush*, soon found work and a place to stay. It was reported in the press that more than fifty of the men on board wished to volunteer for the armed services, although it appears that fewer than twenty were finally accepted, including one Vidal Dezonie, who was to spend his entire working life in the RAF.[45] More than 200 of the passengers who were temporarily housed at the

Clapham South Underground shelter, such as Alan Wilmot's brother, Harold, soon made their own arrangements. Baron Baker, a Jamaican former RAF man who liaised with the government, recalled that he had suggested the idea for the shelter.[46] It was certainly a residence which the government envisaged might discourage other migrants. Within a few weeks it was reported that all those initially housed there had found alternative accommodation.

Sam King, as a former *Windrush* passenger, subsequently did more than most to encourage the commemoration of what has become an iconic moment in post-war British history. He once claimed that 'Immigration to this country really started with that boat'.[47] The *Windrush* has given its name to an entire generation of migrants and their families and more recently to the scandalous state discrimination faced by some, who were subsequently denied full citizenship rights. However, clearly, the *Empire Windrush* was not the first ship to bring migrants from the Caribbean to Britain during this period and cannot be said to have initiated post-war migration. Indeed, June 1948 was not even the first time that the *Empire Windrush* had brought migrants from the Caribbean to Britain. Enrico Stennett is one of those who has spoken about his journey from Jamaica on it in 1947. He claimed that it had no significance, was more a ship of repatriation and wondered 'why we continue to falsify history'.[48] Moreover, before 1950, only six ships had arrived in Britain from the Caribbean, carrying a total of only 1,800 migrants (most of them on the *Empire Windrush*). Large-scale migration was still a few years in the future. King has also pointed out that there was no official encouragement for these early migrants.[49]

Those staying at the shelter in Clapham were welcomed by a small group of MPs, but there was significant disquiet amongst eleven Labour Party MPs, who went so far as to write a letter with strong racist undertones to the Prime Minister, Clement Attlee, to demand immigration controls as the only means to prevent a 'colour racial problem' and Britain becoming 'an open reception centre for immigrants'.[50] Attlee had to reassure them that the *Windrush* passengers were not 'undesirable or unemployables', and were likely to make a 'genuine contribution to our labour difficulties'. However, he concluded: '[T]hey may well find it very difficult to make adequate remittances to their families in Jamaica as well as maintaining themselves over here. On the whole, therefore, I doubt whether there is to be a similar large influx.'[51]

At the time, the Ministry of Labour made a point of announcing that there was no guarantee of jobs, and the Minister of Labour added: 'I hope that no encouragement will be given to others to follow their example.'[52] Government officials had considered whether the *Windrush* might be halted in its journey to Britain, while Attlee is reported to have suggested that its passengers might be diverted to work producing groundnuts in East Africa.[53] The *Windrush* passengers were met by officials from the Colonial Office, including Flight Lieutenant Johnny Smythe and Ivor Cummings, an official of Sierra Leonean heritage, who both reportedly warned the passengers of the difficulties that faced them.[54] Smythe issued a note to all the passengers, telling them:

> I could not honestly paint you a very rosy picture of your future. Conditions in England are not as favourable as you may think. Various reports you have heard about shortage of labour are very misleading. The shortage is not general. Unless you are highly skilled your chances of finding a job are none too good ... Hard work is the order of the day in Britain and if you think you cannot pull your weight you might as well decide to return to Jamaica, even if you have to swim the Atlantic.[55]

THE CARIBBEAN LABOUR CONGRESS

Some of those who arrived on the *Empire Windrush* and faced difficulties turned to the newly formed London branch of the Caribbean Labour Congress (CLC) for help. The CLC was established in September 1945 at a founding conference in Barbados and aimed to unify the trade-union movement in the English-speaking Caribbean (for the most part). It was also strongly in favour of an independent Caribbean based on an economic and political federation, but it was severely handicapped by the onset of the Cold War and the persecution of some of its leading members, such as the Jamaican trade unionist Richard Hart.[56] Despite such difficulties, the London branch, established on 23 May 1948, remained active throughout the late 1940s and 1950s and built links with Caribbean migrants, workers and students in other cities, such as Liverpool, as well as in Birming-ham, where it established another branch.[57] It was created with support from George Padmore and several other notables of Carib-bean heritage, including the future peer Dr David Pitt (1913–1994), Dr Malcolm Joseph-Mitchell of the League of Coloured Peoples (LCP) and Learie Constantine. The London branch also had the sup-port of several Labour MPs.[58]

The London CLC supported the struggle for independence in Africa, as well as in the Caribbean and, in pursuit of its goals for the Caribbean, often collaborated with the American Committee for West Indian Federation. It also supported the struggles of African Ameri-cans, as well as anti-colonialism more generally. In this regard it stated: '[W]e have joined forces for the complete overthrow of coloni-alism and the barbarity that goes with it, towards a goal where all peoples can enjoy a lasting Peace and National Independence.' How-ever, it added, 'We are dangerous, because of the opportunity we had, of exposing British colonial slave conditions at home in the United Kingdom, at the heart of the empire.'[59] Its main focus, therefore, was organizing amongst Caribbean workers in Britain, where it some-times collaborated with the LCP and the Pan-African Federation (PAF). The London branch was led by Billy Strachan (1921–1998) and many of its leading members were active trade unionists, often creating branches of trade unions or establishing new ones.[60]

Strachan, a former RAF pilot, was another of those who returned to Britain in 1947. He had unsuccessfully attempted to establish a post-war career in Jamaica with his English wife and three children. However, the racism he faced there, as well as his growing political awareness, led to his return to London, where he immediately joined the Communist Party, established the London branch of the CLC and was its secretary until 1956.[61] The CLC soon became one of the most important political organizations for Caribbean migrants during the 1940s and 1950s, and attracted many militant members, such as Trevor Carter, Cleston Taylor, Winston Pindar, Lionel and Pansy Jeffrey, as well as others, some of whom had faced Cold War political perse-cution in the Caribbean. Strachan was a key political figure in post-war Britain, the 'Godfather' to many political activists from the Caribbean and later a major contributor to the pioneering *Caribbean News*, published between 1952 and 1956, one of the first post-war papers to focus on the Caribbean and its diaspora in London.[62] Amongst other things, the *Caribbean News* campaigned against the colour bar and called on all workers to fight against racism.[63]

The CLC in London faced persecution for its association with the Communist Party. Of course, Strachan and other CLC members were also members of the Communist Party, which had its own West Indian branch in London.[64] They held an annual 'Emancipation Celebration' and other regular dances and did much to encourage the new West Indian identity that was developing amongst Caribbean migrants in Britain. As Cleston Taylor explained, 'Billy always thought of a Caribbean nation [as] including all territories.'[65] The London branch also did much to clarify to people in Britain that the need for migration was caused by the appalling economic conditions that existed in the colonies.

Caribbean News, February 1953

The CLC's London branch held a welcoming meeting for *Windrush* passengers at Holborn Hall in July 1948 and established a special committee to assist the new arrivals. Strachan received desperate requests for help from several. '. . . I am in bad luck. Can't get a room to live all I try. Can you find me one, I would love a room with just a chair and a bed. See if you can help one who really needs help,' wrote one young Jamaican. From another, 'I am unfortunately one of the 33 Jamaicans sent from Clapham South to work at Stanton Iron Works Co. Finding it difficult to live on the pay and conditions at the hostel. Appealing to you and your organization for help.' Kenneth Levy, one of two brothers, wrote that he was, 'A Windrush arrivee asking CLC for help, 27 years old with four years' service in the RAF in the UK with air traffic control'.[66]

The CLC was one of the first organizations to come to the aid of Caribbean migrants throughout this period. The LCP was much less influential after 1948, following the death of its president, Harold Moody, the previous year, and was finally dissolved in 1951. One of the LCP's major campaigns in the post-war period had been to address another increase in Britain's Black population, children born to white mothers who had been fathered by African Americans, and sometimes other Black men, during the war. The subject had been discussed at the Manchester Pan-African Congress and the LCP estimated that at least 750 of these 'illegitimate' children had been born, but admitted that the figure might be as many as 1,700.[67] It is now estimated that some 2,000 'brown babies' were born in these circumstances.[68] Sexual relations between white women and Black men and the children that resulted from such liaisons had been one of the greatest concerns of the US and British governments during the war. Even though they were powerless to prevent them, it seems likely that the US Army did actively discourage marriages between the parents of such children.[69]

After the war the social stigma attached to such births led to many 'women in distress', who might expect minimal assistance from local welfare organizations, or from a few initiatives such as those set up by Constantine, Padmore, Ekarte and the African Churches Mission in Liverpool.[70] The LCP publicized the situation in the United States and as a result some children were adopted by relatives, or by other 'coloured peoples', although government intervention aimed to prevent such adoptions.[71] The LCP reported that, in Britain, where many of the children were placed in children's homes, they and their mothers were often subjected to discrimination and prejudice.[72] One mother wrote:

> I am shunned by the whole village . . . The inspector for the National Society for the Prevention of Cruelty to Children has told my friend to keep her children away from my house . . . as didn't she know that I had two illegitimate coloured children? Is there anywhere I can go where my children will not get . . . pushed around?[73]

In July 1948, a new British Nationality Act was passed by Parliament. It conferred British citizenship on all those who were colonial subjects, or 'Commonwealth' citizens. Indeed, no distinction was made between citizens of Britain and citizens of the colonies. It was passed in response to changes in related laws in Canada and other 'Dominions' and in order to buttress the conception of a 'New Commonwealth', not in relation to immigration.[74] Although the act simply reaffirmed the pre-war status of British subjects for the most part, it has subsequently been wrongly viewed as facilitating, or even encouraging, migration from the colonies to Britain.

LIVERPOOL

The government made several efforts to stem the flow of seamen and stowaways into Liverpool, where, as you will recall, there was significant unemployment, especially amongst 'coloured seamen', many of whom had become dependent on public funds. At the same time as it closed seamen's hostels, its attempts to discharge and effectively force the deportation of some 25 per cent of all colonial seamen met with opposition from several local organizations during the late 1940s, and, later on, from the Colonial People's Defence Association (CPDA), which had been established under the auspices of the Communist Party in 1950.[75] For its part, the National Union of Seamen (NUS) continued its opposition to the employment of Black sailors, and stowaways in particular, and in August 1948 claimed to have already established its own committees to set 'language tests' and 'vet all coloured entrants to the country who claim to be seamen'. According to the union's Assistant General Secretary, this was 'not colour discrimination but is safeguarding the white seamen and is to save the industry from being flooded with raw labour'.[76] The antagonistic environment created by the government and the NUS, which was often reflected in press reports, contributed to the conditions for the large-scale racist attacks that occurred in Liverpool during the summer of 1948.[77] The League of Coloured Peoples estimated Liverpool's Black population at about 8,000 in 1948. This may be just an approximation, but does suggest the existence of a significant population even before the arrival of post-war Caribbean migrants.

The racist attacks began on the evening of 31 July, when a large crowd of several hundred besieged and wrecked the Anglo-Indian Restaurant in St James Street. When police arrived, about thirty minutes later, only one man, a West African, was arrested (after he had defended himself). It was reported that he had been set upon by the large crowd who had also besieged Colsea House (a 'coloured seamen's hostel'). The following night the hostel and its inhabitants were again attacked by a large crowd, which led to one injured man being admitted to hospital. When the police arrived, they broke in and arrested, not the aggressors, but those who were under attack. On the third night there were further onslaughts on the seamen's hostel which were dispersed by police, followed by an attempted assault on the Technique Club in Upper Parliament Street. The club was apparently defended by a 'larger group of Colonials' who were subsequently set upon by the police and compelled to defend themselves. The police were reported to have attacked and arrested more than thirty 'Colonials' indiscriminately, entering homes and other premises for that purpose. According to some accounts, people sought refuge in a club known as Wilkie's, also in Upper Parliament Street, but the police forced an entry and arrested people there too. Police patrols continued long into the night and there were numerous reports of Black people who were defending themselves, or trying to keep out of harm's way, being arrested and later charged.

In the next few days nearly seventy people appeared in court, but the vast majority were 'coloured men', many of them with injuries received from the police.[78] In addition to the racism of the initial attackers and that of the police, those in the 'coloured quarter' also had to endure the sensational and prejudiced reports that appeared in the local press. These neglected to provide details about any of the attackers, but made much of the alleged violence of those who had been forced to defend themselves and suggested that the 'coloured quarter' was the source of the disturbances.[79] In the aftermath of what were referred to as riots, there were also calls in the national press to restrict the entry of stowaways from West Africa and the Caribbean into Liverpool.[80]

At a public meeting held in the Stanley House Community Centre in the aftermath of the attacks, the Assistant Chief Constable of the city claimed, 'there isn't any colour question in Liverpool at this moment'. He mainly concerned himself with the issue of the 'lawlessness' of those who had been set upon, while at the same time promising 'I will see that you get the protection to which you are entitled.'[81] In these circumstances local Black people, encouraged by Makonnen of the Pan African Federation in Manchester, formed their own Colonial Defence Committee (CDC) and elected Eddie Duplan as its secretary and H. F. Prescod, a long-time resident of Barbadian origin, as chairman. Funds for the legal defence of those arrested were raised locally, with support provided by the PAF and the LCP. Makonnen called for a full investigation into the recent attacks, compensation for personal injuries and damage to property, as well as the prosecution of the perpetrators.[82]

The court cases which followed the attacks were noteworthy in that every effort was made to prevent any discussion of racism. Bail was generally denied and police evidence was used to convict the mainly Black defendants, several of whom were seamen. However, in several cases, the evidence of the police was flimsy. One eyewitness reported:

> The police case was rather thin and though they had all evidently been well-rehearsed, several slips were made and each constable was mauled in turn by the defending solicitor. Each police witness persisted in his story that there was no violence during or before the arrests and 'could not say' how the defendants had received injuries described in picturesque detail by the defence.

The same eyewitness reported that the defendants – a former RAF man, a technician, a dance-band leader and former technician, a saxophonist, a student and a fifteen-year-old boy – still showed evidence of their injuries several weeks later. In this particular case the six defendants were acquitted.[83]

The attacks in Liverpool were significant in that the community was attacked both by racists and by the police and it responded with the organized resistance of the CDC. There was clearly great unity amongst all those of African and Caribbean heritage. One Somali commented on the attacks: '[T]his is as much our business as the West Africans or anyone else. If it can happen to them it can happen to us.'[84] This sense of unity also extended to some other towns and cities, since the CDC travelled to Cardiff and held a joint meeting with the United Committee of Colonial and Coloured People's Organizations (UCCCPO), one of the organizations that was part of the PAF. The CDC's aim was to raise financial and other support in Cardiff and almost certainly, in Manchester, Newcastle and elsewhere, where there were established African and Caribbean communities. The sentiment at the joint meeting was, 'if we do not fight this thing now, we will be beaten one by one'. The UCCCPO subsequently demanded that the government launch an inquiry into police violence in Liverpool. The court cases were notable for another reason, which was that the defence was based on the premise that the police were lying, had, in fact, fabricated evidence, and had violently attacked the defendants. When there were convictions, defendants would lodge appeals against them, with CDC support, sometimes successfully.[85]

Although the CDC was mainly concerned with defending the community in the aftermath of the racist attack, two years later some of its members formed the Colonial People's Defence Association (CPDA), an openly anti-racist organization, established to 'protect individual and collective interests of the coloured race', including, naturally, the employment of seamen, as well as all those of African and Caribbean heritage in Liverpool fighting against a widespread colour bar in general employment.[86] It is interesting to note that as migration from the Caribbean was slowly increasing, many in Liverpool's population of mainly West African heritage were finding it difficult to secure work and the government was proposing that some might be repatriated.[87] The CPDA, largely led by Africans such as Ludwig Hesse, a former seafarer, supported those facing discrimination at work, as well as those assaulted and arrested by the police. It provided advice, as well

as various forms of welfare and, with the support of other organizations, attempted to act as the representative of the entire community. It
also held political meetings related to issues in Britain and abroad, as
well as organizing a special women's committee, in which the activist
Dorothy Kuya played a leading role.[88]

The disturbances in Liverpool were just one example of large-scale
racist attacks that occurred as a result of the hostile environment created during the post-war period. There were attacks on the hostels and
accommodation used by African and Caribbean migrant workers
everywhere. In July 1948 there was a racist assault on Caribbean residents at a Ministry of Labour hostel in Castle Donnington, Nottingham,
by people described as 'Irish and certain foreign elements'. Here, as in
subsequent cases, the victims were seen as creating a problem and were
evicted.[89] Other attacks occurred in Deptford and Birmingham within
a few weeks of each other in the summer of 1949.

DEPTFORD

In Deptford in July, about fifty mainly African men were attacked by
racist crowds reportedly numbering somewhere between 75 and 2,000
people. The men had come to Britain in the aftermath of the war, and
many were skilled workers, or were qualified in various fields, and
some were former servicemen. They had been directed by the Colonial
Office to reside at Carrington House, 'a Common Lodging House' with
hundreds of male occupants in Deptford, where they were subjected to
various forms of discrimination by local employers and in cafés and
public houses, as well as in the lodging house itself. Apparently organized gangs from outside the area had threatened stallholders and others
if they served Africans and it seems likely that post-war fascist groups
were actively involved. One African complained that sometimes racist
occupants of Carrington House even spat in their food. The racism
escalated on 17 July 1949, when the men and their hostel were attacked
by a large crowd following a local incident apparently involving a Black
man and a white woman. A significant police presence then led to fourteen Africans being arrested, many allegedly for attacking policemen,
although several were later acquitted or fined nominal amounts.[90] As in

Liverpool, the local press carried sensational reports of the attacks and the circumstances surrounding them.[91]

A significant feature of these assaults was that local people appear to have been appalled by them. The Africans were also strongly supported by the National Council for Civil Liberties and Deptford Trades Council. In August 1949, the latter declared 'its firm belief in the principles of equality of treatment for all citizens irrespective of their race, colour or creed'. At the end of that year, the two organizations, alongside delegates from twenty-six others, convened a special conference to discuss the attacks. A local committee was established, calls were made for the trade unions to organize against racism, while Desmond Buckle, the veteran African communist, demanded anti-racist legislation. It was reported that most of the Africans were acquitted, or received nominal fines.[92]

In other areas new post-war male migrants from the Caribbean were often housed in National Service hostels which had originally been established during the war, alongside migrants from Ireland and other European countries. Several incidents occurred in the post-war period in such hostels in Letchworth, West Bromwich, Leeds, Derbyshire, Nottingham and elsewhere, in one instance involving a white supremacist and in others most often occasioned by 'racial prejudice' apparently caused by 'black men associating with white women'. Although these were government-run hostels, no action was taken to address the problem of racism, nor that of animosity between those from different European countries, some created by the recent war. The most common reaction was to propose that Caribbean workers should be moved elsewhere or restricted by a quota system.[93]

BIRMINGHAM

In Birmingham, the largest hostel in the city had refused to accept Black residents. However, about sixty-five Jamaican men were accommodated at the Causeway Green Hostel in the suburbs, alongside six hundred other residents, the vast majority men from various European countries. At the start of August 1949 there were several violent incidents within the hostel before the outbreak of large-scale violence on

8 August when Polish residents were reported to have made a raid on bedrooms mainly used by Jamaicans. Police were called to stand guard in the corridors throughout the night to prevent further violence. The hostel authorities and the police wanted to remove the Jamaicans, even though they were the victims of the attacks, arguing that they were the minority and that the other white residents of the hostel and locality were likely to petition the local authorities for their removal. In fact, other hostel residents supported the view that the Jamaicans were constantly subjected to racism. Despite considerable pressure, many of the Jamaicans initially refused to vacate the hostel. One of them, Horace Halliburton, explained their predicament to the press:

> We are little better than nomads, and consider it very unfair that, though we are British, we are the people to suffer. We have put up with a lot from the Poles and did not start the recent fights. The Poles brought reinforcements from local hostels, and we were outnumbered four to one ... It is not easy for us to find work in England. Even though I hold a London Matriculation Certificate and can speak three languages fluently, I still find it impossible to get a skilled job because I'm a coloured man.[94]

Several factors led to such outbreaks of racist violence, with the role of 'white women' often mentioned as a cause once again, but all the factors were created by an environment which presented African and Caribbean men as having fewer rights than European migrant workers and always as being the main cause of any trouble, even though they were British citizens. Moreover, racism was not to be confronted, but appeased, and in the aftermath of the Causeway Green violence, the authorities first proposed that the Jamaicans should be removed and that subsequently quotas for 'West Indians' should be introduced throughout all similar hostels.[95] As elsewhere, the press added to the hostility by spreading sensational and lurid stories regarding sexual relationships between Black men and white women, which effectively condoned (and encouraged) further racism. Opposition to this was led by the resistance of the Jamaican men themselves and by those organizations, often African and Caribbean-led, that supported them, such as the LCP and the Association of Africans and People of African Descent, as well as several Liverpool-based groups.[96]

What such incidents showed was that the government was unable, or unwilling, to address the conditions that gave rise to racism, such as the existence and glorification of the colonial empire. Nor was it able to address the poor economic conditions in the colonies that led to migration. In this period, the numbers of unemployed people in the British West Indies alone were estimated at about 180,000. At the same time, the government would not introduce legislation against racism, nor any public education regarding it or colonial rule. All this in addition to official opposition to large-scale immigration, as well as frequently biased and emotive press coverage, created the conditions for further racism that would only manifest itself more openly as immigrants arrived during the 1950s in much larger numbers. For the powers that be, African and Caribbean people constituted a 'problem', and were largely seen as the cause of racism. So government officials started to consider seriously how to prevent the future arrival of 'coloured persons', who could not be easily assimilated and who were deemed likely to create further social problems.

EVERYDAY RACISM

After the war, official racism was not only directed at immigrants. Britain's governments, both Labour and Conservative, also adopted an openly racialist approach to the marriage in 1948 of Seretse Khama and Ruth Williams, an Englishwoman. Khama, at that time a law student in London, was the heir to the paramount chieftainship of the Bamangwato within the British Protectorate of Bechuanaland, which was encircled by South Africa. The apartheid regime in South Africa opposed the marriage, as well as Khama's and his heirs' entitlement to the chieftainship, while the British government decided to appease the government of South Africa and went further still in 1951 by exiling Khama and his wife from Bechuanaland.[97] The entire affair became a cause célèbre, with public opinion and several campaigning groups in Britain strongly supporting the exiles. A Seretse Khama fighting committee, headed by Learie Constantine and Nii Odoi Annan, a law student from the Gold Coast who was associated with the West African National Secretariat and the Communist Party, met often at the new

WASU hostel in London's Chelsea Embankment. In their turn, the Africa League, originally established by African workers and students in Manchester, organized a protest rally on the issue in Trafalgar Square. African and Caribbean students at Oxford University concluded that 'the acquiescence of the British Government in this policy is an African Munich – a victory for "white" South African fascism'. The West African Students' Club at Oxford wrote a letter to the Prime Minister condemning the government's action, which, it pointed out, could not 'inspire the confidence of Colonial Peoples in Great Britain or help them to see any more clearly the essential difference between the methods of democracy and those of totalitarianism'.[98]

The Seretse Khama affair shone a bright spotlight on the issue of racism, both within Britain and in its colonies, but government and Parliament still rejected any attempts to make any form of discrimination illegal. In 1953 a Private Member's Bill to abolish the colour bar in the colonies introduced by the Labour MP, Fenner Brockway, was defeated in Parliament. Post-war calls for similar legislation in Britain had been made by the PAF from as early as 1945, but a bill to outlaw the colour bar in Britain, introduced by the Labour MP Reginald Sorenson, had been defeated in Parliament in 1950. Brockway continued, on an almost annual basis between 1956 and 1965, to introduce bills against discrimination in Britain on the grounds of 'colour, race or religion', but was defeated time and again, although with increasing support for his proposals on each occasion.[99] In 1954 Winston Churchill had made his government's policy clear. When asked whether he would take action against the colour bar, he replied: 'The laws and custom of this country upon this subject are well known, and I am advised there is no need for new instructions.'[100]

Everyday forms of racism persisted throughout the 1950s and were widely reported in the press.[101] These ranged from mothers being barred from buying children's clothes and hairdressers refusing to cut Black children's hair to problems with accommodation and employment. In 1954, in the so-called Baynes Street Riot, a gang attacked Nigerians in north London, while in 1955 similar attacks were reported in east London.[102] In some parts of the country, African and Caribbean workers and students organized their own opposition to racism. In 1951 the Manchester-based Africa League sent a letter of protest to the Colonial Secretary which demanded 'the appointment of a committee to study the general condition of Colonial workers all over Britain and make recommendations'. The League also argued the case for social and educational centres for colonial workers in Cardiff, Hull, Liverpool, Manchester and Birmingham. In Birmingham the League of Africans and People of African Descent organized public protest meetings against the colour bar.[103]

In public houses and hotels, the colour bar still operated, despite growing criticism. It was in these circumstances that, in 1953, Len Johnson organized a public protest against a public house in Manchester and, with considerable local support, managed to force the landlord to remove the colour bar. As the secretary of the New Internationalist Society (NIS), Johnson had long organized against post-war racism. The NIS had been formed as an anti-racist organization in Dulcie Street, in Moss Side, Manchester, in 1946. It was led by Johnson and others, with the support of the Communist Party. It aimed to 'provide a place where people of all lands could meet fraternally'. It was one of several post-war initiatives involving the Communist Party, which was also active amongst Black people in Liverpool, Cardiff, London and Manchester. Liverpool also had its NIS, led by Ludwig Hesse, a former seaman from the Gold Coast.[104]

MASS MIGRATION

All the conditions that had led to migration to Britain in the 1940s continued in the 1950s. The numbers of migrants from the Caribbean remained relatively small, under 3,000 a year until 1954, with a similar, if not slightly larger number arriving from West Africa. But in 1954 there were over 9,000 new Caribbean migrants, and in 1955 over 27,000, then more than 29,000 the following year. Thereafter numbers declined significantly, but only until 1960, when they climbed to nearly 50,000 and over 60,000 the next year. By 1962, when immigration controls were first introduced, the African and Caribbean population of London alone was reportedly over 130,000. However, the numbers of migrants from the Caribbean and Africa was generally no greater, and often much lower, than the numbers of migrants from

Europe during the same period – while for most of the 1950s more people left the country than entered it, a total of nearly one million migrating to Australia alone.[105] Nonetheless, both Labour and Conservative governments in general remained opposed to the settlement of 'coloured immigrants' and measures were adopted to disperse them 'over as wide an area as possible', purportedly to aid 'assimilation'. Immigration controls were considered by the Cabinet as early as June 1950, when the 'community of colonial people' in Britain was officially estimated at no more than 30,000.[106]

There were official efforts to direct migrants towards areas where there was most unemployment and to those jobs most unpopular with British workers. These also aimed to keep male migrants from employment in close proximity to white women. In those areas where a rigid colour bar in employment had existed, such as in Cardiff and Liverpool, no official efforts were made to remove it.[107] However, the state-led hostile environment failed to prevent migration and could be seen as a major source of racism, which governments did nothing to overcome by 'direct legislative or administrative action'.[108] Migrants from Africa, and especially from the Caribbean, were entering Britain in larger numbers but were forced into the worst-paid and least-skilled jobs by employers, labour exchanges and the policies of trade unions. Employment in the civil service was just one area where there was blatant discrimination that was sanctioned at the highest level.[109]

At the same time as barring African and Caribbean workers from certain jobs and careers, the state was actively recruiting women for the NHS, where there was a shortage both of nurses and domestic workers. Starting in 1948, efforts were intensified to fill some 53,000 nursing vacancies, both by recruiting in the colonies and by encouraging those of African and Caribbean heritage who were training in Britain not to immediately return to the colonies. (From 1949 onwards domestic workers were also directly recruited from Barbados by the NHS, and from Jamaica soon afterwards.[110]) Government policy decreed that 'colonial' nurses were not expected to remain in Britain permanently, nor to be promoted. When it became evident that they might stay, they were often pushed into the role of State Enrolled Nurse, one which offered no prospect of promotion. Such an approach often contributed to antagonism towards African and Caribbean nurses from their fellow nurses.[111] By 1961 there were thousands of African and Caribbean nurses training in Britain, including about 2,500 from Jamaica and more than 1,000 from Nigeria.[112]

From the mid-1950s onwards London Transport also began recruiting migrant workers, from 1956 recruiting directly in Barbados and, from the early 1960s, in Jamaica too, as well as in Trinidad and Tobago. Migrant workers were also hired by bus companies outside London, but they sometimes met with local colour bar policies enforced by trade union leaders. In Birmingham, for example, in the mid-1950s, the local authority effectively operated a colour bar, allegedly because there was strong union opposition to the employment of 'coloured' bus crews, even though there was an acute shortage of as many as 800 bus workers there.[113] Trade union leaders in Birmingham were amongst those to air their views in opposition to the recruitment of migrants in *Has Britain a Colour Bar?* – one of the first British television programme on the subject, which aired in 1955.[114] A similar colour bar also existed among transport employers in Coventry, West Bromwich and elsewhere in Britain, including Bristol. This was just one of the forms of racism which African and Caribbean people faced during this period. In a different form of employment, an African electrician in Birmingham complained that he could not get a job without a union card and that the union would not give him membership if he did not have a job.[115] Indeed, many migrants brought skills with them. It is estimated that about 25 per cent of all male and 50 per cent of female migrants from the Caribbean had professional or managerial experience, nearly half were skilled workers and fewer than a fifth were semi-skilled or manual workers. Yet, by the 1950s, for migrants acquiring employment commensurate with their skills presented a considerable challenge and 63 per cent were employed in unskilled, or semi-skilled jobs, and only 6 per cent of men and 23 per cent of women migrants had found professional or managerial roles.[116]

THE BIRMINGHAM
AFRO-CARIBBEAN ORGANIZATION

In Birmingham in 1952 its entire 'coloured' population was estimated at fewer than 5,000, with only just over one thousand people of African and Caribbean heritage. Unemployment was increasingly a problem in the area, although not only due to the colour bar.[117] Opposition to the colour bar, as well as action on employment and other problems there, was mounted by the Afro-Caribbean Organization (ACO), which grew from a merger of the local branch of the League of Coloured Peoples and the local West Indian Association.[118] The ACO was led by its founder and president, Dr Clarence Piliso, a local GP originally from South Africa, and its vice-president Henry Gunter (1920–2007), a communist from Jamaica, who had trained there as an accountant, but took on factory work when he moved to Britain in 1948. Gunter embraced his new situation, explaining that those from the Caribbean needed to enlighten British workers and that by coming to Birmingham in 1949, 'I have placed myself in the industrial heart of the country so as to meet more of the workers.'[119] He soon became the first Black member of the Amalgamated Engineering Union, then its first Black branch secretary and subsequently the first Black delegate to the Birmingham Trades Council. In August 1951 Gunter started the Birmingham branch of the CLC, known as the CLC Group, and in 1952 he organized protests against the colour bar, as well as a campaign demanding 'Freedom Now for Africa and the West Indies', which gained the support of the Birmingham Trades Council.[120] He also led protests against housing shortages, after discovering that sometimes four migrants were forced to share one room. In December 1952 the Trades Council passed a resolution calling on the TUC to demand that the government provide accommodation for immigrant workers in Birmingham who were living in 'appalling conditions'.[121]

Nevertheless, for some time the colour bar continued in Birmingham, operating in employment as well as accommodation. The ACO first came to public prominence in the summer of 1953 when its members threatened a boycott and picket of hotels in the city that had barred 'coloured' guests, including a Birmingham-trained doctor who had been discriminated against and returned to West Africa 'strongly resentful'. The ACO called on African governments to demand that 'the colour bar which keeps us out of decent jobs and homes here in Britain is ended'. Piliso even made the threat that 'if this protest fails we shall ask for repatriation'. The ACO also complained about commonplace acts of racism in banks, as well as discrimination in employment, accommodation and house purchase.[122] It petitioned the city council for more action against racism and demanded an 'inter-racial council', as well as a 'social centre for coloured people' and their friends.[123]

In 1953 the ACO began to challenge the colour-bar policies of local unions that were attempting to prevent the employment of drivers and conductors on Birmingham's buses on the basis of a variety of racist arguments, including the alleged undesirability of white women working with Black men. The local union claimed that it was only representing the views of its members, but the ACO countered this by demanding action from the council and writing an open letter in the local press, which

The Birmingham Afro-Caribbean Organization.
Henry Gunter is standing at the far left

condemned one local union leader for what it referred to as 'departing from the true principles of British trade unionism'. Amongst other things, the ACO pointed out that 'coloured men' were already employed on buses in London, Manchester and Leeds and that many of those seeking employment were skilled workers or ex-servicemen.[124]

The ACO maintained its campaign for several years and in 1954 Henry Gunter wrote a pamphlet entitled *A Man's a Man: A Study of the Colour Bar in Birmingham and an Answer*, which was published by the Communist Party. Gunter argued that the colour bar was an attempt to divide the workers, which had to be overcome by trade-union unity and fought in the open 'where by exposure to the spotlight of public opinion, it can be seen for the rotten bigotry it is'.[125] He also explained the circumstances that forced people to leave the impoverished conditions created by colonial rule in their homelands, the fact that their skills and qualifications were often ignored in Britain, and the way in which the colour bar operated in housing and other social amenities. As an 'answer' Gunter called on people to take a stand against racism, to assist colonial workers to become more politically organized and effective, for self-government of the colonies and he encouraged them to join the Communist Party.[126]

Gradually, change came to Birmingham, as the city council agreed to demands for a community centre, a specialist welfare officer and an end to the colour bar on the buses. The activism of the ACO prompted government intervention and gained the support of a few local politicians. Bars, hotels and employers began to end their colour ban too, after further threats of boycotts and public shaming in Parliament.[127] The ACO continued its activities in Birmingham, as well as actively supporting the struggles against colonial rule in Kenya and British Guiana. In October 1954 it convened a meeting addressed by Seretse Khama, Fenner Brockway and others, which condemned British colonial rule in Africa and the racial bigotry in Britain. Seretse Khama claimed that he felt like a third-class British citizen and declared that 'If I have to suffer because I am coloured, I will have to keep on fighting'.[128]

As the 1950s wore on, increasingly there were calls, often reported in the press, for an end to the colour bar. However, it persisted, not only in the Midlands, but also in towns and cities throughout the country. There were sometimes 'racial strikes', most notably in the

Midlands, in support of the colour bar, or a cap on the number of Black workers who could be employed, often under the guise of maintaining wage rates and the 'closed shop', or of preventing unemployment and alleged strike-breaking. These and similar arguments had sustained the colour bar since the 1920s, to the detriment of all.[129] At the same time, there were also demands from all the major political parties for immigration to be controlled on the grounds that there was a shortage of accommodation, employment and welfare provision in Britain. The ACO continued to oppose any restriction on immigration, and it also demanded legislation against racism.[130] In this period housing shortages were exacerbated by a 30-per-cent reduction in council-house building and the reluctance of some local authorities, such as Birmingham City Council, to implement redevelopment programmes. As in the case of unemployment, the housing shortage was often blamed on migrants.

Efforts by government to control 'coloured' migration dated back to the period after the First World War and had been modified according to circumstances during the 1940s. In 1950 an investigation by Attlee's Labour government had concluded that further legislative measures to control immigration were unnecessary. No doubt this was the case precisely because there *were* already measures in place, often of dubious legality, to limit migration. These measures were rather more successful in regard to migrants from Africa, but less successfully applied to those from the Caribbean. From 1953 Churchill's government began to gather evidence of the need for immigration controls, even though, as late as 1955, it admitted privately that 'Colonial immigration was not an acute problem', except with regard to housing. At that time the numbers of 'coloured British subjects' were only about 40,000 in total and in 1956 the government admitted that 'coloured immigrants have recently been making a useful contribution to the labour force'.[131] Nevertheless, in 1955 it prepared a draft Immigration Bill, largely in relation to migration from the Caribbean, and in that same year a Conservative MP attempted to introduce a bill into Parliament to restrict immigration.[132]

This approach encouraged the view that 'coloured immigrants' were a problem. This was a view that also appeared in the press (with increasing frequency in parliamentary debates), and informed the surveillance and other activities of the police, in addition to being presented in the publications and public expressions of political parties. The press played a significant role in creating fear and disinformation, presenting migrants as uneducated, living on welfare payments in squalid and overcrowded public housing, and being involved in crime and prostitution. One magazine in the early 1950s went as far as to cautioned its readers: '[S]cientists do not yet know if it is wise for two very different races as whites and blacks to marry, for sometimes children of mixed marriages seem to inherit the worst characteristics of each race.'[133] As early as 1954, the Conservative Commonwealth Group in Liverpool produced a pamphlet called *The Problem of Coloured Immigration* and in 1955 the central council of the Conservative and Union associations passed a motion demanding immigration controls.[134] In 1956 the government concluded in their report on *Colonial Immigrants*: 'the ordinary people of this country seem to be by no means intolerant of coloured people in their midst. There appears to be little prospect therefore of race riots or colour bar incidents on grounds of race alone.'[135] However, the government's conclusion was that more appropriate conditions needed to be created and public opinion changed in order to introduce immigration controls to stem the 'coloured invasion' and to preserve the existing 'racial strain' in Britain.[136] It is in this context that Prime Minister Churchill is reported to have considered the usefulness of 'Keep England White' as a Conservative Party election slogan in 1955.

As you may remember, opposition to racism and the colour bar was often led by those who were members of, or connected with, the Communist Party, such as Henry Gunter and Billy Strachan. Trevor Carter, a communist who had migrated to Britain from Trinidad, explained that many migrants had great political experience based on activism in the trade-union and anti-colonial movements in Africa and the Caribbean, and despite any difficulties, were likely to join unions when they came to Britain. Another Caribbean migrant recalled:

> I was met in London by three friends who were active politically and within their trade unions. They were members of the Communist Party and it seemed natural to me that they were. We grew up in Trinidad during the Second World War when the Soviet Union was one of the

Allied nations fighting against fascism, Nazism and racism. Coming from a colonial country we were generally interested in and attracted by the heroic exploits of the Soviet Union . . . It seemed natural, therefore, for the Communist Party to be the home of black militants.[137]

1958: NOTTINGHAM AND NOTTING HILL

By 1958 the overall numbers of African and Caribbean people in Britain were still modest. The largest African and Caribbean populations were in London – 40,000, Birmingham – 27,000, in Manchester, about 5,000 and Nottingham – 4,000. The total number of those from Africa and the Caribbean was about 125,000.[138] In 1956, in response to labour shortages in certain industries, the British Transport Commission, London Transport and the British Hotels and Restaurants Association began recruiting in Barbados and there was also an increase in recruitment of nurses from the Caribbean and Africa. Such recruitment started and stopped according to the needs of the economy, which began to slow down again in the late 1950s, leading to unemployment, which hit migrants disproportionally. In Nottingham, for example, 13 per cent of those from the Caribbean were unemployed in 1958, although they made up only 1 per cent of the population.[139]

But those who were recruited, or who made their way to Britain independently, still faced all the challenges of the colour bar when they arrived. A survey conducted in London in 1956 found that 90 per cent of landlords would not accept Black students as lodgers. This was the age of the infamous landlords' requirement: 'No blacks, no Irish, no dogs', or, marginally more politely, 'No coloureds'. Leasehold properties commonly included a clause preventing sales to 'non-whites'. In 1958 three African American women were barred from London's prestigious Goring Hotel, despite having already made reservations there.[140] The chain of Mecca dance halls in Nottingham, Birmingham and Sheffield would only admit Black men with female partners, a policy which seems to have been accepted by Dr Winston Pilgrim, Chairman of the West Indian Federation in Birmingham, but which was strongly opposed by the local MP.[141] In 1958 the Musicians Union took a stand in opposition to the colour bar operated by the Scala Ballroom in

Wolverhampton, whose manager had 'ordered that no coloured person was to be admitted'. The boycott was disregarded by the local Wolverhampton branch of the union, and a lengthy dispute ensued, with significant publicity and the involvement of the local council and MP. Eventually, the colour bar was dropped in the Wolverhampton ballroom, as it was in similar venues in east London. Concerns about such blatant racism were expressed in another unsuccessful Private Member's bill opposing 'race discrimination' launched in Parliament in July 1958. The government, however, refused to take any action in regard to accommodation, hotels, pubs or clubs, which all operated a colour bar, or in regard to similar discrimination in the civil service or labour exchanges.[142]

There was bipartisan opposition to legislation against the colour bar, just as both governments had considered whether and how to introduce curbs on 'coloured' immigration. MPs from both major parties, such as George Rogers, the Labour MP for Notting Hill, openly supported immigration controls from the mid-1950s onwards and similar demands were made by the Transport and General Workers' Union at its biennial conference in 1955. Political parties and some trade unions viewed African and Caribbean migrants as a problem, a drain on the welfare state and housing, likely to exacerbate racism, and to become a threat to Britain's 'national way of life'. The difficulty for government was that migrant labour was still needed in some sectors of the economy. The problem was how to introduce immigration controls that did not appear to be openly racist and would not create problems in the emerging New Commonwealth, as well as in the context of the Cold War, wherein Britain and its allies presented themselves as the champions of democracy.[143] The press often presented extremely negative views of migrants, as well as proclaiming that Britain was a country where everyone had 'colour prejudice'.[144]

During the late 1950s, as the economy contracted and unemployment increased, there were increasing demands for immigration controls in Parliament and in the press. These mainstream demands encouraged the emergence and activities of the post-war fascist groups, many of which adopted the slogan 'Keep Britain White'. Despite still-recent memories of the war, during which leading fascists were imprisoned, such groups were not illegal and, on the question of immigration, publicly presented the same racist views that government ministers and officials endorsed behind closed doors.[145] Several such groups were active in the Notting Hill area of west London by 1958 and racist attacks in the area increased accordingly. Such attacks were evidently highly organized and a local magistrate, E. R. Guest, expressed surprise that the police either didn't prosecute the perpetrators or, if they did, would not impose conditions on their being given bail. The violent racist attacks increased to such an extent that a local newspaper, the *Kensington Post*, described them as 'a serious and growing problem', concerned residents organized a petition demanding action, while Guest called for remedies for a situation that was becoming 'extremely dangerous for ordinary citizens'.[146] However, no significant action was taken by the police or the government. The effect of such violence and the hostile environment in general on the 'ordinary citizens' can be judged from the testimonies of those who suffered as a consequence. 'I was threatened, frightened inside, but I know I must go to work,' confessed Tryphena Anderson, a nurse from Jamaica living in Nottingham at the time.[147]

The racist attacks that were launched in Nottingham and Notting Hill in August and September 1958 have gone down in history as some of the worst 'race riots' in Britain's history. The conditions for such attacks had long ago been created, and in London they certainly were fomented by the activities of fascist groups. Investigation into fascist activity also took place in Nottingham.[148] In both places the 'riots' were preceded by racist attacks and what the press openly referred to as 'n—— hunting'. Assaults on individuals began on 23 August 1958 in the St Ann's Well Road area of Nottingham, where a community of about 2,000 Caribbean people resided, and on the same night in Notting Hill. The Nottingham attack soon became a major disturbance with racist crowds, reportedly numbering over a thousand people strong, attacking Caribbean people throughout the St Ann's area.[149] One aspect of the violence was that those who were attacked fought back, and press reports emphasized that as a consequence 'eight Englishmen' had been hospitalized.[150] One Caribbean man used his car as a battering ram and later explained: 'It gave me satisfaction, at least we can fight back, you know, at least we fight back, and people will realise we're not prepared to sit and take this sort of thing any more. If they want to be nasty, we can be nasty too.'[151] In Notting Hill three Black men were hospitalized after being attacked by a racist gang of nine youths who were touring the area in a car. The week that followed the initial attacks was significant for the fact that two Nottingham MPs immediately called for immigration controls, one of whom was given the opportunity to air his views by the BBC. The press added inflammatory comments too, several papers speculating that more attacks would occur in Notting Hill and arguing that such 'race riots' necessitated immigration controls.[152]

On Saturday, 30 August large crowds gathered in St Ann's, as did the police, but few Black people ventured out. The only major disturbance occurred when some in the crowd turned upon others and the police.[153] Some racist attacks did occur in Notting Hill on that night, and BBC reporters witnessed Baron Baker and others being manhandled and arrested by the police even whilst they were being interviewed. Once again, the alleged impartiality of the police was much in question. Edward Scobie, one of the BBC reporters, later wrote, 'It would be no exaggeration to say that the attitude of the British police in the Notting Hill area during those days of riots and violence was unsympathetic and anti-black.'[154] On 1 September, Seymour Manning, described in the press as 'a young West African student' from Derby, was attacked and forced to barricade himself inside a shop before the police arrived.[155] Fascist groups openly encouraged such violence with inflammatory leaflets and street meetings. Violent attacks occurred throughout the area and involved larger crowds, including some sightseers.[156] Once again, Black people in the area defended themselves. According to Baron Baker (1925–1995) a former RAF police officer from Jamaica:

> We had to put our foot down. Our homes were being attacked and we weren't the ones going out in the street looking for trouble. It's only right that one should defend one's home, no matter who or where you are. We really *had* to fight back, which we did [emphasis in original text].

Frances Ezzreco, an activist who worked with women in the area, recalled,

> If someone comes to hit me, I'm going to hit back. If I can't hit back with my fists because they are bigger than me, I'll hit them with anything I can

lay my hands on and that's exactly what happened. We weren't prepared for that kind of fighting but when it came to it, we did it.[157]

Based in the Calypso Club, in Westbourne Park Road, those resisting planned a fightback and then deployed their forces, armed with petrol bombs, into two properties in Blenheim Crescent, one well known as a West Indian café. When the racists attacked, they were counter-attacked in several locations, sometimes with support from Caribbean reinforcements from other parts of London. The resistance was successful, even if some of those who defended themselves, such as Baker, were arrested by the police.[158]

The racist attacks and counter-attacks continued for some days in Notting Hill and also occurred in neighbouring areas, including Paddington and Shepherd's Bush. Press reports include accounts of arson and riot-torn streets, but time and again reports stressed that those who were attacked fought back. Although history has shown otherwise, sections of the press and some politicians expressed the view that such events, and the 'lynch-law madness' of the attackers, were unprecedented and that Britain was becoming more like the USA. The infamous segregationist and governor of Arkansas, Orval Faubus, expressed his sympathy for Nottingham.[159] Although the courts initially made an example of those who had carried out the attacks, they showed some leniency to the fascist agitators who had encouraged them, most often condemning violence and hooliganism while ignoring racism. Sections of the press and some politicians immediately argued that to end the 'colour problem' and avoid such violence, immigration must be controlled or ended. As one fascist leader pointed out at the time – 'The Daily Mirror is expressing our policy. Anyone who says restrict immigration and deport undesirables is repeating parrot-like what we said five years ago.'[160]

Although the Labour Party proposed anti-racist legislation, Rogers (the Labour MP for Notting Hill) sought to condone the racist attacks and to blame Black criminality, a view which endeared him to the local fascists. However, opposing views were expressed too, most notably those of Bishop Trevor Huddleston and the National Council for Civil Liberties (NCCL) which, as reported in The Times, condemned the violence and blamed the government and the courts for condoning the colour bar and refusing to take action against it. The NCCL called for churches and trade unions to take a stand against racism and demanded that the government should 'declare publicly that it is against racial discrimination, racial intolerance and racial violence'.[161] The TUC also condemned what it chose to call 'isolated outbreaks of vicious hooliganism' encouraged by fascist agitators 'fanning the flames of racial violence', but it did not go much further than urging 'further tolerance' of migrants.[162]

The government's public statement acknowledged that it was already 'examining' the existing rights of immigrants to enter Britain.[163] However, government ambition to take advantage of the situation (as a prelude to introducing immigration controls) were tempered by the need not to antagonize Commonwealth governments in what were soon to become newly independent countries in Africa and the Caribbean, where leading politicians had publicly opposed such controls. Several Caribbean governments sent delegations to investigate the attacks and visit the areas affected. The visit most featured in the press was that of Norman Manley, the Chief Minister of Jamaica, whose comments condemning both the violence and immigration controls were widely reported.[164] However, the government, emboldened by strong support for an anti-immigration resolution at the Conservative Party conference, urged the West Indies governments to control migration, continued to plan immigration controls and took no action to outlaw racism.[165] The inaction of the government (as well as the press coverage of racism and the colour bar), which all presented immigration and immigrants as a problem, undoubtedly gave succour to the racists and also led to some 4,500 of those who had migrated to Britain returning to the Caribbean in 1959. Still, most took a contrary view. As Baron Baker explained: 'I was determined to stay to the bitter or sweet end. For me it would have been a terrible blow, having come here to fight in the war, to have the natives kick us out. We were all prepared to challenge it, which we did.'[166]

THE *WEST INDIAN GAZETTE* AND CARNIVAL

The impact of the riots was significant. They were to pave the way for the 1962 Commonwealth Immigration Act, with its stringent restrictions on the entry of Commonwealth citizens into the UK, but they also created the conditions for a much greater unity between those from different Caribbean islands – the West Indians, and, to some extent, between West Indians and Africans too. As a consequence, several new organizations were established, or gained a higher profile: the Afro-West Indian Union (AWIU), in Nottingham, for example, or in London, Baker's United Africa-Asia League, Ashwood Garvey's Association for the Advancement of Coloured People (AACP), as well as the Coloured People's Progressive Association (CPPA) established by Ezzreco who, after being attacked herself, had determined 'we must organize our people against these attacks'.[167] The word 'coloured' became increasingly established as the preferred term for all those who had formerly often been termed 'colonials'. The CPPA soon claimed to be one of the largest of those organizations. It was based in the Notting Hill area, had a membership of over 500 and organized against the colour bar, police harassment, unemployment, poor housing and for the rights of 'coloured' people.[168] One significant attempt to foster unity between the CPPA, WISU and similar organizations was the founding of the Standing Conference of West Indian Organizations in 1958. Another 'Standing Conference' was established in both London and Birmingham by all the high commissions of what was then the Federation of the West Indies.[169] Another significant development was the launch in April 1958 of the *West Indian Gazette and Afro-Asian-Caribbean News*, edited by Claudia Jones.[170]

Originally from Trinidad, Jones had grown up in the United States, where she had become a leading member of the Communist Party. During the 1950s, like many of her comrades, she had been imprisoned under the anti-communist legislation of the time and deported to Britain at the end of 1955. Once in London, she became an activist for the Communist Party of Great Britain, was a member of its 'West Indies Committee', alongside Billy Strachan and Trevor Carter, and also secretary of Ashwood Garvey's AACP. In many ways the *Gazette* built on the work of the CLC's *Caribbean News*. Starting as a 'one-leaf flyer', it gained a reported readership of 15,000, in some places, appearing on news-stands. It was run on a voluntary basis by Jones and others, including Sam King, from its base in two rooms above a record shop at 250 Brixton Road in south London.[171] Just before her death Jones reflected that it had served:

> as a catalyst, quickening the awareness, socially and politically, of West Indians, Afro-Asians and their friends. Its editorial stand is for a united, independent West Indies, full economic, social and political equality and respect for human dignity for West Indians and Afro-Asians in Britain, and for peace and friendship between all Commonwealth and world peoples. It has campaigned vigorously on issues facing West Indians and other coloured peoples. Whether against numerous police frame-ups, to which West Indians and other coloured migrants are frequently subject, to opposing discrimination and to advocating support for trade unionism and unity of coloured and white workers.[172]

It was Jones who proposed that a Caribbean carnival should be organized.[173] Her aim was to encourage pride and unity amongst those of Caribbean origin and to build unity amongst 'other people of colour', as well as 'friendship for all peoples', in response to the racist violence of Notting Hill and Nottingham. Jones wrote at the time in 'A people's art is the genesis of their freedom' that 'our multi-racial culture should be the fount, helping the universal quest to turn the instruments of science everywhere for the good of all mankind, for the freedom of all the world's peoples, no matter what the colour of their skin, for human dignity and friendship of all peoples everywhere'.[174]

Jones and those associated with the *Gazette* began organizing such an event in November 1958 via a Carnival committee whose members included Nadia Cattouse, June Baden-Semper and Pearl Connor-Mogotsi (1924–2005), a Trinidadian-born theatrical and literary agent, actress and cultural activist. The first Carnival was held in St Pancras Town Hall on 30 January 1959 and included performances from Cleo Laine, the Southlanders, Pearl Connor-Mogotsi, Corrine Skinner-Carter, the Mighty Terror and Pearl Prescod.[175] The event was filmed by the BBC, although the recording has apparently been lost. The brochure for the event announced that part of the proceeds 'are to assist the payment of fines of coloured and white youths involved in the Notting Hill events'. This legal fund was also supported by other organizations, such as the AACP, the WISU and the Committee of African Organisations (CAO).[176] In her comments at the time Jones declared the intention of making 'the *West Indian Gazette* Caribbean Carnival an annual event'.[177] For as long as Jones was alive the Carnival was held annually, and always indoors, in London and also in Manchester, and featured steel pans, leading calypsonians such as Lord Kitchener and the Mighty Sparrow, as well as other singers, musicians and performers, including Africans such as Ambrose Campbell (1919–2006), the Nigerian singer, guitarist and founder of the West African Rhythm Boys band. The Carnival held beauty queen contests, to encourage the view that 'Black [wa]s beautiful' in Britain too.[178]

Despite such important developments after the attacks in Notting Hill, the fascists were allowed to continue operating in the area and Oswald Mosley, the leader of the former British Union of Fascists and at this time, the Unity Movement, even stood for election as an MP for Kensington North in the autumn of 1959, but failed to win sufficient votes. Nonetheless, racism was ever present, and manifested itself in tragic circumstances on 17 May 1959, with the murder on the streets of Notting Hill of Kelso Cochrane, a 32-year-old carpenter originally from Antigua.[179] Cochrane, who had only arrived in Britain in 1954, with an ambition to study law, was attacked by six white men in Goulbourne Road. He was fatally stabbed in the chest and died in hospital soon afterwards. Nobody was ever arrested for this crime, which the police denied was a racist attack.[180] Rab Butler, the Home Secretary, who spoke of the murder in Parliament without the courtesy of naming Cochrane, announced that he was not eager to introduce any legislation to combat racism in its wake.[181] Nevertheless, the murder created a sense of public outrage and was widely reported in the press, both in Britain and internationally.[182] The 'riots' and the murder created conditions for the Black communities to be increasingly viewed as either a political problem, or a social problem, and sometimes both. They also led to new efforts to defend themselves from those facing racist attacks.

THE COMMITTEE OF AFRICAN ORGANIZATIONS

After Cochrane's murder, a defence committee for 'the immediate protection' of African and Caribbean people was soon convened by a Nigerian, Alao Aka-Bashorun (1930–2005), Chairman of the Committee of African Organizations (CAO) and also Chairman of the CPPA. The committee, soon known as the Inter-Racial Friendship Co-ordinating Council (IRFCC) demanded 'adequate, unbiased police protection', or African and Caribbean special constables, or failing both, 'full permission to organize our own defence'.[183] The IRFCC included representatives of some twelve organizations, including the *West Indian Gazette,* AACP, the AWIU, the WISU and the Ugandan Association and was established following a meeting held at the CAO headquarters in Gower Street, Bloomsbury. The meeting expressed the view that 'coloured citizens of the UK have lost confidence in the ability of the law-enforcing agencies to protect them', and demanded that the government pass a law making the incitement to racist violence illegal. Although the CAO announced that it rejected 'any suggestion for setting up so-called "defence squads" to protect coloured people', the IRFCC did call for the establishment of 'citizen's committees', in order to protect the 'life and property of coloured residents'.[184]

It was Aka-Bashorun who was the main spokesperson and moving force on this issue and he who signed a letter of protest on behalf of the CAO, AACP, *West Indian Gazette* and '200,000 African, West Indian and other coloured people in the UK', which was sent to the Prime Minister.[185] The letter condemned the racist violence in Nottingham and Notting Hill and expressed the view that Cochrane had been murdered in a racist attack. It concluded by asking the government '[A]re we to be mauled down just because we are black?'[186] It was Aka-Bashorun who called for a 'mammoth demonstration and a memorial march' in protest at Kelso Cochrane's murder, a demand that appears to have been rejected by the authorities, as it was the CAO that convened a memorial meeting for Cochrane at St Pancras Town Hall on 28 May 1959.[187] An IRFCC deputation, including Aka-Bashorun, David Pitt and Claudia Jones, also met with officials at the Home Office at the end of May 1959, to reiterate the demands for action against racist propaganda and to call for new legislation to prevent incitement to racism, as well as racial discrimination.[188] These demands were seen by the council as a clear consequence of 'inactivity by the authorities in the face of organized attempts to stir up racial hatred by fascist groups'.[189]

The IRFCC was formally chaired by Ashwood Garvey and its other leaders included Jones, Ezzreco, John Eber of the Movement for Colonial Freedom (MCF), Connor-Mogotsi and Aka-Bashorun. The council called for 'respect for human rights and fundamental freedoms for ALL without distinctions as to race, colour, sex, language or religion', and was established to work with other organizations 'to oppose all forms of discrimination'.[190] On 1 June 1959 the IRFCC and CPPA held a twelve-hour vigil in Downing Street, with protesters carrying placards with a picture of Kelso Cochrane, condemning the murder and opposing racism.[191] It was the IRFCC that organized and financed Kelso Cochrane's funeral. This became a major public and political event, with thousands lining the streets and accompanying the coffin to Kensal Green Cemetery.[192] The murder made a significant impact on many within the area and further afield and the funeral was attended by Grantley Adams, the Prime Minister of the West Indies Federation. Protest and memorial meetings such as the 'We Mourn Cochrane' event organized by the IRFCC were attended by other leading politicians from the Caribbean, such as Norman Manley and Carl La Corbiniere, Deputy Prime Minister of the West Indies Federation, as well as those in Britain including David Pitt, Fenner Brockway MP, Bishop Trevor Huddlestone, Eslanda Robeson and representatives of all three major political parties.[193]

The CAO, inspired by events in newly independent Ghana, had been formed in early 1958 as a union of African organizations in Britain. It was a Pan-African organization dedicated to 'furthering the struggle against colonialism and imperialism', and to 'assist the struggles of our people for freedom, liberty, equality and national independence'.[194] The CAO grew out of the activities of the WASU and protests concerning the imposition of a colonial Central African Federation on the peoples of Nyasaland, Southern Rhodesia and Northern Rhodesia. Its other founder members included the Nigeria Union, the Kenya Students' Association, the Tanganyika Students' Association, the East and Central African Study Circle, as well the Uganda National Congress and the Uganda Association. Aka-Bashorun, a former law student at the London School of Economics and the CAO's first chairman, was President of both the WASU and the Nigerian Union. Denis Phombeah from Tanganyika also played a leading role and later became the CAO's general secretary.

The CAO developed rapidly and within a few years its membership encompassed over twenty affiliated African organizations, including the Revolutionary Front for the National Independence of Portuguese Colonies and the African National Congress. It was very much an organization connected with the anti-colonial struggles then at their height on the African continent in Kenya, Nyasaland and Southern Rhodesia, and from 1961 onwards, produced its own publication, *United Africa*. It often worked closely with the Movement for Colonial Freedom founded by Fenner Brockway and others in 1954, as well as various Labour Party politicians. The CAO also collaborated with African organizations in Europe and in 1962 established the Union of African Students in Europe to 'unify all African students' organizations in Europe', and 'to act in a common front to fight against Imperialism, Colonialism and Neo-Colonialism'. The union represented students from Britain, Czechoslovakia, France, Holland, the GDR, Hungary, Bulgaria, Poland and the USSR.[195]

The CAO became the centre of African political activity in Britain and, starting in 1959, organized annual African Freedom Day celebrations, the first including a concert performance from Paul Robeson. It organized some of the first national protests against nuclear armament with the Direct Action Committee against Nuclear Weapons. On 26 June 1959, shortly after Cochrane's funeral and in response to calls from the ANC, the CAO initiated a boycott of South African goods on 'South African Freedom Day' via its Boycott Sub-Committee (which included Jones amongst its members), a body that soon developed into the Anti-Apartheid Movement. Many of the CAO's activities and meetings were attacked by fascist organizations, culminating in an arson attack on its Gower Street offices in 1960.[196]

In 1961 the CAO opened its new 'permanent headquarters' following a grant of funds from Kwame Nkrumah's government in Ghana. Africa Unity House stood at 3 Collingham Gardens in Earl's Court, near the neighbouring West Indian Cultural Centre. At the official opening in 1961 Nkrumah stated, 'this House will provide a centre for concentration on the work of African Unity by African students and workers resident in this country'.[197] Africa Unity House soon became an important political centre in London and a meeting place and head-quarters for several different organizations, including the Africa League and Jones' Committee of Afro-Asian Caribbean Organizations (CAACO) formed in 1963. In 1965 the President of the CAO could state with confidence, 'our centre ... is now a centre of activity for all anti-imperialist organizations'.[198]

THE 1962 COMMONWEALTH IMMIGRATION ACT

In April 1962 the new Commonwealth Immigration Act was intro-duced. It limited migration from the 'New Commonwealth', in an openly racist manner for the first time, at the very moment when racism was coming under sustained attack internationally, particularly at the United Nations. As the government admitted, 'the Bill itself applied to all Commonwealth citizens, irrespective of colour; but it would be evident in its operation that the control was being applied in practice only to coloured people'.[199] It was, in the words of Jones, 'a colour-bar bill to restrict the immigration of coloured citizens ... an official colour bar against the coloured and the poor'. She went much further, arguing that the worst feature of the act 'is the green light to the perpetuation, stimulus and encouragement to racialism, that it gives to racialism in theory and practice; to the fascists and "lunatic fringe" and the advocates of apartheid everywhere'. She concluded that the legislation was 'just the old divide and rule tactic to divert the people from the real issues confronting them'.[200]

The act was the culmination of efforts by successive governments since the 1940s to curb immigration, if it appeared to outstrip the labour needs of the economy, and was particularly directed at migrants from the Caribbean. Migration from Africa was about a quarter of the amount of that from the Caribbean in this period, and that from India and Pakistan was only about half the amount.[201] As a result of

Claudia Jones (with handbag) at the head of a demonstration
against the 1962 Commonwealth Immigration Act

this legislation, only those who already had employment, or who had
economically useful skills and professions, would gain rights of residence and citizenship. The act also gave magistrates and the
government power to deport those found guilty of offences punishable by imprisonment. Even some Conservative MPs were concerned
about this legislation and the impact it would have on the country, as
well as on Britain's relations with the Commonwealth.[202]

Opposition to the legislation came from organizations such as the
Communist Party, the MCF, the governments of several Commonwealth countries, including Nigeria and the West Indies Federation
and the Afro-Asian-Caribbean Conference (AACC), established in
early 1962 by Jones, Pitt, and Connor-Mogotsi. The AACC included
the WISU, the CAO, the Indian Workers' Association and many
others. In February 1962 the AACC called on 'thousands of Afro-
Asian-Caribbean citizens', and specifically 'nurses and medical staff
from hospitals in their uniforms, bus train and transport personnel,
factory, canteen and municipal workers in overall and uniforms' to
join in a mass protest against Parliament.[203] In Birmingham, the

Co-ordinating Committee against Racial Discrimination, formed in February 1961, organized the protest not only amongst the African and Caribbean population, but also those from India, Pakistan and all British people who were opposed to a law designed to 'discriminate on racial grounds' and to excite 'racialist and Fascist feelings'.[204]

At the time the Labour Party also voiced opposition to the act and promised to repeal the legislation, but when it returned to office in 1964 the Labour government introduced a new Commonwealth Immigration Act which restricted immigration still further. The basis for such legislation was the view that immigration from certain countries in Africa, the Caribbean and Asia was inherently problematic and needed to be limited, but maintained at a level to suit the needs of Britain's economy.[205] The legislation gave state sanction to such racist views, provided the state with powers to discriminate against and even deport some citizens, and thereby effectively established first- and second-class citizenship.

Jones condemned the Immigration Act in the pages of the *West Indian Gazette* and participated in several protest meetings and demonstrations against it, along with the MCF, the National Council for Civil Liberties, the London branch of the Trinidad People's National Movement and other organizations. She referred to the Immigration Act as 'iniquitous colour-bar legislation', that 'reflected the fear of unity of coloured and white workers and people. It aimed at spreading racialist divisions.' Furthermore, she argued the 'legislation knocks down the very foundation of the Commonwealth, the majority of whose citizens are coloured'. She concluded, 'pandering to vicious racist elements, the Government, through this bill, is throwing the doors wide open to Fascism, against whom [sic] the people of the Commonwealth fought shoulder to shoulder in last World War'. The fascists, including Mosley's Union Movement, openly supported the legislation and attacked those who opposed it.[206]

One immediate consequence of the passing of the act was that it was used to order deportations. In June 1962, Carmen Bryan, a 22-year-old woman of Jamaican heritage, who had been living in Britain since 1960, was found guilty of shoplifting, conditionally discharged by Paddington Magistrates Court, but then detained in Holloway Prison to await deportation. Her case created something of a

parliamentary uproar and, as a result, after six weeks of imprisonment, the deportation order was rescinded by the Home Secretary.
Not surprisingly, Bryan later decided to return to Jamaica.[207]

THE BRISTOL BUS BOYCOTT

Opposition to the Commonwealth Immigration Act, including
attempts to repeal it, as well as protests against other forms of racism
continued throughout the 1960s, not least because racism was still
legal. In 1962 Brockway had again tried, unsuccessfully, to introduce
a bill in Parliament to outlaw racial discrimination. Although his bill
gained increased support, it was defeated in the House of Lords.
Sometimes anti-racism protest was led by organizations such as the
CAACO also acted in support of the civil rights movement in
the United States and other international struggles against racist
oppression.[208]

By this time most migrants had become settlers and a new consciousness was developing, reflecting the fact that Britain was now
becoming 'home'. Such changes were perhaps seen in the further
development of a 'Black press'. In addition to the *West Indian Gazette*
several other publications emerged in the 1960s, including *Link*,
Carib, *Anglo-Caribbean News*, *Cinnamon*, *Sepia* and the *West Indies
Observer*. Some of these publications and others too, such as *Daylight
International*, published in 1963, and *Magnet*, published by Jan Carew
in 1965, lasted only a few months.[209] Edward Scobie, the Dominican-
born journalist and historian who had served in the RAF during the
war, published five issues of *Chequers*, 'Britain's premier Negro magazine', in London from 1948 to 1949. In 1960 he was involved with
the short-lived magazine *Tropic*. From 1961 until 1965 he edited a
new monthly magazine, *Flamingo*, to provide a 'Voice' for 'the 'Negro
citizens of Britain', and to combat the 'prejudiced and harmful view'
that was presented about them elsewhere. *Flamingo* had a significant
impact and sold 20,000 copies in Britain, another 15,000 in the US,
and was distributed there too. It contained a mixture of glamor-
ous young women, music and politics, even carrying an interview
with Malcolm X. Years later it was alleged that *Flamingo* had been

established by MI6 as part of its Cold War anti-communist activities specifically aimed at Britain's African and Caribbean population.[210] Nevertheless, *Flamingo* too campaigned against the Commonwealth Immigration Act, employing the British Market Research Bureau to carry out a survey amongst Caribbean migrants to give their opinions of it, which was referred to in Parliament.[211] Reflecting some years later on this era, Scobie appeared unscathed by any machinations of MI6 when he wrote:

> From the very beginning the only party in Britain which opposed the system of 'quotas' and 'controls' for Commonwealth immigration was the British Communist Party. In 1964 the executive committee of this party issued a statement declaring its opposition to all forms of restrictions on black immigration; declared its readiness to contest every case of discrimination; urged the repeal of the Commonwealth Immigrants Act; and called for equality of opportunity for employment, rates of wages, promotion to skilled jobs, and more openings for apprenticeship and vocational training. The British Communists came out openly on the side of black people and challenged and fought all forms of racial prejudice that cropped up.[212]

At other times opposition to racism involved the heroic stand of individuals such as Paul Stephenson, Roy Hackett, Owen Henry, Audley Evans, Peter Carty, Prince Brown and other leaders of the Bristol Bus Boycott of 1963. At that time the Bristol Omnibus Company maintained a colour bar and refused to employ any non-white bus crews. Hackett and the others were young migrants from the Caribbean who had settled in Bristol in the late 1950s, as part of a community of fewer than a few thousand of mainly Caribbean and some African people, about one per cent of the city's population, although this population had increased to some 7,000 by the early 1960s. Like many migrants at the time, they found it very difficult to get accommodation and were often forced to share rooms in the St Paul's area, at that time one of the most rundown parts of Bristol. They also found that a colour bar existed in pubs, clubs and in employment, even in churches, and so many migrants found security and support by living close to each other. Owen Henry was also one of the first to establish a sound system to play at social events in Bristol. The Africans and Caribbeans began to develop organizations too, such as the West Indian Organization formed in the late 1950s, to campaign against the colour bar.[213]

The Bristol Omnibus Company did employ some Black Bristolians, although not as bus crew, allegedly because of trade-union opposition (although it was clear that many union members, especially those who were 'Christians or Communists', opposed such racism).[214] The Transport and General Workers Union (TGWU) also officially opposed a colour bar yet those Bristolians of Caribbean, African or Asian origin were refused employment even though there was a shortage of bus crews. As in many other cases, this shortage led to overtime pay for Bristol's low-paid bus workers which comprised a significant part of their wages. It seems that fears of an influx of workers ending such overtime pay played at least some part in the support for a colour bar among workers. When Hackett, Henry and others (who were to form the West Indian Development Council (WIDC)), demanded that Bristol City Council abolish the colour bar they were initially rebuffed. They then met Paul Stephenson, Bristol's first Black youth worker, who had recently moved to the city. Stephenson was of West African heritage. He soon became the spokesman for the WIDC, and 'inspired by Rosa Parks and Martin Luther King' during the civil rights movement in the US, he initiated the idea of a bus boycott.

Stephenson arranged a job interview for Guy Bailey, a young and well-qualified Jamaican. When the Omnibus Company refused him even an interview, Stephenson confronted the company and announced the boycott. The boycott initially faced opposition from the council, trade-union officials and the local West Indian Association, which claimed that it might undermine 'racial harmony', but Stephenson and the WIDC gained support from the two local MPs, and from the high commissions of Jamaica and Trinidad. The WIDC also engaged with the local press to expose the racist justifications of the company, which included the view that 'the labour supply gets worse if the labour force is mixed'.[215] Soon the national press and TV stations were reporting on the situation in Bristol, as was the *Jamaican Gleaner*, especially when the Sir Learie Constantine, the High Commissioner for Trinidad, demonstrated his support for the boycott. Local university students also demonstrated in opposition to the colour bar and the indefensible position of the Omnibus Company was condemned by Labour Party leaders. Nevertheless, some Bristol transport workers still refused to work with 'coloureds', and the inaction of the TGWU and Bristol Council was exposed for the world to witness.[216] In the context of the times Bristol was being compared with racist Alabama and South Africa.

The WIDC and its supporters organized marches and meetings. Stephenson was attacked in the press, opposed by local church leaders and libelled by one of the TGWU's local leaders. He sued and won, becoming one of the first Black people to win such a legal case.[217] Such was the national prominence of the threatened boycott that the Omnibus Company and the TGWU were forced to engage in negotiations. After six months of the campaign, on 28 August 1963, the company announced that agreement had been reached on 'the employment of suitable coloured workers as bus crews'. However, two years after the dispute, 'coloured workers' only made up 2.5 per cent of Bristol's bus crews.[218] Still, the Bristol Bus Boycott has become a historic moment which occurred at the same time as the employment of the first Caribbean traffic warden in London, one of two 'coloured' women wardens. Stephenson continued his activities in Bristol and, the following year, he was arrested for refusing to leave a public house that operated a colour bar. The arrest, and subsequent court case, in which the magistrate criticized the police, also made national news and showed how ubiquitous the colour bar still was.[219]

THE CAMPAIGN AGAINST RACIAL DISCRIMINATION

One significant attempt to develop sustained opposition to the racism then in existence was the founding of the Campaign Against Racial Discrimination (CARD) in December 1964.[220] The key figure was Marion Glean, a Trinidadian, who had founded an organization called Multi-Racial Britain and been alarmed at the lack of concern about racism shown by the major political parties during the general election in 1964. This election has now become infamous for the racist political campaign associated with the Conservative Party candidate in Smethwick, which included the slogan 'If You Want a N—— for a Neighbour,

Vote for Labour'. Glean joined others, including C. L. R. James, the Jamaican writer Andrew Salkey and the Kenyan writer Ngumbu Njururi in expressing her view in the pages of *Peace News*. She asserted that 'all major parties agree on a colour-bar in Britain', and concluded: 'It is time that we coloured people of Britain stop this nauseating begging for crumbs ... We have the right to share in the prosperity the three centuries of our labour has helped to build. We have the right to be ordinary citizens of Britain.'[221] Using the occasion of Martin Luther King's visit to Britain in December 1964, Glean arranged for him to meet key members of African, Caribbean and Asian organizations in Britain, including the CAO, the WISU, and the Standing Conference of West Indian Organizations, as well as key individuals such as Pitt and Jones. King called on the 'coloured population' of Britain 'to organize through meaningful non-violent direct-action approaches' to bring the issue of racism 'to the forefront of the conscience of the nation'.[222] Following this meeting, several individuals and organizations continued to meet, and on 10 January 1965 established the CARD. The organization was initially led by Glean and Pitt, who had emerged as a key figure during this period. In 1959 he had unsuccessfully stood as the Labour Party candidate for the parliamentary seat of Hampstead and two years later became the first Caribbean-born member of the London County Council representing Hackney.[223] Other leading members included Richard Small, a law student from Jamaica, as well as those of Indian and English origin.

The CARD was established to 'struggle for the elimination of all racial discrimination against coloured people in the United Kingdom', and to 'oppose all legislation that is racially discriminatory or that is inspired by racial prejudice, for example, the Commonwealth Immigration Act of 1962'. However, although CARD was in touch with the major African and Caribbean organizations such as the CAO, represented by its former president Kojo Amoo-Gottfried, and the Standing Conference of West Indian Organizations, represented by its vice-chairman Frances Ezzreco, it was often out of touch with the communities it was meant to represent and riven by disputes. Nevertheless, it was significant as an organization with a national profile, with local affiliated groups throughout England and Scotland.[224] The CARD did, however, have some influence on one major new law initiated by the Labour government, the Race Relations Act introduced in 1965 (as a prologue to the passing of a new and even more restrictive Immigration Act in 1968). The Labour government's position was encapsulated in the words of a new MP for Birmingham, Roy Hattersley, 'without integration, limitation is inexcusable; without limitation, integration is impossible'.[225]

The Race Relations Act was introduced alongside a Race Relations Board to investigate and mediate the problem of racism in Britain, the latter a proposal championed by the CARD. The act outlawed incitement to 'race hatred' and 'discrimination in public places'. Although these developments are credited for finally recognizing that racism was a problem in society, the notion of 'race relations', an idea borrowed mainly from the US and South Africa, was based on the racist premise that distinct 'races' existed in the world and that the problem in society was that these 'races' could not coexist harmoniously, whether in Britain, or in the empire. Such views were strongly represented amongst social scientists, social workers and within the Institute of Race Relations, established in London in 1958, and gave rise to the call for improved 'community relations', as well as demands for the 'integration' and even 'assimilation' of migrants.[226] However, in the seeming desire for better 'race relations', the sources of racism – colonialism, inequality in society, the actions of governments and the state, such as immigration laws, the actions of the police and judiciary, the education system and the media, as well as the activities of the fascists – were ignored. It was governments, politicians and the media which provoked erroneous fears that immigration led to a deterioration in the general provision of employment, housing, education, health care and welfare payments, the very areas where discrimination was often most acute. Moreover, the 1965 act did not apply to racism in specific areas: housing, employment, policing, or education.

The CARD joined critics of the Race Relations Bill introduced in April 1965. It had the ear of Labour Party leaders and its proposal for the creation of a conciliatory body was eventually adopted in a diluted form, although demands for an extension of the bill to cover employment and housing were not. The act was certainly not a 'victory' for CARD, as claimed in the press, much less a victory for the overall struggle against racism. Pitt referred to the act as 'a sop and not a serious measure', and a ploy to divert attention from the 'reactionary measures' enshrined in the 1968 Immigration Act that followed, which the CARD also opposed.[227] However, Pitt's proximity to the Labour Party and the fact that members of that party joined the government-appointed National Council for Commonwealth Immigrants, led to dissension within CARD and in particular to criticism by the WISC, which began to demand a new form of organization.

In response to racist legislation on immigration and policing, government proposals for segregation in education and threats from white supremacist organizations, the WISC and others increasingly turned their backs on 'integration' and CARD and, alongside other Asian and African organizations, demanded both the right to an existence on their own terms, as well as the right of self-defence. Many of these views were enshrined in publications by prominent WISC members, such as Neville Maxwell, whose *The Power of Negro Action* came out in 1965, and Joseph Hunte, author of the pamphlet *Nigger Hunting in England?* which appeared the following year. Hunte's pamphlet highlighted what he considered the discriminatory behaviour of the police towards Caribbean migrants, mainly in Lambeth, some of which he had personally witnessed. He included the allegation that the police engaged in deliberate efforts to harass, attack and arrest West Indians.[228] Similar complaints were also made by the CARD and by others, including the National Council for Civil Liberties.[229] The most notorious case during this period was the harassment and death of David Oluwale in Leeds, whom we met at the start of this chapter. As you may remember, Oluwale had arrived from Nigeria as a stowaway in 1949, and worked for a time, but then, from 1953 onwards, he spent much of the 1950s and 1960s in and out of psychiatric hospitals, where he was diagnosed as a schizophrenic, or in prison, squatting, or homeless on the streets of Leeds. It was there that he was hounded, racially abused and violently attacked by several Leeds police officers for many months until a final attack by two senior officers led directly to his death in April 1969. Although the police were found guilty of assaulting Oluwale on numerous occasions in 1971, nobody was ever convicted for his death. Nevertheless, the case represents the first and, also, the last time state officials were successfully prosecuted for involvement in the death of a black person.[230]

The experiences of African and Caribbean people in Britain had led many to reject both the notion of 'integration' and the belief that government could defend their interests. A new tone could be heard in the pronouncements in 1967 of one of the CARD's emerging leaders, Johnny James. James, originally from Guyana, had been expelled from the Communist Party of Great Britain for criticizing its adoption of a 'parliamentary road' to socialism. He was also one of the founders of the Caribbean Workers Movement, which engaged in 'anti-colonial, anti-imperialist and anti-fascist activities', and linked the struggle against racism in Britain with the struggles of oppressed people all over the world.[231] These were not dissimilar to the sentiments embraced by Jones, or that were evident at the Manchester Pan-African Congress in 1945. In the mid-1960s James and many others were also inspired by developments in the People's Republic of China and expressed a militancy that heralded the dawning of a new era and its popular slogan of 'Black Power'.

10

Black Liberation

The mid-1960s saw the emergence of significant new political organizations amongst those of African and Caribbean heritage. These reflected global political developments and the new politics of Black Power, a form of Pan-Africanism that has been described as 'a movement for racial solidarity, cultural pride and self-determination'.[1] At the same time, there was an upsurge in the struggles waged against state and other forms of racism in Britain. Often the changes that took place during this period are presented as being initiated by visitors from the United States, especially Malcolm X and Stokely Carmichael (later known as Kwame Ture), without considering the circumstances in which they were invited, nor those who extended the invitations. Many of the organizations and individuals involved had long been politically active in London, Birmingham, Manchester and elsewhere.[2] Although there is no doubt that many of the organizations that emerged during the 1960s and 1970s were influenced by ideas and personalities from the US, they were also inspired by political developments in Africa and the Caribbean. Moreover, they emerged from the struggles of those in Britain who were seeking ways to combat racism and Eurocentrism and to develop the ways and means of empowering themselves. In these struggles, Africans and Caribbeans drew on their own experience and often on political ideas that pre-dated the 1960s.

One of the most significant and most enduring of these organizations, formed in Birmingham in August 1964, was the Afro-Caribbean Self-Help Organization, later renamed the African Caribbean Self-Help Organization (ACSHO). Based at its well-known headquarters at 104 Heathfield Road, it has remained in existence well into the third decade of the twenty-first century and is probably the longest surviving Pan-African organization in Britain's history. The ACSHO was founded by several young people, including Gregory Moon and Aston Walker, who later left Britain, but is most often associated with another of its founders, Bini Brown, sometimes known as Bini But-waka, who arrived in Britain from Jamaica as an eleven-year-old at the beginning of the decade.[3]

The ACSHO emerged out of a youth organization, the Afro-West Indian Study Circle, which Brown joined when he was just fourteen years old. At the same age he was encouraged to read *The Philosophy and Opinions of Marcus Garvey*, and Garvey's principles of self-help and self-reliance, pride in African heritage, history and culture, were a major influence on the ACSHO. As Bini Brown expressed it, ACSHO's politics is based on the 'African philosophy and ideology of the right honourable Marcus Mosiah Garvey . . . we are basically a Black Nation-alist organization'.[4] This politics sets the ACSHO apart from several other organizations that emerged during the 1960s, because it uses the term 'Black' only to refer to those of African heritage, and it maintained a Pan-African orientation throughout. The study circle, too, was inspired by Garveyite principles and established with the help of com-munity elders who were also 'staunch Garveyites', rather than just as a reaction to racism. These elders taught the principles of Garveyism 'to be proud of self, to be proud of your African-ness, to be proud of your black skin, proud of your hair'. Nevertheless, from the earliest days both these organizations were concerned to 'fight the oppression of African people and the police brutality'. The ACSHO placed a great emphasis on self-defence and, as Brown explained, even in confrontations with the police it was known 'that they couldn't mess with us because we could handle ourselves'. The ACSHO also had a clear principle that it would be self-reliant and take no funding from the state.[5]

From its inception the ACSHO engaged in the study of politics and economics to better understand 'who controls what'. By 1965 it was in contact with many of the existing national liberation organizations in Africa, such as FRELIMO, MPLA, PAIGC, SWAPO and the ANC. It invited speakers and raised funds, but never seems to have been influenced by the socialist orientation adopted by many of these organizations. It was also in close contact with organizations in the Caribbean and the United States and favoured those that shared its

'Black Nationalist' perspective. It was, for example, in contact with Maulana Karenga in the US, and it claimed to have first introduced his Kwanzaa celebration to Britain as early as 1972. The ACSHO also claimed to have established the first supplementary school in the country in 1967 and then to have 'spread it country wide'. The ACSHO produced their own publications, including *Harambee* and *The African*, and established many of the key ideas and organizing principles that would be adopted by other black political organizations during the 1960s and 1970s. However, it rejected the socialist leanings that many would later adopt and retained its Black Nationalist perspective, remaining reluctant to organize jointly with those not of African or Caribbean heritage. Others would take a different view and a tension often existed between, and even within, organizations on this key question.

MALCOLM X

Nineteen-sixty-four was also the year that Malcolm X first visited Britain, most notably in December, when he spoke at the Oxford Union, but also in Manchester, Sheffield and London.[6] He returned again in February 1965 to address the first congress of the Committee of African Organizations (CAO) and to speak at the LSE. It was during the latter visit that he met Michael de Freitas (later known as Michael X, 1933–1975), formerly a member of the Coloured People's Progressive Association, a self-confessed pimp and close associate of the notorious property developer and landlord Peter Rachman. It was in 1965 that Malcolm X also made his famous visit to Smethwick, where the local council was buying up property in Marshall Street, 'in order to prevent it becoming a coloured ghetto'. It was there that he was filmed by the BBC and he urged, 'Coloured people must organize themselves'. His visit was strongly condemned by the Mayor of Smethwick, by the local Conservative MP (elected as a result of an infamous racist election campaign in 1964), and even by the local representative of the West Indian Standing Conference (WISC), who was reported as saying, 'The West Indians are not the sort of people who would want to follow Malcolm X.'[7] According to de Freitas, Malcolm

X planned to organize a chapter of his Organization of Afro-American Unity in London but, less than two weeks after he left, he was assassinated in New York.[8]

The fact that Malcolm X was invited and hosted by the CAO tells us something about it and the changing political consciousness at the time. Indeed, the CAO first made contact with Malcolm X during his earlier visits in 1964. The main theme of its congress – 'Charting the path of African Revolution means attacking imperialism, neo-colonialism. Oppressed mankind, organize to achieve unity,' was clearly one which found favour with Malcom X, who spoke alongside the Algerian ambassador, the well-known British historian Basil Davidson, and Mazisi Kunene, who represented the African National Congress (ANC).[9] Malcolm X was also hosted by the Indian Workers' Association and clearly impressed de Freitas, who immediately adopted the name Michael X.[10] There was a general air of militancy produced by the experiences of African, Caribbean and Asian people in Britain. They were also inspired by the struggles against racism in the US and South Africa, as well as by the struggles for liberation throughout Africa and in places like Cuba and Vietnam, which began to be referred to collectively as the Third World. It was an atmosphere that in February 1965 produced a new weekly Black newspaper, *Magnet*, edited by Jan Carew, a Guyanese writer temporarily residing in London, who also met with Malcolm X. One of the directors of this new publication was the famous Guyanese conductor, Rudolph Dunbar.[11]

The newly renamed Michael X and Jan Carew, together with Roy Sawh, a Guyanese accountant living in London who had previously sold the *West Indian Gazette*, and Abdullah Patel, an Indian Muslim worker at the Courtaulds Red Scar Mill in Preston, established the ironically named Racial Adjustment Action Society (RAAS) in 1965.[12] Michael X suggested that the RAAS was 'a child of the 1958 race riots' in London and Nottingham, perhaps highlighting the fact that what became known as the movement for Black Power in Britain grew out of the struggles of those of African and Caribbean heritage against racism, as well as out of a dissatisfaction with existing organizations, such as the Campaign against Racial Discrimination (CARD).[13] The anti-colonial and anti-racist struggles in Britain, as well as the international situation, created the conditions for many younger people to embrace new forms of Pan-Africanism, as well as a new militancy that was influenced by the struggles for Black liberation in the United States and elsewhere. Increasingly they sought alternatives to a society that many considered had totally rejected them.

In May 1965 the RAAS immediately became involved in what was to become a notable strike at Courtaulds Mill in Preston, one of the first to involve a workforce of recent migrants, mostly Indians and Pakistanis, but including more than a hundred from the Caribbean too.[14] The strike concerned a productivity deal concluded by the local union representative behind the backs of the workers in one section of the factory. Sawh and Michael X made numerous statements on behalf of the RAAS that were widely reported in the press, asserting the need for 'immigrants' to become union officials, and attacking British workers as either stupid, or the 'biggest enemy of the black man'.[15] Patel later went on to found the Coloured People's Union, referred to in the press as 'Britain's first all-coloured trade union'.[16] Although the strike at Courtaulds Mill was unsuccessful, the RAAS, and Michael X in particular, were presented as one of the first examples of a new radical demand for 'Black Power'.[17] When de Freitas subsequently adopted a Muslim name, he was often referred to in the press as 'leader of the Black Muslims', an entirely fictional title, and subsequently as the 'leader of the Black Power movement in Britain'.[18] Michael X certainly had a flair for self-publicity, but was soon dismissed by those who saw themselves as serious political activists.

BLACK POWER

In July 1967 when Stokely Carmichael spoke on 'Black Power' at the Dialectics of Liberation Congress, a major 'counter-culture' event at the Roundhouse in London, he made an impression on many. One who was inspired was Zainab Abbas, a young British-born woman of Egyptian heritage from Middlesbrough, who would later become one of the main activists of the London-based Black Liberation Front. She hitchhiked to London to attend her first political meeting and, even before the Roundhouse event concluded, she had to walk all the way to the main road north in order to hitchhike back to Middlesbrough. Over fifty years later she recalled that Carmichael 'was so inspiring. He just had that ability. You know, there's some people who have an ability to get over everything you feel and with such a strength and with such a finger up to the system. He made me incredibly happy.'[19]

Carmichael had by this time already established himself as one of the main proponents of the Black Power movement that emerged in the US in the mid-1960s. Indeed, the term is often associated with him, after he first used it as a political demand in preference to the then more popular term, 'freedom', in a speech in June 1966.[20] It was soon taken up as a political slogan and demand by others in the US, most notably by the Black Panther Party for Self-Defence, established in California in 1966. Abbas recalled that Carmichael was also well known in Britain at the time for other speeches in which he had included the words: 'We have to as a people gather strength to stand up on our feet and say, "[O]ur noses are broad, our lips are thick, our hair is nappy – we are Black and beautiful."' The notion that 'Black is beautiful', formerly embraced by Marcus Garvey and many others, became another key aspect of Black Power.[21]

In London, Carmichael also made an impression on Britain's security services, which considered his arrival the dawn of the 'Black Power' movement in Britain.[22] As a consequence the surveillance of African and Caribbean individuals and organizations, which had existed for decades, was intensified and the Metropolitan Police's Special Branch and MI5 established a 'Black Power desk' to monitor and suppress the movement in Britain.[23]

During an eleven-day visit, Carmichael spoke at numerous other venues, including the West Indian Students' Centre and Africa Unity House, and was interviewed for the BBC. He linked his conception of 'Black Power' not just with the politics of Malcolm X and Franz Fanon, but also with those of Che Guevara and Mao Zedong. He appears to have been somewhat disappointed by the Roundhouse event, apart from a speech on Black Power by C. L. R. James, but was more excited by the Pan-African discussions taking place elsewhere in Britain, to hear that Black Power was 'resonating' in London, and 'to see the raised fists in the Asian communities, especially among Pakistani youth'. Michael X was one of his guides in London and explained that the visits of both Malcolm X and the famous boxer Muhammed Ali had made a big impression in Britain, especially among young Muslims.[24]

The week after the speech at the Roundhouse, Michael X deputized for Carmichael – the latter having left Britain prematurely before an official ban by the Labour government, perhaps the best indication of his impact. Michael X's speech at the RAAS event in Reading reportedly contained the words: '[I]f you ever see a white man laying hands on a Black woman, kill him immediately. If you love your brothers and sisters, you will be willing to die for them.' For that utterance he was arrested and charged under the Race Relations Act with 'attempting to stir up racial hatred', later convicted, and jailed for twelve months, the maximum penalty for this new crime.[25] Michael X, who accused the court of representing 'white justice', became the first 'coloured man' to be convicted under the Race Relations Act, a law that would be used repeatedly against the emerging Black Power movement.[26]

In June 1967 a new 'Black Power' organization was created when the Universal Coloured People's Association (UCPA) adopted 'the Black Power ideology' and elected a Nigerian, Obi Egbuna (1938–2014), as its chairman.[27] Egbuna, who had previously been the editor of *United Africa*, the publication of the Committee of African Organizations, emerged as one of the key figures in the burgeoning movement. This showed just how appealing Black Power could become, even for successful intellectuals.[28] Egbuna was an established novelist and playwright, and his *Wind versus Polygamy* was performed on BBC radio and television and was part of Britain's contribution to the First World Festival of Negro Arts held in Senegal in April 1966, along with the Negro Theatre Workshop's *The Dark Disciples*.

Egbuna was part of an African and Caribbean cultural movement that had long been developing. During the late 1950s, it included the writing of Errol John, Wole Soyinka and Lloyd Reckford, the emergence of the Negro Theatre Workshop, founded by Pearl Connor-Mogotsi in London in 1961, the work of performers such as Yulisa Amadu Maddy, as well as the Caribbean Artists Movement (CAM) founded in London by Kamau Braithwaite (1930–2020), John La Rose (1927–2006) and Andrew Salkey (1928–1995) in 1966. According to the artist Errol Lloyd (1943–), one of its leading members, the CAM was 'the first organized collaboration of artists from the

Caribbean with the aim of celebrating a new sense of shared Caribbean "nationhood", exchanging ideas and attempting to forge a new Caribbean aesthetic in the arts'. The term 'artists' was used in a broad sense to include 'novelists, poets, playwrights, theatre directors and theatre practitioners ... critics, academics, historians, and a range of activists drawn mainly but not exclusively from the Caribbean'. With a central focus on the Caribbean and regular meetings at the West Indian Students' Centre in Earl's Court, the CAM also embraced African music and culture and, for six years, helped create a vibrant atmosphere which inspired and included both established and emerging cultural workers such as C. L. R. James, Pearl Connor-Mogotsi, James Berry (1924–2017), Aubrey Williams (1926–1990), Althea McNish (1924–2020) and Ronald Moody (1900–1984).[29] The West Indian Students' Centre continued to be an important venue for political meetings, as well as cultural and even sporting events during this period, as there were so few other venues available. It was the location for one of the early supplementary schools, named after C. L. R. James, and also provided cultural and political events for the wider community, not just for students.

In 1966 La Rose, who considered Carmichael's visit a 'catalyst in a way that nothing before had been' also founded New Beacon Books, both a pioneering publishing house and one of the first Black bookshops.[30] One of the most significant aspects of the period, and a consequence of the emerging Black Power movement, was an increasing demand for books that related to the history, culture and experience of those of African and Caribbean heritage. Many other bookshops and publishers subsequently emerged, most notably Bogle L'Ouverture, created by Jessica and Eric Huntley in west London in 1969. In 1967, Margaret Busby became one of the country's youngest publishers of Caribbean or African heritage when she co-founded Allison and Busby.[31]

THE UNIVERSAL COLOURED PEOPLE'S ASSOCIATION

Egbuna, as chairman, and Sawh, one of the UCPA's other leaders, had joined Michael X and Carmichael on stage at the Roundhouse, and had encouraged the latter to speak in London's Hyde Park. As a consequence, Egbuna complained, 'the police have been brutalizing us'.[32] Sawh and three other members of the UCPA were arrested and charged for speeches made 'with intent to stir up racial hated' at Speakers' Corner, an outdoor venue in Hyde Park favoured by many Black Power and other political activists and internationally known for its provocative oratory. The prosecutions of UCPA leaders were facilitated by the activities of the security services, which utilized the Race Relations Act for that purpose.[33]

Egbuna also recognized the importance of Carmichael's visit, claiming that it was 'manna from heaven' and was not until that time that 'Black Power got a foothold in Britain'.[34] The UCPA soon produced its own *Black Power Newsletter* and claimed to have recruited over 700 members in London alone.[35] In September 1967, it launched a manifesto: *Black Power in Britain: A Special Statement*. The *Statement* explained that 'Black Power simply reflects a new stage in the revolutionary consciousness of the black man: a change of strategy', and could be defined as 'the totality of economic, cultural, political, and, if necessary, military power which the black people of the world must acquire to get the white oppressor off their backs'.[36]

The UCPA, like the RAAS before it, regularly appeared in the pages of the mainstream press and both organizations used the term 'Black' in exactly the same way as the word 'coloured', to refer to those of Asian, as well as those of African and Caribbean heritage.[37] What the new Black Power organizations voiced was an opposition to notions of integration and assimilation, as well as a pride in being Black. There was also a newfound confidence that, although a minority in Britain, they represented the global majority of the 'coloured' Third World, and the struggles in Cuba, Vietnam, Congo and elsewhere were viewed as inspirational. There was, of course, a strong influence from the United States, from such organizations as the Black Panther Party, as well as from the activities of Angela Davis and George Jackson. British activists were also influenced by all the other well-known cultural aspects of the Black Power movement, from Afro hairstyles to clenched-fist salutes.

In addition, such groups considered that Black Power meant 'that the blacks of this world are out to liquidate capitalist oppression wherever it exists by any means necessary'.[38] The security services,

Jessica Huntley (left) at a meeting in support of Angela Davis (right)

despite heavy surveillance of this new movement, appears to have been contemptuous of it, declaring in 1970 that 'Black Power' in Britain 'is a remedy without a complaint and its advocates are preaching, in the main, to unbelievers'.[39] However, the Black Power movement continued to develop as a consequence of the struggles facing those of Caribbean and African heritage. This was at the same time as the struggle for civil rights in the north of Ireland, widespread student protests, opposition to the war in Vietnam, and strikes and industrial unrest throughout Britain. It was also the era of the Metropolitan Police Special Demonstration Squad, first formed in 1968, that worked with the other security services to infiltrate organizations considered 'extremist'. It was an era of heightened political activity by the defenders of the status quo, as well as those determined to bring about political change.

According to Egbuna, the UCPA was soon plagued by ideological differences and divisions:

> There were members who believed that the answer to the Black man's problems lay in the overthrow of the capitalist system and there were others who felt it lay in the Black man going to the House of Lords; there

were some who saw themselves as part of the international Black revolution and there was a faction who believed that the Black man in this country should only concern himself with what goes on in this country.[40]

Such political differences were often to plague the numerous Black Power organizations that emerged, not just in London but throughout the country, often working in concert with each other. By the early 1970s these organizations were quite numerous and included: a Black Alliance in Cardiff; the Black People's Freedom Movement in Nottingham; the Black People's Liberation Party in Leicester; the United Black People's Organization in Sheffield; and many others.[41]

The UCPA also established a branch in Manchester which was led by activists such as Ron Phillips (1935–1998) and Kath Locke (1928–1992). The Manchester UCPA's most famous action was a demonstration in Manchester Cathedral during a tour of the South African rugby team. Three men and three women 'dressed in black battledress, berets at a military angle' marched into the cathedral, interrupting a service against

The UCPA protest in Manchester Cathedral

apartheid and for 'racial harmony', to read out a statement, the press reported. They then gave clenched fist salutes and shouted 'Power to the People, power to Black People', before marching out. The demonstrators told reporters that they acted on behalf of the UCPA, 'the vanguard party of the black people in their struggle against the white imperialist power structure'. They added, '[W]e recognize that the same international power structure oppresses the black people in this country, too. Therefore, our protest is directed not only against racialism in South Africa, but racialism in Britain, and specifically in Manchester.'[42]

BLACK PANTHERS

In April 1968 Egbuna founded a new publication called *Black Power Speaks*, 'which told Black people the truth about themselves', as well as the new Black Panther Movement (BPM), the first organization formed outside the US with such a title.[43] He also visited Kwame Nkrumah in exile in Guinea, and returned with the latter's famous 'Message to the Black People of Britain' in which the BPM was referred to as 'part of the revolutionary upsurge in the world today'. In his 'Message', Nkrumah also referred to the 'difficulties you are going through in Britain: discrimination, prejudice and racial hostility', and called upon both the BPM and the RAAS to 'mobilize, educate and reawaken the black people of Britain to the full realization of their revolutionary potential'. He argued that '[Y]ou who are in Britain have a significant role to play in the international black revolutionary movement. You live in the very citadel of British imperialism and neo-colonialism.' Nkrumah's 'Message' was subsequently published by the BPM.[44]

In July 1968, Egbuna was arrested, along with two 'Panthers', one Nigerian and one Fijian, for attempting to publish a pamphlet entitled *What to Do When Cops Lay Their Hands on a Black Man at Speakers' Corner*. Those arrested had also been under surveillance by the Special Branch and Egbuna was refused bail and remanded in Brixton Prison for several months. When his case was heard in court, he was given a suspended sentence, a punishment that appeared designed to disrupt the development of Black Power organizations.[45] It was during his incarceration that he wrote his book, *Destroy This Temple:*

The Voice of Black Power in Britain, reflecting on his experiences with both the UCPA and the BPM.

During the trial Egbuna initially refused to recognize the court, but thereafter employed white lawyers to defend him. This severely dented his credibility within the movement and he never regained his former prominence.

The Black Power activists had much to reflect on. In March 1968 the Labour government hurriedly passed a new, openly racist Immigration Act, specifically targeting those with British passports who happened to be of Asian heritage who had been forced to migrate to Britain from Kenya. The new Commonwealth Immigration Act effectively removed citizenship rights from all migrants to Britain who came from Commonwealth countries, unless their parents, or grandparents, had been born in Britain. It demonstrated that racism was government policy. The following month a leading Conservative MP, Enoch Powell, made his infamous 'Rivers of Blood' speech, encouraging the repatriation of migrants and claiming that the government's 'race relations' legislation would bring 'discrimination and deprivation' to the majority of people in Britain. Unlike African and Caribbean activists, Powell was not prosecuted for this under the Race Relations Act. Indeed, it was the proposed 1968 Race Relations Act which he had specifically criticized in his speech. This act expanded previous legislation to cover discrimination in employment and housing. It was allegedly targeted to assist 'coloured youngsters ... who are, and who will be, the product of our own education system, brought up in our own traditions'.[46] However, the act, made law in October 1968, specifically excluded the government from its purview, and therefore any measure relating to immigration, as well as state institutions such as the police.

In response to the growing racism in Britain (which included the founding of the openly fascist National Front), several new organizations took form, including the Black People's Alliance (BPA), 'a militant front for Black Consciousness and against racialism', established in Leamington Spa in 1968. The BPA was closely linked with the Indian Workers' Association in Birmingham, but initially involved twenty other organizations as well, including the WISC, the National Federation of Pakistani Associations, the Black Regional Action Movement, the Group

A poster advertising the Conference on the Rights of Black People in Britain

for Nigerian Revolution and the UCPA. In 1969 the BPA led a national demonstration of 8,000 people to Downing Street demanding the repeal of the immigration acts. Two years later a Conservative government added to that overtly racist legislation with the 1971 Immigration Act, which was, if anything, even more so, since it introduced the notion of 'patrials' – those with the right of abode – and 'non-patrials' – those without that right – creating first- and second-class citizens. Since the definition of a 'patrial' was a person who could trace descent from someone born in Britain, the legislation was widely viewed as openly discriminatory. The response was a mass demonstration in London in March 1971, involving several organizations, including the BPM and the new Black Unity and Freedom Party, which had recently emerged from within the ranks of UCPA. In May 1971 many of these organizations participated in a conference held at London's Alexandra Palace called 'On the Rights of Black People in Britain'.[47]

THE 'MANGROVE NINE'

The climate of racism in the country created by the immigration acts of 1968 and 1971, enhanced by Powell's speeches and the violent activities of the National Front, was made much worse by the racism of the police, which appeared to be particularly directed at young African and Caribbean men. The behaviour of the police was facilitated by the widespread use of what became known as the 'sus' law (Section 4 of the Vagrancy Act 1824), which allowed the police to stop and search any individual they suspected of intent to commit an offence. In practice, it gave the police almost unlimited powers of harassment. Police behaviour that appeared to be openly discriminatory, such as the arrest of the Nigerian diplomat, Clement Gomwalk, for a motoring offence in Brixton in 1969, often led to major resistance.[48] In Brixton six of those who protested against his arrest, including seventeen-year-old Olive Morris, a member of the south London branch of the BPM, were arrested and assaulted by the police.[49]

There were so many incidents that, as early as 1968, the BBC had made a television documentary entitled *Equal Before the Law?* about allegations of police racism, violence and corruption, which the Metropolitan Police tried unsuccessfully to prevent being broadcast.[50] The government of the day was fully aware of police racism, but unwilling to take any measures to prevent it.[51] The scene was set for further clashes between the police and those often referred to as the 'second generation', young people mostly of Caribbean but sometimes continental African heritage, educated and, increasingly often, born in Britain too.

Following Egbuna's arrest, the BPM began to distance itself from him and others it referred to as 'opportunists', such as Sawh and Michael X. It came under the leadership first of David Udah and then of Altheia Jones-Lecointe, a Trinidadian postgraduate student at UCL who became the first woman to lead such an organization in Britain.[52] Like other Black Power organizations of the period, the BPM often based its symbols, such as the black panther, and even its language, on its counterpart in the US. Its British members sometimes sold the newspapers of the United States-based Panthers alongside their own, and often organized in support of Panthers arrested in the US, but there was no formal relationship between the two organizations. The BPM, which established its Youth League in Brixton as a training ground for new recruits, had a political orientation that also included support for Irish Republicanism and British miners, and increasingly it took a strong stand in defence of the rights of women. An important preoccupation was 'the history of black people', as well as various aspects of their music and culture, although, like the Panthers in the United States, the BPM rejected what it referred to as 'cultural nationalism'. The BPM believed that 'it is only by getting to know ourselves and our history that we will be able to effectively fight to liberate ourselves'. The emphasis was therefore on political liberation, and the BPM increasingly adopted the language of Marxism and openly rejected 'the entire capitalist establishment in Britain'.[53]

Jones-Lecointe and other BPM members became involved in one of most famous legal cases of the period following protests against sustained police harassment and arrests of those connected with the Mangrove Restaurant in London's Ladbroke Grove. The BPM was particularly concerned to organize in opposition to what came to be called 'institutional racism' by the Black Power groups, that is to say, racism entwined and deeply connected with state institutions such as the police, the judiciary and the government. London-based but often extending its activities to other towns and cities including Birmingham, Manchester, Leeds, Nottingham and Hull, the BPM reported on numerous examples of state racism in such publications as *Black People's News Service*. Its members demonstrated against police violence, as well as visiting the victims of police assaults in prisons and hospitals, at a time when the notion of 'institutional racism' was not widely accepted at all.[54]

The Mangrove Restaurant was opened in 1968 by Frank Crichlow (1932–2010), a Trinidadian former railway worker and musician. In the 1950s he had previously opened the El Rio Coffee Bar, part of the backdrop to the infamous Profumo scandal, in the same area.[55] The Mangrove soon became a favoured community meeting place, a venue to discuss politics and to get support, but also just a place to hang out and eat. It became well known even to those who lived outside the area and was frequented by a variety of patrons including the local

MP, Bruce Douglas-Mann, and the writer Colin MacInnes. In the words of its owner, it was 'very, very in-crowd'.[56] However, it was obstructed by the local authorities and became a focus for surveillance and the object of nine separate raids by the local police in the space of six weeks.[57] It was in response to this series of police raids, when other forms of protest had been ignored, that Darcus Howe (1943–2017), formerly associated with Michael X and a group known as the Black Eagles, suggested a demonstration, a proposal for community self-defence which was accepted by Crichlow and organized in conjunction with the BPM. The demonstration was formally organized by the Action Group for the Defence of the Mangrove, which sent details of the protest to the Prime Minister, the leader of the Labour Party and several Caribbean governments.[58]

The subsequent march, on 9 August 1970, consisting of about 150 people demanding an end to the harassment of the Mangrove, and 'other places where Black People lawfully gather', was broken up by more than 700 police officers.[59] Resistance from the demonstrators resulted in police injuries and nineteen arrests and was widely reported in the press.[60] The charges against those whom the police viewed as the leaders of the demonstration were initially dismissed by a local magistrate. In a very unusual step, the Director of Public Prosecutions, acting on behalf of the state, reinstated serious charges – including riot and incitement to riot – against those considered leading agitators, including Crichlow, Jones-Lecointe, Howe and six others, who became known as the 'Mangrove Nine'.

The trial of the Mangrove Nine at the Old Bailey lasted eleven weeks, from October to December 1971, and was widely seen as a defining moment. It was also viewed as a 'political trial', both by the government and police, who saw it as an opportunity to neutralize leading figures in the Black Power movement, which they had placed under surveillance, and by those who saw it as an opportunity to put state racism in the dock. The trial occurred after the local press and MP had accused the police in Notting Hill of being 'seriously prejudiced' and called for a public inquiry to 'restore public confidence in the police'. It also followed numerous other incidents, most notably at Caledonian Road Police Station in Islington, in which young Black people in London had been forced to defend themselves against police

Supporters of the Mangrove Nine outside the Old Bailey, London, 1971

violence.[61] Even before the trial began, the Mangrove Nine had established a very public defence campaign, received support from overseas and throughout the country and the case was widely seen as a cause célèbre, comparable to the political trials of Bobby Seale and Angela Davis in the United States.

The Mangrove Nine demanded an all-Black jury and, when that was refused, made sure that they obtained jurors from working-class backgrounds to serve at their trial. They were able to call several prominent character witnesses, including the local MP, and during the trial both Jones-Lecointe and Howe defended themselves advantageously, a radical new departure in such cases. The Mangrove Nine were able to discredit the evidence of the police, expose the bias of the judge and share their experience of police racism with the jury. The jury acquitted five of them of all charges. Although the judge gave suspended sentences to the other four, he also clearly acknowledged the existence of police racism, the first time such a public admission had been made. In the wake of what was considered a defeat for the 'Establishment', measures were taken to restrict the rights of defendants in future court cases. Nevertheless, the case was widely viewed as a victory for 'Black Power' and, as Darcus Howe concluded, 'racism as a basis for the division of the British working class had taken a beating, particularly since our defence was based on the fact that the police were liars and should not be believed'.[62]

In some ways the trial marked something of a high point for the BPM, which, in the early 1970s, included amongst its members Howe, Linton Kwesi Johnson and Farouk Dhondy, who both subsequently became well-known writers; Beverly Bryan, thereafter an academic and co-author of *The Heart of the Race*; and Neil Kenlock, a photographer and co-founder of the radio station Choice FM. The case clearly did not prevent further discriminatory activities by the police. Indeed, a few days after the trial Rothwell 'Roddy' Kentish (1942–2019), one of the defendants, was rearrested, assaulted by the police and sentenced to three years' imprisonment. Frank Crichlow, who later established the award-winning Mangrove Steelband and the Mangrove Community Association, suffered harassment and arrest for more than twenty years after the trial, finally successfully suing the police and winning record damages of £50,000 in 1992.[63]

THE BLACK UNITY AND FREEDOM PARTY AND THE BLACK LIBERATION FRONT

Allegations of police racism became a major focus of other Black political organizations throughout the 1970s. In July 1970 the majority of UCPA's remaining membership, led by George Joseph, Ricky Cambridge, Danny Morrell and Sonia Chang, reconstituted themselves as the Black Unity and Freedom Party (BUFP) with a publication entitled *Black Voice*, launched in September 1970. The BUFP established branches in London and also in Manchester, where Ron Phillips, Kath Locke and Coca Clarke were key organizers.[64] The original members were soon joined by members of the South East London Black Parents Association. Like other organizations at the time, the BUFP declared that it was guided by 'Marxism-Leninism-Mao Tse Tung Thought', although in practice this indicated that it was inspired by the example of the Black Panthers in the US, as well as by the revolutions in China and Cuba. The twenty-sixth of July 'the date on which the organization was launched, was chosen because it was the day set aside to commemorate the Cuban revolution'.[65] The Black Panthers' key demands in the US were often adopted, or adapted, by British organizations and for the BUFP these included, 'an end to police brutality', as well as other forms of state racism, and 'an end to racist education', as well as demands relating to employment, housing and social justice.[66] The BUFP also organized supplementary schooling for children, launching its own summer school in 1971, and 'took the lead in the fight against the miseducation of Black children in British schools', particularly those who, in the racist terms of the period, had been designated 'educationally sub-normal'.[67]

The BPM and the BUFP played a leading role in the National Conference on the Rights of Black People in Britain which was held at London's Alexandra Palace in May 1971, at which Jones-Lecointe gave the opening address. This event was organized in collaboration with the Afro-Caribbean Self-Help Organization (Birmingham), the Afro Carib Circle (Wolverhampton), United Caribbean Association (Leeds) and the West Indian Association (Huddersfield).[68]

Another significant organization was the Black Liberation Front (BLF), established in early 1971 by Tony Soares, together with former members of the north London collective of the BPM.[69] Initially, the BLF felt itself to be not entirely in sympathy with the Marxism of the Black Panthers, but over time it too became increasingly influenced by the US Panthers, by Maoist China's support for 'the complete emancipation of black people', and a vision of a socialist future.[70] The BPM was the British organization nearest in alignment to the US Panthers, and was particularly close to Eldridge and Kathleen Cleaver and the International Section of the Black Panther Party based in Algiers. It was also a member of the US Panthers' Revolutionary Peoples' Communication Network, a means to exchange information and coordinate action among 'oppressed people all over the world'.[71] The BLF established a publication called *Grassroots*, and declared that it adhered to the principles of 'Revolutionary Black Nationalism', but found it difficult to decide on a term that adequately defined its political orientation.[72] It first established its base at 54 Wightman Road in north London, later moving to 61 Goulbourne Road, Ladbroke Grove, and like many organizations founded a youth club and supplementary school, as well as establishing workshops for unemployed young people.[73]

Soares was a veteran of the Black Power movement and had been viewed by the security services as one of its key leaders. He was of Indian heritage, having been born in Goa and grown up in Africa, where he was involved in the movement against colonialism. It was to escape political persecution that he came to Britain in 1961 and, such was the nature of Britain's Black Power movement, that he subsequently became a key figure in the UCPA, joined the BPM and for several years led the BLF. He had attended the conference at the Roundhouse in 1967 and later reflected, 'We were all influenced by events in America, by Malcolm X, by Stokely Carmichael ... that's what politicised a lot of people.'[74] However, Soares was also influenced by other contemporary political events. He was highly involved in anti-Vietnam War activities, for which he was imprisoned, as well as for his anti-imperialist activities in Africa. In addition, he was influenced by contact with leading African American activists such as

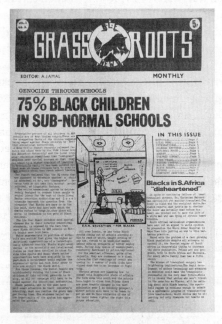

An early edition of the BLF's *Grassroots*

Robert F. Williams, as well as Eldridge and Kathleen Cleaver, and he became a printer and distributor of a variety of revolutionary literature ranging from the *Black Panther* newspaper to Mao Zedong's *Little Red Book*. In 1972, when he republished an article on how to make a 'Molotov cocktail' from the *Black Panther* in the BLF's *Grassroots* he was arrested, after a Special Branch raid, and charged with inciting readers to commit arson and murder. His trial at the Old Bailey in March 1973 became a *cause célèbre* and led to a 'Free Tony Soares' campaign which became a major preoccupation for the BLF and the wider community.[75] To them it made it crystal clear that the state would link political activity with terrorism in order to discredit and disrupt the Black Power movement. Soares was sentenced to community service and bound over for a total of seven years in what was widely seen as an attempt to curtail his political activities.[76]

SUPPLEMENTARY EDUCATION

The BLF established its own youth organization and from 1973 onwards it 'merged' with the south London-based Fasimbas, the 'youth wing' of the South East London Parents Organization (SELPO). The BLF and the SELPO were just two of many organizations during the late 1960s and 1970s that established 'supplementary' or Saturday schools, for young people increasingly facing various forms of racism at school, in employment and from the police and criminal justice system. Although there were increasing numbers of teachers of African and Caribbean heritage in schools and, in 1969, Yvonne Connolly became the first female Black headteacher, Black students still faced many difficulties. Connolly's appointment was greeted with threats against her life and her school. It was partly in response to the opposition to her appointment that she became one of the founders of the Caribbean Teachers' Association.[77]

Some of the earliest attempts to intervene in the miseducation of children had begun in the mid-1960s, with initiatives created by parents and teachers and organizations such as the ACSHO in Birmingham, which established that city's first supplementary school in 1967 and several other initiatives for young people. The ACSHO established its political activity in much the same way as many other Black Power organizations. Placing an emphasis on self-help, it aimed to deal with a range of problems facing local people, including police harassment and homelessness. It often worked in unity with the Harambee Organization founded in 1972 by Fitzmaurice Andrews, a social worker originally from Jamaica, which established a hostel providing accommodation and a community centre focused on young people.[78]

In London, the North London West Indian Association (NLWIA), established in the early 1960s and led by Japheth 'Jeff' Crawford (1932–2003), Jocelyn Barrow (1929–2020) and others, also found it necessary to intervene in education.[79] Crawford, a leading member of the WISC, was a vigorous campaigner against racism and, in 1974, became another of the founders of the Caribbean Teachers' Association. He had already been involved in several successful anti-racist actions, including fighting the National Union of Railwaymen for the right of Asquith Xavier (1920–1980) to become the first Black train guard at Euston Station in 1966, and the NLWIA's campaign against London Transport and the Transport and General Workers' Union for Lionel Franklin's right to become a bus inspector in 1968.[80]

The NLWIA, which also included John La Rose and Jessica Huntley, established the Paul Bogle Youth Movement and later the George Padmore, Albertina Sylvester and other supplementary schools.[81] The NWLIA became involved in education as a result of a campaign in Haringey. During the 1960s the government had already decided upon an educational policy based on the premise that numbers of 'immigrant children' in any one school should be limited because 'as the proportion of immigrant children in a school or class increases, the problems will become more difficult to solve, and the chances of assimilation more remote'.[82] Those referred to as 'West Indian' children were considered to be at best less intelligent, at worst unteachable, and therefore harmful to the education of other children. Schools and local education authorities were therefore encouraged to disperse such children by 'bussing' them to other schools.

The racist notion that students of Caribbean heritage, in particular, were a problem was initially opposed by teachers such as Marina Maxwell, who wrote an article exposing the racism within the education system entitled 'Violence in the toilets in 1969' before returning to

Trinidad. In Haringey, as in many other places, students were assessed by unscientific IQ tests and 'banded' (put in a lower stream) on the racist premise that students of Caribbean heritage had a lower IQ than 'their English contemporaries'. The NWLIA also became heavily involved in the subsequent struggle against the placing of these students in what were so-called schools for the Educationally Sub-Normal (ESN), a practice also based on inadequate and biased IQ tests. The ESN 'problem' existed throughout the country and especially in London, where there were twice the percentage of West Indian children in ESN schools as there were in mainstream education. The NWLIA and the WISC organized a successful campaign against banding and took Haringey Council to the Race Relations Board on the grounds that Black children in ESN schools were being discriminated against.[83]

Another early campaigner on education was Manchester-based Beresford Edwards (1930–2003) who, with his wife, Elouise (1932–2021), was one of the founders of the West Indian Organizations Coordinating Committee in 1964. In 1967 Beresford Edwards was forced to take legal action against his trade union, the Society of Graphical and Allied Trades, after he was wrongfully dismissed from employment as a printer. In 1966 the Edwardses established Manchester's first supplementary school.[84] All these educational efforts included not just work to support children's regular education in state schools, which was often inadequate, but also included a greater emphasis on African and Caribbean history and culture.[85]

Educational problems were most famously highlighted in 1971 by the publication of Bernard Coard's *How the West Indian Child Is Made Educationally Sub-Normal in the British School System*. This small publication sold over 10,000 copies and was itself part of a major community initiative involving a host of organizations led by the Caribbean Education and Community Workers Association (CECWA), which provided funding, New Beacon Books, which published it, and Bogle L'Ouverture, which helped to distribute it. The CECWA was established in 1969 by Jessica Huntley (1927–2013), John La Rose, Winston Best, a teacher and educationalist, and Waveney Bushell, one of the first psychologists of Caribbean heritage, among others. The genesis for the book which Coard came to write was the moment when he read a leaked internal report from the Inner

London Education Authority (ILEA) which showed that 34 per cent of the school students placed in ESN schools were of Caribbean heritage. These placements were based on IQ tests which were clearly discriminatory. The CECWA encouraged Coard to make a presentation at one of their conferences. He had worked in schools for the ESN and with children labelled in this way. His findings contributed to a much greater awareness of these schools as well as racism within the education system more generally.[86] The publication highlighted the low expectations of some teachers, encouraged the growth of more supplementary schools 'to make up for the inadequacies of the British school system' and demanded the mainstream teaching of the history of Africa and the Caribbean and other 'Black studies'.[87] Coard concluded that, for school students, 'Pride and self-confidence are the best armour against the prejudice and humiliating experience they will certainly face in school and society.'[88]

The conditions laid bare by Coard's book existed throughout Britain, and its exposure led to the creation of a supplementary-school tradition that still exists and has been compared to the socialist Sunday-school movement of the later nineteenth and early twentieth centuries.[89] It also led to the activism of parents and teachers throughout the country, as well as to the creation of numerous supportive educational organizations, such as the West Indian Parents and Friends Association in Bristol.[90]

Partly inspired by the activity of the US Panthers, as well as the struggles of students and parents in Britain, many organizations formed their own supplementary schools, often focused on the teaching of English and mathematics, but also on the provision of Black History classes. Such initiatives were common everywhere, with many, like the George Padmore and Albertina Sylvester schools in London and the United Caribbean Association's supplementary school established in Leeds, based in people's homes.[91] The Ahfiwe School established by BLF activists Ansel Wong and Gerlin Bean, along with others in Brixton, developed new approaches to teaching, encouraged creative writing and eventually attracted state funding. Other educational initiatives, such as the Afro-Caribbean Education Resources Project, founded by the Jamaican Len Garrison (1943–2003), also encouraged such writing and, along with many others, also began to develop a particular focus on various aspects of Black history that led to the creation of the Black Cultural Archives in 1981. The 'need for affirmation of dignity and to combat the problem of identity', as well the necessity to struggle against racism and against the capitalist system had also been key features of Sawh's Free University for Black Studies established earlier in Notting Hill in 1968.[92]

The problems of the 'underachievement' of children of Caribbean heritage in schools had long been recognized and some of the earliest official studies and reports were conducted in the 1960s, but there were no major national investigations by the government until 1978. The most significant studies during this period led to the publication of the Rampton report (1981) and the Swann report (1985). The Rampton report recognized that 'West Indian children as a group are indeed underachieving', and concluded with the controversial view that racism 'intentional or unintentional' when taken 'together with, for example negative teacher attitudes and an inappropriate curriculum ... does play a major part in their underachievement'.[93] The Swann report acknowledged the impact of racism and the more general problems of social and economic disadvantage, as well as the need for an 'multicultural' education system that ensured that all pupils reached their potential.[94]

Other initiatives at the time, such as the Harambee Project founded in north London by Herman Edwards, combined education with the provision of accommodation and employment training.[95] Homelessness was another major problem in this period and there were numerous initiatives to address that too, such as Harambee House in Birmingham and George Jackson House in Manchester, both of which collaborated with the BLF. It was also an era when many people were forced to engage in squatting (occupying empty residential property), or assisting others to stay on the right side of the law in order to do so, as, for example, activists Olive Morris, Liz Obi and Zainab Abbas did in Brixton.[96] In London in 1974 BLF activists began establishing the Ujima Housing Association. Operational from 1977, Ujima provided low-rental accommodation, became a model for other such initiatives and, before its demise in the twenty-first century, had acquired some 5,000 properties.[97]

THE 'OVAL FOUR'

Education was only one of many struggles waged at the time. In the early 1970s, young Black men, especially in London, were increasingly being presented in the media and by the state as 'muggers', who were disproportionately responsible for a rise in street robberies. Although this has been described as a 'moral panic', a fear that an American-style crime wave had been unleashed, it was, in many respects, a state-organized campaign that led to young men disproportionately being stopped by police using the 'sus' law.[98] In March 1972, Winston Trew and three other members of the Fasimbas were returning to south London from a meeting planning the defence campaign for Tony Soares when they were attacked at Oval Station by unknown assailants. They defended themselves and subsequently faced arrest by their attackers, who identified themselves as undercover Transport Police officers and accused them of 'nicking handbags'.[99] The Oval Four, as they became known, were beaten by the police (as was often customary), and tortured to make them sign false confessions to various 'unsolved crimes'. They were eventually charged with assaulting the police, robbery, attempted theft from 'persons unknown', and even the theft of a woman detective's handbag.[100]

Their trial at the Old Bailey became another notorious legal case, with a campaign which compared the actions of the police in this case to the proceedings they had employed against the Mangrove Restaurant and its defenders.[101] The aim of the Oval Four and their supporters was to 'call into question the whole idea of "mugging" and suggest that the label was really a shield behind which the police were hiding to criminalise black young people'. They aimed to expose the forced confessions of the four defendants and the violence and criminal behaviour of the police. The trial was, essentially, a question of whether or not the jury believed the police. It resulted in the Oval Four being found not guilty of all robbery charges, but still guilty, by a majority verdict, of assaulting the police, attempted theft from 'persons unknown' and the theft of a policewoman's handbag. The sentences of two years' imprisonment, or in a custodial institution for young offenders, outraged their supporters and a new 'freedom campaign' was organized by the

Fasimbas and SELPO, aided by the BLF, BUFP and BPM, with wide community support. On appeal their sentences were reduced by eight months, due to a legal irregularity, but the judicial system would not permit them to completely clear their names until 2020, even though the police officer at the heart of this and other cases was himself later imprisoned.[102] What was already known at the time, and even broadcast in a BBC television programme in 1973, was that the police team involved in the case was completely corrupt and had fabricated false evidence against other young Black men, who it had claimed were 'muggers', in such cases as the 'Waterloo Four', the 'Stockwell Six' and the 'Tottenham Road Two'. The latter case, involving two Jesuit students from Oxford University, was so preposterous that it was thrown out of court. However, despite clear irregularities in all four cases, no action was taken against the police, nor the judicial system, even though the details were made known to the Home Secretary.[103]

The BLF and other Black Power organizations became nationally known as a result of such high-profile court cases. The BLF was also indirectly linked to the case of the Spaghetti House attempted robbery and kidnapping case in Knightsbridge in 1975, another high-profile event that featured in the national press.[104] The three men who attempted the robbery claimed that it was being undertaken for political purposes, that they were acting on behalf of the 'Black Liberation Army' and asked to speak to a representative of the BLF. Although Zainab Abbas was sent in response to that request, the BLF maintained that it had no political connection with the three men (although one of them had attended some public meetings), and condemned the attempted robbery.[105]

For many people of African and Caribbean heritage, the 1970s were informed by the racism they experienced; in employment, in the education system and at the hands of the police. The decades from 1965 to 1985 are often recalled through the experiences of young Black people, the so-called 'second generation' who were either born or grew up in Britain. Experiences in all three of these areas informed the activities of the Black Power organizations and other community organizations that emerged during that period. The major legal cases, such as those relating to the Mangrove Restaurant and the Oval Four, are just the best-known examples of the actions of the police and

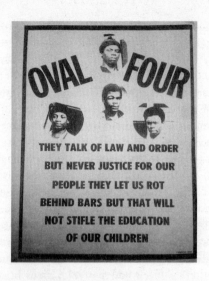

Posters protesting against the arrest of the Oval Four

judiciary, but there were many others. The BUFP, for example, was involved in organizing protests against the police arrests of Black youths at Peckham Rye Fair in September 1971, after the police had failed to prevent an attack on a young man, Radcliffe Carr, who was beaten unconscious by stallholders.[106] It also took up the case of Aseta Simms, a Black woman who died in Stoke Newington Police Station in suspicious circumstances in 1972, and demanded a public inquiry into the circumstances of her death.[107]

In April 1972 the BUFP was involved in the Joshua Francis case, which resulted in Francis' imprisonment for allegedly attacking two police officers. The local community responded with a mass meeting in Lambeth Town Hall, involving not only the BUFP and BPM, but also the WISC and even the legal attaché of the Jamaican High Commission. These and other organizations and individuals formed what became known as the Black People's Defence Committee, initially to support Francis, a transport worker and part-time preacher, who had been severely attacked by the police and then arrested literally in his own backyard. The committee managed to secure Francis' early release, but the actions of the police and courts helped to harden a view that these state institutions acted against the interests of Black communities.[108] Such violent incidents occurred not only in London – in June 1973 at Brockwell Park Fair and in October 1974 at the Carib Club in Cricklewood, where the infamous arrest and subsequent imprisonment of the musician Dennis Bovell took place – but also throughout the country.[109]

It was as a consequence of yet another arrest that the Black Parents Movement (BPM) was founded by La Rose, Huntley and others in 1975. Cliff McDaniel, a seventeen-year-old schoolboy, was arrested outside his school in north London, assaulted by police and charged with stealing a handbag and assaulting *them*. McDaniel was a student at the George Padmore Supplementary School and many of those connected with it came to his defence.[110] The BPM protested against the arrest and arranged McDaniel's legal defence. He was subsequently acquitted. The BPM then determined that it would organize 'the black community to fight its own oppression', especially in education and the criminal justice system. It subsequently formed an alliance with the Race Today Collective, the Bradford Black Collective and the Black Students' Movement. The BPM also established a branch in Manchester with the well-known campaigner and activist Gus John as its co-ordinator.

RESISTANCE, REGGAE AND RASTAFARI

Although some of the political inspiration for the British Black Power organizations of the 1960s and 1970s may have come from the United States, anti-racism was always shaped by conditions in Britain. There was, for example, the very British use of the term 'Black', which might simply be used to refer to anyone previously described as 'coloured', although during the 1970s this term progressively came to be applied to those of African and Caribbean heritage. The development of the supplementary school movement, although partly inspired by initiatives in the US, was particularly aimed at providing support for those 'West Indian' children failed by mainstream British education. There were many other projects aimed at these young people, again mainly of Caribbean heritage, but British from their place of birth and upbringing, whom society could not provide with an adequate education, nor means of employment. By the mid-1970s these young people were often described as 'between two cultures' as if this label helped to explain the many struggles they faced, such as miseducation, unemployment and racist policing.

These young people began to develop their own cultural responses to the oppression that was their everyday reality, which they called 'Babylon', a name drawn from the Jamaican reggae music that became increasingly popular during this period. Jamaicans, the majority migrant population amongst those of Caribbean and African heritage, brought many aspects of their culture with them to Britain, but perhaps the most important one was music. It was a phenomenon that even began to be commented on in the mainstream media.[111] Not only was Jamaican music increasingly popular, but the sound system used to play it on at public gatherings, house parties and various legal and not-so-legal clubs also became a significant British cultural institution.[112] The earliest sound-system operators, men like Vincent 'Duke Vin' Forbes (1928–2012) and Wilbert 'Count Suckle' Campbell (1931–2014) who had arrived in Britain as stowaways, had already established themselves in London by the late 1950s, playing at various venues and in competitive 'sound clashes'. During the next decade the leading sound-system artists established themselves in such clubs as the Roaring Twenties in London's Carnaby Street and Count Suckle's Q Club in Paddington, as well as in other venues throughout the country, such as the Bamboo Club in Bristol. By the early 1970s London clubs such as the Four Aces in Dalston, established by another sound-system operator, Charles 'Sir' Collins (1937–2018), and the Ram Jam in Brixton were just two of the leading venues for the most popular London sound-system artists, such as Sir Coxone and Count Shelley.[113] The production of reggae music generated a network of clubs at which it was played, and other performance venues too, as well as specialist record shops which imported and distributed records from Jamaica. These could be found everywhere. Birmingham had its specialist record shops and record labels too, as well as important sound systems, such as Quaker City and Wassifa. It also had its own music venues, as did every other town and city with a Caribbean population, from small youth clubs such as the Central Club in Reading to the famous West Indian Social Club in Huddersfield's Venn Street.[114]

More importantly, however, reggae contributed to an emerging youth sub-culture of style, language and worldview that was strongly influenced by the Rastafarian or Rastafari movement. The best-known representatives of this movement, for the wider British public, were undoubtedly Bob Marley and the Wailers, who performed in Britain several times in the early 1970s. However, the style, music, language and ideas of the Rastas was influential amongst Black youth in Britain long before Marley became internationally famous.

Rastafarianism, essentially a worldview that considered the Emperor of Ethiopia, Haile Selassie (Ras Tafari), to be a living African deity, was influential in Britain for several reasons. First, because it had such a profound influence on reggae during the 1970s, the music of choice for so many young Black people, and on the leading sound systems which often adopted names influenced by Rastafari. A leading London-based sound system was called Moa Anbessa, using the Amharic words which meant 'Conquering Lion' for its name, one of the titles of Haile Selassie.[115] In addition, Rastafarianism offered an Afrocentric and alternative worldview, one which provided a language to describe the reality of life in Britain, a place which could be seen as 'wicked Babylon' where the exiled 'Children of Israel' underwent various forms of 'sufferation' at the hands of their oppressors. The opposite of the idea of Babylon was that of an African Zion, an ideal place which was in reality most closely connected with Ethiopia, the only African country that had a history of preserving its independence from colonial rule by defeating an invading European army. Rastafarianism was, in this regard, drawing on a wider Pan-African orientation shared by many of the Black Power organizations. It also provided an alternative lifestyle. It encouraged the consumption of healthy food and the smoking of marijuana, as well as reflection upon African history, the teachings of the Bible, and the views of the famous Jamaican Pan-Africanist Marcus Garvey. In short, it provided an entire culture of resistance, most memorably exhibited in the adoption of the 'dreadlocks' hairstyle. Although not all young people adopted these elements of Rastafarianism, its influence, especially through music, was immense. It also fed into other aspects of Pan-Africanism, such as support for the ongoing liberation struggles in Africa, which was a preoccupation for many Black political organizations.

By the mid-1970s British-based reggae musicians and singers were beginning to develop their own form of the music, the most popular being Lovers' Rock, a genre often associated with female performers such as Louisa Mark (1960–2009), Janet Kay and Carol Thompson, as well as vocal groups such as 15, 16 and 17, Simplicity and Brown Sugar.[116] The Lovers Rock style, often with an emphasis on love songs, first came to prominence in 1975, and might be considered a contrast to the 'conscious' lyrics of the Rasta-dominated Jamaican form. However, there was a significant overlap of styles, as is evident from such British songs as 'Black Skin Boys', 'I'm in Love with a Dreadlocks' and 'Black Pride'. What was significant about British Lovers' Rock was that it was produced in Britain by young British-based artists, many of them young women, as well as by more established male performers and musicians, such as Dennis Bovell's vocal group Matumbi. It also heralded the emergence of other British-based reggae performers such as Aswad and Steel Pulse. The new British reggae styles were featured on all the established sound systems and were perhaps a sign of confidence in a new Black British identity. Lovers' Rock was also a musical form with appeal outside the Black communities. In 1979 'Silly Games', sung by Janet Kay and produced by Dennis Bovell, reached Number Two in the UK popular music charts.

RESISTANCE POLITICS

The various political organizations, such as the BLF, BUFP, ACSHO and others, developed a political style and approach that characterized similar organizations well into the 1980s. They often supported the revolutionary overthrow of capitalism, adhered to Maoism, Pan-Africanism, Third World unity, anti-imperialism and various forms of 'Black consciousness', as well as opposing all forms of racism and any dependence on the state. For many reliance on what was viewed as a racist state for funding, or employment, was considered an act of betrayal. The ACSHO's Bini Brown is reported to have once said, 'We don't like going with our hand begging, begging, begging. If you have to keep on begging somebody for something, what kind of human being are you? You have no dignity. When you're self-reliant, you do what you do, you're proud of what you are.'[117] However, some organizations, including Harambee in Birmingham, did accept state funding, arguing '[W]e pay taxes, we are a part of this society.'[118] Some leading anti-racist activists accepted employment in what was often referred to as the race-relations industry, as well as in local government, a trend that would continue in subsequent years.

The organizations focused not just on protests but also on community activism – establishing nurseries, supplementary schools, advice centres, self-defence classes and study groups. Much of this activity was based around the writing and dissemination of publications, pamphlets and leaflets on topical issues of concern.[119] There were many different types. The *Black Liberator*, published from 1973 until 1978 by Alrick 'Ricky' Cambridge (together with Colin Prescod and Cecil Gutzmore) considered itself a 'theoretical and discussion journal for black liberation'. Some publications such as *Race Today*, established by Darcus Howe, Barbara Beese and others in 1973, became an important 'collective' space for the dissemination of published political views. The

BLF established Grassroots Publications and also published material from the US Black Panthers, such as Eldridge Cleaver's *Revolution in the Congo* and Kathleen Cleaver's *On the Vanguard Role of the Black Urban Lumpen Proletariat*. In 1971 Eric and Jessica Huntley's Bogle L'Ouverture produced one of the most widely read publications of the era, Walter Rodney's *How Europe Underdeveloped Africa*.

More generally there was also a particular concern with Black culture – music, poetry, drama, books and films that reflected Pan-African or Black Power themes, as well as a growing interest in Black history.[120] Bookshops such as the BLF's Grassroots Storefront and Headstart, New Beacon Books in London, or the Harriet Tubman Bookshop in Birmingham became key sites of community cultural and political centres, not only providing books, but also music, artwork and other aspects of Black culture, as well as a place to meet and talk. That is why bookshops such as Black Unity and Bogle L'Ouverture in London came under attack by fascist organizations and, given official indifference to their situation, it was necessary for several bookshops and organizations to form Bookshop Joint Action in 1977.[121] A few years later, in 1982, Bogle L'Ouverture Publications, New Beacon Books and Race Today Publications made history by launching the first International Book Fair of Radical Black and Third World Books, designed to be a 'meeting of the continents for writers, publishers, distributors, booksellers, artists, musicians, film makers, and the people who inspire and consume their creative productions'. It linked those in Britain with their counterparts from Africa, the Caribbean, North America and Europe.[122]

Some key cultural figures emerged from within the political organizations. The film-maker Menelik Shabazz (1954–2021), for example, was for a time connected with the BLF and his first films, *Step Forward Youth* (1976) and *Breaking Point* (1978) focused directly on the problems facing young people, including the 'sus' law. The titles of both films (*Breaking Point* was originally entitled *Battering Down Sentence*) were inspired by popular reggae songs.[123] Contributors to *Race Today* included Linton Kwesi Johnson, a former member of the BPM, who developed his own style of Dub Poetry, inspired by reggae as well as the life experiences of West Indian youth. One of his most famous compositions, 'It Dread Inna Inglan', highlighted the ten-year sentence imposed upon George Lindo in 1978, who had been framed by the police in Bradford. His conviction was quashed a year later. Another leading performer in this genre was Benjamin Zephaniah, a Rasta dub poet initially based in Birmingham. One of his popular early compositions entitled 'Dis Policeman Keeps On Kicking Me to Death' was based on personal experience, but reflected widely held sentiments.[124]

Others were inspired by attending the Black Power organizations' events. For Winston Trew, a Black history class attended by his brother in London in 1970 made an immediate impact on them both –

> There was excitement in his voice and a sparkle in his eyes as he began to reel-off all that he had learnt there: that Africa was the cradle of civilization; that the Egyptians were black; the Moors were black; that Timbuctu was a seat of learning in Africa, with a library; that the Greeks learnt philosophy and science from the Egyptians.[125]

The political organizations also established wider Pan-African connections in Africa, the Caribbean and the United States. Most British organizations made efforts to support the liberation struggles in Africa, Zimbabwe, Mozambique and South Africa, and annually, on 25 May organized an appropriate event to celebrate Africa Liberation Day. Several organizations, including the BLF and the BUFP, joined together in 1972 to establish the Africa Liberation Committee, which, amongst other things, published material on various struggles in Africa such as *The Revolution in Congo (Kinshasa)* which highlighted the activity of the People's Revolutionary Party in that country. The Africa Liberation Committee also made links with Caribbean-based organizations such as the Youth Forces for National Liberation in Jamaica.[126] When the organizers of the sixth Pan-African Congress (to be held in Dar es Salaam, Tanzania) visited Britain in preparation for it during 1974 they held discussions with the BPM, the ACSHO, and other organizations in Yorkshire, Manchester, Leicester and Wolverhampton, and apparently found rather more support for Black Power than for Pan-Africanism.[127] Nonetheless, several of the British political organizations sent a joint delegation to Tanzania, which included members of the BLF, BUFP, ACSHO, and several members from Harambee – Gerlin Bean, Zainab Abbas, Ansel Wong, Ron Phillips, Bini Brown and Fitzmaurice Andrews. It was an important occasion for all of them, not least as a means to develop closer relationships with the liberation organizations in Africa.[128] Following the congress, the BLF, Harambee and George Jackson House established a Pan-African exchange scheme which sent volunteers to Africa 'to develop lasting links at the grassroots level between the people living in Africa and their descendants in Britain'.[129]

The political views of leading African American figures, such as Carmichael, Eldridge and Kathleen Cleaver, Angela Davis, Maulana Karenga, and the legacy of Malcolm X, were clearly influential upon young Black people in Britain. But they were strongly drawn to such politics as a result of the racism and other problems that they faced on a daily basis.[130] There were often important discussions about whether Black Power and Pan-Africanism should have a socialist orientation, a Marxist one, or whether they should adopt a largely 'cultural nationalist' perspective.[131] In the early 1970s, the BUFP was one of only a few which would openly declare that, 'The organization is Revolutionary and Socialist. It believes that the major contradiction facing Black people in Britain is that of class.'[132] Such considerations were often connected with the question of whether alliances or joint activities were possible with predominately white organizations.[133]

Socialism became a particularly significant political position because of the inspiring developments in Vietnam and Cuba at the time, the influence of Mao and Amilcar Cabral, leader of the nationalist revolution in Guinea-Bissau and the Cape Verde Islands, the examples of African liberation movements in Angola, Mozambique and Guinea-Bissau and the influence of the US Black Panthers. As the BLF explained: 'It is only natural that countries like Mozambique and Angola should adopt scientific socialism as the guiding ideology, because scientific socialism is a radical improvement on capitalism/colonialism.'[134]

But political differences existed within many organizations and manifested themselves more openly after the sixth Pan-African Congress of 1974. These led to the founding of the Pan-African Committee, a coalition under the leadership of Ron Phillips, and then, in 1977, the creation of a new Pan-Afrikan Congress Movement (PACM), in which Phillips, Brown, former members of the BLF, Lu Garvey and Nkurmah Pepukayi, and others, including Cecil Gutzmore, played a leading role.[135] The PACM became especially associated with meetings that

were publicized as 'strictly an African family occasion', with the promotion of Kwanzaa, an African-inspired festival originating in the
United States, and with a series of annual Africa Liberation Day events
that were first launched in Nottingham in 1975. One of the most notable of these celebrations was held in Handsworth in 1977, with the
crowd estimated at 30,000.[136] It effectively meant that, over time, the
'Black Nationalists' held one celebration for Africa Liberation Day,
whereas organizations such as the BLM and BUFP held another.

During the 1970s and 1980s all organizations were concerned to
develop community welfare programmes. Self-help and community
organizing were two of the main legacies of Black Power in Britain.
For some, anti-imperialist politics also meant supporting the struggle
for national liberation in Vietnam and an end to British rule in Ireland,
as well as a liberated and united Africa. There was, however, often a
tendency among Black Power organizations to support the aim of
socialism and revolution in other countries, especially African and
Caribbean ones, such as Grenada, but to be rather more circumspect
about organizing for it alongside predominately white organizations
in Britain.[137] Nevertheless, views could develop and change. In 1985,

Africa Liberation Day in Handsworth, 1977

471

the BLF's *Grassroots* newspaper, commenting on the lessons of the year-long miners' strike, concluded: '[T]he struggles of Black people must be firmly linked with the struggles of the working class, if we are to successfully fight for all our rights and achieve genuine and lasting freedom.'[138]

FROM RESISTANCE TO REBELLION

Although reggae provided some solace for young Black people, they did not escape the surveillance of the police, even in clubs and dance halls. Some major confrontations took place in, or around, clubs or other places where young people gathered. The Metro Youth Club, in Ladbroke Grove, had been regularly targeted by the police since its opening in 1968, leading to a major incident in May 1971 when police, including members of the notorious Special Patrol Group, attempted to enter the club, clashing with those inside and leading to twelve arrests.[139] In 1970 police forced entry to the Oval House Youth Club in Kennington, during a BPM dance, leading to the arrest and conviction of three Panthers for riotous assembly.

When police raided the Carib Club in Cricklewood in October 1974, for the fifth time in two weeks, it resulted in the arrest of more than forty young people. Twelve of those arrested, the so-called 'Carib 12', were arbitrarily charged with riot and affray and appeared in a well-publicized trial at the Old Bailey.[140] Perhaps the most famous defendant was the musician and sound-system operator, Dennis Bovell, who was sentenced to three years' imprisonment and spent several months in jail before his conviction was quashed on appeal. Indeed, another ten of the Carib 12 were subsequently acquitted.[141] There were also significant clashes between Black youth and police on Bonfire Night in Chapeltown in Leeds in 1975. After a police car had been driven at group of young people, mainly teenagers, 'the Bonfire 12', were arrested and charged with various offences, but all but two were subsequently acquitted by the courts.[142]

Throughout the 1970s there had been warnings that the actions of the police were creating animosity that would find an outlet in the future. In 1973 the National Youth Bureau warned 'that black youths

Supporters of the 'Bonfire 12' protest outside Leeds Crown Court

in particular felt that they were subjected to constant and unnecessary police scrutiny'. In March 1980 even the Commission for Racial Equality, established by the government in 1976, concluded: 'whether the black community's belief that the law enforcement services is discriminatory is justified is irrelevant. What matters is that substantial numbers of blacks of all ages, and particularly young blacks, perceive it to be the case.'[143]

One of the most notable examples of resistance to the police occurred at the Notting Hill Carnival in August 1976.[144] On that occasion police attempts to arrest those who, it was alleged, were pickpockets, led to widescale violent disturbances with more than 250 people hospitalized.[145] The disturbances, at an event that had hitherto been entirely without serious incident, were subsequently labelled 'riots' in the press, but were seen as legitimate self-defence by many in the Black communities.[146] 'The police drew the battle lines and black youth moved to the forefront in the confrontation', opined *Race Today*, adding, 'There would have been no crushing defeat of a well-deployed police army without an event to which young British West Indians flocked in their thousands.' Even the *Financial Times* considered that the actions of the youth 'must surely be seen as expressing a kind of social or political anger, however inarticulate'.[147]

The police had significantly increased their presence at the annual event, deploying some 3,000 officers, an 'unnecessary army', despite warnings that this might be construed as provocative. They had also joined forces with local politicians and others in an attempt to encourage the Home Secretary to ban the event and move the Carnival away from the streets of Notting Hill.[148] In the wake of earlier confrontations, and the widespread misuse of the 'sus' law, many of those attending Carnival in 1976 resented such a heavy police presence and immediately came to the aid of those the police were attempting to arrest. Indeed, the police complained that this was a growing trend and pointed to over forty similar incidents in the previous year.[149] In 1976, there were more than sixty arrests, but at a major trial at the Old Bailey, of seventeen of those arrested, none were convicted of any offences committed during the carnival.[150] Nevertheless, the disturbances, which also occurred on a smaller scale in 1977, were presented in the media as the actions of ferocious and criminal Black youth. Elsewhere, they were seen as an example of violent state repression of the cultural expression of those of Caribbean heritage.[151] *Race Today* concluded: '[W]hen the history of the black community is documented, the skilful resistance which young blacks displayed ... must be registered as a turning point in our struggle for those rights which constantly appear to elude us.'[152]

The large-scale resistance at the Notting Hill Carnival heralded a new era of mass resistance and rebellion by young Black people in Britain that was to continue for the next decade. Provocative actions by the police, as well as the deployment of the Special Patrol Group in areas where there was a high concentration of Caribbean and other oppressed communities, were well documented. Such actions also began to be contrasted with what was widely considered a lack of a police response to racist attacks and with the thousands of police who were deployed to protect the marches of the neo-Nazi National Front, as well as those of other openly racist individuals and organizations.[153] In such circumstances, young people of all nationalities took matters into their own hands with significant anti-fascist actions such as the

'Battle of Lewisham' in August 1977 and the 'Battle of Digbeth' in 1978, in which protesters fought to prevent such racist organizations, which were protected by the police, from provocatively marching through the streets.[154] In this period the police, the mainstream media and the state authorities were even reluctant to admit the existence of racism and racist attacks, whatever their source. In 1978 the future Prime Minister, Margaret Thatcher, made it clear that one of the main sources of racism could be found in the speeches of politicians themselves, with her own infamous remarks that Britain 'might be rather swamped by people of a different culture'.[155]

THE UPRISINGS

The first of the major uprisings, as they became known, broke out in Bristol in April 1980, when the police launched a raid on the popular Black and White Café in Grosvenor Road in the St Paul's district, claiming that it was being used for illegal drinking and marijuana smoking.[156] The raid, carried out in the afternoon, was resisted by local people who felt aggrieved after many years of police harassment. The police were met with bottles and other missiles, forced to defend themselves with milk crates and dustbin lids, and several police vehicles were overturned and set alight, as was the local bank and post office. The so-called 'riots' continued for several hours and involved hundreds (in some reports, thousands) of people who, for a time, forced the police to retreat from the St Paul's area. The uprising led to twenty-five people, mainly police, being hospitalized and subsequently over 140 arrests. Sixteen of those arrested were charged with riot, but all were subsequently acquitted.

St Paul's was the first major uprising of the 1980s and has been seen as an example of a community, mainly of Caribbean heritage, but with support from youth of all nationalities, refusing to accept what was considered further police harassment after years of previous altercations. There was also a background of racism, unemployment and deprivation in the area and the fact that the Black and White Café was widely seen as one of the few community amenities added to community resentment. According to one account, the 'victory against the police was celebrated the following day with an impromptu dance and the singing of the popular reggae song *Beat Down Babylon*'.[157] The St Paul's uprising was unprecedented. Paul Stephenson referred to it as a 'wake-up call for this country', and added that 'The riots were ignited by racist and insensitive policing. It was about young blacks who were born in this country saying that they weren't prepared to be treated as second-class citizens any longer.'[158]

In January 1981 a fire broke out at a house party in New Cross at which thirteen young Black people between the ages of fourteen and twenty-two lost their lives. Twenty-seven other partygoers were seriously injured and a fourteenth young person, traumatized by the events, plunged to his death eighteen months later.[159]Although the tragedy was reported in the mainstream press, it was often done in such a way as to spread disinformation, and this was the case here too.[160] It was a sign of the times that no official statements of condolence and sympathy were issued by the government, nor the head of state.[161] What was worse, there was a strong suspicion locally, and more widely, that the fire had been caused by a racist attack, a firebomb thrown into 439 New Cross Road, following a political campaign against noisy house parties. The authorities appeared to discount such a possibility. There was little trust in the police investigations, which appeared to be focused on investigating those attending the party; with some young people detained and forced to sign statements that the fire was started as a result of a fight at the celebration.[162]

Two days after the fire, the New Cross Massacre Action Committee (NCMAC) was founded by La Rose, Howe, the broadcaster Alex Pascall and Roxy Harris, a founder of the Black Parents Movement. The NCMAC, representing the families and the Black community, began to organize a political response to the tragedy, based on their view that it was a racist attack, and that appropriate measures were not being taken by the state. It also raised money and support for the bereaved families. In March 1981, the NCMAC organized the Black People's Day of Action, a march from New Cross to Hyde Park. It was a unique event, 'the largest and most effective demonstration of black political power in thirty years', according to the Black Parents Movement, Black Youth Movement and Race Today Collective. It involved 20,000 mainly Black youths, as well as other concerned people, marching through the streets of London expressing grief and outrage in equal measure. Perhaps the most popular slogan was '13 Dead, Nothing Said', but there were many others aimed at the racism of the police and the mainstream press. The NCMAC also delivered letters of protest to the government and Metropolitan Police.[163] This tragedy showed that the outrage felt by entire communities could be made visible and articulated as never before. A new Black British personality was emerging.

A month later, in early April 1981, the Metropolitan Police initiated 'Operation Swamp 81', a mass 'stop and search' operation lasting four days in which over 1,000 people were randomly stopped and questioned. The operation began on the streets of Brixton, because of its high crime figures, according to the police, or to harass local Black youth after the Black People's Day of Action, according to the view on the streets. It resulted in three days and nights, from 10 to 12 April, of rebellion and resistance by local youth provoked not only by 'Swamp 81', but also by similar factors to those that had provoked the resistance in Bristol the previous year, including 55 per cent youth unemployment.[164] Police action in April 1981 followed years of provocation and violence, especially by the SPG. The latter had led to an inquiry

The Black People's Day of Action, March 1981

by Lambeth Council on 'community-police relations', which referred to a police 'army of occupation' in the area. The inquiry recommended less use of 'stop and search' and the Special Police Group in Brixton, but was ignored.[165] According to Peter Bletchley, a former police officer in south London, young Black men 'were routinely fitted up, beaten up, tortured and worse'.[166] Herman Ouseley, a community liaison officer in Lambeth at the time, explained, '[T]here was a build-up in which you could sense people saying, "Well we are not prepared to go on taking any more . . . Operation Swamp . . . was really not just pushing people up against the wall, but trying to push them through it . . . It was all about settling scores which were building up over a long period of time." '[167]

Alex Wheatle, the author of the novel *East of Acre Lane*, set against the backdrop of the uprising, who was arrested and imprisoned for his part in the events, illuminated it in this way: 'I had brushed with the police and suffered racist intimidation, so all those bad feelings and experiences I had against the police came out on that weekend . . . For us who experienced it, we saw it as standing up to a racist police force. After these events we believe that society began to start listening to us and taking our concerns seriously.'[168] The BLF's newspaper, *Grassroots*, under the headline 'Uprising inna Brixton', declared: 'It was not just the police that the Black people of Brixton were attacking but all the different layers of rejection they go through daily, these same conditions exist in all the other Black communities up and down the country. Just like Brixton and Bristol, a spark is all that is needed to cause an explosion.'[169]

As was the case with the Notting Hill Carnival disturbances in 1976 and those in Bristol in 1980, scenes from the Brixton Uprising were broadcast on national television and featured prominently in the mainstream press.[170] What was shown to the entire country was a series of running battles between police and mainly young Black people who deployed a variety of missiles, including the first wide-scale use of petrol bombs. over a hundred vehicles and commercial properties were set ablaze or seriously damaged, in an area a few miles away from Parliament and Downing Street. It was estimated that the cost of the damage caused was £7.5m, with more than 300 people, mostly police, injured. There were 200 arrests. However, the impact on the body politic was much greater, not least because the Brixton Uprising inspired other similar acts of rebellion in Liverpool, Manchester, Birmingham, Leeds and in total in more than thirty other towns and cities throughout the country during the summer of 1981. In Liverpool, over four nights in July, 150 buildings were burnt down, more than 250 police needed hospital treatment, 160 people were arrested and one disabled man, David Moore, was killed when he was run over by a police vehicle. The events in Liverpool were apparently sparked when 'a black motorcyclist was arrested by the police. A crowd gathered and stoned the police while the motor cyclist made his escape.'[171] A young man who witnessed the events summed up the sentiments of many at the time:

> To see the power of people, a community united as one with one target. People actually standing together and drawing their line in the sand: 'That's it, we've had enough, this is payback'; to see the people actually succeed. People may call it anarchy, but this was a message from the people ... People still willing to take on the police despite the hi-tech equipment the police had at the time, and they won! Can you imagine that, to see them running, to see officers actually getting up and running away?[172]

The struggles against police and other forms of racism had taken centre stage in Britain's political life. The government of Margaret Thatcher, clearly shocked by such violent and widespread disorder, called for a public inquiry. It was led by Lord Scarman, whose report was published in November 1981. Scarman recommended various reforms, but perhaps the most significant part of his report was his view that 'institutional racism does not exist in Britain: but racial disadvantage and its nasty associate, racial discrimination, have not yet been eliminated'. Scarman concluded that:

> racial disadvantage is a fact of current British life ... Urgent action is needed if it is not to become an endemic, ineradicable disease threatening the very survival of our society ... [Racial disadvantage and racial discrimination] poison minds and attitudes; they are, as long as they remain and will continue to be, a potent factor of unrest.

However, no urgent action was taken and Scarman expressed the view that 'the direction and policies of the Metropolitan Police are not racist', although he accepted that individual officers were guilty of 'racially prejudiced actions'.[173] The overall effect of the report was extremely limited, as recognized in the Macpherson inquiry nearly twenty years later, even though Scarman had accepted that various forms of racism existing over many years had created the condition for the uprisings in Brixton and elsewhere. The government was forced to accept that racism existed, that racist attacks occurred and that the police might act in a racist manner. What was not investigated and not addressed was the source of the racism and other forms of social, economic and political inequality in the country.

The rebellions of 1981, which involved not just young Black people, were to continue throughout the decade, not least because what was considered to be the racism of government and police remained essentially the same. In 1981, the Thatcher government, with the support of the Labour Party, introduced the Nationality Act, which effectively removed citizenship rights from many of African and Caribbean heritage, as well as those classified as Commonwealth citizens who could not establish a relationship of 'patriality' (based on having parents or grandparents born in Britain, as specified by the 1971 Immigration Act), or would not pay a fee for such rights. Even those born in Britain were not automatically eligible for citizenship.

In 1983 there followed the highly suspicious fatal shooting of Colin Roach, a 21-year-old Black man, inside Stoke Newington Police Station. Despite local protests and demands, which led to numerous arrests, there was no official inquiry into the circumstances of his death, which became another notorious case. The Roach Family Support Committee commissioned its own inquiry and subsequently published a report, *Policing in Hackney, 1945–1984*, which strongly criticized the version of events presented by the police and more generally the role of the state in relation to its treatment of all its citizens, and Black citizens in particular.[174] Colin Roach's death created a number of cultural tributes in 1983, including Benjamin Zephaniah's 'Who Killed Colin Roach?' and Isaac Julien's film of the same name. Birmingham-based reggae artist Macka B was later to refer to Roach and several other Black people whose deaths were associated with the police in his song 'We've Had Enough' (1986).[175]

In 1985 the police shooting of Dorothy 'Cherry' Groce in her own home led to further major mass protests and unrest in Brixton, in which one man died, more than fifty people were injured, vehicles and property were set ablaze or destroyed, and over 200 were arrested.[176] Cherry Groce survived the shooting, but was paralysed for the rest of her life. It was a sign of the times that it was not until 2014, twenty-nine years later, three years after her death in 2011, and as a result of an official inquest, that the Metropolitan Police finally publicly apologized unreservedly, both for the shooting and for the time it had taken to issue a public apology (a private apology had been made to the family of Cherry Groce in 2013). In 1985 there was an internal inquiry into the shooting, which concluded that at the very least the police officer responsible 'displayed professional ineptitude'. But this information was kept from the Groce family until 2014. In 1987 the police officer principally involved was charged with 'inflicting unlawful and malicious grievous bodily harm', but was acquitted and no disciplinary action was taken against him.[177]

There were other significant uprisings in south London, Liverpool, Birmingham, in which two people lost their lives, and most notably in north London, on the Tottenham housing estate, Broadwater Farm, on 6 October 1985. The latter uprising was provoked by the death of Cynthia Jarrett, who died of heart failure during a search of her home by the police. It was in the course of violent protests over the death of Mrs Jarrett that a police officer, PC Blakelock, also lost his life.[178] These events led to the occupation of the estate by almost 10,000 police officers. Both deaths were entirely preventable. The police search of Mrs Jarrett's home was made following the arrest of her son for a minor traffic offence. During the independent inquiry, conducted subsequently by Lord Gifford QC, it was revealed that the police had fabricated a justification for his arrest and had no reason for the search of his mother's home. There was even some doubt as to whether the police had a search warrant, and they entered the house using keys illegally acquired. Even official statements issued by the Metropolitan Police after Mrs Jarrett's death were entirely false, since they claimed that she lost her life as a result of a physical struggle with the police.[179]

The actions of the police throughout were strongly condemned by

Cherry Groce, paralysed after a police shooting

Bernie Grant (1944–2000), the first leader of Caribbean heritage of Haringey Council. However, no police officers were disciplined, nor were any held accountable for the death of Cynthia Jarrett. The actions of the Metropolitan Police in Brixton, Tottenham and elsewhere were condemned by Bernard Levin, the famous correspondent of *The Times*, in his article 'Who will defend us against the bullies in blue?'[180] The uprisings in London and Birmingham provided the inspiration for the film *Handsworth Songs* (1985), seen almost as avant-garde at the time, but firmly based within a tradition of films made by Black filmmakers, or those made about the experience of Black youth, such as Horace Ové's *Pressure* (1976), Franco Rosso's *Babylon* (1980), Menelik Shabazz's *Burning an Illusion* (1981) and *Blood Ah Go Run* (1982).

Cynthia Jarrett

WOMEN'S LIBERATION

Women played a significant and often a leading role in many of the organizations formed during this period. This clearly contributed to the political orientation adopted on a range of issues, including the liberation of women. The BUFP declared: 'We believe in the total and unconditional equality of women . . . We believe that women like Black people in general cannot be totally or truly liberated under capitalism. We also understand that Black women form the most oppressed section of society being triply oppressed through class, race and sex.'[181] The BLF declared, 'We stand for total and complete equality between Black women and men and are against all ideas and practices which oppress and degrade Black women.'[182]

Gender sensitivity became one of the most important questions for the Black Power movement in Britain, and several Black women's

483

groups eventually emerged from this movement.[183] Organizations such as the BUFP and BLF often included special pages devoted to the 'woman question' and the triple oppression of women in their publications, while some organizations such as the south London-based Fasimbas had a predominantly female membership.[184] The BLF stated: 'We reject the idea that a woman's place is in the home, and that women cannot play an active part in the fight for Black freedom.'[185] Significantly, Altheia Jones-Lecointe became the leader of the BPM, and she developed a reputation for her opposition to misogyny within the organization.[186] During the 1980s the BLF was also led by a woman, Pauline Machera (née Wilson), who was particularly noted for her commitment to the welfare of those locked up in prison.

The BUFP established the Black Women's Action Group (BWAG) under the direction of Gerlin Bean, who had arrived from Jamaica in the late 1950s, a year after its founding. In 1971 the BWAG published *Black Women Speak Out*, an anthology of earlier writing.[187] Bean, a former nurse, was one of only a few Black women who attended the National Women's Liberation Conference held in Oxford in 1970 and can be considered the leading force in the creation of a Black women's movement in Britain. She and other Black women were, however, more influenced by the leading role that women were taking in the liberation struggles in Africa.[188] After leading the work to establish the BWAG, Bean joined the BLF in 1971 and established a women's section within that organization. As a result, the BLF demanded 'an end to the oppression of black women from all quarters'.[189]

In 1973 Bean led the creation of the Brixton Black Women's Group (BBWG), one of the first such groups in the country, which included Zainab Abbas, Olive Morris and Liz Obi amongst its initial membership, and later produced the publication *Speak Out*. According to Abbas, after Bean's suggestion, five women originally met together informally one evening, 'at the house of another sister called Marcia', to discuss 'issues related to feminism, defining feminism overall, and what it was about and then defining it in relation to black women, and then in relation to our own experiences'. She explained, 'It was a nice evening where we got together to discuss and then agreed to meet the following week because it was interesting enough for us to keep going with it. And we kept going and kept going. And then suddenly it got out about us.'[190] In 1978, Bean was one of the co-founders of the Organization of Women of African and Asian Descent (OWAAD), an umbrella organization for Black women's groups throughout the country. As well as building several important organizations for Black women, Bean has rightly been seen as the mentor of many of the key women activists of the period.[191]

The OWAAD, established in 1978, grew out of the earlier Organization of Women of Africa and African Descent established by members of the BBWG, and African women's organizations such as the Ethiopian Women's Study Group and Eritrean Women's Study Group, as well as those who had formerly been involved with other organizations, such as the African Students' Union.[192] More than 300 women attended its first conference in 1979, which led to other women's groups, or groups dominated by women, being formed throughout the country, some focusing on issues such as education or immigration. The East London Black Women's Organization (ELBWO), for example, was formed in May 1979 after members met at the OWAAD Conference. In a publicity leaflet, it explained that '[W]e have set up a parent/teacher group to increase involvement in children's education and also to run a Saturday school', and concluded, 'the more we learn, the easier it has become to deal with the urgent needs like helping or advising our children on arrest ... helping ourselves in housing, employment, immigration etc.'[193]

OWAAD also provided support for women trying to organize despite local opposition, such as the Black Women's Cooperative in Manchester, which, led by Kath Locke, Coca Clarke and others, organized a nine-day sit-in during 1979 when male members of the George Jackson Housing Trust attempted to lock them out of shared premises.[194] This struggle resulted in the creation in 1980 of the Manchester Black women's group Abisindi, which carried on the tradition of earlier groups such as the Black Women's Co-operative.[195] OWAAD based itself on 'Afro-Asian unity' and was wary of being labelled a 'feminist organization'. It produced its own newsletter, *FOWAAD!*, and in 1985 Stella Dadzie and other leading members co-wrote *Heart of the Race*, often viewed as the seminal text on Black women's experiences and activism in this period.

FOWAAD! Newsletter of OWAAD, July 1980

AFRICAN LIBERATION

The struggles against racism built unity amongst the many organizations established during this period, as did their various efforts to support and contribute to the ending of all forms of colonialism in Africa. These activities occurred throughout the year, but gained a particular focus every 25 May, Africa Liberation Day. Of all the anticolonial struggles, those relating to the ending of the apartheid regime in South Africa occupied a special place. Those fighting against racism in Britain were also concerned about racist oppression in Africa and recognized that they were struggling against common foes. Such sentiments were not limited to Britain and were often featured strongly in the lyrics of reggae songs and other music popular during the 1970s and 1980s.

In 1959, Britain's Anti-Apartheid Movement (AAM) grew out of the efforts of the Committee of African Organizations and, throughout the ensuing years, African and Caribbean political organizations, including the West Indian Standing Conference, Africa Liberation Committee, Black Parents' Movement, Afro-Caribbean Self-Help Organization and Black Action for the Liberation of South Africa, as well as many individuals not affiliated to any organization, continued to provide support for the liberation organizations in South Africa, such as the African National Congress (ANC), the Pan-Africanist Congress (PAC) and the Black Consciousness Movement (BCM). Reports on South Africa even appeared in relatively mainstream publications including *West Indian World*, and later *The Voice*, and the struggle against the apartheid regime was supported by several MPs, most notably by Bernie Grant. However, despite its origins, it was not until the late 1980s that the official AAM made significant efforts to reach out to African and Caribbean communities in Britain.[196]

One important aspect of the struggle to bring about the demise of the racist regime in South Africa was to oppose and expose those who propped up apartheid, including the government in Britain. During the 'Opening Address at Africa Liberation Day' celebrations in Birmingham in 1981, for example, it was pointed out that the British government was amongst those institutions which used the power of veto to limit economic sanctions against South Africa. According to the speaker: 'They protect Apartheid. They defend racism. They are prepared to use continued subjugation and subjection of the Afrikan people, rather than have the White South African minority regime give way to Black majority rule in an independent free Azania.'[197] Many organizations engaged in fundraising activities arranged their own local boycotts of South African goods, or requested speakers and information from the liberation organizations.[198] It could be challenging work, not least because of the tensions between the ANC and the PAC, but by the late 1980s, with the apartheid regime's military defeat in Angola and its retreat from its illegal occupation of Namibia, it was clear that its days were numbered. In 1989 the BUFP's *Black Voice* declared, 'Victory Is Certain', and instructed its readers: 'In Britain, our duty is clear. Step up the boycott of all South African products. Demand the release of all political prisoners and the placing of comprehensive economic sanctions. Give nuff [sic] material and political support to the frontline states (especially Namibia and the Liberation movements).'[199] This was the sentiment of many organizations and, as Mandela acknowledged, such activities made a contribution to his release, and the release of other political prisoners, as well as the eventual demise of the apartheid regime.[200]

There were, of course, many other examples of activities undertaken to support struggles for liberation in Africa. In 1990, for instance, the BLF led the founding of the Committee for Ethiopian and Eritrean Relief (CEER). CEER worked to publicize the struggles of such organizations as the Eritrean Peoples' Liberation Front (EPLF) and the Tigray Peoples' Liberation Front (TPLF), both of which were fighting against the murderous military regime in Ethiopia, which was backed by the Soviet Union. In addition, CEER also worked with the Relief Society of Tigray (REST) and the Eritrean Relief Association (ERA) to raise funds for famine relief and other humanitarian projects.[201]

The period from the mid-1960s onwards is often associated with the experiences of those young people who were the children of post-war migrants, who faced racism in school, employment and at the hands of the police. Many of these young people were born in Britain to families who had long been resident in the country. It was the era of Black Power and Black Liberation, with the emergence of new political organizations that struggled to resist racism and defend the rights of African and Caribbean communities. It was also the period of significant youth uprisings in major cities against racism, disadvantage and disempowerment. The political organizations, publications, bookshops, poetry, music and other manifestations of the period gave rise to a particular Black British culture of resistance and self-expression that had a powerful influence throughout the country.

I I

Into the New Century

One of the most significant changes towards the end of the twentieth and the start of the twenty-first century has been that the population who traced their heritage directly from the African continent became larger than those who traced their immediate heritage to the Caribbean. This change first became statistically apparent in a period of twenty years between 1991, the first time that 'ethnicity' was recorded in British census returns, and 2011. The 2011 census returns showed that the majority of Black British people classified themselves as 'Black-African'. In the 1991 census the total Black population was officially fewer than 900,000 people; over half of them identified as 'Black-Caribbean' and fewer than a third as 'Black-African'. Ten years later, in 2001, the census results suggested a total Black population of over one million, with approximately 49 per cent of Caribbean heritage and 42 per cent of African heritage. By 2011 the census figures showed that there were more than 1.8 million people who identified as 'Black', although this figure does not include almost 600,000 people whom the census records as being of mixed heritage. Of the total Black population, as defined by the census in 2011, 53 per cent were classified Black-African and 31 per cent Black-Caribbean. The figures are in many respects rather misleading, since the term 'Black' may exclude many of those of mixed heritage who generally self-identify as Black. The term also includes those who do not self-identify as Black-African or Black-Caribbean. Nevertheless, what the figures do show is a substantial shift in the population and that the majority trace their immediate heritage to the African continent.[1]

The 2011 census also provides data on countries of birth, which gives some indication of the size of African communities in England

and Wales (although not of those subsequently born in Britain). According to the census birth figures, Nigerians were the largest community (over 191,000), then South Africans (191,000), then those from Kenya (137,000). Other major communities include those from Zimbabwe (118,00), Somalia (101,000), Ghana (nearly 94,000), Uganda (59,000), Mauritius (41,000) and Tanzania (35,000).[2] These figures need to be viewed with caution, since many of those from Kenya and Uganda, for example, might normally be referred to in Britain as being of Asian rather than African origin.[3] Similar caution is required when looking at figures relating to South Africa and Zimbabwe. Even the figures relating to other communities, such as those of Nigerian heritage, may be very unreliable. Some estimates, especially those from organizations representing Nigerians, suggest that in 2020 there were nearly two million people of Nigerian heritage residing in Britain.[4]

Despite now constituting the majority of the Black population, the history and experiences of those of continental African heritage is, at present, poorly documented, especially for the period after 1945.[5] British citizens of Nigerian heritage have long been a significant population in Britain, especially in London. Increased numbers of Nigerians began to arrive in the 1980s, as a result of political and economic problems there, but there have been further migrations since that time and some migrants have been directly recruited by the NHS. Most Nigerians have settled in London, although there are significant numbers in other cities, such as Manchester, and in such concentrations that an area such as London's Peckham has become known as 'Little Lagos'. Two of the area's most famous Nigerian residents were friends. John Adeboyega, better known as the actor John Boyega, looked after ten-year-old Damilola Taylor before he was tragically killed in 2000, just a few months after arriving in Peckham, a crime that shocked the entire country.[6]

A population of Somali heritage has also long existed in Britain and, from the nineteenth century onwards, northern Somali men, often originating from Aden, were working as seafarers and settling in port cities.[7] During the 1930s, Somalis in Cardiff created the British Somali Society, one of the first organizations to voice a demand for Somalia's independence.[8] In the 1960s, some former seafarers found other forms of employment in industry and were often joined by their families in cities such as Sheffield, Manchester and Birmingham. Since 1985 many Somalis, including women and children, have come to Britain as refugees and to seek asylum from the civil war which engulfed the country. During the period from 1986 to 1999 there were more than 31,000 Somalis seeking asylum, the highest number from any African country.[9] Some also came to Britain via other EU countries where they had initially sought asylum, and once here they often faced difficulties relating to their refugee status. As with the population of Nigerian heritage, census figures only provide an approximation as to the size of the Somali population, which has continued to grow in the twenty-first century, especially in London.[10] Migrants from Zimbabwe constitute a newer community, most of whom have settled in Britain since the 1980s and particularly so during the twenty-first century, with increasing numbers claiming political asylum. Under the Immigration and Asylum Act of 1999 many new asylum seekers were dispersed outside London to cities such as Leicester, which has one of the largest Zimbabwean populations in Britain.[11] Like other Africans, Zimbabweans were directly recruited to Britain by such employers as the NHS, and also as teachers, social workers and engineers. Nurses, in particular, could receive funding to train in the UK, and Zimbabweans became the fourth-largest group of nurses in the NHS. Many faced various forms of racism and exploitation when they first arrived in the country.[12]

Another feature of African migration during the 1990s and after was an increase in Africans from Francophone countries such as the Democratic Republic of Congo, Côte d'Ivoire, Rwanda and elsewhere. By the early twenty-first century, London, for example, was considered to have a Congolese population of some 15,000. During the period 1986 to 2003 there were nearly 17,000 Congolese refugees seeking asylum in Britain. In addition to significant numbers of asylum seekers from countries with established colonial ties to Britain, such as Nigeria and Ghana, there were also more than 10,000 asylum applications from Angolans during this time.[13]

Africans in general, and African women in particular, continue to be recruited to the NHS in the twenty-first century, a practice that has often been viewed as a 'brain drain' on Africa's scarce human resources.[14] Those who come to Britain are then in a position to bring their immediate families with them. Between 1998 and 2003, for example, African countries such as South Africa, Nigeria, Zimbabwe, Kenya, Zambia and Ghana provided over 3,000 nurses for Britain, during a period which saw a steady rise in African recruitment to the NHS, either directly, or via the independent health sector and recruiting agencies. Doctors, another scarce resource, are also recruited from Africa. For example, it was reported in 2002 that there was a shortage of doctors in Ghana, with more working outside the country than within it and more than 300 employed in Britain. Thousands of Ghanaian nurses and midwives were also reported to be working in Britain, with over 2,000 seeking verification of Ghanaian qualifications between 1998 and 2003.[15] In 2002, in London alone, well over 2,000 nurses came from just three African countries: South Africa, Nigeria and Ghana.[16]

BLACK BRITISH

The period from the mid-1980s onwards was also the era when the term 'Black British' first began to gain popularity. Before then there was no generally agreed and accepted collective term for Britain's population of those of African and Caribbean heritage, and it was quite usual for most of this population to identify themselves by their own country of origin or that of their parents if they were born in Britain. However, by the 1980s this practice had already begun to change, first of all with the widespread adoption of the term 'Black', replacing the designation 'coloured' (which had often also included those of South Asian descent). The concept of Black British identity had begun to emerge during the 1970s and was clearly evident in the Black People's Day of Action which followed the tragic New Cross massacre in 1981, as well as the major youth uprisings that occurred during the early 1980s. By this time the term 'Black', which had been first adopted as a political term during the mid-1960s, was being more often applied to and adopted by those of African and Caribbean heritage.

One of the first indications of the newly emerging Black British identity was the launch of the *Voice* newspaper in 1982 by Jamaican-born Val McCalla (1943–2002), a former RAF serviceman and accountant. Before the *Voice*, the most widely read weekly paper was the *West Indian World*, started by Aubrey Baynes, published from 1971 until

1985, and at times achieving a readership of 10,000. The *West Indian World* was nearly always in financial difficulties and, although it adopted a campaigning style, was often viewed as being out of step with the needs of younger readers. Still, it provided regular news aimed at African and Caribbean communities, as well as opportunities for journalists from these communities that were not generally available to them in the mainstream press at the time.[17] There was also a British edition of the *Jamaica Gleaner*, described as a 'middle-of-the-road, non-political family newspaper', while those from West Africa often read *West Africa*, a weekly journal first published in Britain in 1917 and initially aimed mainly at colonial expatriates. In 1981, Guyanese publisher Arif Ali started a rival publication to the *West Indian World* entitled *Caribbean Times* and a few years later published *African Times*, the former nationally distributed, with more than 25,000 copies sold a week by the early 1990s.[18]

The *Voice* broke new ground by styling itself 'the voice of Black Britain' rather than having a specifically Caribbean or African focus. Onyekachi Wambu, one of its early editors, who was of Nigerian heritage, explained that 'the *Voice* was being edited by the ones who had been brought up in Britain and this injected a new dimension into Black news reporting in Britain'.[19] The newspaper's initial backers included Alex Pascall, a well-known radio broadcaster responsible for BBC London's *Black Londoners*, a ground-breaking show which ran from 1974 until 1988 and which, in 1978, became Britain's first daily Black radio programme. By the early 1990s the *Voice* was reported to have a circulation of over 50,000 and benefited greatly from job advertisements from local government, especially those in London which were eager to attract a more diverse workforce after the Scarman report into the major uprising in Brixton in 1981.[20]

BLACK SECTIONS

The youth uprisings of the 1980s also created the conditions for changes within the existing political system in Britain. Some trade unions began to establish 'Black Workers' organizations and the Greater London Council supported the creation of such organizations as the

Black Trade Union Solidarity Movement and the Black Media Workers' Association. It also established an Ethnic Minorities Unit which, amongst other things, initiated a London-wide anti-racist initiative. In 1983 a growing demand for 'Black Sections' within the Labour Party led to an unofficial national grouping under the leadership of future MPs Diane Abbott, Paul Boateng and others and a first national conference in Birmingham in 1984. Those arguing for such changes believed that they would lead to political advances, especially greater political representation, for those of African, Caribbean and South Asian heritage in Britain. Critics argued that such developments would do nothing for the majority of Black British people, but merely advance the careers of a handful of individuals.[21]

Certainly, in the next few years such initiatives contributed towards the election of Merle Amory, Linda Bellos and Bernie Grant as leaders of London councils in 1986. St Kitts-born Merle Amory was the first woman of Caribbean heritage to became a council leader when elected to office in the London borough of Brent. Bellos was the first woman of African heritage to be so employed, when she was elected leader of Lambeth Council. There followed the selection and then election of four Black Labour Party MPs, Diane Abbott, Paul Boateng, Bernie Grant and Keith Vaz, in 1987. Keith Vaz followed in the footsteps of previous MPs of South Asian origin, including Dadabhai Naoroji, Manchergee Bhownaghree and Shapurji Salatvala. They also followed previous, but largely long-forgotten MPs of Caribbean origin, including Richard Beckford (d. 1796) and Peter McLagan (1823–1900).[22]

The fact that four Black MPs from minority communities were elected in the same Parliament was seen as an historic event of unprecedented significance, not least because Abbott became the first woman of Caribbean origin to be elected to Parliament. However, there were still many difficulties for such prospective MPs. In 1989 Martha Osamor, a woman of Nigerian heritage who was the vice-chair of the Labour Party's Black Sections (and is now Baroness Osamor) was prevented from standing for election in the Vauxhall constituency by the leadership of the Labour Party, even although she had strong support.[23]

In 1997 Boateng became the first Black government minister as Parliamentary Under-Secretary for Health, in 2002, the first Black cabinet minister when he was appointed Chief Secretary to the Treasury and

the first Black ambassador with his appointment as High Commissioner to South Africa in 2005. Valerie Amos was the first Black woman
to be appointed a cabinet minister, when she became Secretary of State
for International Development in 2003. In 2009, she also became the
first Black woman ambassador when she was appointed High Commissioner to Australia.

BLACK HISTORY

Black History Month was first launched as a celebration in October
1987 by the London Strategic Policy Unit (LSPU), successor to the
recently abolished Greater London Council (GLC), and representing
several Labour-controlled boroughs. Originally devised by Akyaaba
Addai-Sebo, a political exile from Ghana who had worked in the
GLC Ethnic Minorities Unit led by Ansel Wong, it was from its inception almost entirely devoted to the history of those of African and
Caribbean heritage. Addai-Sebo later explained that he initiated it
partly because he was concerned about 'the identity crisis that Black
children faced as some brazenly would not identify with Africa and
shrank when called an African'. While it was based on similar celebrations in the United States, Addai-Sebo was particularly concerned to
engage with young people and chose October as a month when 'the
weather was not cold and children were fresh after the long summer
vacation and had less to worry about exams and tests and the camaraderie was stronger as they shared experiences'.[24]

The first Black History Month was also part of a wider initiative of
the London Strategic Policy Unit, led by Linda Bellos, for an African
Jubilee year, 1987 to 1988, celebrating the centenary of the birth of
Marcus Garvey, 150 years since the abolition of slavery in Britain's
Caribbean colonies and twenty-five years since the founding of the
Organization of African Unity. African Jubilee Year was officially
launched on 31 July 1987 with an address by Sally Mugabe, standing
in for Robert Mugabe, the president of Zimbabwe, at Central Hall,
Westminster. The first Black History Month commemoration in Britain
was addressed by Maulana Karenga, an African American academic,
the Kenyan activist Wanjiru Kihoro and the leader of the Inner London

Education Authority, Bernard Wiltshire. Addai-Sebo explained that 'we were determined to let Londoners, especially the children, know about the contributions Africa and Africans had made to London and the world, through the talks, concerts and exhibitions'.[25] One of these exhibitions led to an important publication, *A History of the Black Presence in London*, which was first published by the GLC in 1986. It was one of the first attempts to bring the history of African, Caribbean and South Asian people in Britain to a wide audience and reflected a growing body of work by historians, including Peter Fryer's ground-breaking *Staying Power: The History of Black People in Britain* (1984), as well as File and Power's *Black Settlers in Britain* (1981). The latter had arisen out of the demands of students and teachers at Tulse Hill School in London during the 1970s, where File was head of history. It was part of several initiatives in the 1970s to develop Black studies and Black history courses and exams, in London and Birmingham in particular. The early 1980s was also a period in which important conferences in this field were first held, including the International Conference on the History of Blacks in Britain held at the University of London Institute of Education in 1981 and, at the same venue in 1984, the Conference on the History of Blacks in London.[26]

Black History Month can therefore be seen as arising out of this new emphasis on the history of African and Caribbean people in Britain, as well as the same political environment as other initiatives in local government in that period, particularly those connected with Black sections in the Labour Party. These initiatives, often led by those of African and Caribbean heritage, devised in the aftermath of the uprisings of the early 1980s and targeted at African and Caribbean communities. Launched in London, Black History Month spread throughout the country, frequently with support from local authorities. Even before this, in the early 1980s, Len Garrison (1943–2003), an educationalist and historian, as well as others, including Gloria Cameron, Amelda Inyang, Makeda Coaston and Askala Miriam, founded the African People's Historical Monument Foundation (APHMF).[27] This was the body which worked to create what would become the Black Cultural Archives (BCA), formed in response to the lack of history reflecting the experiences of those of African and Caribbean heritage and partly inspired by the African American reparations activist, Queen Mother Moore, who visited Britain in 1982. Garrison had already founded the African Caribbean Educational Research (ACER) project, working with the Inner London Education Authority to create a library and provide 'multi-cultural resources' for the use of all schoolchildren. Garrison and the APHMF had a vision and voiced a demand that was shared by very few others at the time. They established the BCA as a community organization, for many years based in Coldharbour Lane, Brixton, that was dedicated to collecting and preserving material relating to the history of African and Caribbean people in Britain.[28] It took the work of many others to realize this vision some years after Garrison's premature death. The BCA was a small community project for many years, with some initial funding from the Greater London Council and the Commission for Racial Equality, before receiving substantial Heritage Lottery and local authority funding that enabled it to move into a purpose-built archive in Brixton in 2014.[29] The early twenty-first century was a period for many other important initiatives relating to history, such as the London Mayor's Commission on African and Asian Heritage, which first met in 2003. The aim was to 'celebrate and champion London's hidden history'. According to London's mayor of the time, Ken Livingstone, that meant 'ensuring that we tell the full story about London's history. It also means ensuring that London's African, Caribbean and Asian communities are able to see their achievements, contributions and historical presence reflected in our museums, archives, galleries and text books.'[30] The Mayor's Commission made many important recommendations to government and the heritage sector, most of which, sadly, went unheeded.

BLACK FIRSTS

The emergence of a new Black British identity was accompanied by numerous historic breakthroughs for Britain's citizens of African and Caribbean heritage around that time. In 1981 Moira Stuart became the BBC's first woman of Caribbean heritage to become a newscaster for the BBC, and went on to present all the BBC's major television news programmes. By the end of the 1980s, Trinidad-born Trevor

McDonald was occupying a similar role for ITV News and went on to become the most famous presenter of ITV's flagship *News at Ten*. Both literally changed the face of British television. Another key appointment was that of Jamaican-born Bill Morris, who, in 1991, was elected General Secretary of the Transport and General Workers' Union (TGWU), and thereby became the first Black leader of a major trade union. Morris had, in 1985, been elected Deputy General Secretary of the TGWU, at that time the country's largest trade union. Characteristically he said at the time:

> I did not stand as a black candidate. I was a candidate who happens to be black. My appointment will be of added value to the T and G and in the union movement as a whole because it demonstrates that the system works and ethnic people can come forward to take positions of responsibility.[31]

There were also many sporting firsts during this period. In 1993 Paul Ince became the first Black captain of the England football team, when he led his country in a match against the United States. Ince's captaincy and his tenacious role in the team were a fitting riposte to the racism that was endemic in the sport. In 1991, two years before Ince's appointment, the Chairman of Crystal Palace had made his infamous racist comments about Black players: 'I don't think too many of them can read the game. When you're getting into the mid-winter you need a few of the hard white men to carry the athletic black players through.'[32] In 1994 Ellery Hanley, who had already captained the Great Britain rugby league team, was appointed the team's coach and became the first Black coach, or manager, of any national team in British sport.

In 2006 Ugandan-born John Sentamu became the Church of England's first Black archbishop when he was appointed Archbishop of York.[33] In 2019 Bernadine Evaristo became the first Black British woman to win the Booker Prize for her novel *Girl, Woman, Other*, following a distinguished career which included establishing the Theatre of Black Women with Paulette Randall and Patricia Hilaire in 1982. The theatre was 'about the lives and struggles of Black women and provides an opportunity for Black women's voices to be heard positively through theatre'.[34] There are many other examples of those who individually and collectively contributed to a distinctive Black British sense of achievement in the period since the 1980s. However, whatever the successes of individuals, particular challenges and many struggles remained for those of African and Caribbean heritage.

STEPHEN LAWRENCE

The murder of Stephen Lawrence, a nineteen-year-old teenager who was returning home with a friend one evening in Eltham, south London, in April 1993, became not just a tragedy for his family and all who knew him, but also one of the most infamous examples of racism in Britain's history. This was not only because of the completely unprovoked actions of his murderers, five young men to whom Stephen Lawrence was a complete stranger. Perhaps even more horrifying than their actions were those of the Metropolitan Police and other state agencies in the aftermath of the murder. As a consequence, the legal and other investigations into the murder, as well as the activities of the police, have continued into the third decade of the twenty-first century.[35] The murder told the world about the state of racism in Britain.

Stephen Lawrence was born in Greenwich to parents Doreen and Neville, who migrated to Britain from Jamaica during the 1960s, and was brought up in Plumstead. He was much like any other teenager, apart from his ambition to become an architect and the fact that he was a friend of Rolan Adams, who had been murdered by a racist gang in Thamesmead in 1991. Rolan, then aged fifteen and his younger brother Nathan, aged fourteen, who survived, were attacked on their way home. Although the large gang of attackers were well known in the area, and already known to the police, only one man was eventually convicted for Rolan Adams' murder. The police and the Crown Prosecution Service were reluctant to accept that the murder of Rolan Adams constituted a racist attack.[36] The mainstream press were more concerned about the involvement of the African American activist Reverand Al Sharpton, who came to Britain to campaign on behalf of the Adams family, than whether the attack was a racist murder.[37] It was revealed many years later that the Metropolitan Police Special Demonstration Squad had placed the Rolan

Adams Family Campaign group, formed to combat state indifference and to support other victims of racism, under surveillance, as well as harassing members of the Adams family and those supporting them. At the same time the police did little to protect and support the family, who were receiving racist threats, and were forced to leave their home three months after the murder of their son. The Adams family continue to maintain that the police did more to harass the victims of a racist attack and murder than they did to prevent further attacks of the same kind in the area.[38]

On 22 April 1993 Stephen Lawrence was fatally assaulted in front of witnesses while waiting for a bus and, even when police arrived, was not given appropriate first aid.[39] Five suspects, well known for previous racist attacks, were soon identified but not arrested for several weeks, allegedly because the police officer leading the investigation was not aware that the law permitted him to make arrests on the grounds of reasonable suspicion.[40] The actions of the police throughout the investigation have since been described as 'bungling' and 'disturbing'. The evidence shows that not only were the main suspects not arrested expeditiously, but also that the police did not gather appropriate evidence, nor heed the many tip-offs that were offered to them. It seems probable that at least one of the detectives was corruptly in league with a local criminal, the father of one of the chief suspects, a fact first revealed in the national press nearly twenty years later, in 2012.[41] In addition, the police were extremely reluctant to view the murder as a racist attack and initially took the view that Stephen Lawrence was 'a criminal belonging to a gang'. As Doreen Lawrence later wrote, 'My son was stereotyped by the police – he was black then he must be a criminal – and they set about investigating him and us.'[42] The family of Stephen Lawrence began to express concern and frustration concerning the police investigation within weeks of his murder and held a well-publicized meeting with Nelson Mandela to further highlight the situation. Doreen Lawrence subsequently explained: 'It struck me as incredible that a foreign dignitary as important as Nelson Mandela had made time for us, whereas there had been no statement by any British Conservative government official about the death of our son.'[43] Even the Home Secretary of the time refused to meet with the Lawrence family.

Anti-racist campaigners in Britain criticized the inaction of the police. Although the main suspects were subsequently charged, by July 1993, the Crown Prosecution Service (CPS) dropped the charges, claiming that there was insufficient evidence. In response to growing criticism, the police turned their attention to investigating Stephen's friend, Duwayne Brooks, who was the main witness to the murder, and mounted a campaign to discredit him. Stephen's grieving parents and family quickly began to despair of the indifference of the police and mounted their own campaign to achieve justice. It has since been established that the police paid more attention to gathering secret information about the Lawrence family, Duwayne Brooks, and those campaigning against racism than they did to investigating his murder. A member of the Metropolitan Police's Special Demonstration Squad was deployed to collect 'disinformation' on family members and those supporting them and to find 'any intelligence that could have smeared the campaign'.[44]

Although new evidence was found by the end of 1993, the CPS again declined to prosecute, without consulting or advising the Lawrence family of its decision. As Doreen Lawrence wrote at the time, 'it was an act as hurtful and painful in its effects as the news that Stephen had been killed ... We have been brought into the public spotlight not by our own acts, but by the failure of others who were under a public duty to act.'[45] In September 1996 the family of Stephen Lawrence attempted to bring private prosecutions against two of the suspects, but the case collapsed when the judge ruled that the evidence of Duwayne Brooks was inadmissible. In 1997, following an inquest that concluded that 'Stephen Lawrence was unlawfully killed in a completely unprovoked racist attack by five white youths', Doreen and Neville Lawrence complained to the Police Complaints Authority which, in its own investigation 'roundly criticized' the actions of the Metropolitan Police.[46] The murder and subsequent legal process became so notorious that, in 1997, in response to demands from the Lawrence family, the new Labour government was forced to launch a public inquiry. It appeared that a Black teenager could be murdered in front of witnesses by a gang of known racists, but that the police and state were unable to hold anyone to account. Moreover, there was a growing view that not only was this a racist murder, but a similar prejudice was also preventing the successful prosecution and conviction of those responsible for it. The state itself was on trial. The public inquiry was led by Sir William Macpherson, a retired judge.

Macpherson's report was published in February 1999 and was seen as a landmark, not only for what it said about the circumstances of Stephen's Lawrence's murder, but especially for its comments on the racism of the Metropolitan Police and the police in general. The report concluded:

> We believe that the immediate impact of the Inquiry, as it developed, has brought forcibly before the public the justifiable complaints of Mr & Mrs Lawrence, and the hitherto underplayed dissatisfaction and unhappiness of minority ethnic communities, both locally and all over the country, in connection with this and other cases, as to their treatment by police.[47]

The inquiry concluded that the racism highlighted by the Scarman Inquiry in 1981 was just as prevalent nearly twenty years later. The Macpherson Inquiry noted that what it termed 'institutional racism' 'exists both in the Metropolitan Police Service and in other Police Services and other institutions countrywide'.[48] However, Macpherson did not go any further than this and made it clear that this recognition did not mean that the Metropolitan police could be considered racist 'in its policies'. This was the case even though the inquiry had evidence about the activities of the police since the 1960s, particularly in relation to police powers to 'stop and search', as well as arrests and deaths in custody, that demonstrated beyond doubt the existence of 'discrimination'. Although the inquiry indicated that other institutions, such as education, needed reform and criticized some aspects of the investigation by the Crown Prosecution Service, it did not make any criticism of the state in general for its failure to combat racism, or indicate that it might be held accountable for the existence of racism in society. As a result of the Macpherson Inquiry, the Metropolitan Police agreed to pay the parents of Stephen Lawrence £320,000 in an out-of-court settlement in compensation for the failures during the investigation into their son's murder, a figure significantly below that demanded by the family's lawyers.[49]

One of the recommendations of the Macpherson Inquiry was to lead to a change in the law on double jeopardy, in the Criminal Justice

Act of 2003, which stipulated that an accused person might be tried more than once for the same crime. A fresh investigation into the murder of Stephen Lawrence commenced in 2006 and produced new forensic evidence. As a consequence, two of the original suspects were re-tried in 2011 and convicted of the murder in early 2012. After the case Doreen Lawrence commented: 'Had the police done their job properly, I would have spent the last 18 years grieving for my son rather than fighting to get his killers to court.' Neville Lawrence welcomed the conviction, but added, 'I'm also conscious of the fact that there were five or six attackers that night. I do not think I'll be able to rest until they are all brought to justice.'[50]

Investigations continued and, in 2014, the findings of the *Stephen Lawrence Independent Review* into police corruption and undercover policing were published. The review established by the government was led by Mark Ellison, the British barrister who had led the prosecution against Stephen Lawrence's murderers in 2012. Ellison's review established that police corruption had indeed been present in the initial investigation into the murder of Stephen Lawrence, that some information relating to it was withheld from the Macpherson inquiry and that relevant information had been destroyed since that inquiry. It also concluded that the Lawrence family and Duwayne Brooks had been spied upon by the Metropolitan Police, even at the time of the Macpherson Inquiry, and that such activity was kept secret from that inquiry.[51] Much of this information had already been disclosed in the press and on television in statements by a former undercover police officer.[52] In addition, Ellison criticized the previous investigations into police corruption by the Metropolitan Police and the Police Complaints Authority, and the fact that the Metropolitan Police had destroyed important records relating to corruption. Ellison concluded that the police could not be trusted to investigate itself. A former Home Secretary suggested that had Macpherson had all the facts at his disposal, he might have also concluded that the Metropolitan Police was 'institutionally corrupt'.[53] In the light of the Ellison review, the government commissioned further investigations in 2014 in the form of a public inquiry into police corruption and undercover policing. That inquiry was initially due to report its findings in 2018. However, its final report has been delayed, by efforts to keep details of undercover policing as secret as possible, until 2023. The way in which this latest inquiry is being conducted has been criticized by many, including Stephen Lawrence's mother, Baroness Lawrence.

An opening statement made on her behalf to that inquiry in 2020 expressed the following:

> Baroness Lawrence is losing confidence, if she has not already lost it, in this Inquiry's ability to get to the truth. The truth as to why she, her family and supporters were spied upon by the police. This Inquiry is not delivering on what she was promised and is not achieving what she expected. To say that Baroness Lawrence is disappointed is to understate her position. Baroness Lawrence is also disappointed by the approach of the Metropolitan Police Service in its Opening Statement with its suggestion that there has been 'widespread and lasting change' in the police. The reality is that there has been very little change. What change there has been was forced upon the MPS. It has never welcomed it or embraced it . . . The racism which continues to be rife in our police and society was the racism which led to the murder of Stephen Lawrence and which resulted in his killers not being convicted for 18 years.[54]

The statement went to on to detail how the Lawrence family had continued to be denied justice and closure nearly thirty years after the murder of their son, as well as how they had been failed by numerous inquiries. It emphasized that it was vital to expose the nature and extent of undercover police work, not only in this case, but also in regard to other Black justice campaigns, and to clearly expose the involvement not only of the leadership of the Metropolitan Police but also of the Home Office. It pointed out that it appeared to Baroness Lawrence 'that this inquiry is more interested in protecting the alleged perpetrators than the victims'. And it concluded with her own words, 'I am just an ordinary person. I have nothing special that deserves public attention or acclaim. I simply ask for justice.'[55] In fact the inquiry has highlighted the fact that many other ordinary people have been the subjects of secretive undercover policing: those connected with Rolan Adams, Cherry Groce, Roger Sylvester, who was killed in hospital while being restrained by police in London in 1999, and the Broadwater Farm Defence Committee, established in the wake of the major uprising in Tottenham in 1985. The police have also spied on MPs, including Diane Abbott and Bernie Grant.[56]

THE WINDRUSH SCANDAL

If the scandal surrounding the murder of Stephen Lawrence exposed the inadequacies of public prosecutions and public inquiries, as well as the racism and subterfuge of the police, the so-called Windrush scandal, which first came to the attention of the public in 2017, revealed more fully the role of the Home Office and government in overt acts of racism. It led to the resignation of one Home Secretary.[57] The scandal has been a tragedy for many hundreds of people who had arrived in Britain from the Caribbean, and some other Commonwealth countries such as Kenya and Sierra Leone, prior to 1 January 1973, and who were fully entitled to British citizenship. By the twenty-first century those who arrived from the Caribbean after the Second World War have increasingly been referred to as the 'Windrush generation', a term which was sometimes used to describe all who migrated from the former colonies to Britain in the post-war period.

However, from the early years of the twenty-first century, many of these migrants, who may have arrived as young children on their parents' passports, found that, despite living in Britain for decades, they had no proof of such citizenship and began to lose employment, as well as housing, welfare, banking and other rights, including the right to drive, and to obtain access to the NHS. Such cases were referred to in a Home Office circular in 2006 and were well known to civil servants. After 2010 the Coalition government led by David Cameron began to champion what it referred to as a 'hostile environment' policy in regard to 'illegal migrants' – a policy that had originated under the previous Labour government and had been implemented from 2006 onwards. From about 2009, the Home Office began to destroy landing cards and other historical immigration documents that could prove the citizenship rights of Caribbean and other former migrants from the Commonwealth. New immigration legislation was introduced in 2014 and 2016 to make it even more difficult for people without documentation to remain in the country. Moreover, from a historical perspective, a case could be made that for those of African and Caribbean heritage either entering or living in Britain, a 'hostile environment' existed in some form throughout most of the twentieth century.

Although the government received warnings and criticisms about its approach, both inside and outside Parliament, these went largely unheeded. As early as 2014, for example, the Legal Action Group published a report, *Chasing Status*, highlighting the plight of what it referred to as 'surprised Brits', while others raised concerns in Parliament.[58] The plight of those British citizens whose origins were in the Caribbean and elsewhere was well known. Having destroyed the evidence of citizenship, the Home Office began to ask people to produce it. In one case, it took a 58-year-old woman, who had come to the country at the age of ten from St Kitts, seven years to prove her identity, even with the assistance of her MP. She lost her job and nearly lost her house on numerous occasions. Some people were forced to leave the country, 164 were detained, or deported, and in some cases both. One 61-year-old woman, who had even worked in the House of Commons and made tax payments for over thirty years, was detained and nearly deported. Often documentary evidence such as school and NHS records, and even National Insurance numbers, held for many years by the individuals concerned were declared by the Home Office to be insufficient evidence and, so officials said, produced 'no trace' of the individual who possessed them. Even a former serviceman was told by the Home Office that his service record was insufficient evidence of citizenship. He had refused entreaties by his wife to take foreign holidays for years, concerned that he would not be allowed back in the country. He simply told her that he was afraid of flying. A 63-year-old man was forced to spend years of destitution in Jamaica before being allowed back to Britain. There were also cases of those who 'voluntarily' returned to the Caribbean, because they did not wish to be a burden on their families in Britain.[59]

By 2017 such cases were appearing in the press, most notably those of three long-term residents, originally from Jamaica, all threatened with deportation. Anthony Bryan, who had come to Britain as a child in 1965 and had been in the country fifty-two years; Edwin Burton, who had lived in Britain for over fifty-three years but was held in detention, and Paulette Wilson, who was only released from detention after the intervention of her MP. Anthony Bryan's case was later turned into a television drama by the BBC. Paulette Wilson's story was especially important: when it appeared in the *Guardian*, where journalist Amelia Gentleman had begun to investigate the scandal, it encouraged many others to come forward.[60] The government was required to explain why it was deporting its citizens who had arrived before 1973. By early 2018, there was significant press coverage of many of these cases. However, even in Parliament, the government refused to provide detailed answers to questions from MPs about the scandal and publicly stated its view that the onus was on individuals to prove their status. It demanded: 'Those who have resided in the UK for an extended period but feel they may not have the correct documentation confirming their leave to remain should take legal advice and submit the appropriate application with correct documentation so we can progress the case.'[61]

No legal aid of any kind was provided and many found their situation almost impossible and a severe strain on their mental health. By early 2018 there were so many cases being presented in the press, and so many questions in Parliament, that representatives of Caribbean governments requested a meeting with the Prime Minister, a request that was initially rejected. The Home Secretary, Amber Rudd, denied that there were government targets for deportations. When it became apparent that there were such targets, she was forced to resign and the new Home Secretary ordered a review into the entire scandal. The existence of targets for removals, raids on premises and arrests meant that 'anything to put pressure on migrants was seen as a good thing', as one former civil servant expressed it.[62] In April 2018 Theresa May, the Prime Minister who as Home Secretary had been most associated with the hostile-environment policy, was forced to issue apologies to the leaders of Caribbean countries, as well as in Parliament. She promised to compensate those who had lost jobs and benefit entitlements, or had been forced to take legal advice to prove that they were British citizens.[63]

The Windrush scandal emerged from successive governments' attempts to control immigration from what became known as the new Commonwealth, Britain's former colonies in Africa, the Caribbean and South Asia. However, as we have seen, these attempts to control and discourage the settlement of 'coloured' migrants began long before 1948. There is no doubt that migration to Britain from these countries increased in the post-war period, as did attempts to discourage it by successive governments, as well as by sections of the mass media. It became a major political issue, often exploited by the neo-Nazi organizations that existed as legal entities in Britain.

The plight of those who migrated from the Caribbean and other parts of the world after the Second World War arose because of a series of immigration acts, starting in 1962, which were openly racist. Even such legislation as the 1965 and 1968 race relations acts were introduced by Labour governments in such a way as to suggest that limiting migration was a key means to improve 'race relations'. The inference was that migrants provoked racism. Later immigration acts, such as those of 1968 and 1971, were also openly racist, and viewed as such by the European Commission of Human Rights. Government ministers at the time were well aware of the discriminatory nature of the acts, the main aim of which was to stem 'coloured immigration'. The Cabinet Secretary, Sir Burke Trend, claimed that the main aim of the 1971 act was 'to avoid the risk of renewed "swamping" by immigrants from the new Commonwealth'.[64] The 1971 Immigration Act had introduced the racist term 'patriality' to decide who had rights to stay and who didn't, on the basis of descent. The act also established that Commonwealth citizens already in the UK before 1973 had the right of abode and leave to remain. However, those citizens were given no documentation and the onus was placed on the individual to prove their citizenship status.

When Thatcher's Conservative government came to office in 1979, it immediately set out to tighten citizenship law with the introduction of the 1981 Nationality Act, which went so far as to remove citizenship rights from those born and raised in Britain. Those who had come from Africa and the Caribbean and had been living in Britain legally for many years were required to register and apply for a newly defined 'British citizenship' and to pay for the privilege. At least 8,000 people who were entitled to register declined and saw no reason to do so, as the Home Office informed them, 'your position under immigration law is unchanged'.[65] Numerous other immigration laws and controls were enacted at the end of the twentieth century and beginning of the twenty-first century. Some concerned those seeking political asylum, or coming to Britain as refugees, but all were designed to prevent migrants coming to Britain. By 2006 the government was starting to develop what would become the hostile-environment policy, initially by targeting employers who employed those declared 'illegal migrants'. What subsequent history shows is that even when there was legislation ostensibly enacted to prevent discrimination, such as the 2010 Equalities Act, the Home Office largely ignored it, and took no measures to safeguard citizens subsequently affected by the Windrush scandal.[66] In 2019 the Home Office's 'right to rent' scheme, which was introduced under the 2014 and 2016 immigration acts and required landlords to check tenants' citizenship status, was itself declared unlawful under the Equalities Act and the Human Rights Act of 1998, since its implementation led to discrimination.

After the exposure of the Windrush scandal in 2018, there were government promises of investigation, compensation for victims and pledges to overhaul the immigration system. However, reparatory justice was slow. In 2020 it was reported that just over one thousand people had applied for compensation but only thirty-six people had been compensated. At that time Home Office officials suggested that as many as 15,000 might be eligible for compensation. Many complained that the procedure was too complicated and too slow, while payments were insufficient. In November 2020 it was announced that nine applicants had died before being compensated.[67] Many others had died in the course of the scandal. Dexter Bristol almost certainly died as a result of stress after being made redundant and being denied welfare payments because he had no passport, and then having to find evidence to prove that he was British. He had come to Britain as a child in 1968 to join his mother, who was a nurse. She had tried to obtain a passport for him in 1970 but her application had been rejected by the Home Office. Following his tragic death his mother Sentina Bristol simply stated:

> This is racism. He was the victim of their policies, and it is a tragedy. I'm hoping no one will go through what I'm going though now. There was a lot of racism when I came here, but I was young, I could handle

it. People would call you 'black'; I just ignored it. This is worse, this is the government. They are intelligent people, they are people of power. We expect better from them.[68]

Perhaps even more scandalously, some people born and raised in Britain, but with links to the Caribbean, continued to be denied their citizenship rights. In 2019 the *Guardian* reported that three generations of one family were so affected. When a 25-year-old British-born mother who was homeless went to apply for emergency accommodation for herself and her son in east London, she was asked by the local authority to prove that she was British, by producing either her own passport, or that of her parents. Her parents had arrived in Britain as children from the Caribbean over half a century previously. Her father had been living in Britain for more than sixty years and neither parent had ever applied for a passport.[69]

In March 2021 the *Guardian* reported the case of Trevor Donald, who had initially arrived in Britain from Jamaica as an eleven-year-old in 1967. He remained in Britain for forty-three years, until 2010, when he returned to Jamaica to visit his dying mother. Forced to travel to her funeral with emergency documents, he was then refused re-entry to Britain for nine years and had to survive in Jamaica separated from his family in Britain. In 2019 the Windrush taskforce established by the government to investigate such cases invited him back and paid his return fare. On his return he applied for citizenship, which was then denied on the basis that he had not been resident in Britain continuously for five years before the application. The Home Secretary, Priti Patel, wrote to Donald to say that his treatment was 'shameful', but that nothing could be done because of the stipulations of the 1981 Nationality Act. In 2018 he had received a letter from a previous Home Secretary who wrote: 'In its handling of your case, the department should have demonstrated more flexibility, common sense and empathy. I wish to assure you that the Home Office is making sure lessons have been learned and changes are being made to the approach it takes.' In 2021 the Home Office agreed that Donald could remain in Britain and reapply for citizenship in 2023.[70]

BLACK LIVES MATTER

The Black Lives Matter (BLM) movement became well known to the entire country following the nationwide protests that erupted in the summer of 2020 in the wake of the media reports of the horrific police killing of George Floyd, an unarmed African American man, in Minnesota, in April of that year. BLM activists in Britain first came to public prominence in August 2016, when a series of protests were organized in London, Nottingham, Manchester and elsewhere by activists from Black Lives Matter UK (UKBLM), a loose coalition that had been in existence since 2015.[71] The August 2016 protests were held on the fifth anniversary of the fatal shooting by police of 29-year-old Mark Duggan in Tottenham, in 2011, an event which led to wide-scale public disorder, described by the media as riots, on a scale not seen since the 1980s. Black Lives Matter protests had previously been organized in London in July 2016, following the deaths of two other African Americans, Philando Castile and Alton Sterling, in the United States. Two eighteen-year-old students, Maryam Ali and Capres Willow, were credited as the main London organizers of those protests.[72] At the same time, BLM protesters in Birmingham were highlighting the 2011 killing in that city of 29-year-old Kingsley Burrell, after a recent inquest into his death. Burrell had been detained by police under the Mental Health Act and died after being violently restrained in an ambulance. The inquest in May 2015 found that he had been left handcuffed in hospital for hours and had not received vital medical attention which, together with the force used by the police, had contributed to his death.[73]

According to a video released by UKBLM in August 2016, the protests, or 'nationwide shutdown' as the media termed it, sought to bring to public attention the deaths of Sarah Read, Jermaine Baker and Mzee Mohammed, who had all died in suspicious and violent circumstances, as well as other forms of policing which disproportionately affected people of African and Caribbean heritage, such as the divergent numbers of arrests and convictions. The protests also grew out of concern for the 3,000 asylum seekers whose lives were lost crossing the Mediterranean from North Africa at that time.

UKBLM also wished to highlight inequalities in employment and in school exclusions. Sarah Reed (1984–2016) was a young Black woman who suffered from mental health problems following the sudden death of her nine-month-old daughter from muscular atrophy in 2003. In 2012 she was falsely arrested and viciously assaulted by a police officer, who broke two of her ribs. This attack added to her health problems and she was subsequently admitted to a psychiatric hospital. There she was forced to defend herself from a sexual assault and subsequently sent to Holloway Prison for psychiatric assessment at a time when, although vulnerable and needing medical help, she had begun to show signs of recovery. Her death in prison was widely seen as the result of a failure of the health and criminal justice systems.[74] Jermaine Baker (1987–2015) was fatally shot by a police officer in 2015, allegedly while he was part of an attempt to free another man who was being transported from prison. He was shot through a car window and it was claimed that he had his hands raised at the time.[75] Mzee Mohammed was an eighteen-year-old Liverpudlian who suffered from autism and ADHD. In a distressed state, he was killed while being detained by police and security guards at a Liverpool shopping centre. His death led to public protests in both Liverpool and London and was one of the first occasions when the slogan 'Black Lives Matter' was used in Britain.[76]

A spokesperson for UKBLM explained that the August 2016 protests were organized because 'we are in a crisis about the brutality inflicted on black people ... We are seeing people talking about how they are being attacked, abused in the streets. Other forms of protests have been exhausted and so the disruption today is bringing back to the mainstream discussions around black lives and the racist structures and inequalities we know about.'[77] Protesters blocked the roads to Heathrow Airport and disrupted traffic in Nottingham city centre, as well as roads leading to Birmingham Airport.[78] The UKBLM also reached out to those who had long campaigned about deaths at the hands of the police, such as Marcia Rigg, the sister of Sean Rigg, a forty-year-old musician who, although suffering from mental health problems, had been killed during violent police restraint in 2008.[79]

Marcia Rigg had dedicated herself to securing justice for her brother and refused to accept that the police could kill with immunity from prosecution.[80] She became a prominent member of the United Friends and Family Campaign, formed in 1997, which campaigned over deaths in police custody and state institutions.[81] It was started by the families of those of African and Caribbean heritage, including the families of Roger Sylvester (1968–1999), Joy Gardner (1953–1993), Christopher Alder (1960–1998), David Emmanuel (a.k.a. Smiley Culture, 1963–2011) and Olaseni Lewis (1986–2010), but subsequently included the families of people of all nationalities who had died at the hands of the state. Sean Rigg's family found that they had to struggle to find out how their loved one was killed. When the Independent Police Complaints Commission (IPCC) was compelled to investigate the circumstances of his death, it merely concluded that police had acted 'reasonably and proportionately'. But Marcia Rigg and others refused to give up and their persistence led to an independent external review of the IPCC itself, which was highly critical of its investigation into Sean Rigg's death.[82]

Marcia Rigg also worked particularly closely with the family of Olaseni Lewis, a 23-year-old man of Nigerian heritage, who was killed by eleven police officers, who handcuffed and violently restrained him for forty minutes whilst he was an outpatient in Bethlem Royal Hospital in London in 2010. Together with others, the family forced the government to produce a review into this by Dame Elish Angiolini, and to produce the *Report of the Independent Review of Deaths and Serious Incidents in Police Custody*, which was finally published by the Home Office in 2017. Amongst other conclusions, the review found that in the twenty-first century nobody had ever been successfully prosecuted in connection with a death in police custody. The government had already accepted that there was a 'significant overrepresentation of Black, Asian and minority ethnic (BAME) individuals in the criminal justice system', and that young Black men were six times more likely to be stopped and searched by the police than others of a similar age, but the review also found 'disproportionate deaths of BAME people in restraint-related deaths' whilst in police custody.[83] Such conclusions were hardly a surprise, and in 2016 the government commissioned a review into racism in the criminal justice system which was conducted by the MP David Lammy. This review showed that 'Black people make up around 3%

of the general population but accounted for 12% of adult prisoners in 2015/16; and more than 20% of children in custody.'[84]

The family of Olaseni Lewis were also failed by the IPCC, which claimed that no charges should be brought against the police. In 2013 the family took their case to the High Court, arguing that the investigation should be reopened, a demand which was even supported by the IPCC itself. A second investigation in 2013 concluded with the Crown Prosecution Service arguing that there was insufficient evidence to level charges against the police.[85] Subsequent inquiries by the coroner and the police raised concerns about the actions of hospital staff and police, but did not lead to anybody being held to account for the death of Olaseni Lewis.[86] It was, once again, left to his family to take further action and to draft a proposed change to the law to prevent such restraint being used in hospitals. The Mental Health Units (Use of Force) Act, or 'Seni's Law', received royal assent in 2018.[87]

The concerns that had been expressed by the United Friends and Family Campaign for many years, as well as others, over racist violence by the police, were confirmed by Angiolini's *Report of the Independent Review of Deaths and Serious Incidents in Police Custody* in 2017. The review concluded, 'Deaths of people from BAME communities, in particular young black men, resonate with the black community's experience of systemic racism, and reflect wider concerns about discriminatory over-policing, stop and search, and criminalisation.'[88] In 2018 the IPCC reported that of the eleven people that had died in police custody in the previous year, six were of African or Caribbean heritage. One of those killed was twenty-year-old Rashan Charles, the great-nephew of a chief inspector in the Metropolitan Police, innocent of any offence, who was killed by a police officer in Hackney.[89]

Such statistics were released as the IPCC was replaced by the Independent Office for Police Conduct after being widely criticized for its inability to investigate the police and its lack of independence. Later in 2018 experts from the UN Human Rights High Commission expressed concern about the number of deaths of people of African descent in Britain 'as a result of excessive force by State security'. The experts added that: 'The deaths reinforce the experiences of structural racism, over-policing and criminalisation of people of African descent and other minorities.' They also raised the important issue 'that there has never been a successful prosecution for manslaughter ... despite unlawful killing verdicts in coroner's inquests'.[90] In 2021 it was reported that since 1990 there had been 190 'Black, Asian and minority ethnic' people killed through contact with the police.[91]

SUMMER 2020

From the end of May and then throughout the summer of 2020, Black Lives Matter protests were held in London, Manchester, Cardiff, Newcastle, Glasgow, Belfast, Londonderry, Leicester, Milton Keynes, Sheffield, Watford and more than 200 villages, towns and cities throughout Britain. On the weekend of 8 June alone, there were 200 such protests and, the following weekend, another 160.[92] It was an unprecedented demonstration of anti-racist activity involving hundreds of thousands of people from Land's End to John o'Groats.[93]

Although initially in response to events in the United States, protesters made it clear that 'the UK is not innocent' and that they were also concerned about the Windrush Scandal, deaths at the hands of the police and other state agencies, and racism more generally, especially in the education system. The protests included well-known figures such as the musician Stormzy, the boxer Anthony Joshua and the actor John Boyega and they occurred in the midst of the Covid epidemic and against the wishes of the police and the government. Ironically, it also happened at a time when the government included a Minister of Equalities of African heritage, Kemi Badenoch, who had once claimed 'We don't have all the horrible stuff that's happened in America here.'[94]

The protests were organized by a variety of groups and individuals including UKBLM and All Black Lives UK. A significant number of the protesters were, as the *Guardian* noted, 'Young, British and Black'. The newspaper poignantly captured the views and experiences of fifty of them. They told remarkably similar stories of facing racism from a young age, or being made aware of the extent of racism by the killing of Mark Duggan in 2011, and also indicated that in many cases protests were organized by a handful of individuals inspired by what was happening elsewhere. Natasha, a

21-year-old student and Aima, an eighteen-year-old student, organized one of the early London protests via social media. 'We couldn't just be silent,' Aima recalled. 'We posted tweets about our protest and it just skyrocketed.'[95] Natasha recalled her experiences of racism at school at the age of eight and concluded: 'Being black in this country, especially a black woman, is a political statement. You've seen just within the past six weeks, how much more confident black people have been, how much more outspoken – they realise their opinions are valid.'[96]

One of the most notable protests occurred in Bristol where, after many years of having requests for removal rejected, protesters toppled the statue of the infamous seventeenth-century human trafficker Edward Colston and deposited it in the harbour. This one event came to symbolize the protests and the need for the country to come to terms with the racist crimes of the past, as well as those still being perpetuated. The toppling of the statue was immediately condemned by the government but contributed to a reassessment of the appropriateness of statues, place names, and other examples of public history, which glorified those responsible for acts of racism, slavery and colonialism.[97] Subsequently many institutions in Bristol, including schools and the Bristol Beacon concert hall, removed the name of Colston from their titles, which had connected Bristol with a legacy of slavery and racism dating back to the eighteenth century.[98]

In March 2021 Bristol City Council passed a motion urging a parliamentary commission of inquiry be set up to investigate reparations for Britain's role in trafficking enslaved Africans across the Atlantic Ocean. The council also called for the city to make reparation for its own role in this great crime, and Bristol thereby became the first city in Britain to give support for international calls for reparations to be made for the historic enslavement and trafficking of Africans.[99] Previous demands for reparations and a parliamentary commission of inquiry had been passed in motions by the councils of the London boroughs of Lambeth and Islington in July 2020.[100]

REPARATIONS

The motion passed by Bristol Council was historic in the sense that it was the first city council to adopt such a stance. It was also notable that the demand for a parliamentary commission grew out of the work of the Pan-Afrikan Reparations Coalition in Europe (PAR-COE), formed in 2001, which describes itself as a 'UK-based grassroots reparations advocacy alliance in Europe working to amplify the voices of African communities of reparations interest all over the world'. It was founded by two British-based activists, Kofi Mawuli Klu and Esther Stanford-Xosei. PARCOE played a leading role in organizing an annual 'Afrikan Emancipation Day Reparations March' in London, every 1 August, and the 'Stop the Maangamizi: We Charge Genocide/Ecocide' campaign.[101] They made it clear that 'holistic reparatory justice' that is 'repairing the harm done' should be viewed not only in relation to slavery and colonialism in the past but also as part of a 'continuum of unbroken struggle for emancipation and restitution in the present'. PARCOE viewed its own activity as being part of a continuum of struggle in Britain and other parts of the world that can be traced back to at least the eighteenth century and the Sons of Africa. In the late-twentieth century such activity was further developed by Bernie Grant MP, who established the African Reparations Movement UK (ARMUK) and, in 1993, tabled a motion in Parliament urging 'all those countries that were enriched by enslavement and colonization to review the case for reparations, to be paid to Africa and Africans in the Diaspora'.[102]

The ARMUK, which included activists such as Dorothy Kuya, Linda Bellos and Sam King, convened a reparations conference in Birmingham in December 1993, and began to demand the return to Africa of stolen cultural artefacts, an official apology for the crimes of the past and a development of the 'Reparations Movement'. Grant recognized that many other organizations had demanded reparations and hoped that they would all come under the ARMUK umbrella. During his famous 'Reparations or Bust' speech he argued that it was an issue that could 'unite all people of African origin'.[103] Its activities were brought to an end with the premature death of Grant in 2000.

Since 2001 PARCOE has carried forward the campaign for reparative justice in Britain, alongside others, with one of its principal demands being an all-party parliamentary commission of inquiry for truth and reparative justice. One of the key features of the annual August march is the delivery of a petition to the Prime Minister 'charging the British state with the crimes of genocide and econocide'.[104]

In early June 2020, UKBLM and other related groups started to publicly fundraise and within days announced that over one million pounds had been raised from individual donations throughout the country.[105] In early 2021, the organization announced that it had raised £1.2m in total and that it would assist in funding related organizations and causes. One of the leaders of UKBLM, Adam Elliot Cooper, explained what they would do with the funds:

> Around 10% to 15% will be donated straight away to black-led campaigns and organizations that we're already familiar with and have been working with over the last five years. These are groups that include educational projects, campaign groups, police monitoring projects, as well as some of the new protest groups, which helped organize at the demonstrations in the summer of last year ... One of the things we're really invested in is making sure that the money that we've been able to raise can build sustainable projects, campaigns, and movements in this country that go beyond simply protest in individual cities or individual communities, but can build a broad-based national network, campaign and movements for anti-racism in this country.[106]

The protests in the summer of 2020 highlighted a variety of ongoing concerns, but one of the key demands articulated by those who spoke to the *Guardian* was the need to address the neglect throughout the education system of what was often referred to as 'Black history' and particularly 'Black British history'. This was connected with what many considered a reluctance by the powers-that-be to recognize the legacy of Britain's history of colonialism, the exploitation of people of African and Asian heritage in particular and the continuing legacy of that exploitation, the racism and Eurocentrism that still exists throughout society in the twenty-first century, as well as the economic and political system that exploitation has created. In regard to the teaching of history in schools, one young woman from Sunderland complained: 'The curriculum is ridiculous. They just teach you that there was slavery for a little bit and it was really bad, then the slaves were freed and that was that, Martin Luther King did a speech and racism was over. It's only from reading black authors that I realised how much of my own history I was shielded from.' A young woman from Newmarket reflected on her own experience of history lessons: 'The only thing I was taught about black people in school was that we were slaves, which when you're 12 is very upsetting.' Another commented on the importance of history: 'It really helps people manifest and grasp their identity ... It shouldn't be a young person's task to have to learn these things themselves.'[107]

Such views often gave rise to demands to 'decolonise the curriculum', recognizing that too often history has been taught and presented from 'a colonial perspective', that 'what we learn is the victor's story', and what is required is 'challenging the power structures that we live in'.[108] Some campaigners argue that the 'History National Curriculum systematically omits the contribution of Black British history in favour of a dominant White, Eurocentric curriculum, one that fails to reflect our multi-ethnic and broadly diverse society' (although in the twenty-first century, with the emergence of academies, fewer schools are required to follow the National Curriculum).[109]

Such Eurocentrism has resulted in young people of African and Caribbean heritage being alienated from the history studied in schools and even in universities. Many of them expressed their concerns at a special History Matters conference held in London in 2014, which led to the creation of the Young Historians Project (YHP), which is dedicated to encouraging young people of African and Caribbean heritage to discover and research history for themselves and to present it for their peers. One member related her experience:

> Before joining YHP, I associated studying History with thick textbooks with black and white photographs, boring essays and most importantly, a lack of representation. The YHP project I worked on was about the British Black Power movement. This was of particular importance to me as I had only ever studied the Civil Rights Movement before and despite the importance of learning such a subject, it often used to make me feel like I did not have my own history, my own heroes and I longed for

that ... The YHP was an experience that greatly differed from my course at university. It was an interactive and creative process of bringing History to life; for the first time in years, I felt a passion for History again ... The main skill I learned from the YHP was inquisitiveness. When approaching History, one must always be curious, it makes you ask the right questions to paint an accurate picture. I also learned the responsibility we have to document our history, to empower ourselves and to never forget the work we have inherited from our elders. All of these things reignited my passion for History and even though I was not always fortunate in having riveting histories to study in my course.[110]

However, this history is not just important for young people of African and Caribbean heritage. It is important that a full picture of Britain's history is available to all. It is not just a history of the white men of property, but one that includes those who, like Cheddar Man and other early Britons, either migrated to Britain from other parts of the world or had ancestors who were migrants. It is also a history of Britain's relationship with other parts of the world, with Africa, the Caribbean and the Americas, a relationship that was often an unequal and exploitative one. We should all have a fuller understanding of the past, not just for celebration, or condemnation, but because it provides us with an understanding of the present too. In many respects, history is the study of change. It demonstrates that change is not just possible but inevitable and that we are the agents of that change.

Acknowledgements

It has often been remarked that the writing of history is a collective rather than an individual effort. Consequently, the author has to accept criticism for shortcomings, but any praise should be equally shared between all those who have contributed. I take this opportunity to thank all those who have helped to bring into being this publication. What is presented here has been developed over many years of teaching and discussion with students, most recently at the University of Chichester and initially at Middlesex University, where I was first appointed a lecturer in 'Black British History' in 1996. I have also benefited from questions and comments posed over an even longer period by those who kind enough to attend my lectures, as well as classes and discussions in numerous other places, many of them having nothing to do with universities. I remember, in particular, those valuable contributions and questions from guests and patients at Broadmoor Hospital, HMP Manchester and HMP Ashfield.

I would especially like to thank my editor at Penguin, Casiana Ionita, who first approached me with the idea of writing such a book and has seen it through to completion. For the first time I've had an editor who has actually edited my work and made many useful suggestions. I would also like to thank Louisa Watson, an indefatigable copy editor, who also make many helpful suggestions and corrections. My thanks also to Edward Kirke for finding all the photos with great speed and efficiency.

At the University of Chichester, I received continual and important support from Prof. Hugo Frey and from all those colleagues associated with the university's Research and Innovation Fund, which generously contributed to the cost of photos. I would also like to thank Karen Lloyd, Gail Graffham, Sue Booker, Jane Rackstraw and other librarians at the University of Chichester. In addition, I received support from the staff at many libraries and archives who fulfilled my many requests for articles, books and documents. I would particularly like to thank Hannah Ishmael, Rhoda Boateng at the Black Cultural Archives in London, Geoff Burns at Birmingham Archives and Collections, as well as Safina Islam and Joanne Robson at the Ahmed Iqbal Ullah Education Trust in Manchester for their help in supplying important archival material.

Several colleagues and friends, including those who might be considered my students, have generously shared the results of their knowledge and research with me. I would particularly like to thank Zainab Abbas, Cleo Blyden, Makeda Coaston, John Ellis, David Featherstone, Amelia Francis, Hannah Francis, Kelly Foster, Trevor Getz, Sonia Grant, David Horsley, Askala Miriam, Marika Sherwood, Adisa Stevens, Laura Tabili, Claudia Tomlinson, and Elizabeth Williams.

I am also very grateful to my friends Zainab Abbas, Marika Sherwood and Tee White who were kind enough to read drafts of this book. Thank you for correcting errors as well as making many very helpful suggestions.

Last, but certainly not least, many thanks to Esther, always a rock in bad times and in good.

Notes

PREFACE

1. P. Fryer, *Staying Power: The History of Black People in Britain* (London: Pluto, 1984).

2. R. Visram, *Ayahs, Lascars and Princes: The Story of Indians in Britain 1700–1947* (London: Pluto, 1986) and *Asians in Britain: 400 Years of History* (London: Pluto, 2002).

3. W. Armistead, *A Tribute for the Negro: Being a Vindication of the Moral, Intellectual, and Religious Capabilities of the Colored Portion of Mankind; with Particular Reference to the African Race* (Manchester: William Irwin, 1847), Documenting the American South, https://docsouth.unc.edu/neh/armistead/armistead.html#armistead267, accessed 1 March 2020.

4. N. File and C. Power, *Black Settlers in Britain 1555–1958* (London: Heinemann, 1981); J. Walvin, *Black and White: The Negro and English Society 1556–1945* (London: Allen Lane, 1973) and *The Black Presence: A Documentary History of the Negro in England, 1550–1860* (London: Orback and Chambers, 1971).

5. See, e.g., https://research.sas.ac.uk/search/fellow/181/ms-marika-sherwood/, accessed 1 November 2020.

6. D. Olusoga, *Black and British: A Forgotten History* (London: Pan Macmillan, 2016).

7. J. A. Rogers, *World's Great Men of Color*, Vol. II (London: Touchstone, 1996); J. A. Rogers, *Nature Knows No Color-Line* (St Petersburg FL: Helga M. Rogers, 1980).

8. F. Shyllon, *Black People in Britain, 1555–1833* (Oxford: Oxford University Press, 1977); F. Shyllon, *Black Slaves in Britain* (Oxford: Oxford University Press, 1974).

9. R. Ramdin, *The Making of the Black Working Class in Britain* (Aldershot: Gower, 1987).

10. G. Gerzina, *Black England: Life Before Emancipation* (London: John Murray, 1995); also G. Gerzina (ed.), *Black Victorians/Black Victoriana* (London: Rutgers University Press, 2003); G. Gerzina (ed.), *Britain's Black Past* (Liverpool: Liverpool University Press, 2020).

11. 'The Project', Runaway Slaves in Britain, University of Glasgow, https://www.runaways.gla.ac.uk/, and Black Cultural Archives, https://artsandculture.google.com/project/black-cultural-archives, both accessed 1 November 2020.

12. The Mayor's Commission on African and Asian Heritage, *Delivering Shared Heritage* (London: GLA, 2005), p. 55.

13. See J. Green's website at https://jeffreygreen.co.uk, accessed 1 November 2020.

14. The Young Historians Project is at https://www.younghistoriansproject.org/; the Black Coal Miners Project at https://www.blackcoalminers.com/archives; African Stories in Hull and East Yorkshire is at https://www.africansinyorkshireproject.com/, all accessed 1 November 2020.

CHAPTER 1: THE EARLY AFRICAN PRESENCE

1. S. Boyle, 'Plans to teach GCSE pupils Africans came to Britain before the English branded as "pro-immigration propaganda" by critics', 11 January 2016, *Daily Mail*, http://www.dailymail.co.uk/news/article-3393189/Plans-teach-GCSE-pupils-Africans-came-Britain-English-branded-pro-immigration-propaganda-critics.html, accessed 24 January 2018.

2. V. Ward, 'New GCSE history course on migration branded as "disturbing" and "dangerous"', 10 January 2016, *Daily Telegraph*, http://www.telegraph.co.uk/education/12091770/New-history-GCSE-course-on-migration-branded-disturbing-and-dangerous.html, accessed 24 January 2018.

3. M. Branagan and N. Craven, 'GSCE pupils to be taught that the nation's earliest inhabitants were Africans who were in Britain before the English', 10 January 2016, *Daily Mail*, http://www.dailymail.co.uk/news/article3392088/GCSE-pupils-taught-nation-s-earliest-inhabitants-Africans-Britain-English.html, accessed 24 January 2018.

4. P. Fryer, *Staying Power: The History of Black People in Britain* (London: Pluto, 1984), p. 1.

5. P. Edwards, 'The early African presence in the British Isles', in J. S. Gundara and I. Duffield (eds.), *Essays on the History of Blacks in Britain* (Aldershot: Avebury, 1992) pp. 9–29 (quotation, pp. 10–11).

6. S. Oppenheimer, *The Origin of the British: The New Pre-history of Britain from Ice Age Hunter Gatherers to Vikings as Revealed by DNA Analysis* (London: Robinson, 2007).

7. C. Green, 'Some oxygen isotope evidence for long-distance migration to Britain from North Africa and southern Iberia, c.1100 BC to AD 800', 24 October 2015, at http://www.caitlingreen.org/2015/10/oxygen-isotope-evidence.html, accessed 30 January 2018.

8. J. I. McKinley, M. Lievers, J. Schuster, P. Marshall, A. J. Barclay and, N. Stoodley, *Cliffs End Farm, Isle of Thanet, Kent: A Mortuary and Ritual Site of the Bronze Age, Iron Age and Anglo-Saxon Period* (Salisbury: Wessex Archaeology, 2014) and Dr Caitlin Green, 'Thanet, Tanit and the Phoenicians: place-names, archaeology and trading settlements in Eastern Kent', 21 April 2015, http://www.caitlingreen.org/2015/04/thanet-tanit-and-the-phoenicians.html, accessed 31 January 2018.

9. See e.g., A. Ali and I. Ali, *The Black Celts: An Ancient African Civilization in Ireland and Britain* (Cardiff: Punite Publications, 1992) and *England Affric: An Ethnological Survey* (Cardiff: Punite Publications, 1995) and D. MacRitchie, *Ancient and Modern Britons: A Retrospect*, 2 vols. (London: Kegan Paul, Trench & Co, 1884).

10. H. Bodkin, 'Cheddar Man: The first Britons were black, Natural History Museum DNA study reveals', 8 February 2018, *Daily Telegraph*, http://www.telegraph.co.uk/science/2018/02/07/first-britons-black-natural-history-museum-dna-study-reveals/, accessed 8 February 2018.

11. K. Lotzof, 'Cheddar Man: Mesolithic Britain's blue-eyed boy', Natural History Museum website, http://www.nhm.ac.uk/discover/cheddar-man-mesolithic-britain-blue-eyed-boy.html, accessed 7 February 2017.

12. L. Thompson, 'Africans in Roman Britain', *Museum Africum: West African Journal of Classical and Related Studies*, Vol. I (1972), pp. 28–39.

13. R. W. Davies, 'Roman Cumbria and the African Connection', *Klio*, 59 (1977), pp. 155–77.

14. Thompson, 'Africans in Roman Britain', p. 36; A. Birley, *Septimius Severus: The African Emperor* (London: Routledge, 1999), pp. 184–5.

15. V. G. Swan, 'Builders, suppliers and supplies in the Tyne-Solway region and beyond', in P. Bidwell (ed.), *Understanding Hadrian's Wall: Papers from a Conference Held at South Shields*, 3–5 November 2006, to mark the publication of the fourteenth edition of the *Handbook to the Roman Wall* (South Shields: Tyne and Wear Archives and Museums, 2008) pp. 49–82.

16. V. G. Swan, 'Legio VI and its men: African legionaries in Britain', *Journal of Roman Pottery Studies*, 5 (1992), pp. 1–33; V. G. Swan and

J. Monaghan, 'Head-pots: a North African tradition in Roman York', *Yorkshire Archaeological Journal*, 65 (1993), pp. 21–38.

17. Swan, 'Legio VI and its men', p. 4.

18. S. Leach, H. Eckardt, C. Chenery, G. Müldner and M. Lewis, 'A lady of York: migration, ethnicity and identity in Roman Britain', *Antiquity*, 84 (2010) pp. 131–45.

19. A. Watson, 'The ivory-bangle lady', Our Migration Story, https://www.ourmigrationstory.org.uk/oms/roman-britain-the-ivory-bangle-lady, accessed 25 January 2018; 'Ivory bangle lady', York Museums Trust website, https://www.yorkshiremuseum.org.uk/collections/collections-highlights/ivory-bangle-lady/, accessed 25 January 2018.

20. Leach et al., 'A lady of York: migration, ethnicity and identity in Roman Britain'.

21. P. Ghosh, 'DNA study finds London was ethnically diverse from start', 23 November 2015, BBC News, http://www.bbc.co.uk/news/science-environment-34809804, accessed 24 January 2018.

22. J. Seaman, 'The mystery of Beachy Head lady: a Roman African from Eastbourne', 5 April 2018, Museum Crush, https://museumcrush.org/the-mystery-of-beachy-head-lady-a-roman-african-from-eastbourne/, accessed 14 February 2018.

23. Geoffrey of Monmouth, *The History of the Kings of Britain* (London: Penguin, 1973), pp. 263–70.

24. M. Wood, 'The African who transformed Anglo-Saxon England', 28 September 2020, https://www.historyextra.com/period/anglo-saxon/hadrian-clerk-libya-african-who-anglo-saxon-england/, accessed 1 February 2021.

25. British Library, Medieval manuscripts blog, 'An African abbot in Anglo-Saxon England', 27 October 2016, http://blogs.bl.uk/digitisedmanuscripts/2016/10/an-african-abbot-in-anglo-saxon-england.html; S. Lin, 'The mystery of Stephen the African', in the series Race, Racism, and the Middle Ages, *The Public Medievalist*, 2 May 2017, https://www.publicmedievalist.com/mystery-stephen-african/, both accessed 8 February 2018.

26. S. Lucy et al., 'The burial of a princess? The later-seventh-century cemetery at Westfield Farm, Ely', *The Antiquaries Journal*, 89 (2009), pp. 81–141; S. E. Groves et al., 'Mobility histories of 7th–9th century-AD people buried at early medieval Bamburgh, Northumberland, England', *American Journal of Physical Anthropology*, 151/3 (2013), pp. 462–76; K. A. Hemer et al., 'Evidence of early medieval trade and

migration between Wales and the Mediterranean Sea region', *Journal of Archaeological Science*, 40/5 (2–13), pp. 2352–9.

27. D. Gover, 'The first black Briton? 1,000-year-old skeleton of African woman discovered by schoolboys in Gloucestershire river', 2 October 2013, *International Business Times*, http://www.ibtimes.co.uk/fairford-sub-sahara-africa-skeleton-gloucestershire-507102, accessed 31 January 2018.

28. P. Rich, 'The history of blacks in Britain', *History Today*, 31/11 (1 September 1981), p. 33; Edwards, 'The early African presence in the British Isles', p. 13.

29. Edwards, 'The early African presence in the British Isles', pp. 11–14.

30. C. Green, 'A great host of captives? A note on Vikings in Morocco and Vikings in medieval Ireland and Britain', 12 September 2015, http://www.caitlingreen.org/2015/09/a-great-host-of-captives.html, accessed 8 February 2018.

31. P. Wade-Martins, 'Excavations in North Elmham Park, 1967–72', *East Anglian Archaeology Report*, 9 (1980), especially pp. 259–62, http://eaareports.org.uk/publication/report9/, accessed 8 February 2018.

32. A. Petersen, 'The archaeology of Islam in Britain: recognition and potential', *Antiquity*, 82/318 (December 2008), pp. 1080–92.

33. O. Nubia, *Blackamoores: Africans in Tudor England, Their Presence, Status and Origins* (London: Narrative Eye, 2013), p. 47.

34. M. Sherwood, 'Black people in Tudor England', *History Today*, 53/10 (October 2003), pp. 40–42.

35. O. Nubia, 'Who was the Ipswich Man?', Our Migration Story, https://www.ourmigrationstory.org.uk/oms/the-ipswich-man, accessed 31 January 2018.

36. 'Patent rolls of the reign of Henry III, preserved in the public record office', Hathi Trust Digital Library, https://catalog.hathitrust.org/Record/000270470, accessed 8 February 2018. See also M. Ray, 'A black slave on the run in thirteenth-century England,' *Nottingham Medieval Studies*, LI (2007), pp. 111–19.

37. R. Redfern and J. Hefner, '"Officially absent but actually present": bio-archaeological evidence for population diversity in London during the Black Death, AD 1348–50', in M. Mant and A. Holland (eds.), *Bio-archaeology of Marginalised Peoples* (Cambridge: Academic Press, 2019), pp. 69–114.

38. Redfern and Hefner, '"Officially absent but actually present"'.

CHAPTER 2: AFRICAN TUDORS AND STUARTS

1. F. Shyllon, *Black People in Britain, 1555–1833* (London: Oxford University Press, 1977), p. 1; P. Fraser, 'Slaves or free people? The status of Africans in England, 1550–1750', in R. Vigne and C. Littleton (eds.), *From Strangers to Citizens: The Integration of Immigrant Communities in Britain, Ireland and Colonial America, 1550–1750* (Portland, OR: Sussex Academic Press and the Huguenot Society of Great Britain and Ireland, 2001), pp. 254–60.

2. G. Ungerer, *The Mediterranean Apprenticeship of British Slavery* (Madrid: Editorial Verbum), 2008.

3. Ungerer, *Mediterranean Apprenticeship*, pp. 16–28.

4. I. Elbl, 'The volume of the early Atlantic slave trade, 1450–1521', *Journal of African History*, 38 (1997), pp. 31–75.

5. B. Davidson, *Discovering Africa's Past* (London: Longman, 1978), p. 62.

6. I. Shoval, *King John's Delegation to the Almohad Court (1212): Medieval Interreligious Interactions and Modern Historiography* (Belgium: Brepols, 2016).

7. T. F. Earle and K. J. P. Lowe (eds.), *Black Africans in Renaissance Europe* (Cambridge: Cambridge University Press, 2005), pp. 115–16, 229; I. Habib, *Black Lives in the English Archives, 1500–1677: Imprints of the Invisible* (Aldershot: Ashgate, 2008), p. 22.

8. M. Kaufmann, *Black Tudors: The Untold Story* (London: Oneworld, 2017), p. 35; O. Nubia, *Blackamoores: Africans in Tudor England, Their Presence, Status and Origins* (London: Narrative Eye, 2013), p. 111.

9. Nubia, *Blackamoores*, pp. 20, 109–10; Kaufmann, *Black Tudors*, p. 49.

10. E. Weissbourd, '"Those in their possession": race, slavery and Queen Elizabeth's "Edicts of expulsion"', *Huntingdon Library Quarterly*, 78/1 (2015), p. 16.

11. Nubia, *Blackamoores*, pp. 107–37.

12. O. Nubia, *England's Other Countrymen: Black Tudor Society* (London: Zed Books, 2019), pp. 146–7.

13. Kaufmann, *Black Tudors*, p. 144.

14. Weissbourd, '"Those in their possession"', pp. 1–20.

15. Fraser, 'Slaves or free people?', p. 256.

16. Habib, *Black Lives in the English Archives*, p. 66.

17. Quoted in H. Thomas, *The Slave Trade: The History of the Atlantic Slave Trade, 1440–1870* (London: Papermac, 1997), p. 156.

18. Nubia, *Blackamoores*, pp. 172–4.

19. P. Fryer, *Staying Power: The History of Black People in Britain* (London: Pluto, 1984), p. 5.

20. Nubia, *Blackamoores*, p. 173.

21. Ibid., 178.

22. Kaufmann, *Black Tudors*, pp. 180–81.

23. Ibid., p. 185.

24. Ibid., p. 182.

25. Nubia, *Blackamoores* and Kaufmann, *Black Tudors*. See also Habib, *Black Lives in the English Archives* and M. Sherwood, 'Black People in Tudor England', *History Today*, 53/10 (October 2003), pp. 40–42.

26. Kaufman, *Black Tudors*, pp. 101–2.

27. Ibid., pp. 56–78; Nubia, *Blackamoores*, pp. 155–9.

28. Kaufmann, *Black Tudors*, p. 124; Habib, *Black Lives in the English Archives*, pp. 135–6.

29. Kaufmann, *Black Tudors*, pp. 125–6.

30. Nubia, *Blackamoores*, p. 72.

31. R. L. Knutson, 'A Caliban in St. Mildred Poultry', in T. Kishi, R. Pringle and S. W. Wells (eds.), *Shakespeare and Cultural Traditions: The Selected Proceedings of the International Shakespeare Association World Congress, Tokyo, 1991* (Newark: University of Delaware Press, 1994), pp. 110–26.

32. Kaufmann, *Black Tudors*, p. 163.

33. Habib, *Black Lives in the English Archives*, p. 3.

34. Knutson, 'A Caliban', pp. 113–14. Nubia, *Blackamoores*, p. 132.

35. Kaufmann, *Black Tudors*, pp. 219–42.

36. Ibid., pp. 243–59.

37. Ibid., p. 60.

38. M. Corlett, 'Between colony and metropole: empire, race and power in eighteenth-century Britain', in H. Adi (ed.), *Black British History: New Perspectives* (London: Zed Books, 2019).

39. Knutson, 'A Caliban', p. 116.

40. Nubia, *Blackamoores*, p. 112.

41. See, for example, https://www.johnblanke.com/, accessed 27 February 2018.

42. Kaufmann, *Black Tudors*, pp. 8–31; Nubia, *Blackamoores*, pp. 120–25.

43. Kaufmann, *Black Tudors*, p. 29.

44. Quoted in Nubia, *Blackamoores*, p. 114.

45. L. Johnson, 'A life of Catalina, Katherine of Aragon's Moorish servant', English Historical Fiction Authors, 21 March 2015, https://englishhisto ryauthors.blogspot.co.uk/2015/03/a-life-of-catalina-katherine-of-aragons.html, accessed 27 February 2018; Kaufmann, *Black Tudors*, pp. 15–16; Nubia, *Blackamoores*, pp. 117–18.

46. Knutson, 'A Caliban,' pp. 110–26.

47. Nubia, *Blackamoores*, pp. 118–19.

48. Habib, *Black Lives in the English Archives*, pp. 30–32.

49. Quoted in P. Edwards, 'The early African presence in the British Isles', in J. S. Gundara and I. Duffield (eds.), *Essays on the History of Blacks in Britain* (Aldershot: Avebury, 1992) p. 16.

50. Edwards, 'The early African presence', p. 17.

51. *Accounts of the Lord High Treasurer of Scotland*, Vol. III (Edinburgh: 1901), pp. 108, 118, 190, 197, 206, 330 and 377; Habib, *Black Lives in the English Archives*, p. 42.

52. *Accounts of the Lord High Treasurer of Scotland*, Vol. IV (Edinburgh: 1902), pp. 62, 112, 139, 178, 191.

53. Fryer, *Staying Power*, p. 3.

54. *Accounts of the Lord High Treasurer of Scotland*, Vol. III (Edinburgh: 1901), p. xlix.

55. Fryer, *Staying Power*, p. 4.

56. Knutson, 'A Caliban', pp. 110–26.

57. Ibid., p. 120.

58. Nubia, *Blackamoores*, pp. 166–70.

59. Ibid., pp. 132–5.

60. Kaufmann, *Black Tudors*, pp. 32–55.

61. Nubia, *Blackamoores*, pp. 155–9.

62. Kaufmann, *Black Tudors*, pp. 196–218.

63. O. Nubia, 'Henrie Anthonie Jetto', *Oxford Dictionary of National Biography*, https://www.oxforddnb.com/view/10.1093/ref:odnb/9780198614128.001.0001/odnb-9780198614128-e-112805, accessed 1 February 2021.

64. Nubia, *Blackamoores*, pp. 4–9.

65. Kaufmann, *Black Tudors*, p. 109; M. Kaufmann, 'Caspar van Senden, Sir Thomas Sherley and the "Blackamoor" Project', *Historical Research*, 81/212 (May 2008), pp. 366–71.

66. Nubia, *Blackamoores*, pp. 10–11.

67. Ibid., p. 12.

68. E.g., E. C. Bartels, 'Too many Blackamoors: deportation, discrimination, and Elizabeth I', *Studies in English Literature*, 36/2 (Spring 2006), pp. 305–22.

69. See, for example, Weissbourd, '"Those in their possession"'.

70. Nubia, *Blackamoores*, pp. 12–29.

71. See, for example, A. T. Vaughan and V. M. Vaughan, 'Tales from the vault: in search of slavery's English roots', *Common-Place*, 1/4 (July

2001), http://www.common-place-archives.org/vol-01/no-04/tales/, accessed 5 July 2018. Habib, *Black Lives in the English Archives*, p. 60.

72. W. D. Jordan, *White over Black: American Attitudes Toward the Negro, 1550–1812* (Baltimore: Penguin, 1971), pp. 3–43.

73. Quoted in Habib, *Black Lives in the English Archives*, p. 102.

74. D. Salkeld, *Shakespeare Among the Courtesans* (London: Ashgate, 2012), pp. 120–42; also D. Salkeld, 'Black Lucy and the "Curtizans" of Shakespeare's London', *Signatures*, 2 (2000) 1.1–1.10, https://www.academia.edu/1951732/Black_Luce_and_the_Curtizans_of_Shakespeares_London_for_Black_Luce_see_Courtesans_book_above_, accessed 5 July 2018.

75. Habib, *Black Lives in the English Archives*, p. 12.

76. Nubia, *England's Other Countrymen*, pp. 131–64.

77. O. Nubia, '"Blackamoores" have their own names in early modern England', in H. Adi (ed.), *Black British History: New Perspectives* (London: Zed Books, 2019), pp. 15–36.

CHAPTER 3: THAT INFAMOUS TRAFFIC

1. P. Fryer, *Staying Power: The History of Black People in Britain* (London: Pluto, 1984), p. 20.

2. E. Williams, *Capitalism and Slavery* (London: André Deutsch, 1967), p. 13; D. Brion Davis, *The Problem of Slavery in Western Culture* (London: Penguin, 1966), p. 271.

3. Williams, *Capitalism and Slavery*, pp. 9–19.

4. H. Fuller, *The Holy State and the Profane State* (London: Thomas Tegg, 1841), p. 121.

5. Williams, *Capitalism and Slavery*, p. 19.

6. I. Habib, *Black Lives in the English Archives, 1500–1677* (London: Routledge, 2007), p. 126.

7. H. Thomas, *The Slave Trade: The History of the Atlantic Slave Trade, 1440–1870* (London: Papermac, 1998) p. 198.

8. Thomas, *The Slave Trade*, p. 201.

9. 'America and West Indies: July 1677, 16–31', in *Calendar of State Papers*, Colonial Series, *America and West Indies: Vol. X: 1677–1680*, ed. W. Noel Sainsbury and J. W. Fortescue (London: 1896), pp. 116–38, British History Online, http://www.british-history.ac.uk/cal-state-papers/colonial/america-west-indies/vol10/pp116-138, accessed 3 May 2020.

10. Thomas, *The Slave Trade*, p. 236.

11. Ibid., p. 235.

12. P. Scanlan, *Slave Empire: How Slavery Built Modern Britain* (London: Robinson, 2020), p. 25.

13. Williams, *Capitalism and Slavery*, p. 104.

14. Ibid., pp. 98–102.

15. Scanlan, *Slave Empire*, p. 50; H. Beckles, 'Caribbean anti-slavery: the self-liberation ethos of enslaved blacks', *Journal of Caribbean History*, 22/1 (January 1988) pp. 1–19.

16. Williams, *Capitalism and Slavery*, p. 102.

17. S. Mullen, 'James Watt and slavery in Scotland', *History Workshop Journal*, 17 August 2020, https://www.historyworkshop.org.uk/james-watt-and-slavery-in-scotland/, accessed 1 February 2021.

18. A. Hochschild, *Bury the Chains: The British Struggle to Abolish Slavery* (Oxford: Pan Books, 2005), pp. 67–8.

19. S. Huxtable, C. Fowler, K. Cefalas and E. Slocombe (eds.), 'Interim report on the connections between colonialism and the properties now in the care of the National Trust, including links with historic slavery' (Swindon: National Trust, 2020), https://nt.global.ssl.fastly.net/documents/colonialism-and-historic-slavery-report.pdf; M. Dresser and A. Han (eds.), *Slavery and the British Country House* (London: Historic England, 2013), https://historicengland.org.uk/images-books/publications/slavery-and-british-country-house/; M. Dresser and M. Wills, 'The transatlantic slave economy and England's built environment: a research audit', 19 August 2020, Historic England, https://historicengland.org.uk/research/results/reports/247-2020.

20. Scanlan, *Slave Empire*, p. 143.

21. Thomas, *The Slave Trade*, p. 241.

22. I. Law, 'White racism and black settlement in Liverpool', PhD thesis, University of Liverpool (1985), pp. 31–2.

23. Hanlan, *Slave Empire*, p. 60.

24. Thomas, *The Slave Trade*, pp. 264–5.

25. C. Shaw, 'Liverpool's slave trade legacy', *History Today*, 70/3 (March 2020), https://www.historytoday.com/history-matters/liverpool%E2%80%99s-slave-trade-legacy, accessed 1 February 2021.

26. Law, 'White racism and black settlement in Liverpool', p. 32.

27. D. Brion Davis, *Inhuman Bondage: The Rise and Fall of Slavery in the New World* (Oxford: Oxford University Press, 2006), p. 80.

28. K. Marx, *The Poverty of Philosophy*, Chapter 2, 'The Metaphysics of Political Economy', https://www.marxists.org/archive/marx/works/1847/poverty-philosophy/ch02.htm, accessed 1 February 2021.

29. H. Thomas, *The Slave Trade*, p. 198, and Habib, *Black Lives in the English Archives*, p. 127.

30. Habib, *Black Lives in the English Archives*, p. 162.

31. P. Linebaugh and M. Rediker, *The Many-Headed Hydra: Sailors, Slaves, Commoners, and the Hidden History of the Revolutionary Atlantic* (Boston: Beacon Press, 2000), pp. 71–103.

32. C. Hill, *The World Turned Upside Down* (Harmondsworth: Penguin, 1975), pp. 17, 171.

33. Habib, *Black Lives in the English Archives*, pp. 169–70.

34. M. Kaufmann, *Black Tudors: The Untold Story* (London: Oneworld, 2017), pp. 196–218; 'James I: March 1620' in *Calendar of State Papers, Domestic Series, James 1, Vol. CXIII: 1619–1623*, ed. M. A. Everett Green (London: 1858), pp. 127–35, British History Online, http://www.british-history.ac.uk/cal-state-papers/domestic/jas1/1619-23/pp127-135, accessed 17 March 2022.

35. Fryer, *Staying Power*, p. 22.

36. Ibid., p. 21.

37. Habib, *Black Lives in the English Archives*, p. 179.

38. Ibid., p. 179; F. Shyllon, *Black People in Britain, 1555–1833* (London: Oxford University Press, 1977), p. 11.

39. Habib, *Black Lives in the English Archives*, pp. 123, 176 and 178.

40. Ibid., p. 184.

41. 'America and West Indies: July 1677, 16–31', *Calendar of State Papers*.

42. 'For Sale', Runaway Slaves in Britain, University of Glasgow, https://www.runaways.gla.ac.uk/for_sale/, accessed 1 March 2021.

43. Shyllon, *Black People in Britain*, p. 11.

44. 'The Project', Runaway Slaves in Britain, University of Glasgow, https://www.runaways.gla.ac.uk/, accessed 12 July 2018.

45. *Edinburgh Evening Courant*, 13 February 1727, Runaway Slaves in Britain, University of Glasgow, https://www.runaways.gla.ac.uk/database/display/?rid=2, accessed 12 July 2018.

46. K. Chater, *Untold Histories: Black People in England and Wales during the Period of the British Slave Trade, c.1660–1807* (Manchester: Manchester University Press, 2009).

47. *Weekly Journal or British Gazetteer*, 9 October 1725.

48. S. Drescher, *Capitalism and Antislavery: British Mobilization in Comparative Perspective* (Oxford: Oxford University Press, 1987), p. 188, n. 24.

49. 'Slave Grave at Oxhill', https://www.avondassett.com/wp-content/uploads/2014/06/Slave-grave.pdf, accessed 15 July 2018.

50. Charles Dickens, 'The Black Man', *All the Year Round*, 3 March 1875, p. 491.

51. M. Kaufmann, 'English Common Law and Slavery', *Encyclopedia of Blacks in European History and Culture*, Vol. 1, pp. 200–203, http:// www.mirandakaufmann.com/common-law.html, accessed 15 July 2018.

52. T. Carthew, *Reports of Cases Adjudged in the Court of King's Bench from the Third Year of King James the Second to the Twelfth Year of King William the Third* (London: Carthew, 1728), pp. 396–7, http:// lawlibrary.wm.edu/wythepedia/library/CarthewReportsOfCases AdjudgedInTheCourtOfKingsBench1728.pdf, accessed 19 July 2018.

53. Davis, *The Problem of Slavery*, p. 233.

54. Quoted in Fryer, *Staying Power*, p. 114; G. Van Cleve, 'Somerset's Case and its Antecedents in Imperial Perspective', *Law and History Review*, 24/3 (Fall 2006), pp. 601–45.

55. Quoted in V. C. D. Mtubani, 'African Slaves and English Law', *Botswana Journal of African Studies*, 3/2 (1983), pp. 71–5; W. Salkeld, *Report of Cases Adjudg'd in the Court of the King's Bench*, Vol. 2 (London, 1718), pp. 666–8, http://lawlibrary.wm.edu/wythepedia/library/ SalkeldReportsOfCasesAdjudgedInTheCourtOfKingsBench1718Vol2. pdf, accessed 19 July 2018.

56. 'Examples of "For Sale" advertisements', Runaway Slaves in Britain, University of Glasgow, https://www.runaways.gla.ac.uk/for_sale/ Runaway%20Slaves%20in%2018th%20C%20Britain%20-%20 For%20Sale.pdf, accessed 13 July 2018.

57. Law, 'White racism and black settlement in Liverpool', p. 45.

58. 'Examples of "For Sale" advertisements', Runaway Slaves in Britain.

59. Ibid.

60. Ibid.

61. 'A black servant sues her employers, 1690', Middlesex County Records, Sessions Books, no. 472, February 1690, Black Presence, National Archives, http://www.nationalarchives.gov.uk/pathways/blackhistory/ rights/docs/middlesex.htm, accessed 15 July 2018.

62. Van Cleve, 'Somerset's Case', p. 616; See also 'London Lives 1690– 1800', https://www.londonlives.org/browse.jsp?div=LMSMPS50165 PS501650126, accessed 19 July 2018.

63. T. Glasson, '"Baptism doth not bestow Freedom": Missionary Anglicanism, Slavery and the Yorke-Talbot Opinion, 1701–1730', *The William and Mary Quarterly*, 67/2 (April 2010), pp. 279–318.

64. Mtubani, 'African Slaves', p. 73.

65. 23–25 December 1762, *St James's Chronicle, Or The British Evening Post*.

66. R. H. Eden, *Reports of Cases Argued and Determined in the High Court of Chancery from 1757 to 1766*, Vol. 2 (London, 1818), p. 127, http://www.mindserpent.com/American_History/reference/eng_reports/1818_eden_reports_of_cases_in_the_high_court_of_chancery_vol_02_of_02.pdf, accessed 19 July 2018.

67. Glasson, '"Baptism doth not bestow Freedom"', pp. 279–318; Pulicola, 'To the Printer', 27–29 January 1763, *St James's Chronicle; Or the British Evening Post.*

68. *Country Journal or the Craftsman*, 9 May 1730.

69. Pulicola, 'To the Printer'.

70. *Daily Post*, 28 October 1732.

71. Quoted in D. Lorimer, 'Black resistance to slavery and racism', in J. S. Gundara and I. Duffield (eds.), *Essays on the History of Blacks in Britain* (Aldershot: Avebury, 1992), pp. 58–80 (quotation, p. 60).

72. Anglicus, 'To the Printer', *London Chronicle*, 29 September–2 October 1764.

73. F. Freeman, 'To the Printer', *London Chronicle*, 19–22 October 1765.

74. Quoted in Lorimer, 'Black resistance', p. 60.

75. Quoted in Fryer, *Staying Power*, p. 71.

76. Quoted in C. Midgely, *Women Against the Slave Trade: The British Campaigns, 1780–1870* (London: Routledge, 1992), p. 12.

77. Fryer, *Staying Power*, p. 118.

78. Quoted in Lorimer, 'Black resistance', p. 62.

79. E. Long, *Candid Reflections Upon the Judgment Lately Awarded by the Court of King's Bench, in Westminster-Hall, on What is Commonly Called the Negro-Cause, by a Planter* (London: T. Lowndes, 1772), pp. 47–8, https://repository.library.northeastern.edu/downloads/neu:m041092oh?datastream_id=content, accessed 25 July 2018.

80. Quoted in Shyllon, *Black People in Britain*, p. 76.

81. Lorimer, 'Black resistance', p. 61.

82. M. Sherwood, 'Blacks in the Gordon Riots', *History Today*, 47/12 (December 1997), pp. 24–8.

83. Lorimer, 'Black resistance', p. 61.

84. Chater, *Untold Histories*, p. 31.

85. J. Northcote, *Memoirs of Sir Joshua Reynolds: Comprising Original Anecdotes of Many Distinguished Persons, His Contemporaries; and a Brief Analysis of His Discourses, to Which Are Added Varieties on Art* (London: 1813), pp. 117–19; Trial of Thomas Windsor, 21 October 1776, Old Bailey Proceedings Online, https://www.oldbaileyonline.org/browse.jsp?id=t17671021-44-defend479&div=t17671021-44, accessed 25 July 2018.

86. 17 February 1764, *London Chronicle*.

87. Shyllon, *Black People in Britain*, p. 81.

88. Ibid., p. 81.

89. Public Ledger, 23 October 1772.

90. M. L. Miller, *Slaves to Fashion: Black Dandyism and the Styling of Black Diasporic Identity* (Durham, NC: Duke University Press, 2009), pp. 27–76.

91. Prince Hoare (ed.), *Memoirs of Granville Sharp, Esq: Composed from His Own Manuscripts, and Other Authentic Documents in the Possession of His Family and of the African Institution* (London: Henry Colburn and Co., 1820), p. 50, https://archive.org/stream/memoirsof granviloohoar/memoirsofgranviloohoar_djvu.txt, accessed 27 July 2018.

92. Hoare (ed.), *Memoirs of Granville Sharp*, p. 59.

93. J. Oldfield, 'New light on Mansfield and slavery', *Journal of British Studies*, 27/1 (January 1988), pp. 45–68.

94. Ibid., pp. 53–4.

95. Hoare (ed.), *Memoirs of Granville Sharp*, pp. 90–91; *London Magazine*, June 1772, pp. 267–8.

96. Quoted in V. Carretta, *Equiano, the African: Biography of a Self-Made Man* (London: Penguin, 2005), p. 208.

97. Shyllon, *Black People in Britain*, p. 80, and Carretta, *Equiano, the African*, p. 208.

98. Carretta, *Equiano, the African*, p. 209.

99. Oldfield, 'New light on Mansfield and slavery', pp. 45–68; C. L. Brown, *Moral Capital: Foundations of British Abolitionism* (Durham, NC: University of North Carolina Press, 2012), pp. 97–100.

100. G. Horne, *The Counter-Revolution of 1776: Slave Resistance and the Origin of the United States of America* (New York: New York University Press, 2014).

101. Shyllon, *Black People in Britain*, pp. 25–6; C. Durnford and E. Hyde East (eds.), *Reports of Cases Argued and Determined in the Court of King's Bench from Michaelmas Term 31st George III to Trinity Term 32nd George III Inclusive*, Vol. 4 (Dublin: 1793), pp. 301–2.

102. Shyllon, *Black People in Britain*, p. 25.

103. Carretta, *Equiano, the African*, pp. 210–12.

104. Hoare, *Memoirs of Granville Sharp*, p. 93.

105. Drescher, *Capitalism and Antislavery*, p. 40: Carretta, *Equiano, the African*, pp. 212–13.

106. Long, *Candid Reflections*, pp. 36–7.

107. I. Whyte, *Scotland and the Abolition of Black Slavery, 1756–1838* (Edinburgh: Edinburgh University Press, 2006); J. Cairns, 'Freeing

from slavery in 18th-century Scotland', in A. Burrows and D. Johnstone (eds.), *Judge and Jurist: Essays in Memory of Lord Rodger of Earlsferry* (Oxford: Oxford University Press, 2013), pp. 367–83.

108. Whyte, *Scotland and the Abolition of Black Slavery*, p. 12.

109. *Edinburgh Evening Courant*, 13 February 1727, Runaway Slaves in Britain, University of Glasgow, https://www.runaways.gla.ac.uk/database/display/?rid=2, accessed 1 June 2019.

110. See 'James Mongomery, Runaway Slave', Legacies of Slavery in Glasgow Museums and Collections, https://glasgowmuseumsslavery.co.uk/2018/08/14/jamie-montgomery-runaway-slave/, accessed 30 July 2018.

111. 'A bid for freedom', National Archives of Scotland, 6 January 2017, https://webarchive.nrscotland.gov.uk/20170106021747/http://www.nas.gov.uk/about/061010.asp, accessed 30 July 2018.

112. Whyte, *Scotland and the Abolition of Black Slavery*, pp. 9–10; 'A bid for freedom', National Archives of Scotland.

113. Whyte, *Scotland and the Abolition of Black Slavery*, p. 10.

114. S. Cunningham, *Rambles in the Parishes of Scoonie and Wemyss* (Leven: Purves and Cunningham, 1905), pp. 154–6; Whyte, *Scotland and the Abolition of Black Slavery*, p. 22.

115. 'Laws relating to coal workers in Scotland – 1775 Act', http://www.hoodfamily.info/coal/law1775act.html, accessed 30 July 2018.

116. 'A bid for freedom', National Archives of Scotland.

117. Quoted in Whyte, *Scotland and the Abolition of Black Slavery*, p. 18.

118. 'A narrative of the most remarkable particulars in the life of James Albert', Project Gutenberg, http://www.gutenberg.org/ebooks/15042?msg=welcome_stranger, accessed 31 July 2018.

119. R. Hanley, 'Calvinism, Proslavery and James Albert Ukawsaw Gronniosaw,' *Slavery and Abolition*, 36/2 (2015), pp. 360–81; *Chester Chronicle*, 2 October 1775.

120. Y. Taylor (ed.), *I Was Born a Slave: An Anthology of Classic Slave Narratives* (London: Payback Press, 1999), p. 3.

121. A useful bibliography of Phillis Wheatley's work can be found at https://www.poetryfoundation.org/poets/phillis-wheatley, accessed 3 August 2018.

122. *London Magazine*, March 1772, pp. 134–5.

123. M. A. Isani, 'The British reception of Wheatley's poems on various subjects', *Journal of Negro History*, 66/2 (Summer 1981), pp. 144–9.

124. J. C. Shields, 'Phillis Wheatley', *Oxford Dictionary of National Biography*, https://doi.org/10.1093/ref:odnb/53405, accessed 3 August 2018.

125. *Gentlemen's Magazine*, September 1773, p. 456.

126. Quoted in Isani, 'The British reception', p. 148.

127. Ibid., pp. 145–6.

128. W. Harris, 'Phillis Wheatley: a Muslim connection', *African American Review*, 48/1–2 (Spring–Summer 2015), pp. 1–15.

129. 'Phillis's Reply to the Answer', J. C. Shields (ed.), *The Collected Works of Phillis Wheatley* (Oxford: Oxford University Press, 1988), p. 144.

130. Phillis Wheatley, 'To the Right Honorable William, Earl of Dartmouth', https://www.poetryfoundation.org/poems/47706/to-the-right-honorable-william-earl-of-dartmouth, accessed 2 August 2018.

131. V. Caretta (ed.), *Ignatius Sancho: Letters of the Late Ignatius Sancho, An African* (London: Penguin, 1998), pp. ix–x; see also 'Introduction' in P. Edwards and P. Rewt, *The Letters of Ignatius Sancho* (Edinburgh: Edinburgh University Press, 1994), pp. 1–22.

132. *London Chronicle*, 3–5 October 1782.

133. Caretta, *Ignatius Sancho*, p. xi.

134. Ibid., pp. 73–4, 331–6.

135. Ibid, pp. xxviii–xxxi; Edwards and Rewt, *The Letters*, pp. 262–3.

136. Sancho to Fisher, 27 January 1778, in Carretta, *Ignatius Sancho*, pp. 111–12.

137. Quoted in Edwards and Rewt, *The Letters*, p. 4.

138. See, e.g., *Chester Chronicle*, 11 December 1775.

139. See for examples, *General Evening Post*, 28 October 1776; *London Evening Post*, 17 October 1776.

140. See e.g., *Whitehall Evening Post*, 14 December 1780.

141. *Public Advertiser*, 9 August 1782.

142. *London Chronicle*, 1 October 1782.

143. J. Oldfield, 'New light on Mansfield and slavery', *Journal of British Studies*, 27/1 (January 1988), pp. 45–68.

144. N. Myers, *Reconstructing the Black Past: Blacks in Britain 1780–1830* (London: Frank Cass, 1996), pp. 18–37; S. Braidwood, *Black Poor and White Philanthropists: London's Blacks and the Founding of the Sierra Leone Settlement 1786–1791* (Liverpool: Liverpool University Press, 1994), pp. 23, 52, n. 114.

145. Braidwood, *Black Poor and White Philanthropists*, pp. 22–33, 149–58.

146. T. Bluett, *Some Memoirs of the Life of Job, the Son of Solomon, the High Priest of Boonda in Africa; Who Was a Slave about Two Years in Maryland; and Afterwards Being Brought to England, Was Set Free, and Sent to His Native Land in the Year 1734* (London: R. Ford, 1734), Documenting the American South, https://docsouth.unc.edu/neh/bluett/menu.html, accessed 1 February 2021.

147. W. Sypher, 'The African prince in London', *Journal of the History of Ideas*, 2/2 (April 1941), p. 238.

148. F. Moore, *Travels into the Inland Parts of Africa* (London: Edward Cave, 1738), p. 203, Library of Congress, https://www.wdl.org/en/item/650/view/1/5/#q=Solomon, accessed 1 February 2021.

149. *Gentleman's Magazine*, XIX (1749), pp. 89–90.

150. Shyllon, *Black People in Britain*, pp. 45–6; *The Royal African: or, Memoirs of the Young Prince of Annamaboe* (London: 1750), Documenting the American South, https://docsouth.unc.edu/neh/royal/royal.html, accessed 10 February 2022; Sypher, 'The African prince in London', pp. 237–47; ; V. Carretta, 'William Ansah Sessarakoo', *Oxford Dictionary of National Biography*, https://www.oxforddnb.com/view/10.1093/ref:odnb/9780198614128.001.0001/odnb-9780198614128-e-97280, accessed 1 February 2021.

151. *Gentleman's Magazine*, XX (1750), p. 273.

152. C. Wadström, *An Essay on Colonization Particularly Applied to the West Coast of Africa, with Some Free Thought on Cultivation and Commerce: Also Brief Descriptions of the Colonies Already Formed, or Attempted in Africa, Including Those of Sierra Leone and Bulama* (London: Darton and Harvey, 1794), Part 1, pp. 94–5, Internet Archive, https://archive.org/details/essayoncolonizatoowads/page/n107, accessed 9 April 2019.

153. Ibid., Part 2, pp. 269–70, Internet Archive.

154. Shyllon, *Black People in Britain*, pp. 46–8.

155. Ibid., pp. 49–54.

156. Ibid.

157. Letter from the Secretary to the Society for Propagating the Gospel in Foreign Parts, no. 3, no date, pp. 98–9, Hathi Trust Digital Library, https://bit.ly/3Jl8KdY, accessed 13 February 2022; B. L. Mouser, 'African Academy Clapham – 1799–1806', *History of Education*, 33/1 (January 2004), pp. 87–103, n. 12.

158. Shyllon, *Black People in Britain*, pp. 57–8; M. Priestly, 'Philip Quaque of Cape Coast', in P. Curtin (ed.), *Africa Remembered: Narratives by West Africans from the Era of the Slave Trade* (London: University of Wisconsin Press, 1967), pp. 99–142.

159. Letter from the Secretary to the Society for the Propagation of the Gospel in Foreign Parts, no. 3, no date; Letter from the delegates from Liverpool, in answer to the enquiry made by the committee respecting the natives of Africa who have been sent to England for education, addressed to John Tarleton, Esquire, Liverpool, 17 April 1788, no. 4,

Hathi Trust Digital Library, pp. 98–100, https://bit.ly/3Jl8KdY, accessed 13 February 2022.

160. M. Priestly, 'Philip Quaque of the Gold Coast: Introduction', in Curtin (ed.), *Africa Remembered*, pp. 99–112.

161. Mouser, 'African Academy,' p. 93.

162. Ibid., p. 101.

163. J. Gilmore, 'Francis Williams', *Oxford Dictionary of National Biography*, https://www.oxforddnb.com/view/10.1093/ref:odnb/9780198614128. 001.0001/odnb-9780198614128-e-57050, accessed 1 February 2021.

164. Shyllon, *Black People in Britain*, pp. 40–41.

165. C. Eickelmann, 'Within the same household: Fanny Coker', in G. Gerzina (ed.), *Britain's Black Past* (Liverpool: Liverpool University Press, 2020), pp. 141–59.

166. M. Dresser and P. Fleming, *Bristol: Ethnic Minorities and the City: 1000–2001* (Chichester: Phillimore, 2007), pp. 85–92; C. Eickelmann and D. Small, *Pero: The Life of a Slave in Eighteenth-Century Bristol* (Bristol: Redcliffe Press, 2004).

167. M. Corlett, 'Between colony and metropole: empire, race and power in eighteenth-century Britain', in H. Adi (ed.), *Black British History: New Perspectives* (London: Zed Books, 2019), pp. 37–51.

168. Chater, *Untold Histories*, pp. 269–70.

169. Exeter Working Papers in British Book Trade History, The London Book Trades, 1775–1800, https://bookhistory.blogspot.com/2007/01/london-1775-1800-s.html, accessed 1 March 2020.

170. Trial of Catherine Burk, 26 February 1746, https://www.oldbaileyonline.org/print.jsp?div=t17460226-13, accessed 23 August 2018.

171. Sherwood, 'Blacks in the Gordon Riots', pp. 27–8.

172. M. Moss, 'Scipio Kennedy', *Oxford Dictionary of National Biography*, https://www.oxforddnb.com/view/10.1093/ref:odnb/97801986 14128.001.0001/odnb-9780198614128-e-107129#odnb-9780 198614128-e-107129, accessed 1 February 2021.

173. K. Chater, 'George John Scipio Africanus', *Oxford Dictionary of National Biography*, https://www.oxforddnb.com/view/10.1093/ref:o dnb/9780198614128.001.0001/odnb-9780198614128-e-112802, accessed 1 February 2021.

174. Alltud Eifion, *John Istumyllyn, or 'Jack Black': The History of His Life and Traditions about Him, Since His Capture in the Wilds of Africa Until His Death; Together with a Picture of Him in the Year 1754*, (Tremadoc: R. Isaac Jones, 1888), http://www.black-boy-inn.com/wp-content/uploads/2012/11/blackJackHistoryEnglish.pdf, accessed 1 February 2021.

175. H. Farmer, *The Rise and Development of Military Music* (London: W.M. Reeves, 1912) p. 74.

176. Ibid., p. 75.

177. Ibid., pp. 77–8.

178. J. Ellis, 'Black soldiers in the British Army – 18th and 19th century', 2 March 2009, The Black Presence in Britain, https://blackpresence.co.uk/black-soldiers-in-the-british-army-john-ellis/, accessed 10 February 2022.

179. P. Edwards and D. Dabydeen (eds.), *Black Writers in Britain 1760–1890* (Edinburgh: Edinburgh University Press, 1991), p. 16.

180. J. Ellis, synopsis of MA thesis, 'The visual representation, role and origin of black soldiers in British Army regiments during the early nineteenth century', 3 March 2009, https://blackpresence.co.uk/the-visual-representation-role-and-origin-of-black-soldiers-in-british-army-regiments-during-the-early-nineteenth-century/, accessed 10 February 2022.

181. C. Foy, 'The Royal Navy's employment of black mariners and maritime workers, 1754–1783', *International Journal of Maritime History*, 28/1 (2016), pp. 6–35, and 'Britain's Black Tars', in Gerzina (ed.), *Britain's Black Past*, pp. 63–79.

182. Foy, 'The Royal Navy's employment', p. 16, n. 42.

183. R. Boser, 'The Creation of a Legend', *History Today*, 52/10 (1 October 2002), pp. 36–7.

184. *London Chronicle*, 6–9 March 1779; Oldham, 'New light on Mansfield and slavery', p. 65.

185. C. Foy, '"Unkle Somerset's" freedom: liberty in England for black sailors', *Journal of Maritime Research*, 13/1 (May 2011), pp. 21–36.

186. Foy, '"Unkle Somerset's" freedom', pp. 24–31.

187. M. Sherwood, 'Shall we ever learn the full story of blacks in the Royal Navy?', *BASA Newsletter*, 57 (July 2010), pp. 8 and 12.

188. Trial of Sarah Jones and Mary Smith, September 1736, Old Bailey Proceedings Online, https://www.oldbaileyonline.org/print.jsp?div=t17360908-39, accessed 23 August 2018.

189. Sherwood, 'Shall we ever learn', p. 9.

190. Trial of Ann Read, September 1781, Old Bailey Proceedings Online, https://www.oldbaileyonline.org/print.jsp?div=t17810912-52, accessed 23 August 2018.

191. R. McGrady, *Music and Musicians in Early Nineteenth-Century Cornwall: The World of Joseph Emidy – Slave, Violinist and Composer* (Exeter: University of Exeter Press, 1991), pp. 25–6.

192. McGrady, *Music and Musicians*, p. 145.

193. Ibid., p. 148.
194. V. Carretta, 'Introduction' in Q. O. Cugoano, *Thoughts and Sentiments on the Evil of Slavery and Other Writings* (London: Penguin, 1999), pp. ix–xxviii.
195. Quoted in Carretta, 'Introduction', in Cugoano, ibid., p. xiv.
196. Ibid., p. xviii; Hoare, *Memoirs*, pp. 261–2.
197. O. Equiano, *The Interesting Narrative and Other Writings* (London: Penguin, 2003), p. 32.
198. S. Scharma, *Rough Crossings: Britain, the Slaves and the American Revolution* (London: BBC Books, 2005), pp. 187–236.
199. See, for example, *Morning Post and Daily Advertiser*, 7 November 1777 and 4 March 1778; Shyllon, *Black People in Britain*, pp. 245–66.
200. *Public Advertiser*, 5 February 1788 and 28 April 1788.
201. *Morning Chronicle and London Advertiser*, 15 July 1788.
202. H. Adi, 'African resistance, activism and the Sons of Africa', in A. Torrington, R. McLean, V. Osborne and L. Grosvenor (eds.), *Equiano: Enslavement, Resistance and Abolition* (Birmingham: Birmingham Museum and Art Gallery, 2008), pp. 78–84.
203. *Morning Chronicle and London Advertiser*, 28 May 1773.
204. T. Day, Fragment of an original letter on the slavery of the Negroes, written in the year 1776, Internet Archive, https://archive.org/details/fragmentoforiginoodayt, accessed on 15 August 2018.
205. Drescher, *Capitalism and Antislavery*, pp. 59–60; Hoare, *Memoirs*, pp. 184–94.
206. Davis, *The Problem of Slavery in Western Culture*, pp. 423–56.
207. J. Walvin, *England, Slaves and Freedom, 1776–1838* (Jackson, MS: University Press of Mississippi, 1986), p. 98.
208. 'Baxter's directions to slave holders, revised', first printed in London in the year 1673, Evans Early American Imprint Collection, https://quod.lib.umich.edu/e/evans/N34072.0001.001?rgn=main;view=fulltext, accessed 1 March 2019.
209. W. Snyper, 'Hutcheson and the "classical" theory of slavery', *Journal of Negro History*, 24/3 (July 1939), pp. 263–80.
210. R. Blackburn, *The Overthrow of Colonial Slavery: 1776–1848* (London: Verso, 2011), p. 50.
211. D. Brion Davis, 'New sidelights on early antislavery radicalism', *William and Mary Quarterly*, 28/4 (October 1971), pp. 585–94.
212. Walvin, *England, Slaves and Freedom*, p. 103.
213. Ibid., pp. 101–2.
214. Shyllon, *Black People in Britain*, pp. 245–6.

215. T. Tryon, *The Negro's Complaint of Their Hard Servitude, and the Cruelties Practised Upon Them by Divers of their Masters Professing Christianity in the West-Indian Plantations*, the Second Part, Early English Books Online, https://quod.lib.umich.edu/e/eebo/A63791.000 1.001/1:3?rgn=div1;view=fulltext, accessed 1 March 2019.

216. P. Rosenberg, 'Thomas Tryon and seventeenth-century dimensions of anti-slavery', *William and Mary Quarterly*, 61/4 (October 2004), pp. 609–42.

217. Carretta, *Equiano the African*, p. 246.

218. G. Turnbull, *An Apology for Negro Slavery: Or the West-India Planters Vindicated from the Charge of Inhumanity* (London: pub. 1786), pp. 32–4.

219. E. Long, *A History of Jamaica*, Vol. 2 (London: T. Lowndes, 1774), pp. 442–75, https://archive.org/details/historyofjamaica02long/page/442/mode/2up?view=theater, accessed 1 March 2019.

220. Carretta, *Equiano, the African*, pp. 257–61.

221. S. Braidwood, *Black Poor and White Philanthropists: London's Black and the Foundation of the Sierra Leone Settlement, 1786–1791* (Liverpool: Liverpool University Press, 1994); C. Pybus, *Epic Journeys of Freedom: Runaway Slaves of the American Revolution and Their Global Quest for Liberty* (Boston: Beacon Press, 2006), pp. 75–87 and 103–19.

222. Carretta, 'Introduction', in Cugoano, *Thoughts and Sentiments*, p. xvi.

223. P. Linebaugh and M. Rediker, *The Many-Headed Hydra: Sailors, Slaves, Commoners, and the Hidden History of the Revolutionary Atlantic* (Boston: Beacon Press, 2000), p. 273.

224. J. Wilson (ed.), *The Songs of Joseph Mather* (Sheffield: pub. 1862), p. 1.

225. K. Morgan, *Slavery and the British Empire: From Africa to America* (Oxford: Oxford University Press, 2007), p. 157.

226. See, e.g., *Diary or Woodfall's Register*, 13 May 1789.

227. Drescher, *Capitalism and Antislavery*, pp. 214–15, n. 44; *Gazetteer and New Daily Advertiser*, 21 February 1788.

228. Shyllon, *Black People in Britain*, p. 82.

229. A. Hochschild, *Bury the Chains: The British Struggle to Abolish Slavery* (London: Pan, 2005), p. 137.

230. Drescher, *Capitalism and Antislavery*, pp. 67–88.

231. *Gazetteer and New Daily Advertiser*, 14 January 1790.

232. Quoted in Carretta, *Equiano, the African*, p. 343.

233. A. Osborne, *Equiano's Daughter: The Life and Times of Joanna Vassa* (Cambridge: Momentum Arts, 2007), pp. 3–4.

234. Letter from Cugoano to G. Sharp, in Cugoano, *Thoughts and Sentiments*, p. 196.

235. Carretta, 'Introduction', in Cugoano, *Thoughts and Sentiments*, pp. xix–xx, and ibid., pp. 195–6.

236. Ibid., p. 19.

237. *Gazetteer and New Daily Advertiser*, 21 February 1788.

238. *Oracle Bell's New World*, 12 August 1789.

239. V. Caretta, 'Introduction', in O. Equiano, *The Interesting Narrative and Other Writings* (London: Penguin, 1995), p. xxvi. Also Carretta, *Equiano, the African*.

240. V. Carretta, 'Olaudah Equiano or Gustavus Vassa? New light on an eighteenth-century question of identity', *Slavery and Abolition*, 20/3 (1999), pp. 96–105; P. Lovejoy, 'Autobiography and Memory: Gustavus Vassa alias Olaudah Equiano, the African', *Slavery and Abolition*, 27/3 (2006), pp. 317–47; V. Carretta, 'Response to Paul Lovejoy's "Autobiography and Memory: Gustavus Vassa alias Olaudah Equiano, the African"', *Slavery and Abolition*, 28/1 (2007), pp. 115–19.

241. J. Bugg, 'The other interesting narrative: Olaudah Equiano's public book tour', *PMLA*, 120/5 (October 2006), pp. 1424–42.

242. J. Uglow, *The Lunar Men: The Friends Who Made the Future* (London: Faber & Faber, 2002).

243. J. Priestley, 'A sermon on the subject of the slave trade, delivered to a society of Protestant dissenters at the New Meeting, in Birmingham, and published at their request', 1788, Internet Archive, https://archive.org/stream/sermononsubjectoooprie#page/n1, accessed 15 August 2018.

244. Uglow, *The Lunar Men*, pp. 410–14.

245. N. Rogers, 'Equiano in Belfast: A study of the anti-slavery ethos in a northern town', *Slavery and Abolition*, 18/2 (1997), pp. 73–89; N. Rogers, *Equiano and Anti-Slavery in Eighteenth-Century Belfast* (Belfast: Belfast Society, 2000).

246. Bugg, 'The other interesting narrative', p. 1430.

247. Adi, 'African resistance, activism and the Sons of Africa', pp. 78–84.

248. Shyllon, *Black People in Britain*; Cugoano, *Thoughts and Sentiments*, pp. 187–8, 189–95.

249. Equiano to Hardy, 28 May 1792, in Equiano, *The Interesting Narrative and Other Writing*, p. 347.

250. T. Hardy, *Memoir of Thomas Hardy* (London: James Ridgeway, 1832), p. 15, Internet Archive, https://archive.org/details/memoirofthomashaoohard, accessed 15 August 2018.

251. R. N. Buckley, *Slaves in Red Coats: The British West India Regiments, 1795–1815* (London: Yale University Press, 1979), pp. 76–7.

252. J. Stephen, *Buonaparte in the West Indies, or the History of Toussaint L'Ouverture, the Hero* (London: J. Hatchard, 1803), Internet Archive, https://archive.org/details/buonaparteinwestoostep/page/2, accessed 27 February 2019.

253. D. Geggus, 'British opinion and the emergence of Haiti', in J. Walvin (ed.), *Slavery and British Society: 1776–1846* (London: Macmillan Press, 1982), pp. 123–49.

254. R. Anstey, *The Atlantic Slave Trade and British Abolition* (New Jersey: Humanities Press, 1975), pp. 373–4.

255. Walvin, *England, Slaves and Freedom, 1776–1838*, p. 121.

CHAPTER 4. FREEDOM STRUGGLES

1. J. Walvin, *Black and White: The Negro and English Society 1555–1945* (London: Penguin, 1973), p. 189.

2. Ibid., p. 196.

3. G. Gerzina (ed.), *Black Victorians/Black Victoriana* (London: Rutgers University Press, 2003) and *Britain's Black Past* (Liverpool: Liverpool University Press, 2020); J. Green, *Black Americans in Victorian Britain* (Barnsley: Pen & Sword History, 2018).

4. C. Bressey, 'The next chapter: the black presence in the nineteenth century', in Gerzina (ed.), *Britain's Black Past*, pp. 315–30.

5. Charles Dickens, 'The Black Man', *All the Year Round*, 6 March 1875, p. 492.

6. R. Blackburn, *The Overthrow of Colonial Slavery 1776–1848* (London: Verso, 2011), especially pp. 293–329.

7. M. Sherwood, *After Abolition: Britain and the Slave Trade Since 1807* (London: I. B. Tauris, 2007).

8. D. Eltis, 'The British contribution to the nineteenth-century transatlantic slave trade', *Economic History Review* 32/2 (1979), pp. 211–27 (quotation, p. 211).

9. Sherwood, *After Abolition*, pp. 23 and 83–110.

10. R. Hussey, *Freedom Burning: Anti-Slavery and Empire in Victorian Britain* (London: Cornell University Press, 2012), pp. 132–76.

11. H. Beckles, *Natural Rebels: A Social History of Enslaved Black Women in Barbados* (New Brunswick: Rutgers University Press, 2000), pp. 161–2.

12. E. Wong, *Neither Fugitive nor Free: Atlantic Slavery, Freedom Suits and the Legal Culture of Travel* (New York: New York University Press,

2009), pp. 37–8; H. T. Catterall (ed.), *Judicial Cases Concerning American Slavery and the Negro*, Vol. 1 (Washington, DC: Carnegie Institute, 1926), pp. 23–5.

13. Catterall, *Judicial Cases Concerning American Slavery and the Negro*, p. 34. Also F. Shyllon, *Black People in Britain, 1555–1833* (London: Oxford University Press, 1977), p. 27.

14. Ibid., p. 35.

15. C. Midgley, *Women Against Slavery: The British Campaigns 1780–1870* (London: Routledge, 1992), p. 91.

16. P. Scully, 'Peripheral visions: heterography and writing the transnational life of Sara Baartman', in D. Deacon, P. Russell and A. Woollacott (eds.), *Transnational Lives: Biographies of Global Modernity, 1700–Present* (London: Palgrave, 2010), pp. 27–40; R. Holmes, *The Hottentot Venus: The Life and Death of Saartjie Baartman – Born 1789 – Buried 2002* (London: Bloomsbury, 2008).

17. T. Ngcukaitobi, *The Land Is Ours: South Africa's First Black Lawyers and the Birth of Constitutionalism* (Cape Town: Penguin, 2018), p. 49.

18. B. Lindfors, *Early African Entertainments Abroad: From the Hottentot Venus to Africa's First Olympians* (Madison: University of Wisconsin Press, 2014), pp. 10–33.

19. *The Times*, 26 November 1810, p. 3.

20. Lindfors, *Early African Entertainments*, p. 15.

21. Holmes, *Hottentot Venus*, pp. 57–9.

22. Lindfors, *Early African Entertainments*, p. 199, n. 19.

23. Ibid., p. 22.

24. Ibid., p. 23.

25. P. Scully and C. Crais, 'Race and erasure: Sara Baartman and Hendrik Cesars in Cape Town and London', *Journal of British Studies*, 47/2 (2008), pp. 301–23.

26. Ibid., p. 319.

27. S. Quereshi, 'Displaying Sara Baartman, the "Hottentot Venus"', *History of Science*, 42/2 (2004), pp. 233–57.

28. Jeffrey Green, 'The English "Hottentot Venus", 1840', http://www.jeffreygreen.co.uk/159-the-english-hottentot-venus-1840, accessed 14 August 2019.

29. J. Marsh, 'The black presence in British art 1800–1900: introduction and overview', in J. Marsh (ed.), *Black Victorians: Black People in British Art 1800–1900* (Aldershot: Lund Humphries, 2005), pp. 12–34.

30. R. Ferrari, 'Fanny Easton: the "other" Pre-Raphaelite model', Columbia University Libraries, 10.7916/D8X92900, accessed 7 August 2019;

J. Marsh, 'Pictured at work: employment as art (1800–1900)', in C. Bressey and H. Adi, *Belonging in Europe – the African Diaspora and Work* (London: Routledge, 2011), pp. 50–59; P. Gerris Nunn, 'Artist and model: Mary Jane Boyce's *Mulatto Woman*', *Journal of Pre-Raphaelite Studies*, 2 (Fall 1993) pp. 12–15; J. Richmond, 'Fanny Eaton: forgotten beauty', https://www.caribbean-beat.com/issue-143/forgotten-beauty#axzz5vvpjO9ci, accessed 7 August 2019.

31. M. Prince, *The History of Mary Prince* (London: Penguin, 2004), p. 3.

32. Ibid., p. 55.

33. Ibid., pp. 62–3.

34. J. Grant, 'William Brown and other women: black women in London c.1740–1840', in H. Grant (ed.), *Women, Migration and Empire* (Oakhill: Trentham Books, 1996), pp. 51–72.

35. A. Rainsbury, 'Nathaniel Wells: The making of a black country gentleman', in G. Gerzina, *Britain's Black Past* (Liverpool: Liverpool University Press, 2020), pp. 253–74.

36. J. A. H. Evans, 'Nathaniel Wells', *Oxford Dictionary of National Biography*, https://doi.org/10.1093/ref:odnb/74450, accessed 21 August 2019.

37. Will of William Wells, owner of West Indian plantations, Black Presence, National Archives, http://www.nationalarchives.gov.uk/pathways/black history/work_community/transcripts/william_wells.htm, accessed 23 August 2019.

38. Rainsbury, 'Nathaniel Wells', p. 261.

39. J. Farington, *The Farington Diary*, p. 94, Internet Archive, https://archive.org/details/b3135970x_0002/page/94, accessed 21 August 2019.

40. Ibid., p. 154, Internet Archive, https://archive.org/details/b313597 0x_0002/page/154; ibid., p. 110, Internet Archive, https://archive.org/details/b3135970x_0004/page/110, both accessed 21 August 2019; D. Livesay, *Children of Uncertain Fortune: Mixed-Race Jamaicans in Britain and the Atlantic Family, 1733–1833* (Chapel Hill: University of North Carolina Press, 2018), p. 311.

41. 'Work and community: the wealthy few', Black Presence, National Archives, http://www.nationalarchives.gov.uk/pathways/blackhistory/work_community/wealthy.htm, accessed 23 August 2019.

42. *London Gazette*, 19 January 1819, https://www.thegazette.co.uk/London/issue/17442/page/132, accessed 23 August 2019.

43. *London Gazette*, 8 April 1823, https://www.thegazette.co.uk/London/issue/17912/page/564, accessed 23 August 2019.

44. 'Nathaniel Wells', Centre for the Study of the Legacies of British Slavery, University College London, https://www.ucl.ac.uk/lbs/person/view/25474, accessed 21 August 2019.

45. Sherwood, *After Abolition*, pp. 19–26, 83–110.

46. C. Perreira, 'Black liberators: the role of African and Arab sailors in the Royal Navy within the Indian Ocean 1841–1941', United Nations Educational, Scientific and Cultural Organization, The Slave Route, http://www.unesco.org/new/fileadmin/MULTIMEDIA/HQ/CLT/dialogue/pdf/Black%20Liberators.pdf, accessed 1 May 2021.

47. L. Asa-Asa, *Narrative of Louis Asa-Asa, a Captured African* (London: F. Westley and A. H. Davies, 1831), Northeastern University Library, https://repository.library.northeastern.edu/files/neu:mo4150611, accessed 1 March 2019.

48. Sherwood, *After Abolition*, pp. 111–42.

49. Ibid., p. 121.

50. A. Elebute, *The Life of James Pinson Labulo Davies: A Colossus of Victorian Lagos* (Lagos: Prestige, 2013), pp. 31–49; cf. W. Dean Myers, *At Her Majesty's Request: An African Princess in London* (New York: Scholastic, 1999) and J. Van Der Kiste, *Sarah Forbes Bonetta: Queen Victoria's African Princess* (South Brent: A&F, 2018).

51. F. Forbes, *Dahomey and the Dahomeans: Being the Journals of Two Missions to the King of Dahomey, and Residence at This Capital, in the Years 1849 and 1850*, Vol. II (London: Longman, Brown, Green and Longmans, 1851), p. 207, Internet Archive, https://archive.org/details/dahomeydahomansbooforb/page/206, accessed 8 August 2019.

52. Ibid., pp. 208–9.

53. C. Bressey, 'Of Africa's brightest ornaments: a short biography of Sarah Forbes Bonetta', *Social and Cultural Geography*, 6/2 (April 2005), pp. 253–66.

54. Queen Victoria, journal entry, 11 January 1851, Royal Collection Trust, https://www.rct.uk/collection/themes/trails/black-and-asian-history-and-victorian-britain/queen-victorias-journal-ra, accessed 8 August 2019.

55. Bressey, 'Of Africa's brightest ornaments', pp. 255–6.

56. J. Anim-Addo, 'Sarah Forbes Benetta', *Oxford Dictionary of National Biography*, https://doi.org/10.1093/ref:odnb/75453, accesssed 11 February 2022; Myers, *Her Majesty's Request*, pp. 106–8.

57. Bressey, 'Of Africa's brightest ornaments', p. 259.

58. Captain Speedy and Prince Alemayehu, son of Emperor Tewodros II of Ethiopia, Royal Collection Trust, https://www.rct.uk/collection/

2800864/captain-speedy-and-prince-alemayehu-son-of-emperor-tewodros-ii-of-ethiopia, accessed 1 March 2019.

59. J. Walvin, *England, Slaves and Freedom, 1776–1838* (London: University Press of Mississippi, 1986), p. 126.

60. Quoted in Beckles, *Natural Rebels*, p. 172.

61. P. Scanlan, *Slave Empire: How Slavery Built Modern Britain* (London: Robinson, 2020), p. 210.

62. Ibid., pp. 202–3.

63. Quoted in A. Hochschild, *Bury the Chains: The British Struggle to Abolish Slavery* (London: Pan Books, 2005), p. 320.

64. M. Craton, 'Slave culture, resistance and the achievement of emancipation in the British West Indies, 1783–1938', in J. Walvin, *Slavery and British Society, 1776–1846* (London: Macmillan, 1982), p. 120.

65. R. Sheridan, 'The condition of the slaves on the sugar plantations of Sir John Gladstone in the colony of Demerara, 1812–49', *New West Indian Guide*, 76/3–4 (2002), pp. 243–69.

66. Walvin, *England, Slaves and Freedom*, pp. 140–41.

67. K. Corfield, 'Elizabeth Heyrick: Radical Quaker', in G. Malmgreen (ed.), *Religion in the Lives of English Women, 1760–1930* (London: Croom Helm, 1986), pp. 41–67.

68. E. Heyrick, *Immediate not Gradual Abolition* (Philadelphia: Philadelphia Anti-Slavery Society, 1837), p. 4, https://archive.org/details/immediatenotgradooheyr/page/4, accessed 30 April 2019.

69. Corfield, 'Elizabeth Heyrick', p. 49.

70. Ibid., p. 6.

71. Elizabeth Heyrick, 'An enquiry: which of the two parties is best entitled to freedom? The slave, or the slave holder?' (London: 1824), Recovered Histories, http://www.recoveredhistories.org/pamphlet1.php?page=1&orderby=date&catid=86, accessed 3 June 2019.

72. Ibid., p. 10; Corfield, 'Elizabeth Heyrick', p. 42.

73. Corfield, 'Elizabeth Heyrick', p. 41.

74. R. Blackburn, *The Overthrow of Colonial Slavery 1776–1848* (London: Verso, 2011), p. 439.

75. Blackburn, *The Overthrow of Colonial Slavery*, p. 426.

76. H. Bleby, *Death Struggles of Slavery: Being a Narrative of Facts and Incidents in a British Colony, During the Two Years Immediately Preceding Negro Emancipation* (London: W. Nichols, 1868), p. 129, Internet Archive, https://archive.org/details/b24870109/page/128, accessed 30 April 2019.

77. Ibid., pp. 130–31.

78. E. Williams, *Capitalism and Slavery* (London: Andre Deutsch, 1945), p. 169.

79. N. Draper, *The Price of Emancipation: Slave-Ownership, Compensation and British Society at the End of Slavery* (Cambridge: Cambridge University Press, 2009).

80. Scanlan, *Slave Empire*, pp. 253–4.

81. R. Huzzey, *Freedom Burning: Anti-Slavery and Empire in Victorian Britain* (London: Cornell University Press, 2012), pp. 10–12.

82. J. Williams, *A Narrative of Events since the First of August 1834* (London: J. Rider, 1834), Documenting the American South, https://docsouth.unc.edu/neh/williamsjames/williams.html, accessed 3 June 2019.

83. Sherwood, *After Abolition*; p. 2; Huzzey, *Freedom Burning*, pp. 186–98.

84. Huzzey, *Freedom Burning*, pp. 2–4.

85. A. Highmore, *Philanthropic Metropolitana: A View of the Charitable Institutions Established in and Near London* (London: Longman et al., 1822), p. 71.

86. Ibid., p. 73.

87. N. Myers, *Reconstructing the Black Past: Blacks in Britain, 1780–1830* (London: Frank Cass, 1996), pp. 118–38.

88. J. Marryat, *More Thoughts, Occasioned by Two Publications etc.* (London: 1816), pp. 99–117, Hathi Trust Digital Library, https://babel.hathitrust.org/cgi/pt?id=nyp.33433075912877;view=1up;seq=15 , accessed 29 January 2019.

89. *The First Report of the Society for the Suppression of Mendicity* (London: 1819), p. 21, Hathi Trust Digital Library, https://babel.hathitrust.org/cgi/pt?id=umn.31951t000852030;view=1up;seq=3, accessed 21 January 2019.

90. Shyllon, *Black People in Britain*, p. 160.

91. *Report from the Select Committee on the State of Mendicity in the Metropolis* (London: House of Commons, 1816), p. 15; *Report from the Select Committee on the State of Mendicity in the Metropolis* (London: House of Commons, 1814–1815), p. 50.

92. Shyllon, *Black People in Britain*, p. 161.

93. Ibid., p. 163.

94. Ibid., pp. 163–4.

95. H. Mayhew et al., *London Labour and the London Poor: A Cyclopedia of the Condition and Earnings of Those That Work, Those That Cannot Work and Those That Will Not Work*, Vol. 4 (London: Griffin, Bohn and Co., 1851), p. 425.

96. I. Duffield, 'Skilled workers or marginalized poor? The African population of the United Kingdom, 1812–52', in D. Killingray (ed.), *Africans in Britain* (Ilford: Frank Cass, 1994), pp. 49–87.

97. Communication from John Ellis to the author, 28 August 2019.

98. Duffield, 'Skilled workers or marginalized poor?', p. 53.

99. Ibid., p. 61.

100. Trial of Jacob Morris, 13 September 1815, Old Bailey Proceedings Online, https://www.oldbaileyonline.org/browse.jsp?id=t18150913-90&div=t18150913-90&terms=jacob_morris#highlight, accessed 24 January 2019.

101. Trial of George Barrett, 20 May 1801, Old Bailey Proceedings Online, https://www.oldbaileyonline.org/browse.jsp?id=t18010520-6-defend77&div=t18010520-6#highlight, accessed 24 January 2019. With thanks to John Ellis.

102. Trial of Marian Mitchell, 17 September 1838, Old Bailey Proceedings Online, https://www.oldbaileyonline.org/browse.jsp?id=t18380917-2204&div=t18380917-2204&terms=Marian_mitchell#highlight, accessed 24 January 2019.

103. Trial of John Henry Neville, Sarah Neville, Sarah Chapman and Elizabeth Jones, August 1838, Old Bailey Proceedings Online, https://www.oldbaileyonline.org/browse.jsp?div=t18380820-1831, accessed 17 March 2022.

104. Trial of William Berry, 16 September 1801, Old Bailey Proceedings Online, https://www.oldbaileyonline.org/browse.jsp?id=t18010916-19&div=t18010916-19&terms=Ann_Holman#highlight, accessed 24 January 2019.

105. Duffield, 'Skilled workers or marginalized poor?', especially pp. 71–3.

106. C. Bressey, 'Looking for work: the black presence in Britain 1860–1920', in C. Bressey and H. Adi (eds.), *Belonging in Europe – The African Diaspora and Work* (London: Routledge, 2011), pp. 67–71.

107. C. Bressey, 'Forgotten histories: three stories of black girls from Barnardo's Victorian archive', *Women's History Review*, 11/3 (2002), pp. 351–74.

108. J. Ellis, 'A revolutionary activist in his own cause: William Afflick of the 10th Hussars', *Westminster History Review* 5 (2007), pp. 24–9. My thanks to John Ellis for supplying a copy of this article.

109. J. Ellis, 'Thomas Rackett from Demerara to St Giles', Academia, https://nottingham.academia.edu/JohnDEllis, accessed 3 September 2019.

110. J. Ellis, 'The travels of Israel Waterford: free-born seaman, prisoner of war and soldier', Academia, https://nottingham.academia.edu/JohnDEllis, accessed 5 September 2019.

111. 'Black prisoners of war at Portchester Castle', English Heritage, https://www.english-heritage.org.uk/visit/places/portchester-castle/history-and-stories/black-prisoners-at-portchester/, accessed 5 September 2019.

112. R. Buckley, 'The British Army's African recruitment policy, 1790–1807: some further thoughts on the abolition issue', *Contributions in Black Studies: A Journal of African and Afro-American Studies*, 5/2 (2008), https://scholarworks.umass.edu/cibs/vol5/iss1/2, accessed 22 August 2019; R. Buckley, *Slaves in Red Coats: The British West India Regiments, 1795–1815* (London: Yale University Press, 1979).

113. Buckley, 'The British Army's African recruitment policy'.

114. Buckley, *Slaves in Red Coats*, p. 62.

115. J. Ellis, 'Drummers for the devil? The black soldiers of the 29th (Worcestershire) Regiment of Foot, 1759–1843', *Journal of the Society for Army Historical Research*, 80 (2002), pp. 186–202.

116. J. Ellis, '"Left to the streets and the workhouse": the life, visual representation and death of John Baptist, 3rd Scots Fusilier Guards', *Journal of the Society for Army Historical Research*, 82/331 (Autumn 2004), pp. 204–9.

117. J. Ellis, '"Distinguished in action . . ." The black soldiers of the 4th Dragoons, 1715–1842', *The Chronicle*, 1/3 (2003), pp. 1–9.

118. J. Ellis, 'George Rose – an exemplary soldier, 73rd and 42nd Foot, 1809–1837', Academia, https://www.academia.edu/37844331/George_Rose_An_Exemplary_Soldier_73rd_and_42nd_Foot_1809_1837, accessed 17 March 2022.

119. Ellis, 'Drummers for the devil'.

120. Ibid., p. 201.

121. 'High Court of Justiciary', 20 January 1808, *Aberdeen Journal*, and 'The Murder of the Black Drummer', *Aberdeen Journal*, 1 January 1840.

122. Ellis, 'Drummers for the devil', p. 199.

123. J. Ellis, 'The black, the red and the green: black red-coats and Ireland in the eighteenth and nineteenth centuries', *The Irish Sword*, XXIII/94 (Winter 2003), pp. 409–24.

124. J. Ellis, 'Stephen Blunman: black soldier and resident of London', Academia, https://nottingham.academia.edu/JohnDEllis, accessed 17 March 2022.

125. *Lancaster Gazette*, 3 October 1807, p. 1.

126. Ellis, '"Distinguished in action . . ."' and 'Thomas Rackett from Demarara to St Giles'.

127. J. Ellis, 'Soldiers of African origin in British Army regiments in England and Yorkshire, 1700s to 1840s', Academia, https://nottingham.academia.edu/JohnDEllis, accessed 17 March 2022.

128. J. Ellis, 'An incumbrance on the regiment: the black soldiers of the 78th Foot', *Journal of the Society for Army Historical Research*, 81/328 (Winter 2003), pp. 381–2.

129. G. Wolsey, 'The Negro as a Soldier', *Fortnightly Review*, 4 September 1888, pp. 689–703.

130. *Standard*, 4 May 1886, p. 3.

131. 'Negro musicians in our army', *Northern Echo*, 21 April 1896; Dickens, 'The Black Man', p. 495.

132. 'The story of Jimmy Durham', Durham County Record Office, http://www.durhamrecordoffice.org.uk/article/10689/The-Story-of-Jimmy-Durham, 29 August 2019; J. Green, *Black Edwardians: Black People in Britain 1901–1914* (London: Frank Cass, 1998), pp. 68–70.

133. A. Cobley, 'Black West Indian seamen in the British Merchant Marine in the mid-nineteenth century', *History Workshop Journal*, 58/1 (2004), pp. 259–74.

134. B. Joyce, *Black People in Medway* (Rochester: Pocock Press, 2010).

135. M. Sherwood, 'Shall we ever learn the full story of blacks in the Royal Navy?', *BASA Newsletter*, 57 (July 2010), pp. 8–12.

136. B. Joyce, *Black People in Medway* (Rochester: Pocock Press, 2010)

137. Sherwood, 'Shall we ever learn', pp. 8–12.

138. R. Costello, *Black Salt: Seafarers of African Descent on British Ships* (Liverpool: Liverpool University Press, 2012), p. 72.

139. L. Tabili, *"We Ask for British Justice": Workers and Racial Difference in Late Imperial Britain* (London: Cornell University Press, 1994), p. 43; M. Sherwood, 'Lascar struggles against discrimination in Britain 1923–1945: the work of N. P. Upadhyaya and Surat Alley', *Mariner's Mirror*, 90/4 (November 2004), pp. 438–55.

140. *Bridgewater Mercury*, 14 July 1858, p. 3.

141. A. Cobley, 'Harrison's from Liverpool and seafarers from Barbados: a case study of sea-borne colonial labour', *Journal of Caribbean History*, (January 1995), pp. 71–95.

142. A. Cobley, 'That turbulent soil: seafarers, the "Black Atlantic" and the shaping of Afro-Caribbean identity', History Co-operative's Conference Proceedings, http://webdoc.sub.gwdg.de/ebook/p/2005/

history_cooperative/www.historycooperative.org/proceedings/sea scapes/cobley.html, accessed 2 September 2019.

143. 'Africans in England', *Liverpool Mercury*, 5 March 1841.

144. N. Roger, *The Wooden World: An Anatomy of the Georgian Navy* (London: Fontana Press, 1986), p. 272; N. Roger, 'John Perkins', *Oxford Dictionary of National Biography*, https://doi.org/10.1093/ref:odnb/50232, accessed 29 August 2019.

145. 'In the guise of a man: defying female convention to serve in the Royal Navy', Royal Navy: The National Museum, https://www.nmrn.org.uk/news-events/nmrn-blog/guise-man-defying-female-convention-serve-royal-navy, accessed 17 March 2022; R. Boser, 'The creation of a legend', *History Today*, 52/10 (2002), pp. 36–7.

146. Costello, *Black Salt*, p. 62.

147. M. Sherwood, 'The multi-ethnic Royal Navy and Merchant Marine from the seventeenth century onwards', *Topmasts*, 27 (August 2018), pp. 10–12.

148. Costello, *Black Salt*, p. 64.

149. J. Ellis, 'A black "Jack Tar": Samuel Michael, an Afro-American sailor late of the Napoleonic Royal Navy and in-pensioner of Greenwich Hospital', Academia, https://nottingham.academia.edu/JohnDEllis, accessed 3 September 2019.

150. Costello, *Black Salt*, pp. 119–21; 'William Hall, VC', Info, Nova Scotia Museum, https://web.archive.org/web/20060203183824/http://museum.gov.ns.ca/infos/william-hall-info.pdf, accessed 2 September 2019.

151. *Liverpool Echo*, 11 June 1884, p. 4.

152. Biographical sources are available at 'Mary Seacole: 1805–1881', National Libraries Jamaica, https://nlj.gov.jm/biographies/mary-seacole-1805-1881/, accessed 30 July 2019.

153. 'Annie Brewster, the Royal London's "nurse ophthalmic"', East End Women's Museum, https://eastendwomensmuseum.org/blog/annie-brewster-the-london-hospitals-nurse-ophthalmic?rq=Annie%20Brewster, accessed 31 July 2019.

154. R. Hill, *A Week at Port Royal* (Montego Bay: Cornwall Chronicle, 1855), pp. 2–4.

155. Hill, *Port Royal*, p. 4.

156. M. Seacole, *Wonderful Adventures of Mrs Seacole in Many Lands* (London: Penguin, 2005), pp. 34–5.

157. Ibid., p. 71.

158. Ibid., pp. 73–4.

159. J. Robinson, *Mary Seacole: The Charismatic Black Nurse Who Became a Heroine in the Crimea* (London: Robinson, 2005).

160. Ibid., p. 131.

161. *Illustrated London News*, 25 July 1857, p. 125.

162. Seacole, *Wonderful Adventures*, Appendix, p. 173.

163. Robinson, *Mary Seacole*, p. 168.

164. Seacole, *Wonderful Adventures*, p. 5.

165. The last will and testament of Mary Seacole, National Library of Jamaica, https://nlj.gov.jm/wp-content/uploads/2017/05/bn_seacole_mj_023.pdf, accessed 31 July 2019.

166. Fryer, *Staying Power*, pp. 446–53.

167. L. Williams, *Richmond Unchained: The Biography of the World's First Black Sporting Superstar* (Stroud: Amberley, 2015).

168. Ibid., p. 82; 'Pugilism', *Morning Chronicle*, 25 May 1805.

169. Williams, *Richmond Unchained*, p. 98.

170. Ibid., pp. 138 and 147.

171. P. Egan, *Boxiana: Or, Sketches of Ancient and Modern Pugilism*, Vol. 1 (London: George Virtue, 1812), p. 406.

172. Ibid., p. 390.

173. Williams, *Richmond Unchained*, pp. 156–7.

174. Ibid., pp. 159–60; *Morning Chronicle*, 24 December 1810.

175. Williams, *Richmond Unchained*, pp. 161–2; 166.

176. *Caledonian Mercury*, 3 October 1811, p. 2.

177. Williams, *Richmond Unchained*, pp. 214, 222–9.

CHAPTER 5: STRUGGLES FOR THE RIGHTS OF ALL

1. P. Linebaugh and M. Rediker, *The Many-Headed Hydra: Sailors, Slaves, Commoners, and the Hidden History of the Revolutionary Atlantic* (Boston: Beacon Press, 2000), pp. 248–86.

2. *Chester Chronicle*, 1 March 1799, p. 4.

3. Linebaugh and Rediker, *The Many-Headed Hydra*, p. 253.

4. Letter from F. Engels to M. Hyndman, 13 March 1882, https://www.marxists.org/archive/marx/works/1882/letters/82_03_13.htm, accessed 29 January 2019.

5. T. Spence, *Property in Land Every One's Right* (Newcastle: 1775), in A. Bonnett and K. Armstrong (eds.), *Thomas Spence: The Poor Man's Revolutionary* (Bristol: Breviary Publications, 2014), Marxists

Internet Archive, https://www.marxists.org/history/england/britdem/people/spence/property/property.htm, accessed 17 March 2022.

6. I. McCalman (ed.), *The Horrors of Slavery and Other Writings by Robert Wedderburn* (Edinburgh: Edinburgh Press, 1991), pp. 1–35.

7. Quoted in I. McCalman, 'Anti-slavery and ultra-radicalism in early nineteenth-century England: the case of Robert Wedderburn', *Slavery and Abolition* (1986), pp. 99–117. See T. M. Parssinen, 'The revolutionary party in London, 1816–1820', *Bulletin of the Institute of Historical Research*, 45 (1972), pp. 266–82.

8. R. Wedderburn, *The Axe Laid to the Root*, issue nos. 4 and 6 in McCalman (ed.), *The Horrors of Slavery*, pp. 96–110; I. McCalman, *Radical Underworld: Prophets, Revolutionaries and Pornographers, 1795–1840* (Cambridge: Cambridge University Press, 1988), p. 69; M. Cazzola, '"All shall be happy by land and by sea": Thomas Spence as an Atlantic Thinker', *Atlantic Studies*, 15/4 (2018), pp. 431–50; Linebaugh and Rediker, *The Many-Headed Hydra*, pp. 287–326.

9. Linebaugh and Rediker, *The Many-Headed Hydra*, p. 304.

10. I. Duffield, 'Skilled workers or marginalized poor? The African population of the United Kingdom, 1812–52', in D. Killingray (ed.), *Africans in Britain* (Ilford: Frank Cass, 1994), p. 83, n. 64.

11. McCalman, *The Horrors of Slavery*, pp. 15–16.

12. 'The Statutes of the United Kingdom of Great Britain and Ireland', 57 George III 1817 (London, 1817), p. 43.

13. McCalman, *The Horrors of Slavery*, pp. 81–110; McCalman, 'Anti-slavery', p. 108.

14. M. Scrivener, *Seditious Allegories: John Thelwall and Jacobin Writing* (University Park, PA: Pennsylvania State University Press, 2001), pp. 129–66.

15. McCalman, *The Horrors of Slavery*, p. 113; McCalman, 'Anti-slavery', p. 112.

16. McCalman, *The Horrors of Slavery*, pp. 114–15.

17. Ibid., pp. 116–28.

18. Papers relating to the prosecutions: (i) for high treason (arising from the riots in London in 1816); (ii) for a misdemeanour (sending a challenge to Lord Sidmouth to fight a duel in 1818); (iii) for high treason and other offences (arising from the 'Cato Street conspiracy' of 1820), National Archives, TS 11/205.

19. M. Sherwood, 'William Davidson', *Oxford Dictionary of National Biography*, https://doi.org/10.1093/ref:odnb/57029, accessed 27 February 2019.

20. McCalman, 'Anti-slavery', pp. 109–10.

21. H. Mackey, '"The complexion of the accused": William Davidson the black revolutionary in the Cato Street conspiracy of 1820', *Negro Educational Review*, 23/4 (1972), pp. 132–47.

22. Ibid., p. 110.

23. Trial of Arthur Thistlewood, William Davidson, James Ings, John Thomas Brunt, Richard Tidd, James William Wilson, John Harrison, Richard Bradburn, John Shaw Strange, James Gilchrist, Charles Cooper, 16 April 1820, Old Bailey Proceedings Online, https://www.oldbaileyonline.org/browse.jsp?id=t18200416-1-defend199&div=t18200416-1&terms=Cato_Street#highlight, accessed 27 February 2019.

24. G. Wilkinson, *An Authentic History of the Cato-Street Conspiracy* (London: Thomas Kelly, c.1820), pp. 406–14, https://archive.org/stream/authentichistoryoowilkiala#page/n5/mode/2up, accessed 31 January 2019.

25. William Davidson, 'Speech from the Dock', in P. Edwards and D. Dabydeen (eds.), *Black Writers in Britain 1760–1890* (Edinburgh: Edinburgh University Press, 1991), pp. 127–36.

26. Letter to Mr James Paul Cobbett at New York on the death of Arthur Thistlewood, James Ings, William Davidson etc., *Cobbett's Weekly Political Register*, 6 May 1820, pp. 537–667; 'Cato Street Conspiracy – George Edwards', House of Commons, debated 2 May 1820, Vol. 1, cols. 54–63, *Hansard historic record*, https://api.parliament.uk/historic-hansard/commons/1820/may/02/cato-street-conspiracy-george-edwards#S2V0001P0_18200502_HOC_14, accessed 17 March 2022.

27. Treasonable and Seditious Practices Act (36 George III, c. 7), 18 December 1795, The Napoleon Series, https://www.napoleon-series.org/research/government/british/c_gagging3.html, accessed 27 February 2019.

28. M. Chase, 'Robert Wedderburn', *Oxford Dictionary of National Biography*, https://doi.org/10.1093/ref:odnb/47120, accessed 28 February 2019.

29. McCalman, *The Horrors of Slavery*, p. 80.

30. Ibid., p. 83.

31. 'Mr William Cuffay', *Reynold's Political Instructor*, 23/1 (1850), p. 177.

32. 'The People's Charter' (1836), https://cuffay.blogspot.com/2011/01/peoples-charter.html, accessed 4 March 2019.

33. A. L. Morton, *A People's History of England* (London: Lawrence and Wishart, 1979), pp. 429–40.

34. 'Mr William Cuffay', *Reynold's Political Instructor*.

35. M. Hoyles, *William Cuffay, The Life and Times of a Chartist Leader* (London: Hansib, 2013), p. 28.

36. 'Mr William Cuffay', *Reynold's Political Instructor*.

37. Ibid.

38. Hoyles, *William Cuffay*, pp. 113–14.

39. Ibid., p. 127.

40. Ibid., p. 130.

41. 'Mr William Cuffay', *Reynold's Political Instructor*.

42. N. Gossman, 'William Cuffay: London's black Chartist', *Phylon*, 44/1 (1983), pp. 56–65.

43. Hoyles, *William Cuffay*, p. 132.

44. Ibid.

45. Ibid., p. 171; M. Chase, *Chartism: A New History* (Manchester: Manchester University Press, 2007).

46. P. Fryer, *Staying Power: The History of Black People in Britain* (London: Pluto, 1984), p. 239.

47. *The Times*, 17 March 1848, p. 7; 4 April 1848, p. 8; 10 April 1848, p. 7; 11 April 1848, p. 7.

48. Trial of Anthony Finlay, Thomas Howlett, James Taylor, Henry Brown, David Anthony Duffy, George Lower, Thomas Walker, Robert Archer, Thomas Horssey, Richard Webster, Joseph Burden, Samuel Mayney, Thomas Snead, George Payne, William Bailey, 3 April 1848, Old Bailey Proceedings Online, https://www.oldbaileyonline.org/browse.jsp?div=t18480403-1165, accessed 1 March 2019.

49. Chase, *Chartism: A New History*, pp. 303–4.

50. P. Fryer, 'William Cuffay', *Oxford Dictionary of National Biography*, https://doi.org/10.1093/ref:odnb/71636, accessed 14 March 2019.

51. D. Frost, *Forty Years' Recollections: Literary and Political* (London: Sampson Low etc., 1880), p. 162.

52. The Chartists' trial, CRIM 10/28, pp. 792, 822 & 852, Black Presence, National Archives, http://www.nationalarchives.gov.uk/pathways/black history/rights/transcripts/state_trial_reports.htm, accessed 15 March 2019.

53. Frost, *Forty Years' Recollections*, p. 165.

54. Fryer, 'William Cuffay'.

55. 'Cuffay found guilty and sentenced', Reports of State Trials, new series, Vol. 7, cols. 467–8, 478, 480–82, Black Presence, National Archives, http://www.nationalarchives.gov.uk/pathways/blackhistory/rights/ transcripts/extract_cuffey.htm, accessed 15 March 2019.

56. Gossman, 'William Cuffay', p. 63.

57. Hoyle, *William Cuffay*, p. 244.

58. David Ramshaw, 'A look into Carlisle's past', *History Matters*, https://www.p3publications.com/NewP3/Pictures/John%20Kent.pdf, accessed 1 March 2020.

59. D. Killingray, 'Tracing peoples of African origin and descent in Victorian Kent', in G. Gerzina (ed.), *Black Victorians/Black Victoriana* (London: Rutgers University Press, 2003), pp. 51–67.

60. D. Frost, *Work and Community among West African Migrant Workers since the Nineteenth Century* (Liverpool: Liverpool University Press, 1999), p. 15.

61. C. Wadström, *An Essay on Colonization Particularly Applied to the West Coast of Africa, with Some Free Thought on Cultivation and Commerce: Also Brief Descriptions of the Colonies Already Formed, or Attempted in Africa, Including Those of Sierra Leone and Bulama* (London: Darton and Harvey, 1794), Part 1, pp. 94–5; Part 2, pp. 15, 269, https://archive.org/details/essayoncolonizatoowads/page/n107, accessed 9 April 2019.

62. F. Shyllon, *Black People in Britain 1555–1833* (Oxford: Oxford University Press, 1977), pp. 48–9.

63. R. Costello, *Black Salt: Seafarers of African Descent on British Ships* (Liverpool: Liverpool University Press, 2012), pp. 73–5; R. Costello, 'The making of a Liverpool community', in G. Gerzina (ed.), *Britain's Black Past* (Liverpool: Liverpool University Press, 2020), p. 101.

64. I. Law and J. Henfrey, *A History of Race and Racism in Liverpool, 1660–1950* (Liverpool: Merseyside Community Relations Council, 1981), p. 9.

65. F. Shyllon, *Black People in Britain 1555–1833* (London: Oxford University Press, 1977), p. 32. *Fourth Report of the Directors of the African Institution* (London: Ellerton and Henderson, 1810), pp. 24–5, Hathi Trust Digital Library, https://babel.hathitrust.org/cgi/pt?id=nyp.33433075935126;view=1up;seq=38, accessed 15 April 2019.

66. Shyllon, *Black People in Britain*, p. 60; *Sixth Report of the Directors of the African Institution* (London: Ellerton and Henderson, 1812), p. 15, Hathi Trust Digital Library, https://babel.hathitrust.org/cgi/pt?id=nyp.33433075935142;view=1up;seq=29, accessed 15 April 2019.

67. *Seventh Report of the Directors of the African Institution* (London: Ellerton and Henderson, 1813), pp. 19–20, Hathi Trust Digital Library, https://babel.hathitrust.org/cgi/pt?id=nyp.33433075935159;view=1up;seq=34, accessed 15 April 2019.

68. Costello, *Black Salt*, pp. 86–90.

69. P. Hamer, 'Great Britain, the United States and the Negro Seaman Acts, 1822–1848', *Journal of Southern History* 1/822 (1935), pp. 3–28.

70. C. Ripley (ed.), *The Black Abolitionist Papers*, Vol. 1: *The British Isles 1830–1865* (Chapel Hill, NC: University of North Carolina Press, 1985), p. 376, n. 1.

71. I. Law, 'White racism and black settlement in Liverpool', PhD thesis, University of Liverpool (1985), p. 68.

72. D. Lorimer, *Colour, Class and the Victorians: English Attitudes to the Negro in the Mid-Nineteenth Century* (Leicester: Leicester University Press, 1978), p. 39.

73. *Liverpool Mercury*, 21 January 1857, p. 3, 23 January 1857, p. 3. Also *Morning Chronicle*, 27 January 1857, p. 3; *New York Herald*, 11 April 1857, p. 3 and *Isle of Wight Observer*, 11 April 1857, p. 3.

74. J. Brown, *Slave Life in Georgia: A Narrative of the Life, Sufferings and Escape of John Brown, a Fugitive Slave Now in England* (London, 1855), pp. 31–44, Internet Archive, https://archive.org/details/06374405.4802.emory.edu/page/n49, accessed 16 April 2019.

75. Ibid., p. 170.

76. Quoted in Law and Henfrey, *A History of Race and Racism in Liverpool*, p. 15.

77. Ibid.

78. Ripley (ed.), *Black Abolitionist Papers*, p. 284, n. 3.

79. R. Law and P. Lovejoy (eds.), *The Biography of Mohommah Gardo Baquaqua: His Passage from Slavery to Freedom in Africa and America* (Princeton: Marcus Wiener, 2001), pp. 1–84.

80. J. Green, *Black Americans in Victorian Britain* (Barnsley: Pen and Sword History, 2018), pp. 32–35; Ripley (ed.), *Black Abolitionist Papers*, pp. 237–8, n. 10 and p. 476, n. 9.

81. Frost, *Work and Community*, pp. 18, 34–5.

82. D. Frost, 'Ethnic identity, transience and settlement: the Kru in Liverpool since the late nineteenth century', in D. Killingray (ed.), *Africans in Britain* (London: Frank Cass, 1994), pp. 88–106; Costello, *Black Salt*, p. 92.

83. Ibid.

84. H. Mayhew, *London Labour and the London Poor: A Cyclopedia of the Condition and Earnings of Those That Will Work, Those That Cannot Work, and Those That Will Not Work* (London, 1861), p. 425, https://archive.org/details/cu31924092592793/page/n505, accessed 11 April 2019.

85. Costello, *Black Salt*, pp. 93–4.

86. C. Bressey, 'Looking for work: the black presence in Britain 1860–1920', in C. Bressey and H. Adi (eds.), *Belonging in Europe: The African Diaspora and Work* (London: Routledge, 2011), pp. 60–78.

87. S. Creighton, '"I am a Lancastrian bred and born": the life and times of John Archer, 1863–1932', *North West Labour History*, 20 (1995/6), pp. 73–85.

88. Costello, *Black Salt*, pp. 108–9; J. Green, 'George William Christian: Liverpool merchant', in R. Lotz and I. Pegg (eds.), *Under the Imperial Carpet: Essays in Black History 1780–1950* (Crawley: Rabbit Press, 1986), pp. 69–83.

89. *Liverpool Mercury*, 25 August 1880, p. 5.

90. R. Fyson, *The Struggle for Manx Democracy* (Douglas: Culture Vannin, 2016), pp. 94–5. Cf. R. Costello, *Black Liverpool: The Early History of Britain's Oldest Black Community 1730–1918* (Liverpool: Picton Press, 2001), pp. 36–7; Costello, *Black Salt*, p. 61.

91. Fyson, *The Struggle for Manx Democracy*, p. 95.

92. Ibid., pp. 97–101.

93. Ibid., pp. 155, 160.

94. Ibid., p. 174.

95. Ripley (ed.), *Black Abolitionist Papers*, p. 33.

96. D. Davis, *The Problem of Slavery in the Age of Emancipation* (New York: Alfred A. Knopf, 2014), p. 297.

97. Ripley (ed.), *Black Abolitionist Papers*, p. 5.

98. *Story of Mary Ann Macham, Afterwards Mary Ann Blyth*, http://www. newcastle-antiquaries.org.uk/clearsight/documents/uploaded/Mary_ Ann_Macham_s_story.pdf, accessed 1 May 2020.

99. Ripley, *Black Abolitionist Papers*, pp. 472–3, n. 3, 497–9.

100. D. B. Davis, *The Problem of Slavery in the Age of Emancipation* (New York: Alfred A. Knopf, 2014), p. 298.

101. R. Blackett, *Building an Antislavery Wall: Black Americans in the Atlantic Abolitionist Movement 1830–1860* (London: Louisiana State University Press, 1983), p. 17.

102. Ripley, *Black Abolitionist Papers*, pp. 481–7.

103. H. Murray, '"My name is not Tom": Josiah Henson's fight to reclaim his identity in Britain 1876–1877', in D. Gottshe (ed.), *Memory and Post-Colonial Studies: Synergies and New Directions* (Oxford: Peter Lang, 2019).

104. R. Blackett, 'Fugitive slaves in Britain: the odyssey of William and Ellen Craft', *Journal of American Studies*, 12/1 (1978), pp. 41–62.

105. Ripley, *Black Abolitionist Papers*, p. 511.

106. Blackett, 'Fugitive Slaves', p. 53.

107. Ripley, *Black Abolitionist Papers*, pp. 494–6.

108. C. Midgley, *Women Against Slavery: The British Campaigns 1780–1870* (London: Routledge, 1992), p. 181.

109. Ripley, *Black Abolitionist Papers*, pp. 58–9, n. 9; pp. 117–19, n. 1.

110. Ibid., p. 257, n. 3.

111. Ibid., pp. 440–41, n. 1.

112. Green, *Black Americans in Victorian Britain*, p. 35.

113. Ripley, *Black Abolitionist Papers*, p. 251, n. 2.

114. Ibid., pp. 258–9, n. 1.

115. See the photograph of Dr George Rice and his staff outside Belmont Workhouse, Whitehall Historic House, 'Object of the Month', https://whitehallmuseum.wordpress.com/2018/10/05/object-of-the-month-october/, accessed 1 March 2020.

116. Ripley, *Black Abolitionist Papers*, pp. 537–43.

117. Blackett, *Building an Antislavery Wall*, p. 193.

118. W. Wells Brown, *Three Years in Europe: or Places I Have Seen and People I Have Met* (London: Charles Gilpin, 1852), Documenting the American South, https://docsouth.unc.edu/neh/brown52/brown52.html, accessed 4 June 2019.

119. Ripley, *Black Abolitionist Papers*, pp. 568–9.

120. R. Bradbury, 'Frederick Douglass and the Chartists', in A. Rice and M. Crawford (eds.), *Liberating Sojourn: Frederick Douglass & Transatlantic Reform* (London: University of Georgia Press, 1999), pp. 169–86, Davis, *The Problem of Slavery*, pp. 401–2, n. 57.

121. Ripley, *Black Abolitionist Papers*, pp. 304–5.

122. P. Jefferson (ed.), *The Travels of William Wells Brown* (Edinburgh: Edinburgh University Press, 1991), pp. 203–7.

123. J. McCarthey, *Selim Aga: A Slave's Odyssey* (Edinburgh: Luath Press, 2006), p. 7.

124. S. Aga, *Incidents Connected to a Life of Selim Aga, a Native of Central Africa* (Aberdeen: 1846), Documenting the American South, https://docsouth.unc.edu/neh/aga/aga.html, accessed 5 June 2019; Hakluyt Society, https://www.hakluyt.com/downloadable_files/Journal/Selim_Aga.pdf, accessed 17 March 2022.

125. M. Pickering, '"A jet ornament to society": black music in nineteenth-century Britain', in P. Oliver, *Black Music in Britain* (Milton Keynes: Open University Press, 1990), pp. 25–6.

126. Green, *Black Americans in Victorian Britain*, pp. 81–90; Pickering, '"A jet ornament to society"', pp. 30–33.

127. S. Meer, 'Competing representations: Douglass, the Ethiopian Seren-aders and Ethnic Exhibition in London', in A. Rice and M. Crawford (eds.), *Liberating Sojourn: Frederick Douglass & Transatlantic Reform* (London: University of Georgia Press, 1999), pp. 141–68.

128. E. Lott, '"The seeming counterfeit": racial politics and early black min-strelsy', *American Quarterly*, 43/2 (June 1991), pp. 223–54.

129. F. Douglass, 'Hutchinsons versus Minstrels', *North Star*, 27 October 1848, Minstrelsy: Contemporary Accounts, http://utc.iath.virginia.edu/minstrel/miar03bt.html, accessed 5 June 2019.

130. F. Douglass, 'The reason for our troubles', speech on the war delivered in National Hall, Philadelphia, 14 January 1862, River Campus Librar-ies, University of Rochester, Frederick Douglass Project, https://rbscp.lib.rochester.edu/4381, accessed 1 March 2019.

131. T. Barley, *Myths of the Slave Power: Confederate Slavery, Lanca-shire Workers and the Alabama* (Liverpool: Coach House Press, 1992), pp. 97–8.

132. 'The Manchester workmen and emancipation', [Manchester] *Daily News*, 2 January 1863.

133. Jason M. Kelly, 'The Civil War, Abraham Lincoln and antislavery among Manchester textile workers', https://jasonmkelly.com/jason-m-kelly/2014/12/18/the-civil-war-abraham-lincoln-and-antislavery-among-manchester-textile-workers, accessed 1 March 2019.

134. Abraham Lincoln, 'To the workingmen of Manchester, England', 19 January 1863, https://quod.lib.umich.edu/l/lincoln/lincoln6/1:117?rgn=div1;view=fulltext, accessed 14 February 2022.

135. Barley, *Myths of the Slave Power*, p. 98.

136. K. Marx, 'A London workers' meeting', in K. Marx and F. Engels, *Arti-cles on Britain* (Moscow: Progress Publishers, 1975), pp. 330–34.

137. Ripley, *Black Abolitionist Papers*, p. 505, n. 4.

138. J. Green, 'Thomas Lewis Johnson: the Bournemouth evangelist', in Lotz and Pegg (eds.), *Under the Imperial Carpet*, pp. 55–68.

139. D. Killingray and J. Edwards (eds.), *Black Voices: The Shaping of Our Christian Experience* (Nottingham: Inter-Varsity Press, 2007), p. 69.

140. Reverend Paul Walker, 'American slavery to English ministry: The Reverend Peter Thomas Standford (1860–1909)', Connecting Histo-ries, https://www.search.connectinghistories.org.uk/details.aspx?ResourceID=1042&ExhibitionID=1042&SearchType=2&ThemeID=50, accessed 1 March 2019.

141. P. Thomas Stanford, *The Tragedy of the Negro in America: A Con-densed History of the Enslavement, Sufferings, Emancipation, Present*

Condition and Progress of the Negro Race in the United States of America (Boston, MA: Charles A. Wasto, 1897), Documenting the American South, https://docsouth.unc.edu/church/stanford/stanford. html, accessed 1 March 2020.

142. C. Bressey, *Empire, Race and the Politics of Anti-Caste* (London: Bloomsbury, 2015), p. 143.

143. 'George Cousins: 1805–1881', My Primitive Methodists, https://www. myprimitivemethodists.org.uk/content/people-2/primitive_methodist_ ministers/c-2/cosens-george-1805-1881, accessed 1 March 2020.

144. See F. Walker, *Thomas Birch Freeman: The Son of an African* (London: Student Christian Movement, 1929); 'Thomas Birch Freeman, Son of an African', 11 September 2017, Missiology Blog, https://missiology.org. uk/blog/thomas-birch-freeman/; accessed 14 February 2022; J. Milum, *Thomas Birch Freeman: Missionary Pioneer to Ashanti, Dahomey and Egba* (New York: Fleming Revell Co., c.1893), Internet Archive, https:// archive.org/details/thomasbirchfreemoomiluuoft/page/12, accessed 5 August 2019; and John Flint, 'Thomas Birch Freeman', *Oxford Dictionary of National Biography*, https://doi.org/10.1093/ref:odnb/47629, accessed 5 August 2019.

145. R. Birch Freeman, *Journal of Various Visits to the Kingdom of Ashanti, Aku and Dahomi, in Western Africa* (Cambridge: Cambridge University Press, 2010).

146. H. Marshall and M. Stock, *Ira Aldridge: The Negro Tragedian* (Washington, DC: Howard University Press, 1993), pp. 48–9.

147. Ibid., pp. 291–2.

148. B. Lindfors, 'Mislike me not for my complexion: Ira Aldridge in whiteface', *African American Review*, 50/4 (Winter 2017), pp. 1005–12.

149. Marshall and Stock, *Ira Aldridge*, p. 80.

150. Anon, *Memoir and Theatrical Career of Ira Aldridge, the African Roscius* (London: Onwhyn, 1849), quoted in B. Lindfors (ed.), *Ira Aldridge: The African Roscius* (Rochester: University of Rochester Press, 2007), pp. 7–38.

151. T. Saxon, 'Ira Aldridge in the north of England: provincial theatre and the politics of abolition', in Gerzina (ed.), *Britain's Black Past*, pp. 275–93.

152. B. Lindfors, '"Nothing extenuate, nor set down aught in malice": new biographical information on Ira Aldridge', *African American Review*, 28/3 (Autumn 1994), pp. 457–72; E. Scobie, *Black Britannia: A History of Blacks in Britain* (Chicago: Johnson Publishing Co., 1972), p. 132.

153. H. Waters, 'Ira Aldridge and the battlefield of race', *Race and Class*, 45/1 (2003), pp. 1–30; Marshall and Stock, *Ira Aldridge*, p. 103.

154. *Memoir and Theatrical Career of Ira Aldridge*, pp. 31–7.

155. Vanessa Thorpe, 'From 19th-century black pioneer to cultural ambassador of Coventry', 13 November 2016, *Guardian*, https://www.theguardian.com/uk-news/2016/nov/13/black-theatre-ira-aldridge-coventry-slavery, accessed 28 May 2019.

156. Marshall and Stock, *Ira Aldridge*, p. 198; also M. Hoyles, *Ira Aldridge: Celebrated 19th-Century Actor* (London: Hansib, 2008), p. 55.

157. Scobie, *Black Britannia*, p. 132.

158. Pickering, '"A jet ornament to society"', pp. 16–33.

159. Bressey, 'Looking for work: the black presence in Britain', pp. 318–19.

160. S. Bourne, 'Amy Height', *Oxford Dictionary of National Biography*, https://doi.org/10.1093/ref:odnb/101390, accessed 15 August 2019.

161. See J. Turner, 'Pablo Fanque, black circus proprietor', in G. Gerzina (ed.), *Black Victorians/Black Victoriana* (London: Rutgers University Press, 2003), pp. 20–38; G. Davies, *Pablo Fanque and Victorian Circus* (Lowestoft: Poppyland Publishing, 2017); M. Dash, 'Pablo Fanque's fair', https://www.smithsonianmag.com/history/pablo-fanques-fair-71575787/, accessed 7 August 2019.

162. J. Turner, 'Black circus performers', *BASA Newsletter* 27 (April 2000), p. 8.

163. C. Bressey, 'Looking for work: the black presence in Britain 1860–1920', pp. 60–78.

164. 'Heroines of the circus – the iron jaw acrobat', Circus Girl Blog, https://thecircusgirlblog.wordpress.com/tag/miss-lala/, accessed 15 August 2019.

165. Turner, *Pablo Fanque*, p. 23

166. Ibid. p. 25

167. Ibid. p. 34

168. *The Era*, 29 March 1868, p. 13; 6 September 1868, p. 7.

169. Ibid., 27 February 1886, p. 8.

170. Fryer, *Staying Power*, pp. 165–90.

171. Cecil Rhodes, 'Confession of Faith', in John E. Flint, *Cecil Rhodes* (Boston: Little, Brown, 1974), https://www.pitt.edu/~syd/rhod.html, accessed 1 June 2020.

172. C. Bolt, *Victorian Attitudes to Race* (London: Routledge & Kegan Paul, 1971), p. 76.

173. C. Buxton, 'The outbreak in Jamaica', *The Times*, 7 December 1865, p. 5.

174. Lorimer, *Colour, Class and the Victorians*, pp. 178–200.

175. *Western Daily Press*, 5 December 1866, p. 2.

176. P. Handford, 'Edward John Eyre and the conflict of laws', *Melbourne University Law Review*, 26 (2008) 32/3, http://www.austlii.edu.au/au/journals/MelbULawRw/2008/26.html#fn127, accessed 1 March 2020.

177. N. Kelvin (ed.), *The Collected Letters of William Morris*, Vol. 2, Part B: *1885–1888* (Princeton, NJ: Princeton University Press, 1987), p. 399, n. 4.

178. W. Armistead, *A Tribute for the Negro: Being a Vindication of the Moral, Intellectual, and Religious Capabilities of the Coloured Portion of Mankind; with Particular Reference to the African Race* (Manchester: William Irwin, 1847), Documenting the American South, https://docsouth.unc.edu/neh/armistead/armistead.html#armistead267, accessed 1 March 2020.

179. *African Times*, 23 December 1862, p. 68.

180. I. Geiss, *The Pan-African Movement: A History of Pan-Africanism in America, Europe and Africa* (New York: Africana Publishing House, 1974), pp. 166–9.

181. A. Kirk-Greene, 'America in the Niger Valley: a colonization centenary', *Phylon*, 23/3 (1962), pp. 225–39.

182. C. Fyfe, *Africanus Horton: West African Scientist and Patriot* (London: Oxford University Press, 1972), pp. 23–4.

183. J. Derrick, *Africa, Empire and Fleet Street: Albert Cartwright and 'West Africa' Magazine* (London: Hurst & Co, 2018), p. 16; *African Times*, 23 April 1866, p. 115.

184. *African Times*, 23 April 1866, ibid.

185. J. Horton, *West African Countries and Peoples, British and Native, with the Requirements Necessary for Establishing That Self-Government Recommended by the Committee of the House of Commons, 1865; and a Vindication of the African Race* (London: W. J. Johnson, 1868).

186. *African Times*, 23 April 1866, pp. 113–14.

187. Horton, *West African Countries and Peoples*, p. 66.

188. Ibid., pp. 1–2.

189. Ibid., p. 202.

190. Fyfe, *Africanus Horton*, pp. 95–110. H. Wilson, *Origins of West African Nationalism* (London: Macmillan, 1969), pp. 198–207.

191. Fryer, *Staying Power*, p. 277.

192. H. Lynch, *Edward Wilmot Blyden: Pan-Negro Patriot 1832–1912* (London: Oxford University Press, 1967), p. 248.

193. H. Adi and M. Sherwood, *Pan-African History: Political Figures from Africa and the Diaspora since 1787* (London: Routledge, 2003), pp. 11–15.

194. E. Holden, *Blyden of Liberia*: *An Account of the Life and Labors of Edward Wilmot Blyden, LL.D. – As Recorded in Letters and in Print* (New York: Vantage Press, 1966), pp. 65–9. I am indebted to Cleo Blyden for making this rare publication available to me.

195. Ibid., p. 65.

196. Ibid., pp. 69–72.

197. Ibid., p. 981, n. 40.

198. Ibid., pp. 950–95, 1. 39.

199. Ibid., p. 154.

200. 'Ministerial plan for the abolition of slavery', Vol. 18, debated on 3 June 1883, http://bit.ly/2k8oFDy, accessed 16 July 2019; R. Quinault, 'Gladstone and slavery', *Historical Journal*, 52/2 (2009), pp. 363–83.

201. Holden, *Blyden of Liberia*, pp. 125, 150.

202. Lynch, *Edward Wilmot Blyden*, p. 56; Holden, *Blyden of Liberia*, pp. 152, 772.

203. Holden, *Blyden of Liberia*, p. 232.

204. Adi and Sherwood, *Pan-African History*, pp. 11–15; Lynch, *Edward Wilmot Blyden*, pp. 248–52.

205. Holden, *Blyden of Liberia*, p. 599.

206. Ibid., pp. 376–7.

207. Ibid., p. 397.

208. H. Lynch, *Edward Wilmot Blyden*, p. 186; *Looking for Aunt Martha's Quilt*, 8 July 2017, BBC Sounds, https://www.bbc.co.uk/sounds/play/po57ht6d, accessed 17 July 2019.

209. Holden, *Blyden of Liberia*, p. 641.

210. Ibid., pp. 790–91.

211. Adi and Sherwood, *Pan-African History*, pp. 11–15.

212. Bressey, *Empire, Race and the Politics of Anti-Caste*, p. 93, n. 46; D. Lorimer, 'Legacies of slavery for race, religion and empire: S. J. Celestine Edwards and the hard truth (1894)', *Slavery and Abolition*, 39/4 (2018), pp. 731–55.

213. Bressey, *Empire*, pp. 31–2, 81.

214. Lorimer, 'Legacies of slavery', p. 734.

215. C. Edwards, *Political Atheism: A Lecture* (London: J. Kensit, 1890); C. Edwards, *Does God Answer Prayer? A Lecture* (Portsmouth: G. Hawkins, 1895); see also Appendix 1: Tamsin Lily, 'Remembering slavery: Sunderland's links to the Atlantic slave trade', 2008, http://collectionsprojects.org.uk/slavery/_files/research-zone/Sunderland_slinkstothetrans-atlanticslavetrade.pdf, accessed 22 July 2019.

216. J. Schneer, 'Celestine Edwards', *Oxford Dictionary of National Biography*, https://doi.org/10.1093/ref:odnb/71088, accessed 22 July 2019.

217. S. J. Celestine Edwards, Preface, *From Slavery to a Bishopric or the Life of Bishop Walter Hawkins* (London: John Kensit, 1891), Documenting the American South, https://docsouth.unc.edu/neh/edwardsc/edwards.html, accessed 22 July 2019.

218. Bressey, *Empire*, pp. 86–9; J. Schneer, *London 1900: The Imperial Metropolis* (London: Yale University Press), pp. 204–12.

219. T. Zackodnik, 'Ida B. Wells and "American Atrocities in Britain"', *Women's International Studies Forum*, 28 (2005), pp. 259–73; N. King, '"A colored woman in another country pleading for justice in her own: Ida B. Wells in Great Britain', in Gerzina (ed.), *Black Victorians*, pp. 88–109.

220. A. Duster (ed.), *Crusader for Justice: The Autobiography of Ida B. Wells* (London: University of Chicago Press, 1972), pp. 85–124. I. Wells, *United States Atrocities – Lynch Law* (London: Lux Newspaper and Publishing Co., 1893).

221. Bressey, *Empire*, pp. 192–4; Duster (ed.), *Crusader*, p. 214.

222. Duster (ed.), *Crusader*, pp. 216–17.

223. Bressey, *Empire*, p. 153.

224. Ibid., pp. 157–8.

225. Ibid., p. 185.

226. Lorimer, 'Legacies of slavery', pp. 731–55.

227. Ibid., p. 731.

228. B. Brereton, *Race Relations in Colonial Trinidad 1870–1900* (Cambridge: Cambridge University Press, 2002), p. 96; J. De Barros, '"Race" and Culture in the Writings of J. J. Thomas', *Journal of Caribbean History*, 27 (1993), pp. 36–53.

229. J. Thomas, Preface, *Froudacity: West Indian Fables by James Anthony Froude*, Project Gutenberg, http://www.gutenberg.org/files/4068/4068h/4068-h.htm, accessed 23 July 2019.

230. Ibid., p. 234.

231. C. Fyfe, 'Sierra Leoneans in English schools in the nineteenth century', in Lotz and Pegg, *Under the Imperial Carpet*, pp. 25–31.

232. D. Killingray, 'Significant black South Africans in Britain before 1912: Pan-African organisations and the emergence of South Africa's first black lawyers', *South African History Journal*, 64/3 (September 2012), pp. 393–417.

233. J. Davis, 'Family trees: roots and branches – the dynasty and legacy of the Reverend Tiyo Soga', *Studies in World Christianity*, 21/1 (April 2015), pp. 20–37.

234. P. Curtin, 'Joseph Wright of the Egba', in P. Curtin (ed.), *Africa Remembered: Narratives by West Africans from the Era of the Slave Trade* (London: University of Wisconsin Press, 1967), pp. 317–34.

235. J. Ade Ajayi, 'Samuel Ajayi Crowther of Oyo', in Curtin (ed.), *Africa Remembered*, pp. 289–316.

236. F. Cundall, 'Richard Hill', *Journal of Negro History*, 5/1 (January 1920) pp. 37–44.

237. M. Campbell, *The Dynamics of Change in a Slave Society: Sociopolitical History of the Free Coloureds of Jamaica 1800–1865* (Rutherford, NJ: Fairleigh Dickinson University Press, 1976), p. 107.

238. R. Hill, *Haiti and Spain: A Memorial* (Kingston: De Cordova & Co., 1862).

239. Campbell, *The Dynamics of Change*, p. 195.

240. Cundall, 'Richard Hill', p. 40.

241. R. Freeman, 'Darwin's Negro bird-stuffer', *Notes and Records of the Royal Society of London*, 33/1 (August 1978), pp. 83–6.

242. Ibid.

243. Ibid.

244. M. Pandika, 'John Edmonstone: the freed slave who inspired Charles Darwin', 31 May 2014, OZY, https://www.ozy.com/flashback/john-edmonstone-the-freed-slave-who-inspired-charles-darwin/31600, accessed 4 August 2019.

245. 'Extraordinary History of Mr Thomas Jenkins', *Chambers' Edinburgh Journal*, 46 (15 December 1832), pp. 361–2, https://randomscottishhis tory.com/2020/12/11/chambers-edinburgh-journal-extraordinary-history-of-mr-thomas-jenkins-saturday-december-15-1832-pp-361-362/, accessed 14 February 2022.

246. M. Sherwood, 'Two Pan-African political activists emanating from Edinburgh University: Drs John Randle and Richard Akiwande Savage', in A. Adogame and A. Lawrence (eds.), *Africa in Scotland, Scotland in Africa* (Leiden: Brill, 2014), pp. 101–36.

247. P. Casey and T. Pilgrim, 'The incredible tale of Tom Jenkins, Britain's "first black teacher"', Brunel University London, https://www.brunel.ac.uk/news-and-events/news/articles/The-incredible-tale-of-Tom-Jenkins-Britains-first-black-teacher#, accessed 10 June 2019.

248. C. Cole, *Reflections on the Zulu War, By a Negro, B.A., of University College, Oxford, and the Inner Temple* (London: Glaisher, 1879), University College Oxford, https://www.univ.ox.ac.uk/news/reflections-on-zulu-war/, accessed 24 July 2019.

249. Quoted in M. Mendelssohn, *Making Oscar Wilde* (Oxford: Oxford University Press, 2018), p. 38.

250. Quoted in P. Roberts, *Black Oxford: The Untold Stories of Oxford University's Black Scholars* (Oxford: Signal Books, 2013), p. 3.

251. Ibid., pp. 82–3; Also 'Joseph Renner Maxwell', *Dictionary of African Christian Biography*, https://dacb.org/stories/gambia/maxwell-josephr/, accessed 24 July 2019.

252. R. Jenkins, 'In pursuit of the African past: John Mensah Sarbah (1864–1903), historian of Ghana', in Lotz and Pegg, *Under the Imperial Carpet*, pp. 109–29; J. M Sarbah, *Fanti Customary Laws, A Brief Introduction to the Native Principles and Customs of the Fanti and Akan Sections of the Gold Coast* (London: W. Clowes, 1897), Internet Archive, https://archive.org/details/fanticustomarylaoosarb/page/n4/mode/2up, accessed 31 January 2020.

253. R. Jenkins, 'Gold Coasters overseas, 1880–1919: with special reference to their activities in Britain', *Immigrants and Minorities*, 4 (1995), pp. 5–52.

254. J. E. Casely Hayford, *Gold Coast Native Institutions, with Thoughts upon a Healthy Imperial Policy for the Gold Coast and Ashanti* (London: Sweet and Maxwell, Limited, 1903), https://archive.org/details/goldcoastnativeioohayfiala/page/n4/mode/2up, accessed 31 January 2020.

255. P. Vasili, *The First Black Footballer: Arthur Wharton 1865–1930* (London: Frank Cass, 1998).

256. S. Tenkorang, 'John Mensah Sarbah, 1864–1910', *Journal of the Historical Society of Ghana*, 14/1 (June 1973), pp. 65–78; A. Cromwell, *An African Victorian Feminist: The Life and Times of Adelaide Smith Casely Hayford, 1868–1960* (Washington, DC: Howard University Press, 1992).

257. A. Adeloye, 'Some early Nigerian doctors and their contribution to medicine in West Africa', *Medical History,* 18 (1974) pp. 275–93.

258. C. Draper and J. Lawson-Reay, *Scandal at Congo House: William Hughes and the African Institute, Colwyn Bay* (Llanrwst: Gwasg Carreg Gwalch, 2012), pp. 181–217.

CHAPTER 6: WAR, RIOT AND RESISTANCE: 1897–1919

1. M. Sherwood, *Origins of Pan-Africanism: Henry Sylvester Williams, Africa and the African Diaspora* (London: Routledge, 2011), pp. 38–44; D. Killingray, 'Significant black South Africans in Britain before

1912: Pan-African organisations and the emergence of South Africa's first black lawyers', *South African Historical Journal*, 64/3 (September 2012), pp. 393–417; H. Adi, *Pan-Africanism: A History* (London: Bloomsbury, 2018), pp. 19–23.

2. Sherwood, *Origins of Pan-Africanism*, p. 42.

3. T. Ngcukaitobi, *The Land Is Ours: South Africa's First Black Lawyers and the Birth of Constitutionalism* (Cape Town: Penguin, 2018), pp. 43, 49.

4. Sherwood, *Origins of Pan-Africanism*, pp. 41, 252–3; Killingray, 'Significant black South Africans in Britain before 1912', pp. 401–4.

5. Ngcukaitobi, *The Land Is Ours*, pp. 41, 44.

6. G. Colenso and C. Saunders, 'New light on the Pan-African Association: Part I', *African Research & Documentation*, p. 107 (2008), pp. 27–46.

7. J. Schneer, *London 1900: The Imperial Metropolis* (London: Yale University Press, 1999), pp. 220–21.

8. Sherwood, *Origins of Pan-Africanism*, p. 43; Schneer, *London 1900*, p. 202.

9. Ibid., p. 39.

10. Ibid.

11. Schneer, *London 1900*, p. 221.

12. Sherwood, *Origins of Pan-Africanism*, pp. 56, 60–61.

13. Ibid., p. 73.

14. Ibid., p. 70.

15. Ibid., p. 76.

16. http://docsouth.unc.edu/neh/walters/walters.html#walt253, accessed 21 January 2020; Schneer, *London 1900*, pp. 222–5.

17. Sherwood, *Origins of Pan-Africanism*, pp. 75–97.

18. Ibid., pp. 277–80.

19. Ibid., pp. 98–121.

20. Colenso and Saunders, 'New light on the Pan-African Association: Part I', pp. 33–4.

21. Sherwood, *Origins of Pan-Africanism*, pp. 124–55; G. Colenso and C. Saunders, 'New light on the Pan-African Association: Part II', *African Research & Documentation* (2008), pp. 89–110.

22. Adi, *Pan-Africanism: A History*, pp. 19–23.

23. Sherwood, *Origins of Pan-Africanism*, p. 133.

24. R. C. Maguire, 'Allan Gleisyer Minns', *Oxford Dictionary of National Biography*, ttps://doi.org/10.1093/ref:odnb/109662, accessed 21 January 2020.

25. S. Creighton, 'John Archer and the politics of labour in Battersea (1906–1932)', in C. Bressey and H. Adi (eds.), *Belonging in Europe: The African Diaspora and Work* (London: Routledge, 2011), pp. 79–98.

26. *Crisis*, January 1914, p. 120; March 1914, pp. 225–6.

27. Creighton, 'John Archer', p. 84.

28. S. Coleridge-Taylor, *Twenty-Five Negro Melodies Transcribed for the Piano* (Boston: T. Ditson, 1905), Hathi Trust Digital Library, https://babel.hathitrust.org/cgi/pt?id=hvd.32044040402273&view=1up&seq=21, accessed 31 January 2020.

29. W. C. Berwick Sayers, *Samuel Coleridge-Taylor, Musician: His Life and Letters* (London and New York: Cassell and Company Limited, 1915), Internet Archive, https://archive.org/details/samuelcoleridget002424mbp/page/n305/mode/2up, accessed 31 January 2020.

30. I. Duffield, 'Dusé Mohamed Ali and the development of Pan-Africanism, 1866–1945', PhD thesis, University of Edinburgh (1971), Vol. 1, p. 397.

31. R. C. Maguire, 'Allan Gleisyer Minns', *Oxford Dictionary of National Biography*, ttps://doi.org/10.1093/ref:odnb/109662, accessed 21 January 2020.

32. J. Green, *Black Edwardians: Black People in Britain 1901–1914* (London: Frank Cass, 1998), pp. 70–73.

33. With thanks to Ed Keazor.

34. Green, *Black Edwardians*, pp. 42–67.

35. P. Panayi, *An Immigration History of Modern Britain: Multicultural Racism since 1800* (London: Routledge, 2010), p. 23.

36. T. Weir, 'James Peters: the man they wouldn't play. England's first black international and the 1906 Springboks', MA thesis, De Montfort University (2015).

37. P. Vasili, 'Walter Daniel John Tull', *Oxford Dictionary of National Biography*, https://doi.org/10.1093/ref:odnb/62348, accessed 29 January 2020.

38. P. Vasili, *Walter Tull, 1888–1918: Footballer and Officer* (London: Raw Press, 2010).

39. 'Walter Tull: the first black officer in the British Army and a professional footballer', Walter Tull, https://waltertull.org/, accessed 1 March 2019.

40. Green, *Black Edwardians*, pp. 80–81.

41. E. F. Ahovi and N. W. Kponou, 'Kathleen Mary Easmon Simango: reflections', Easmon Family History, http://www.easmonfambuldem.com/index.html#, accessed 1 March 2019.

42. M. Sherwood, 'Two Pan-African political activists emanating from Edinburgh University: Drs John Randle and Richard Akiwande Savage', in A. Adogame and A. Lawrence (eds.), *Africa in Scotland, Scotland in Africa* (Leiden: Brill, 2014), pp. 101–36.

43. Ibid.

44. H. Adi, *West Africans in Britain 1900–1960: Nationalism, Pan-Africanism and Communism* (London: Lawrence and Wishart, 1998), p. 10.

45. Ibid., p. 10.

46. Ibid., p. 11.

47. *Constitution of the Ethiopian Progressive Association* (Liverpool: D. Marples & Co., 1905), https://credo.library.umass.edu/view/pageturn/mums312-b002-i204/#page/2/mode/1up accessed 27 January 2020.

48. H. Adi, 'Bandele Omoniyi – a neglected Nigerian nationalist', *African Affairs*, 90/361 (1991), p. 583, n. 9.

49. Green, *Black Edwardians*, pp. 151–2.

50. D. Jones, *An African in Imperial Britain: The Indomitable Life of A. B. C. Merriman-Labor* (London: Hurst, 2018), pp. 82, 164.

51. Green, *Black Edwardians*, pp. 7, 115–37.

52. Jones, *An African in Imperial Britain*, pp. 24, 28.

53. Ibid., pp. 68–9.

54. H. Adi, 'Bandele Omoniyi – a neglected Nigerian nationalist'.

55. K. Blake, 'T. E. S. Scholes: the unknown Pan-Africanist', *Race and Class*, 49/1 (2007), pp. 62–80.

56. T. E. S. Scholes, Preface, *Glimpses through the Ages; or, the 'Superior' and 'Inferior' Races, So-Called, Discussed in the Light of Science and History* (London: John Long, 1908), pp. viii–ix, Internet Archive, https://archive.org/details/glimpsesagesors03schogoog/page/n16/mode/2up, accessed 28 January 2020.

57. Ibid., p. 392, Internet Archive, https://archive.org/details/glimpsesofageso1schoiala/page/392/mode/2up, accessed 28 January 2020.

58. Ibid., pp. xvi–xv, Internet Archive, https://archive.org/details/glimpsesofageso1schoiala/page/xiv/mode/2up, accessed 28 January 2020.

59. Blake, 'T. E. S. Scholes', pp. 73–4.

60. Ngcukaitobi, *The Land is Ours*, pp. 84–5.

61. Ibid., pp. 87–9.

62. Ibid., p. 223.

63. Green, *Black Edwardians*, p. 199.

64. Ibid., p. 214.

65. J. E. Casely Hayford, *Ethiopia Unbound: Studies in Race Emancipation* (London: C. M. Phillips, 1911), Internet Archive, https://archive.org/details/ethiopiaunboundsoohayf/page/n3/mode/2up, accessed 31 January 2020.

66. J. M. Sarbah, *Fanti Customary Laws, A Brief Introduction to the Native Principles and Customs of the Fanti and Akan Sections of the Gold Coast* (London: W. Clowes, 1897), Internet Archive, https://archive.org/details/fanticustomarylaoosarb/page/n4/mode/2up, accessed 31 January 2020; J. M. Sarbah, *Fanti National Constitution: A Short Treatise on the Constitution and Government of the Fanti, Asanti and Other Akan Tribes of West Africa etc.* (London: Frank Cass, 1968).

67. M. Abdelwahid, *Dusé Mohamed Ali (1866–1945): The Autobiography of a Pioneer Pan-African and Afro-Asian Activist* (Tenton: Red Sea Press, 2011); R. Bowen, 'Dusé Mohamed Ali's *The African Times and Orient Review* and its Pan-Africanism in Britain, 1910–1920', Master's by Research (MRes) thesis, University of Chichester (2019), p. 5; Duffield, 'Dusé Mohamed Ali', pp. 1–22; M. Sherwood, 'Dusé Mohamed Ali', *Oxford Dictionary of National Biography*, https://doi.org/10.1093/ref:odnb/59530, accessed 3 February 2020.

68. 'Dusé Mohamed Ali: actor, writer, businessman, entrepreneur and political activist (1866–1945)', African Stories in Hull and East Yorkshire, https://www.africansinyorkshireproject.com/duse-mohamed-ali.html, accessed 4 February 2020.

69. Duffield, 'Dusé Mohamed Ali', pp. 55–85.

70. Ibid., pp. 120–59.

71. 'The Races Congress', *Crisis*, 2/5 (September 1911), pp. 196–209; S. Pennybacker, 'The Universal Races Congress, London political culture and imperial dissent 1900–1939', *Radical History Review*, 92 (2005), pp. 103–17.

72. 'The Races Congress', *Crisis*, 2/4 (August 1911), pp. 157–9.

73. Duffield, 'Dusé Mohamed Ali', p. 173.

74. Ibid., pp. 176–7.

75. Bowen, 'Dusé Mohamed Ali's *The African Times and Orient Review*', p. 38.

76. Duffield, 'Dusé Mohamed Ali', p. 181.

77. Bowen, 'Dusé Mohamed Ali's *The African Times and Orient Review*', p. 40.

78. Duffield, 'Dusé Mohamed Ali', pp. 233, 236.

79. Bowen, 'Dusé Mohamed Ali's *The African Times and Orient Review*', pp. 8–9.

80. Ibid., pp. 55–9.

81. Duffield, 'Dusé Mohamed Ali', pp. 406–415.

82. Adi, *West Africans in Britain*, p. 13.

83. Ibid., pp. 14–15.

84. Ibid., pp. 15–16.

85. D. Olusoga, *The World's War* (London: Head of Zeus, 2014), p. 101; R. Costello, *Black Tommies: British Soldiers of African Descent in the First World War* (Liverpool: Liverpool University Press, 2015), p. 1; S. Bourne, *Black Poppies: Britain's Black Community and the Great War* (Cheltenham: The History Press, 2014), pp. 29–30.

86. M. Sherwood, 'An information "black hole": World War I in Africa', 9 May 2018, https://everydaylivesinwar.herts.ac.uk/2018/05/an-information-black-hole-world-war-i-in-africa/, Everyday Lives in War, accessed 1 May 2020.

87. G. Shepperson and T. Price, *Independent African: John Chilembwe and the Nyasaland Rising of 1915* (Edinburgh: Edinburgh University Press, 1958), pp. 234–5.

88. Bourne, *Black Poppies*, p. 29; Private Bai, died 15 August 1914, Commonwealth War Graves Foundation, https://www.cwgc.org/find-war-dead/casualty/417255, accessed 19 February 2020.

89. D. Killingray, 'All the king's men? Blacks in the British Army in the First World War, 1914–1918', in R. Lotz and I. Pegg (eds.), *Under the Imperial Carpet: Essays in Black History 1780–1950* (Crawley: Rabbit Press, 1986), pp. 164–81; R. Smith, *Jamaican Volunteers in the First World War: Race, Masculinity and the Development of National Consciousness* (Manchester: Manchester University Press, 2004), p. 55.

90. Bourne, *Black Poppies*, p. 83.

91. G. Howe, *Race, War and Nationalism: A Social History of West Indians in the First World War* (Oxford: James Currey, 2002), pp. 91–4.

92. Ibid., pp. 79–80.

93. Ibid., pp. 164–7.

94. Costello, *Black Tommies*, p. 18.

95. J. Siblon, '"Race", rank, and the politics of inter-war commemoration of African and Caribbean servicemen in Britain', in H. Adi (ed.), *Black British History: New Perspectives* (London: Zed Books, 2019), pp. 52–70.

96. '*SS Mendi*: We die like brothers', education resource pack, Historic England, https://historicengland.org.uk/content/docs/education/explorer/

ssmendi-we-die-like-brothers-education-resource-pack-pdf/, accessed 20 February 2020; B. Willan, 'The South African native labour contingent, 1916–1918', *Journal of African History*, 19/1 (1978), pp. 61–86, https://www.sahistory.org.za/sites/default/files/willan_the_sanlc.pdf, accessed 20 February 2020.

97. Costello, *Black Tommies*, pp. 29–30; E. Marke, *Old Man Trouble* (London: Weidenfeld & Nicolson, 1975), pp. 24–5; Smith, *Jamaican Volunteers in the First World War*, pp. 64–5.

98. Green, *Black Edwardians*, p. 266.

99. Costello, *Black Tommies*, p. 72.

100. Ibid., p. 89.

101. Killingray, 'All the king's men?', p. 170; Smith, *Jamaican Volunteers in the First World War*, pp. 60–61.

102. Costello, *Black Tommies*, pp. 84–8.

103. Killingray, 'All the king's men?', pp. 168–71.

104. Ibid.

105. Ibid., pp. 180–81.

106. Ibid., p. 171.

107. Smith, *Jamaican Volunteers in the First World War*, p. 64; *Daily Mirror*, 8 November 1915; *Daily Sketch*, 7 March 1916.

108. *Western Mail*, 5 May 1915, p. 7.

109. Costello, *Black Tommies*, pp. 45–7.

110. M. Miller, R. Laycock, J. Sadler and R. Serdiville, *As Good as Any Man: Scotland's Black Tommie* (Cheltenham: The History Press, 2014).

111. Ibid., pp. 85–6.

112. Ibid., pp. 120–21.

113. Marke, *Old Man Trouble*, pp. 24–5.

114. Costello, *Black Tommies*, p. 56.

115. *Western Mail*, 5 May 2015, p. 7; 6 May 1915, p. 4.

116. Ibid., 5 September 1914, p. 3.

117. Ibid., 25 May 1915, p. 9.

118. Ibid., 26 May 1915, p. 6.

119. Ibid.

120. Ibid., 2 June 1915, p. 5.

121. Ibid., 26 May 1915, p. 6.

122. Ibid., 31 May 1915, p. 7.

123. Ibid., 14 October 1915, p. 6

124. Ibid., 19 October 1915, pp. 5–6.

125. Ibid., 5 November 1915, p. 6.

126. Ibid., 25 October 1915, p. 6.

127. *Evening Despatch*, 27 May 1915, p. 6; *Western Daily Express*, 27 May 1915, p. 5.

128. Bourne, *Black Poppies*, pp. 47–51.

129. Ibid., pp. 96–101.

130. Costello, *Black Tommies*, pp. 49–58.

131. Ibid., pp. 136–7.

132. Bourne, *Black Poppies*, p. 35–6.

133. C. McKay, *A Long Way from Home* (London: Pluto Press, 1985), p. 67.

134. Killingray, 'All the king's men?', p. 176.

135. Ibid.

136. P. Vasili, *Colouring Over the White Line* (Edinburgh: Mainstream Publishing, 2000), p. 51.

137. Killingray, 'All the king's men?', pp. 176–7; Bourne, *Black Poppies*, p. 37; M. Page, *The Chiwaya War: Malawians in the First World War* (Abingdon: Routledge, 2019).

138. Bourne, *Black Poppies*, pp. 61–4.

139. *Sportsman*, 8 March 1915, p. 3.

140. *Western Mail*, 14 April 1915, p. 6.

141. Costello, *Black Tommies*, pp. 61–2.

142. Smith, *Jamaican Volunteers in the First World War*, p. 63.

143. Killingray, 'All the king's men', pp. 177–8.

144. Costello, *Black Tommies*, pp. 98–100.

145. Ibid., pp. 101–2.

146. Ibid., pp. 102–3.

147. 'The officer who refused to lie about being black', BBC News, 27 April 2015, https://www.bbc.co.uk/news/magazine-31796542, accessed 4 March 2020.

148. Costello, *Black Tommies*, pp. 104–5; Violet Sphinx, 'David Louis Clemetson', Trinity College Library, Cambridge, https://trinitycollegelibrarycambridge.wordpress.com/2014/07/09/wwi-clemetson/, accessed 4 March 2020.

149. Killingray, 'All the king's men', pp. 172–3.

150. Smith, *Jamaican Volunteers in the First World War*, p. 65.

151. C. Fyfe, 'McCormack Charles Farrell Easmon', *Oxford Dictionary of National Biography*, https://doi.org/10.1093/ref:odnb/76276, accessed 4 March 2020.

152. Killingray, 'All the king's men', p. 155.

153. J. Green, 'James Samuel Risien Russell', *Oxford Dictionary of National Biography*, https://doi.org/10.1093/ref:odnb/96832, accessed 4 March 2020.

154. Howe, *Race, War and Nationalism*, pp. 114–15.

155. Ibid., pp. 150–51.

156. *Dundee People's Journal*, 14 July 1917, p. 1.

157. Howe, *Race, War and Nationalism*, pp. 142–3.

158. *Western Mail*, 21 November 1916, p. 4.

159. P. Fryer, *Staying Power: The History of Black People in Britain* (London: Pluto, 1984); *Western Mail*, 14 April 1919, p. 3.

160. R. Lawless, *From Ta'izz to Tyneside: An Arab Community in the North-East of England during the Early Twentieth Century* (Exeter: University of Exeter Press, 1995), p. 271, n. 20.

161. E. Scobie, *Black Britannia: A History of Blacks in Britain* (Chicago: Johnson Publishing Co., 1972), p. 159.

162. Marke, *Old Man Trouble*, pp. 9–16.

163. 'Butetown and Tiger Bay seafarers took a heavy toll', Tiger Bay and the World: The Heritage and Cultural Exchange, https://www.tigerbay.org.uk/butetown-seafarers, accessed 2 March 2020.

164. I. Broad, 'Marcus Bailey, 1883–1927', African Stories in Hull and East Yorkshire, https://www.africansinyorkshireproject.com/marcus-bailey.html, accessed 25 February 2020.

165. Bourne, *Black Poppies*, p. 93.

166. J. Ellis, 'Black ratings of the Royal Naval Division', Academia, https://www.academia.edu/49056048/Black_Ratings_of_the_Royal_Naval_Division_1914_to_1918?email_work_card=view-paper, accessed 1 June 2020.

167. 'Black History Month: commemorating World War 1 West African merchant seamen', Royal Commission on the Ancient and Historical Monuments of Wales', https://rcahmw.gov.uk/commemorating-wwi-west-african-merchant-seamen/, accessed 25 February 2020.

168. 'Forgotten wrecks of the First World War', Maritime Archeology Trust, https://forgottenwrecks.maritimearchaeologytrust.org/uploads/images/Booklets/BME_booklet_v2.pdf, accessed 3 March 2020.

169. Costello, *Black Salt*, p. 144; Bourne, *Black Poppies*, pp. 93–4; D. Frost, *Work and Community among West African Migrant Workers since the Nineteenth Century* (Liverpool: Liverpool University Press, 1999), p. 74.

170. 'Remarkable affair at Milford Haven: sixteeen men refuse to go to sea', People's Collection Wales, https://www.peoplescollection.wales/items/1184441, accessed 2 March 2020.

171. Sylvester Leon, The Famous Jamaica Choir, http://thefamousjamaicachoir.weebly.com/--sylvester-leon.html, accessed 12 March 2020.

172. Thanks to Sonia Grant for all this information.

173. Thanks to Sonia Grant for all this information; William Savory, 'Statement of treatment and conditions at Wilhelmshaven, Emden, Sennelager and Ruhleben camps', National Archives, FO 383/156.

174. F. Brockway, *Bermondsey Story: The Life of Alfred Salter* (London: Allen and Unwin, 1951), p. 67.

175. House of Commons, 'Conscientious objectors', debated 13 November 1918, Vol. 110, cols. 2654–9W, *Hansard historic record*, https://api.parliament.uk/historic-hansard/written-answers/1918/nov/13/conscientious-objectors, accessed 14 February 2020.

176. Brockway, *Bermondsey Story*, p. 68.

177. 'October 1916', Remembering the Men Who Said No: Conscientious Objectors, 1916–1919, https://menwhosaidno.org/tribunal/tribunals/10october/TribunalTextOctober1916.html, accessed 14 February 2020.

178. Brockway, *Bermondsey Story*, p. 67.

179. *Cambria Daily Leader*, 14 September 1916, p. 1.

180. Siblon, '"Race", rank, and the politics of inter-war commemoration', pp. 55–63.

181. Ibid., p. 65.

182. *Report of the Special Committee to Review Historical Inequalities in Commemoration*, Commonwealth War Graves Foundation, https://www.cwgc.org/media/noantj4i/report-of-the-special-committee-to-review-historical-inequalities-in-commemoration.pdf, accessed 1 May 2021.

183. *Dundee Evening Telegraph*, 24 January 1919, p. 5.

184. *Liverpool Mercury*, 25 August 1880, p. 5.

185. M. Daunton, 'Jack ashore: seamen in Cardiff before 1914', *Welsh History Review* 9/2 (1978), pp. 176–203.

186. Letter to the Colonial Secretary, 13 April 1919, National Archives, CO 323/818.

187. W. Elkins, 'Hercules and the Society of African Origin', *Caribbean Studies*, 11/4 (1972) pp. 47–59.

188. *Yorkshire Evening Post*, 1 April 1919, p. 5.

189. J. Jenkinson, *Black 1919: Riots, Racism and Resistance in Imperial Britain* (Liverpool: Liverpool University Press, 2019), p. 19.

190. R. Lawless, *From Ta'izz to Tyneside: An Arab Community in the North-East of England during the Early Twentieth Century* (Exeter: University of Exeter Press, 1995), p. 269, n.5.

191. Smith, *Jamaican Volunteers in the First World War*, p. 112–13.

192. *Exeter and Plymouth Gazette*, 30 November 1916, p. 3.

193. House of Commons, 'Native labour', debated 4 December 1916, Vol. 88, col. 652, *Hansard historic record*, https://api.parliament.uk/

historic-hansard/commons/1916/dec/04/native-labour, accessed 12 March 2020.

194. J. Jenkinson, 'Black sailors on Red Clydeside: rioting, reactionary trade unionism and conflicting notions of "Britishness" following the First World War', *Twentieth Century British History*, 19/1 (2007), pp. 29–60.

195. Smith, *Jamaican Volunteers in the First World War*, p. 114.

196. *Western Mail*, 21 July 1917, p. 4.

197. J. Jenkinson, 'The 1919 race riots in Britain: a survey', in R. Lotz and I. Pegg (eds.), *Under the Imperial Carpet: Essays in Black History 1780–1950* (Crawley: Rabbit Press, 1986), pp. 182–207.

198. Jenkinson, *Black 1919*, p. 42.

199. Ibid., p. 74.

200. *Dundee Courier*, 25 January 1919, p. 4.

201. Jenkinson, *Black 1919*, p. 139.

202. *Dundee Evening Telegraph*, 31 January 1919, p. 1; *Newcastle Daily Chronicle*, 25 January 1919, p. 5.

203. L. Tabili, *Global Migrants Local Culture: Natives and Newcomers in Provincial England 1841–1939* (London: Palgrave, 2011), especially pp. 200–235.

204. L. Tabili, *"We Ask for British Justice": Workers and Racial Difference in Late Imperial Britain* (London: Cornell University Press, 1994), p. 9.

205. Lawless, *From Ta'izz to Tyneside*, pp. 75–6.

206. Jenkinson, *Black 1919*, pp. 86–7.

207. Ibid., p. 75.

208. *Shields Daily News*, 5 February 1919, p. 3; Lawless, *From Ta'izz to Tyneside*, pp. 74–5.

209. *Hartlepool Northern Daily Mail*, 13 February 2019, p. 3; Lawless, *From Ta'izz to Tyneside*, pp. 82–3.

210. Jenkinson, *Black 1919*, pp. 134–5.

211. Jenkinson, 'The 1919 race riots', p. 205.

212. Jenkinson, *Black 1919*, p. 79.

213. *Aberdeen Press and Journal*, 28 July 1919, p. 6.

214. Jenkinson, 'The 1919 race riots', p. 204.

215. Jenkinson, *Black 1919*, p. 79.

216. *Taunton Courier and Western Advertiser*, 23 April 1919, p. 1.

217. *Scotsman*, 17 April 1919, p. 6.

218. *Illustrated Police News*, 22 January 1919, p. 2.

219. *Taunton Courier and Western Advertiser*, 23 April 1919, p. 1.

220. *Yorkshire Evening Post*, 17 April 1919, p. 8; *Newcastle Evening Chronicle*, 17 April 1919, p. 5; *Illustrated Police News*, 22 January 1919, p. 2.

221. *Western Mail*, 21 April 1919, p. 3; *Taunton Courier and Western Advertiser*, 23 April 1919, p. 1.

222. *Taunton Courier and Western Advertiser*, 23 April 1919, p. 1.

223. *Blyth News*, 17 April 1919, p. 3; *Shields Daily News*, 17 April 1919, p. 3.

224. *Newcastle Daily Chronicle*, 21 April 1919, p. 3.

225. *Globe*, 2 July 1917, p. 3.

226. *Dublin Daily Express*, 4 July 1917, p. 6.

227. *Western Mail*, 21 April 1919, p. 3.

228. *Illustrated Police News*, 8 May 1919, p. 2.

229. *Daily Herald*, 8 May 1919, p. 11.

230. Ibid., 1 May 1919, p. 8.

231. *Dundee Evening Telegraph*, 30 May 1919, p. 3.

232. Jenkinson, 'The 1919 race riots', p. 192.

233. Jenkinson, *Black 1919*, pp. 78, 208; *Nottingham Evening Post*, 17 June 1919, p. 3.

234. A. Murphy, *From the Empire to the Rialto: Racism and Reaction in Liverpool 1918–1948* (Birkenhead: Liver Press, 1995), especially pp. 1–64; R. May and R. Cohen, 'The interaction between race and colonialism: a case study of the Liverpool race riots of 1919', *Race and Class*, XVI/2 (1984), pp. 111–26; J. Belchem, *Before the Windrush: Race Relations in 20th-Century Liverpool* (Liverpool: Liverpool University Press, 2014), especially pp. 39–55.

235. Belchem, *Before the Windrush*, p. 39; Murphy, *From the Empire to the Rialto*, pp. 159–160.

236. *Liverpool Daily Post*, 20 December 1918, p. 7.

237. Fryer, *Staying Power*, p. 297.

238. May and Cohen, 'The interaction between race and colonialism', p. 113.

239. Murphy, *From the Empire to the Rialto*, p. 14

240. Jenkinson, *Black 1919*, pp. 79–80.

241. Belchem, *Before the Windrush*, p. 46.

242. Jenkinson, *Black 1919*, pp. 79–82; Murphy, *From the Empire to the Rialto*, p. 17.

243. *Pall Mall Gazette*, 6 June 1919, p. 4; *Yorkshire Evening Post*, 6 June 1919, p. 7.

244. Jenkinson, *Black 1919*, p. 86.

245. Belchem, *Before the Windrush*, pp. 44–5.

246. *Derby Daily Telegraph*, 12 June 1919, p. 3

247. Marke, *Old Man Trouble*, p. 31.

248. Belchem, *Before the Windrush*, p. 42.

249. Ibid., p. 43.

250. *Daily Gazette for Middlesbrough*, 18 June 1919, p. 4; *Nottingham Evening Post*, 17 June 2019, p. 3.

251. J. Chapman, *Early Black Media 1918–1924: Print Pioneers in Britain* (Cham: Palgrave Macmillan, 2019), p. 44.

252. Chapman, *Early Black Media*, p. 44.

253. *Hartlepool Northern Daily Mail*, 12 June 1919, p. 2.

254. Belchem, *Before the Windrush*, pp. 48–53.

255. Marke, *Old Man Trouble*, pp. 33–9.

256. Jenkinson, *Black 1919*, pp. 135–6.

257. Ibid., pp. 142–3.

258. Quoted in Fryer, *Staying Power*, p. 298.

259. Letter to the Colonial Secretary, 13 April 1919.

260. Daunton, 'Jack ashore', p. 191.

261. B. Hirson and L. Vivian, *Strike Across the Empire – The Seamen's Strike of 1925: In Britain, South Africa and Australasia* (London: Cleo Publications, 1992), pp. 39–40.

262. N. Evans, 'The South Wales race riots of 1919', *Llafur*, 3/1 (1980), pp. 3–29.

263. *Yorkshire Evening Post*, 7 June 1919, p. 6.

264. Evans, 'The South Wales race riots', p. 14.

265. J. Jenkinson, 'The 1919 race riots in Britain: their background and their consequences', PhD dissertation, University of Edinburgh (1987), pp. 241–56.

266. Evans, 'The South Wales race riots', p. 14.

267. Jenkinson, 'The 1919 race riots in Britain', pp. 256–66.

268. K. Little, *Negroes in Britain: A Study of Racial Relations in English Society* (London: Kegan Paul, 1947), pp. 57–60; Jenkinson, *Black 1919*, p. 83; Evans, 'The South Wales race riots of 1919', p. 5; Jenkinson, 'The 1919 race riots in Britain', pp. 210–39.

269. T. Lane, 'The political imperatives of bureaucracy and empire: the case of the Coloured Alien Seamen Order, 1925', *Immigrants and Minorities*, 13/2–3 (July/November 1994), pp. 104–29.

270. Jenkinson, *Black 1919*, p. 123.

271. Jenkinson, 'The 1919 race riots in Britain', p. 215.

272. N. Sinclair, *The Tiger Bay Story* (Cardiff: Butetown History and Arts Project, 1993), pp. 32–6.

273. *Dundee Courier*, 13 June 1919, p. 5.

274. R. Pankhurst, 'An early African Autobiography (II)', *Africa: Rivista Trimestrale Di Studi e Documentazione Dell'Istituto Italiano per l'Africa e l'Oriente*, 32/ 3, (1977), pp. 355–84.

275. Elkins, 'Hercules and the Society of African Origin', p. 50.

276. Evans, 'The South Wales race riots of 1919', p. 16.

277. Jenkinson, 'The 1919 race riots in Britain', p. 222.

278. Jenkinson, *Black 1919*, pp. 120–23.

279. Evans, 'The South Wales race riots of 1919', p. 20; N. Evans, 'The South Wales race riots of 1919: a documentary postscript', *Llafur* 3/4 (1983), pp. 76–87.

280. *Dundee Courier*, 3 June 1919, p. 5.

281. *Taunton Courier and Western Advertiser*, 18 June 1919, p. 6.

282. *Daily Herald*, 13 June 1919, p. 4.

283. N. Evans, 'Across the universe: racial violence and the post-war crisis in imperial Britain, 1919–1925', *Immigrants and Minorities*, 13/2–3 (July/November 1994), pp. 59–88.

284. 'Board of Trade circular', February 1919, National Archives, CO 323/798.

285. Confidential letter to Chief Constable, Salford, 25 June 1919, National Archives, CO 323/803.

286. Board of Trade circular, February 1919.

287. Jenkinson, *Black 1919*, pp. 155–89.

288. Letter to the Colonial Secretary, 13 April 1919.

289. Tabili, *"We Ask for British Justice"*, pp. 47–57.

290. Lane, 'The political imperatives of bureaucracy and empire', pp. 116–19.

291. Hirson and Vivian, *Strike Across the Empire*, p. 41.

292. Aliens Restriction (Amendment) Act 1919, http://www.legislation.gov.uk/ukpga/Geo5/9-10/92/enacted, accessed 30 March 2020.

293. *Nottingham Evening Post*, 17 June 1919, p. 3.

294. L. Tabili, 'The construction of racial difference in twentieth-century Britain: the Special Restriction (Coloured Alien Seamen) Order, 1925', *Journal of British Studies*, 33/1 (January 1994), pp. 54–98.

295. P. Rich, *Race and Empire in British Politics* (Cambridge: Cambridge University Press, 1990), pp. 122–30; Lane, 'The political imperatives of bureaucracy and empire', and Tabili, 'The construction of racial difference', ibid.

296. Tabili, *"We Ask for British Justice"*, pp. 121–2.

297. Lane, 'The political imperatives of bureaucracy and empire', p. 113; Little, *Negroes in Britain*, pp. 65–7.

298. Tabili, *"We Ask for British Justice"*, p. 127.

299. Rich, *Race and Empire*, p. 128.

300. Smith, *Jamaican Volunteers in the First World War*, pp. 189–90.

301. Elkins, 'Hercules and the Society of African Origin', p. 53.

CHAPTER 7: THE INTERWAR YEARS

1. H. Adi, *West Africans in Britain 1900–1960: Nationalism, Pan-Africanism and Communism* (London: Lume Books, 2019), p. 19; J. Green and R. Lockhart, '"A brown alien in a white city" – black students in London, 1917–1920', in R. Lotz and I. Pegg, *Under the Imperial Carpet: Essays in Black History 1780–1950* (Crawley: Rabbit Press, 1986), pp. 208–16.

2. J. Chapman, *Early Black Media 1918–1924: Print Pioneers in Britain* (Cham: Palgrave Macmillan, 2019), p. 20.

3. Ibid.

4. *Report of the Foreign Students' Work of the Student Christian Movement (SCM)*, December 1918, M.128, Student Christian Movement Archive, University of Birmingham.

5. R. Lapiere, 'Race prejudice: England and France', *Social Forces*, 7/1 (September 1928), pp. 102–11.

6. *Daily Herald*, 17 August 1935, p. 2.

7. *African Telegraph*, December 1918, pp. 89–90.

8. M. Sherwood, 'Robert Broadhurst', *Oxford Dictionary of National Biography*, https://doi.org/10.1093/ref:odnb/67910, accessed 9 April 2020.

9. J. Green, 'Kwamina Faux Tando (Chief Kofi Amoah)', *Oxford Dictionary of National Biography*, https://doi.org/10.1093/ref:odnb/97932, accessed 9 April 2020.

10. J. Green, 'John Alexander Barbour James', *Oxford Dictionary of National Biography*, https://doi.org/10.1093/ref:odnb/57362 and J. Green, 'John Alcindor', *Oxford Dictionary of National Biography*, https://doi.org/10.1093/ref:odnb/57173, both accessed 9 April 2020.

11. *West Africa*, 4 January 1919, pp. 840–42.

12. *African Telegraph*, December 1918, p. 89.

13. *West Africa*, 18 January 1919, pp. 882–4.

14. Ibid., 1 February 1919, p. 16.

15. *African Telegraph*, December 1918, p. 90.

16. J. Langley, *Pan-Africanism and Nationalism in West Africa 1900–1945* (Oxford: Oxford University Press, 1973), pp. 124, 245.

17. I. Duffield, 'John Eldred Taylor and West African opposition to indirect rule in Nigeria', *African Affairs*, 280 (1971), pp. 252–68; *Westminster Gazette*, November 1919, pp. 4, 7; *The Crisis*, 20/2 (June 1920), p. 96.

18. W. Elkins, 'Hercules and the Society of Peoples of African Origin', *Caribbean Studies*, 11/4 (1972), pp. 47–59.

19. *African Telegraph*, March 1919, p. 139.

20. Ibid., p. 142.

21. *The Crisis*, 17/6 (April 1919), p. 273.

22. *African Telegraph*, January–February 1919, p. 122 and *African Telegraph*, April 1919, p. 170.

23. J. Jenkinson, *Black 1919: Riots, Racism and Resistance in Imperial Britain* (Liverpool: Liverpool University Press, 2019), pp. 7–8.

24. Chapman, *Early Black Media 1918–1924*, pp. 45–6.

25. Jenkinson, *Black 1919*, p. 8; *Glasgow Forward*, 3 March 1923, p. 3.

26. J. Starfield, 'A dance with the empire: Modiri Molema's Glasgow years, 1914–1921', *Journal of Southern African Studies*, 27/3 (2001), pp. 479–503.

27. Jenkinson, *Black 1919*, p. 8.

28. Ibid., pp. 117–18; S. Davies, 'Edward Theophilus Nelson', *Oxford Dictionary of National Biography*, https://doi.org/10.1093/ref:odnb/57262, accessed 9 April 2020.

29. Jenkinson, *Black 1919*, pp. 118–19.

30. Elkins, 'Hercules', p. 51.

31. Communication from Director of Intelligence to Major Thornton, 4 December 1919, National Archives, CO 318/352; J. Derrick, *Africa, Empire and Fleet Street* (London: Hurst & Co., 2018), p. 153.

32. Derrick, *Africa, Empire and Fleet Street*, pp. 155–6.

33. C. Høgsbjerg, 'Rufus E. Fennell: a literary Pan-Africanist in Britain', *Race and Class*, 56/1 (2014), pp. 56–80.

34. Ibid., p. 65.

35. Ibid., pp. 66–7; Elkins, 'Hercules', p. 52; Jenkinson, *Black 1919*, pp. 120–23.

36. *Report of the London Committee for the Repatriation of Coloured Men*, September 1919, National Archives, CO 323/803.

37. The African Progress Union to J. Harris, 23 April 1919, MSS. Brit. Emp. S23 H2/56, Oxford, Bodleian Library.

38. Chapman, *Early Black Media*, p. 48.

39. Adi, *West Africans in Britain*, pp. 18–19.

40. Chapman, *Early Black Media*, p. 28.

41. Ibid., p. 32.

42. Ibid.

43. See, for example, House of Commons, 'Trinidad', debated 2 March 1920, Vol. 126, col. 286, *Hansard historic record*, https://bit.ly/34P9lS8, and again, House of Commons, 'Trinidad and Tobago (Disturbances)', debated 15 December 1919, Vol. 123, col. 37, *Hansard historic record*, https://bit.ly/3coanon, both accessed 19 April 2020.

44. Elkins, 'Hercules', pp. 47–59.

45. Langley, *Pan-Africanism and Nationalism*, pp. 245–6, 252–3.

46. Ibid., p. 72.

47. *The Crisis*, 23/2 (December 1921), pp. 68–9.

48. H. Adi, *Pan-Africanism: A History* (London: Bloomsbury, 2019), pp. 51–2.

49. *The Crisis*, 27/3 (January 1924), p. 120.

50. Langley, *Pan-Africanism and Nationalism*, p. 86.

51. I. Duffield, 'Dusé Mohamed Ali and the development of Pan-Africanism, 1866–1945', PhD thesis, University of Edinburgh (1971), Vol. 2, p. 548.

52. *West Africa*, 20 September 1924, p. 991; 4 October 1924, p. 1073.

53. Adi, *West Africans in Britain*, p. 24.

54. Ibid.; M. Matera, *Black London: The Imperial Metropolis and Decolonization in the Twentieth Century* (Oakland: University of California Press, 2015), pp. 24–9.

55. Adi, *West Africans in Britain*, pp. 24–5.

56. D. Stephen, '"The white man's grave": British West Africa and the British Empire Exhibition of 1924–1925', *Journal of British Studies*, 48/1 (January 2009), pp. 102–28.

57. Ibid., p. 126.

58. Adi, *West Africans in Britain*, p. 26.

59. P. Garigue, 'The West African Students' Union: a study in culture contact', *Africa*, 23/1 (January 1953), pp. 55–69.

60. Adi, *West Africans in Britain*, p. 28.

61. H. Adi, 'Amy Ashwood Garvey and the Nigerian Progress Union', in J. Byfield, L. Denzer and A. Morrison, *Gendering the African Diaspora: Women, Culture and Historical Change in the Caribbean and Nigerian Hinterland* (Bloomington: Indiana University Press, 2010), pp. 203–5.

62. Ibid., pp. 199–218.

63. Adi, *West Africans in Britain*, p. 29.

64. Ibid., pp. 29–30.

65. Letter from P. Giles (Emmanuel College, Cambridge) to Colonial Office, August 1923, National Archives, CO 554/161/8864.

66. Stephen, '"The white man's grave"', p. 115.

67. G. Olusanya, *The West African Students' Union and the Politics of Decolonisation, 1925–1958* (Ibadan: Daystar Press, 1982), pp. 6–7.

68. Adi, *West Africans in Britain*, pp. 34–9.

69. L. Solanke, *United West Africa (or Africa) at the Bar of the Family of Nations* (London: African Publications Society, 1969); J. de Graft

Johnson, *Towards Nationhood in West Africa: Thoughts of Young Africa Addressed to Young Britain* (London: Frank Cass & Co., 1971).

70. Adi, *West Africans in Britain*, p. 41.

71. Ibid., p. 44; House of Commons, 'North East Coast Exhibition (African Village)', debated 8 May 1929, Vol. 227, *Hansard historic record*, https://bit.ly/3cC83N2, accessed 23 April 2020.

72. Adi, *West Africans in Britain*, p. 53.

73. Ibid., pp. 45–7; S. Onakomaiya (ed.), *Mama Wasu – a Village Girl Turned International Personality, Guardian and Counsellor: The Autobiography of Chief (Mrs) Opeolu Solanke-Ogunbiyi* (Lagos: 2009), pp. 14, 21.

74. Adi, *West Africans in Britain*, p. 54.

75. Ibid., p. 116.

76. *Portsmouth Evening News*, 12 June 1935, p. 9.

77. D. Killingray, '"To do something for the race": Harold Moody and the League of Coloured Peoples', in B. Swarz (ed.), *West Indian Intellectuals in Britain* (Manchester: Manchester University Press, 2003), pp. 51–70.

78. D. Vaughan, *Negro Victory: The Life Story of Dr Harold Moody* (London: Independent Press, 1950), p. 28.

79. Killingray, '"To do something for the race"', p. 59.

80. Matera, *Black London*, pp. 37–45; *The Keys*, 1/2 (October 1933), p. 32.

81. *The Keys*, 2/3 (January–March 1935), p. 62.

82. Matera, *Black London*, p. 40.

83. *The Keys*, 1/1 (July 1933), pp. 1–2.

84. *The Keys*, 2/1 (July–September 1934), p. 17.

85. D. Jarrett-Macaulay, *The Life of Una Marson* (Manchester: Manchester University Press, 1998).

86. *Daily Herald*, 16 January 1934, p. 3; 10 March 1934, p. 11.

87. Jarrett-Macaulay, *The Life of Una Marson*, p. 51; *The Keys*, 1/1 (July 1933), pp. 8–9.

88. *The Keys*, 2/1 (July–September 1934), p. 17.

89. Ibid., 2/2 (October–December 1934), p. 42.

90. Adi, *West Africans in Britain*, pp. 193–7.

91. Ibid., pp. 62–7.

92. *Negro Worker*, 3/2 (March 1932), pp. 2–3.

93. Ibid., pp. 30–31; N. Cunard, *Colour Bar: An Anthology* (New York: Frederick Ungar Publishing Co., 1970), pp. 344–5.

94. N. Sharpe, 'Report on the Negro population in London and Cardiff', 1932, Cardiff Local Studies Library.

95. P. Rich, *Race and Empire in British Politics* (Cambridge: Cambridge University Press, 1986), pp. 120–44; R. Lawless, 'Religion and politics among Arab seafarers in Britain in the early twentieth century', *Islam and Christian-Muslim Relations*, 5/1 (1994), pp. 35–56.

96. R. Lawless, *From Ta'izz to Tyneside: An Arab Community in the North-East of England in the Early Twentieth Century* (Exeter: University of Exeter Press, 1995), p. 107.

97. Ibid., p. 124.

98. H. Adi, *Pan-Africanism and Communism: The Communist International, Africa and the Diaspora, 1919–1939* (Trenton: Africa World Press, 2013), pp. 260–63; M. Sherwood, 'The Comintern, the CPGB, colonies and black Britons, 1920–1938', *Science and Society*, 60/2 (Summer 1996), pp. 137–63.

99. D. Byrne, 'The 1930 "Arab riot" in South Shields: a race riot that never was', *Race and Class*, 18/3 (Winter 1977), pp. 261–77; Lawless, 'Religion and politics', pp. 37–8.

100. Lawless, *From Ta'izz to Tyneside*, p. 114.

101. L. Tabili, *"We Ask for British Justice": Workers and Racial Difference in Late Imperial Britain* (London: Cornell University Press, 1994), pp. 105–10; Lawless, *From Ta'izz to Tyneside*, pp. 251–3.

102. Lawless, *From Ta'izz to Tyneside*, p. 137.

103. Byrne, 'The 1930 "Arab riot"', pp. 261–77; Lawless, *From Ta'izz to Tyneside*, p. 124.

104. Lawless, 'Religion and politics', p. 39.

105. Byrne, 'The 1930 "Arab riot"', pp. 261–77.

106. K. Little, *Negroes in Britain: A Study of Race Relations in English Society* (London: Kegan Paul, 1947), p. 67.

107. Ibid., p. 74.

108. Rich, *Race and Empire in British Politics*, p. 129.

109. M. Sherwood, 'Racism and resistance: Cardiff in the 1930s and 1940s', *Llafur*, 4/5 (1991), pp. 51–70.

110. 'Seamen's Welfare Board Progress Report', 1941, National Archive, LAB 26/177.

111. Interview with Coka Clarke, 1982, Roots Family History Project, Iqbal Ullah Race Relations Resource Centre, Manchester.

112. *The Keys*, 1/1(July 1933), p. 10.

113. *Negro Worker*, 4/5 (April–May 1933), pp. 24–5.

114. Rich, *Race and Empire in British Politics*, pp. 127–8.

115. Ibid., p. 128.

116. Ibid., p. 131; *Western Mail*, 8 May 1930, p. 12.

117. M. Christian, 'The Fletcher Report, 1930: a historical case study of contested black mixed heritage Britishness', *Journal of Historical Sociology*, 21/2–3 (2008), pp. 213–41.

118. Rich, *Race and Empire in British Politics*, p. 132; J. Belchem, *Before the Windrush: Race Relations in 20th-Century Liverpool* (Liverpool: Liverpool University Press, 2014), p. 62.

119. N. Sharpe, 'Cardiff's coloured population', *The Keys*, 1/3 (January 1934), pp. 44–5, 61.

120. Sherwood, 'Racism and resistance', p. 59.

121. *Western Mail*, 8 July 1935, p. 9.

122. *The Keys*, 2/2 (October–December 1934), p. 43.

123. *Negro Worker*, 5/9 (September 1935), pp. 10–11 and 18.

124. D. Featherstone, 'Harry O'Connell, maritime labour, and the racialised politics of place', *Race and Class*, 57/3 (2016), pp. 71–87; Sherwood, 'Racism and resistance', pp. 58–61.

125. Sherwood, 'Racism and resistance', p. 61; *Colonial Information Bulletin*, 11 (15 September 1937), p. 10.

126. *Negro Worker*, 5/9 (September 1935), pp. 10–11 and 18.

127. Adi, *Pan-Africanism and Communism*, p. 258.

128. Ibid., pp. 251–91.

129. S. Pennybacker, *From Scottsboro to Munich: Race and Political Culture in 1930s Britain* (Princeton: Princeton University Press, 2009), p. 47.

130. *Negro Worker*, 5/2–3 (February–March 1935), pp. 25–6.

131. Adi, *Pan-Africanism and Communism*, p. 264.

132. *The Keys*, 3/1 (July–September 1935), p. 3.

133. L. Tabili, 'The contradictions of economic nationalism: the National Union of Seamen, colonized workers, and the British Shipping (Assistance) Act, 1935', paper delivered at North American Labor History Conference, Detroit, October 2002.

134. *Western Mail*, 10 July 1935, p. 10.

135. *The Keys*, 3/2 (October–December 1935), pp. 15–24.

136. Ibid., 3/3 (January–March 1936), p. 42.

137. Tabili, 'The contradictions of economic nationalism', p. 13.

138. Lawless, *From Ta'izz to Tyneside*, p. 167.

139. Tabili, 'The contradictions of economic nationalism', p. 16.

140. Lawless, *From Ta'izz to Tyneside*, p. 169.

141. Sherwood, 'Racism and resistance', p. 61.

142. *Western Mail*, 11 July 1935, p. 11; N. Evans, 'Regulating the reserve army: Arabs, blacks and the local state in Cardiff, 1919–1945', in

K. Lunn (ed.), *Race and Labour in Twentieth-Century Britain* (London: Routledge, 1986), p. 98.

143. 'Labour imperialists and the colonial seamen', *Colonial News* (April 1934), pp. 4–5.

144. *Western Mail*, 17 April 1935, p. 10.

145. *Negro Worker*, 9/5 (September 1935), pp. 10–11, 18.

146. M. Sherwood, *Pastor Daniels Ekarte and the African Churches Mission* (London: Savannah Press, 1994), p. 7.

147. E. Marke, *Old Man Trouble* (London: Weidenfeld & Nicolson, 1975), pp. 51 and 62.

148. Belchem, *Before the Windrush*, p. 55.

149. D. Frost, 'Racism, work and unemployment: West African seamen in Liverpool, 1880s–1960s', *Immigrants and Minorities*, 13/2–3 (July–November 1994), pp. 22–33.

150. House of Commons, 'Home Office', debated 11 July 1928, Vol. 219, col. 2370, *Hansard historic record*, https://api.parliament.uk/historic-hansard/commons/1928/jul/11/home-office, accessed 1 May 2020.

151. Tabili, *"We Ask for British Justice"*, pp. 68–77.

152. Belchem, *Before the Windrush*, p. 56.

153. Tabili, *"We Ask for British Justice"*, p. 157.

154. Adi, *Pan-Africanism and Communism*, pp. 256–8.

155. Sherwood, *Pastor Daniels Ekarte*, p. 117.

156. Ibid., p. 11.

157. *The Keys*, 4/3 (January–March 1937), p. 34.

158. Sherwood, *Pastor Daniels Ekarte*, passim.

159. Belchem, *Before the Windrush*, p. 65.

160. *The Keys*, 2/2 (October–December 1934), p. 21.

161. Ibid., 1/3 (January 1934), p. 58.

162. Ibid., 2/2 (October–December 1934), p. 21.

163. J. Derrick, *Africa's 'Agitators' – Militant Anti-Colonialism in Africa and the West, 1918–1939* (London: Hurst, 2008), pp. 332–46.

164. H. Adi, *Pan-Africanism: A History* (London: Bloomsbury 2018), pp. 107–8.

165. Adi, *Pan-Africanism and Communism*, p. 179.

166. Adi, *Pan-Africanism: A History*, p. 108; D. Whittall, 'Creolising London: black West Indian activism and the politics of race and empire in Britain, 1931–1948', PhD thesis, Royal Holloway, University of London (2012), pp. 22–3.

167. Adi, *Pan-Africanism and Communism*, pp. 152–61; L. James, *George Padmore and Decolonisation from Below: Pan-Africanism, The Cold War and the End of Empire* (London: Palgrave, 2015).

168. C. Høgsbjerg, *C.L.R. James in Imperial Britain* (London: Duke University Press, 2014), pp. 67–84.

169. Ras Makonnen, *Pan-Africanism from Within* (London: Oxford University Press, 1973), pp. 110–16.

170. Adi, *West Africans in Britain*, pp. 63–4.

171. G. Padmore, *Pan-Africanism or Communism? The Coming Struggle for Africa* (London: Denis Dobson, 1956), pp. 122–3.

172. Høgsbjerg, *C.L.R. James in Imperial Britain*, p. 90.

173. Makonnen, *Pan-Africanism from Within*, p. 117.

174. T. Martin, *Amy Ashwood Garvey: Pan-Africanist, Feminist and Mrs Marcus Garvey no. 1 or, A Tale of Two Amies* (Dover: Majority Press, 2007), pp. 140–41; M. Makalani, *In the Cause of Freedom: Radical Black Internationalism from Harlem to London, 1917–1939* (Chapel Hill, University of North Carolina Press, 2011), p. 202–3.

175. M. Sherwood, 'An emperor in exile, Part 2: Ethiopia and black organisations in the UK 1935–1936', *Black and Asian Studies Newsletter*, 43 (September 2005), pp. 18–23.

176. Derrick, *Africa's 'Agitators'*, p. 337.

177. *Negro Worker*, 5/11 (December 1935), p. 25.

178. Sherwood, 'An emperor in exile, Part 2: Ethiopia and black organisations', pp. 20–21; *Labour Monthly*, 17/9 (September 1935), pp. 532–6.

179. C. L. R. James, 'Abyssinia and the imperialists', *The Keys*, 3/3 (January–March 1936), pp. 32, 39–40.

180. *The Keys*, 3/3 (January–March 1936), p. 31.

181. *West Africa*, 19 October 1935, p. 1229; *Wāsù*, 4/5 (November 1935), p. 70; *Wāsù*, 5/1 (May 1936), p. 21.

182. Adi, *West Africans in Britain*, pp. 67–70.

183. Adi, *Pan-Africanism: A History*, p. 111.

184. *Negro Worker*, 5/7–8 (July–August 1935), pp. 35–7; 5/9 (September 1935), p. 23.

185. Ibid., 7/2 (February 1937), p. 4.

186. M. Sherwood, 'Lascar struggles against discrimination in Britain 1923–45: the work of N. J. Upadhyaya and Surat Alley', *Mariner's Mirror*, 90/4 (November 2004), pp. 438–55.

187. D. Featherstone, *Solidarity: Hidden Histories and Geographies of Internationalism* (London: Zed Books, 2012), pp. 96–7; Adi, *Pan-Africanism*

and Communism, pp. 279–81 and C. Høgsbjerg, *Mariner, Renegade and Castaway: Chris Braithwaite Seamen's Organiser, Socialist and Militant Pan-Africanist* (London: Socialist History Society, 2014); *Communism and the West Indian Labour Disturbances*, National Archives, CO 295/606/4.

188. Padmore, *Pan-Africanism or Communism?*, p. 123.

189. See Chapter 5.

190. R. Scott, 'Black Nationalism and the Italo-Ethiopian conflict 1934–1936', *Journal of Negro History*, 63/2 (April 1978), pp. 118–34.

191. C. L. R. James, 'Black intellectuals in Britain', in B. Parekh (ed.), *Colour, Culture and Consciousness: Immigrant Intellectuals in Britain* (London: George Allen & Unwin, 1974), pp. 154–63; Padmore, *Pan-Africanism or Communism?*, p. 123; Makalani, *In the Cause of Freedom*, p. 210.

192. S. Asante, *Pan-African Protest: West Africa and the Italo-Ethiopian Crisis 1934–1941* (London: Longman, 1977), p. 60.

193. M. Garvey, 'Editorial', *The Black Man*, March–April 1937.

194. Padmore, *Pan-Africanism or Communism?*, p. 124.

195. Adi, *Pan-Africanism: A History*, pp. 114–15.

196. *Communism and the West Indian Labour Disturbances*, National Archives, CO 295/606/4; Makalani, *In the Cause of Freedom*, p. 215.

197. Padmore, *Pan-Africanism or Communism?*, p. 124; Derrick, *Africa's 'Agitators'*, p. 389; Makonnen, *Pan-Africanism from Within*, pp. 117–20.

198. Letter from Padmore to Crichlow, July 1934, National Archives, KV 2/1787.

199. Whittall, 'Creolising London', p. 23.

200. Ibid., p. 234.

201. Ibid., p. 238.

202. Padmore, *Pan-Africanism or Communism?*, p. 125.

203. Makonnen, *Pan-Africanism from Within*, pp. 117–18.

204. Makalani, *In the Cause of Freedom*, pp. 212–14; P. Von Eschen, *Race Against Empire: Black Americans and Anticolonialism, 1937–1957* (London: Cornell University Press, 1997), p. 18.

205. International African Service Bureau, *Hands off the Protectorates* (London: International African Service Bureau, 1938).

206. Adi, *Pan-Africanism: A History*, p. 119.

207. A. Lewis, *Labour in the West Indies: The Birth of a Workers' Movement* (London: New Beacon Books, 1977), pp. 18–19.

208. Matera, *Black London*, pp. 93–4.

209. L. James and D. Whittall, 'Ambiguity and imprint: British racial logics, colonial commissions of enquiry and the Creolization of Britain in the 1930s and 1940s', *Callaloo*, 39/1 (Winter 2016), pp. 166–84.

210. R. Hill (ed.), *The Marcus Garvey and UNIA Papers*, Vol. VIII (London: University of California Press, 1990), p. 664, n. 1.

211. Pennybacker, *From Scottsboro to Munich*, p. 94; Whittall, 'Creolising London', p. 323.

212. R. Hill (ed.), *The Marcus Garvey and UNIA Papers*, Vol. X (London: University of California Press, 2006), pp. 646–8.

213. Matera, *Black London*, p. 94.

214. D. Whittall, 'The conference on African peoples', *History Today*, 65/7 (July 2015), pp. 49–55 and *The Keys*, 5/4 (April–June 1938) p. 84; Adi, *Pan-Africanism and Communism*, p. 288.

215. National Archives, CO 323/1697/5.

216. Makonnen, *Pan-Africanism from Within*, pp. 160–61.

217. Quoted in Whittall, 'Creolising London', p. 282.

218. C. L. R. James, *The Black Jacobins: Toussaint L'Ouverture and the San Domingo Revolution* (New York: Vintage Books, 1989), Appendix, p. 402.

219. C. Posgrove, *Ending British Rule in Africa: Writers in a Common Cause* (Manchester: Manchester University Press, 2009), p. 5.

220. S. Bourne, *Black in the British Frame: Black People in British Film and Television, 1896–1996* (London: Cassell, 1998), p. 13.

221. M. Duberman, *Paul Robeson* (London: Pan Books, 1989), pp. 109–27.

222. Pennybacker, *From Scottsboro to Munich*, p. 47.

223. Ibid., p. 58.

224. C. Høgsbjerg, *C.L.R. James in Imperial Britain* (London: Duke University Press, 2014), pp. 159–60.

225. Duberman, *Paul Robeson*, p. 627, n. 59.

226. P. Robeson, *Here I Stand* (London: Cassell, 1998), p. 33.

227. Bourne, *Black in the British Frame*, pp. 43–65.

228. Marke, *Old Man Trouble*, p. 136.

229. R. Visram, *Asians in Britain: 400 Years of History* (London: Pluto Press, 2002), pp. 259–60; Adi, *Pan-Africanism and Communism*, p. 279; *Daily Herald*, 11 March 1939, p. 16.

230. Matera, *Black London*, pp. 48–9; Pennybacker, *From Scottsboro to Munich*, p. 49; *The Keys*, 1/3 (January 1934), p. 47.

231. J. Southern, 'W. Rudolph Dunbar: pioneering orchestra conductor', *The Black Perspective in Music*, 9/2 (Autumn 1981), pp. 193–225.

232. Matera, *Black London*, pp. 107 and 146.

233. Makonnen, *Pan-Africanism from Within*, p. 130.

234. J. Cowley, 'London is the place: Caribbean music in the context of empire 1900–60', in P. Oliver (ed.), *Black Music in Britain: Essays on Afro-Asian Contributions to Popular Music* (Milton Keynes: Open University Press, 1990), pp. 61–2.

235. Martin, *Amy Ashwood Garvey*, p. 137; *Hull Daily Mail*, 17 December 1934, p. 3.

236. Matera, *Black London*, p. 168; J. Walkowitz, *Nights Out: Life in Cosmopolitan London* (London: Yale University Press, 2012), pp. 232–46.

237. *Sunday Post*, 2 November 1919, p. 12.

238. H. Rye, 'Fearsome means of discord: early encounters with black jazz', in P. Oliver (ed.), *Black Music in Britain: Essays on Afro-Asian Contributions to Popular Music* (Milton Keynes: Open University Press, 1990), pp. 46–53.

239. J. Green, 'Afro-American symphony: popular black concert hall performers 1900–40', in P. Oliver (ed.), *Black Music in Britain*, p. 40; Val Wilmer, 'Rita Cann', Obituaries, *Guardian*, 10 May 2001, https://www.theguardian.com/news/2001/may/10/guardianobituaries1, accessed 3 June 2020.

240. 'The Deniz Dynasty', Gypsy Jazz UK, https://gypsyjazzuk.wordpress.com/36-2/the-deniz-dynasty/, accessed 28 May 2020.

241. C. Tackley, 'Tiger Bay and the routes/roots of black British jazz', in J. Toynbee, C. Tackley and M. Doffman (eds.), *Black British Jazz: Routes, Ownership and Performances* (London: Ashgate, 2014), pp. 43–62.

242. Ibid., p. 59.

243. Cowley, 'London is the place', p. 63.

244. Tackley, 'Tiger Bay', p. 62; Rye, 'Fearsome means of discord: early encounters with black jazz', pp. 56–7.

245. R. Makonnen, *Pan-Africanism from Within, As Recorded and Edited by Kenneth King* (London: Oxford University Press, 1973), p. 127.

246. Matera, *Black London*, pp. 55–8.

247. M. Herbert, *Never Counted Out: The Story of Len Johnson, Manchester's Black Boxing Hero and Communist* (Manchester: Dropped Aitches Press, 1992), pp. 1–7.

248. Ibid., p. 21, n. 42.

249. Ibid., p. 41.

250. Ibid., p. 19.

251. Ibid.

252. Ibid., p. 15.

253. J. Turpin and W. Fox, *Battling Jack: You Gotta Fight Back* (Edinburgh: Mainstream Publishing, 2005), p. 280.

254. *The Keys*, 1/1 (July 1933), pp. 11–13; 1/2 (October 1933), p. 26; 2/2 (October–December 1934), pp. 30, 44.

255. P. Vasili, *Colouring Over the White Line: The History of Black Footballers in Britain* (Edinburgh: Mainstream Publishing, 2000), p. 62; The Jack Leslie Campaign, https://jackleslie.co.uk/, accessed 5 June 2020.

256. Vasili, *Colouring Over the White Line*, p. 63; 'King' Charles: Everton (Trinidad and Tobago), Everton FC Heritage Society, http://efcheritagesociety.com/?p=4296, accessed 8 June 2020.

257. Vasili, *Colouring Over the White Line*, pp. 64–5.

258. Ibid., pp. 63–4.

259. *Gloucestershire Echo*, 7 April 1938, p. 7; 5 April 1938, p. 7.

260. *Glamorgan Advertiser*, 28 January 1938, p. 6.

CHAPTER 8: THE SECOND WORLD WAR AND AFTER

1. K. John, '"You ask for bread, they give you hot lead": When Caribbean radicals protested against conscription for colonial subjects', in H. Adi (ed.), *Black British History: New Perspectives* (London: Zed Books, 2019), pp. 71–89; National Archives, MEPO 38/91; *The Crisis* (November 1939), pp. 327–8.

2. *Crisis* (November 1939), pp. 327–8.

3. G. Padmore, 'England's West Indian slums', *Crisis*, October 1940, pp. 317–18 and 322.

4. M. Sherwood, *World War II Colonies and Colonials* (London: Savannah Press, 2013), p. 9; G. Padmore, 'Democracy not for colored races', *Crisis* (January 1940), pp. 13 and 25.

5. G. Padmore, 'Fascism invades West Africa', *The Crisis* (October 1939), pp. 297–8.

6. L. James, *George Padmore and Decolonization from Below: Pan-Africanism, the Cold War and the End of Empire* (London: Palgrave Macmillan, 2015), p. 50.

7. Sherwood, *World War II*, p. 20; D. Whittall, 'The conference on Africans', *History Today*, 65/7 (1 July 2015), pp. 49–55.

8. *Wāsù*, 7/1 (May 1940), p. 15.

9. James, *George Padmore*, pp. 52–3.

10. H. Moody and W. Mumford, 'Colored peoples in the British Empire', *Crisis* (June 1940), pp. 174 and 186.

11. Obituaries: 'Major Seth Anthony: The first black African commissioned into the British Army', 19 March 2009, *Independent*, https://www.independent.co.uk/news/obituaries/major-seth-anthony-the-first-black-african-commissioned-into-the-british-army-1648287.html, accessed 22 June 2020.

12. J. Buggins, 'West Indians in Britain during the Second World War: a short history drawing on Colonial Office papers', in *Imperial War Office Review*, no. 5 (1990), pp. 86–97.

13. Sherwood, *World War II*, pp. 36–8.

14. Ibid., pp. 48–51.

15. Ibid., pp. 5–6.

16. R. Sawyer and A. Bagshaw, *Colour Bar: by a White Woman and a Black Man* (London: no date).

17. Sherwood, *World War II*, pp. 15–17.

18. M. Sherwood, *Many Struggles: West Indian Workers and Service Personnel in Britain, 1939–1945* (London: Karia Press, 1985), p. 1.

19. Ibid., pp. 4–6; R. Wellesley Cole, *An Innocent in Britain* (London: Campbell Matthews & Co., 1988), p. 151.

20. Sherwood, *Many Struggles*, p. 15.

21. E. Jones to Capt. H. Fagnani, 25 September 1939, Solanke Papers (SOL 58), University of Lagos, Nigeria. *Wāsù*, 7/1 (May 1940), p. 16; *West Africa*, 28 October 1939, p. 1453.

22. H. Adi, *West Africans in Britain 1900–1960: Nationalism, Pan-Africanism and Communism* (London: Lawrence and Wishart, 1998), p. 91; Moody and Mumford, 'Colored peoples in the British Empire', pp. 174 and 186.

23. K. Little, *Negroes in Britain: A Study of Racial Relations in English Society* (London: Kegan Paul, 1947), p. 117, n. 1; S. Bourne, *Mother Country: Britain's Black Community on the Home Front, 1939–45* (London: The History Press, 2010), p. 66.

24. E. I. Ekpenyon, *Some Experiences of an African Air-Raid Warden*, West End at War series, City of Westminster and the Heritage Lottery Fund, http://westendatwar.org.uk/documents/E._Ita_Ekpenyon_download_version_.pdf, accessed 6 July 2020.

25. Ibid., p. 16.

26. Ibid., p. 20.

27. *LCP Newsletter*, 7 (April 1940), p. 13.

28. *Daily Herald*, 11 January 1940, p. 7; Sherwood, *Many Struggles*, p. 7; House of Commons, 'Royal Navy', debated 24 January 1940, Vol. 356, *Hansard historic record*, https://hansard.parliament.uk//Commons/ 1940-01-24/debates/0c074adf-5f9d-4d09-aabd-6e200f871145/Royal-Navy#contribution-b358a7ea-7719-4d14-b5a7-f8e875e01f5c, accessed 22 February 2022; *Daily Record*, 11 January 1920, p. 5; 25 January 1940, p. 4.

29. Sherwood, *Many Struggles*, pp. 6–7.

30. Ibid., p. 11.

31. *Crisis* (March 1941), p. 72.

32. Bourne, *Mother Country*, pp. 19–21.

33. Sherwood, *World War II*, p. 17.

34. R. Lambo, '*Achtung! The Black Prince*: West Africans in the Royal Air Force, 1929–46', in D. Killingray (ed.), *Africans in Britain* (London: Frank Cass, 1994), pp. 145–63.

35. Sherwood, *Many Struggles*, p. 4; Moody and Mumford, 'Colored peoples in the Empire', p. 174.

36. Lambo, 'West Africans in the Royal Air Force', pp. 148–9.

37. Sherwood, *Many Struggles*, p. 6.

38. Ibid., pp. 30–31; Buggins, 'West Indians in Britain', pp. 86–97.

39. *Crisis* (March 1941), pp. 72–5, 82.

40. Ibid.

41. *LCP Newsletter*, 15 (December 1940), p. 49.

42. J. Bourne, *The Motherland Calls: Britain's Black Servicemen and Women* (London: The History Press, 2012), pp. 97–101; *Lancashire Evening Post*, 29 January 1945, p. 3; Lambo, 'West Africans in the Royal Air Force', p. 156.

43. Ibid., pp. 152–3.

44. Ibid., p. 154.

45. 'Johnny Smythe', Memorial Gates 1914–18 | 1939–45; https://memori algates.org/history/ww2/participants/african/johnny-smythe.html, accessed 17 June 2020; 'From Sierra Leone to Stalag Luft I; remembering Johnny Smythe', Museum of London, https://www.museumoflondon. org.uk/discover/sierra-leone-stalag-luft-i-remembering-johnny-smythe, accessed 17 June 2020.

46. Lambo, 'West Africans in the Royal Air Force', pp. 154–6.

47. Ibid., pp. 158–9.

48. Buggins, 'West Indians in Britain', p. 92.

49. Lambo, 'West Africans in the Royal Air Force', pp. 161–2; Sherwood, *World War II*, p. 29.

50. D. Thompson, *From Kingston to Kenya: The Making of a Pan-Africanist Lawyer* (Dover: The Majority Press, 1993); C. Grant, *'A Member of the RAF of Indeterminate Race': WW2 Experiences of a former RAF Navigator and POW* (Bognor Regis: Woodfield, 2006); E. Martin Noble, *Jamaican Airman* (London: New Beacon Books, 1984). Also M. Johnson, *Caribbean Volunteers at War: The Forgotten Story of Britain's Tuskegee Airmen* (Barnsley: Pen and Sword Books, 2014); R. Murray, *Lest We Forget: The Experiences of World War II West Indian Ex-Service Personnel* (Nottingham: Nottingham West Indian Combined Ex-Services Association, 1996).

51. Johnson, *Caribbean Volunteers at War*, p. 3.

52. Murray, *Lest We Forget*, pp. 13, 55.

53. Ibid., p. 75.

54. D. Horsley, *Billy Strachan, 1921–1998: RAF Officer, Communist, Civil Rights Pioneer, Legal Administrator, Internationalist and Above All Caribbean Man* (London: Caribbean Labour Solidarity, 2019), pp. 11–12.

55. 'Pilots of the Caribbean: volunteers of African heritage in the Royal Air Force', https://www.rafmuseum.org.uk/research/online-exhibitions/pilots-of-the-caribbean.aspx accessed 23 June 2020.

56. Murray, *Lest We Forget*, p. 80.

57. Thompson, *From Kingston to Kenya*, p. 23.

58. Ibid., p. 30.

59. Johnson, *Caribbean Volunteers at War*, pp. 126–34.

60. 'Pilots of the Caribbean: volunteers of African heritage in the Royal Air Force', accessed 23 June 2020.

61. Johnson, *Caribbean Volunteers at War*, pp. 123–5.

62. Interview with Josephine Florent, June 1994.

63. Sherwood, *World War II*, p. 74.

64. B. Bousquet and C. Douglass, *West Indian Women at War: British Racism in World War II* (London: Lawrence and Wishart, 1991), p. 130.

65. Ibid., pp. 127–40.

66. Ibid., p. 2.

67. Ibid., pp. 82–106.

68. Buggins, 'West Indians in Britain,' pp. 93–4.

69. Audrey Dewgee, 'Nadia Cattouse', Historycal Roots, http://historycal-roots.com/nadia-cattouse#_ftnref2, accessed 10 July 2020.

70. S. King, *Climbing Up the Rough Side of the Mountain* (London: Minerva Press, 1998).

71. Murray, *Lest We Forget*, p. 78.

72. Ibid., pp. 97–123.

73. *Manchester Evening News*, 28 September 1946, p. 5.

74. Murray, *Lest We Forget*, pp. 107–9.

75. R. Makonnen, 'Pan-Africanism from within', as recorded and edited by Kenneth King, *Journal of African History* (Nairobi: Oxford University Press, 1973), pp. 141–3.

76. Sherwood, *Many Struggles*, p. 99; A. Ford, *Telling the Truth: The Life and Times of the British Honduras Forestry Unit in Scotland, 1941–44* (London: Karia Press, 1985); Buggins, 'West Indians in Britain', pp. 87–8. Vicki Allan, 'The last lumberjack: Sam Martinez left his homeland of British Honduras in 1941', 15 January 2006, *Herald*, https://www.heraldscotland.com/news/12443406.the-last-lumberjack-sam-martinez-left-his-homeland-of-british-honduras-in-1941-bound-for-a-new-life-as-a-woodcutter-in-scotland-now-96-he-shares-his-wisdom-with-vicky-allan-and-talks-about-changed-times-staying-positive-and-life-as-a-local-celebrity/, accessed 24 June 2020.

77. Ford, *Telling the Truth*, p. 50.

78. Sherwood, *Many Struggles*, p. 109.

79. Quoted in A. Forbes, 'The British Empire and the war effort: a comparative study of the experiences of the British Honduran Forest Unit and the Newfoundland Overseas Forestry Unit', BA dissertation, University of East Anglia, p. 22, https://www.uhi.ac.uk/en/t4-media/one-web/university/research/centre-for-history/students/Angela-Forbes-Dissertation.pdf, accessed 29 June 2020.

80. Ford, *Telling the Truth*, pp. 81–3.

81. Ibid., pp. 88–96.

82. Sherwood, *Many Struggles*, p. 121; Ford, *Telling the Truth*, pp. 79–80.

83. A. Richmond, *Colour Prejudice in Britain: A Study of West Indian Workers in Liverpool, 1941–1951* (London: Routledge & Kegan Paul, 1954); Buggins, 'West Indians in Britain', pp. 88–90.

84. C. Wilson, 'Liverpool's black population during World War II', *Black and Asian Studies Newsletter* (January 1998), pp. 6–18.

85. Sherwood, *Many Struggles*, p. 61.

86. Ibid., pp. 63–4.

87. Wilson, 'Liverpool's black population during World War II', pp. 6–18.

88. Sherwood, *Many Struggles*, p. 66.

89. Ibid., p. 69.

90. Letter from representative of colonial employees to J. C. Hyland, 14 August 1942. Solanke Papers, University of Lagos, Nigeria.

91. Sherwood, *Many Struggles*, pp. 73–8.

92. J. Belchem, *Before the Windrush: Race Relations in 20th-Century Liverpool* (Liverpool: Liverpool University Press, 2014), pp. 82–3.

93. Belchem, *Before the Windrush*, p. 86.

94. Sherwood, *Many Struggles*, p. 80.

95. Ibid., p. 79.

96. J. Southern, 'W. Rudolph Dunbar: pioneering orchestra conductor', *The Black Perspective in Music*, 9/2 (Autumn 1981), pp. 193–225; M. Matera, *Black London: The Imperial Metropolis and Decolonization in the Twentieth Century* (Oakland: University of California Press, 2015), pp. 306–7.

97. Bousquet and Douglass, *West Indian Women at War*, pp. 166–9.

98. D. Buckle, 'Colour Bar', *World News and Views*, 22/47 (21 November 1942), pp. 453–4.

99. *Daily Mirror*, 4 September 1943, pp. 1, 8; P. Rich, *Race and Empire in British Politics* (Cambridge: Cambridge University Press, 1990), pp. 161, 252–5, n. 94.

100. *Birmingham Daily Gazette*, 24 September 1943, p. 1; *Newcastle Journal*, 24 September 1943, p. 4; *Daily Herald*, 11 September 1943, p. 3; *Daily Mirror*, 24 September 1943, pp. 1, 8.

101. 'They Tried Putting a Colour Ban on Harvests', Holborn Trades Council, 1943, Modern Records Centre, Warwick, MSS.292/805.9/1/140.

102. R. Costello, *Black Salt: Seafarers of African Descent on British Ships* (Liverpool: Liverpool University Press, 2012), p. 176.

103. Bourne, *The Motherland Calls*, p. 27.

104. Ibid., p. 28.

105. Costello, *Black Salt*, p. 172.

106. Abbie Wightwick, 'Tiger Bay legend Patti Flynn has died', 12 September 2020, Wales Online, https://www.walesonline.co.uk/news/wales-news/patti-flynn-cardiff-tiger-bay-18923700, accessed 6 July 2020.

107. M. Sherwood, 'Blacks in the Royal Navy', *BASA Newsletter*, 23 (January 1999), pp. 13–15.

108. Ibid.

109. Bourne, *The Motherland Calls*, p. 83; Annie Kean, 'Allan Wilmot: making a difference – experiences of a black British serviceman', 27 October 2003, WW2 People's War, https://www.bbc.co.uk/history/ww2peopleswar/stories/96/a1921196.shtml, accessed 6 July 2020.

110. Sherwood, *Many Struggles*, pp. 133–7; Buggins, 'West Indians in Britain', p. 87.

111. M. Sherwood, 'Strike! African Seamen, Elder Dempster and the government 1940–1942', *Immigrants and Minorities*, 13/2–3 (July-November 1994), pp. 130–45.

112. Ibid., p. 141.

113. L. Thompson with J. Green, *Swing from a Small Island: The Story of Leslie Thompson* (London: Northway Publications, 2009), p. 119.

114. Bourne, *Mother Country*, p. 69.

115. M. Herbert, *Never Counted Out: The Story of Len Johnson, Manchester's Black Boxing Hero* (Manchester: Dropped Aitches Press, 1992), pp. 63–4.

116. J. Wood, *Bill Miller – Black Labour Party Activist in Plymouth: A Biographical Sketch* (London: History and Social Action, 2006).

117. Bourne, *Mother Country*, pp. 56–62; N. Sinclair, *The Tiger Bay Story* (Cardiff: Butetown History and Arts, 1993), p. 45.

118. *Springtime in a British Village*, 1944, Colonial Film: Moving Images of the British Empire, http://www.colonialfilm.org.uk/node/1923 and https://www.youtube.com/watch?v=6QbHhm4620I, both accessed 15 July 2020; *Daily Mirror*, 2 May 1944, p. 1; *Northampton Mercury*, 5 May 1944, p. 5.

119. *Shields Daily News*, 14 April 1942, p. 2; Vanessa Mongey, 'Spaces of solidarity: the International Coloured Mutual Aid Association and the Colonial House in North Shields', https://pathswaters.wixsite.com/tyne/spaces-of-solidarity, accessed 15 July 2020.

120. Adi, *West Africans in Britain*, p. 106.

121. D. Jarrett-Macauley, *The Life of Una Marson* (Manchester: Manchester University Press, 1998), pp. 144–56.

122. 'A hidden history: African women and the British health service in the 20th century', 2019, Young Historians Project, https://www.younghistoriansproject.org/african-women-and-the-health-service, accessed 16 July 2020.

123. Matera, *Black London*, p. 305.

124. C. Wilson, 'Liverpool's black population during World War II', *Black and Asian Studies Association Newsletter* (January 1998), pp. 6–15; C. Caballero and P. Aspinall, *Mixed Race Britain in the Twentieth Century* (London: Palgrave Macmillan, 2018), p. 200.

125. P. Rich, *Race and Empire in British Politics* (Cambridge: Cambridge University Press, 1990) pp. 149–55; Buggins, 'West Indians in Britain,' pp. 95–6.

126. *Crisis* (March 1943), pp. 76–7.

127. Caballero and Aspinall, *Mixed Race Britain in the Twentieth Century*, pp. 199–236; L. Bland, *Britain's Brown Babies: The Stories of Children Born to Black GIs and White Women in the Second World War* (Manchester: Manchester University Press, 2019).

128. Caballero and Aspinall, *Mixed Race Britain in The Twentieth Century*, p. 206.

129. Ibid.

130. Richmond, *Colour Prejudice in Britain*, pp. 88–9.

131. Ibid., p. 90. Wilson, 'Liverpool's black population', pp. 14–15.

132. G. Schaffer, 'Fighting racism: black soldiers and workers in Britain during the Second World War', in C. Bressey and H. Adi (eds.), *Belonging in Europe: The African Diaspora and Work* (London: Routledge, 2011), pp. 142–61.

133. Ibid., 149.

134. J. Walkowitz, *Nights Out: Life in Cosmopolitan London* (London: Yale University Press, 2012), pp. 248–50.

135. Matera, *Black London*, pp. 308–12; Adi, *West Africans in Britain*, p. 108.

136. Adi, *West Africans in Britain*, p. 111.

137. Ibid., p. 96.

138. Ibid., pp. 101–2.

139. Ibid., pp. 96–101.

140. *West Africa*, 20 February 1943, p. 144.

141. C. Polsgrove, *Ending British Rule in Africa: Writers in a Common Cause* (Manchester: Manchester University Press, 2009), p. 58; L. James, *George Padmore and Decolonization from Below: Pan-Africanism, the Cold War and the End of Empire* (Basingstoke: Palgrave Macmillan, 2015), pp. 52–3.

142. League of Colored Peoples, 'Charter for Colored Peoples', February 1945, UMassAmherst, Special Collections and University Archives, https://credo.library.umass.edu/view/full/mums312-b106-i209, accessed 24 July 2020.

143. H. Adi and M. Sherwood, *The 1945 Manchester Pan-African Congress Revisited* (London: New Beacon, 1995), p. 13.

144. P. Blackman, *Footprints: Poems by Peter Blackman* (London: Smokestack Books, 2013), pp. 31–6.

145. G. Padmore, 'Industrialised Soviet backs Red Army', *The Crisis* (June 1943), pp. 173–4, 179, 186.

146. G. Padmore and D. Pizer, *How Russia Transformed Her Colonial Empire: A Challenge to the Imperialist Powers* (London: Dennis Dobson, 1946).

147. M. Sherwood, *Manchester and the 1945 Pan-African Congress* (London: Savannah Press, 1995), pp. 72–4.

148. Adi and Sherwood, *The 1945 Manchester Pan-African Congress Revisited*, p. 13.

149. Ibid., p. 27, n. 9.

150. Letter from G. Padmore to W. E. B. Du Bois, 17 August 1945, UMass-Amherst, Special Collections and University Archives, https://credo.library.umass.edu/view/full/mums312-b107-i440, accessed 20 July 2020.

151. Sherwood, *Manchester and the 1945 Pan-African Congress*, pp. 7–10.

152. Ibid., pp. 65–71.

153. Makonnen, 'Pan-Africanism from within', p. 131.

154. E. Marke, *Old Man Trouble* (London: Weidenfeld & Nicolson, 1975), pp. 136–7.

155. P. Weiler, *British Labour and the Cold War* (Stanford: Stanford University Press, 1988), p. 54.

156. Adi and Sherwood, *The 1945 Manchester Pan-African Congress Revisited*, pp. 14–15; G. Padmore (ed.), *The Voice of Coloured Labour* (Manchester: Panaf, 1945).

157. Adi and Sherwood, *The 1945 Manchester Pan-African Congress Revisited*, p. 15.

158. Ibid., pp. 28–9, n. 18.

159. World Federation of Trade Unions, *A Call to All the Peoples* (London: World Federation of Trade Unions, 1945), p. 3.

160. Adi and Sherwood, *The 1945 Manchester Pan-African Congress Revisited*, pp. 16–17.

161. Ibid.

162. Ibid., p. 18.

163. M. Sherwood, 'The All Colonial Peoples' conferences in Britain, 1945', 1 May 2018, *Leeds African Studies Bulletin*, 79 (2017–2018), https://lucas.leeds.ac.uk/article/the-all-colonial-peoples-conferences-in-britain-1945/, accessed 1 May 2020.

164. M. Sherwood, '"There is no new deal for the black man in San Francisco": African attempts to influence the founding conference of the United Nations, April–July 1945', *International Journal of African Historical Studies*, 29/1 (1996), pp. 71–94.

165. Adi and Sherwood, *The 1945 Manchester Pan-African Congress Revisited*, pp. 19–21.

166. Padmore, *The Voice of Coloured Labour*, pp. 44–5.

167. Adi and Sherwood, *The 1945 Manchester Pan-African Congress Revisited*, pp. 23–4.

168. Ibid., pp. 25–6.

169. Adi, *Pan-Africanism: A History*, p. 125.

170. K. Nkrumah, *The Autobiography of Kwame Nkrumah* (London: Panaf Books, 1979), pp. 43–4.

171. Sherwood, *Manchester and the 1945 Pan-African Congress*, pp. 42, 52; Adi and Sherwood, *The 1945 Manchester Pan-African Congress Revisited*, pp. 141–2.

172. W. E. B. Du Bois, 'Report on the fifth Pan-African Congress', October 1945, UMassAmherst, Special Collections and University Archives, https://credo.library.umass.edu/view/full/mums312-b107-i460, accessed 24 July 2020.

173. Sherwood, *Manchester and the 1945 Pan-African Congress*, p. 32.

174. Adi and Sherwood, *Manchester Pan-African Congress*, p. 98.

175. Ibid., pp. 55–6.

176. Ibid., pp. 57–9.

177. *Picture Post*, 10 November 1945.

178. Adi and Sherwood, *Manchester Pan-African Congress*, p. 32, n. 51.

179. A. Francis, 'Committed black women: Britain's black women radicals 1965–1985', PhD thesis, University of Chichester (forthcoming), p. 17.

180. Nkrumah, *The Autobiography of Kwame Nkrumah*, p. 45.

181. M. Sherwood, *Kwame Nkrumah and the Dawn of the Cold War: The West African National Secretariat 1945–48* (London: Pluto Press, 2019).

182. Ibid., p. 52.

183. *Aims and Object of the West African National Secretariat* (London: West African National Secretariat, 1946).

184. Nkrumah, *Autobiography*, pp. 46–7.

185. Adi, *West Africans in Britain*, pp. 130.

186. Correspondence from Nii Odoi Annan to M. Sherwood, 9 February 1996. (I'm very grateful to Marika Sherwood for sharing this important correspondence with me.) See also M. Sherwood, 'Kwame Nkrumah: The London Years, 1945–1947', in D. Killingray (ed.), *Africans in Britain* (London: Frank Cass, 1994), pp. 164–95.

187. Nkrumah, *Autobiography*, p. 50.

188. Sherwood, *Kwame Nkrumah and the Dawn of the Cold War*, p. 125.

189. Ibid., p. 130.

190. Ibid., p. 70.

191. Makonnen, 'Pan-Africanism from within', p. 145.

192. Adi and Sherwood, *The Manchester Pan-African Congress Revisited*, pp. 47–9; C. Posgrove, *Ending British Rule in Africa: Writers in a Common Cause* (Manchester: Manchester University Press, 2009), pp. 76–7.

193. L. James, *George Padmore and Decolonization from Below: Pan-Africanism, The Cold War and the End of Empire* (London: Palgrave, 2015), pp. 98–103.

194. *Western Daily Press*, 25 October 1946, p. 3.

195. R. Costello, *Black Salt: Seafarers of African Descent on British Ships* (Liverpool: Liverpool University Press, 2012), pp. 181–5; K. King (ed.), *Ras Makonnen: Pan-Africanism from within* (London: Oxford University Press, 1973), pp. 139–40.

196. *Western Daily Press*, 18 November 1946, p. 1.

197. Makonnen, 'Pan-Africanism from within', pp. 139–41.

198. *Pan-Africa*, 1/2 (February 1947), p. 4.

199. *Pan-Africa, Nigerian Prospect* (October–December 1947); G. Padmore, *Pan-Africanism or Communism: The Coming Struggle for Africa* (London: Dennis Dobson, 1956), p. 153.

200. *Pan-Africa*, 1/2 (February 1947), p. 30; J. Hooker, *Black Revolutionary: George Padmore's Path from Communism to Pan-Africanism* (London: Pall Mall Press, 1967), p. 103.

201. Polsgrove, *Ending British Rule in Africa*, pp. 88–9; Padmore, *Pan-Africanism or Communism*, p. 152; G. Shepperson and S. Drake, 'The fifth Pan-African conference, 1945 and the All-African People's Congress, 1958', *Contributions to Black Studies*, 8/5 (1986), pp. 35–66.

202. 'Aircraft – Swift Scale Prosecution', 1941, National Archives, LAB 10/125.

CHAPTER 9: THE POST-WAR WORLD

1. David Clover, 'Dispersed or destroyed: archives, the West Indian Students Union, and public memory', Annual Conference Papers, *Society for Caribbean Studies*, Vol. 6 (2005), https://sas-space.sas.ac.uk/3117/1/olvol6p10.PDF, accessed 1 March 2020.

2. H. Adi, *West Africans in Britain: Nationalism, Pan-Africanism and Communism* (London: Lawrence and Wishart, 1998), p. 121.

3. Political and Economic Planning, *Colonial Students in Britain: A Report by PEP* (London: PEP, 1955), p. 213.

4. Ibid., p. 213.

5. J. Bailkin, 'The postcolonial family? West African children, private fostering and the British state', *Journal of Modern History*, 81 (March 2009), pp. 87–121.

6. 'A hidden history? African women and the British health service in the 20th century', Young Historians Project, https://www.

younghistoriansproject.org/african-women-and-the-health-service, accessed 1 March 2020.

7. R. Hackett, 'The history of workforce policy and planning in British nursing, 1939–1960', PhD thesis, University of London (2005), p. 11.

8. H. Adi, *West Africans in Britain: Nationalism, Pan-Africanism and Communism* (London: Lawrence and Wishart, 1998), pp. 144–5, 176–7; M. Matera, *Black London: The Imperial Metropolis and Decolonization in the Twentieth Century* (Oakland: University of California Press, 2015), pp. 115–20.

9. Bailkin, 'The postcolonial family?', p. 88; *Times*, 4 June 1966, p. 10; P. Williams, *Precious* (London: Bloomsbury, 2010).

10. Clover, 'Dispersed or destroyed: archives, the West Indian Students Union, and public memory'; L. Braithwaite, *Colonial West Indian Students in Britain* (Jamaica: UWI Press, 2001), pp. 127–81.

11. P. Rich, *Race and Empire in British Politics* (Cambridge: Cambridge University Press, 1990), p. 159.

12. K. Aspden, *The Hounding of David Oluwale* (London: Vintage, 2007), pp. 19–20.

13. SuAndi, *Afro Solo UK: 39 Life Stories of African Life in Greater Manchester 1920–1960* (Manchester: artBlacklive, 2014), pp. 36–41.

14. D. Manley, 'The social structure of the Liverpool Negro community with special reference to the formation of formal associations', PhD thesis, University of Liverpool (1958), p. 71.

15. J. Thakoorin, *Our Lives, Our History, Our Future* (Jim Thakoorin, 2012), pp. 30, 60–68.

16. H. Adi, 'West Africans and the Communist Party in the 1960s', in G. Andrews, N. Fishman and K. Morgan (eds.), *Opening the Books: Essays on the Social and Cultural History of the British Communist Party* (London: Lawrence and Wishart, 1995), pp. 176–94.

17. E. Smith, 'National liberation for whom? The postcolonial question, the Communist Party of Great Britain, and the party's African and Caribbean membership', *International Review of Social History*, 61/2 (August 2016), pp. 283–315.

18. Thakoorin, *Our Lives*, p. 86.

19. *Dundee Evening Telegraph*, 1 April 1947, p. 3; *The Times*, 2 April 1947, p. 2.

20. J. Belchem, *Before the Windrush: Race Relations in 20th-Century Britain* (Liverpool: Liverpool University Press, 2014), pp. 134–5; *Liverpool Echo*,

30 April 1940, p. 2; K. Searle, 'Before Notting Hill: the Causeway Green "riots" of 1949', in H. Adi, *Black British History: New Perspectives* (London: Zed Books, 2019), p. 90.

21. *Western Daily Press*, 23 December 1949, p. 3.

22. Quoted in C. Wills, *Lovers and Strangers: An Immigrant History of Post-War Britain* (London: Penguin Books, 2018), p. 10.

23. C. Harris, 'Post-war migration and the industrial reserve army', in W. James and C. Harris (eds.), *Inside Babylon: The Caribbean Diaspora in Britain* (London: Verso, 1993), p. 19.

24. Searle, 'Before Notting Hill', p. 91.

25. S. Drake, 'The "colour problem" in Britain: a study in social definitions', *Sociological Review*, 3/2 (December 1955), pp. 197–217.

26. *Liverpool Echo*, 30 April 1947, p. 2; 19 February 1949, p. 3; 23 May 1949, p. 3; *Shields Daily News*, 22 January 1947, p. 10.

27. *Southern Daily Echo*, 22 December 1947, p. 1; A. Wilmot, *Now You Know: The Memoirs of Allan Charles Wilmot, WWII Serviceman and Post-war Entertainer* (London: Liberation Publishers, 2015), p. 32.

28. *Daily Mirror*, 11 August 1948, p. 5.

29. Wilmot, *Now You Know*, p. 32.

30. *Liverpool Echo*, 16 March 1957, p. 29.

31. *Daily Herald*, 22 July 1941, p. 4.

32. J. Turpin and W. Fox, *Battling Jack – You Gotta Fight Back* (London: Mainstream Publishing, 2005), pp. 115–21.

33. Belchem, *Before the Windrush*, p. 133.

34. S. Milne, 'Accounting for the hostel for "coloured colonial seamen" in London's East End, 1942–1949', *National Identities*, 22/4 (2020), https://www.tandfonline.com/eprint/IDIXMXPXARGBRXKMFNP4/full?target=10.1080/14608944.2019.1600484, accessed 10 November 2020; *The Times*, 4 May 1949, p. 2.

35. Belchem, *Before the Windrush*, pp. 134–5.

36. Drake, 'The "colour problem" in Britain', pp. 197–217; A. Richmond, *The Colour Problem* (Harmondsworth: Penguin, 1955), pp. 230–92.

37. D. Renton, 'The attempted revival of British Fascism and Anti-Fascism, 1945–1951', PhD thesis, University of Sheffield (1998).

38. E. Marke, *Old Man Trouble* (London: Weidenfeld & Nicolson, 1975), pp. 136–7; R. Matthews, *Progress: Organ of the Coloured Workers' Association of Great Britain and Ireland, 1948*, pp. 3–4; R. Matthews, *The Man That Speaks the Truth: A Symposium on the Colour Question* (London: Coloured Workers Welfare Association, 1953).

39. S. Milne, 'Accounting for the hostel for "coloured colonial seamen."'

40. *Times*, 31 January 1950, p.2 and 3 February 1949, p. 5.

41. Milne, 'Accounting for the hostel for "coloured colonial seamen"'; Transcription of interview with Kathleen Wrasama, 30 November 1984, Black Cultural Archives (BCA), Myth of the Motherland Collection (Oral 7/20).

42. Harris, 'Post-war migration and the industrial reserve army', p. 24.

43. Angela Cobbinah, 'Mona's musical journey after Windrush', 11 October 2018, http://camdennewjournal.com/article/monas-musical-journey-after-windrush, accessed 11 September 2020.

44. Black Coal Miners Museum Project, https://www.blackcoalminers.com/archives, accessed 11 September 2020.

45. S. King, *Climbing Up the Rough Side of the Mountain* (Peterborough: Upfront Publishing, 1998), pp. 96–113; *Bradford Observer*, 22 June 1948, p. 1; *Forty Winters On: Memories of Britain's Post-war Caribbean Immigrants* (London: Lambeth Council, 1988), p. 11.

46. *Forty Winters On*, pp. 17–18.

47. Ibid., p. 7.

48. Thakoorin, *Our Lives*, pp. 43–9.

49. *Forty Winters On*, pp. 7–10; S. Joshi and B. Carter, 'The role of Labour in the creation of a racist Britain', *Race and Class*, 25/3 (Winter 1984), pp. 53–70.

50. Harris, 'Post-war migration', pp. 24–5.

51. Letter from Clement Attlee to Labour MPs, 5 July 1948, National Archives, https://www.nationalarchives.gov.uk/wp-content/uploads/2014/03/ho-213-715-v2.jpg, accessed 18 September 2020; *Forty Winters On*, p. 5.

52. E. Pilkington, *Beyond the Mother Country: West Indians and the Notting Hill Riots* (London: I. B. Tauris, 1988), p.19.

53. D. Dean, 'Coping with colonial immigration, the Cold War and colonial policy: the Labour government and black communities in Great Britain, 1945–1951', *Immigrants and Minorities*, 6/3 (1987), pp. 305–34.

54. *Bradford Observer*, 22 June 1948, p. 1; *Sphere*, 3 July 1948, p. 22.

55. *Daily Mirror*, 22 June 1948, p. 8.

56. T. Carter, *Shattering Illusions: West Indians in British Politics* (London: Lawrence and Wishart, 1986), pp. 45–7.

57. See, for example, Manley, 'The social structure of the Liverpool Negro community', pp. 208–9.

58. *CLC Monthly Bulletin*, March 1948. (Thanks to Kelly Foster for sharing this important publication with me.)

59. *Federation & Self-Government NOW or Colonialism & Slavery FOR EVER* (London: CLC, n.d.), p. 5.

60. Carter, *Shattering Illusions*, pp. 53–5; D. Horsley, *Billy Strachan, 1921–1998: RAF Officer, Communist, Civil Rights Pioneer, Legal Administrator, Internationalist and Above All Caribbean Man* (London: Caribbean Labour Solidarity, 2019), pp. 13–15.

61. B. Strachan, *Sugar: The Story of a Colony* (London: CLC, 1955).

62. Horsley, *Billy Strachan*, pp. 13–18.

63. Carter, *Shattering Illusions*, pp. 48–55.

64. Ibid., p. 56.

65. Horley, *Billy Strachan*, p. 15.

66. Ibid., p. 20.

67. *LCP Newsletter*, 16/93 (July 1947), pp. 142–5. H. Adi and M. Sherwood, *The Manchester Pan-African Congress Revisited* (London: New Beacon Books, 1995), p. 75.

68. L. Brand, *Britain's 'Brown Babies': The Stories of Children Born to Black GIs and White Women in the Second World War* (Manchester: Manchester University Press, 2019).

69. C. Caballero and P. Aspinall, *Mixed Race Britain in the Twentieth Century* (London: Palgrave Macmillan 2018), pp. 213–14.

70. M. Sherwood, *Pastor Daniels Ekarte and the African Churches Mission* (London: Savannah Press, 1994), pp. 51–76.

71. Caballero and Aspinall, *Mixed Race Britain*, pp. 213–35.

72. https://credo.library.umass.edu/view/pageturn/mums312-b114-i151/#page/7/mode/1up accessed 20 September 2020.

73. Caballero and Aspinall, *Mixed Race Britain*, p. 215.

74. K. Hammond Perry, *London Is the Place for Me: Black Britons, Citizenship and the Politics of Race* (New York: Oxford University Press, 2015), pp. 54–9.

75. Belchem, *Before the Windrush*, pp. 129–31; R. Ramdin, *The Making of the Black Working Class in Britain* (Aldershot: Gower, 1987), pp. 384–7.

76. *Yorkshire Post and Leeds Intelligencer*, 10 August 1948, p. 4.

77. A. Murphy, *From the Empire to the Rialto: Racism and Reaction in Liverpool 1918–1948* (Birkenhead: Liver Press, 1995), pp. 131–51; A. Richmond, *Colour Prejudice in Britain* (London: Routledge and Kegan Paul, 1954), pp. 102–8.

78. *The Times*, 4 August 1948, p. 3.

79. M. Young, 'Racism, tolerance and identity: responses to black and Asian migration into Britain in the national and local press, 1948–72',

PhD thesis, University of Liverpool (2012), pp. 220–26; Murphy, *From the Empire to the Rialto*, p. 34.

80. *Daily Herald*, 4 August 1948, p. 3.
81. Murphy, *From the Empire to the Rialto*, pp. 134–5.
82. Ibid., pp. 135–6, 146.
83. Richmond, *Colour Prejudice in Britain*, pp. 104–7.
84. Ibid., p. 108.
85. C. Fevre, '"Race" and resistance to policing before the "Windrush years": the Colonial Defence Committee and the Liverpool "race riots" of 1948', *Twentieth-Century British History*, 32/1 (2021), pp. 1–23.
86. Manley, 'The social structure of the Liverpool Negro community', PhD thesis, University of Liverpool (1959), p. 230.
87. Belchem, *Before the Windrush*, pp. 143, 147–8.
88. Ibid., pp. 165–9.
89. Pilkington, *Beyond the Mother Country*, p. 49.
90. *The Times*, 2 August 1949, p. 2.
91. *Civil Liberty*, 10/2 (February–March 1950), pp. 1–6; *The Mail*, 23 July 1949.
92. *Civil Liberty*, 10/2 (February–March 1950), pp. 1–6.
93. Searle, 'Before Notting Hill', pp. 91–2.
94. Ibid., p. 94.
95. Pilkington, *Beyond the Mother Country*, p. 51.
96. Searle, 'Before Notting Hill', pp. 95–6.
97. M. Phillips and T. Phillips, *Windrush: The Irresistible Rise of Multi-Racial Britain* (London: HarperCollins, 1998), p. 98.
98. Adi, *West Africans in Britain*, p. 159; *Seretse Khama: A Background Study of the South African Crisis* (Oxford: Oxford University Socialist Club, West African Students Club and West Indian Club, 1950).
99. F. Brockway, *Outside the Right* (London: George Allen & Unwin, 1963), pp. 165–7.
100. House of Commons, 'Colour bar', debated 8 February 1954, Vol. 523, cols. 521–5, *Hansard historic record*, https://api.parliament.uk/historic-hansard/commons/1954/feb/18/colour-bar, accessed 2 October 2020.
101. *Bradford Observer*, 22 August 1951, p. 3.
102. E. Scobie, *Black Britannia: A History of Blacks in Britain* (Chicago: Johnson Publishing Co., 1972), pp. 206–7.
103. Adi, *West Africans in Britain*, pp. 159–60.

104. P. Britton, 'The shameful history of the racist "colour bar" in Manchester: and how a local boxing hero made history by ordering a round in the pub', *Manchester Evening News*, 24 February 2019, https://www.manchestereveningnews.co.uk/news/greater-manchester-news/len-johnson-hulme-colour-bar-15859656, accessed 14 March 2022; M. Herbert, *Never Counted Out: The Story of Len Johnson, Manchester's Black Boxing Hero and Communist* (Manchester: Dropped Aitches Press, 1992), pp. 80–100.

105. A. Chater, *Race Relations in Britain* (London: Lawrence and Wishart, 1966), pp. 33–5; *Forty Winters On: Memories of Britain's Post-war Caribbean Immigrants*, p. 13; Pilkington, *Beyond the Mother Country*, p. 83.

106. *Coloured People from British Colonial Territories*, June 1950, National Archives, CAB 128/17 and *Coloured People from British Colonial Territories*, May 1950, National Archives, CAB 129/40.

107. Harris, 'Post-war migration and the industrial reserve army', p. 28.

108. *Coloured People from British Colonial Territories*, May 1950.

109. Harris, 'Post-war migration and the industrial reserve army', pp. 31–3.

110. Ibid., pp. 38–40.

111. Hackett, 'The history of workforce policy and planning in British nursing, 1939–1960', pp. 165–6; *Yorkshire Post and Leeds Intelligencer*, 18 November 1955, p. 1.

112. Hackett, 'The history of workforce policy and planning in British nursing, 1939–1960', p. 196.

113. *Daily Herald*, 26 February 1954, p. 7.

114. *Birmingham Daily Gazette*, 1 February 1955, p. 1.

115. *Birmingham Daily Gazette,* 10 August 1953, p.1.

116. Pilkington, *Beyond the Mother Country*, pp. 23, 32–3.

117. *Birmingham Daily Gazette*, 10 October 1952, p. 3.

118. *Birmingham Daily Post*, 11 June 1954, p. 11; *Birmingham Daily Gazette*, 8 October 1953, p. 3.

119. *Jamaica Arise*, June 1949, p. 9, Library of Birmingham Archives (LBA), MS 2165/2/1.

120. Emma Hancox, 'Henry Gunther and the campaign for equality', 5 October 2016, the Iron Room, the Library of Birmingham @ Collections and Archives, https://theironroom.wordpress.com/2016/10/05/henry-gunter-and-the-campaign-for-equality/, accessed 30 September 2020.

121. H. Gunter, 'End Colour Bar in Britain', *Caribbean News*, 1/4 (February 1953), pp. 1 and 6, LBA, MS 2165/2/4.

122. *Birmingham Daily Gazette*, 13 July 1952, p. 1.

123. *Birmingham Daily Gazette*, 8 October 1953, p. 3.

124. *Birmingham Daily Gazette*, 25 November 1953, p. 3.

125. F. Tait, 'Henry Charles Gunter', *Oxford Dictionary of National Biography*, https://doi.org/10.1093/ref:odnb/105624, accessed 30 September 2020.

126. H. Gunter, *A Man's a Man: A Study of the Colour Bar in Birmingham and an Answer*, LBA MS 2165/2/5.

127. *Birmingham Daily Post*, 10 November 1954, p. 23; *Birmingham Daily Gazette*, 15 November 1954, p. 1.

128. *Birmingham Daily Gazette*, 18 October 1954, p. 5.

129. Pilkington, *Beyond the Mother Country*, pp. 26–30; *Daily Herald*, 1 March 1955, p. 1.

130. *Birmingham Daily Post*, 14 March 1955, p. 26.

131. *Colonial Immigrants*, June 1956, National Archives, CAB 129/81.

132. B. Carter, C. Harris, S. Joshi, 'The 1951–55 Conservative government and the racialization of black immigration', in James and Harris, *Inside Babylon*, pp. 55–67; *Colonial Immigrants*, November 1954, National Archives, CAB 129/72; *Colonial Immigrants*, June 1955, National Archives, CAB 129/75.

133. Pilkington, *Beyond the Mother Country*, pp. 87–8, 92.

134. F. van Hartesveltd, 'Race and political parties in Britain 1954–1965', *Phylon*, 44/2 (1983), pp. 126–34; Carter, Harris, Joshi, 'The 1951–55 Conservative government', pp. 62–3.

135. *Colonial Immigrants*, June 1956.

136. Ibid., November 1956, National Archives, CAB 129/81.

137. Carter, *Shattering Illusions*, p. 44.

138. Pilkington, *Beyond the Mother Country*, p. 38.

139. Ibid., p. 39.

140. Ibid., pp. 41–52.

141. *Birmingham Daily Post*, 7 July 1958, p. 16.

142. Pilkington, *Beyond the Mother Country*, pp. 41–52; House of Commons, 'Race discrimination: no. 2', debated 8 July 1958, Vol. 591, cols. 205–7, *Hansard historic record*, https://api.parliament.uk/historic-hansard/commons/1958/jul/08/race-discrimination-no-2, accessed 2 October 2020.

143. Pilkington, *Beyond the Mother Country*, pp. 68–9.

144. *Daily Herald*, 26 August 1958, p. 4.

145. Pilkington, *Beyond the Mother Country*, pp. 98–100.

146. Ibid., pp. 104–5.

147. Phillips and Phillips, *Windrush*, p. 166.

148. *Daily Herald*, 26 August 1958, p. 3; Phillips and Phillips, *Windrush*, p. 158.

149. Scobie, *Black Britannia*, pp. 210–13.

150. *Daily Herald*, 25 August 1958, p. 1.

151. Phillips and Phillips, *Windrush*, p. 169.

152. Pilkington, *Beyond the Mother Country*, pp. 109–11; *Daily Herald*, 26 August 1958, p. 1.

153. *People*, 31 August 1958, p. 1.

154. Scobie, *Black Britannia*, p. 217.

155. Hammond Perry, *London Is the Place for Me*, p. 122.

156. Pilkington, *Beyond the Mother Country*, pp. 112–20; Phillips and Phillips, *Windrush*, pp. 172–3.

157. Pilkington, *Beyond the Mother Country*, p. 121.

158. D. Howe, 'Fighting back: West Indian youth and the police in Notting Hill', *Race Today* (December 1974), pp. 335–7.

159. Pilkington, *Beyond the Mother Country*, p. 126.

160. Ibid., p. 131.

161. *The Times*, 3 September 1958, p. 7; 4 September 1958, p. 11.

162. *Birmingham Post*, 5 September 1958, p. 13.

163. *The Times*, 4 September 1958, p. 10.

164. Pilkington, *Beyond the Mother Country*, p. 142.

165. 'Racial disturbances', 8 September 1958, National Archives, CAB 128/32.

166. Pilkington, *Beyond the Mother Country*, pp. 140–41.

167. M. Sherwood, *Claudia Jones: A Life in Exile* (London: Lawrence and Wishart, 1999), p. 93.

168. Pilkington, *Beyond the Mother Country*, p. 142; Sherwood, *Claudia Jones*, pp. 93–4.

169. B. Heinemann, *The Politics of the Powerless: A Study of the Campaign Against Racial Discrimination* (London: Oxford University Press, 1972), pp. 65–75.

170. D. Hinds, 'The *West Indian Gazette*: Claudia Jones and the black press in Britain', *Race and Class*, 50/1 (2008), pp. 88–97.

171. Ibid.; Sherwood, *Claudia Jones*, pp. 125–49, 196–203.

172. C. Jones, 'The Caribbean community in Britain', in B. Johnson, *"I Think of My Mother" – Notes on the Life and Times of Claudia Jones* (London: Karia Press, 1985), p. 152.

173. Hinds, '*West Indian Gazette*: Claudia Jones', p. 92.

174. C. Jones, 'A people's art is the genesis of their freedom', in C. Boyce Davies, *Claudia Jones: Beyond Containment* (Banbury: Ayuba Clarke Publishing, 2011), p. 166.

175. Sherwood, *Claudia Jones*, pp. 150–62.

176. Hammond Perry, *London Is the Place for Me*, p. 133.

177. Sherwood, *Claudia Jones*, p. 157.

178. Ibid., p. 159.

179. Phillips and Phillips, *Windrush*, pp. 181–8.

180. Scobie, *Black Britannia*, pp. 231–5.

181. House of Commons, 'Racial discrimination', debated 4 June 1959, Vol. 606, cols. 369–72, *Hansard historic record*, https://bit.ly/2T2j7eF, accessed 16 October 2020.

182. *The Times*, 18 May 1959, p. 6; *Daily Herald*, 12 June 1959, p. 1.

183. *The Times*, 22 May 1959, p. 7.

184. *Report*, 21 July 1959, National Archives, HO 325/9.

185. Letter from Aka-Bashorun to Harold Macmillan, 18 May 1959, National Archives, CO 1028/50.

186. Hammond Perry, *London Is the Place for Me*, p. 128. Sherwood, *Claudia Jones*, p. 94.

187. *Daily Herald*, 20 May 1959, p. 7.

188. *Report*, 28 May 1959, National Archives, HO 325/9.

189. Sherwood, *Claudia Jones*, pp. 95–6.

190. Ibid., p. 95.

191. Ibid., p. 96; Hammond Perry, *London Is the Place for Me*, pp. 143–6.

192. *Kensington Post*, 12 June 1959, p. 1; Hammond Perry, *London Is the Place for Me*, pp. 147–52.

193. *Kent and Sussex Courier*, 5 June 1959, p. 16; Hammond Perry, *London Is the Place for Me*, pp. 139–43.

194. H. Adi, 'The committee of African organisations', unpublished paper.

195. *United Africa*, December 1965, p. 11.

196. Adi, 'The committee of African organisations'.

197. *United Africa*, June 1961, p. 4.

198. Sherwood, *Claudia Jones*, p. 100; K. Amoo-Gottfried, *What Is CAO?* (London: CAO, 1965).

199. 'Commonwealth immigrants', October 1961, National Archives, CAB 128/35.

200. C. Jones, 'Butler's colour-bar bill mocks Commonwealth', *Race and Class*, 58/1 (2016), pp. 118–21.

201. 'Commonwealth immigrants', October 1961; S. Patterson, *Immigration and Race Relations, 1960–1967* (Oxford: Institute of Race Relations and Oxford University Press, 1969), p. 133.

202. Hammond Perry, *London Is the Place for Me*, pp. 163–8.

203. Sherwood, *Claudia Jones*, pp. 98–9; Hammond Perry, *London Is the Place for Me*, p. 154; Scobie, *Black Britannia*, p. 253.

204. *Birmingham Daily Post*, 18 December 1961, p. 13.

205. Hammond Perry, *London Is the Place for Me*, p. 165.

206. Sherwood, *Claudia Jones*, pp. 98–9.

207. *The Times*, 24 July 1962, p. 14; Hammond Perry, *London Is the Place for Me*, pp. 181–3.

208. Sherwood, *Claudia Jones*, pp. 100–103.

209. Hinds, 'The *West Indian Gazette*: Claudia Jones', p. 90.

210. N. Oppenheim, 'Popular history in the black British press: Edward Scobie's *Tropic* and *Flamingo*, 1960–64', *Immigrants and Minorities*, 37/3 (2019), pp. 136–62; J. Doward, 'Sex, ska and Malcolm X: MI6's covert mission to woo 1960s West Indians', *Guardian*, 26 January 2019, https://www.theguardian.com/world/2019/jan/26/west-indians-flamingo-magazine-m6-anti-communist-mission, accessed 4 November 2020.

211. Scobie, *Black Britannia*, pp. 256–8.

212. Ibid., pp. 267–8.

213. M. Dresser, *Black and White on the Buses: The 1963 Colour Bar Dispute in Bristol* (Bristol: Bristol Broadsides, 1986), pp. 4–12, 36; P. Stephenson, *Memoirs of a Black Englishman* (Bristol: Tangent Books, 2011), p. 46.

214. Dresser, *Black and White on the Buses*, p. 13.

215. Ibid., p. 18.

216. Ibid., pp. 19–23; *Birmingham Daily Post*, 4 May 1963, p. 1; *Daily Herald*, 8 May 1963, p. 5.

217. Stephenson, *Memoirs*, p. 59.

218. Dresser, *Black and White on the Buses*, p. 46.

219. Stephenson, *Memoirs*, pp. 66–8.

220. Patterson, *Immigration and Race Relations*, pp. 308–12.

221. Hammond Perry, *London Is the Place for Me*, pp. 189–90.

222. Ibid., p. 191.

223. Ibid., pp. 216–17.

224. Patterson, *Immigration and Race Relations*, p. 310.

225. A. Sivanandan, *A Different Hunger: Writings on Black Resistance* (London: Pluto, 1982), p. 114.

226. *The Times*, 3 June 1960, p. 35.

227. Hammond Perry, *London Is the Place for Me*, pp. 210–14.

228. J. Hunte, *Nigger Hunting England* (London: West Indian Standing Conference, 1966).

229. Patterson, *Immigration and Race Relations*, pp. 368–71.

230. K. Aspden, *The Hounding of David Oluwale* (London: Vintage, 2007); H. Athwal, 'The racism that kills', *Guardian*, 18 October 2010, https://www.theguardian.com/commentisfree/2010/oct/17/racism-asylum-seekers-uk-laws, accessed 9 November 2020.

231. Heinemann, *The Politics of the Powerless*, pp. 187–8.

CHAPTER 10: BLACK LIBERATION

1. H. Adi, *Pan-Africanism: A History* (London: Bloomsbury, 2018), p. 163.

2. The Times News Team, *The Black Man in Search of Power: A Survey of the Black Revolution Across the World* (London: Nelson, 1968), p. 144; R. Wild, '"Black was the colour of our fight": the transnational roots of British Black Power', in R. Kelley and S. Tuck (eds.), *The Other Special Relationship: Race, Rights, and Riots in Britain and the United States* (New York: Palgrave Macmillan, 2015), pp. 25–46.

3. A. Richardson, 'Bullied and caned, how Bini Brown escaped beatings to form African Caribbean Self-Help Organisation', 19 June 2018, https://www.birminghammail.co.uk/news/midlands-news/bullied-caned-how-bini-brown-14800450, accessed 1 March 2020, K. Connell, *Black Handsworth: Race in 1980s Britain* (London: University of California Press, 2019), p. 154.

4. A. Steven, interview with Elder Bini Brown, 15 February 2016. I am very grateful to Adisa Steven for sharing this interview.

5. A. Steven, interview with Elder Bini Brown.

6. M. Sherwood, *Malcolm X – Visits Abroad, April 1964–February 1965* (Oare: Savannah Press, 2010).

7. *The Times*, 13 February 1965, p. 6.

8. Sherwood, *Malcolm X*, pp. 144–55.

9. Ibid., p. 138.

10. J. Williams, *Michael X: A Life in Black and White* (London: Century, 2008), p. 112.

11. J. Carew, *Ghosts in Our Blood: With Malcolm X in Africa, England and the Caribbean* (Chicago: Lawrence Hill, 1994), p. 8.

12. Williams, *Michael X*, p. 113; R. Waters, *Thinking Black: Britain 1964–1985* (Oakland: University of California Press, 2019), p. 14.

13. K. Hammond Perry, *London Is the Place for Me: Black Britons, Citizenship and the Politics of Race* (New York: Oxford University Press, 2015), pp. 239–43.

14. R. Ramdin, *The Making of the Black Working Class in Britain* (Aldershot: Gower, 1987), pp. 269–71.

15. *Daily Mirror*, 30 August 1965, p. 20; *The Times*, 1 September 1965, p. 10.

16. *The Times*, 20 September 1967, p. 2.

17. Williams, *Michael X*, p. 153.

18. *The Times*, 29 August 1967, p. 2; M. Phillips and T. Phillips, *Windrush: The Irresistible Rise of Multi-Racial Britain* (London: HarperCollins, 1998), pp. 230–41.

19. Interview with Z. Abbas, 1 April 2021.

20. H. Adi, *Pan-Africanism: A History* (London: Bloomsbury, 2018), p. 164.

21. See, e.g., Stokeley Carmichael, Speech given at Garfield High School, Seattle, Washington, 19 April 1967, https://www.aavw.org/special_features/speeches_speech_carmichael01.html, accessed 1 March 2020.

22. S. Carmichael, *Stokely Speaks: From Black Power to Pan-Africanism* (Chicago: Lawrence Hill, 2007), pp. 77–100.

23. *Black Power in the UK*, Special Branch report, 11 August 1970, contributed by E. Lubbers, Special Branch Files Project, https://www.documentcloud.org/documents/6204822-1970-BP-HO-376-154-BP-Intelligence-Reports.html#document/p17/a519890; E. Lubbers, 'Black Power – 4. The Black Power desk', 17 September 2019, http://specialbranchfiles.uk/black-power-4-black-power-desk/, both accessed 20 November 2020.

24. S. Carmichael, *Ready for Revolution: The Life and Struggles of Stokely Carmichael (Kwame Ture)* (London: Scribner, 2003), pp. 572–81.

25. *The Times*, 25 July 1967, p. 1; *Belfast Telegraph*, 11 August 1967, p. 10.

26. Williams, *Michael X*, p. 162; *The Times*, 10 November 1967, p. 3.

27. O. Egbuna, *Destroy This Temple: The Voice of Black Power in Britain* (London: MacGibbon & Kee, 1971), p. 18.

28. J. Wyver, 'Obi Egbuna and the BBC: the story continued', 10 July 2020, Illuminations Blog, https://www.illuminationsmedia.co.uk/obi-egbuna-and-the-bbc-the-story-continued/, accessed 17 November 2020.

29. E. Lloyd, 'Caribbean Artists Movement: 1966–1972', 4 October 2018, British Library, https://www.bl.uk/windrush/articles/caribbean-artists-movement-1966-1972, accessed 1 March 2020.

30. J. Wyver, 'Earl Cameron and a lost play', 6 July 2020, Illuminations Blog, https://www.illuminationsmedia.co.uk/earl-cameron-and-a-lost-play/; N. Bonnelame, 'Black British theatre, 1950–1979', 7 September

2017, British Library, https://www.bl.uk/20th-century-literature/articles/black-british-theatre-1950-1979; C. Chambers, 'Black British plays post World War II–1970s', Black Plays Archive, National Theatre, https://www.blackplaysarchive.org.uk/featured-content/essays/black-british-plays-post-world-war-ii-1970s-professor-colin-chambers, accessed 17 November 2020.

31. H. Goulbourne, *Caribbean Transnational Experience* (London: Pluto, 2002), pp. 136–59.

32. *The Times*, 29 August 1967, p. 2.

33. Ibid., and 20 October 1967, p. 3; interview with Roy Sawh, Sounds from the Park, https://soundsfromthepark.org.uk/people/roy-sawh/, accessed 14 March 2022; 'Watson, Sawh, Ghose et al. charged', contributed by E. Lubbers, Special Branch Files Project, https://www.documentcloud.org/documents/6200123-01081967-BP-DPP-2-4428-Watson-Sawh-Ghose-Et-Al.html, accessed 20 November 2020.

34. Egbuna, *Destroy This Temple*, p. 16.

35. R. Bunce and P. Field, 'Obi B. Egbuna, C. L. R. James and the birth of Black Power in Britain: Black radicalism in Britain 1967–1972', *Twentieth Century British History*, 22/3 (2011), pp. 391–414.

36. *The Times*, 11 September, p. 3; A. Angelo, 'The Black Panthers in London, 1967–1972: a diasporic struggle navigates the Black Atlantic', *Radical History Review*, 103 (2009), pp. 21–2.

37. A. Sivanandan, 'Black Power: the politics of existence', in A. Sivanandan, *A Different Hunger: Writings on Black Resistance* (London: Pluto Press, 1982), pp. 57–66; *The Times*, 14 March 1968, p. 10.

38. Sivanandan, *A Different Hunger*, p. 21; *The Times*, 16 November 1967, p. 4.

39. *Black Power in the UK*, Special Branch Report.

40. Egbuna, *Destroy This Temple*, pp. 19–20.

41. Waters, *Thinking Black: Britain 1964–1985*, p. 35.

42. R. Wild and E. Lubbers, 'Black Power – 2. Main groups', 17 September 2019, Special Branch Files Project, http://specialbranchfiles.uk/2182-2/, accessed 26 November 2020; K. Locke, Transcript of video interview with Paul Okojie, Ahmed Iqbal Race Relations Centre (Manchester: 1992), p. 20; B. Hickman, 'From the archive, 26 November 1969: Black Power group interrupts Manchester Cathedral service', *Guardian*, 26 November 2014, https://www.theguardian.com/world/2014/nov/26/black-power-manchester-cathedral-service-1969, accessed 1 March 2020. Interview with C. Clarke, Roots Family History Project (4 June 2000), Ahmed Iqbal Race Relations Resource Centre, Manchester.

43. Egbuna, *Destroy This Temple*, p. 21; Angelo, 'The Black Panthers in London', pp. 17-35.

44. Egbuna, *Destroy This Temple*, p. 23; K. Nkrumah, 'Message to the Black People of Britain', *Revolutionary Path* (London: PANAF, 2001), pp. 429-35.

45. *The Times*, 26 July 1968, p. 1; 13 August 1968, p. 2; Egbuna, *Destroy This Temple*, p. 10.

46. House of Commons, 'Race Relations Bill', debated 23 April 1968, Vol. 763, *Hansard historic record*, https://bit.ly/2EA99Np, accessed 24 November 2020.

47. R. Wild, '"Black was the colour of our fight": Black Power in Britain 1955-1976', PhD thesis, University of Sheffield (2018), pp. 133-5; Sivanandan, *A Different Hunger*, pp. 25-7; *The Times*, 22 March 1971, p. 2.

48. *The Times*, 17 November 1969, p. 2.

49. T. Ford, *Liberated Threads: Black Women, Style and the Global Politics of Soul* (Chapel Hill: University of North Carolina Press, 2015), pp. 123-57.

50. R. Bunce and P. Field, 'Mangrove 9: Darcus Howe and the extraordinary campaign to expose racism in the police', *New Statesman*, 7 January 2014, https://www.newstatesman.com/politics/2014/01/darcus-howe-and-extraordinary-campaign-expose-racism-police, accessed 24 November 2020; R. Bunce and P. Field, *Darcus Howe: A Political Biography* (London: Bloomsbury, 2014), pp. 51-7.

51. 'Race relations legislation', 8 January 1968, National Archives, CAB 129/135; 'Callaghan: I was wrong on police and race', BBC News, 8 January 1999, http://news.bbc.co.uk/1/hi/special_report/1999/01/99/1968_secret_history/244320.stm, accessed 27 November 2020.

52. 'Benedict Obi Egbuna, Peter Martin and Gideon Turagalevu Dolo: charged with circulating writings at Speakers' Corner, Hyde Park, threatening to kill and maim police officers, involvement of the above-named with "Black Panther" Party', National Archives, MEPO 2/11409; H. Goulbourne, 'Africa and the Caribbean in Caribbean consciousness and action in Britain', 2000, David Nicholls Memorial Lectures, http://www.dnmt.org.uk/wp-content/uploads/2018/06/2000-DNMT-Lecture-Harry-Goulbourne.pdf, accessed 1 March 2020.

53. Wild, '"Black was the colour of our fight"', pp. 100-103; A. Angelo, '"Black oppressed people all over the world are one": the British Black Panthers' grassroots internationalism, 1969-1973', *Journal of Civil and Human Rights*, 4/1 (2018), pp. 64-97.

54. Angelo, '"Black oppressed people all over the world are one"'.

55. Bunce and Field, *Darcus Howe: A Political Biography*, pp. 94–5.

56. Phillips and Phillips, *Windrush*, p. 279.

57. Bunce and Field, *Darcus Howe: A Political Biography*, pp. 100–101.

58. 'Relationship between police and immigrants: Black Power movement; demonstration and march in Notting Hill, London, August 1970 in support of restaurant, Notting Hill; allegations of police discrimination; police sustained injuries; arrests', January 1970–December 1972, National Archives, HO 325/143.

59. P. Brook, 'When cops raided a hip 1970s London café, Britain's Black Power movement rose up', 5 February 2018, Timeline, https://timeline.com/cops-raided-a-1970s-london-cafe-britains-black-power-movement-ff855e7b23f0, accessed 26 November 2020.

60. *The Times*, 10 August 1970, p. 1; 11 August 1970, p. 3; 15 August 1970, p. 2.

61. Bunce and Field, *Darcus Howe: A Political Biography*, p. 120.

62. Ibid., p. 135.

63. L. Jasper, Obituary: Frank Crichlow, founder of Mangrove Community Association, 17 September 2010, Operation Black Vote, https://operationblackvote.wordpress.com/2010/09/17/obituary-a-tribute-to-frank-crichlow-founder-of-mangrove-community-association/ and M. Busby, Obituary: Frank Crichlow, *Guardian*, 26 September 2010, https://www.theguardian.com/world/2010/sep/26/frank-crichlow-obituary-civil-rights-activist, both accessed 26 November 2020.

64. Wild, '"Black is the colour"', p. 90.

65. H. Goulbourne, *Caribbean Transnational Experience* (London: Pluto, 2002), pp. 79–111; H. Goulbourne, *Introducing the Black Unity and Freedom Party 1970–85* (London: BUFP, 1985).

66. Goulbourne, *Introducing the Black Unity and Freedom Party 1970–85*.

67. Ibid.

68. Wild, '"Black is the Colour"', p. 136; Waters, *Thinking Black: Britain 1964–1985*, p. 72.

69. W. C. Johnson, '"The spirit of Bandung" in 1970s Britain: the Black Liberation Front's revolutionary transnationalism', in H. Adi (ed.), *Black British History: New Perspectives* (London: Zed Books, 2019), pp. 125–43; 'The Black Liberation Front', Young Historians Project, https://www.younghistoriansproject.org/blackliberationfront, accessed 1 March 2020.

70. Mao Zedong, 'Statement supporting the American Negroes in their just struggle against racist discrimination by US imperialism', *Peking Review*, 8 August 1963.

71. Johnson, '"The spirit of Bandung"', p. 130.

72. A. Hassan, *Revolutionary Black Nationalism – Unity and Struggle Against Domination* (London: BLF, 1977).

73. *Working Platform of the BLF* (London: Blacklash Publications, 1977).

74. A. Angelo, '"We all became Black": Tony Soares, African American internationalists, and anti-imperialism', in R. Kelly and S. Tuck (eds.), *The Other Special Relationship: Race, Rights, and Riots in Britain and the United States* (London: Palgrave Macmillan, 2015), pp. 95–102.

75. Ibid., p. 100.

76. *Police against Black People: Evidence Submitted to the Royal Commission on Criminal Procedure by the Institute of Race Relations* (London: Institute of Race Relations, 1979).

77. C. Fraser and T. Foot, 'How Yvonne wrote history as UK's first black headteacher', *Camden New Journal*, 5 February 2021, http://islington-tribune.com/article/how-yvonne-wrote-history-as-uks-first-black-headteacher, accessed 1 March 2020.

78. Connell, *Black Handsworth: Race in 1980s Britain*, passim; J. Rex and S. Tomlinson, *Colonial Migrants in a British City* (London: Routledge & Kegan Paul, 1979), pp. 257–62.

79. T. Carter, *Shattering Illusions: West Indians in British Politics* (London: Lawrence and Wishart, 1986), pp. 87–103.

80. Ibid., p. 88.

81. M. Stevens, *Doing Nothing Is Not an Option: The Radical Lives of Eric and Jessica Huntley* (Middlesex: KrikKrak, 2013), pp. 94–5; 'Black Education Movement', George Padmore Institute, https://www.georgepadmoreinstitute.org/collections/the-black-education-movement-1965-1988, accessed 1 March 2020.

82. Carter, *Shattering Illusions: West Indians in British Politics*, p. 85.

83. W. Best, 'John La Rose: The man and the idealist and the shrewd political operator', in *Foundations of a Movement* (London: John La Rose Tribute Committee, 1991), pp. 12–19; 'Black Education Movement', George Padmore Institute.

84. 'The life of a Pan-African community activist in Manchester, UK', Nana Bonsu Oral History Project, https://nanabonsu.com/, accessed 1 March 2020.

85. W. Trew, *Black for A Cause . . . Not Just Because: The Case of the 'Oval 4' and the Story of Black Power in 1970s Britain* (London: Trew Books, 2015), pp. 148–9, 184–286.

86. B. Coard, 'Why I wrote the "ESN book"', *Guardian*, 5 February 2005, https://www.theguardian.com/education/2005/feb/05/schools.uk, accessed 1 March 2020.

87. B. Coard, *How the West Indian Child Is Made Educationally Sub-Normal in the British School System: The Scandal of Black Children in Schools in Britain* (London: New Beacon Books, 1971); F. Dhondy, 'The Black explosion in schools', *Race Today* (February 1974), pp. 44–7.

88. Carter, *Shattering Illusions*, p. 92.

89. Ibid., p. 93.

90. M. Dresser and P. Fleming, *Bristol: Ethnic Minorities and the City 1000–2001* (Chichester: Phillimore, 2007), pp. 170–71.

91. Waters, *Thinking Black: Britain 1964–1985*, pp. 143–51; O. Wyatt, 'The enemy in our midst: "community" and African Caribbean women's provisions for Black youths in Leeds in the 1970s', undergraduate essay, University of Leeds (2020).

92. Waters, *Thinking Black: Britain 1964–1985*, pp. 154–63.

93. *West Indian Children in Our Schools: The Rampton Report* (London: Her Majesty's Stationery Office, 1981), Education in England, http://www.educationengland.org.uk/documents/rampton/rampton1981.html#04 accessed 5 February 2020.

94. *Education for All: The Swann Report* (London: Her Majesty's Stationery Office, 1985), Education in England, http://www.educationengland.org.uk/documents/swann/swann1985.html#18, accessed 5 February 2020.

95. K. Couvée, 'The Black House: photographer looks back at 1970s black youth project', *Camden New Journal*, 22 September 2017, http://islingtontribune.com/article/the-black-house accessed 1 March 2020.

96. Interview with Z. Abbas, 1 April 2021.

97. P. Hetherington, 'In ruins: Britain's oldest and biggest housing association has gone bust, sending shockwaves through the social homes sector', *Guardian*, 16 January 2008, https://www.theguardian.com/society/2008/jan/16/housing.communities, accessed 5 February 2020.

98. *The Times*, 14 November 1969, p. 2; 26 September 1972, p. 4; S. Hall et al., *Policing the Crisis: Mugging, the State and Law and Order* (Basingstoke: Palgrave Macmillan, 2013).

99. Trew, *Black for a Cause*, pp. 23–36.

100. Ibid., pp. 56–7.

101. *The Times*, 13 October 1972, p. 2; 31 July 1973, p. 3; Trew, *Black for a Cause*, p. 53.

102. D. Campbell, 'Final member of the "Oval Four" has 1972 conviction overturned', *Guardian*, 24 March 2020, https://www.theguardian.com/law/2020/mar/24/final-member-oval-four-1972-conviction-overturned-constantine-omar-boucher, accessed 20 December 2020.

103. Trew, *Black for a Cause*, pp. 86–101.

104. *Daily Mirror*, 29 September 1975, p. 15.

105. Interview with Z. Abbas, 1 April 2021; *Liverpool Echo*, 30 September 1975, p. 1.

106. Goulbourne, *Caribbean Transnational Experience*, pp. 79–111; *Black Revolutionary*, 1/1 (December 1971), p. 11.

107. *Who Killed Aseta Simms?*, Black Unity and Freedom Party, no. 1, 1972, Radical History of Hackney, https://hackneyhistory.wordpress.com/2016/09/11/who-killed-aseta-simms-1972/, accessed 3 November 2020.

108. Goulbourne, *Caribbean Transnational Experience*, pp. 107–10.

109. L. Bradley, *Bass Culture: When Reggae Was King* (London: Penguin, 2000), pp. 422–7; M. Farrar, 'Rioting or protesting? Losing it or finding it?', *Parallax*, 18/2 (Summer 2012), pp. 72–91; *Sunday Mirror*, 10 June 1973, p. 15; 13 October 1974, p. 5.

110. 'Black Parents Movement', George Padmore Institute, https://www.georgepadmoreinstitute.org/collections/black-parents-movement-1969-1993, accessed 23 March 2022; Stevens, *Doing Nothing*, pp. 92–4.

111. C. McGlashan, 'The sound system: reggae and the culture of West Indians in London', *Sunday Times Magazine*, 4 February 1973; B. Troyna, 'The reggae war', *New Society*, 10 March 1973, pp. 491–2; 'Dub conferences', *New Society*, 23 March 1978, p. 655.

112. Bradley, *Bass Culture*, pp. 111–32.

113. C. Gayle, 'The reggae underground', *Black Music* 1/8 (July 1974), https://forum.speakerplans.com/reggae-sound-system-list-back-in-the-real-days_topic17036_page3.html, and S. Gelder, 'Charlie Collins: reggae pioneer and founder of Dalston's legendary Four Aces Club dies age 81', *Hackney Gazette*, 28 March 2018, https://www.hackneygazette.co.uk/news/charlie-collins-reggae-pioneer-and-founder-of-dalston-s-legendary-3589042, accessed 25 December 2020.

114. D. Simpson, 'Champion sound! When Huddersfield ruled the British reggae scene', *Guardian*, 31 July 2014, https://www.theguardian.com/music/2014/jul/31/champion-sound-huddersfield-ruled-british-reggae-scene, accessed 25 December 2020; P. Ward, 'Sound system culture:

space and identity in the United Kingdom, 1960–1989', *Historia Contemporanea*, 57 (2018), pp. 349–76.

115. Trew, *Black for a Cause*, p. 199.

116. Bradley, *Bass Culture*, pp. 438–46.

117. Connell, *Black Handsworth: Race in 1980s Britain*, p. 151.

118. Ibid., p. 149.

119. Trew, *Black for a Cause*, pp. 190–94.

120. Ibid., pp. 149–50.

121. C. Beckles, '"We shall not be terrorized out of existence": the political legacy of England's Black bookshops', *Journal of Black Studies*, 29/1 (September 1998), pp. 51–72.

122. Andrews, *Doing Nothing*, pp. 142–6.

123. 'Stories behind the films', Menelik Shabazz, https://menelikshabazz.co.uk/stories-2-2/, accessed 1 March 2020.

124. B. Zephaniah, 'Dis Policeman Keeps On Kicking Me to Death', https://www.youtube.com/watch?v=n_PRL1Z_Li4, accessed 1 March 2020.

125. Trew, *Black for a Cause*, p. 145.

126. Ibid., pp. 200–201.

127. J. Garrett, 'A historical sketch: the sixth Pan-African Congress', *Black World* (March 1975), p. 11.

128. Interview with Z. Abbas, 26 January 2021.

129. Johnson, '"The spirit of Bandung"', pp. 136–7.

130. Trew, *Black for a Cause*, pp. 145–60.

131. R. Walters, *Pan-Africanism in the African Diaspora (An Analysis of Modern Afrocentric Political Movements* (Detroit: Wayne State University Press, 1993), p. 182; Hassan, *Revolutionary Black Nationalism*, p. 1.

132. Goulbourne, *Introducing the Black Unity and Freedom Party 1970–85*, p. 2.

133. Ibid., pp. 5–6.

134. Hassan, *Revolutionary Black Nationalism*, p. 1.

135. C. Steven, 'The evolution of ideas and practices amongst African-centred organisations in the UK, 1975–2015', in H. Adi, *Black British History: New Perspectives* (London: Zed Books, 2019), pp.144–61.

136. Ibid.

137. Wild, '"Black is the colour"', pp. 143–56.

138. *Grassroots* (April–May 1985), pp. 3–4.

139. *Police against Black People*, p. 7.

140. Ibid.

141. Bradley, *Bass Culture*, pp. 422–9.

142. *Police against Black People*, p. 6; *Race Today*, September 1976, pp. 180–83.

143. *The Commission for Racial Equality's Submission to Lord Scarman's Inquiry into Brixton Disorders* (London: CRE, 1981), p. 4.

144. *Race Today*, September 1976, pp.170–79.

145. *The Times*, 31 August 1972, p. 1.

146. Ibid., pp. 1–2.

147. *Race Today*, September 1976, p.170.

148. *Police Against Black People*, pp. 5–6.

149. *The Times*, 1 September 1976, p. 2.

150. *The Times*, 12 August 1977, p. 2.

151. C. Gutzmore, 'Carnival, the state and the black masses in the United Kingdom', in W. James and C. Harris (eds.), *Inside Babylon: The Caribbean Diaspora in Britain* (London: Verso, 1993), pp. 207–30; *The Times*, 30 August 1977, pp. 1–2.

152. *Race Today*, September 1976, p. 171.

153. *Police against Black People*, passim.

154. *The Times*, 15 August 1977, p. 1; 20 February 1978, p. 4.

155. Margaret Thatcher, 'TV interview for Granada, *World in Action*', 27 January 1978, Margaret Thatcher Foundation, https://www.margaretthatcher.org/document/103485, accessed 25 December 2020.

156. *The Times*, 3 April 1980, p. 1.

157. S. Reicher, 'The St Pauls' riot: an explanation of the limits of crowd action in terms of a social identity model', *European Journal of Social Psychology*, 14 (1984), pp. 1–21.

158. L. Churchill, 'The St Paul's riots 37 years on', *Bristol News*, 3 April 2017, https://www.bristolpost.co.uk/news/bristol-news/st-pauls-riots-37-years-17634, accessed 25 December 2020.

159. C. Pierre, 'The New Cross fire of 1981 and its aftermath', in H. Adi, *Black British History: New Perspectives* (London: Zed Books, 2019), pp. 164–75.

160. *The New Cross Massacre Story: Interviews with John La Rose* (London: George Padmore Institute, 2020), pp. 62–3.

161. *The Times*, 14 May 1981, p. 17.

162. *The New Cross Massacre Story*, p. 8; *The Times*, 24 April 1981, p. 2.

163. *The New Cross Massacre Story*, pp. 58–61.

164. *The Times*, 13 April 1981, p. 1.

165. Bunce and Field, *Darcus Howe: A Political Biography*, p. 209.

166. Ibid., pp. 210–11.

167. Phillips and Phillips, *Windrush*, pp. 357–8.

168. 'Brixton riots 1981: What happened 40 years ago in London?', *Newsround*, BBC, 12 April 2021, https://www.bbc.co.uk/newsround/5003 5769, accessed 25 December 2020.

169. *Grassroots* (June–July 1981), p. 3.

170. 'How smouldering tension erupted to set Bristol aflame – archive, 1981', *Guardian*, 13 April 1981, https://www.theguardian.com/theguard ian/1981/apr/13/fromthearchive, accessed 25 December 2020.

171. D. Frost and R. Phillips (eds.), *Liverpool '81: Remembering the Riots* (Liverpool: Liverpool University Press, 2011), pp.1–2.

172. Ibid., p. 9.

173. Stephen Cook, 'Scarman report into Brixton riots published – Archive, 1981', *Guardian*, 6 November 2021, https://www.theguardian.com/world/2021/nov/26/scarman-report-into-brixton-riots-published-archive-1981.

174. *Policing in Hackney, 1945–1984: A Report Commissioned by the Roach Family Support Committee*, Radical History of Hackney, https://hackneyhistory.wordpress.com/2011/03/12/policing-in-hackney-1945-1984/ and *Bulletin of the Roach Family Support Committee*, no. 3, 1983, Radical History of Hackney, https://hackneyhistory.wordpress.com/2015/11/20/roach-family-support-committee-bulletin-3-1983/, accessed 4 February 2020.

175. 'Deaths in custody: songs for Colin Roach', Radical History of Hackney, https://hackneyhistory.wordpress.com/2014/05/18/deaths-in-custody-songs-for-colin-roach/ accessed 4 February 2020.

176. *The Times*, 30 September 1985, pp. 1–3; 9 October 1985, p. 2.

177. 'Jury concludes multiple police failures led to 1985 shooting of Cherry Groce', 10 July 2014, Inquest: Truth, Justice & Accountability, https://www.inquest.org.uk/cherry-groce-inquest-conclusions, accessed 29 January 2021.

178. *The Times*, 7 October 1985, p. 1.

179. T. Gifford, *The Broadwater Farm Inquiry* (London: Karia Press, 1986), pp. 55–86.

180. *The Times*, 17 December 1985, p. 10.

181. Goulbourne, *Introducing the Black Unity and Freedom Party 1970–85*, p. 4.

182. *Working Platform of the BLF* (undated pamphlet in the author's private collection).

183. B. Bryan, S. Dadzie and S. Scarfe, *The Heart of the Race: Black Women's Lives in Britain* (London: Virago Press, 1985), pp. 140–64.

184. B. Bryan, S. Dadzie and S. Scarfe, 'Chain reactions: Black women organising', *Race and Class*, XXVII/1 (Summer 1985), pp. 1–27.

185. *Working Platform of the BLF*, p. 4.

186. A. S. Francis, '"Committed Black Woman": a history of Britain's Black women radicals from 1965–1985', PhD thesis, University of Chichester (forthcoming).

187. Johnson, '"The spirit of Bandung"', p. 129.

188. Bryan, Dadzie and Scarfe, 'Chain reactions', p. 12.

189. Johnson, '"The spirit of Bandung"', p. 129.

190. Interview with Z. Abbas.

191. Francis, '"Committed Black Woman"'.

192. Bryan, Dadzie and Scarfe, *The Heart of the Race*, p. 165.

193. East London Black Women's Organization publicity leaflet.

194. Interview with C. Clark.

195. Francis, '"Committed Black Woman"'; D. Watt and A. Jones, *Catching Hell and Doing Well: Black Women in the UK – the Abasindi Cooperative* (Stoke-on-Trent: Trentham Books, 2015).

196. E. Williams, *The Politics of Race in Britain and South Africa: Black British Solidarity and the Anti-Apartheid Struggle* (London: I. B. Tauris, 2014).

197. Pan-African Congress Movement, *Africa Liberation Day 1981: The Struggle for the Survival of the Black Race* (Birmingham: Pan-African Congress Movement, 1981), p. 7.

198. Williams, *The Politics of Race in Britain and South Africa*, p. 192.

199. *Black Voice*, 20/1 (1989), p. 11.

200. Williams, *The Politics of Race in Britain and South Africa*, p. 233.

201. *Committee for Ethiopian and Eritrean Relief Bulletin*, 1/1 (Spring 1990), p. 2.

CHAPTER 11: INTO THE NEW CENTURY

1. See *Population of England and Wales*, GOV.UK, https://www.ethnicity-facts-figures.service.gov.uk/uk-population-by-ethnicity/national-and-regional-populations/population-of-england-and-wales/latest#main-facts-and-figures, accessed 15 February 2021.

2. In 'Country of Birth', 2011 Census, Office for National Statistics, http://www.nomisweb.co.uk/census/2011/QS213EW/view/2092957703?cols=measures, accessed 15 February 2020.

3. P. Daley, 'Black Africans in Great Britain: spatial concentration and segregation', *Urban Studies*, 35/10 (1998), pp. 1703–8.

4. Central Association of Nigerians in the UK (CANUK), https://www. canukonline.com/about-us, accessed 1 March 2021.

5. Afro Solo UK, http://www.afrosolouk.com/home; 'A hidden history: African women and the British health service in the 20th century', 2019, Young Historians Project, https://www.younghistoriansproject. org/african-women-and-the-health-service, accessed 1 March 2021.

6. Damilola Taylor Trust, https://www.damilolataylortrust.co.uk/about/ damilola-taylor/, accessed 1 March 2021.

7. *The Somali Sailors*, Ethnic Communities Oral History Project, https:// hamunitedcharities.org.uk/wp-content/uploads/2017/06/Somali-Sailors.pdf, accessed 15 March 2021; H. Harris, *The Somali Community in the UK: What We Know and How We Know It* (London: ICAR, 2004).

8. M. Sherwood, 'Racism and resistance: Cardiff in the 1930s and 1940s', *Llafur*, 5/4 (1991), pp. 51–70.

9. D. Styan, 'La Nouvelle Vague? – recent Francophone African settlement in London', in K. Koser (ed.), *New African Diasporas* (London: Routledge, 2003), pp. 17–36.

10. *Somalis in London*, 9 October 2014, Open Society Foundations, https:// www.opensocietyfoundations.org/publications/somalis-london?utm_ source=feedburner&utm_medium=feed and *Appendix One: Supporting New Communities: Case Study of the Somali Community*, May 2011, London Borough of Tower Hamlets, https://democracy.towerhamlets. gov.uk/mgConvert2PDF.aspx?ID=29979, accessed 1 March 2021.

11. C. Zembe, 'Quest for a cohesive African Diaspora community: reliving historic experiences of black Zimbabweans in Britain', in H. Adi, *Black British History: New Perspectives* (London: Zed Books, 2019), pp. 199–217.

12. See J. McGregor, 'Professionals relocating: Zimbabwean nurses and teachers negotiating work and family in Britain', Geographical paper no. 178, University of Reading, February 2006, https://www.reading. ac.uk/web/files/geographyandenvironmentalscience/GP178_Profes sionals_relocating_JAMcGregor_2a.pdf, accessed 1 March 2021.

13. Styan, 'La Nouvelle Vague?', p. 22.

14. 'A hidden history: African women and the British health service in the 20th century', Young Historians Project.

15. J. Buchan and D. Dovlo, *International Recruitment of Health Workers to the UK: A Report for DFID* (London: DFID, 2004).

16. J. Buchan, R. Jobanputra and P. Gough, 'London calling? The recruitment of international health workers to the capital', July 2004, King's

Fund, https://www.kingsfund.org.uk/sites/default/files/field/field_publi
cation_file/london-calling-international-recruitment-health-
workers-to-the-capital-james-buchan-renu-jobanputra-pippa-gough-
kings-fund-1-july-2004.pdf, accessed 1 March 2021.

17. I. Benjamin, *The Black Press in Britain* (Stoke: Trentham Books, 1995),
pp. 47–54.

18. Benjamin, *The Black Press*, p. 68.

19. Ibid., p. 69.

20. A. Chrisafis, 'McCalla, publisher who gave black people a voice, dies',
Guardian, 24 August 2002, https://www.theguardian.com/uk/2002/aug/
24/arts.raceandreligion?INTCMP=SRCH, accessed 20 February 2021.

21. *Marxism Today* (September 1985), pp. 31–7.

22. 'Who were the first MPs from ethnic minority backgrounds?', 28 October 2020, House of Commons Library, https://commonslibrary.
parliament.uk/who-were-the-first-mps-from-ethnic-minority-
backgrounds/, accessed 20 February 2021.

23. H. Athwal and J. Bourne, 'Martha Osamor: unsung hero of Britain's
black struggle', 17 November 2015, Institute of Race Relations, https://
irr.org.uk/article/martha-osamor-unsung-hero-of-britains-black-
struggle/, accessed 20 February 2021.

24. 'Londoners hear about the history of Black History Month in the UK',
African Voice, 7 December 2018, http://africanvoiceonline.co.uk/
londoners-hear-about-the-history-of-black-history-month-in-the-uk/,
accessed 20 February 2021.

25. 'Wandsworth borough changes Diversity Month back to Black History
Month after criticisms of erasure', 30 October 2019, https://london-
newsonline.co.uk/wandsworth-borough-changes-diversity-month-
back-to-black-history-month-after-criticisms-of-erasure/, accessed 20
February 2021.

26. J. Gundara and I. Duffield (eds.), *Essays on the History of Blacks in
Britain* (Aldershot: Avebury, 1992), pp. 1–7.

27. *West Indian Digest*, September 1982, pp. 27–33.

28. Black Cultural Archives, https://blackculturalarchives.org/, accessed 20
February 2021.

29. H. Ishmael, 'The development of black-led archives in London', PhD
thesis, University College London (2020), pp. 119–26.

30. The Mayor's Commission on African and Asian Heritage, *Delivering
Shared Heritage* (London: GLA, 2005), p. 3.

31. Archive, 1985: 'Bill Morris becomes first black person to win position
of power in a British union', *Guardian*, 18 September 1985, https://

www.theguardian.com/politics/2020/sep/18/bill-morris-elected-deputy-general-secretary-tgwu-union-1985, accessed 5 March 2021.

32. T. Wigmore, 'By being blinded by colour, racist sports teams are hampering themselves', *i*, 8 February 2018, https://inews.co.uk/sport/football/racist-sports-teams-hampering-themselves-124512, accessed 5 March 2021.

33. S. Jeffrey and agencies, 'First black Church of England archbishop appointed', *Guardian*, 17 June 2005, https://www.theguardian.com/world/2005/jun/17/religion.immigrationpolicy, accessed 1 March 2021.

34. 'Theatre of Black Women', Unfinished Histories: Recording the History of Alternative Theatre, https://www.unfinishedhistories.com/history/companies/theatre-of-black-women/ accessed 1 March 2021.

35. D. Lawrence, *And Still I Rise: A Mother's Search for Justice* (London: Faber & Faber, 2007); B. Cathcart, *The Case of Stephen Lawrence* (London: Penguin, 2000).

36. *Opening Statement on Behalf of Tariq Ali, Norman Blair, Piers Corbyn, Ernie Tate, Myk Zeitlin, Advisory Service for Squatters, Friends of Freedom Press Limited, Audrey Adams, Nathan Adams, Richard Adams, Duwayne Brooks OBE and Ken Livingstone*, Undercover Policing Inquiry, 25 October 2020, https://www.ucpi.org.uk/wp-content/uploads/2020/11/20201025-Opening_Statement-Saunders_DPG_CP_clients-RMQC.pdf, accessed 15 March 2022.

37. J. West, 'Roil Britannia! Al Sharpton, the British press and the 1991 murder of Rolan Adams', *Immigrants and Minorities*, 37/3 (2019), pp. 184–210.

38. P. Peachey, 'Police spied on family of boy killed in a racist attack', *Independent*, 24 July 2014, https://www.independent.co.uk/news/uk/crime/police-spied-family-boy-killed-racist-attack-9627202.html, accessed 25 February 2021.

39. *The Stephen Lawrence Inquiry: Report of an Inquiry by Sir William MacPherson of Cluny*, February 1999, 46.5, https://assets.publishing.service.gov.uk/government/uploads/system/uploads/attachment_data/file/277111/4262.pdf, accessed 15 March 2022.

40. D. Pallister, 'Police bungling that betrayed Stephen Lawrence', *Guardian*, 18 July 1998, https://www.theguardian.com/uk/1998/jul/18/lawrence.ukcrime, accessed 25 February 2021.

41. M. Gillard and L. Flynn, 'The copper, the Lawrence killer's father and secret police files that expose a corrupt relationship', *Independent*, 6 March 2021, https://www.independent.co.uk/news/uk/crime/copper-

lawrence-killer-s-father-and-secret-police-files-expose-corrupt-relationship-7537762.html, accessed 1 March 2021; *The Stephen Lawrence Independent Review: Report and Summary of Findings from Mark Ellison's Independent Review*, March 2014, pp. 13–14, https://www.gov.uk/government/publications/stephen-lawrence-independent-review, accessed 15 March 2022.

42. Lawrence, *And Still I Rise*, p. 168.

43. Ibid., p. 91.

44. T. Symonds, 'Police "spied on" Stephen Lawrence family, says Guardian newspaper', BBC, 24 June 2013, https://www.bbc.co.uk/news/uk-23022634, accessed 25 February 2021.

45. Lawrence, *And Still I Rise*, p. 153.

46. *The Stephen Lawrence Inquiry*, 2.6.

47. Ibid., 2.15.

48. Ibid., 6.39.

49. N. Hopkins and V. Dodd, 'Lawrence family accepts £320,000 payout from Met', 20 December 2000, https://www.theguardian.com/uk/2000/dec/20/lawrence.ukcrime, accessed 1 March, 2021.

50. Press Association, 'Stephen Lawrence verdict: statements from Doreen and Neville Lawrence', *Guardian*, 3 January 2012, https://www.theguardian.com/uk/2012/jan/03/statements-doreen-neville-lawrence, accessed 1 March 2021.

51. *The Stephen Lawrence Independent Review: Report and Summary of Findings*.

52. Press Association, 'Stephen Lawrence verdict: statements from Doreen and Neville Lawrence'.

53. R. Evans and V. Dodd, 'Stephen Lawrence: Theresa May orders inquiry into police spies', *Guardian*, 6 March 2014, https://www.theguardian.com/uk-news/2014/mar/06/stephen-lawrence-theresa-may-inquiry-police, accessed 15 March 2021.

54. *Opening Statement on Behalf of Baroness Doreen Lawrence of Clarendon, OBE*, in the Undercover Policing Inquiry, https://www.ucpi.org.uk/wp-content/uploads/2020/11/20201109-Opening_Statement-Baroness_Doreen_Lawrence_OBE.pdf, accessed 1 March 2021.

55. Ibid.

56. *Opening Submissions on Behalf of Core Participants*, Undercover Policing Inquiry, https://www.ucpi.org.uk/wp-content/uploads/2020/11/20201026-Opening_Statement_CPs_represented-by_HJA_BM_Bindmans-MRQC.pdf, accessed 1 March 2021.

57. A. Gentleman, *The Windrush Scandal: Exposing the Hostile Environment* (London: Faber & Faber, 2020).

58. Legal Action Group, *Chasing Status: If Not British, Then What Am I?*, https://www.lag.org.uk/document-downloads/204756/chasing-status--if-not-british--then-what-am-i-, accessed 1 March 2021.

59. House of Commons, *Windrush Lessons Learned Review*, an independent review by Wendy Williams, HC 93, 19 March 2020, https://assets.publishing.service.gov.uk/government/uploads/system/uploads/attachment_data/file/874022/6.5577_HO_Windrush_Lessons_Learned_Review_WEB_v2.pdf, accessed 1 March 2021.

60. A. Gentleman, 'The Windrush generation deserves justice: not video chats with the home secretary', *Guardian*, 12 June 2020, https://www.theguardian.com/commentisfree/2020/jun/12/windrush-generation-justioce; A. Gentleman, 'I can't eat or sleep: the woman threatened with deportation after 50 years in Britain', *Guardian*, 28 November 2017, https://www.theguardian.com/uk-news/2017/nov/28/i-cant-eat-or-sleep-the-grandmother-threatened-with-deportation-after-50-years-in-britain, both accessed 1 March 2021.

61. House of Commons, *Windrush Lessons Learned Review*, pp. 22–40.

62. Ibid., p. 105.

63. P. Walker and A. Gentleman, 'Theresa May apologises for treatment of Windrush citizens', *Guardian*, 17 April 2018, https://www.theguardian.com/uk-news/2018/apr/17/uk-still-uncertain-about-windrush-era-deportations, accessed 1 March 2021.

64. A. Travis, 'Minister says law's racism was defensible', *Guardian*, 1 January 2002, https://www.theguardian.com/politics/2002/jan/01/uk.race, accessed 10 March 2021.

65. House of Commons, *Windrush Lessons Learned Review*, p. 59.

66. Ibid., pp. 84–7.

67. A. Gentleman and P. Walker, 'Windrush claimants "tip of the iceberg" as payments scandal continues', *Guardian*, 9 February 2020, https://www.theguardian.com/uk-news/2020/feb/09/windrush-scandal-wrongly-designated-illegal-immigrants and Jack Fenwick, 'Windrush: At least nine victims died before getting compensation', 2 November 2020, BBC News, https://www.bbc.co.uk/news/uk-politics-54748038, both accessed 1 March 2021.

68. A. Gentleman, 'Mother of Windrush citizen blames passport problems for his death', *Guardian*, 18 April 2018, https://www.theguardian.com/uk-news/2018/apr/18/mother-of-windrush-citizen-blames-passport-problems-for-his-death, accessed 1 March 2021.

69. A. Gentleman, 'Three generations of Windrush family struggling to prove they are British', *Guardian*, 18 December 2019, https://www.theguardian.com/uk-news/2019/dec/18/three-generations-of-windrush-family-struggling-to-prove-they-are-british, accessed 1 March 2021.

70. A. Gentleman, 'Windrush victim denied UK citizenship despite Home Office admitting error', *Guardian*, 5 March 2021, https://www.theguardian.com/uk-news/2021/mar/05/windrush-victim-denied-uk-citizenship-home-office-admitting-error-trevor-donald, accessed 11 March 2021.

71. N. White, 'Revealed: who will get first Black Lives Matter UK grants after £1M fundraiser', *Huffington Post*, 18 February 2021, https://www.huffingtonpost.co.uk/entry/black-lives-matter-uk-funding-revealed_uk_602ba983c5b6741597e48b2f, accessed 15 March 2021.

72. R. Sigee, 'The 18-year-old Black Lives Matter protester who closed Oxford Street', *Evening Standard*, 14 July 2016, https://www.standard.co.uk/lifestyle/london-life/the-18yearold-black-lives-matter-protester-who-closed-oxford-street-a3295836.html and Y. Jeffery, 'Meet the 18-year-old student behind Black Lives Matter London', *Vice*, 14 July 2016, https://www.vice.com/en/article/nnknpd/black-lives-matter-london-marayam-ali-interview, accessed 15 March 2021.

73. J. Halliday, 'Student restrained by police died from neglect', *Guardian*, 15 May 2015, https://www.theguardian.com/uk-news/2015/may/15/kingsley-burrell-restrained-by-police-died-from-neglect-inquest-finds, accessed 15 March 2021.

74. Lee Jasper Official Blog, 'Sarah Reid: a black woman victim of vicious police assault found dead in her cell', 2 February 2016, http://leejasper.blogspot.com/2016/02/sarah-reid-black-woman-victim-of.html, accessed 15 March 2021.

75. D. Shaw, 'Jermaine Baker was "complying with police" when shot', 7 July 2020, BBC News, https://www.bbc.co.uk/news/uk-england-london-53321648, accessed 15 March 2021.

76. N. Parveen, 'Death of black teenager sparks protests in Liverpool', *Guardian*, 17 July 2016, https://www.theguardian.com/uk-news/2016/jul/17/death-of-black-teenager-in-police-custody-sparks-protests-in-liverpool, accessed March 2021.

77. H. Siddique, 'Black Lives Matter protests block roads around UK', 5 August 2016, https://www.theguardian.com/uk-news/2016/aug/05/black-lives-matter-protest-sparks-heathrow-traffic-chaos, accessed 15 March 2021.

78. 'Black Lives Matter protests stop trains and cars across England', BBC News, 5 August 2016, https://www.bbc.co.uk/news/uk-england-nottinghamshire-36983852, accessed 15 March 2021.

79. O. Blair, 'Marcia Rigg: you think police brutality is just a US issue? Think again', *Elle*, 2 June 2020, https://www.elle.com/uk/life-and-culture/a32742001/marcia-rigg-anti-racism/, accessed 15 March 2021.

80. 'Marcia Rigg addresses UN Human Rights Council on importance of family voices', Inquest: Truth, Justice & Accountability, 15 October 2021, https://www.inquest.org.uk/news-marcia-rigg-un-address, accessed 23 March 2021.

81. United Families and Friends Campaign, https://uffcampaign.org/, accessed 15 March 2021.

82. *Report of the Independent External Review of the IPCC Investigation of Sean Rigg's Death*, https://www.seanriggjusticeandchange.com/Review%20Report%20FINAL.pdf, accessed 15 March 2021.

83. Dame E. Angiolini, *Report of the Independent Review of Deaths and Serious Incidents in Police Custody* (London: Home Office, 2017), pp. 83–95, https://assets.publishing.service.gov.uk/government/uploads/system/uploads/attachment_data/file/655401/Report_of_Angiolini_Review_ISBN_Accessible.pdf, accessed 15 March 2021.

84. *The Lammy Review: An Independent Review into the Treatment of, and Outcomes for, Black, Asian and Minority Ethnic Individuals in the Criminal Justice System* (London: Home Office, 2017), p. 3, https://assets.publishing.service.gov.uk/government/uploads/system/uploads/attachment_data/file/643001/lammy-review-final-report.pdf, accessed 15 March 2021.

85. Justice for Seni: The Olaseni Lewis Campaign for Justice and Change, https://www.justiceforseni.com/about/, accessed 15 March 2021.

86. *Inquest Touching the Death of Olaseni Lewis*, 28 June 2017, https://www.judiciary.uk/wp-content/uploads/2017/07/Olaseni-Lewis-2017-0205.pdf, accessed 15 March 2021.

87. 'Today the Mental Health Units (Use of Force) Bill – also known as Seni's Law – has received royal assent and has become an act', *Mind*, 1 November 2018, https://www.mind.org.uk/news-campaigns/news/mental-health-units-use-of-force-bill-becomes-law/, accessed 15 March 2021.

88. V. Dodd, 'IPCC concerned about rise in minority ethnic deaths following police restraint', *Guardian*, 7 January 2018, https://www.theguardian.com/uk-news/2018/jan/07/ipcc-concerned-about-rise-in-ethnic-

minority-deaths-following-police-restraint, accessed 15 March 2021; Angiolini, *Report of the Independent Review of Deaths and Serious Incidents in Police Custody*.

89. C. Sambrook and R. Omonira Oyekanmi, *Accidental Death of a Young Black Londoner: The Case of Rashan Charles*, a short documentary film on a death by police restraint, openDemocracy, https://www.open-democracy.net/en/tagged/rashan-charles/, accessed 15 March 2021.

90. 'UN human rights experts say deaths in custody reinforce concerns about "structural racism" in UK', press release, 27 April 2018, United Nations, Human Rights: Office of the High Commissioner, https://www.ohchr.org/EN/NewsEvents/Pages/DisplayNews.aspx?NewsID=22997&LangID=E, accessed 15 March 2021.

91. D. Coles, 'BAME deaths in police custody: the disproportionality in the use of force against Black people adds to the irrefutable evidence of structural racism embedded in policing practices', Inquest: Truth, Justice & Accountability, https://www.inquest.org.uk/bame-deaths-in-police-custody, accessed 15 March 2021.

92. A. Mohdin, '"We couldn't be silent": the new generation behind Britain's anti-racism protests', *Guardian*, 29 July 2020, https://www.theguardian.com/uk-news/2020/jul/29/new-generation-behind-britain-anti-racism-protests-young-black-activists-equality, accessed 15 March 2021.

93. A. Mohdin, G. Swann and C. Bannock, 'How George Floyd's death sparked a wave of British anti-racism protests', *Guardian*, 29 July 2020, https://www.theguardian.com/uk-news/2020/jul/29/george-floyd-death-fuelled-anti-racism-protests-britain, accessed 15 March 2021.

94. R. Urwin, 'Kemi Badenoch: I'm black, but I'm also a woman, a mum and an MP', *Evening Standard*, 14 June 2017, https://www.standard.co.uk/lifestyle/london-life/kemi-badenoch-i-m-black-but-i-m-also-a-woman-a-mum-and-an-mp-a3564851.html, accessed 15 March 2021.

95. Mohdin, '"We couldn't be silent": the new generation behind Britain's anti-racism protests'.

96. A. Mohdin and L. Campbell, 'Young, British & Black: The death of George Floyd in the US sparked the UK's biggest anti-racism protests in centuries. We spoke to 50 young Britons at the heart of these rallies', *Guardian*, 29 July 2020, https://www.theguardian.com/uk-news/ng-interactive/2020/jul/29/young-british-black-voices-behind-uk-anti-racism-protests-george-floyd, accessed 15 March 2021.

97. H. Siddique and C. Skopeliti, 'BLM protesters topple statue of Bristol slave trader Edward Colston', 7 June 2020, https://www.theguardian.com/uk-news/2020/jun/07/blm-protesters-topple-statue-of-bristol-slave-trader-edward-colston, accessed 15 March 2021.

98. Countering Colston: Campaign to Decolonise Bristol, https://counteringcolston.wordpress.com/, accessed 15 March 2021.

99. *Full Council Agenda*, 2 March 2021, Bristol City Council, https://democracy.bristol.gov.uk/documents/g8692/Agenda%20frontsheet%2002nd-Mar-2021%2016.00%20Full%20Council.pdf?T=0, accessed 15 March 2021.

100. Stop the Maangamizi, https://stopthemaangamizi.com/2020/07/; 'Lambeth Council pass motion to demand government reparations for slavery', Lambeth Council/News, https://www.brixtonbuzz.com/2020/07/lambeth-council-pass-motion-to-demand-government-reparations-for-slavery/, both accessed 25 March 2021.

101. E. Stanford-Xosei, 'The Long Road of Pan-African Liberation to Reparatory Justice', in H. Adi (ed.), *Black British History: New Perspectives* (London: Zed Books, 2019), pp. 176–198.

102. Ibid., p. 186.

103. Bernie Grant, MP, 'Reparations or Bust!', Africa Reparations Movement UK, http://berniegrantarchive.org.uk/wp-content/uploads/2014/05/Reparations-or-Bust-Speech.pdf, accessed 15 March 2021.

104. Stanford-Xosei, 'The Long Road', p. 195.

105. H. Siddique, 'Donations to Black Lives Matter UK and other groups top £1m', *Guardian*, 9 June 2020, https://www.theguardian.com/uk-news/2020/jun/09/donations-to-black-lives-matter-uk-and-other-groups-top-1m, accessed 15 March 2021.

106. A. Mohdin, 'Black Lives Matter UK to start funding groups from £1.2m donations', *Guardian*, 11 January 2021, https://www.theguardian.com/world/2021/jan/11/black-lives-matter-uk-to-start-funding-groups-from-12m-donations, accessed 15 March 2021.

107. L. Campbell, '"I was shielded from my history": the changes young black Britons are calling for', *Guardian*, 30 July 2020, https://www.theguardian.com/uk-news/2020/jul/30/history-young-black-britons-race-schools-policing, accessed 15 March 2021.

108. 'Decolonising the curriculum', BBC Bitesize, https://www.bbc.co.uk/bitesize/articles/z7g66v4, accessed 15 March 2021.

109. J. Arday, *The Black Curriculum: British Black History in the National Curriculum – Report 2021*, 2020, https://static1.squarespace.com/

static/5f5507a237cea057c5f57741/t/5fc10c7abc819f1cf4fd0eeb/
1606487169011/TBC+2021++Report.pdf, accessed 15 March 2022.

110. BantuScribe, 'How YHP changed my relationship with my degree', 4 May
2020, Young Historians Project, https://www.younghistoriansproject.org/
single-post/2020/05/04/how-yhp-changed-my-relationship-with-my-
degree, accessed 15 March 2021.

Index

Page numbers for illustrations are in *italics*.

Abbas, Zainab 438–9, 459, 461,
    469, 484
Abbot, Diane 494, 505
Abdallah, Tewfik 324
Abdullah, Mohamed 267
abolitionism 51–5, 78–96, 117–21
    African 45–9, 62–3, 78–9, 89–93
    American 163–4, 168–71, 174–6
    Caribbean 200–1
    economic argument for 79, 82,
        94, 95–6, 98–9, 121
    opposition to 88–9
    propaganda 86–7, 88, 91–2
    support for 56–7, 86, 118–19,
        174–6
Abrahams, Peter 375, 376
accommodation 266
    attacks on 398–400
    and citizenship 509
    colour bar and 288–9, 406–7,
        411–12
    hostels 289, 322, 346–7, 356,
        361, 379
    housing associations 459
    for seafarers 386–8, 394, 395
    segregated 346–7
    shortages 393, 409
    squatting 459

student 229–30, 289, 292, 380, 385
Acham-Chen, Sylvia 274
activism
    beginnings of 47–8
    suppression of 148, 150–1,
        184, 328
actors 173, 178–81, 215, 224,
    318–19
Adams, Grantley 421
Adams, Robert 358
Adams, Rolan 499–500, 504
Adams, Sarah 138
Addai-Sebo, Akyaaba 495–6
Ademola, Aderemi 252, 310, 322
Ademola, Adetokunbo 288
Ademola, Princess Adenrele 252,
    322, 357, 357
Adeniyi-Jones, Ayo 379
Adeniyi-Jones, Curtis 285
Admiralty 73, 74–5, 137, 237, 252,
    352–3
Adrian of Canterbury
    (Abbot Hadrian) 6–7
advertisements 39, 41–3, 42, 46, 52,
    86–8, 105
Aelane, Yahne (George Sanders) 92
Afflick, Charles 128
Afflick, William 128

Africa 183–98
  armed forces recruitment in
    336–8, 339
  diplomatic relations with 14–15
  imperialism in 99–100, 183–4,
    192, 197–8
  military bases in 330
  protests in 315, 328
Africa and Orient Review (*AOR*,
    journal) 227, 272–3
Africa and the World (journal) 314
Africa House (hostel) 322, 361, 379
Africa League 402–3
Africa Liberation Committee 469
Africa Liberation Day 471, 471,
    486, 487
Africa Unity House 422–3
African Academy, London 69–70
African Aid Society 170, 187, 188
African and Asiatic Society 122–3
African Association 187–8, 207–11
African Caribbean Educational
    Research (ACER) project 497
African Caribbean Self-Help
    Organization (ACSHO) 434–6,
    455–6, 467, 469
African Churches Mission 311
African in London, An (film) 357–8
African Institution 104, 160–1
African Jubilee Year (1987–88)
    495–6
African National Congress (ANC)
    223, 279, 422, 487
African Opinion (journal) 314
African People's Historical
    Monument Foundation
    (APHMF) 496–7
African Progress Union (APU)
    274–5, 278, 280–2
African Races Association 277–8
African Reparations Movement UK
    (ARMUK) 517

African Sentinel (newspaper) 274,
    314, 316
African Society and the Anti-Slavery
    and Aborigines' Rights
    Protection Society (ASARPS)
    228–9
African Students' Association 206
African Students' Union 229
African Telegraph (journal) 275–6,
    277, 281
African Times and Orient Review
    (*ATOR*, journal) 224–8
African Times (newspaper) 187,
    188–9, 493
African Unity Society (Oxford
    University) 220
African-American people 168–76,
    358–60
Africanus, George Scipio 72
Afro-Asian-Caribbean Conference
    (AACC) 424
Afro-Caribbean Organization (ACO)
    406–11, 407
Afro-West Indian Society (Edinburgh
    University) 218
Afro-West Indian Union (AWIU)
    417
Aga, Selim 173
Agbebi, Mojola 225
agriculture 29–30, 350–1
Aguirra, Joseph 129
Aka-Bashorun, Alao 420–1,
    421, 422
Alakija, Babatunde O. 335, 336
Alakija, Oluwale 289
Alcindor, John 210, 218, 223, 274,
    281–2
Alder, Christopher 513
Aldridge, Ira 173, 178–80
Aleifasukure Toumananah, D. T.
    259, 261–2
Alemayehu, Prince 116–17

Algeria 3, 4
Ali, Arif 493
Ali, Dusé Mohammed 217, 224–8,
  225, 229, 274
Ali, Maryam 511
Ali, Surat 311
All the Year Round (journal)
  97–8, 133
Allen, William G. 171
Almanzora, SS (ship) 382–3
Alvarez, Pedro 18
amelioration 80, 92, 118, 121
American Colonization Society
  (ACS) 190
American Revolution 61, 65, 74,
  82, 85
Ammere, Cojoh (George Wallace)
  81, 92
Amoo-Gottfried, Kojo 430
Amory, Merle 494
Amos, Valerie 494
Anchoy, Louis 245
Anderson, Cliff 384
Anderson, Francis 171
Anderson, John 170, 174
Anderson, Tryphena 413
Andrews, Fitzmaurice 456, 469
Angiolini, Dame Elish 513, 514
Annan, Nii Odoi 373, 374, 401
Anne, Queen of Great Britain 31
Annerby, Walter 15
Annis, John 54, 78
Anthonie (Tudor African) 15
Anthony, John 24, 36–7
Anthony, Seth 330
Antia, Stephanie and Connie 355
Anti-Apartheid Movement (AAM)
  422, 487–8
anti-capitalism 365–6, 442–3
Anti-Caste (journal) 196
anti-colonialism 208–11, 227, 306,
  309–10, 453, 486–8

Caribbean 272–3
  conferences on 316, 366, 367–9
  post-war 391, 421, 422, 433
anti-fascism 317, 328, 359–60, 433,
  474–5
Antigua 29, 101–2, 108
anti-imperialism 184–6, 194–8,
  218–19, 222–3, 313, 327–9
Anti-Lynching Committee 196
anti-racism 194–6, 288–93, 348,
  385–6
  colonialism, motivated by 228–9
  of Communist Party 410–11, 427
  legislation 402, 412, 415, 426
  and 'pseudo-scientific' racism
  189–90
  publications 177, 185–6, 196
  religious 176–7
  and trade unions 411–12,
  456, 457
Anti-Slavery Society 108–9, 118–19,
  200–1
Apapa, SS (ship) 246
appeasement
  of Nazi Germany 328
  of racism 335, 358, 400
apprenticeships 71–2, 122
Arbuckle, Sir William 223
archaeology x, 2–10
Archer, John 165, 210, 211, 211–12,
  274–5
archives ix-x, 496–7
Armistead, Wilson viii, 185–6
army, British 72–3, 127–33, 330,
  335–6
army, USA 358–60
Army Council 234
arrests 146, 151, 445–6
  of Chartists 155, 156, 157
  vs. convictions 254, 262, 375,
  463, 472, 511
  protests against 448–9

arrests – *cont'd.*
  under Race Relations Act 1965
    440, 442
  and social disorder 48, 251,
    259–60, 264, 475, 478–9
art and artists 106–8, 440–1
Arundell, Charles 131
Asa-Asa, Louis 113
Ashwood Garvey, Amy 285–6,
    306–7, 307, 309–12, 319–20,
    370–2, 417–18, 421
Askins, Peter 131
assimilation 382, 404, 431,
    442, 456
Associated Negro Press 348
Association for the Advancement of
    Coloured People (AACP) 359,
    417, 418
Athenaeum Club 192
Atlantic Charter (1941) 361
Atta, Nana Sir Ofori 305
Attlee, Clement 369, 389–90
August, George (Thomas Lewis)
    52–3, 73
Aukur, Katherine 43, 45
Auxiliary Territorial Service (ATS)
    343–4
awards and honours 203, 308
  military 137, 238, 239, 338, 339,
    341
Awolowo, Obafemi 370
Awooner-Renner, Bankole 363, 373,
    374
Awooner-Renner, Olabisi 373
Axe Laid to the Root (journal) 148
Azikiwe, Nnamdi 313, 376

Baartman, Sara (Saartjie) 102–6,
    105, 174
Baden-Sepmer, June 418
Bader, Lilian (née Bailey) 343, 351,
    354

Bai, Private (Gold Coast Regiment)
    232
Bailey, Marcus 236, 244–5, 343
Bainkie, William 173
Baker, Baron 389, 414, 415, 416,
    417
Baker, Jermaine 511, 512
Banda, Hastings 370
Banes, Edward 24
Bank of England 31, 32
banking system 32–3
Bankole-Bright, Herbert R. 218, 287
Banks, Aaron (comedian) 173
baptism 15–17, 21, 39–40, 44, 56,
    67, 77
Baptiste, Mona 388
Baquaqua, Mohommah Gardo 163
Barbados 29, 33, 100, 117–18
Barber, Francis 50, 70–1
Barbour-James, John 214, 274, 282
Barbour-James, Muriel 274
Barnardo, Thomas 127
Barr, Richard Dickie 238
Barrett, George 126
Barrow, Errol 342, 380
Barrow, Jocelyn 456
Bartels-Kodwo, C. 220
Bartholemew (medieval African) 9
Baskerville, Sir Thomas 24, 25
Bastian, Aidi 313
Baxter, Richard 81
Baynes, Aubrey 492
'Beachy Head Lady' 5
Bean, Gerlin 458, 469, 484–5
Beard, Donald Gerald 344
beauty 439
beauty contests 228, 419
Bechuanaland (Botswana) 401–2
Beckford, Richard 494
Beese, Barbara 467
Beethoven, Ludwig van 77
begging 51, 123–5

Belle, Dido Elizabeth 70
Belle, Maria 70
Bellerophon, HMS (ship) 136
Bellos, Linda 494, 495, 517
Belsaco, Aby 129
Bemand, George 241
Benezet, Anthony 53, 79, 82
Benin 78, 113
Beoku-Betts, E. S. 230
Berber people 3–4
Berkeley, George, Bishop of
    Cloyne 44
Berry, James 441
Besant, Annie 227
Best, George (1555–84) 27
Best, Winston 457
Bhownaghree, Manchergee 494
Bicknell, John, 'The Dying Negro' 80
Binne (Tudor African) 15
Birmingham 399–401, 406–11, 436
Bishop, Francis 163
Bishop, Maurice 380
Bissett, James, 'The Negro Boy' 179
Black Cultural Archives (BCA) x
Black Liberation Front (BLF) 438,
    453–5, 454, 461, 468, 469–70,
    483–4
Black Liberator (journal) 467–8
Black Lives Matter (BLM)
    movement 511–16
Black Lives Matter UK (UKBLM)
    511–12, 515, 518
Black Londoners (TV programme)
    493
'Black Loyalists' 65, 69, 74, 85
Black Man (journal) 315
Black Nationalism 435–6
Black Panther Movement 445–53
Black Parents Movement (BPM)
    463–4, 469, 484
Black People's Alliance (BPA)
    446–7

Black Peoples' Defence Committee
    463
'Black Poor' 65, 75, 85
Black Power movement 434,
    438–47, 451, 461–3, 469–70
Black Power Speaks (journal) 445
Black Society 51
Black Unity and Freedom Party
    (BUFP) 447, 452–3, 463, 483–4
Black Women Speak Out (book)
    484
Black Women's Action Group
    (BWAG) 484
Black Women's Cooperative,
    Manchester 485
blackface 85, 173–4, 182–3, 197–8
Blackman, Peter 291, 315, 316, 319,
    362
Blackman, Reasonable 16
Blair, John J. 341
Blake, Cyril 321, 322
Blake, George 322
Blakelock, Keith 481
Blanke, John 18–19
Bluett, Thomas 66
Blunman, Stephen 131–2
Blunt, Catherine 68
Blyden, Edward 190–3, 288
Boateng, Paul 494–5
bodies, Black 102–6, 221, 288, 419
Bogle L'Ouverture (publisher) 441,
    457, 468
Bonetta, Sarah Forbes (Aina)
    112–16, 115, 171
Bonfire 12 472
booksellers 71, 468
Botswana (Bechuanaland) 401–2
Bovell, Dennis 463, 466–7, 472
Bovell, Edward 332
Bowfry, Benjamin 48
Boyega, John (John Adeboyega) 490,
    515

Bracken, Brendan 348–9
Braithwaite, Kamau 440
Branch, Sammy 382
Brewster, Annie 138
Bridgetower, George Polgreen 76–7
Bristol 34, 41, 67, 71, 475–6
  Bus Boycott 1963 427–9
Bristol, Dexter 509–10
Bristol, Sentina 509–10
British Boxing Board of Control
    (BBBC) 323, 383–4
British Broadcasting Corporation
    (BBC) 332, 334, 341, 356,
    418–19, 448, 493, 497–8
British Honduran Forestry Unit
    345–6, 370
British Legion 239–40
Brixton Black Women's Group
    (BBWG) 484–5
Broadhurst, Robert 274, 275, 280,
    281–2, 312, 370
Broadwater Farm uprising 481–2,
    504–5
Brockway, Fenner 402, 408, 421,
    422, 426
Brooks, Duwayne 501, 503
brotherhood (human/of man) 80–1,
    91, 227
Brougham, Henry 95, 96, 188, 191
Brown, Albertina (Miss LaLa) 181–2
Brown, Bini (Butwaka) 435, 467,
    469
Brown, Eugene 239, 325
Brown, George 300
Brown, Harold 238
Brown, James (1815–81) 165, 166–7
Brown, James Jackson 242
Brown, John (c.1810–76) 162
Brown, John (d.1914) 239, 325
Brown, Prince 427
Brown, Roy 324–5
Brown, Vincent 381–2

Brown, William 294
'Brown, William' (disguised woman
    sailor) 73–4, 136
Bruce, John Edward 212, 220, 227
Bryan, Anthony 506–7
Bryan, Beverly 452
Bryan, Carmen 425–6
Bryan, Charles 243
Buckle, Desmond 291, 292, 349,
    367, 399
Buckley, Eva 388
Burke, Edmund 50, 80
Burnham, Forbes 380
Burrell, Kingsley 511
Burton, Edwin 506–7
Burton, Richard (explorer) 173, 189
Busby, Margaret 441
Bushell, Waveney 457
Butler, Rab 419
Butler, Uriah 328, 386

Caddi-biah, King 22
Caeser, Elizabeth 44
Caeser, John 44
Callander, W. S. 278
Cambridge, Alrick ('Ricky') 452,
    467
Cameron, David 505
Cameron, Gloria 496
Campaign against Racial
    Discrimination (CARD)
    429–33, 437
Campbell, Ambrose 419
Campbell, Robert 170, 187
Campbell, Wilbert 'Count Suckle'
    464–5
Campbell-Bannerman, Henry 219
Canada 69–70, 233
Cann, Rita 321
Cardiff 135, 265, 296–302, 321–2,
    325, 332
Cardiff Coloured Association 270–1

Cardiff Coloured Seamen's Committee 299
Carew, Jan 426, 437
Cargill, Gilbert 370
Carib 12 472
Caribbean
    anti-colonialism 272–3
    armed forces recruitment in 337, 339–40, 343–6
    colonization of 29–30, 94
    military bases in 330
    strikes in 314–15, 328
    unemployment in 401
    uprisings in 49, 94–5, 314–15
    war funding from 330–1, 336
    see also Barbados; Jamaica
Caribbean Artists Movement (CAM) 440–1
Caribbean Education and Community Workers Association (CECWA) 457
Caribbean Labour Congress (CLC) 390–4, 406
Caribbean News (newspaper) 391–2, 392
Caribbean Teachers' Association 455–6
Caribbean Times (newspaper) 493
Caribbean Workers Movement 433
Carmichael, Stokely (Kwame Ture) 434, 438–42, 454, 470
Carnival (Notting Hill) 418–19, 473–5
Carr, John 188
Carr, Radcliffe 463
Carter, Trevor 391, 410, 417
Carty, Peter 427
Casely Hayford, J. E. 193, 196, 204, 205, 217, 224, 226
Castillo, William 74–5
Catalina (Tudor African) 19–20
Catherine of Aragon, Queen of England 18–20

Cato Street conspiracy 149, 151
Cattelena (Tudor African) 17
Cattouse, Nadia 343–4, 418
Cecil, William, 1st Baron Burghley 16
cemeteries see graves
Central Emancipation Committee 122
Cesar, Hendrik 103, 104, 106
Chalmers, William 57
Chamberlain, Joseph 222
Chang, Sonia 452
charity 78, 85, 122–3, 144, 488
Charles, Alfred 324
Charles, Rashan 514
Charles I, King of England 31
Charlotte, Queen of England 92, 112, 117
'Charter for Coloured Peoples' 362
Cheddar Man 2–3
Chen, Percy Acham 283
Chequers (journal) 426
children 20, 21, 77
    adopted/fostered 379, 393–4
    advertisements for sale of 41–3, 52
    emancipation of 100
    evacuees 355
    as hostages 68
    labour of 133–4
    of mixed heritage 297–8, 393–4
    as 'pets' 37, 41
    in poverty 123, 127
    as 'presents' 113–14
    as soldiers 131
Chilembwe, John 231–2
Christian, George William 165
Christian, Jacob 165
Christian Endeavour Federation 289–90
Christian Evidence Society 195
Christianity 6–7, 13, 27, 58, 82–4, 336
    baptism 15–17, 21, 39–40, 44, 56, 67, 77

Christianity – *cont'd.*
　Baptists 36, 176–7
　Church of England 33–4, 68–9,
　　83–4
　churches, segregation in 304–5
　conversion to 13, 16–17, 22, 69
　Methodism 78, 82, 177, 194
　missions 69, 114, 177–8, 304–5
　Quakers 82–3, 85–6, 92, 102,
　　119–20
　see also clergy
Christopher, George (Herr Christoff)
　181
Churchill, Winston 361, 383, 402, 410
cinema *see* film
circus 181–2, 215
citizenship 179, 425, 446–7, 480,
　505–10
civil service 204, 214, 404
Clarke, Coca 296, 452, 485
Clarkson, Thomas 80, 82, 83, 86,
　88, 200
class, social 8–9
　elite 4, 65–8, 78, 111–17, 202, 241
　working 91–2, 120, 145, 152,
　　174–5, 349, 451–2, 472
Cleaver, Eldridge 453, 455, 468, 470
Cleaver, Kathleen 453, 455, 468, 470
Clemetson, David Louis 241
clergy 21, 68–9, 176–8, 200, 498
　missionaries 69, 114, 118, 177–8,
　　199–200, 205
clothing 18–22, 40
Clough, Joe 238
Coard, Bernard 457–8
Coaston, Makeda 496
Cobbie, Anne 17
Coboro, Thomas 68
Cochrane, Kelso 419, 420–1, 422
Coker, Frances 71
Coker, Kate 71
Cole, A. M. 310

Cole, Gilbert 375
Cole, Irene 379
Colebourne, Walter 236
Colenso, Frank 208
Coleridge-Taylor, Samuel 210, 211,
　212–13, 214, 218, 226, 227, 348
Coles, Obadiah 240
Collier, Bob 239
Collins, Charles 'Sir' 465
Collins, Reginald 241
Colonial Defence Association 299
Colonial Defence Committee (CDC)
　396, 397
Colonial Film Unit (CFU) 336, 357–8
Colonial Immigrants (government
　report) 410
Colonial Office 192, 227, 267, 285,
　289, 292, 356, 385
Colonial People's Defence Association
　(CPDA) 394, 397–8
Colonial Seamen's Association (CSA)
　310–11
colonialism 13, 28–9, 31–5, 88,
　281–2, 329
　see also anti-colonialism;
　　imperialism
colour bar
　Edwardian 221
　in First World War 233, 234,
　　236–8, 240, 242
　interwar 282, 290
　in Second World War 331–5,
　　339–40, 348–51, 352–3
　post-war 383–7, 402–3, 405, 406–8
　in accommodation 288–9, 406–7,
　　411–12
　in armed forces 128, 134, 137,
　　330–40, 352–3, 358–60
　in employment 186, 342–3, 347,
　　427–9
　in entertainment industry 359,
　　411–12

in hospitality industry 359, 403,
    411–12, 429
legislation against 402, 412
opportunist removal of 335–6
protests against 332, 335–6, 351,
    360–2, 402–3
in social organizations 228
in sport 323–4, 349, 383–4
support for 408–9
and trade unions 405, 407–8
Coloured Film Artistes Association
    328–9
Coloured Nationals Mutual Social
    Club 310
Coloured People's Progressive
    Association (CPPA) 417,
    420–1
Coloured People's Union 438
Coloured Workers/Worker's
    Welfare Association (CWWA)
    365, 386
Colston, Edward 34, 516
Colwyn Bay Institute 205–6, 223
Commission for Racial Equality
    473, 497
Committee for Ethiopian and
    Eritrean Relief (CEER) 488
Committee for the Relief of the Black
    Poor 78, 85
Committee of African Organizations
    (CAO) 420–3, 436–7, 487
Committee of Afro-Asian Caribbean
    Organizations (CAACO) 423,
    426
Commonwealth 30, 394, 508
Commonwealth War Graves
    Commission 250
communism 291–4, 299, 302,
    307–8, 349, 384–5
Communist Party of Great Britain
    (CPGB) 304, 309, 374–5,
    410–11, 427, 433

migrants, support for 381, 391–2,
    403
at Pan-African Congress 370, 373
community 50–1, 132, 172, 280,
    282, 321–2, 467
Company of Merchants Trading to
    Africa 69, 74
compensation
    of enslaved people 119, 121–2
    for failures of policing 502
    of slave owners 112, 121–2
    for war dead 246
    for Windrush scandal 509
    see also reparations
composers 63, 76–7, 212–13, 348
conferences
    African Peoples, Democracy and
        World Peace (1939) 316, 328–9
    Bandung Conference (1955) 226
    on Black history 496, 519–20
    Conference for Africans (1913) 229
    Dialectics of Liberation Congress
        (1967) 438–9
    International Conference of
        Negroes and Arabs (1936) 311
    League of Coloured Peoples
        305–6, 328–9, 362
    Pan-African 209–11, 276, 282,
        323, 365–73, 372, 469–70
    'On the Rights of Black People in
        Britain' 1971 447, 447, 453
    Subject Peoples' Conferences
        (1945) 367–8, 369
    Universal Races Congress (1911)
        225–6
    women's 485
    World Trade Union Conference
        (1945) 365–6
Connoll, William 280
Connolly, Yvonne 455
Connor-Mogotsi, Pearl 418, 421,
    424, 440, 441

conscientious objectors 247–9, 332

conscription 231–2, 247–9, 328, 330, 361–2

conservatism 62–3

Conservative Commonwealth Group 410

Conservative Party 211, 404, 410, 416, 429–30, 447–8, 508–9

Constantine, Sir Learie (Baron Constantine)
  activism 367, 391, 393, 401, 428
  cricketer 324
  Imperial Hotel, court case against 349, 351
  Learie Constantine (film) 357
  peerage 308
  welfare officer 347, 354, 356

convicts 29, 125–7

Cooper, Adam Elliot 518

Cooper, Elizabeth 123

co-operation, activist 334, 367–8, 374–5, 391, 417, 470–2

Co-ordinating Committee against Racial Discrimination 425

Coote, Lulu 205, 215

Coree (South African man) 15

Corker, Elizabeth 181

Cornwallis, Cubah 138

Corydon, Christopher 46

Cosens, George 177

Cosway, Maria 77

Cosway, Richard 77–8

cotton 35, 99, 112, 149, 174

'Count Suckle' (Wilbert Campbell) 464–5

Country Journal or the Craftsman 45

court, royal 18–20

court cases 36, 125–7, 278, 344
  abolitionism and 51–5
  Black people and 71
  Butts v. Penny (1677) 38
  Chamberlain v. Harvey (1696) 40
  against Edward Eyre 184–5
  fabricated evidence in 288, 396–7, 481
  Gelly v. Cleve (1694) 40
  Jonathan Strong 51–2
  Knight v. Wedderburn (1774) 57–8
  on legality of slavery 38, 40–1
  libel 429
  Lowe v. Elton (1677) 40
  Mangrove Nine 450–2
  Newton, Elizabeth (Mrs Miler) 100
  Oval Four 460–1
  Pearne v. Lisle (1749) 44
  of Sara Baartman 104
  Shanley v. Harvey (1762) 44
  Smith v. Brown and Cooper (1701) 40
  Smith v. Gould (1706) 40
  Somerset v. Stewart (1772) 45, 53–5, 100
  on status of enslaved people 43–4, 47, 48, 55–6, 101–2
  Stephen Lawrence murder 501, 503
  testimony 17–18, 19–20, 23, 501
  Williams v. Brown 1802 100

Cowan, E. A. 364

Cowper, William, 'The Negro's Complaint' 86, 147

Craft, Ellen 168, 170–1, 185

Craft, William 168, 170–1, 185

Crane, Walter 226

Crawford, Japheth 'Jeff' 456

Creech Jones, Arthur 314, 316, 329, 362

Cribb, Tom 142–3

Crichlow, Frank 449–50, 452

crime 71, 72, 124–7, 422, 499–500
  false accusations of 460–1
  theft 50, 75, 126–7, 128, 129
  treason 146, 151–2
  see also murder

Cripps, Stafford 314
Crisis, The (journal) 212, 336
Cromwell, Oliver 30
Cross, Ulric 340, 341, 344
Crown Prosecution Service (CPS)
499, 501, 514
Crowther, Samuel Ajayi 171, 200
Cruikshank, George 152
Cruikshank, Isaac 65
Crummell, Alexander 168, 169, 170
Cudjo, William 68–9
Cuffay, Chatham 133, 154
Cuffay, Lynda Myra 154
Cuffay, Mary Ann 155, 157, 158
Cuffay, William 133, 152–8, 153,
172
Cugoano, Quobna Ottobah 59,
77–9, 89–91, 92, 145, 185
Cullen, Susanna 93
Cumbria 1, 3–5
Cummings, Ivor 356, 390
Cunard, Nancy 314, 329, 362
Cunard, Sir William 137
Cuvier, Georges 105

Dadzie, Stella 485
Dahomey 113
Dalrymple, David 56–7
dance halls 359–60
dancers 173, 218
Daniels, Leo 277–8
Danquah, J. B. 288, 308
Darby, John 181
Darby, Mary 181
Darby, William (Pablo Fanque) 181–2
Darwin, Charles 184, 201–2
Darwin, Erasmus 91
Davidson, Basil 437
Davidson, William 133, 148,
149–52, 150
Davies, Captain James 115–16
Davis, Angela 442, 443, 451, 470

Dawe, George 106
Day, Thomas (1748–89) 80, 91
Day, Thomas (Mary Seacole's
business partner) 139
de Clare, Richard 8
de Freitas, Michael (Michael X)
436–8, 439–40, 441, 448, 450
death
of children 70
executions 48, 75, 146, 151
in police custody 432, 463, 480,
511–15
by police shooting 481, 511
poverty and 127
racist violence and 259–60, 264–5
of seafarers 245–6
suicide 61
in war 233–4, 244–6, 330, 337,
339, 342, 346, 352
see also murder
Defoe, Daniel 31
dehumanization 31, 84
Delany, Martin 168, 187–8
Demane, Harry 78
Demerette, John ('Demetrius') 259
demonstrations 156–7, 317
Africa Liberation Day 471, 471
Black Lives Matter 511–12,
515–16
Black People's Day of Action
(1981) 476–7, 492
Bonfire 12 473
against Immigration Acts 424–5,
424
Mangrove Nine 450, 451
neo-fascist 474–5
Spa Fields, London 147
Deniz, Clare 321
Deniz, Frank 321
Deniz, Joe 321
Deniz, Laurie 321
dentists 216, 335

deportation 295, 301, 303, 425–6, 506
  see also transportation
Deptford 398–9
Deptford Trades Council 399
De'Souza, Ivor 341
Despard, Catherine 145–6
Despard, Edward 145–6
Dezonie, Vidal 388
Dhingra, Madan Lal 229
Dhondy, Farouk 452
Diallo, Ayuba Suleiman (Job Ben
  Solomon) 66, 67
Dickens, Charles 98, 133, 164
Diderot, Denis 81
Diego (African seafarer) 16, 23–4
Dinah 'the Black' (servant) 36
Diogo (Tudor African) 17
diplomacy 14–15, 22, 178, 192–3,
  494–5
disease/illness 9, 63, 68, 116, 134,
  138, 154, 232–3
  psychological 36, 68–9, 512–14
doctors 137–41, 163–4, 188, 205,
  214, 223–4, 492
  racism, experience of 218, 289–90
  in wartime 242–3, 334, 335–6
documentation
  citizenship, destruction of 505–6
  manumission 100
  passports 168, 303–4, 346
Dolben, Sir William 79, 92
Domesday Abbreviato 8–9
domestic servants
  Tudor 16–22
  eighteenth century 46, 49, 50, 68,
  70–2
  nineteenth century 100, 109, 124–7
  Edwardian 215
  unemployment of 123
Donald, Trevor 510
Douglass, Fredrick 119, 168–9, 172,
  174, 185

Dove, Frank 239
Drake, Sir Francis 11, 16
Dreadnought Seamen's Hospital,
  London 134, 137
Du Bois, W. E. B. 212, 220, 227,
  365, 367
  Pan-African Congress 1900 210
  Pan-African Congress 1919 276
  Pan-African Congress 1921 282
  Pan-African Congress 1945
  370–2, 375
  Universal Races Congress 1911
  225–6
Dudley, Robert, 1st Earl of
  Leicester 16
Duffield, Ian 126
Duffy, David Anthony 156
Duggan, Mark 511, 515
'Duke Vin' (Vincent Forbes) 464–5
Dunbar, Paul Laurence 213
Dunbar, Rudolph 319–20, 345–6,
  348
Dunbar, William, 'Ane Blak Moir'
  21–2
Duncan, Private 'Darkie' 240
Duncan, Elsie 313
Dungala 15
Dunlop, Alexander 103, 104
DuPlan, Eddie 364, 396
Durham, Charles 207
Durham, Jimmy (Mustapha) 133

Easmon, John 242
Easmon, Kathleen 217–18
Easmon, M. C. F. 242
East India Company 15
East London Black Women's
  Organization (ELBWO) 485
Eaton, Fanny 106–8, *107*
Eber, John 421
Edmonstone, John 201–2
education 69–70, 113–14, 456–9

in Africa 190–1, 193
of Africans in England 14, 15,
  22–3, 66–72, 159, 186–7
Colwyn Bay Institute 205–6, 223
decolonization of curriculum
  518–20
Educationally Sub-Normal (ESN)
  category 457–8
Edwardian 217–19
of enslaved people 59, 61–2
Rampton Report 459
refusal of 61–2
school 170–1, 200, 217–18
supplementary 453, 455–9
Swann Report 459
see also universities
Edwards, Beresford 457
Edwards, Celestine 193–8, *194*
Edwards, Herman 459
Edwards, Passmore 196
Edwards, Paul 1–2
Egbado (Yewa) people 113
Egbuna, Obi 440, 441–2, 443–6, 448
Egypt 224–5
Ekarte, Daniels 304–5, 353, 393
Ekpenyon, E. I. 332–3
Elder Dempster (shipping company)
  164, 191, 303, 353–4
Eldred Taylor, John 226, 274–82
elections 211–12, 224, 386, 429–30,
  494–5
Elizabeth Tudor (Elizabeth I, Queen
  of England) 14–15, 20, 24–6
Ellis, John 125–6
Ellison, Mark 503
emancipation 82, 118, 119–20,
  121–2, 174–5
Emidy, Joseph 76
Emmanuel, Charles 264
Emmanuel, David (Smiley Culture)
  513
Emmet, Robert 145–6

Empire Exhibition (1924) 284–5,
  290
Empire Windrush, HMT (ship) xi,
  339, 387–90, *388*, 393
employment 24–5, 71–2, 125,
  251–2
colour bar in 186, 342–3, 347,
  427–9
post-war 388, 390, 404–5
see also occupations;
  unemployment
Engels, Frederick 146
England
invasions of 5–6
as 'safe haven' 167–8
Enlightenment 80–1
enslaved people 4, 9, 37–9
escaped 37, 38–9, 46–8, 164, 168,
  169–70
habeas corpus rights of 41, 45
popular support for 56–7
as property 38, 40
proposed registration of 118
seafarers 161–2
soldiers 129–30
state confiscation of 101–2
enslavement 11–16, 38–9
legal status of 17–18, 20, 43–5,
  57–8
re-enslavement 74–5, 78, 100
entertainment industry 127, 165,
  178–83, 215–18, 296, 318–22,
  359–60
colour bar in 359, 411–12
racism in 102–6, 173–4, 179, 183
see also film; musicians; television;
  theatre
Entertainment National Service
  Association (ENSA) 354–5
Equal Before the Law? (TV
  programme) 448
equality 80–1, 123

Equiano, Olaudah 33, 54, 65, 73,
    77–9, 82–3, 85, 88–93
  biographies of 185
  in London Corresponding
    Society 88
  Narrative 89, 90, 91–2
Eritrea 488
Esin, Daniel Ekanem 285
Este, Harriet 111
Ethalion, HMS (ship) 137
Ethiopia 9, 116, 210, 211, 305–11,
    488
Ethiopian Association 304
Ethiopian Progressive Association
    (EPA) 205–6, 220–1
Ethiopian Review (journal) 220
Ethiopianism 220–1, 228–9
eugenics 84, 297–8
Evans, Audley 427
Evaristo, Bernadine 498
Evening News (newspaper) 283–4
Ewusi, Kwesi 205–6, 220
exhibition, of Black people 102–6,
    105, 221, 288
exoticism 26, 102–6, 108, 221
expulsion *see* transportation
Eyre, Edward John 184–5
Ezzreco, Frances 414–15, 417, 421,
    430

Fabian Society 211
Fairchild, E.G. 165
Falaba, SS (ship) 246
fame 63–4, 67, 104–5, 115–16, 179
Fanimokun, Aurora (later Kayode)
    276, 283
Fanque, Pablo (William Darby) 181–2
Fanti Confederacy 190
fascism, post-war 385, 419, 425,
    446, 474, 508
  racist violence of 412–13, 415,
    422

Fasimbas 455
Faubus, Orval 415
feminism 449, 483–5
Fennell, Rufus 279
Ferguson, William 57
Fergusson, William 188
Fielding, Sir John 46, 48, 49
Figaro, Alex 130
File, Nigel viii, 496
Fillis, Marye 17
film 318–19, 328–9, 355, 468
  activist 480, 482
  propaganda 336, 357–8, *357*,
    360–1
First World War 216–17, 231–50
  'Black Battalion,' proposed 236–7
  British West India Regiment
    (BWIR) 232–4
  colour bar in 233, 234, 236–8,
    240, 242
  conscientious objectors 247–9
  doctors in 242
  enlistment, voluntary 233–9
  memorials 250, 280
  munitions workers 243
  mutinies 233
  officers 241–3
  opposition to 231–2
  prisoners-of-war 246–7
  seafarers 237, 244–6
  South African Native Labour
    Contingent 233
Fisk Jubilee Singers 173
Fitzgerald, Ferdinand 187
Flamingo (journal) 426–7
Fletcher Report (1930) 297–8
Florence Mills Social Parlour 319–20
Florent, Napoleon 215, 342
Florent, Vivian 342, 354
Flying Officer Peter Thomas (film)
    357
Forbes, Frederick 113–14

Forbes, Vincent 'Duke Vin' 464–5
Forbes Bonetta, Sarah (Aina)
    112–16, 115, 171
Forlorn Hope (journal) 148
Fortuyn, Tobias 46
Foster, Matilda 107
Foster Jones, Claude 337
FOWAAD! (newsletter) 485, 486
France 32, 49, 88, 94, 105, 117
Francis (African woman, Bristol
    C17) 36
Francis, Alexander 133–4
Francis, Jacques 23
Francis, Joshua 463
Francis, Martin 36
Francklyn, Gilbert 48, 49, 64
Franklyne, Gladys 310
Fraternity (journal) 196–7, 208
freedom 59–60, 74–5, 80–1, 130
    emancipation 82, 118, 119–20,
        121–2, 174–5
    purchase of 66, 100, 108–9, 111
    see also liberation; self-liberation
Freeman, John 131
Freeman, Patrick 239
Freeman, Thomas Birch 177–8
French Revolution 82, 88
Froude, J. A. 199
Fryer, Peter vii, viii, 1–2, 156, 183,
    244, 496
Fulani 59, 66
Fuller, Henry 30
Fye, John 255

Gainsborough, Thomas, Portrait of
    Sancho 62
Gambia 61
Gardner, Joy 513
gardeners 177–8
Gardiner, Charlotte 48
Garnet, Henry Highland 168, 169,
    170, 176

Garrick, David 63
Garrison, Len 458–9, 496–7
Garvey, Marcus 227–8, 289,
    311–12, 315, 495
    influence of 286, 435, 439, 466
Gentleman, Amelia 507
Geoffrey of Monmouth 6
George (Tudor African) 15
George III, King of England 95
George IV, King of England 77, 112
Germany 246–7, 315
Gerzina, Gretchen ix
Ghana 66, 67, 77, 178, 492
Gifford, Anthony, 6th Baron Gifford
    481
Gill, Margaret 179
Gilroy, James 255
Gittens, Rupert 370
Gladstone, Jack 118
Gladstone, Quamina 118
Gladstone, Sir John 118
Gladstone, William 118, 190–2, 203
Glasgow, John 162
Glean, Marion 429–30
Gleaner (ship) 135
Glossop, George 321
Glover, John 48
Godwin, James 130
Godwyn, Morgan 81
Gold Coast 122, 177–8, 204–5
Gold Coast Students' Association
    328–9
Gollancz, Victor 314
Gomwalk, Clement 448
Gordon, George William 184
Gordon, Lord George 48, 65
Gordon, Sarah 146
Gormund, 'King of the Africans' 5–6
Graham, Sid 351–2
Grant, Bernie 482, 487, 494, 505,
    517
Grant, Cy 342

Grassroots (journal) 453, 454, 455, 472, 478
Grassroots Publications 468
graves 4, 7, 8, 9, 116
  for war dead 234, 250
Greater London Council (GLC) 493–7
Green, Jeffrey x
Green, Oreoluwa 215
Green, William 78
Grenada 56, 77, 101
Gresham, Frederick (Frederick Njilima) 239
Grigg, James 360
Grigg, Nanny 117, 121
Groce, Cherry 481, 482, 504
Gronniosaw, James Albert Ukawsaw 58–9, 73
Gross, Theodore 169
Grunshi, Alhaji 231
Guardian (newspaper) 507, 510
Guest, Carmel Haden 300
Guest, E.R. 413
Guinea Company 35
Gunter, Henry 406, 407, 408, 410
Gurney, Samuel 191
Guy, John 75
Guy, Thomas 34

Hackett, Roy 427, 428
Hadrian, Abbot (Adrian of Canterbury) 6–7
Hadrian's Wall 3–5
Haile Selassie 311–12
Haiti 88, 89, 94–5, 96, 200–1, 211
Halifax, 2nd Earl of, George Montagu-Dunk 66–7
Hall, Adelaide 354–5
Hall, Charles 126
Hall, Isaac 247–9
Hall, William 137
Halliburton, Horace 400

Hammon, Briton 58, 73
Hanley, Ellery 498
Harambee Organization 456, 459, 469–70
Hardie, Keir 196, 218
Hardy, Thomas (political reformer) 92–3
Harford, George 75
Harlem Nightbirds (revue) 320
Hart, Richard 390
Harvey, Joseph 44–5
Has Britain a Colour Bar? (TV programme) 405
Hastings, Selina, Countess of Huntingdon 58, 59
Hatch, Isaac (Ike) 299, 319, 320
Hattersley, Roy 431–2
Hawkins, John 14–15, 28
Hawkins, Walter 195
Hawkins, William 12, 14
Hayfron-Benjamin, H. A. 283
Headley, Jim 294
Height, Amy 181
Henderson, John 56–7
Henley, Robert, 1st Earl of Northington (Lord Chancellor) 45
Henriques, Fernando 355
Henry, Owen 427, 428
Henry III, King of England 9
Henry VII, King of England 18, 19
Henry VIII, King of England 18, 19
Henson, James 237
Henson, Josiah 169
Hercules, Felix 274, 275, 276, 277, 278–9, 280–1
heredity 84, 297–8, 410
Hesse, Ludwig 397, 403
Heyrick, Elizabeth 119–20, 121
Hill, Ken 328, 366, 370
Hill, Richard 200–1
Hiller, Joseph 181

*History of the Black Presence in
    London, A* (book) 496
history/historiography vii-xi, 1,
    195-6, 457-8, 469, 495-7,
    518-20
Hodgkin, Thomas 187, 191
Holman, Ann 127
Holt, Sir John (Lord Chief Justice)
    40-1
Home Office 303-4, 420-1, 505-6,
    509-10
Horton, Africanus 188-90, 288
hospitality industry
    colour bar in 359, 403, 411-12,
        429
    International Afro Restaurant 309
    Mangrove Restaurant 449-50
    publicans 142, 164
    see also nightclubs
Houston, William 161
Howe, Charlotte 54
Howe, Darcus 450, 451-2, 467, 476
Howe, Irene 310
Huddleston, Trevor 415, 421
Huggins, Willis 311
Hughes, Samuel 275-6
Hughes, Thomas 187
Huiswoud, Otto 299, 305
Hull 255-6
humanity 64, 81-2, 175
Hume, David 81, 83
Hunt, James (1833-69) 171, 189
Hunte, Joseph 432
Huntley, Eric 441, 468
Huntley, Jessica 441, 443, 456, 457,
    463, 468
Hutcheson, Francis 81
Hutchinson, W. F. 275
Hutchinson Family Singers 174
Hyde, Ade 338-9
Hylas, John 47
Hylas, Mary 47

identity
    Black British 492-3
    national 3
Imperial War Graves Commission
    (IWGC) 250
imperialism 99-101, 116, 183-4,
    187, 192, 197-8
    see also anti-imperialism;
        colonialism
Impey, Catherine 196
imprisonment 129, 160-1, 166-7,
    248-9, 375, 440, 506
    political 328, 366, 445-6
Ince, Paul 498
Independent Labour Party (ILP) 313
Independent Office for Police
    Conduct 514
Independent Order of Good
    Templars (IOGT) 194
Independent Police Complaints
    Commission (IPCC) 513, 514
India League 313
Indian Home Rule Society 229
industrial action *see* strikes
Institute of Race Relations 431
integration 431, 432, 433
intelligence services 227, 426-7,
    439, 442
International African Friends of
    Abyssinia/Ethiopia (IAFA/E)
    306-11
International African Opinion
    (journal) 327-8
International African Service Bureau
    (IASB) 312-15, 316-17, 327-8
International Coloured Mutual Aid
    Society 356
internationalism 313-14, 316-17,
    375
Inter-Racial Friendship Co-
    ordinating Council (IRFCC)
    420-1

Inyang, Amelda 496
'Ipswich Man' 8
Ireland 5–6, 91–2, 145–6, 154–5, 156
Islam 12, 66, 160, 227
Isle of Man 166–7
Ismaa'il, Ibrahim 266
'Ivory Bangle Lady' 4

Jackson, George 442
Jackson, Thomas H. 274, 279
Jackson, William A. 174
Jacobs, Harriet 168
Jamaica 30, 49, 69, 70, 246, 382,
    464–6
    Baptist War 1831 120–1
    Morant Bay rebellion 172, 184–5
Jamaica Gleaner (newspaper) 493
James, Albert 236
James, C. L. R. 313, 324, 439
    and CAM 441
    and CARD 430
    and IAFE 306–10, 311
    and LCP 291
    writings of 317, 318
James, Daniel 108
James, Johnny 433
James, William 236
James I, King of England 36
James II, King of England (Duke of
    York) 30–1, 31
James IV, King of Scotland 20–2
James L. Bogart, USS (ship) 161–2
Jaquoah, Prince Dederi (John) 22–3
Jarrett, Cynthia 481–2, 483
Jeffers, Audrey 274, 276
Jeffrey, Lionel 391
Jeffrey, Pansy 391
Jemmott, Lily 321
Jenkins, Joseph (Selim) 172–3
Jenkins, Thomas (Tom) 202–3
Jetto, Henrie Anthonie 24
John, Errol 440

John, Gus 464
John, King of England 8, 12
Johnson, Akinpelu 339
Johnson, Bill 322–3
Johnson, Don 321
Johnson, Frank 180
Johnson, Isaac Augustus 220
Johnson, J. W. de Graft 288
Johnson, John 259
Johnson, Joseph 124
Johnson, Ken 'Snakehips' 319,
    322, 354
Johnson, Len 217, 323, 355, 370,
    384, 403
Johnson, Linton Kwesi 452,
    468–9
Johnson, Obadiah 205
Johnson, Dr. Samuel 50, 63
Johnson, Thomas Lewis 176
Johnson, Tom 253
Johnson, William 217
Johnston, Sir Harry 229
Jones, Alfred Lewis 191
Jones, Chris (Braithwaite) 294, 299,
    307, 310, 313
Jones, Claudia 417–18, 421, 423,
    424, 424
Jones, E. N. (Laminoh Sankoh) 332
Jones, Edward 234
Jones, Elizabeth 127
Jones, Grace (C19 enslaved woman)
    101–2
Jones, Pero 71
Jones-Lecointe, Altheia 448, 449,
    450, 451, 453, 484
Jonson, Ben 27
Jordan, Edward 120
Jordan, William 134
Joseph, George 452
Joseph, Henry Mason 207
Joseph-Mitchell, Malcolm 391
Joshua, Anthony 515

journalism 166–7, 192, 195–8, 345–6, 348
Julien, Isaac 480
Julyane (Tudor African woman) 17

Karenga, Maulana 436, 470, 495
Kay, Janet 466, 467
Kayode, Aurora (née Fanimokun) 276, 283
Keane, Henry Perry 161
Kenlock, Neil 452
Kennard, Sydney 335
Kennedy, Scipio (Douglas) 72
Kent, John ('Black Kent') 158–9
Kentish, Rothwell 'Roddy' 452
Kenyatta, Jomo 299–300, 305, 376
  and IFAE 307, 309
  and PAF 312, 319, 363, 367, 374
  Pan-African Congress 1945 370, 372
Kessie, Kobina 299
Keys, The (journal) 290–1, 296, 300, 309–10
Khama, Seretse 401–2
kidnapping 15, 29, 32, 37, 47, 49, 76, 161–2
Kihoro, Wanjiru 495
Kildare, Dan 321
King, Amelia 349–51, 350
King, Henry 350
King, Martin Luther 428, 430, 519
King, Nathaniel 205
King, Sam 344, 388, 389, 418, 517
Kinloch, Alice Victoria 207–8
Klu, Kofi Mawuli 517
Knight, Joseph 57–8
Knox, Robert 189
Koutaté, Garan 313
Kru 164
Kunene, Mazisi 437
Kuya, Dorothy 375, 398, 517
Kuya, Joseph 375

Kwanzaa 436, 471
Kyd, Thomas 27

La Corbiniere, Carl 421
La Rose, John 440, 441, 456, 457, 463, 476
LaBadie, Alma 370
Labour Party 212, 361, 369, 404, 480
  Black Sections 494, 496
  migration policy 253, 389–90, 409, 425, 505, 508
  racism and 401–2, 415, 430–2
labour shortages 382, 388
Lacton, Frank 321
Laine, Cleo 418
LaLa, Miss (Albertina Brown) 181–2
Lammy, David 513–14
Lananmi, Oladipo 206
Lane, William Henry (Master Juba) 173
Lang, Cosmo, Archbishop of Canterbury 336
language use 6–7, 23, 113, 115, 191, 200
  Arabic 66
  Dutch 104
  English 42
  French 491
  Twi 110
  see also terminology
'Lant Street Teenager' 5
Lapiere, Richard 273
Lashley, Joe 141
Latif, Mohamed 324
Lawrence (ship) 75
Lawrence, Doreen, Baroness Lawrence 499–504
Lawrence, Neville 499–504
Lawrence, Stephen 499–504
Lawrence, Sir Thomas 36
laws see legislation

Lawson, H. 370

League against Imperialism (LAI) 292, 293, 299, 312

League of Coloured Peoples (LCP) 289–93, 311, 315–16, 324, 335, 393–4
and CLC 391
conferences 305–6, 328–9, 362
founding 224, 240
and PAF 363
seafarers, support for 296–7, 300–1
and WASU 298

League of Nations 275, 306, 309, 311, 315

Learie Constantine (film) 357

lectures and public speaking 87, 89, 90–2, 148, 154–5, 169–71, 194–6

Legal Action Group 506

legal profession 196, 201, 203–4, 208, 215, 285
barristers 223–4, 278
women in 291

legislation 45, 51–5, 121, 385, 420–1, 430–3, 505, 508–9
Act of Union, 1709 31
Aliens Order 1920 270
Aliens Restriction (Amendment) Act 1919 270
British Nationality Act 1948 382, 394
British Nationality Act 1981 480, 508
British Shipping (Assistance) Act 1935 300, 301, 302
Coloured Alien Seamen Order 296, 300, 303
Commonwealth Immigration Act 1962 417, 423–6
Commonwealth Immigration Act 1964 425
Commonwealth Immigration Act 1968 431, 432, 446

Criminal Justice Act 2003 502–3
Foreign Slave Trade Act 1806 94, 96, 99
Fugitive Slave Law 1850 163
'Gagging Acts' (Treason Act and Seditious Meetings Act 1817) 148
Immigration Act 1971 447
Lascar Act 1823 135
Mental Health Units (Use of Force) Act 2018 514
Merchant Shipping Act 1894 135
Navigation Acts 31, 38, 135
Negro Seamen's Act (South Carolina 1822) 161
Parliamentary Reform Act 1832 152–3
Race Relations Act 1965 431–3, 440
Race Relations Act 1968 446
'Six Acts' 1819 150–1
Slave Trade Act (Abolition Act) 1807 93, 96, 98–102, 130
on slavery 13, 17–18, 20, 31, 38
Slavery Abolition Act 1833 93, 99
Special Restriction (Coloured Alien Seamen) Order 1925 270–1
'sus' law 448
Vagrancy Act 1824 448

Leigh, William 337

Leigh-Sodipe, Akinsipe 205

Leslie, Jack 324

Levin, Bernard 482

Lewis, Olaseni 513, 514

Lewis, P. Cecil 300

Lewis, Sir Samuel 203–4

Lewis, Thomas (George August) 52–3, 73

Lewis, W. Arthur 291, 315

Liberal Party 208–9, 211

liberation 117–21, 129, 435–6

liberation politics 437–8, 486–8

Liberia 22, 68, 190–1, 202, 211
Libya 3, 4
Lincoln, Abraham 174–5
Lincoln, Charles 63
Lindsay, Sir John 70
Linton, Joseph 370
literacy 59, 104, 117
literature 27, 63, 440–1, 468–9,
    498
  abolitionist 80–3, 89–93
  anti-racist 177, 185–6
  dub poetry 468–9, 480
  fiction 178
  memoirs 67, 138, 178, 235–6
  North African 7
  poetry 86, 145, 203–4
  revolutionary 455
  'slave narratives' 58–9, 109, 113,
    169, 200
litigation see court cases
Little, Kenneth viii
Liverpool 32–5, 71, 134–5, 158–67,
    303–5
  Black population of 67–8, 164–5
  racial violence in 258–62, 278–9,
    394–8
  sale of enslaved people in 41, 43
  uprising 479
Lloyd, Errol 440–1
Lloyd George, David 279, 288
Locke, Alain 220, 223
Locke, John 31, 81
Locke, Kath 373, 444, 452, 485
Lok, John 14, 15
Lollius Urbicus, Quintus, Governor
    of Britain 3
London
  medieval 8–9
  Tudor 16–17
  seventeenth century 35–6
  eighteenth century 34, 41, 43, 45,
    61–2, 64–5, 69–72

nineteenth century 107–9, 122–5,
    127
  interwar 256–8
  Second World War 357–8
  post-war 386–7, 413–19, 456–7,
    476–7
  Brixton 448, 477–9
  GLC 493–7
  Haringey 456–7
  Metropolitan police 443, 445,
    499–504
  New Cross fire 476–7
  Notting Hill 413–19, 473–5
  racial violence in 398–9, 413–16,
    476–7
  uprisings and unrest 256–8,
    477–9, 481–2, 511
London Anthropological Society
    (LCS) 171, 189
London Corresponding Society
    (LCS) 88, 92–3, 145
London Emancipation Committee
    (LEC) 170
London Mayor's Commission on
    African and Asian Heritage 497
London Strategic Policy Unit (LSPU)
    495
London Transport 404–5, 411, 456
London University Graduates' Club
    228
Long, Edward 47–8, 49, 50, 55, 84
Longman, Frederick 264
'Lord Kitchener' (Aldwyn Roberts)
    387–8, 419
'Lord Woodbine' (Harold Phillips)
    387–8
Loudin, Frederick 210, 211
Loudin, Harriet 210
Loudin Jubilee Singers 210
L'Ouverture, Toussaint 94–5, 145,
    185, 213, 318, 348
Lucas, F. O. 285

Lucette, Tom 182–3
Lunar Society 91
Lux (journal) 195–6
lynching 196, 210, 261
Lyntin, Roger de 9

Macaulay, Thomas Babington 69
Macaulay, Zachary 104, 122
Macauley, Tommy 236
MacDonald, Malcolm 308, 329, 337
Macdonald, Ramsay 219
MacDonald, Trevor 497–8
Macham, Mary Ann 168
Machera, Pauline 484
Macka B (Christopher MacFarlane)
    480
Macnell, John 73
Macpherson Inquiry and Report
    480, 502–3
Maddy, Yulisa Amadu 440
Magnes, Elizabeth ('Kaitus Vessula')
    106
Magnet (newspaper) 426, 437
Mahomet, Hadji 266
Mainwaring, Sir Henry 24, 36, 37
Makippe (Watteau, George) 71
Makonnen, Ras 315, 316, 320, 322,
    344, 370, 396
    and IASB 312–14
    and IFAE 307–9
    and PAF 364–6, 374–6
    Pan-African Congress (1945) 367,
    369–70
Malcolm X 426, 434, 436–7, 439,
    440, 454, 470
Manchester 364–5, 444
Manchester Union and Emancipation
    Society 175–6
Mandela, Nelson 106, 488, 500
Mangena, Alfred 223
Mangrove Nine 449–52
Manley, Michael 380

Manley, Norman 234, 344, 416, 421
Manley, Roy 234
Mann, Tom 196
Manning, Sam 307, 320, 322
Manning, Seymour 414
Mansfield, William Murray, 1st Earl
    48, 52, 64, 70, 74, 78
    Somerset v. Stewart (1772) 45, 51,
    52–4, 78, 100
manumission 44, 56, 66, 100,
    108–9, 111
Manx Times (journal) 166
Maoism 452–3
March, Leo 335–6
Margeret Lucy (C17 African) 40
mariners *see* seafarers
Marke, Ernest 236, 244, 319
    and Coloured Workers' (Welfare)
    Association 365, 386
    in Liverpool 260, 303
    repatriation of 262, 269
Marley, Bob 465
Marlowe, Christopher 27
marriage 46–7, 59, 108
marriage, 'mixed' 15, 16, 50, 57, 68,
    165, 243, 401–2
    opposition to 253, 410
    racial violence and 264–5
    and repatriation 269
Marryat, Joseph 123
Marryshaw, T. Albert 307
Marson, Una 291–2, 305, 341,
    356
Martin, J. L. 386
Martin, John Sella 169–70, 176
Martin, Tommy 384
Marx, Eleanor 185
Marx, Karl 35, 176
Marxism 452–3, 470
Mary Rose (ship) 23
Mary Tudor (Mary I, Queen of
    England) 20

Mather, Joseph 86
Matthews, Robert 386
Mauritius 203
Maxwell, Joseph Renner 204
Maxwell, Marina 456–7
Maxwell, Neville 432
May, Theresa 507
Mayhew, Henry 125, 164
Mayo, Isabella 196
McCalla, Val 492
McCune Smith, James 170
McDowall, J. 242–3
McKay, Claude 238–9
McKay, Peter Karl ('Prince
    Monolulu') 246
McLagan, Peter 494
McNish, Althea 441
medicine see doctors
memorials 250, 280, 352, 389,
    420–1, 516
Men of Two Worlds (film) 361
Mendi, SS (ship) 184, 233, 246
Merriman-Labor, Augustus 221–2
Meyer, William 218
M'Gee, Charles 124
Michael, Samuel 137
Michael X (Michael de Freitas)
    436–8, 439–40, 441, 448, 450
Mighty Sparrow (Slinger Francisco,
    singer) 418, 419
migrants
    direct recruitment of 404–5, 411,
        491–2
    dispersal of 404
    settlement of 426
migration
    early Britain 2–5
    nineteenth century 186, 188
    opposition to 252–3, 385, 389–90
    post-war 378–83, 387–90, 403–5
    Tudor 24–6
migration controls 385, 399

Commonwealth Immigration Acts
    423–6, 446
    'hostile environment' 505–10
    opposition to 424–5, 424
    support for 401, 408–10, 412,
        414–17
Miler, Elizabeth (née Newton) 100
militancy 309, 437–8, 446–7, 452–4
military service 3–4, 72–5, 78, 112,
    124–5, 127–37, 268, 388
    commissions/promotions 130–1
    demobilization from 251–2, 260–1
    labour units 330
    officers 216–17, 330, 331–2,
        338–9, 340, 342
    veterans of 381–2, 383
    see also conscription
Miller, Bill 355
Milliard, Peter 307, 364, 367, 374,
    375
Mills, John (C17 churchwarden) 71
Ministry of Information 356–7
Ministry of Shipping 352–3
Minns, Allan Glaisyer 211, 212, 214
Minto, Charles 356
Miriam, Askala 496
Mitchell, Marian 126–7
models, artists' 106–8
moderateness 292–3
Mohammed (C19 former enslaved
    person, Liverpool) 160
Mohammed, Mzee 511, 512
Molema, S. M. 278
Molineux, Tom 141, 142–3
Montagu, Edward, 1st Earl of
    Sandwich 37
Montagu, George, Duke of
    Montagu 62
Montagu, John, 2nd Duke 62, 70
Montagu, Mary, Duchess of
    Montagu (formerly
    Churchill) 62

Montesquieu (Charles Louis de Secondat) 80, 81
Montgomery, Jamie 55–6
Montsioa, George 223
Moody, Harold 224, 316, 329, 334, 356, 393
  and LCP 289–93, 298, 302, 305, 315
Moody, Joe 334–5
Moody, Ronald 441
Moon, Gregory 435
Moore, David 479
Moore, Egbert ('Lord Beginner') 387–8
Moore, George 308, 312
Moore, Queen Mother 497
Moore, Susannah 181
Moore, Walter 245
'Moors' 8
More, Elen 21
More, Hannah 69
More, Margaret 21
More, Sir Thomas 19
Moriana, Maria 12–13
Morier, David 72–3
Moriscos 13
Morocco 14
Morrell, Danny 452
Morris, Bill 498
Morris, Jacob 126
Morris, Olive 448, 459, 484
Morris, William 185
Mosley, Oswald 419
Movement for Colonial Freedom (MCF) 421, 422
Mugabe, Robert 495
Mugabe, Sally 495
Muhammad an-Nāsir, Caliph 12
munitions workers 243, 346–7, 351, 361
murder 75, 78, 131, 264, 266–7, 432, 490

  of Kelso Cochrane 420–1
  of Stephen Lawrence 499–504
music
  blues 320
  calypso 320, 322, 387–8
  jazz 320, 321
  Lovers' Rock 466–7
  recordings 320
  reggae 464–7, 468, 480
musicians 12, 20–1, 76–7, 127, 180–1, 218, 321–2, 354–5
  calypsonians 387–8
  at Carnival 418–19
  conductors 348
  drummers 20–1, 72–3, 131
  for films 358
  military bandsmen 72–3, 126, 128, 129, 131, 132–3
  minstrels 173–4, 197–8
  singers 173–4, 210, 318–19
  sound-systems artists 464–6
  trumpeters 18–19, 72–3, 128
mutinies 161–2, 233, 268

Naggi, Abdul 253
Naimbana, John (Henry Granville) 68
Naipaul, V. S. 1–2
names 27–8, 78, 92
Namibia 487–8
Naoroji, Dadabhai 196, 208–9, 494
Naronje, Robert 337
National Congress of British West Africa (NCBWA) 218, 280–2, 287
National Council for Civil Liberties (NCCL) 292, 308, 399, 415–16
National Council of Nigeria and the Cameroons (NCNC) 376
National Reformer (journal) 166
nationalism 288, 435–6
nationality 382, 383, 394, 480

naturalization 301
Navy, Merchant 125, 133–7, 237, 244–5, 350–4
Navy, Royal 13, 24, 59, 73–5, 78, 125, 133–7, 161
  Anti-Slave Trade (West Africa) Squadron 99, 113
  colour bar 134, 331, 352–3
  enslaved men in 130
  in First World War 244–7
  promotions and ranks 135–6, 137
  in Second World War 330
needle-makers 16, 23
Negro, Fraunces 20
Negro, Lucy (Black Luce) 27
Negro Association 364
Negro Theatre Workshop 440
Negro Welfare Association (NWA) 292, 299, 304–5, 310, 312, 315, 318, 328–9
Negro Welfare Centre 364–5
Negro Worker (journal) 292, 299–300, 307, 312
Neilson, Samuel 91, 92
Nelson, Edward T. 224, 278, 364
Nelson, Frank 240
Nelson, Horatio 73, 136, 138
Nevis 29, 71
New African (newspaper) 373–4
New Beacon Books 457
New Cross Massacre Action Committee (NCMAC) 476–7
New Internationalist Society (NIS) 403
Newton, Elizabeth (Mrs Miler) 100
NHS (National Health Service) 404–5, 491–2
Nigeria 58, 115–16, 178, 286, 336, 376
Nigerian Progress Union (NPU) 285–6, 286

nightclubs 319–20, 365, 411–12, 464–5, 472–3
Nightingale, Florence 139
Njilima, Frederick (Frederick Gresham) 239
Njururi, Ngumbu 430
Nkrumah, Kwame 306, 370, 373–4, 422–3, 445
Nollekens, Joseph 63, 78
North London West Indian Association (NLWIA) 456
Nottingham 72, 411, 413–16
Nurse Ademola (film) 357
nursing 137–41, 205, 291–2, 378–9, 404–5, 491–2
  in Second World War 334, 357, 357
Nylander, Susannah 292

Obasa, Orisadipe 205
Obi, Liz 459, 484
Obisanya, Opeulu 289
occupations 16–24, 70–2, 124–5, 203–4
  see also employment
O'Connell, Harry 294, 298–9, 302, 305, 309, 316
O'Connor, Fergus 155–6
Odunsi, Olabode 375
Olusoga, David viii–ix
Oluwale, David 380, 432
Omoniyi, Prince Bandele 218–19, 219, 222
O'Neill, Eugene 318
Organization of Women of African and Asian Descent (OWAAD) 485
Ormonde, SS (ship) 381, 385
orphanages 215, 216
Osamor, Martha, Baroness 494
Osborn, Robert 120
Osborne, Anne (later Sancho) 62, 71

Ouseley, Herman 478
Oval Four 460–1, 462

pacifism 327–9
Padmore, George 292, 299, 307–8,
  318, 393
  and CLC 391
  on colour bar 334, 336
  *How Russia Transformed Her
    Colonial Empire* 362
  and IASB 311–13, 315, 317
  'Manifesto against War' 327–9
  and PAF 362–4, 366–7, 374–5,
    376
  Pan-African Congress (1945) 367,
    370
  'White Man's Duty' 329, 362
Paine, Thomas 92, 149
PANAF Service Ltd 374–5
Pan-Africa (journal) 376–7
Pan-African (journal) 211
Pan-African Association 208–11
Pan-African Committee 470
Pan-African Conference (1900)
  209–11
Pan-African Congresses 276, 282,
  323, 365–73, 372, 469–70
Pan-African Federation (PAF) 312,
  363–72, 374–7, 391
Pan-Africanism 92, 187–8, 189–90,
  199, 207–11, 272, 434–5
  Ethiopianism 220–1, 228–9
  interwar 306–7, 309–17
  manifesto 282
  nationalism 373
  networks of 223, 316
  newspapers 205, 316–17
  post-war 369–71, 421–3
  protests of 314–17
  Rastafarianism 465–6
  see also Black Power movement
Pan-Africanist Congress (PAC) 487

Pan-Afrikan Congress Movement
  (PACM) 470–1
Pan-Afrikan Reparations Coalition
  in Europe (PARCOE) 517–18
Panah, Peter 68
Pankhurst, Sylvia 314, 329
Paris, Eddie 324
Parker, Victor 321
Parliament
  and abolition 88–9, 93–4, 95
  House of Commons 80
  petitions to 86, 109, 153–4
  Privy Council 24, 25, 36, 86, 89
  reform, campaigns for 120, 121,
    147–8, 152–4, 166–7
Pascall, Alex 476, 493
passing 241
passports 168, 303–4, 346
Patel, Abdullah 437, 438
Patel, Priti 510
patriality 447, 480, 508
Paul, Nathaniel 168
Paul Bogle Youth Movement 456
Payne, John 308
Peart, Henry 381
Pennington, J. W. C. 169, 170
pensions 129, 130, 137, 239–40, 342
Pepys, Samuel 31, 37
Percy, Hugh 141
performers *see* actors; entertainment
  industry; musicians
Perkins, Captain John ('Jack Punch')
  135–6
Perry, John 141
Perth, Mary 69
Peter the More 21
Peter the Saracen 8
Peterloo Massacre 150
Peters, James 'Jimmy' 215–16
Peters, John 61
Phal, Louis 323
Phillip, John (African sailor) 24

Phillips, Harold ('Lord Woodbine') 387–8
Phillips, Ron 444, 452, 469, 470
Phombeah, Denis 422
Picton, Cesar 71
Pilgrim, Winston 411–12
Piliso, Clarence 406, 407
Pindar, Winston 391
Pinney, John 71
piracy 24, 36
Pitt, David 391, 420, 421, 424, 430, 431–2
Pitt, Thomas, 2nd Baron Camelford 142
Pitt, William, the Younger 86, 96
Pizer, Dorothy 362, 375
plantations 32–4, 121
police
  Black 71, 158–9, 420
  corruption 460–1, 503–4
  deaths caused by/in custody 432, 463, 480, 481, 511, 511–15
  entrapment 151
  harrassment 448, 452, 463–4, 500
  Metropolitan 443, 445, 499–504
  'Operation Swamp 81' (stop and search) 477–8
  racism of 262, 272, 303, 414, 432, 448, 450–1, 479–81
  and racist violence 255, 266–7, 395–6, 414–15
  raids 320, 472–3
  registration with 270–1, 293
  resistance against 473–5
  Special Patrol Group 472, 474, 477–8
  violence of 328, 432, 448, 450–1
  see also arrests
Police Complaints Authority 501
political organizations 207, 283–93
  Black sections 493–4
  co-operation of 334, 367–8, 374–5, 391, 417, 470–2
  disputes 292, 315, 431–2, 443–4
  transnational work of 280–2, 286–7
politicians 199, 205–6, 211–12, 224, 386, 494–5, 505
Polly (enslaved person) 102, 110–11
Pope, Alexander 34
populations
  prehistoric 1–3
  Roman 1–5
  medieval 11–14
  Tudor 11–22, 24–6
  Stuart period 30–2
  eighteenth century 46, 64–5, 67–8, 71, 164–5, 256, 262
  nineteenth century 98, 123, 134–6, 198–9
  Edwardian 215
  interwar 293
  post-war 380–1, 403–4, 411, 423–4
  twenty-first century 489–92, 513–14
Portugal 11–12, 18, 32
Post Man and the Historical Account (journal) 42
Postlethwayte, Malachy 35
poverty 59, 84, 100, 108, 122–7, 163, 247
  among seafarers 267, 295, 296–7, 300
  of military veterans 124–5, 130
Powell, Enoch 446, 448
Powell, William 163–4, 167
Power, Chris viii, 496
Prescod, H. F. 396
Prescod, Pearl 418
press 63–4, 76, 79, 97–8, 234, 272–4
  on abolitionism 86–7
  Black 426–7, 467–8, 492
  censorship 152, 227, 377
  disinformation in 409–10

press – *cont'd.*
  pamphlets 314, 317
  on racist violence 255–8, 260–1,
    267, 395–6
Price, George 332–4
Priestley, Joseph 91
Prince, Mary 108–9, 113, 140
'Prince Monolulu' (Peter Karl
    McKay) 246
Pringle, Thomas 109
printing industry 167
prisoners-of-war 129, 338, 361
prisons 48, 125–6, 129
privateering 13–14, 21, 24
Progress (journal) 386
Progressive Party 211
Prophett, Benjamin 156
prostitution 17, 27, 126–7
protests 277, 422
  boycotts 427–9, 487–8
  against British Shipping
    (Assistance) Act 1935 301, 302
  suppression of 184, 328
  UCPA, Manchester Cathedral
    444–5, 444
  see also demonstrations; strikes
public office roles 111–12, 167
publishing industry 71, 374–5, 457,
    467–8

Quamina (leader of Demerara
    rebellion) 118
Quaque (Kewku), Philip 68–9
Quarcoopome, Solomon 380
Queens' College, Taunton 217

race, concepts of 431
Race Relations Board 431
Race Today (journal) 467–8, 473–4
Racial Adjustment Action Society
    (RAAS) 437–8, 445
racism 83–5, 138–9
  medieval 8
  Tudor 19, 21–2
  eighteenth century 46–7, 64
  Stuart 26–7
  interwar 272–3
  in criminal justice system 151,
    156, 157–8, 513–14
  critique of 83–4, 197–9
  and employment 71–2, 218, 291–2
  in entertainment industry 102–6,
    173–4, 179, 183
  epithets/names and 28
  everyday 401–3
  growth of 221–5
  and imperialism 183–4, 336, 385
  institutional 449, 479–80, 502
  in military service 131–3, 135,
    240, 245–6, 251–3
  towards mixed heritage children
    297–8
  opinion polls on 273
  physiological 105–6
  of police 262, 272, 303, 414, 432,
    448, 450–1, 479–81
  'pseudo-scientific' 171–2, 183,
    189–90
  in public life 188
  refutation of 70, 222–3
  and sexism 105–6
  slavery, justified by 83–4
  in sport 142, 143, 498
  of trade unions 252–3, 255,
    258–9, 269–70, 277, 407–8
  in universities 221, 286
  see also colour bar
Rackett, Margaret 129
Rackett, Thomas 128–9
radicalism 36, 48, 82, 87–8, 91–3,
    119–20, 145–6
  Chartism 152–8, 166–7
  revolutionary 148–51
  Spencean Philanthropists 147, 148

Rainy, William 187
Raleigh, Sir Walter 16
Ramdin, Ron ix
Ramsey, James 82–3
Randle, John 205
ransoms 161–2
Raynal, Guillaume 81
Read, Ann 75
rebellions 49, 82, 84–5, 88, 95, 96,
     148–9, 161, 231–2
  La Amistad 185
  Bambatha 223
  Baptist War, Jamaica 1831 120–1
  Bussa's Rebellion, Barbados 117–18
  Demerara 1823 118, 119
  Morant Bay 172, 184–5
  Newport Rising 154
  Tacky's Rebellion 84–5
  see also uprisings
'recaptives' 178, 188
Reckford, Lloyd 440
Reed, Sarah 512
re-enslavement 74–5, 78, 100
Reeves, George 245
religion 176–8
  atheism 195
  faith 58–9
  Islam 8
  Rastafarianism 465–6
  see also Christianity; clergy
Remond, Charles Lenox 168
Remond, Sarah Parker 168, 170,
     171, 172
reparations 516–18
repatriation 102, 261–2, 267–9,
     279–80, 302, 346, 397
  of artifacts and human remains
     106, 117
  voluntary 123, 160, 187, 259
representations 8–9, 18, 34–5
  in art 62, 67, 72, 77, 106–8, 141,
     440–1

media 65, 460, 478–9, 493, 497–8
  see also press; television
resettlement 85, 162–4, 188
resistance
  against policing 473–5
  of slavery 9, 38–9
  uprisings 475–82, 511
resistance politics 467–72
revolutions 95, 96, 148–51
  American 61, 65, 74, 82, 85
  French 82, 88
  Haiti 88, 89, 95
Reynolds, Sir Joshua 50, 78
Rich, Robert 43
Richard of Devizes 8
Richardson Report (1935) 297–8, 302
Richmond, Bill 141–4
Rickman, Thomas 145
Ricks, Martha 193
Rigg, Marcia 512–13
Rigg, Sean 512–13
rights 80, 82, 87–8, 175, 447, 449
riots see social disorder
Risien Russell, James 200, 242
Roach, Colin 480
Roberts, Aldwyn ('Lord Kitchener')
     387–8, 419
Roberts, Arthur 234–5, 248
Roberts, George 239–40, 359
Robeson, Eslanda 421
Robeson, Paul 290, 318–19, 422
Robinson, Jemmy 141
Robinson, Sam 141
Robinson, Sugar Ray 383
Rocha, Moses Da 220
Rogers, George 412, 415
Rogers, J. A. ix
Roman era 1–5
Roper, Moses 168
Roscoe, William 160
Rose, George 130–1
Rossetti, Dante Gabriel 108

Rowland, Clement 381
Royal Africa Company (RAC) 30,
    31, 34, 66–7
Royal Air Force (RAF) 331, 335–44,
    340
Rudd, Amber 507
Rushdie-Gray, G. O. 242
Russell, James Risien 200, 242
Russell, William 139–40
Ryan, George 136

Said, Mohammed 307, 312
sailors *see* seafarers
Saklatvala, Shapurji 282, 288, 494
Salford 255–6
Salkey, Andrew 430, 440
Salter, Alfred 248, 249
salvage divers 23
Sampson, John 131
Sancho, Anne (née Osborne) 62, 71
Sancho, Charles Ignatius 61–4,
    70–1, 76, 185
Sancho, William 71
Sanders, George (Yahne Aelane) 92
Sanders of the River (film) 318, 319
Sapara, Oguntola 196, 205
'Saracens' 8–9
Sarbah, Eve Nancy 205
Sarbah, John Mensah 204, 224
Satia, John 72
Savage, Richard Akinwande 210, 218
Savory, William 247
Sawh, Roy 437, 438, 441–2, 448, 459
Sawyer, Rowland 299, 331
Saxons 2, 4, 5–6
Scarman Inquiry 479–80, 502
Schoen, Dr James 115
Scholes, T. E. S. 222–3, 224
Scobie, Edward ix, 244, 414, 426–7
Scotland 92, 235, 253–4, 345
    Roman 3–5
    Tudor 13, 20–2

eighteenth century 55–8
    Edinburgh 41, 56
    Glasgow 39, 72, 253–4, 277–8
Scott, William, Baron of Stowell 102
Scottsboro case 299–300, 318, 319
Seacole, Mary 137–41
seafarers
    Tudor 23–4
    seventeenth century 36–7
    eighteenth century 73–5, 78
    nineteenth century 124–5, 133–4,
        159–65
    Edwardian 215
    in First World War 250, 251
    interwar 258–70, 277, 293–305
    in Second World War 351–4
    post-war 386
Seaford, Sussex 232–3
Seamen's Minority Movement
    (SMM) 294, 295, 298–9
seamen's mission, London 386–7
seamstresses 17, 71, 108
Secker, Thomas, Archbishop of
    Canterbury 33–4
Second World War
    Air Raid Precautions (ARP)
        services 332–3, 355
    colonies' service in 329–31
    D-Day landings 352
    declaration of 327
    funding contributions to 330–1,
        336
    Home Front 354–5
    munitions workers 346–7
    propaganda 356–8
segregation 343–4, 346–7, 353, 358,
    404, 407
self-defence 254, 257, 414–16, 432,
    435, 450–1, 473
self-determination 229, 275, 276,
    281, 288, 316
    rights to 361, 362

self-government
  of Africa 189–90, 361–2
  demands for 328, 361–3
  support for 391
self-help 467, 471
self-liberation 9, 33, 39–40, 46–8,
  54, 56, 100–2, 108–9
Seme, Pixley 220, 223
Senden, Caspar Van 25–6
Senegal 66
Sentamu, John 498
servitude 29–30
Sessarakoo, William Ansah 66–7
Sessay, Abdul 386
Severus, Septimius, Roman emperor
  3–4
sex work 17, 27, 126–7
sexual relationships, 'mixed' 35–6,
  84, 229, 256–7, 344
  acceptance of 360
  criticism of 278–9, 393
  as justification for racism 399,
  400
  policing of 271, 297
  prevention of 404
sexuality 322
Shabazz, Menelik 468, 482
Shakespeare, William 22, 27,
  178–80, 180
Sharp, Granville 47, 51–3, 60, 68–9,
  78–9, 82, 85–8
Sharpe, Nancie 298
Sharpe, Samuel 120–1
Sharpton, Al 499
Shenbanjo, Akin 338
Sheridan, Richard 142
Sherwood, Marika viii
Shinwell, Emmanuel 253
Shirley, Walter 58
Shropshire, John 50
Shyllon, Folarin ix, 50
Shyngle, J. Egerton 239

Sierra Leone 65, 69, 85, 113, 114,
  188, 192
Sierra Leone Company 69
Silver Falcon (ship) 36
Simmonds, John 137
Simmonds, Richard 147
Sinclair, Henry 133–4
Skelhorn, Norman 450
skin colour 2–3, 27, 111
Skinner-Carter, Corrine 418
slave auctions 41, 45
slave owners 47–8, 54–5, 57–8, 83, 96
  Caribbean 70, 111–12
  compensation of 112, 121–2
slave ships 74, 159, 185
  Brooke 87, 110
  Zong 78, 80
slavery
  in British colonies 122
  defences of 83–5
  English trade in 29–35
  legal status of 17–18, 20, 43–5,
  53–4, 57–8
  in medieval period 9, 12–13
  post-abolition, continuation of
  99–103, 109–11
  proposed reform of 80–1
  support for 123
  'triangular trade' 32
Slim, James 240
Sloane, Hans 66
Small, Richard 430
Smiley Culture (David Emmanuel)
  513
Smith, Adam 82
Smith, Adelaide (later Casely
  Hayford) 205, 217
Smith, Bob 141
Smith, John (missionary) 118
Smith, John Thomas 124
Smith, Lewis 169
Smith, Morgan 180

Smith, R. B. 191
Smyth, John 241
Smythe, Johnny 337–8, 339, 340, 388, 390
Soares, Tony 453–5
sociability 50–1, 54–5, 218, 230, 280, 282, 305, 321–2
  see also nightclubs
social disorder 265, 278
  1919 251–67, 277–80
  1958 413–16
  2016 511
  see also rebellions; uprisings
social organizations 228, 238–9, 291
socialism 185, 194–5, 373–4, 470–2
Socialist Labour Party 253
Society for Promoting Constitutional Reform 87
Society for the Abolition of the Slave Trade 85–6
Society for the Furtherance of the Brotherhood of Man (SFBM) 196
Society for the Mitigation and Gradual Abolition of Slavery see Anti-Slavery Society
Society for the Propagation of the Gospel in Foreign Parts 33–4, 68, 69
Society for the Recognition of the Brotherhood of Man (SRBM) 177, 196–7, 207
Society for the Suppression of Mendicity 123–4
Society of African Peoples (SAP) 279
Society of Peoples of African Origin (SPAO) 275–7, 278–9, 280–1
Society of United Irishmen 91–2
Soga, A. K. 199
Soga, J. F. 199
Soga, Jessie Margaret 199
Soga, Tiyo 199

Solanke, Ladipo 283–9, 311
Solanke, Olu 322
Solomon, Henry 238
Solomon, Simeon 107
Somali people 164, 301, 490–1
Somerset, James 53–5, 100
Sons of Africa (organization) 51, 77–9, 89, 92
Sorenson, Reginald 402
Soubise, Julius 70–1
South Africa 14, 103, 199, 208, 221, 314, 401–2
  African National Congress (ANC) 223, 279, 422
  anti-apartheid campaign 422, 486–8
  First World War 233
South America 118, 119, 200
South Place Ethical Society 225
South Sea Company 31, 34
South Shields 254–5, 295, 301
Sowande, Fela 289, 321, 358
Soyinka, Wole 440
Spain 8, 11–14, 19, 31–2
Spence, Thomas 146, 147
Spens, David (Black Tom) 56–7
spies/spying see surveillance
Spiller, Gustav 225
sport 215–17
  athletics 240
  boxing/prize-fighting 131, 141–4, 217, 239–40, 322–4, 383–4
  colour bar in 323–4, 349, 383–4
  cricket 324
  football 205, 216–17, 216, 324–5, 498
  racism in 142, 143, 498
  rugby 215–16, 498
Springtime in An English Village (film) 355
St Augustine's Missionary Training College, Canterbury 199–200

St Kitts 111, 112
Standing Conference of West Indian
    Organizations 417
Stanford, Peter 176–7
Stanford-Xosei, Esther 517
statues, removal of 516
status 21–2, 24–8
    enslaved 37–8, 40–1, 43–5, 108–11
    free 23, 37–8, 70, 75, 108–11
    legal 27–8, 43–5
    servile 41
    wage-earners 23–4, 36–7
Stead, W. T. 221
Stephen, James 95, 96, 123
Stephen Lawrence Independent
    Review 503
Stephenson, Paul 427, 428, 429, 476
Stepney Coloured People's
    Association 387
Sterne, Laurence 62
Steuart, Private 240
Steward, Henry 161
Stewart, Margaret (1598–1600) 21
Still, William Grant 348
Stock, Dinah 376
Stormzy (Michael Ebenezer Kwadjo
    Omari Owuo Jr.) 515
stowaways 237, 244, 337, 380–3,
    387, 388, 394, 396
Stowe, Harriet Beecher, *Uncle Tom's
    Cabin* 169, 173, 181, 217
Strachan, Billy 340–1, 391–3, 410,
    417
Strickland, Susanna 109
strikes 148, 246, 328, 354, 368, 377
    of migrant workforces 437–8
    by seafarers 295, 353–4, 375–6
    in Second World War 330–1, 345,
    347
Strong, Jonathan 51–2
Stuart, John 126
Stuart, Moira 497

Student Christian Movement (SCM)
    229
students
    seventeenth century 22–3
    eighteenth century 68–9
    nineteenth century 206
    Edwardian 217–19
    First World War 228–30
    interwar 277–8, 283–9
    post-war 378–80, 379, 428
    see also West African Students'
    Union
sugar boycott 87
surveillance 15, 151, 227, 281
    of Black Power movement 442–3
    of Mangrove Restaurant 450
    of murder victims' families
    499–500, 501, 503–5
    Pan-African Congress (1945)
    372–3
    police 503–5
    of young people 472–3
Sutton, Henry 141
Sweeney, Joe 180–1
Sylvain, Benito 210
Sylvester, Noel (Sylvester Leon) 246
Sylvester, Roger 504, 513

Talbot, Charles 44, 52, 102
Tandoh, Kwamina F. 274, 275, 282
tattooists 165
taxidermy 201–2
Taylor, Cecilia Amado 274, 276
Taylor, Cleston 391, 392
Taylor, Damilola 490
Taylor, George 352
Taylor, James 367
Taylor, Jimmy 364–5
teachers 171, 191, 194–5, 202–3,
    213, 455–6
television 405, 448, 461, 478, 493,
    497–8, 507

terminology
'Black' vii, 442, 464
'Black British' 492
'coloured' 417, 464
names 27–8, 78, 92
racist, campaigns against 334
racist, criticism of 62, 275, 288
racist, usage of 221, 222, 247
Tewedros II of Abyssinia 116
Thatcher, Margaret 474–5
theatre 142, 178–81, 291, 318, 440,
498
Thistlewood, Arthur 150–2
Thomas, John Jacob, *Froudacity*
198–9
Thomas, Peter Adeniyi 336–7
Thomas, Stella 291
Thomas, Theodore, *Hard Truth*
197–8
Thompson, Ann 57
Thompson, Dudley 341–2
Thompson, Egbert 321
Thompson, Eugene 381
Thompson, Leslie 321, 322, 354–5
Thompson, Montacute 274, 275
Thompson, Thomas J. 207
Tillett, Ben 196
Tiptoft, Robert 8
Tobin, James 84–5
Togoland (Togo/Ghana) 231
Torbotoh, John Liverpool 246
Tottenham 481–2, 511
tournaments 21–2
trade 13–14, 22–3, 34, 94, 96, 97, 121
see also trafficking
trade unions 186, 316, 391, 412,
438
and anti-racism 411–12, 456, 457
Black sections 493–4
British Seafarers' Union 252, 253
Coloured Film Artistes Association
319

International Trade Union
Committee of Negro Workers
(ITUCNW) 305, 307
Musicians Union 411–12
National African Sailors and
Fireman's Union 304
National Sailors and Fireman's
Union (NSFU) 237, 252,
267–8, 269–70, 277
National Union of Seamen (NUS)
294–5, 300, 302, 353, 354, 375,
385, 394–5
racism of 252–3, 255, 258–9,
269–70, 277, 407–8
Transport and General Workers
Union (TGWU) 427–9, 498
World Federation of Trade Unions
366
Trades Union Congress (TUC) 406,
416
trafficking 7, 11–16, 28, 29–35
African 65–7, 68, 78
financing of 31–3, 121, 122
French 88, 117
increased, post-abolition 99, 112
prohibition of 96, 97
transport industry 404–5, 411, 456
transportation 24–6, 427–9
of convicts 29, 50, 126, 128
of fugitive enslaved people 47, 49
resettlement 85, 162–4, 188
see also repatriation
Trend, Sir Burke 508
trials *see* court cases
Tryon, Thomas 83–4
Tucker, David 293
Tull, Walter 216–17, 216, 241, 248
Tull-Warnock, Edward 216
Tunisia 3, 4, 8
Tupper, Edward 237
Ture, Kwame (Stokely Carmichael)
434, 438–42, 454, 470

Turnbull, Gordon 84–5
Turpin, Jackie 238, 384, *384*
Turpin, Lionel ('Dick') 238, 324, 383, *384*
Turpin, Lionel (senior) 234, 238
Turpin, Randolph 234, 383, *384*
Two Dialogues on the Man-trade (pamphlet) 81–2

Udah, David 448
UKBLM *see* Black Lives Matter UK
unemployment 24–5, 59, 303, 397
    Black workers, blamed on 253
    in Caribbean 401
    of domestic servants 123
    of military veterans 124–5
    of seafarers 165, 268, 353
    wartime 342, 347, 353
Union of Students of African Descent (USAD) 229, 282–3
United Africa (journal) 422, 440
United Africa-Asia League 417
United Committee of Colonial and Coloured People's Organizations (UCCCPO) 397
United Friends and Family Campaign 514
United Irish League 212
United Nations 366, 368, 371–2, 514–15
United States of America (USA) 29, 56, 59, 78, 174–5, 210, 358–60
unity 305–6, 315, 316, 368, 397, 417
Universal Coloured People's Association (UCPA) 440, 441–5, 444, 447, 454
universities 170–1, 188, 198–206, 218, 220, 287
    Cambridge 70, 77
    Glasgow 199
    racism in 221, 286
uprisings 475–82, 511

in Caribbean 49, 94–5, 95, 96, 314–15
    Gordon Riots 48, 63, 147
    see also rebellions
Utrecht, Treaty of (1713) 31
Uxbridge, Joseph 126

Vanloo, Robert Ebenezer 249
Vassa, Gustavus *see* Equiano, Olaudah
Vaughan, James 278
Vause, Anne 16
Vause, Anthonie 16
Vaz, Keith 494
veterinary surgeons 199, 242
Victoria, Queen of Great Britain 113–16, 169, 193
Victory, HMS (ship) 136
vigils 421
Vincent, F. O. 285
violence
    activist responses to 277–80
    'Battle of Bamber Bridge' 358
    police 395, 397
    popular opposition to 399
    in suppression of protest 184
violence, racist 258, 259–60, 394–403, 413–16, 420–1
    assaults 12, 51, 129, 131–2, 135
    flogging 276
    justification of 253
    in Liverpool 258–62, 278–9, 394–8
    lynching 196, 210, 261
    see also murder
Visram, Rozina vii
Vivour, Bankole 339
Voice, The (newspaper) 487, 492–3
Voice of Africa (journal) 312
Voltaire (François-Marie Arouet) 71, 80
Voluntary Aid Detachments (VAD) 334

voting rights 61, 72, 87, 92, 112,
    152–3, 175–6, 228

Wachuku, Jaja 370
Wadström, Carl 67–8, 159
wage inequality 135, 164–5, 246,
    270, 294
  in Merchant Navy 331, 353–4
  for war service 330, 345
wages 19, 21, 23, 268, 270, 428
  legal pursuit of 100, 134
  petitions for 24, 36, 45
Walcott, Lewis 245
Wales 72, 92, 111–12, 205–6, 223,
    236–7, 262–7, 265
  see also Cardiff
Walker, Aston 435
Walker, George 217
Walker, Thomas 88, 92
Wallace, George (Cojoh Ammere)
    81, 92
Wallace-Johnson, Isaac
  and IASB 312–13, 315
  internment of 328, 366
  and PAF 363, 366–7
  Pan-African Congress (1945) 369,
    370
  and WANS 373
Wallen, Otto 335–6
Walpole, Horace 67
Walters, Alexander 210, 211
Walvin, James viii, 98
Wambu, Onyekachi 493
war loans 330–1, 336
Ward, Arnold 299, 300, 305, 319
Ward, K. A. 334
wars
  American War of Independence
    61, 65, 74, 82, 85
  Anglo-French 31, 88, 98, 129–30
  Anglo-Spanish 13–14, 26
  Battle of Trafalgar 136

Battle of Waterloo 128
Cold War 390, 391
Crimean War 137–40
English Civil War 35
between enslaved and enslavers
    33, 49
  of liberation 117–21, 129
  Napoleonic 124, 128, 136–7
  see also First World War; Second
    World War
Washington, Booker T. 210, 213,
    220, 227
Wāsù (journal) 288
Watchman and Jamaica Free Press
    120
Waterford, Israel 129
Waters, Billy 124
Waterton, Charles 201
Watkins, James 163, 171
Watt, James 33, 91
Watteau, George (Makippe) 71
wealth 17, 21–2, 32–4, 62, 111, 124,
    141
weavers 16, 59
Webb, Alfred 209
Wedderburn, John 57–8
Wedderburn, Robert 133, 146–52
Wedgwood, Josiah 86–7, 91
welfare work 347, 393–4
Wellesley-Cole, Robert 331
Wells, Ida B. 168, 196
Wells, Joardine (Juggy) 111
Wells, Nathaniel 111–12
Wells, William 111
Wells Brown, William 168, 169,
    171–3, 185
Wesley, Charles 290
Wesley, John 82
West, Frederick 381
West Africa (newspaper) 283–4, 493
West African and West Indian
    Christian Union 276, 283

West African Medical Service 218
West African National Secretariat
(WANS) 373–4
West African Students' Union
(WASU) 218, 287–9, 292–3,
298, 305, 310, 316
in *An African in England* (film)
358
anti-colonialism of 329
and CAO 422
colour bar, protests against 332
hostels 322
and PAF 363
Paul Robeson and 318–19
in Second World War 360–1
wartime broadcasts 357
West African Women's Association
(WAWA) 379
West Indian Development Council
(WIDC) 428–9
West Indian Gazette (newspaper)
417–18, 425
West Indian Standing Conference
(WISC) 430–2, 436
West Indian Student Centre 380, 441
West Indian Students' Union (WISU)
380
West Indian World (journal) 487,
492–3
Wharton, Arthur 205
Wharton, Clara 205
Wharton, James 141
Wheatley, Phillis 59–61, 60, 63, 185
Wheattle, Alex 478
Whiston, John George 160–1
White, Percy 264
white supremacism 412–13
whiteness 410, 470–2
Wilberforce, William 71, 86, 92,
122, 148
abolition bills 88–9, 93–5
and African Academy 69

and Richard Hill 200
and Robert Wedderburn 152
Wilkes, John 48
Wilkinson, Ellen 314
Willcocks, Sir James 233
William (Dennis), Ann 71
Williams, Aubrey 243, 441
Williams, Bert 217
Williams, Dave 'Baba' 354
Williams, Elizabeth 127
Williams, Eric 30, 33, 94, 96, 121
Williams, Francis 70
Williams, George 239
Williams, Henry Sylvester 207, 208,
210–11, 222, 223
Williams, James 122
Williams, John 75, 238
Williams, Joseph 126
Williams, Ruth 401–2
Willow, Capres 511
Wilmot, Allan 353, 383
Wilson (artists' model) 106
Wilson, Paulette 507
Wiltshire, Bernard 496
Wiltshire, Edward 237
Windrush (ship) *see Empire
Windrush, HMT* (ship)
Windrush scandal 505–10
Windsor, Thomas 50
Winnington, Sir Francis 31, 38
Winters, Mary 376
Wise, George 131
Wollstonecraft, Mary 91
women
early Britain 4–5
Tudor 16–17, 19–22
seventeenth century 36
abolitionist 87, 119–20, 170
activism of 274, 276, 282, 291–2
advertisements for sale of 41, 42, 42
Chartists 153
convicts 126–7

women – *cont'd.*
  education of 70, 205
  enslaved status of 101–2
  escaped 39
  and liberation 55, 117, 483–5
  men, disguised as 73–4, 136
  munitions workers 243
  politicians 207–8, 494–5
  students 68, 217–18, 378–9
  voting rights 153, 228
  war service 339, 343–4, 349–51, 357, 357
  white 256–7, 268, 344
  writing by 109, 376, 484
Women's Auxiliary Air Force (WAAF) 339, 370
Women's Land Army (WLA) 350–1
Women's League (NWL) 379
Wong, Ansel 458, 469, 495
Wood, Samuel 308, 312
Woodburn, Arthur 333
Woolman, John 82
Wootton, Charles 258, 259–60, 278–9
Wordsworth, William 145
Workers' Socialist Federation 253
working conditions 345–6
World War I *see* First World War
Wrasama, Kathleen 386–7

Wrasama, Suleiman 386–7
Wright, Ada 299
Wright, Ernest Jenner 242
Wright, Joseph 200
writers 58–64, 195–8, 440–1
Wyllie, Sir William Curzon 229
Wyndham, Thomas 14

Xavier, Asquith 456

Yemeni people 253–4
yeomen 24
York, Duke of *see* James II, King of England
Yorke, Sir Phillip (Lord Hardwicke) 44, 52
Young, Arthur 342
Young, Wilmot 352
Young Historians Project (YHP) 519–20
young people 455, 456, 461–5, 471–82
Ystumllyn, John 72

Zarlia, John 303
Zephaniah, Benjamin 469, 480
Zouche, Edward la, 11th Baron Zouche 36